MAX BEAVERBROOK
NOT QUITE A GENTLEMAN

CHARLES WILLIAMS

Biteback Publishing

First published in Great Britain in 2019 by
Biteback Publishing Ltd
Westminster Tower
3 Albert Embankment
London SE1 7SP
Copyright © Charles Williams 2019

Charles Williams has asserted his right under the Copyright, Designs and Patents Act 1988 to be
identified as the author of this work.

Every reasonable effort has been made to trace copyright holders of material reproduced
in this book, but if any have been inadvertently overlooked the publisher would
be glad to hear from them.

ISBN 978-1-84954-746-8

10 9 8 7 6 5 4 3 2 1

A CIP catalogue record for this book is available from the British Library.

Set in Adobe Garamond Pro

Printed and bound in Great Britain by
CPI Group (UK) Ltd, Croydon CR0 4YY

MIX
Paper from
responsible sources
FSC® C020471
FSC
www.fsc.org

For Jane

CONTENTS

When the Devil wants to make major mischief,
he sends for Max Beaverbrook.

When he wants to make minor mischief,
he sends for Evelyn Waugh.

PROLOGUE

Lady Diana Cooper, in her day one of London's leading society lionesses, described Max Beaverbrook as 'this strange attractive gnome with an odour of genius about him'.[1] She was far from alone in her admiration. Many others were similarly captivated: a good number of minor lionesses, more than a few journalists and historians, a scattering of politicians and, above all – but perhaps with a greater sense of realism – Winston Churchill himself. They all succumbed to the charm, sense of mischief and sheer ebullience of the man.

By contrast, there were also those who saw the darker side of the character. Indeed, had she been less mesmerised by him even Lady Diana might have been forgiven for adding 'and from time to time with more than a hint of malice'. Certainly, the list of those who openly disliked him is impressive: Kings George V and VI, Clement Attlee, Stanley Baldwin, Lords Alanbrooke and Curzon, Hugh Dalton, Ernest Bevin, as well as a large segment of the Canadian political and industrial establishments. Furthermore, Clementine Churchill's attitude towards him, unlike that of her husband, was one of 'lifelong mistrust'.[2] (She also, by the way, thought him an unreconstructed lecher.) As one of the few still alive who knew Beaverbrook in person, if only in her capacity as Churchill's secretary in his later years, my wife still describes him as 'somebody you would instinctively walk away from'.[3]

It is not for the biographer to take sides in such a controversy, however animated it was and, to some extent, still is. His task is to tell the story of a life and, in doing so, to illustrate – and, if possible, explain – how and why it gave rise to the sometimes explosive expressions of opinion which his subject has provoked. As it happens, there is no shortage of material to hand. The Beaverbrook story is, after all, one of continuing fascination: over eighty years of high (and low) finance, political dogfights, wars, conspiracy, media wrangles, sex and grand living, all of it threading through the dramatic years of the first half of the twentieth century. Yet the biographer, any biographer, has to be careful. It is too easy to slip into other rhythms, either too laudatory or too critical or – worst of all – simply too boring. Caution thrown aside, following Beaverbrook has been an absorbing journey on a human roller-coaster. But from time to time the author, while carefully fastening his seatbelt, has had to prepare himself for moments of queasiness. It may be that the reader will now have to do the same.

CHAPTER 1

THE BRUNSWICKER

Spem reduxit[1]

For the King's Men, 1783 was the decisive year. They had remained loyal to the British Crown through the turbulent early years of the American Revolutionary War, had fought in militias alongside the Redcoats, had been scorned by the Revolutionaries ('Patriots', they called themselves) and had seen their houses burnt down, their property confiscated and their friends tarred and feathered. But, as much as the Revolutionaries were aggressive and unforgiving, the King's Men had no great love for the British. Like the Patriots, they, too, objected to the arrogance of their colonial masters and to the taxes they were obliged to pay without the possibility of argument. Nevertheless, King George III was still the King to whom they had sworn allegiance, and therein lay their problem. As it happened, a Maryland lawyer, Daniel Dulany, was ready with a solution. 'There may be a time when redress may not be obtained,' he wrote. 'Till then, I shall recommend a legal, orderly, and prudent resentment.'[2] The language suited its purpose. What was offered was a fence of procrastination to be sat on; and the King's Men, or Loyalists as they became known, duly sat on it.

Although they were joined under one metaphorical flag, the Loyalists were far from a homogeneous group. There were tenant farmers in upper New York, Dutch traders in New Jersey, German smallholders in Pennsylvania, Quakers and Anglican clergy in Connecticut, a few Presbyterians in the southern colonies and a large number of Iroquois Indians, in all amounting to around one fifth of the total non-slave population of the Thirteen Colonies of some two and a half million. For such a disparate bunch it is no surprise to find that there was little

I

formal organisation. In short, the only glue that kept them together was caution, tenuous loyalty to the British Crown – and fear.

Fear became the major element in the glue after the surrender of Lord Cornwallis at Yorktown, Virginia, in October 1781. Word spread quickly that the British were to sue for peace. The question then for the Loyalists was how the victorious Revolutionaries would treat their defeated compatriots. At first, the outlook was promising. In April 1782, negotiations between representatives of Great Britain and the nascent United States opened in a small hotel in what is now the Rue Jacob in the Saint-Germain quarter of Paris. It was quickly agreed that the United States should be free and sovereign. There was then an extended argument over boundaries – the American negotiators wished to swallow up the Province of Quebec – much wrangling over fishing rights off the coast of Newfoundland, debate about the validity of contracts on either side and agreement about the release of prisoners of war.

The debates, as might be imagined, were more than usually protracted, and little percolated through to the anxiously waiting transatlantic audience. It took weeks for news to travel, by post coach, then sailing ship and then coach again. But by early 1783 the main lines of agreement had become clear. In particular, the provisions of what became Article 5 of the final treaty started to circulate as rumour – that the Congress of the Confederation of the United States would agree to recommend to state legislatures that they should provide for the restitution of confiscated properties to their rightful owners, the Loyalists. That was all very well. The difficulty was that this was to be no more than a recommendation. State legislatures were free to ignore it. Indeed, as the year went on, it became apparent that a number of states would be exercising their right to do so.

By the time the Treaty of Paris was signed in September 1783, some Loyalists were already deciding that their future did not lie within the newly independent Thirteen Colonies. The majority, in fact, remained, particularly those who had acquired property and social status – or family ties with Patriot relations. However, some sixty thousand, according to one estimate, emigrated, half to the south and the friendlier political climate of Florida and half to the north. The Iroquois Indians were summarily expelled from the state of New York and ended up in the west of what became Canada. The white émigrés (together with their slaves) made moves to settle in the British colonies of Upper Quebec and Nova Scotia.

Those who made for Nova Scotia immediately encountered a problem. The past had been troubled and Nova Scotia itself was only just in the process of calming down. The century to date had witnessed six wars between the British colonists and the French and Indians. Subsequently, the Treaty of 1763 had ceded most of the old French colony of Acadia and all of the peninsula of Nova Scotia to Britain. That gave the signal for the British to remove the remaining Acadians from the peninsula and to invite some 2,000 families of British descent in the colonies of New England to leave their homes there to take the Acadians' place. That done, the new settlers had hardly built their homes and set up their farms when the Thirteen Colonies to the south declared independence. At first, they were minded to join the Patriots, to the point where some called them 'the Fourteenth Colony'. But during the Revolutionary War American privateers made such devastating raids on Nova Scotia ports that opinion swung decisively against the Patriot cause. Reluctantly, the New Planters, as they came to be called, decided to dig in and nurse their resentment against the British within the boundaries of allegiance to the Crown.

At that moment, the last thing they wanted was a straggling army of some thirty thousand Loyalist refugees arriving on their doorstep. They were vociferous in their objections to the point where there was a good deal of random and unprovoked violence – and even official persecution. The Loyalists, wrote Colonel Thomas Dundas, 'have experienced every possible injury from the old inhabitants of Nova Scotia'.[3] The upshot was that in 1784 the British had to intervene to create a new colony to accommodate those Loyalists who had found shelter on the Acadian mainland and who wished to leave behind the unhappy experience of the peninsula – and the abuse of the New Planters.

The new colony, it was decided, was to be called New Brunswick (the name was an anglicisation of the German city of Braunschweig, one of the ducal titles of King George III). Furthermore, the British Governor of Quebec, Lord Dorchester, announced that all those who had remained faithful to the Empire – and their descendants – were to be distinguished by the letters U. E. after their names, 'alluding to their great principle The Unity of the Empire'.[4] The Loyalist motto in turn duly became the motto of the new colony. Its imperial vocation was thus established at its birth.

New Brunswick is now one of Canada's three Maritime Provinces, perched somewhat uneasily at the north-eastern corner of the American continent. To the north it is bounded by the Gaspé Peninsula of the province of Quebec and Chaleur Bay, to the east by the Gulf of Saint Lawrence and Northumberland Strait, to the south by the Bay of Fundy and to the west by the American state of Maine. Unlike its sister provinces, Prince Edward Island and Nova Scotia, which are wholly or largely surrounded by water and hence climatically defined by the Atlantic, New Brunswick, although it has a long sea coast, is sheltered from the great ocean by its neighbour Nova Scotia, with the result that its climate, particularly in the interior, is to a large extent continental. The winters are cold to the marrow and the summers are hot, fierce and dry. Frozen rivers – its wide rivers and its spruce forests are the dominant characteristics of the province – make travel difficult in the dark months of the year and are given to flooding as the ice melts, bringing debris down from the hills and the logs which have been cut by the shivering woodsmen. Then it is the time for the Atlantic salmon, running in with the tide to make their way to spawn in the reeds in the source streams.

As is frequently the case in inhospitable climates, the weather and geography have determined both the spread and the activity of the population. In fact, the spread has hardly changed in the 200 years of the province's history. Of a total population of 751,171 recorded in the census of 2011, a third were Francophone, living where their Acadian ancestors lived after being bundled out by the British. The central area around the river Miramichi provided a haven for the Scots of the Lowland diaspora of the eighteenth and nineteenth centuries and the Irish fleeing the potato famine of 1845. To the south lies the redoubt of the old Loyalists in the port of St John and the capital Fredericton over 100 kilometres to the north on the St John River. Today it has all the conveniences – and inconveniences – of modern life. One hundred and fifty years ago it was a 'land for the huntsman, the fisherman, of lumber and saw-mills and possessed of a tiny coasting trade, and in the distant past a ship-building industry, where great ships were launched'. But for William Maxwell

Aitken, the first Lord Beaverbrook, the land, the province, the New Brunswick of his childhood, had 'always been home'. It was 'the nursery rather than the career of prominent Canadians. It has indurated [*sic*] the brood and sent it forth to richer climes to conquer.' For Beaverbrook, the induration, whatever that meant, was the legacy of Loyalism.[5]

In his later years, he may indeed have thought of New Brunswick as some sort of spiritual home. The extent of his benefactions, a library here, a university endowment there, carillons for churches, an art gallery with the most sumptuous works of European masters almost thrown in as a bonus, testify to his efforts to secure his reputation – even his immortality – in the province. Yet Max Aitken, as he was known until his elevation to the British peerage, left New Brunswick as soon as he could. As he wrote himself, he was one of the brood who went forth to richer climes to conquer.

This comes as no surprise. He had, after all, arrived there in the first place by a tortuous route. The Aitkens (the name was quite common in their original home) lived in the rolling countryside of West Lothian in Scotland. Max's own grandfather was a man of substance – a tenant farmer on the estate of the Marquis of Linlithgow and a lime merchant with property in the market town of Bathgate. The main farm itself, known as Silvermine after the earlier silver workings which had subsequently given way to lime works before these too reached exhaustion, lay in the extreme corner of the parish of Linlithgow, abutting the parishes of Torphichen and Bathgate. In fact, it was at Torphichen that the Aitkens worshipped and where, at least from the middle of the eighteenth century, they were buried.

Torphichen itself is an attractive enough place of about five hundred inhabitants, with rows of miners' houses running alongside steep and rather narrow roads. Situated some thirty kilometres west of Edinburgh, its main feature is the ruin of the Preceptory, or Headquarters, of the Knights Hospitaller of the Order of St John of Jerusalem. Built originally in the twelfth century, it was expanded over the years to include a cruciform church, living quarters and, to complete the complex, a hospital. Before the Reformation its history was colourful. William Wallace held his parliament here before the Battle of Falkirk in 1298 and after the battle King Edward I was brought to the hospital for treatment for an injury sustained when his horse unseated him and then, for good measure, trod on him. The Hospitallers then made the mistake of fighting on the English side at Bannockburn but were allowed to return to the Preceptory by Robert the Bruce. They were unable to survive the Reformation. In 1560 the Order was disbanded and the buildings, apart from the nave of the church which was used as a kirk, allowed to fall into disrepair. In the eighteenth century a new kirk, unfortunately of little architectural merit, was built around the ruins. Yet for all its history, today's visitor finds it a tranquil, even sleepy, place.

Not far from Torphichen Church is the old parish school. Although it is not known precisely where he was born, it is almost certainly here that Max Aitken's father, William Cuthbert Aitken, received his early education. The third child of ten, and the first son, he was enrolled at Bathgate Academy at the age of eight in 1842. He 'matriculated at two shillings in the Rector's Department',[6] a class reserved for the brighter pupils, and went on to study humanities at the University of Edinburgh. This was followed by a further four years of Divinity also at Edinburgh. By 1858 he was ready to be examined and received in the Presbytery of Linlithgow as a probationer to the Holy Ministry. That done, he was looking to a steady future in the domestic Church of Scotland. But there was a problem. In short, there was no job open to him. All the posts in the Presbytery of Linlithgow, and in the neighbouring ones, had their incumbents, all of them years away from retirement. Probationers had to occupy themselves as they might with casual preaching engagements and the odd hour of teaching. As far as money was concerned, there was no alternative for him but to live at home at Silvermine.

It was the schism in the Church of Scotland, known as the Disruption of 1843, that, indirectly, rescued William Aitken's career and, in doing so, resulted in Canadian birth and nationality for his son. In May of that year the row which had simmered for some ten years over who had the right to appoint ministers of the church came to a head. Tradition and practice had it that the right to do so lay with the patron, normally the landowner of the district. Objectors held that this infringed the right of spiritual independence of the church, claiming the overriding 'Crown right of the Redeemer' as justification. As with most arguments of this sort, the dispute was conducted with a good deal of heat and very little Christian charity. The upshot was that about a third of the ministers walked out of a stormy meeting of the General Assembly of the Church of Scotland in St Andrew's Church in Edinburgh to form the Free Church of Scotland.

St Andrew's Presbyterian Church, Maple, where Rev. William Aitken served as minister, c. 1908.

The schism, painful as it was, led to a number of results. The first was that the remaining majority in what liked to call itself the Established Church of Scotland became very much less rigorous in the application of Calvinism in the face of the vigour of the dogmatic assertions of its Free Church opponents. The position of saints, for instance, precarious since the Reformation after the thunder of Calvin himself and now subject to Free Church anathema, was covertly reinforced – new churches were named after the saints of old such as St Andrew, not least because it proved loyalty to Scotland's patron saint and hence to the civil establishment. The doctrine of predestination, equally, started to be viewed with a good deal of caution. Yet whatever the theological wrangles, it was the undignified scramble for congregations that had the greatest effect on the ground. If ministers defected to the Free Church, it was only natural that they would try to take their congregations with them. If the congregation agreed, the money went with them, as well as, in all probability, the church building and the accompanying manse.

The effect was far reaching. Even in the North American colonies there were defections. The small lakeside town of Cobourg, for instance, in what was to become the Canadian province of Ontario, there was one such. True, Cobourg was essentially a Loyalist town – named after another Hanoverian title – but among the 3,500 residents recorded in the 1851 census there was a sizeable number of Scottish descent. In 1844, when the news of the Disruption reached them, the congregation, who had previously adhered to what they had thought to be the true faith, defected. It was obvious, so it was argued, that the right to appoint a minister must lie with the congregation and not with a civil patron – particularly one who might owe his right to some dim and distant British legacy. The minister and congregation switched their allegiance as one and took over both the church building and the manse. Uneasily, since they were not entirely clear about the theological divide, they declared themselves true followers of Presbyterian principles as set out by Calvin and his Scottish acolyte John Knox. All remained calm until 1859, when the official Church of Scotland took legal action against the Free Church to recover the church building. Judgment was given in its favour. Undismayed, the Free Church congregation simply built its own church. That done, the congregation sat back to await events.

By that time the dispute at Cobourg, together with all the parallel defections in other parts of the colony – and, indeed, in other colonies – had triggered alarms in Edinburgh. The Colonial Committee of the General Assembly of the Church of Scotland had been forced into action. A trawl was made for candidates who might be willing to serve abroad. One of the names that came up was that of Mr William Aitken, an unemployed probationer in Linlithgow. At the same time a request was received in August 1862 from a Dr Barclay of the Presbytery of Toronto for 'two or more missionaries [sic], one Gaelic speaking'.[7]

Given the nature of the request, the mills of the Colonial Committee ground at a remarkably slow pace. In March 1864 Dr Barclay was obliged to reiterate his request. This was laid on the table at a further meeting of the committee on 31 May but 'consideration ... was postponed until further information was received'.[8] It was not until July that the decision was made. 'The Rev William Aitken', the minutes read, 'was appointed to the charge of Cobourg, Toronto, with a salary of One hundred and fifty pounds a year for one year the circumstances of the congregation to be considered at the end of the first year of incumbency.'[9] In other words, Aitken was given a year to sort Cobourg out.

It was not much of an offer but at least it was a job. The salary was, for the time, not ungenerous – worth some £13,000 in today's values. In addition, he was to be paid £25 for clothing and £22 for the passage across the Atlantic. Yet in terms of job security it was about as precarious as could be. There was also one further hurdle. Aitken had yet to be ordained. This meant a return to Linlithgow Presbytery to complete his trial discourses and to undergo a question-and-answer session in Divinity and Church History. All that completed satisfactorily, he 'received from the brethren the right hand of fellowship...', listened to the Moderator of the Presbytery addressing to him 'suitable admonitions as to his pastoral duties ... signed the Confession of Faith and the Formula of the Church of Scotland'.[10] He was now free to make his way, by himself, to a new home, a new job – and a new continent. In short, both in his own life and geographically he was going to a New World.

As it turned out, the whole venture was something of a fiasco. He made his way along the various stages of the laborious journey – the details are not recorded but at the time the preferred shipping route was from Glasgow to Liverpool, from there on the uncomfortable winter crossing of the Atlantic to Boston, on to Halifax, and then by land to Montreal and Toronto – to arrive in Cobourg before Christmas 1864. Once there, he found the congregation unrepentant, the manse dilapidated beyond possible occupation and the church of which he had by law acquired charge almost a ruin. His only recourse was to find lodgings, uncomfortable as they turned out to be, and summon his younger sister Ann to cross the Atlantic and join him in his lonely misfortune. This she dutifully did.

The stand-off could not last. Nor did it. Well before the completion of his one-year assignment, Aitken was thrown a lifeline. On 3 October

1865 the congregation of Vaughan, 'desirous of promoting the glory of God and the good of the church, being destitute of a fixed pastor … have agreed to invite, call and entreat … you to undertake the office of Pastor among us and the charge of our souls…'[11] Not only was the call a career lifeline but it came with pledges of financial support. At their meeting the previous June at which the elders of the congregation decided to make their call, no less than $115 in half-yearly payments to the management committee of the parish had been signed up. Furthermore, the elders and managers of the congregation promised that they and their successors would use their best efforts to raise $500 every year of Aitken's incumbency in consideration of his services. Finally, they promised him the use of the manse and the glebe and held out the prospect of an increase in his stipend as might be suitable in the future. The call could not possibly be refused – and was duly accepted.

But there was a snag. Vaughan itself was little more than a small township on the fringe of the growing conurbation of Toronto. Straggling along the boundaries of a swamp, a road had been built in 1829 to encourage settlement to the north. In the course of time, the settlement developed into a community. The community then grew to the point where it became the seat of Vaughan's – admittedly little – civil administration. With that came, naturally, given the nature of the community, the foundation and subsequent oversight of a church. William Aitken, having accepted – and been accepted for – the post of minister, now found himself in charge of a congregation rather smaller than the one he had left behind. Nevertheless, it existed – and the congregation had resisted the blandishments of the Free Church.

The main feature on the ground was the profusion of trees which lined its uneven streets. Disregarding the soft, feminine implications, the inhabitants had decided, after much discussion and renaming, to call their parish Maple in honour of the trees. This they were conveniently able to do since there had been little time for local tradition to take hold. Maple, and its sister village Nobleton, were indeed recent foundations. The two heads of the founding family, Joseph Noble and his elder brother Thomas, had been born in Strathblane, on the north-eastern fringe of County Tyrone, in what was a largely Catholic area. Without jobs or prospects, in their thirties they had taken the long voyage across the Atlantic and arrived in Toronto at some point in the 1830s. They bought land – marshy at best – just outside the Toronto boundary and still available under the Crown concession.

Thomas farmed the land and Joseph started a pub. The pub did so well that Joseph was not only granted the licence to be postmaster but was also able to buy additional land and start marketing the produce from his brother's farm. Not content with that, in 1844 he married the daughter of a close neighbour, Sarah McQuarrie, whose family had migrated to New York from the Scottish island of Mull early in the century. On 19 July 1845, their first child – Jane, sometimes known as Jennie – was born. Two years later their first son – Arthur – joined her. They were not to know it, but both of them were to play their parts in the Aitken family story.

Maple was, as a community, modest but by no means impover-ished. Along Kemble Street, rough as it was, the houses were well built of brick with steep tiled gables, upper rooms and chimneys to release the smoke from the wood burners heating the floors below. Sanitation, of course, was primitive – outdoors – and water had to be collected. Yet it was a friendly place and William and Ann soon settled down. The congregation, such as it was, 'from 90 to 100 of us, chiefly from Scotland',[12] had in 1829 asked for permission to acquire a house in which they would be licensed to worship. That granted, they asked for a minister, who duly arrived in 1832. Ministers then came and went, but by 1865 the faithful had built both a proper church – named after the patron saint of Scotland, St Andrew – and a manse. It was this combination, apart from the relief of being free of Cobourg, which had attracted William to accept the call.

As it happened, romance – if it can be called that – was in the air. In 1866 Arthur, Joseph Noble's eldest son, courted and then married William's sister Ann. Soon afterwards, William solved the problem of his consequent loneliness by repeating the exercise with Arthur's elder sister Jane. In truth, there was not much romance in either arrange-ment. In fact, of the two marriages, the second was by far the more successful. Arthur drank too much and was unfaithful to the point of contracting venereal disease, which he passed on to his wife and of which he died at an early age. So far, as it were, so bad. William and Jane in their turn settled down – but without obvious enthusiasm.

There was little in the way of marital warmth. Jane 'invariably spoke of her husband and to him as Mr Aitken'[13] and William replied in kind. Yet in a formal sense, marital relations were productive. Six children were born in Maple; the last, seeing the light of day on 25 May 1879, was William Maxwell Aitken – soon to be known universally as 'Max'.

By then William was getting restless, a situation that was exacerbated by the life of dissipation led by his brother-in-law Arthur, of which he, as a man of God, profoundly disapproved. Accordingly, when in April 1880 he received a call from the Presbytery of Miramichi in New Brunswick he was minded to respond favourably. After all, it was not just a matter of moving out of a difficult environment. The congregation of St James in Newcastle to which he was called was both well-endowed and had a thriving – mainly Scottish – membership. They certainly appeared eager to have him as their minister. When various candidates presented themselves for scrutiny he was given a particularly friendly reception and on 16 April the call was finalised. William, Jane and their young children prepared to move.

William Cuthbert Aitken must have appeared to his small children as resembling a particularly grim Old Testament prophet. Photographs of the time show him with a mass of facial hair – an unkempt white moustache and long white beard covering the whole of his lower face and collar – and above it a square, intransigent face with staring eyes below a square, intransigent forehead. His manner of life was equally daunting. His main – it seems almost his only – passion was a large library of books which were kept in a special room to which he would retire to smoke his pipe and ponder no doubt on the sins of the world. Discipline in his house was, as might be imagined, severe. On Sundays, the family was to show evidence of their 'purity of heart' by abstaining from anything which might give enjoyment or relaxation,[14] and Monday was not much better since it was the day when Mrs Aitken did the washing and ironing – and the children were there to bring buckets of water as and when required. On other days there was little family joy. Meals were solemn affairs with prayers before and after eating. Occasionally, the father would indulge himself, after supper at six-thirty, by singing 'without any grasp of tune' some old Scottish folk songs.[15] This sudden burst of warmth, of course, never occurred on a Saturday evening, when his mind was concentrated on the extended sermon exhorting the virtues of Calvinism which he was to deliver to the faithful the following morning.

Portrait of Rev. William Aitken, father of Max Aitken, c. 1880s.

Jane Aitken was no great beauty. Her face had the simian features that she passed on to her third son and although in her young days her figure was trim it soon filled out with the burden of carrying and bearing her many children. Her wardrobe reflected her upbringing and the position into which she married, as well as the social norms of the day: long black dresses with high white collars and white cuffs, simple black hats with white trimmings and, in winter, a heavy black fur coat and black muff. Like her husband, she was a disciplinarian. She may have been marginally more light-hearted than him, but her Ulster parentage did not allow much room for jollity – only for a shrewd and caustic gift of repartee. Her one affliction, which regularly struck when least expected, was asthma. The attacks were brutal, lasting hours and at times most of a day. When they occurred, 'discipline was abandoned, and rules of conduct were relaxed'.[16] Her daughter was called on to bake bread and biscuits, to do the washing and to clean the house. For the rest of the family, those times were both worrying and depressing.

Mrs William Aitken (Jane Noble), mother of Max Aitken, late 1800s.

The Aitken family, William, Jane and their six children (Sarah, nicknamed Rahno; Annie, known as Nan; Robert, the eldest son, who was known by his middle name Traven, after the Scottish farm over which the Aitkens had at times held a lease; Rebecca Catherine, known as Katie; Joseph Magnus, known as Mauns; and Max himself), left Maple in the spring of 1880 on the long trek to the north-east and to their new home in Newcastle. Max, aged eleven months, had, of course, no knowledge of the journey or of what had caused it. But without him knowing it, he was about to become what he was subsequently so proud of: a Brunswicker – or, as he would say himself, adding the extra spin, a New Brunswicker.

CHAPTER 2

MISCHIEF MAKER

'A small, white faced little boy'[1]

'The town of Newcastle', according to one account, 'might not impress the casual tourist.'[2] Nowadays this goes without saying, since Newcastle, as a separate community with its own distinctive name, has ceased to exist. What was once an independent town is now no more than an annexe of the City of Miramichi, known prosaically and with hardly a nod to its past as Miramichi West. Moreover, regrettable as it may be, it is unlikely that any tourist, casual or otherwise, would put the suburb of Miramichi West high on his or her agenda for an uplifting cultural visit.

It was not ever thus. The account refers, of course, to the Newcastle of the nineteenth century and, even so, is perhaps unduly harsh. In 1880, when the Aitken family arrived, Newcastle had its own identity, and its own pride, as the shire town of what was then Northumberland County. There were, in addition to some elegant clapboard houses, a courthouse, local government offices, a railway station to serve the Intercolonial Railroad, a fine church and, to accompany them all, a newly built manse able to accommodate a large and intermittently noisy family. It was certainly a place of reasonable substance; a tourist, however casual, would have done well to take note and might, after all, have been impressed.

The town itself, in its prime, lay in a commanding position on a hill above the north bank of the Miramichi River. It overlooked the point just where the river runs downstream to the north-east in a wide bend out of the rough water which has made it unnavigable even in summer. The course of the river, and the guarantee in the warm months of a clear access to the sea, gave the site, and its accompanying port on the riverside, a ready advantage. To exploit it, in the late

15

eighteenth century the Scottish forester William Davidson, along with a group of fellow Scots, settled the site and built a small river port. From that beginning Newcastle, as they called it, grew into a bustling centre for lumber exports, from there into shipbuilding and then, with the advent of steel-hulled ships, into the production and export of pulp and paper. As a spring or autumn sideline, of course, there was always the catch of the prolific Atlantic salmon.

Newcastle's glory days, such as they were, did not last long. The lumber and pulp export trade fell off. Competition from the ports of Nova Scotia and New England, with ready access to the Atlantic all year round, proved too difficult to handle. Small wooden ships no longer found a market. In time, what was a thriving community in the early 1800s contracted steadily to the point where in the census of 1871 only some 1,500 residents were recorded in the town itself.

The decline in population was mirrored in the decline in church-going. Of the 1,500 declared souls, not more than 700 or so declared their religion as Presbyterian of one form or another. Of those, the Free Church, if the average of the period is applied, would have re-cruited half, leaving perhaps some 350 loyal to St James on the Hill. Proud they may have been and determined in signalling themselves in the 1871 census as Scottish, with or without the affiliation to the 'established' church, this was the somewhat meagre congregation to which the Reverend William Aitken was in 1880 invited to minister.

The Old Manse, Newcastle, New Brunswick c. 1950s.

The manse, the Aitkens' new home, had only been built in the year before their arrival. In fact, they were its first occupants. It stood in the most salubrious part of Newcastle, surrounded by the houses of what passed for the gentility of the town. It was sufficiently spacious to provide a large family room on the ground floor while upstairs the bedrooms were large enough for two children to share; there was a study for William and a boudoir for Jane, attics for servants, two kitchens, a sizeable veranda in the front for fresh air when the weather was hot and a barn in the back for livestock. Furthermore, there were spare rooms available as the family continued to grow – Arthur was born in 1883, Jean (nicknamed 'Gyp') in 1885, Allan ('Buster' or 'Bud' according to preference) in 1887 and Laura in 1892. Tragically, one of Max's elder sisters, Katie, was to die of diphtheria at the age of seven in 1881, shortly after the family settled in Newcastle.

It was, nevertheless, not the easiest house to manage. Commodious and comfortable as it may appear in description, there was in the days of Max's childhood and adolescence no electricity, no running water, no indoor lavatory, lighting only by paraffin lamps and no heating other than wood fires in the main family room and in the minister's study – with the consequent hazard of wood smoke and potential fire. (Yet, in the march of progress, as one of the most important buildings in the town it was among the first to have a telephone installed. Unfortunately, it turned out to be useless as there were no other subscribers.)

About five minutes' walk from the manse stood the church of St James on the Hill, a fine, if for its purpose overlarge, example of colonial ecclesiastical architecture. It was regarded as a jewel by its congregation, who apparently volunteered in numbers to take turns for its maintenance. There was the normal, and in winter dreary, business of cleaning the church, sweeping away the results of the attendance, particularly in winter when boots brought in snow and mud, and preparation for the services. Special attention was needed to prepare the church for each event of the liturgical agenda: there was Morning Prayer on weekdays and Morning Service on Sundays, with Communion on the first Sunday of the month and at the major points of the Church's calendar. For these there had to be perfect tidiness without undue and distracting decoration, as Calvinist custom and practice required. In the services themselves the family also lent a hand. Max's job, much to his irritation, was to work the hand pump on the organ, which he did until, in a bout of inattention, he fell asleep at his post.

Max Aitken as a small boy of about ten years old, in a sailor suit, c. 1890.

All in all, apart from a certain rigour imposed by the father's position, family life for the Aitkens in Newcastle was not much different to family life elsewhere. The children had regular fights, Max was bored from time to time and took refuge with various playmates in the neighbourhood, there were punishments for misbehaviour and rewards for virtue, childhood accidents – Max fell down one day and was nearly run over by a mowing machine – and, most important, there were the elements of childhood education of basic reading and writing taught at home by the parents, to make sure that the children were properly equipped before each in his or her turn started formal schooling. As the years went by, of course, the house gradually emptied, as each child went off to school and later to different careers.

In 1884, it was time for Max, at the age of five, to cross the threshold from home to formal education. As it happened, he was fortunate.

The main school in Newcastle, affiliated to the church and named, perhaps rather portentously, Harkins Academy, was by all accounts a school of high standard. It was modelled on the Scottish pattern of primary and high schools, with a grading system as pupils advanced. Furthermore, it was comprehensive, accepting boys and girls from all sections of society (including illegitimate children); and it provided an education which was 'wholesome, sound, non-religious and common to all'.[3] In later life, Max was to claim that the education provided at Harkins 'surpass[ed] that given at public schools (Eton, etc.) in England'.[4] (As a matter of fact, he may well have been right, given the low academic reputation of English public schools of the day compared to their Scottish counterparts.)

Max Aitken's class at Harkins Academy, Newcastle, New Brunswick, 1893.
Max can be seen top left.

At his new school Max made what seems to be an almost comically bad start. A note dated 30 June 1885 from his primary school teacher records that in his first year he was present on only eleven and a half days out of a possible total of 156. This led to a caustic addendum by a senior teacher that 'perhaps hooky was a compulsory subject in Grade 1 in 1885'.[5] His performance was not much better as he moved up the grades and into the high school in 1890. According to the school records he was by a wide margin the worst offender for attendance in all his grades. Furthermore, he seemed wholly uninterested in the education on offer – apart from mathematics, at which he was surprisingly attentive. He was also recalcitrant to the point of rebellion. When his class was invited 'to do such and such a problem in arithmetic or some other subject', complained one teacher, 'Max would promptly fold his arms, sit back and not raise his pencil'.[6] 'During his last year at the school he paid no attention whatever to any subject of the school. He sat in a little chair by himself up in front. He was placed there to prevent him from annoying the other pupils and distracting their attention from their work.'[7]

Max's record as a pupil at school was bad enough, but worse still was his extracurricular activity. There were, to be sure, some harmless pranks, and a wayward career as a newspaper salesman and gossip writer for the *St John Daily Sun*, but it went well beyond that. He 'organised parties to play tricks' not only on the teachers but on 'unpopular persons in the town'. (What his father thought of that is anybody's guess.) He refined a device known as a 'pin-trap' so that it was invisible to anybody sitting down on the bench on which it was placed. 'It proved very successful and was the means of shooting many a surprised boy screaming into the air. His victims were invariably the dull, more studious pupils…'[8]

Photo of young Max (seated bottom right) at the Sunday school picnic, on Beaubears Island, near Miramichi, New Brunswick, c. 1889–92.

If there was a redeeming feature it was in Max's interest in English literature and the English language. True to his father's love of books, he read avidly and, on the whole, with discretion – Walter Scott, Thackeray and Stevenson (but not, apparently, Dickens). His reading clearly helped him with the language since, at the age of sixteen, he produced a critique of Macaulay's essay on Warren Hastings which took both the Principal and his father by surprise in its quality. But it was not enough to gain redemption with his father. William understandably disapproved of Max selling newspapers as a sideline, of his attempt to start an irreverent student newspaper and, after the school was burnt down in 1890, of his leading role in organising a protest of pupils at the unsatisfactory temporary conditions in which they were required to study. Indeed, by the time Max left school (without completing his course of studies), his father had 'almost despaired of him'.[9]

But William Aitken persevered. Max's ability in English and mathematics was enough to encourage his parents to send him, following the example of his elder brothers and sisters, to university. After much debate, the chosen destination was Dalhousie University in Halifax, where his brother Traven had studied law. It was not a happy choice. In fact, Dalhousie was lucky to be there at all. It had a history of financial trouble and by the time Max was sent there in 1895 to sit his entrance examination it was still far from final recovery. Founded as a college in 1818 by George Ramsay, Earl of Dalhousie and Lieutenant-Governor of Nova Scotia at the time, it was funded by the customs receipts collected (almost certainly illegally) after the British had captured the Maine port of Castine during the war of 1812 and operated it as a port of entry. When these funds ran out, the institution collapsed, to be re-founded in 1863 from local donations 'with six professors and one tutor ... in 1866 the student body consisted of 28 students working for degrees and 28 occasional students'.[10] There was a further near collapse in 1879 until a New York publisher by the name of George Munro, from a Scottish Nova Scotia family, provided a lifeline. Thus rescued, the college managed to find its own building in 1886 on what is now Carleton campus.

In the event, Max arrived at this somewhat rickety institution in his most truculent mood. He sat through two days of the entrance examination complainingly but without too much difficulty. On the third day, however, he was required to sit a paper on Greek and Latin languages. In his own later account, he claimed that he was suddenly repelled by the whole exercise. 'The paper was solemnly returned to the examiner with my declaration that a university career held no attractions as it involved unnecessary and even useless labour in futile educational pursuits.'[11] Needless to say, he failed. But it was not just failure. He had offended the examiners and he had, specifically and intemperately, rebelled against his parents. But the truth is that, such was his mood at the time, he simply could not be bothered one way or the other.

His father again displayed all the virtues of Christian patience. After what was no doubt an embarrassing scene on Max's return home to Newcastle, he suggested that a post as a clerk in the Bank of Nova Scotia could be arranged. The suggestion was met with blank refusal, followed by 'passive resistance', until the plan collapsed.[12] It was a low point in Max's adolescent rebellion, and his parents, obviously dismayed and upset, decided that there was little more they could do.

Max, in face of this clearly expressed parental disapproval, did what many rebellious adolescents do. He escaped from his home each morning to find life on the streets. But selling newspapers was no longer enough. It was too unreliable as a steady source of income. Almost as a last resort he took a job with a local pharmacist at a salary of one dollar a week. Although boring and menial, the job at least allowed him to gather gossip about the pharmacy's customers, gossip which, in diluted form, he wrote up for the *Daily Sun*. Furthermore, while he was kept busy washing empty bottles he was able to reflect on the pharmacist's profit and loss account. For the first time in his life he took an interest in the mechanics of business.

None of this, of course, added up to what Max wanted: an opening to a serious career which would take him away from a frustrating life at home in Newcastle. As luck would have it, however, it was when he was at his most frustrated and depressed that he was presented with just such an opportunity by the man who was to become one of the most influential role models in his young life.

Richard Bedford Bennett had been born in 1870 of a family of New Planters, originally from the state of Connecticut. He had grown up at his family's small farm in Hopewell Cape, New Brunswick, had been educated locally and had studied law at Dalhousie, graduating in 1893. Taken on as an assistant by Lemuel J. Tweedie, a lawyer in Chatham, a settlement of a few thousand people on the opposite bank of the Miramichi to Newcastle, Tweedie soon recognised his ability and invited him to become a partner in his firm, to be renamed as Tweedie and Bennett. Bennett's ability was undoubted. As a lawyer he was sharp, ruthless and to the point. As a person, however, he was not to everybody's taste. He was a bachelor, a teetotaller, a strict Methodist, conservative in all senses of the word and a resolute British imperialist. He also had a fiery temper, was dismissive of those he thought inferior, frequently almost monosyllabic in conversation and intolerant of sin in any form. Unlikely as it seems, Max came to feel for him the calf love that only an adolescent boy can feel for an older man.

Bennett had first met Max when he was a teacher at a small school in Douglastown, a kilometre or so downriver from Newcastle. Although he was nearly ten years older than Max, the two seem to have struck up a friendship. Certainly, Bennett was much liked by Max's parents and was a frequent guest to Sunday dinner at the manse. In the summer of 1895 Max came across Bennett on the Miramichi ferry. He told him about his troubles and asked whether he should take up the law as a career and, if so, whether he could join Tweedie and Bennett as an articled clerk. Bennett agreed to help his young friend and convinced his partner Tweedie to accept Max as a law student with duties as a clerk to pay his way.

There was, of course, a difficulty about money. Max was in the middle of negotiating an agency agreement to sell life insurance, as well as writing a column for the *Sun*, and he had also agreed to become a local correspondent for the *Montreal Star*. But the income all told hardly amounted to much. Always persuasive, he was able to borrow some money from a customer of the pharmacy, a lumberman by the name of Edward Sinclair. It was enough, if only just, to pay for lodgings and food in Chatham. At the age of sixteen, for the first time, he left home.

Contrary to Max's expectations, the job at Tweedie and Bennett turned out to be suffocatingly boring. In fact, it was little more than typing a succession of legal documents. Max needed much more excitement than that and soon set about finding it. His first idea was nothing if not ingenious. He persuaded his friend H. E. Borradaile, a fellow guest at the hotel where he lived and a clerk at the Bank of Montreal next door, to use the bank's writing paper (quite improperly) to write to the Chicago firm of Armour with a request to act as its agent for the sale of tinned meats and beans. No doubt encouraged by the respectability lent by the bank writing paper, Armour agreed. 'Borradaile and Aitken' was to be formed, but 'when we came to discussing terms we were almost at once at loggerheads' and the project fizzled out.[13]

More exciting was his excursion into local politics. In early 1896 Chatham was incorporated as an independent town. Elections to the town council were to follow. Max persuaded Bennett to put himself forward as a candidate for alderman and volunteered to run his campaign. This he did with great energy. There was much door-to-door canvassing, many leaflets sent out and, of course, promises of future performance freely made. It was only when Bennett was elected, by a narrow margin, that he found out that many of Max's promises on his behalf were wholly reckless and could not possibly be redeemed. Bennett was furious – but Max was duly elated.

The elation did not last long. At the age of twenty-six Bennett was ambitious to move on with his career. Chatham was, after all, no more than a small local practice. The real business was to be found in the fast-developing west. Moreover, Tweedie was not an easy person to work with. When, in January 1897, Bennett was offered a partnership with Senator James Lougheed in Calgary he accepted without hesitation. Leaving Chatham and Tweedie was easy enough, but he did feel guilty about leaving Max behind, since he had a good idea what would happen to him without the protection of a senior figure in the firm. Max, it was true, had been an unsatisfactory apprentice, fooling around and apparently unable to concentrate to Tweedie's satisfaction on the business at hand.

That was Tweedie's main complaint. Max was still rebellious and bored. To quote just one example of his mood, in the days before Christmas 1896 he wrote to Bennett:

The office is very dull today, and an air of tranquillity rests on all the town. A disconsolate face and a ruffeted pink dress passed the window today. The lines on her face clearly showed that a young life had been blighted. I told her that it was better to have loved and lost than never to have loved at all. Her only reply was a sigh. Fred Tweedie spent the morning in the office and not much work was done … This ink is frozen, this pen is bad, and this office is cold. As it was in the beginning, is now, and ever shall be. Amen. Yours truly…[14]

In Adams House, where Max was staying, there was a back room at which he and others met to enjoy what they called 'a gay time'.[15] In other words, there was drinking, card playing and smoking. Tweedie – and Bennett, for that matter – was vocal in his disapproval. In return, Max refused to work overtime. 'Mr Tweedie gets no free typing from me.'[16]

Bennett tried to persuade Max to try again to enrol in law school, but still without success. The suggestion was of little interest. Yet when Tweedie refused to promote him and offered his job to another aspiring apprentice, Max changed his mind. He walked out of his job and, for lack of an alternative, decided to have another try at a formal legal education. On the advice and recommendation of a friend of his father, a judge no less, he took the train to St John, found a place as an assistant in a law office – more typing of legal documents – and enrolled in St John Law School. But it turned out to be yet another mistake. After no more than a few weeks of boring work and loneliness in St John society, Max decided that he had had enough.

At just about the same time, Max's father was pondering a reply to a letter he had received from Bennett soon after the latter's arrival in Calgary. It reiterated the advice that he had given to Max, by then many times, that he should pursue a formal legal training. Confronted with what was a difficult choice for his son, William Aitken took his time to reply. After learning of Max's experiences in St John, he sent a long letter to Bennett explaining why he could not accept the advice. Max had spoken to him about the matter, he wrote, and he had agreed to think about it. Hence the delay in his reply. 'Would a College course be now a benefit to Max?' was the question he asked. 'My deliberate opinion is that it would not. His nature is such as would never make a first-class student. It is too eager to grasp the practical. And now that he has got a taste for business and the business intercourse of the world I believe that he could no more set himself down to a course of theoretical study', the father concluded in a unexpected flight of fancy, 'than he could take (or rather think of taking) a journey to the moon.'[17]

William's judgement of his son proved, perhaps surprisingly, to the point. Max had already discovered a taste for selling whatever he had opportunity to sell, whether newspapers or life, accident or fire insurance. Yet he still believed that fortunes were to be made in the west. St John was not for him, so he decided to follow his hero Bennett and seek what he hoped would be his own fortune in Calgary. By the spring of 1898 he had sold enough insurance policies and written enough gossip for his newspapers that he had in his pocket the price of a train ticket for the long journey across continental Canada. Thus equipped, he set off west to Calgary.

The Calgary that Max was to discover in the autumn of 1898 was in its early adolescence. The Canadian Pacific Railway had come to Fort Calgary in 1883. The population of the surrounding plains and Calgary itself rose exponentially. True, what became known as the prairie wheat boom had hardly got under way by 1898 (together with the discovery of oil in 1903 it was to transform the town by the time of the outbreak of the First World War), but there was excitement enough for young arrivals from the east to feed their ambition.

It was also enough to promise well for the legal partnership of Lougheed and Bennett, the largest and most influential in the town when Max arrived in 1898. In fact, not only was there business to be done but the two partners were well equipped to do it. Both were from the east; Lougheed from Toronto and Bennett from New Brunswick. Both had been brought up as strict Methodists, although Lougheed in his youth had added affiliation to the Orange Young Britons (he 'wore a white gown and carried a Bible at Parades').[18] Both were supremely intelligent, hardworking, deeply conservative, charming, courteous when required but competitive by nature, at times aggressive and arrogant to the point of rudeness. Both also transferred smoothly from the law into politics.

Lougheed had arrived in Calgary in late 1883. 'The only landmarks of civilization to be then found that antedated the arrival of the railway', he later said, 'were the old Hudson's Bay Company Post on the east bank of the Elbow, the Northwest Mounted Police stockade, and the trading post of I. G. Baker & Co., on the west bank.'[19] Around these wooden buildings was a village of some four hundred people living in tents. Everybody expected the railway to build its station, marshalling yard and sheds on the same patch of ground. Lougheed knew better. He had inside information from his position as the railway's legal adviser that they were going to build their permanent station some two kilometres to the west. In January 1884 he bought five pieces of land close to the site. When the railway offered to donate land for a new town hall and fire station, the villagers realised what was going on and 'got up suddenly one morning and moved itself westwards across the Elbow – 200 tar-papered shacks, half a hundred unpretentious wooden buildings and a few log structures'.[20] Lougheed had made his first fortune.

His second fortune came a few months later. In September 1884 he married Belle Hardisty, a self-confident and attractive girl who had the additional advantage of being extremely rich. Her father, William Hardisty, had been Chief Factor of the Hudson's Bay Company in the Mackenzie River Valley and had, on his death in 1881, left his family a sizeable fortune. Not only that, but his younger brother Richard soon thereafter became Chief Factor for the company in the North Saskatchewan River Valley, a territory larger than the British Isles. The opportunities for enrichment, it need hardly be said, were multiple, and Richard Hardisty, like his elder brother, took full advantage. In 1883 Richard moved his headquarters and his family to Calgary and invited Belle, his niece, to stay with them. On her marriage the following year Belle and her money became, such was the law at the time, the sole and unchallenged property of James Alexander Lougheed.

By 1888 Lougheed, enjoying his marriage, his new wealth and the social position in Calgary they brought with them, was foremost in supporting his uncle by marriage, Richard, in his nomination as the first Senator for the District of Alberta to the Canadian Senate. Almost immediately there was one more incident that favoured Lougheed. In 1889, Richard was killed in an accident. All, apart from a few exceptions who were quickly bought off, agreed that Lougheed was the only possible candidate as his replacement and, at the age of thirty-five, he became a Canadian Senator. That done, and almost by way of celebration, Lougheed and his wife commissioned and built a large sandstone house on the edge of town and called it Beaulieu. Such as Calgary was, which by modern standards was not very much, they had become its uncrowned king and queen.

It was into the shadow of this royalty, with astonished admiration of this new phenomenon, that the young Max Aitken intruded. It was the first time that he had met a true grandee. Certainly, here was a good model for him, but he was unsure how he could learn from Lougheed's spectacular career. Bennett was not at all helpful. He had finally abandoned his attempt to persuade Max to settle down and article for a career as a lawyer but, given that, could not find anything for the impatient young man to do. As a result, Max started to mix with some of the roughnecks in town. Together with a new-found business partner called Jack Maclean, he borrowed enough money to buy a bowling alley across the street from the office of Lougheed and Bennett. There was drinking and smoking, bowling and billiards. The Senator did not approve. Even Bennett went so far as to distance himself from his wayward protégé.

It was not until the late summer of 1898 that Bennett and Max were, at least to some extent, reconciled. Bennett had accepted nomination for membership of the assembly of the Northwest Territories and needed help with his campaign. Remembering Max's success at Chatham, and forgetting the unhappy fallout, Bennett recruited Max to run his campaign. True to form, Max showed the same enthusiasm and ingenuity that he had previously shown in Chatham. As before, a good deal of whisky was dispensed, and many promises made. The result was as before. Bennett won his seat (easily this time) and found himself burdened with promises he could not possibly keep. But at least he had won and, somewhat grudgingly, he gave Max the credit.

It was still not enough to keep Max in Calgary. In the face of Bennett's coolness and Lougheed's overt disapproval, Max sold the bowling alley in exchange for a tobacco shop, sold that and looked elsewhere for a change in his luck. It so happened that a boyhood friend from New Brunswick, James Dunn, who had had, like Max, a wandering, unsettled career but had at least qualified as a lawyer at Dalhousie, had been sent by his employer in Halifax to advise a group of railway promoters in Edmonton. When Max heard of Dunn's arrival there, he jumped at the idea of working with him. Almost immediately after Bennett's election Max made the journey to Edmonton, almost 500 kilometres to the north.

Nevertheless, leaving Calgary was not at all easy. His former partner Maclean seemed to have reneged on a debt which Max had to make up. He could only do this by calling yet again on Bennett's goodwill to discount a draft. (Somewhat cheekily, he was now starting his letters 'Dear Bennett'.)[21] All in all, Max's undignified exit from Calgary, and, indeed, his whole stay there of no more than a few months, had been an embarrassing failure. Later in life he did his best to cover it up: 'My sojourn in Calgary gave me many opportunities to establish myself in professional or commercial enterprise [presumably referring to the bowling alley and the tobacco shop!] … but … there was no evidence of stability or fixity of purpose.'[22] All that he had truly achieved was knowledge of how a grandee looked and behaved, and, more to the immediate point, of the advantages of insider information as a sure way of making money and of the right marriage.

Worse was to follow in Edmonton. Dunn proved a disappointment. Soon after Max arrived Dunn had decided that trading and selling securities was a better bet than advising railway promoters, and that this was best done in the east, in particular in Montreal. He left Max without a partner and without a job. In some desperation Max embarked on a much riskier exercise, buying meat wholesale and delivering it in lots to the camps of railway workers. There was much profit to be made but the business was highly capital intensive – and Max had no capital. The only way to meet the ever-rising financial re-quirements of the project was to borrow, using the meat as collateral. It was bad business, and the crash was not long in coming. One large consignment of meat was delayed by weather and went bad. Heavily indebted to, among others, the Merchants Bank of Canada, Max had to leave Edmonton in a hurry.

He then chose the classic way to avoid impatient creditors: sign up for the Army and hope to be posted to serve overseas. It so happened that this way suddenly became available. In October 1899 the Second Boer War had broken out. There was, among Empire Loyalists, at least in eastern Canada, an outbreak of populist frenzy. Signing up to fight for the Empire against a group of renegade Dutchmen was the thing to do, and Max, with at least one of his brothers, Mauns, duly did so. At the recruiting office, however, Max was rejected. It seems that his asthma disqualified him, although he himself later claimed that by the time the recruiting officer got round to him the quota of volunteers was full. On 30 October the troopship sailed from Quebec amid general rejoicing. But 'the soldiers were the lucky fellows; the spectators were condemned to remain at home'.[23]

Max was not only condemned to stay at home, as he put it. He was also condemned to find a way out of his money troubles. Yet again, he turned to the long-suffering Bennett for help. As so often, Bennett's patience again did not fail. With his help and with the money he made from sales of insurance policies, Max was able to discharge his debt to the Merchants Bank and recover the papers, books and furniture which the bank had been holding as security for their loan.

In December 1898, after stopping in Toronto and Montreal to firm up his position as a full-time insurance agent, Max arrived back in St John. His failures in both Calgary and Edmonton weighed heavily. Not only that, he found the business of insurance agency boring and the margins thin. He made friends, of course, but none that could point him to or help him in a more profitable career. In short, he drifted. He drank too much, played too much poker, tried too often to defeat the odds at dice and wasted too much time at the billiard table.

It was on his twenty-first birthday in May 1900 that, according to his memoirs, Max had what he claimed to be a Damascene conversion. He and some friends had organised a three-day fishing trip at a lake in a forest near Truro in Nova Scotia. 'There was', he later wrote, 'an ample supply of whisky to make the party go.'[24] Apparently, someone who was not in the original party unexpectedly joined in. He (his identity is not recorded) had spent time in the United States in business and during the evenings around the camp fire talked at length about his experiences there. Max was so impressed that he cut short his stay and returned to St John. 'The idler became a demonic worker,' he went on. 'The spendthrift [became] a rigid economist; the man of casual habits punctual, exact and unswerving in attention to business.'[25]

Some at the time thought that the 'conversion' was overblown and would disappear round the next poker table. Others have cast doubt on the whole account as written. Be that as it may, and whatever the doubts, Max certainly did turn some sort of corner. It is clear that around that time he drew up a balance sheet of himself as he saw it. He noted carefully the result and did become more serious in his lifestyle (poker was apparently abandoned). Furthermore, he made the decision to move again, this time to where the real money was, in Halifax, Nova Scotia.

In his personal balance sheet, Max could record, on the asset side, a robust, if small, physique, five foot seven inches in height and spare in body; a lively if unfocused mind; great charm when needed, evidenced by his much-admired wide grin; sensitivity to the emotional and, more and more, financial demands of his family (Mauns had asked him for money when he was in Calgary and then joined up to go to South Africa without paying him back); and loyalty to his friends. On the liabilities side, he would have to admit to a serious health problem (sporadic but, when they occurred, debilitating asthma attacks); restless indulgence in the frivolities of adolescence; difficulty in relations with the opposite sex other than the occasional fruitless attempt; inability to concentrate on or even enjoy anything intellectual bar mathematics and English literature; and a powerlessness to resist gambling.

Much of that, particularly on the liabilities side, was to change over the next few years. In short, Max was growing up. Furthermore, his luck was changing. It was in Halifax that he met another role model who was to point him both to a business in which his talent could flourish and, as a bonus, to the possibility of entering the political game. In achieving his majority, Max was, almost without knowing, about to realise his true potential as a deal maker of something, leaving aside the morality, near to genius. It is fitting, therefore, that in this story the mischief-making, white-faced little boy 'Max' should become the calculating and sharp businessman 'Aitken'.

CHAPTER 3

FROM DRIFTER
TO GENIUS

'Royal Securities Corporation was me'[1]

John Fitzwilliam Stairs, as he would have himself admitted with becoming modesty, was a true Haligonian gentleman. His social status, given his wealth backed by his family history, could not possibly be challenged. Moreover, as a devout Presbyterian, he not only did his duty in his congregation but, as befitted his position, grew effortlessly into roles of responsibility and influence both in his church and in a city which itself, like him, respected old money, Ulster ancestry, Loyalist roots and success in business. As though all that were not enough, he was also blessed with a particularly imaginative financial mind.

Physically, however, he was not at all strong. Of medium height and spare of figure, with a small head fronted by carefully trimmed moustache and beard, he is shown in a photograph of the time almost submerged by the winter fur coat and fur hat he habitually wore when the weather grew cold. But it was not just a matter of cold Halifax winters. His overall health was never as good as his family and friends would have liked. Indeed, in the course of time it was to undo him.

Born in 1848, Stairs had been carefully groomed through his childhood and adolescence to take over the family interests. For somebody less prepared, the prospect would have been daunting. His grandfather had founded the provisioning firm of William Stairs, Son and Morrow with offices in Halifax in a strategic position overlooking the long Stayner's Wharf where the big Atlantic ships docked. His father had extended the business into industry and finance, buying a share in the Union Bank of Halifax of which he soon became president.

At the age of twenty-one Stairs himself had become a partner in the family firm and general manager of one of its associate companies, Dartmouth Ropeworks. While he was learning his trade as a manager, his family's portfolio continued to expand through the acquisition of small companies and limited but carefully planned holdings in local banks. John Fitzwilliam was set to inherit one of the dominant commercial empires of the Maritime Provinces.

Financier and Conservative John F. Stairs at his desk, 1867.
He was a patron to Max Aitken as a young man.

Stairs himself was not satisfied even with that. He soon embarked on a political career, first in Halifax and then in the Canadian capital of Ottawa. His political views, as might be imagined, were deeply conservative. They were also robustly imperialist. In this he was by no means alone, either in Halifax or in Ottawa. Those were the days of the Imperial Federation League, a body of determined enthusiasts which advocated full military and political federation of the British white

Dominions, with Britain at its head, along the lines of the United States or, in some variants, a looser confederation along the lines of Canada. The League, although founded in England, had quickly taken root in Canada, first in Toronto then spreading east to the Maritime Provinces of New Brunswick and Nova Scotia. There the main base of the League was Fredericton, where the leader, and, so it was said, the most eloquent speaker, was the New Brunswicker George Parkin. Parkin preached the virtues of imperialism, Christian education and the old values of Loyalism with a powerful rhetoric which reached beyond New Brunswick, beyond even Canada to England itself. It was heady stuff, delivered, for those who heard it, with memorable conviction. Apart from all else, it earned Parkin a reputation in England – and a knighthood – which put him in the same bracket as the great imperialist himself, Cecil Rhodes.

Stairs, although himself not a member of the League, certainly subscribed with enthusiasm to Parkin's message, though not with the High Church Christianity with which Parkin surrounded it. In fact, he was true to the twin faiths of imperialism and the Presbytery throughout his life. Yet his political career turned out to be long in years but unsuccessful in achievement. A good man on committees, he was not a natural orator. Furthermore, the occasionally bruising side of national politics, with continued accusations of corruption, personal sniping and squalid bargaining for position, was not at all to his taste. As it happened, not only did he find national politics, in all its aspects, difficult and unpleasant, but his life was blighted by family misfortune. In May 1886, Charlotte, his wife of sixteen years, died of scarlet fever, leaving him with six children between the ages of fifteen and one. As he wrote sadly to the Canadian Prime Minister, Sir John Macdonald, who had offered condolences, 'It is hard to come home and find no wife to talk to about the events of the day.'[2]

It was nine years before Stairs married again, this time to a widow, and acknowledged beauty, Helen Bell Gaherty ('Nellie'). By then, Stairs had given up his ambition to prominence in national politics and had taken again to business in Halifax. True, he did not give up his devotion to the imperialist cause. If anything, it became more firmly rooted. Moreover, it was shared by his two, and by then closest, business associates in Halifax, Robert Harris and Charles Cahan. In fact, Cahan had at one point served as the honorary secretary of the Halifax branch of the Imperial Federation League. In that sense, they were all political birds of a feather.

Yet it was not their political views but their diverse characters and joint business acumen that made them such successful partners. Harris and Cahan were, like Stairs, grounded in the law. Both also had their family origins, quite unlike Stairs, not in the Haligonian élite but in small Nova Scotia towns; Harris in Annapolis Royal and Cahan in Yarmouth. That said, in character the two could hardly have been more different. Harris, the son of a blacksmith, was conservative, certainly very able but apt to be stuffy, more a small-town lawyer than an adventurer. Cahan, on the other hand, was open to friends and opportunities alike, ranging from politics to business, journalism and speculative ventures in the West Indies. An unlikely partnership, the two had joined forces in 1894 when Harris, by then the senior partner in a Halifax law firm, invited Cahan to join the practice following the loss of the latter's Shelburne County seat in the Nova Scotia General Assembly election, which was to mark the end of his political career. Now operating as Harris, Henry and Cahan, they quickly made a reputation for themselves and soon secured the Stairs account together with his major undertaking, Nova Scotia Steel and Coal, known familiarly simply as 'Scotia'. The three men went on to establish a close personal relationship; so close in fact that they were informally known as the 'Scotia Group'.[3] The relationship, to be fair, was not exclusive. They were quite ready to work with allies, such as William B. Ross, who had taught Aitken the business of selling securities rather than insurance, particularly bonds in the growing utilities of the West Indies and Latin America, and James Dunn's former backer, Benjamin Franklin Pearson. Nevertheless, the Scotia Group remained the kernel while others formed no more than the outer shell. (Ross and Pearson, for instance, were both Liberals and anti-imperialist, useful for business but not part of the political family.)

There is no agreed account of how Max Aitken and Stairs first came into contact. Aitken's own version was that they had met on a train. Another version is that Aitken tried to sell Stairs a typewriter, a third that Stairs found him one day sitting in his office. What is common to all these versions is that Aitken, thanks to Ross pointing his way, was unrelenting in his targeting of Stairs and that Stairs not only was impressed by that but also saw, in Aitken's enthusiasm and sharpness of mind, material that he could work with. As for Aitken himself, he was not altogether satisfied with his modest home in the Roy Building in Halifax (not that he spent much time there) and with his career as a peddler of life insurance. He thought he could do better. Be all that as it may, the result was that in the late spring of 1902 Stairs engaged Aitken as his executive assistant.

As it turned out, both had chosen well. Stairs was a good teacher and Aitken was a sharp and willing pupil. The intricacies of financial dealing, of flotations, underwriting, margins, short and long positions, mergers and acquisitions, all was grist to Aitken's capacious mill. At the same time, Aitken, apart from more mundane secretarial duties, was encouraged to deal for his own account, particularly in the bonds and stock of companies within the ambit of the Scotia Group, above all Scotia itself. (It almost goes without saying that Stairs gave him titbits of information about the group's companies to help him on his way.) True, he was not yet dealing in large amounts. In his notebook for early September, for instance, he records that he 'sold to A. G. Collar 25 shares N. S. Steel and Coal at 115 for which he gave me note $250 on demand'.[4] Yet he was quite comfortable dealing on margin and, as the example shows, accepting a note of hand in payment.

Aitken's first major task was to take on the marketing of a bond issue of the Trinidad Electric Company, a concern which had been acquired by Stairs, Harris, Cahan, Ross and Pearson in 1901. The issue was large but not unmanageable: $730,000 nominal value. The purpose was announced to be financing the construction in Port of Spain of a new electric tramway with accompanying rolling stock. It was a challenge Aitken was happy to meet. He used the techniques that he had used many times before in selling insurance. He called in all his contacts, from individuals dabbling in the deep waters of investment to the retired ship captains, professional men and religious ministers throughout the Maritime Provinces and even into central Canada. Time and again he pointed out that the bonds would yield a higher rate of return than government bonds, that both principal and interest were payable in gold and that the demand for transport on the island was so great that the security was undoubted. It was by no means an easy sell. But Aitken's sales methods worked. In fact, such was the success that less than a third of the issue was left with the promoters for a further, secondary, offer when the time was ripe.

So far, so good. But the real excitement came with his first bank merger. Stairs and Harris had decided to use what had become in essence the family bank, the Union Bank of Halifax, as a vehicle for the consolidation of banks in the Maritime Provinces against the threat of domination by the powerhouses of central Canada. The immediate target was the Commercial Bank of Windsor. Following his policy of giving the young man his opportunity, in August 1902 Stairs deputed the 23-year-old Aitken to keep a watch over the negotiations on his behalf. It was another success. On 8 September he was able to note, 'Shareholders met at 11 a.m. Adjourned at 9 p.m. For amalgamation 8970 votes Against 522 votes.'[5]

The merger proved profitable to all concerned, as Aitken was quick to note. Whether he was paid a fee of $10,000 for the transaction, as he claimed later, is open to doubt. What is not open to doubt is that it was his first experience both of the excitement of merger negotiations and of the profit which their success could quickly bring. But he was soon to learn that not all deals went smoothly. Harris and Cahan brought him into their plot to take over the London and Lancashire Life Insurance Company of Montreal. Their plan, however, was botched as the approach to management was badly handled and came to nothing. As though by contrast, Aitken's standby, selling securities, brought compensating satisfaction: 'Met R. E. Harris and C. N. Cahan and discussed Mexican Light and Power. I am to have right to dispose of $85,000 bonds and stock at 95, with 2½% commission to me. After that probably 85,000 further on same terms ... Will make a pot of money...'[6] Mergers were all great fun and full of profit, but the mundane business of selling bonds and stock paid for the daily bread.

It was on this wave of success that Aitken received a visit from his father. William Aitken had for some time been suffering from aphasia. In the middle of his sermons he had developed the habit of falling silent for up to a minute, while the agonised congregation, including his wife, looked on in dismay. By the spring of 1902 there was a good deal of muttering in the Newcastle congregation and even a vote to remove him, which he won by a distressingly small majority. He made the best of it by deciding to retire to a small house in Newcastle, spending his winters, with Aitken's financial support, at a hotel in the Florida sun. In September he took the trouble to visit his son in Halifax, staying a number of days in the Roy Building and wandering about the old city. He was particularly pleased at Aitken's success but not shy of delivering lectures on probity and principle, which Aitken, of course, heartily endorsed. Irony apart, however, Aitken treated his father with sincere and affectionate respect.

Probity and principle had not been high on the agenda in the failed plot to take over London and Lancashire, in which Aitken had apparently tried to suborn a senior employee into a scheme to buy the company's shares 'secretly'.[7] Nor were they evident in his attempts to cajole the 89-year-old Alexander Gibson to give up control of his large cotton manufacturing interests in return for a sizeable injection of fresh capital. Aitken was quickly learning the ways of the financial world – and, not to put too fine a point on it, the adjustment of his moral compass.

By the end of 1902, Stairs was treating Aitken almost like another son. In fact, he treated Aitken rather better than his sons Gilbert and Jim. Sunday lunch at the Stairs' opulent house at 170 George Street became almost a ritual. The Stairs daughters, Geraldine and Ethel, were regular companions on visits to the theatre. There was even speculation that Aitken and Ethel might be moving beyond friendship and towards marriage. There was, however, competition. On 14 February 1903, for instance, Aitken paid a visit to Pictou for the purpose of seeing 'Miss Glover', with whom he 'spent [the] evening'. The following day he stayed in Pictou, not leaving until the following morning.[8] The names of other women make fleeting appearances in his diary, but they had to compete with evenings spent playing poker or bridge and days idled away enjoying games of golf.

Yet social life, hectic as it was at times, never interfered with Aitken's almost frenetic business life. As 1902 gave way to 1903, things were going well enough for him to be able to engage a secretary, which in turn allowed him to keep a more organised diary of each day's events. The filing of documents became more systematic, letters less telegraphic in style and appointments recorded more rigorously. But if anything, the tempo became even more intense. He travelled hither and thither, often accompanying Stairs and Harris (always reverentially referred to as 'Mr Stairs' and 'Mr Harris'), in pursuit of deals to do or securities to sell.

At the same time, he was revealing a swift grasp of the complexities of the operations in which Stairs and his partners were engaged – so swift, indeed, that even Stairs was surprised. It was this speed of mind, and a capacity for invention which started to accompany it, that led Stairs to give Aitken a new, and decisive, opening. The capital requirements of Nova Scotia Steel and Coal were large and growing. Stairs concluded that a new financial institution was needed to mediate between the company and lenders or investors. In early 1903 Stairs decided that a securities corporation, or 'bond house', would be set up to handle the issues of the steel company. It would also act as underwriter and broker for government and municipal bonds and other companies in the Scotia Group's portfolio.

Stairs had already seen an example. In 1901 such a company, the Dominion Securities Corporation, had been set up in Toronto and had thrived. The technique Dominion had developed was simple but, for those with a financial turn of mind, little short of brilliant: to borrow short-term from banks on the basis of a limited capital input from the bond house, to buy an issue outright (the bonds or stock to be used as collateral for the bank borrowings) and subsequently sell it on to other brokers and investors. The bond house's own liability in the transaction was limited, due to the legal protection of incorporation, while the issue was in practice underwritten in full by the lending banks. Any unsold securities could be left with the bond house and its holding financed by rolling over the short-term bank loans until the remainder of the issue could be disposed of. Interest on the bank loans was met from the return on the underlying securities. Commissions on sales and underwriting fees were, of course, collected by the bond house.

The formula was, without a doubt, attractive, not least because bond houses, unlike banks and trust companies, were unregulated. Stairs duly decided early in 1903 to set up a similar bond house in Halifax. No doubt using his political contacts and citing the precedent of the Royal Bank of Canada, which had renamed itself two years earlier, he managed to persuade the authorities to allow him to use the name of Royal Securities Corporation (RSC). The house was duly incorporated on 18 April 1903 under the Nova Scotia Companies Act with a nominal capital of $50,000 and five shareholders: Stairs himself, his brother George, Harris, Cahan and Aitken. Its Memorandum of Association stated that it was to act as 'investors, capitalists, financiers, concessionaires, brokers and agents'.[9] Initially the shareholders subscribed a total of only $10,000, Aitken himself putting up $1,900 for nineteen shares (possibly helped by Stairs as a reward for his role in the Windsor affair). Stairs was president and, since there was no one else to run it, Aitken was given the job of secretary and manager at a salary of $750 for the remainder of 1903, to rise to $1,500 the following year. On 26 May Aitken was able to record in his diary, 'Played golf this afternoon. Organised Royal Securities Co. Ltd today.'[10] For the first time in his life he had real managerial responsibility.

The first task was to organise the sales force. Aitken again used all the contacts he had made as a bond and insurance salesman. He pressured others to develop and expand their own list of clients, and, if necessary, to cut out intermediary brokers. 'Please keep me advised', he wrote to one of his contacts, 'of buyers and sellers in Scotia, and also any information you can get concerning clients of brokers buying and selling, for which … I am indebted to you…'[11] The mailing list soon expanded to some 1,500 names, with salesmen required to fill in a printed form for each individual, listing name, address, business and net worth. In practice, of course, such information was not easy to come by and the form often contained no more than a name. But at least the names were on RSC's record. As it happened, the largest group consisted of merchants of one form or another. It was followed by doctors, then lawyers, then retired ship captains, then bank managers, clergymen, insurance agents and pharmacists. In all, members of these professions made up some two thirds of the list. This is hardly surprising. It was, after all, a business for the relatively affluent.

There was also the back office to put in place, needing recruits who either knew what to do or could learn very quickly. In all this it became clear that Aitken, as well as an inventive mind, also had a talent for management. Although he was only twenty-four, he was not at all shy about giving terse, sometimes abrasive, orders to older employees. He also expected them to work as hard as him. The days of drifting were finished for good.

In its early days, once its basic infrastructure had been set up, RSC concentrated on familiar territory. A further tranche of Trinidad Electric 5 per cent bonds was successfully marketed, as was an issue of Scotia common stock. Aitken was also successful in obtaining a listing for Scotia common stock on the Boston Stock Exchange through the long-established Boston investment bank Hayden, Stone & Co. In fact, it was to be more than just a listing. Aitken suggested that

> the best method of procedure [sic] would be for me to obtain out-side of the market at a price to be agreed upon a certain number of shares of Scotia common and form a pool to be controlled and operated by you on the Boston market, you receiving a percentage of the pool profits.

Not content with that, Aitken went on: 'For purpose of manipulation [sic] it might be necessary for you to operate in Toronto and Montreal also, through agents there, and if so I can give you accurate information as to ... the holdings in those markets.'[12] The offer, disreputable as it appears today, was not one Hayden, Stone was minded to refuse, particularly since it put them in privileged touch with the brokers in Montreal and Toronto whom Aitken had been assiduously cultivating in his campaign to expand RSC's underwriting reach.

The offer to Hayden, Stone was not unique. Aitken was organising other 'pools' as and when he thought desirable. One was to control the market price of Trinidad Electric 5 per cent bonds (not least because Aitken himself held $50,000 nominal value of the bonds which he wished to dispose of). 'You will understand', he wrote to a potential investor,

> that it is our intention to judiciously handle this security ... With

this in view we will endeavour to govern the advances and declines in market quotations ... All the directors of Trinidad Electric Co Ltd ... have agreed not to sell or buy in the market until after the first day of July 1904 when this pool will be dissolved.[13]

Furthermore, Aitken was showing great agility in jobbing in and out of the smaller concerns, coal companies, timber land and pulp mills for whom RSC was raising seed capital.

By such means, fair or foul as they may have been, Aitken could by the end of 1903 with justification claim that RSC had built up a substantial business. The links with provincial clientele had been cemented; and he had established links in central Canada which rivalled those of Dominion Securities. There seemed to be no barriers to RSC's sustained and rapid progress. But barriers there were, and the first was thrown up by the very company which had been at its origin and which provided its life blood. The recession of 1902–04 badly affected demand for steel just when the Scotia board, led by Stairs, had decided to construct a new facility at Sydney Mines, Cape Breton, where there were large deposits of coal and iron ore. At first the financing had gone well, some $4 million being raised in common stock and bonds by the middle of 1902. But the price of Scotia common stock then suffered badly. The Sydney Mines project, on the other hand, could not be stopped or even temporarily mothballed. Graham Fraser, Scotia's general manager, suggested cancelling all dividends for the foreseeable future. Stairs and Aitken rightly saw that this would do unavoidable damage to Scotia's financial standing for years to come, and perhaps even permanently. Fraser's proposal was turned down, whereupon he promptly resigned and leaked his resentment through an anonymous letter to the press.

Fortunately, by the middle of 1904 the financial outlook was healthier, and the Scotia board decided to issue $1.5 million of second mortgage bonds, to be underwritten and placed by a syndicate organised by RSC. In mid-September Stairs and Aitken travelled to Toronto to try to put together a syndicate for the purpose. Aitken, for the first time, was uneasy. Before he left he wrote a long letter to Harris detailing his doubts. His letter concluded:

I do not recommend the value of this deal to the Royal Securities and I do not intend to take the responsibility of saying that it could be carried successfully to completion, but if the Directors decided to go in for it they can depend on hard work and effort on the part of the Secretary.[14]

At the same time he had the temerity to suggest that two more directors be nominated to the RSC board to balance the preponderance of Scotia representatives. Harris and George Stairs were both quick to slap him down. 'Your proposition of nomination', Harris replied by telegram, 'cannot be considered and even its suggestion after agreeing to underwrite without any such condition is calculated to shake everybody's confidence in you. For your own sake withdraw your telegram at once and stick to your agreement.'[15]

It was at that point that the blow fell. Stairs had been unwell for some time. He suffered badly from sciatica, the pain taking its toll on his whole system. By the time he arrived, accompanied by Aitken, at the newly built King Edward Hotel in Toronto he had a bad cold and looked grey and out of sorts. At breakfast on 9 September he had his first heart tremor. His cold had developed into pneumonia. He was immediately admitted to Toronto General Hospital, Aitken staying with him on the journey and thereafter at his bedside. At first it was not thought that his condition was serious, but it soon deteriorated. Nellie and his brother George were sent for. The hospital would not allow Nellie to stay with him overnight. In protest she demanded to be admitted as a patient. But it was all to no avail. Stairs, after the first signs that he would recover, slipped into a coma, his kidneys failed and finally his heart gave out. At 12.45 p.m. on 26 September 1904 he died. 'A man of large enterprises', mourned the *Halifax Herald*,

wide sympathies, varied activities, he was withal, and best of all, genuine, sincere, without an atom of affectation, pride or conceit … The shock of his death has been a terrible blow to his relatives. The deepest sympathy of the community will be extended to his widow and family for the loss of an idolized husband and father.[16]

Certainly, the family were deeply affected by their loss, but there is equally no doubt that Aitken himself was in a state of shock. Later in life he still was able to recall 'the night ... of sorrow, of utter and extreme misery ... A sense of loneliness and futility overcame me.'[17] A sad figure, he returned to Halifax in a private railway carriage with Stairs's body, Nellie and the rest of the family.

Stairs was buried on 29 September. In a letter to his friend W. D. Ross, Aitken wrote that his mentor had been laid to rest 'in Fairview Cemetery on the side of a little hill, where his evening sunsets, which he loved so well, will fall upon his grave'. He added that the remedy for his own personal distress at Stairs's death was to be hard work in order to dispel the melancholia: 'My own usefulness seems to be ended, although it will only be too soon when I will have recovered from this way of thinking and devote myself as strenuously as ever to our business affairs.'[18] His one consolation was the way the Stairs family responded. Nellie invited him to choose the epitaph for Stairs's grave and George Stairs made sure that he walked with the family in the funeral procession to Fort Massey Presbyterian Church.

In truth, it did not take too long for him to snap out of it. Aitken fully realised that without Stairs's protective umbrella he was vulnerable. He was not popular in Halifax. Many of the more traditional businessmen thought him cheeky, believed that success had come too early to him, and now that Stairs was dead he would be shown to be a mere trickster. Aitken's response was simple. First, he became much tougher in his dealings with others. 'In these years', he recalled, 'the "good companion" side of my nature vanished altogether.'[19] Secondly, in his determination to show what he was made of he devoted himself almost obsessively to his work. In the six months following Stairs's death he managed the issue of Scotia bonds, sold a further tranche of Trinidad Electric bonds to bring the company's finances back to health, took control of Demerara Electric, successfully marketed a tranche of the manufacturers Robb-Mumford which had been left with him and Harris as underwriters a year earlier and was sketching out plans for utility investments in Cuba and Puerto Rico. In spite of all this, George Stairs did not agree to his becoming managing director of RSC until March 1905, at a salary of no more than $4,000 per annum. Even then, and seemingly by way of insurance, later in the year three new directors were appointed, including W. D. Ross and Will B. Ross (no relation), the general manager of the Metropolitan Bank of Toronto.

Max Aitken, president of the Royal Securities Corporation (RSC), in 1905, nearly twelve months after the death of John F. Stairs.

This amounted to a clear demonstration that neither George Stairs nor Robert Harris fully accepted Aitken, as John Stairs almost had, as an equal partner for the future. Both thought him too young, inexperienced and full of rash ideas. Harris, in particular, still thought of Aitken as the elder Stairs's secretary and now that he was gone, Aitken's role in Scotia, at least, should certainly not be elevated. Aitken, of course, was aware of this latent antagonism, so much so that in May 1905 he even flirted with the idea of resuming his previous half-hearted attempt at qualifying for the New Brunswick Bar. But this was only a fleeting spasm and, apart from the occasional grouse that he was not being paid enough, his response was to work even harder on the projects that his mentor and patron had left behind him.

This was not altogether easy. The important projects, mostly only half begun, were, first, to arrange a consolidation of banking interests in the Maritime Provinces with the Metropolitan Bank of Toronto to give a foothold in central Canada, in a new holding company called the Alliance Bank of Canada; second, to form a shipbuilding venture based on the acquisition of a shipyard in Halifax; and, third, to bring Scotia's finances into proper order while continuing to satisfy its voracious need for capital. Of these, the ambitious proposal for banking consolidation was the first to turn sour. One of the proposed constituent banks, the People's Bank of Halifax, control of which had been bought by Stairs and Harris in early 1904, turned out to have made a large loan to one of its directors secured on a number of ships which did not exist. In their panic at the prospect of the fraud being discovered and the bank collapsing, the managers sought the help of the general manager of the Bank of Montreal, Edward Clouston. Without telling the majority shareholders (George Stairs, Harris, Aitken and RSC had bought the shares previously held by the Stairs estate), they negotiated the sale of their bank at a price well below the current market price, but which reflected its real residual value.

Needless to say, Aitken, Harris and George Stairs were horrified at the revelations. There was now a double fraud, the first against the bank and the second against the majority shareholders. George Stairs wanted to sue the bank directors and officers immediately. The other two, however, were more cautious. All three took a train to Montreal to see Clouston and try to negotiate a better price. Clouston, when they saw him, would not move. When their meeting broke up in acrimony, Clouston decided to recall Aitken. He pointed out that if they refused his offer, the People's Bank would collapse. They might win a lawsuit for fraud but there would be almost no assets left to seize. The best he could do, he said, was to arrange for them to receive Bank of Montreal shares at a price slightly better than that proposed for the People Bank's other shareholders. Aitken, realising the weakness of his negotiating position, accepted the (somewhat dubious) offer and managed to convince his fellow shareholders that they too should accept. 'Our loss will amount to about $11,000 each,' as Aitken reported to W. D. Ross.[20]

The project was then quietly put to sleep. Aitken had lost money which at the time he could ill afford. His only compensation was that he had been spotted by Clouston. The reward came when Clouston invited him to take management control of yet another Caribbean utility company in difficulty, the Demerara Electric Company, in what was then British Guiana. The invitation was an act of confidence in the 26-year-old to take on the management of a complex utility in the way he had taken on the management control of Trinidad Electric. Aitken's acceptance was a matter of course.

Shipbuilding was a different problem. The British firm of Swan Hunter had agreed to invest in Stairs's idea. That was all to the good. The support of a well-established British shipbuilder was essential to the project. The Shipbuilding Investment Company was formed, and a search made for a suitable shipyard to buy. None came on the market. There were consequently no contracts to build any ships. Aitken was able to put that project quietly to sleep as well.

Much more difficult was the Scotia financing. By early 1905 Aitken was worried that 'the company is not in good shape and the Sydney Mines works must be finished before the earnings will improve'.[21] Part of the problem was the continuing wrangle over who should take over the presidency of the company. The vice-president, Senator James D. McGregor, thought that he was entitled to succeed, but Aitken, Harris and Cahan all had doubts about his ability. Aitken promised his support to Harris in return for a place on the Scotia board. Harris was duly appointed but failed to make Aitken a director. 'It was a bitter setback and a real betrayal,' Aitken wrote later.[22] In return, Aitken claims to have interposed himself between the issuer and the underwriting syndicate which he and Stairs had been putting together in Toronto at the time of Stairs's death, borrowed up to his personal maximum and bought the whole issue in his own name. The bonds were then marketed by the syndicate to investors in eastern Canada and Toronto. 'My profit', he recalled, 'amounted to short of $200,000.'[23] Not content with that, Aitken founded the Commercial Trust Company of Halifax to handle all RSC's trust business, in spite of the competing presence of the Eastern Trust, which Stairs had founded and of which Harris was president.

If Aitken worked hard, he also played hard. He drank too much, smoked too many cigars and spent too many evenings playing poker.

But there was another side. Almost by way of precaution, he was building a cottage for himself on the other side from Halifax of the inlet from the sea known as the Arm. At first, it was intended to be a place for relaxation, with a launch, a dingy and a canoe. In fact, it came not a moment too soon. 1904 and 1905 had placed a severe strain on his health. The asthma attacks were more frequent and were accompanied by worrying palpitations. They had got to the point where he needed some serious medical attention.

On his return from Montreal in mid-June 1905 he wrote to a friend in Newcastle inviting him to come and stay since 'I ... spent some days in Dr Finlay's disecting [sic] room. As a result, I have given up smoking and do not drink any stimulants, even such mild drinks as coffee and tea ... I have given up sleeping at night also.'[24] In short, Dr Finlay had put him on a course of detoxification and he was suffering consequent withdrawal symptoms. In the event, however, the treatment did not go entirely according to plan. Aitken found life in his cottage lonely, particularly on days when he did not feel well. By the end of July, however, he was feeling much better and was even planning a house party. Yet business was business. It was not long before he broke his agreement with Dr Finlay and returned to his office. True, he still had some bad days, but by the autumn he claimed to be much better.

Nevertheless, the whole experience had left its mark. From then on, he became much more conscious of the fragility of his health, even from time to time to the point of something close to hypochondria. Mindful of the risks and of the feelings of isolation at his cottage on the Arm, it was in the late autumn of 1905 that he decided to get married. The decision made, it was then a question of finding an appropriate candidate for the role of his wife. His eye then fixed on Gladys Henderson Drury. It was time not just for marriage but for a step up the social ladder.

Lieutenant-Colonel Charles William Drury, Gladys's father, ranked high in Halifax society. His military career had been, and continued to be, of the highest distinction. Commissioned in 1874, he had had an active career, culminating in distinction at the battle of Magersfontein in 1899 during the Second Boer War. He was mentioned in

Despatches and became a Commander of the Order of the Bath. On his return to Canada he was appointed military commander of the Maritime Provinces region. He was then further promoted to be the first Canadian to command the Halifax garrison when the British left. It was the largest military installation in Canada and as its commander Drury was entitled to live, with his wife and three charming daughters, in one of the grandest houses in Halifax. But Drury's problem was that he had very little money and could not afford either the upkeep of the house or the lifestyle demanded of his rank and position. He moved into the Halifax Hotel. Aitken soon took to dining there and spending the evening with Drury's daughter Gladys, admiring no doubt her long auburn hair and green Irish eyes.

Gladys Henderson Drury in Halifax, Nova Scotia, c. 1900–06.

Socially, the Drury family were a notch, and perhaps more than a notch, above the son of a Presbyterian minister. There was, however, a large and unpleasant skeleton in the Drury cupboard. Colonel Drury's father, Ward, had lived with his brothers in the family farm, near St John in New Brunswick, which he had inherited ahead of his elder brother John. John was apparently consumed with resentment, which turned to rage one night in 1880. Obviously inflamed by drink,

John drew a gun and fired at Ward. But he was clearly not in a state to shoot accurately and the bullet missed. John then went up to his room, trashed it and set fire to it. The third brother, Edward, rushed upstairs to put the flames out. John, still furious, turned his gun on Edward and shot him dead. Immediately, and in clear desperation, John committed suicide.

'The Drury Tragedy', as it was called, was widely reported in the *St John Globe*, but Ward seems to have survived the incident without harm. Indeed, five years later he was still alive and well enough to welcome the birth of his granddaughter Gladys. In Halifax, of course, it was a story people continued to whisper about. But Aitken was obviously unworried. He was fixed on the idea that marriage with one of the Drury daughters, whatever the murky family background, would give him a social standing that would be beneficial to his business. For his part, of course, Colonel Drury was aware that Aitken had already, at the age of twenty-six, accumulated a substantial fortune and looked set fair to accumulate much more. A marriage to Gladys would be most convenient.

The Garrison Chapel, Halifax, Nova Scotia, venue for the marriage of Max Aitken and Gladys Henderson Drury – seen here with a parade and memorial service for Queen Victoria, 1901. General Charles Drury (father of Gladys) had taken over the command of the Halifax Garrison from the British.

When it came to it, the wedding took place in an atmosphere of some confusion. Aitken was too busy tidying up his affairs to pay much attention to the arrangements. Social events were missed as well, which even the good-tempered Gladys found trying. On 23 January, for instance, he noted in his diary that 'Walter Black gave a dance tonight. Gladys went. I didn't. Gladys and everybody else offended.'[25] Nor was he showing much aptitude in recruiting ushers. On 19 January he wired an architect friend of his in Montreal, Sam Finley, inviting him to act as usher without giving him the date. 'I will be on deck to see you through all right,' Finley wrote back, 'but for Heaven's sake let us know the day if you know it yourself! But I would not be in the least surprised if you didn't definitely decide till about an hour before!!'[26] Finally, on 29 January 1906, the deed was done, in the chapel of the Halifax Garrison. Aitken's mother and his brother Traven were present, along with forty-three other guests. Aitken himself worked in his office until 4 p.m. His diary entry does not portray a besotted groom: 'Will be married at 6 and a half at the Garrison Church. Leaving tonight at nine o'clock. Won't write any more.'[27] But, as a last wistful afterthought, he wrote, 'I hope the experiment will be successful … Years will tell.'

CHAPTER 4

HALFWAY THERE

'My wife had a lively interest in me'[1]

The newly wed Mrs Maxwell Aitken may have been rather surprised to learn that the first days of her honeymoon were to be taken up with a visit by her husband to the office of the Royal Securities Corporation in St John. She may have been even more surprised to find out that the main part of her honeymoon in the romantic island of Cuba was to be spent not on the white sandy beaches of the Caribbean but on expeditions to explore business opportunities. Surprise or not, it was, whatever she might have imagined on plighting her troth, no more than the first signpost on what turned out to be the rocky road of her marriage.

Aitken himself, of course, carried on as before. His visit had in fact been scheduled before the date of his wedding had been finally decided. Whatever the circumstances of his marriage and the froth that surrounded it, there were in his mind certain imperatives to be respected: the welfare of his parents, his siblings, his mentors and his new wife. Nevertheless, overriding all these, at this stage in his life the matter of making money was in place at the top of the list.

It was this that had taken him, with his new bride in tow, to St John on 30 January 1906. To realise his financial ambitions it was essential, at least as a first step, to make sure that his chosen vehicle for the purpose was properly organised. In fact, since John Stairs's death in 1904 Aitken had been building a supporting team in RSC to his liking, and, even at his young age, in doing so he had shown a rare ability both in picking future talent as his subordinates and then, having picked them, in motivating them by a suitable mixture of bribing and bullying.

His first important addition to RSC's staff had been a 21-year-old teller in the Union Bank of Halifax, Izaak Walton Killam. Killam's job was to assist in opening a branch office in St John and to use his talent as a salesman to expand the range of RSC's clientele in southern New Brunswick. Then there was the task, towards the end of 1905, of opening a branch office in Montreal. Aitken's first choice for this assignment was another contemporary, Gerald Farrell, already on the staff of RSC in Halifax. Farrell came from a respected, and affluent, Irish Catholic family and seemed at first sight to be the ideal candidate. It soon turned out, however, that Farrell was rather too fond of what Aitken considered to be an overactive social life. It would obviously be wrong to let him loose in Montreal. On interview, he was told abruptly that he would be staying on the Halifax staff in overall charge of sales.

Aitken then looked elsewhere. Another contemporary caught his eye, Arthur Nesbitt, a travelling salesman for a wholesale business in St John. 'At two o'clock in the morning', Aitken wrote later, '[in the Halifax Hotel] … the notion of engaging him for the Royal Securities Corporation occurred to me.'[2] Since Nesbitt was staying in the same hotel, Aitken immediately sent him a message asking him to come without delay. Nesbitt replied that he was in bed and that he wanted to stay there. Aitken insisted. Nesbitt finally agreed. They talked about the wholesale business and other subjects and 'when he was exhausted I asked "how much are you getting?". He said "$2,100". I said: "I will give you $1,800 if you will go to Montreal and open up there a branch of the Royal Securities Corporation".'[3] In other words, Aitken was offering a share in profits as a trade for reduced salary. Nesbitt took a weekend to decide, agreed to Aitken's proposal and in December 1905 the Montreal office was opened. Two other appointments completed Aitken's support team: Blake Burrill as secretary, Aitken's old job, running the office in Halifax, and Horace Porter as manager of the St John office.

All this seemed to have gone well. But Aitken was, as always, without any sentimentality in the supervision of the staff he employed. The reason for his visit to St John on the day after his wedding was news that Killam was not performing as he should. Farrell, as manager of sales, had reported that Killam had become addicted to playing bridge well into the night, arriving late for work and spending too much time sitting around in the office. He needed, according to Farrell, 'a good blowing up, one like I get from your Royal Highness occasionally'.[4] It was this 'good blowing up' that Aitken went to St John to deliver. He told Killam that once his contract for the year expired his salary was to be halved but he would be given a share of RSC's profits. It was up to him. 'A change came over him the next day. The bridge table was forsaken; the club life was forgotten.'[5]

A political meeting with J. C. Buckley (Max Aitken's Conservative Party agent in Ashton-under-Lyne), R. B. Bennett (who became Canadian Prime Minister in 1930), Max Aitken and Izaak Walton Killam (financier, who succeeded Aitken as head of the Royal Securities Corporation), c. 1913.

The first days of the honeymoon completed, without, apparently, much involvement of the bride, the couple moved on. The next stop was Boston, where Aitken and Gladys went shopping, an evening cloak costing, as Gladys rather acidly pointed out, some nine times more than her wedding ring. From there they sailed to Cuba, arriving at Havana on 13 February. Once there, Aitken sent for the chief engineer of Trinidad Electric, Fred Teele, who was at the time in British Guiana sorting out the affairs of Demerara Electric. Immediately abandoning his current task as soon as summoned, Teele joined the honeymoon couple at Matanzas, a port about 100 kilometres east of Havana. Following the information they had from the Royal Bank of Canada branches on the island, the two men studied a project for a tramway and accompanying electricity generating plant at Matanzas itself. At first, it looked promising, but it soon turned out that a competitor already held the franchise and would not sell at a price which Aitken was prepared to pay.

The honeymoon caravan, now swollen to three principals and an accompanying lawyer, then made the long journey of some 800 kilometres to the south-eastern corner of the island and its second city, Santiago de Cuba. Another tramway route was studied and deemed promising. Heads of agreement were signed with the local authority for RSC to buy the franchise and promote the venture in Canada. That done, the party took the train back to Havana with a view to returning immediately to Halifax to start preparations for the Santiago flotation. Teele, in the meantime, was to travel to Georgetown, British Guiana, to finish his work on the Demerara Electric with a view to taking managerial control of the Santiago project. En route, they stopped at Camagüey, then a small town about halfway along on the Santiago–Havana railway line in the middle of the island. Intrigued, Aitken and Teele got out of the train and stayed to have a quick look at a small electricity generating system which served the town. They noted that it was well maintained and that the owner wanted to sell. It was certainly something to look at if the Santiago project did not materialise.

Back in Halifax in early March 1906, Aitken heard that the Santiago principals had indeed reneged on their agreement and were now demanding that they retain a controlling interest in whatever company was to be set up. He hurried back to Cuba, taking with him a lawyer from Harris, Cahan and Henry. By the end of April, Aitken had concluded that he was negotiating with an unreliable and, in his view, distinctly shifty group of people. He withdrew and accordingly wrote to Teele that he was giving up on the project. Things went no better at Matanzas. Not only was the franchise too expensive but it turned out that Aitken would have to buy an old and inefficient generating plant as well. This he refused to do. But the owner had insisted and had enough political influence in the community to force the sale. Aitken had no option but to withdraw. The next opportunity was at Camagüey. Here he had better luck. The owner of the generating plant (which Aitken was willing to buy) was so keen to sell that he offered to include some land he owned. Since the franchise to build a tramway was available from the local authority, Aitken quickly decided on an immediate purchase. Seeking confirmation for his decision, he cabled Teele in Georgetown. Teele replied, 'I really think it is a bit unfair on your part to ask me to express an opinion regarding Camaguey without my having the slightest idea as to what the output of the present plant was, the number of lights it supplies, its present capitalization etc...'[6]

Undaunted, Aitken went ahead. By early June, following his usual formula, he had assembled his syndicate of Halifax supporters to act in their personal capacity as promoters alongside RSC and had signed up the Union Bank of Halifax to take the sub-underwriting. The RSC sales force then went out and sold the bonds of the newly formed Camaguey Electric Company. The issue was successful enough for the purpose, although not fully subscribed. At least the project could go ahead as planned, and Aitken could feel satisfied with his share of the profits from RSC's underwriting and sales commissions, with his ability to deal with insider information in the securities allocated to him as promoter and remain as part owner of what turned out to be a successful company. All in all, it was a satisfactory arrangement.

That done, and with his personal finances more than reasonably secure, Aitken decided that RSC's business was becoming too extensive to be run out of Halifax. He needed to have an established presence in central Canada. Nesbitt had set up the branch office in Montreal. Aitken now decided that he himself should back that up by setting up residence there. Gladys was given notice that they would take a flat in the centre of Montreal near the new RSC office. 'Halifax', she was told, 'was [to be] a memory of the past. There would be no return except as a visitor.'[7]

Almost immediately, things started to go wrong. On 11 June, Aitken wrote to W. D. Ross that he was 'suffering from severe attacks of intestinal trouble. I have dropped in weight to 122 pounds and if I can possibly get away from my business in the near future I expect to take a good long holiday.'[8] Doctors were summoned but could not arrive at a clear diagnosis or a recommendation for treatment. Moreover, whatever the state of his intestines, Aitken was not deterred from pursuing another, and greater, Caribbean venture. The target was another prosperous island, recently acquired by the United States under the terms of the Treaty of Paris in 1898, and given an anglicised name, Porto Rico.

Puerto Rico (it would eventually recover its Spanish title in 1932), along with the Philippines, Cuba and the island of Guam, had been among the spoils of victory gathered up by America following the successful conclusion of their war with Spain. Uncertain how to manage its new colony, the United States had passed the Foraker Act in 1900 to set up an American-dominated civilian government and to give the island its new name. Legislation from that government in turn ensured that American companies were given privileged access to the island's business.

There was a stampede. Everybody in American business seemed to want a piece of what was potentially some very profitable action. Among those was the New York engineering firm of J. G. White & Co. Even before the Treaty of Paris was signed J. G. White had bought not just a steam railway in the capital San Juan but soon after a generating plant, a tramway and two franchises, one to build a hydroelectric plant and the other to build a steam railway leading out of the capital.

Aitken already had contacts with the company through purchases of equipment but it came as something of a surprise when in March 1906 he had been asked whether he would be interested in buying all White's Puerto Rico assets in one package. With the Camaguey bond issue safely under way, Aitken went to New York for preliminary discussions. He liked what he saw. Yet it was not just a question of the White assets. It turned out that the hydroelectric plant at Comerío Falls, in the uplands which formed the spine of the island, could be expanded to provide enough electricity to power all the trams, the railway and the whole of the San Juan lighting system. Enthusiasm ran high when Aitken, W. D. Ross, the Toronto stockbroker A. E. Ames, and Teele visited the island to inspect the properties. By the end of July, the deal was done and the promoting vehicle, the Porto Rico Railways Company, set up. RSC and its Halifax backers were joined by J. G. White in person and A. E. Ames as promoters. It was by some distance the largest operation that RSC had undertaken so far.

For a moment it seemed as though Aitken had discovered a new El Dorado. But on 14 September 1906 he complained of stomach pains. The following day a doctor was summoned to his Montreal apartment. The diagnosis was firm: acute inflammation of the appendix. He was immediately admitted to the Royal Victoria Hospital in Montreal and prepared for what in those days was a very dangerous operation. This took place and was successfully accomplished (although Aitken continued to complain about the size of the fee charged by the surgeon). Gladys, according to Aitken's later account, 'watched over me devotedly'.[9]

Though her attentiveness was undoubtedly genuine, she was not really given a choice. Her husband, as might be imagined, was a far from ideal patient. Only a few days after emerging from the anaesthetic he was firing off cables and letters demanding to know what was going on in his now widespread network of businesses. In the letters he received in return there were expressions of genuine sympathy for him in his illness but also some veiled comment (and some not so veiled) that it served him right. James Harding, for instance, one of the senior RSC salesmen in St John, who had been sent to London in an effort to interest British brokers in the issue of Porto Rico Railway bonds, mixed reporting disappointing results with a terse comment that 'I have been thinking for some months that you were burning the candle at both ends, and the result generally is trouble in the middle, and that is evidently where it has hit you hard'.[10] Gerald Farrell was even less tactful. 'Although it seems unkind to say so,' he wrote on 6 October,

> I was very glad that you had this attack of appendicitis as you certainly were not well and the fact of your having an operation would give the doctors a chance to discover what was the matter, and probably would frighten you sufficiently to make you live a little more regular life than you have done in the past...[11]

It was all to no avail. Aitken had already written a furious letter to Blake Burrill in Halifax saying that he had

> not yet received a letter from you advising me of the progress at the office. I sincerely urge you to undertake this work ... It will enable you in writing these letters to review the office work of the day and give you a better grasp of the organization and control of the office, which I am most desirous you should undertake.[12]

He was expecting to be out of bed by 12 October and to be discharged soon thereafter. His doctors, however, had other ideas for his convalescence and on that day he was writing mournfully to George Stairs (still addressing him as 'Mr Stairs' and eliciting a reply starting 'Dear Aitken') that 'I expect to go away for six months: I do not know where I shall go, but some place where there are not any trains'.[13]

It took almost the whole of the autumn of 1906 for him to recover fully. Once out of hospital he travelled to New York to complete the Porto Rico transaction by signing the final contracts. While there he had another setback as he began to suffer severe abdominal pains. He was convinced that they related to his previous appendicitis. There were more consultations. Neither of the two doctors involved, Dr St John Ross and Dr Edward Quintard, could find any symptoms which supported the patient's theory. Two more doctors were duly summoned, Drs Saunders and Halsey, and the four of them, in something of a huddle, arrived at a diagnosis. In a letter to his own doctor in Halifax, a Dr Curry, Aitken described how they had concluded he was suffering from 'gastritis of the stomach and intestines, with some special condition of the intestines which I have forgotten but which consisted of a disposition to adhesions'.[14]

All four doctors recommended complete rest. The patient was duly admitted on 23 October to Quintard's private hospital in Katonah, a small town in Westchester County at the southern end of New York state. He was to remain in bed for four weeks while Dr Quintard treated him. (Treatment apparently involved liberal and unpleasant use of a stomach pump.) Furthermore, he was not allowed to conduct any business. To make matters worse, Gladys, who had previously been treated by Dr Curry for an unspecified ailment, suffered a relapse aggravated by the stress of her husband's operation and subsequent serious illness which was sufficient for Dr Quintard to insist that she should also enter his care for an extended period.

By mid-November 1906, Aitken was feeling better. He wrote to W. D. Ross on 22 November that he found 'the present enforced idleness ... very hard' although his 'very exacting doctor allows me to go downtown for a little while occasionally and the rest of the day I spend in walking and reading'. He did not expect to be out 'of the clutches of my doctor until 15 December at the very earliest. Unfortunately for me he has obtained some hypnotic influence over my wife and, when I determine to go home he gets at me through her and upsets my plans.'[15]

Aitken managed finally to manoeuvre himself and Gladys out of Dr Quintard's care by arranging a suitable transfer to Halifax for treatment by Dr Curry. Nevertheless, he agreed to report regularly to Dr Quintard, particularly on the continued use of the stomach pump, and to return to New York for a review of his progress. As 1906 gave way to 1907 he was putting a brave face on it. 'I go out every day at three o'clock and ride for an hour and a half. I do not come to my office until eleven in the morning and I am on the whole a wonderfully behaved person.'[16]

Wonderfully behaved or not, it was not until the early spring of 1907 that Aitken felt that he really was on the mend. He had spent some time during the winter at Hot Springs, Virginia, and, although he found the place boring beyond measure, to the point where he swore that he would never go there again, the warmer weather seems to have done him good. Moreover, the enforced idleness of which he so vehemently complained had the advantage of allowing him to think about his businesses in a way that was all but impossible when he was dealing with day-to-day problems.

As a result of this process, he had come to two main conclusions. The first was that he should gradually break his relations with George Stairs, Robert Harris and the Scotia Group. The reason was clear in his mind: he wanted to move beyond the limited financial world of Halifax. Furthermore, he felt unappreciated. The previous June he had complained to W. D. Ross that Harris had refused to raise his salary unless he stayed in Halifax and devoted his whole time to RSC. That was out of the question if he was to continue to operate for his personal account alongside RSC, which was the only way to make what he regarded as his true reward. Although their correspondence continued to be courteous (it was still 'Mr Stairs' and 'Mr Harris' while he remained 'Aitken' to them), there were all the signs of under-lying tension.

The second conclusion was that the collection of businesses within the RSC family had been founded or acquired on a seemingly hap-hazard basis, taking advantage of opportunities as they arose. This was particularly true of the portfolio of Caribbean utilities. In addition, their ultimate management lay in Canada, a long way from their op-erational centre. That was not good enough. The disparate businesses had to be brought together in some form of central organisation. Aitken's solution to this was innovative, unusual and cunning. At the RSC annual general meeting in March 1907 he proposed that their engineering department be spun out into a separate company. The new company would not only give engineering advice but would also be the vehicle for central purchasing. Although he did not spell it out with precision, his intention was to add a management account-ing capability to set up proper systems in affiliated businesses. With these three functions in place the new company would in practice be the management centre for the whole empire. Aitken was moving the business beyond that of a traditional investment bank to follow what had already become an established model in the United States, in essence a modern conglomerate.

At first, the project was resisted by Stairs and Harris, suspecting, rightly, that Aitken's true motive was to take RSC away from its Hal-ifax base and the close ties with the Scotia Group. A compromise was reached, that the new company should be a subsidiary of RSC, and on that basis the project was agreed. On 1 March 1907 the Montreal Engineering Company was born, to 'take over the duties of RSC's Engineering Department'.[17] Apart from RSC, the shareholders were Aitken and his brother Traven, Killam, Nesbitt, Carl Giles from the Camaguey Company and Fred Clarke from the Trinidad Electric

Company. It was a formidable team, but there was no doubt about who had the commanding voice.

Not content with that, Aitken had already started to manoeuvre in a different direction. He had already set up the Commercial Trust Company of Halifax. He had stolen an important client from Harris's Eastern Trust as well as finding other clients who had not yet farmed out their trustee and registry roles to an independent trust company. Once he was satisfied that Commercial Trust was operating profitably, he aimed higher. On 15 February he had received a letter from Richard Wilson-Smith, the president of the distinguished but increasingly lacklustre Montreal Trust Company, suggesting that Commercial Trust might act as Montreal Trust's agent in Halifax. Aitken saw his opportunity. He wrote a long reply to Wilson-Smith explaining that Commercial Trust had decided to open an office in Montreal to service companies listed and traded on the Montreal Stock Exchange, since trust company law required a presence in the province for permission to be granted to do so. Aitken also added that they would be starting a real estate department for which he depended on Wilson-Smith for 'assistance and support'.[18]

It was all a ruse. What Aitken was really after was a merger of the two companies, with himself emerging as controlling shareholder and chief executive. Since Montreal Trust had ten times the capital of Commercial Trust, Wilson-Smith thought the whole idea ridiculous. Aitken's response was to resort to bribery. He had by then assembled a syndicate of mainly Halifax investors led by W. B. Ross and including George Stairs, Charles Cahan and Almon Lovett, the lawyer who had helped Aitken over the Caribbean utility investments (of course excluding Harris). He offered Wilson-Smith a place in the syndicate and the guarantee of an immediate capital gain of $5,000 when the merger was completed.

Wilson-Smith took the bait and, suddenly convinced of the merits of the merger, set about persuading his fellow directors. Aitken added some practical help by offering selling shareholders a premium of 10 per cent over the current Montreal price. Montreal's directors voted immediately to proceed. But now that he was in control of events Aitken started to lay out his conditions. Wilson-Smith would stay as president for one year; the present general manager would be dismissed before the merger was consummated; he, Aitken, would become vice-president and chief executive officer with 'absolute jurisdiction over the staff';[19] W. B. Ross would also be vice-president; Cahan would be a director; Lovett would be corporate counsel.

There were, however, assurances given to satisfy both the law and Montreal pride. The Aitkens already planned to become fully resident in Montreal; the other three would now likewise, as soon as was convenient, move there from Halifax. 'Montreal Gains Three Good Halifax Men', mourned the *Halifax Herald* at the news.[20] By contrast, however, Aitken could be content that his move was warmly welcomed by, among others, Edward Clouston. There were other pluses too. Aitken had come out with a profit of $22,500 and, by clever manipulation of the share price during the negotiations, had met his guarantee to Wilson-Smith.

At the age of twenty-eight Aitken was outplaying almost all the others in the corporate game. He was also freeing himself from the constraints of his erstwhile patrons in Halifax. 'I see', wrote George Stairs in May 1907, 'that you are centering everything in Montreal, so that after a while Halifax will be but a branch office.'[21] That was certainly Aitken's intention. It was also his own, very personal, decision. As a matter of fact, however unsurprising, there is no record of consultation with Gladys on the final and decisive move to Montreal, even though her family and the majority of her friends would be left behind in Halifax.

Although Aitken said that he found life in Montreal very much more stimulating than life in Halifax, he was referring to business rather than social life. Montreal society was stuffy and excluding. Gladys, even though her health had recovered, had little to do, at least until the autumn of 1907. It was then that, for the first time, she became pregnant.

The timing could hardly have been worse. In fact, Aitken showed none of the enthusiasm normal for first-time fathers. Nor, for that matter, did he show much patience with his brothers and sisters, who were asking for financial help. He simply turned family matters over to his secretary to deal with, which she did with admirable tact and efficiency. In June, for instance, Traven had asked for assistance. 'Your favor of the 8th June addressed to Mr Aitken has been received at this office', Miss de Gruchy replied, 'and I am taking the liberty of replying to same as I am at present attending to all matters of this nature for him.' The excuse was that 'Mr Aitken is not in the best of health and as I understand it [he] anticipates leaving Halifax about the first of July for an indefinite period in order to recover his health'.[22]

None of this was true. Aitken was by then in reasonable health and in Montreal. The truth was that he was already absorbed in dealing with what he, and many others, saw as an impending crisis. 1907 was about to see the worst financial panic of the new century. In fact, the financial world had recognised the likelihood of an impending crisis but very few individuals were as skilled as Aitken in preparing for it. As far back as March the US stock market had shown sharp falls. In May, the Halifax branch of the Bank of Montreal called in its loan to RSC. The signs became rapidly more worrying. Aitken realised that he would have to quickly liquidate RSC's substantial portfolio, which was largely financed with short-term borrowing. Cash would be at a premium. He immediately went into defensive action: he cut the price of utility bonds, bullied his salesmen even more fiercely, sent Nesbitt to London to try to offload stock onto British investors, demanded payment from the remaining Camaguey underwriters and threatened to stop construction in Cuba if they did not pay up. In the meantime, Montreal Trust would fill the cash hole in RSC when the short-term debt could no longer be rolled over at a reasonable price.

The climax came on 18 October with a run on the Knickerbocker Trust Company of New York. The panic spread to other New York trusts and banks. One of Aitken's New York lawyers, Kingsbury Curtis, wired Aitken to tell him to take an overnight train to the city since the run was threatening the Trust Company of America, where Montreal Trust had a sizeable deposit of monies destined for the Puerto Rico project. Aitken took his advice and arrived to find that the Knickerbocker Trust had closed its doors and that its president, Charles T. Barney, had shot himself in his New York home. Queues were forming outside the Trust Company of America's head office. There was not much that Aitken could do other than look on with horror. As a gesture, after securing financial support from another trust, albeit at a punitive rate, he wrote to the Trust Company of America's president to say that Montreal Trust would not be making a withdrawal until the situation had stabilised. But it was no more than a gesture. As a spectator, in fact, he witnessed at first hand the intervention of the commanding figure of J. Pierpont Morgan running up and down the lines of despairing depositors trumpeting, 'Don't sell the United States short.' Morgan, legend has it, duly saved the day.[23] The crisis passed. But it had a profound effect on Aitken. The sight of queues forming in the streets in panic about their savings convinced him that the risks of deposit-taking were too great. 'No more inside the bank. It was more comfortable to be in the queue, not behind the grille.'[24]

*Investors storming Wall Street, New York, in 1907. The bankruptcy
of one of the largest banks in New York, the Knickerbocker Trust Company, and the
awkward disposition of the Trust Company of America triggered a severe financial crisis.
To the right is the Federal Hall with the George Washington Monument.*

The first step along the new path was the reorganisation of RSC. Aitken not only argued that RSC's bank accounts should in future be managed out of Montreal; he further proposed the establishment of an executive committee which would include George Stairs but exclude Harris. Stairs urged caution, provoking an outburst from Aitken. 'I suppose that Mr Harris is opposed to this plan,' he wrote on 31 October. 'Mr Harris sees out of a very small window: viz. the Eastern Trust Company. We did more business with the Commercial Trust than the Eastern could do...'[25] Not content with that, he proposed a further share exchange between the Montreal Trust and RSC to strengthen the relationship (and further isolate Harris).

At an otherwise inconclusive meeting in Halifax in November, Aitken made another move. RSC, he argued, should be wound up. It was the only way to resolve obvious differences between himself and the older, more cautious, Haligonians. Stairs and Harris agreed with his argument but insisted that RSC's assets should first be liquidated, and the proceeds distributed to the shareholders. Aitken then sold the portfolio that had remained in RSC, after a $50,000 write-off due to the October crisis, to its RSC sales manager Gerald Farrell. By early 1908 Farrell had agreed to buy the RSC name as well. As Aitken wrote to Stairs towards the end of January:

> I am delighted at the prospect of liquidating, and while the price we have accepted is entirely too low, still the purposes for which the Corporation was organised have now really disappeared. My only regret is that the association which I have had with you as President will be terminated.[26]

There was no mention of regret about Harris. In fact, Aitken was still pursuing him to pay up in full his share of the Puerto Rico underwriting. The sale of RSC to Farrell was completed at the end of March 1908. Battered by all the ill-tempered disputes and already suffering from a weak heart, on 1 April George Stairs died suddenly of cardiac arrest. Aitken, who had been so badly shaken by the death of John Stairs in 1904, hardly paused to pay his respects to the younger brother, other than to note that his death had severed another important link with Halifax. There was another, more serious, crisis to be dealt with. The sale of RSC had left a gap in Aitken's underwriting armoury. To fill it, he created the Utilities Securities Company, which was to function as a supplier of seed capital for utilities in the West Indies and Latin America, and ensured that he held the controlling interest. Parallel to that he formed, again with himself as the majority share-holder, the Bond and Share Company, which was to act as promoter and underwriter (but not distributor) of mainly domestic securities. But these companies were only in their infancy when it became evi-dent that Farrell was proving himself incapable of managing RSC. In the summer of 1908 it became clear to Aitken that he should prepare to buy RSC back. The new companies would have to wait.

The timing was complicated by the arrival of the Aitkens' first child on 9 July. Gladys had decided that she wanted the baby to be born in the cottage on the Arm at Halifax which Aitken had built for himself a few years earlier. 'My wife insisted on this out-of-the-way place for the birth of her baby,' Aitken unpaternally wrote later. 'It is difficult to explain why she was allowed her own way...'[27] He had a point. The building was small and uncomfortable and its remote setting, combined with the frequent summer thunderstorms which made nav-igation treacherous, meant that Dr Curry failed to make the crossing from Halifax in time to assist in the labour. Fortunately, the Aitkens had brought with them the couple who looked after them in Montre-al. The wife was able to manage the birth without incident and Gladys was successfully delivered of a daughter, whom they named Janet.

Mother and daughter were then left in the cottage to convalesce while Aitken returned to Montreal. On his arrival, he discovered that Farrell was nearly bankrupt and that RSC was in disarray. Aitken was able to convince the Montreal Trust directors and shareholders that a rescue of the company would turn out to be profitable; with their agreement he paid off Farrell's debts and bought the corporation back, with 75 per cent parked in Montreal Trust and 25 per cent in his own account. Now that he controlled RSC through both his holding in the trust and by his direct share, Aitken was able to move RSC in whatever direction he chose without any interference from Halifax. He invited Clouston (by then Sir Edward), Cahan and Lovett to take up shares and sit on the board. RSC then took over Aitken's holding in the Utilities Securities Company, which in turn bought a controlling interest in the Bond and Share Company. By that sleight of hand Aitken had manoeuvred himself into overall control of the whole group. Outside shareholders were left with no option but to follow or sell to him.

The interior of Edward Clouston's office at the Bank of Montreal, 1886.

In early September, Gladys had arrived back in Montreal with their baby daughter, but there was little opportunity to settle down into a domestic family routine. Later that month Aitken decided that it was time to go to London to test the market there for high-quality Canadian investments. He expected Gladys to accompany him. It seems, yet again, that she was not given a choice. On their arrival in London, Aitken did the usual round of brokers while Gladys had her first taste of English social life. Before leaving Canada, Aitken had arranged to meet the City financier and politician Ion Hamilton Benn. That introduction led in turn to his first meeting with a fellow New Brunswicker, Andrew Bonar Law. At first sight the two had much in common, although Bonar Law was the older by some twenty years. Also the son of a Presbyterian minister (but Free Church), Bonar Law had left Canada as a young child following the death of his mother and his father's remarriage, accompanying his aunt, Janet Kidston, to Scotland in order to enter its education system with the aim of bettering his start in life. He attended Glasgow High School, leaving at sixteen to join the family merchant bank of Kidston and Sons. When that was sold, he bought a partnership in the Glasgow firm of iron merchants William Jack & Co. By the turn of the century he had made enough money to be able to turn his attention to a career in Conservative politics. He won the seat of Glasgow Blackfriars and Hutchesontown at the 1900 general election and moved quickly up the parliamentary ranks to become a minister at the Board of Trade in 1902. His rise was only momentarily hampered by the loss of his seat in the Liberal election landslide of 1906; his growing promise and popularity led to him being invited to contest the safe Unionist constituency of Dulwich, where he was comfortably returned at a by-election three months later.

They may have had a common background in New Brunswick, but their respective characters could hardly have been less alike. Bonar Law was personally shy, liked playing chess by way of relaxation and took no obvious pleasure in the social life of London clubs. Aitken, on the other hand, was ebullient, impulsive, full of enthusiasm and, above all, enjoying the business of making money and relishing the power it gave him. As a result, their first meeting, according to Aitken in later life, did not go well. 'Bonar Law was not interested in me,' he wrote. In return, Aitken did not think much of Bonar Law. 'His head was too small, his conversation too narrow and his interest in Canada too obviously negligible.'[28] Yet Bonar Law was still prepared to put up $5,000 to buy the bonds Aitken was trying to peddle. Aitken in turn thought that this gesture was made only to get rid of him, but $5,000 was a generous amount of money and Bonar Law, when it came to money, was no fool.

Aitken and Gladys sailed back to Canada in time for Christmas. On his return he had to address the problems he had left behind in the summer. Burrill had felt very much excluded when the head office of RSC had been moved to Montreal, so much so that he had resigned to set up his own firm. Nesbitt had been the next to go. He had been dealing on his own account with RSC funds. This had led to an acrimonious correspondence: 'You evidently are not satisfied with the way I am carrying on the business,' Nesbitt had written tersely.[29] 'You are not giving as great efforts to your business today as you were two years ago,' Aitken had then replied with heightened asperity.[30] Finally, Nesbitt had walked out to start his own firm. Killam, too, although his skin was thicker than Burrill's or Nesbitt's, had got tired of Aitken's bullying. Alarmed, Aitken did his best to persuade Killam to stay. Despite his entreaties, however, he could not prevent Killam from leaving to set up his own business in Quebec City. Nonetheless, after a few unsuccessful months in the financial wilderness, the prodigal son returned and was welcomed back into the company.

Such turmoil served to convince Aitken to change direction once again. Selling bonds had become routine. Running the Montreal Trust to perform mundane tasks for corporate clients, accepting deposits and lending on call to brokers, had become a question of mechanics. Besides, he had not forgotten the panic of 1907 and his resolve to leave the banking business to others. It was time to sell the Montreal Trust itself. In April the Royal Bank of Canada had made an offer, but it was not until the arrival of Sir Herbert Holt as the bank's president that Aitken felt comfortable with the relationship. The deal was duly done. Aitken stayed as a vice-president of the trust and Holt became a shareholder and director of RSC. The decks were now clear for him to set about making the kind of money which he now believed was there for the taking. He had been halfway there. It was time to go the whole way.

CHAPTER 5

'POTS OF MONEY'

'Please don't tell anybody that I admitted that I had organized any trusts'[1]

The timing could hardly have been better. By the beginning of 1909, the storm clouds had fully lifted and Canada was set again on its previous path of accelerating economic growth. This in turn provoked a wave of industrial mergers as companies adjusted to the new and ever more promising market opportunities. The stronger thrived, but those with weaker cash flows sought refuge in amalgamations with their competitors. By September 1909, they were occurring at such a rate the *Monetary Times* was complaining that 'mergers are falling upon the investor in Canada as thick as autumn leaves'.[2] As a matter of statistical fact, during the years 1896–1913, known, after the Prime Minister of the day, as the Laurier boom, more than forty major consolidations were put in place. Of these, the three largest, one of which was to be the most controversial – even to some the most notorious – of all forty, were promoted by Max Aitken.

Aitken was far from the only promoter at the time. Others tried their hand as well. In truth, the promotion of a merger, whoever was running it, followed a consistent pattern. The promoter identified a particular sector where a number of small firms competed for business but in which none of them had the cash flow needed to invest in up-to-date technology or the market strength to be the price leader. He then proceeded to negotiate options over the target firms, explaining to their owners the benefits of a merger with competitors (together with personal inducements, in other words bribes, where necessary). The promoter then gathered together a syndicate of banks and individuals to form a new holding company which would be the vehicle for the merger. That done, the options were exercised using the securities, common stock and bonds as the case required, of the holding company as currency. They would then be listed on one of the major stock exchanges and marketed to the public. The syndicate by that time would have awarded itself a substantial tranche of securities (usually the common stock) in the holding company, which could be sold or retained as necessary. Members of the syndicate could also take part in underwriting the public offering to provide them with an extra reward. This may appear as a process little short of mechanical. But it was the skill at spotting the opportunities and driving through the deal which marked out the most successful, and in these two skills the thirty-year-old Aitken was the undoubted master.

The first, and most controversial, of Aitken's three mergers was in the Canadian cement industry. So contentious did it turn out to be that the reputation of all the participants, including Aitken himself, was in one way or another severely damaged. To cap it all, the whole affair blew up, ending in litigation between the parties involved and, finally, in Canadian anti-trust legislation. To be fair, none of this could have been foreseen at the outset. The origin lay in a relatively insignificant company, the Western Canada Cement and Coal Company. It had been founded in 1905 by Joseph Irvin, the general manager of the International Portland Cement Company in Quebec. Irvin had persuaded one of the most distinguished figures in Canadian engineering and finance, Sir Sandford Fleming, to invest heavily in a new plant to be built in Exshaw, in the province of Alberta. Irvin had then without consultation paid himself a commission of $500,000 before the plant had even been completed. When he found out about it, Fleming, horrified at what appeared to be a clear fraud on investors, tried to recoup the money by arranging for an issue of a tranche of the company's bonds in London. When that failed, and with the company now facing bankruptcy, Fleming consulted his friend Edward Clouston. Clouston in turn advised sending for Aitken to see what could be done.

Sir Sandford Fleming, 1903.

In April 1909, Irvin and Aitken met in Montreal to discuss a rescue plan. It was to take the form of a merger of a number of firms to make a viable unit. The promoting syndicate would include both Irvin and Fleming, with Irvin as the principal player. He was deputed to go out to negotiate options over those firms which he had suggested should be part of the amalgamation. Yet, in spite of Irvin's efforts, which turned out to be successful beyond Aitken's initial expectations, Aitken soon realised that Irvin's new, amalgamated unit would have less than 50 per cent of Canadian productive capacity and would therefore be unable to establish price leadership. In other words, the amalgamation would not achieve its purpose. Aitken then took over the project. He convinced Irvin that his original scheme would not work and persuaded him to transfer the options he had collected to the Bond and Share Company (while still guaranteeing Irvin his share of the final reward) and then, behind Irvin's back, started negotiations with other companies not on Irvin's list. He brought in Cahan for the detailed legal work. Together, they drafted a new agreement between the promoters. Finally, to shore up the financing, at the same time he took pains to reassure Clouston and the Bank of Montreal that they were not ignored by offering both of them generous terms in return for the necessary financial back-up.

Following two weeks of uneasy negotiation between 27 August and 10 September, eleven companies signed up to the merger. Missing in the deal, however, was the Western Cement Company, which had been deliberately left out because Aitken thought its valuation was too high. The deal signed, the new Canada Cement Company was then incorporated and immediately applied for listing on the Montreal Stock Exchange. The Bond and Share Company duly exercised its options at a value of $14.8 million. In return, as part of Cahan's revised promotion agreement, the company delivered to the Bond and Share Company bonds, preferred stock and common stock at par value $29 million. On 14 September, Canada Cement issued a prospectus for the sale of 5 million preferred shares at $93 per share. On 15 September, the Bond and Share Company duly transferred its Canada Cement securities to RSC. The Bond and Share Company was then dissolved. Aitken came out of the whole transaction with a personal profit of some $600,000. Everything had happened almost in the twinkling of an eye.

In fact, for many of those involved, and for surprised onlookers, the twinkling had been far too sharp. Allegations and accusations began to mount: there had been a bloated overvaluation of the stock; a hurried prospectus completed without proper audits of the underlying companies and clearly designed for a quick flotation; large amounts of supposedly valuable paper shunted around in obscure deals between shadowy companies which then disappeared; deceitful negotiations in hotel rooms; clear conflicts of interest of senior officials in the Bank of Montreal; and manifest insider trading. The size of Aitken's personal commission was also the subject of animated comment and speculation. Almost everybody complained. There would eventually be an apocalyptic storm.

Aitken, however, was yet to be buffeted by these ill winds and had instead also been busy putting together two large, if less spectacular, mergers in, as he later put it, 'that wonderful year of 1909'.[3] The first was a merger of manufacturers making rolling stock for the ever-expanding railway network. Some years before he had seen the opportunity when he had tried to buy into the Nova Scotia company known informally as Rhodes Curry and formally as the Railway Carriage Company, but it was not until early 1909 that the owner, Nathaniel Curry, agreed to the increase in the company's capital which let Aitken in. By the summer, Rhodes Curry had been relaunched as a much larger enterprise. In October, when the new company's securities were waiting to be listed in Montreal, Aitken heard of another project to consolidate two competitors. He immediately suggested that the three companies should merge into Canadian Car and Foundry Limited and do so at speed. So quick were the negotiations that at the end of October 1909 the merger was announced.

That done, Aitken turned his attention to the Canadian steel industry. Immediately after the completion of the Car and Foundry merger he was invited to join a syndicate to promote a merger between Dominion Iron and Steel and Dominion Coal. This went ahead for completion at the end of 1909. Yet Aitken saw that this was not enough to meet the competition from the giant US Steel, the product of the first wave of US mergers, which was planning an entry into the Canadian market. What was needed was a Canadian equivalent of US Steel, and he set about creating it. Other candidates for amalgamation were identified: Montreal Rolling Mills, Hamilton Steel and Iron, Dominion Wire Manufacturing Company of Montreal, Lake Superior Corporation, Canada Screw and Canada Bolt and Nut Company. Early in 1910 he duly made the rounds to test their willingness to merge and to assess their financial ability to do so. The one company missing from the list, however, was Nova Scotia Steel and Coal.

It was an obvious target, but it also held a special place in Aitken's mind. He had not forgotten – he would never forget – that Harris had not lived up to his agreement to appoint Aitken a director of Scotia in return for supporting his bid to succeed John Stairs as president, nor that Harris had resisted all attempts Aitken had made to carve out a future for RSC away from Halifax. It was now the moment, after having been both deferential and on the defensive for so long, for Aitken to go on the attack. What he planned was no less than the first hostile takeover in Canadian financial history.

Harris and the general manager of Scotia had for some time been nervous about the company's position. Much depended on the newly discovered source of iron ore lying under the sea bed off Newfoundland. If this was viable, and if the cost of extraction was not prohibitive, Scotia could rely on a secure future. In March 1909, on the back of this prospect, Harris had induced the Nova Scotia legislature to permit the exchange of Scotia preference shares into bonds, which in turn would give the company a welcome increase in capital funds. Harris wrote to Aitken, as a shareholder, to explain his intentions. Aitken was not impressed and wrote back to Harris to say so. But his letter was more than just a rejection. It was tantamount to a declaration of war. 'It is due to myself', his letter ran, 'to let you know where I stand so that we may eliminate the possibility of any personal animosity in doing everything we can to make our respective views effective.'[4] Animosity, of course, was precisely what it was. To cap it, Aitken had by then taken to referring to Harris as 'that podgy gentleman'.[5]

Aitken was even then organising a syndicate to launch an attack on Scotia. The customary band of Aitken's Montreal allies were there, not least Rodolphe Forget, the Montreal stockbroker who had led other merger promotions. They were all active in the market buying up Scotia stock. Aitken, however, was cautious. He needed to know more about the mysterious undersea source of iron ore. He therefore commissioned a report from Frank Jones, the general manager of Canada Cement, whose previous career had been in the steel industry. But the market activity in Scotia had alerted Harris. He realised that Scotia was under threat and persuaded his board to sanction a 20 per cent stock bonus dividend to shareholders to reduce its cash holdings as a defence against the raiders. Undeterred, Aitken's syndicate continued buying, to the point where in January 1910 they could claim to hold a majority. By then, however, Jones had reported to Aitken that the submarine iron ore deposits were too far out to sea and possibly 'no longer commercially viable'.[6] Aitken immediately stopped buying Scotia shares for his own account, but concealed Jones's report from the other members of the syndicate. Forget was encouraged to take the lead and did so with enthusiasm. Although he now suspected that the raid would fail, Aitken was determined in his revenge – even at the expense of his allies.

In the middle of this bruising contest there was some family news. In July 1909, Gladys had announced her second pregnancy and had taken to her bed in the Aitkens' large house in Drummond Street in the Square Mile, the most elegant quarter of Montreal. This time there was to be no question of her opting to go back to the cottage in Halifax where she had given birth to Janet. There would be a more dignified, and more carefully supervised, delivery at home. That duly happened, and a son, John William Maxwell, was born on 15 February 1910. 'He was a comfort and joy,' Aitken later wrote, 'and for the first time in his life, though not the last, he was a unifying influence in our family.'[7] Gladys had been complaining that Janet had not been properly looked after while she was confined to bed, and that had not been 'conducive to the tranquillity of our domestic relations'.[8]

Six weeks after the baby's arrival, on 30 March, the decisive Scotia shareholders' meeting was held at the plant in New Glasgow. For once, Harris moved quickly and unexpectedly turned the tables on the raiders. It was a neat trick. He had employed a friendly Halifax stockbroker to borrow as many shares as he could on that morning to be held overnight and returned the following day. When the syndicate members arrived at the meeting, they found that they were 1,500 votes short – votes Harris had in his pocket. The rest of the day was spent in counting the votes and bad-tempered squabbling. But the issue was not in doubt. Harris had triumphed. Furthermore, he was not slow to crow about his triumph in Halifax, particularly noting in his celebratory announcements that Aitken had not even bothered to attend the crucial meeting.

The Scotia raid may have failed, but it left Scotia itself badly weakened, with a large minority of disaffected shareholders. Aitken decided that he could safely leave Scotia out of his plans, as the ultimate snub to Harris, and concentrate on his own plan for the amalgamation of the remainder of the industry. In March 1910, at Clouston's invitation, Aitken met William McMaster, the largest shareholder and managing director of the Montreal Rolling Mills Company. McMaster was getting on in years and was looking to retirement. He was not interested in mergers. He wanted cash. Specifically, he valued the company at $4.2 million. In support of his figure, McMaster gave Aitken a copy of an accountant's report and invited him to visit the plant for an onsite inspection. Aitken duly brought Frank Jones with him. Together, they came to the conclusion that McMaster's estimated value was realistic. After a conversation with Herbert Holt, Aitken's partner in the Montreal Trust and by then president of the Royal Bank of Canada, the offer was made, conditional on McMaster withdrawing from all other discussions and on the availability of what was a large sum of money.

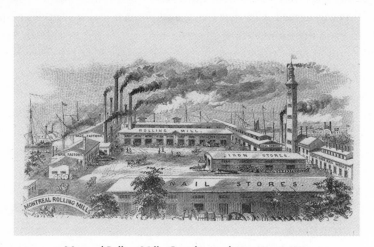

Montreal Rolling Mills, Canada, wood engraving, c. 1885.

Aitken then made contact again with William Farrell, the controlling shareholder in the Dominion Wire Company. Farrell's discussions with Hamilton Steel and Iron Company, together with the Canada Screw Company, run by Charles Wilcox, and Canada Bolt and Nut Company, run by Lloyd Harris, had run into trouble when Farrell held out for a cash payment of $1 million. Aitken not only agreed this in principle but went on to suggest that the other companies should join in his merger plan with Montreal Rolling Mills. In the ferment of the moment, all of them became enthusiastic for the idea and, at the end of March, they met at the Windsor Hotel in Montreal.

The meeting ended without a conclusion. The various opinions on the value of their respective companies, and that of their proposed partners, were so wide apart that there was no possibility of a conclusion, however great the enthusiasm, in one meeting. They did agree with Aitken's suggestion that they should meet again in New York, at the Waldorf-Astoria Hotel, and stay there until a deal had been reached. When the day came, the problem of relative valuations was as intractable as ever. All agreed that they would take bonds and preference shares to a value of the underlying net worth of each participant and common stock for the goodwill based on earnings. In the end the stumbling block was the valuation of Montreal Rolling Mills. Aitken suggested that they commission a review from independent appraisers. This was agreed. On that basis, and conditional on Aitken being able to raise the money to pay McMaster and his fellow shareholders by the end of May, the merger document was signed on 9 April 1910.

The difficulty was that only five days previously the war over the Canada Cement issue had moved into a new and explosive phase. On 4 March, the first general meeting of the company's shareholders had endorsed the opinion of the directors that the opening accounts represented an accurate view of the company's financial position. On 24 March, the directors, in a report compiled at Fleming's request, had written to him that in their opinion the company's promotion had been 'legally and properly carried out'.[9] Aitken had then written to Fleming to suggest a way of bringing Western Canada Cement into the new company, the proviso being that Fleming should put in writing an endorsement of the directors' conclusion. Under pressure from a group of British bondholders, Fleming wrote back that 'with unanimity on the part of [the directors] it remains for me to accept their decision as over-ruling. The responsibility must rest with them.'[10]

It did not stop there. Fleming's acceptance was no more than grudging. Furthermore, he went on to issue a circular criticising both Aitken and Canada Cement, demanding a government inquiry. He sent it to the Prime Minister, Sir Wilfrid Laurier, with an accompanying letter that he had on legal advice 'omitted the name of the person who has pocketed so many millions wrongly (viz. William Maxwell Aitken)'.[11] Laurier hedged in his reply to the request for a government inquiry, knowing that some of his party colleagues were directors of the company and might be seriously embarrassed by its conclusions. Fleming then submitted a further inflammatory letter to a parliamentary committee which was investigating the matter. That brought the whole row into the open. There was an explosion in the popular press. Aitken and his fellow financiers were immediately branded as villains.

Nevertheless, Fleming's case had a flaw. He had not given any assurance about taking further action in the courts or making a further public fuss. On hearing of Fleming's now public attacks, Irvin, Hugh Fleming (Fleming's son) and Frank Dunsford (representing the British bondholders) finally agreed that enough was enough. On 9 April, the day on which the steel merger was being signed at the Waldorf-Astoria in New York, they signed an agreement accepting Aitken's proposal to bring Western Cement Company into Canada Cement provided that the Bank of Montreal agreed. Fleming denounced the agreement and continued to demand easier conditions for the company to join the merger. Clouston decided immediately that the Bank of Montreal should call in its loan covenant and send Western Canada Cement into receivership. Fleming then lost what was left of his temper. He demanded access to all the papers relating to the Canada Cement promotion. Furthermore, he demanded that his own lawyer should review them. Almon Lovett, by then the chief counsel for Canada Cement, thought it prudent to accede to the request in the hope that it would calm Fleming down. Disconcertingly, however, Fleming's lawyer ended his review of the documentary evidence by concluding that the directors had been right in their conclusion that everything had been done within the law. Fleming refused to accept even his view. He was not prepared to give up. The war would continue.

In the meantime, Aitken had to raise some $5 million by the end of May. It was obvious that the Montreal market had reached capacity with Aitken-sponsored securities. New York had also been heavily involved in the Canada Cement issue and was taking time to digest it. The alternative, improbable as it might have seemed, was London. 'I informed my wife', Aitken wrote later, 'that I was leaving on a journey to London. She informed me that her duty to her husband conflicted with her devotion to her young daughter and newborn son.' The response was decisive to the point of cruelty. 'She must make a sacrifice. And I was not the victim. Care of my daughter and her brother was turned over to my mother, brought from New Brunswick.'[12]

On 30 April 1910, after a rough crossing on the liner *Lusitania*,

Aitken and Gladys arrived in London to stay at the Savoy. On arrival, he went to see Bonar Law. It was not a happy meeting. Bonar Law's dearly loved wife Annie had died the previous October at the age of forty-two, leaving him with six children. It is little wonder that he was grieving, but all that Aitken could say about their meeting was, 'I did not succeed in arousing his enthusiasm.'[13] Undeterred, Aitken tried unsuccessfully to see the old Joseph Chamberlain, who, in spite of his debilitating stroke some years earlier, had been leading a campaign for a united Empire which had filled Aitken with enthusiasm. Then it was back to business. Aitken's partner this time was to be the merchant bank Lazard Brothers, who not only subscribed to a shareholding in RSC but led a syndicate to underwrite a tranche of the proposed Canadian Steel Company's securities. At the same time, Aitken had arranged a bridging loan from another well-established City name, Parr's Bank, to exercise his and Holt's option over Montreal Rolling Mills.

It had been an extremely slick money-raising operation, taking only a week to complete. On 7 May (as it happened, the day after the death of King Edward VII), Aitken and Gladys sailed back across the Atlantic. On arrival in Montreal he lost no time in exercising the option over Montreal Rolling Mills. As Clouston was mired in several conflicts of interest, he was politely told to resign as the company's president and Holt was appointed in his place. Since the valuation of the company by the independent appraisers under the Waldorf-Astoria agreement had come out nearly $1 million higher than expected, the promoters were obliged under the agreement to pay up. Aitken immediately declared a dividend to himself and Holt as the new owners of the company. Their shares were then duly transferred, at a full valuation, for securities in what had now been named the Steel Corporation of Canada. As his daughter Janet later recalled, 'When he had finished, on the morning of 17 July, the Steel Company of Canada was an established fact, and my father was a multimillionaire.'[14] Indeed he was. He himself estimated his fortune at 'more than five million dollars'.[15]

At nightfall on the same day, Gladys met Aitken at RSC's office in Montreal and, accompanied by two friends but leaving their two children behind, they set off in an open-top touring car to drive to New York. Aitken admitted that he was tired and needed a holiday. In fact, so tired was he that he lost control of the car he was driving and it ended up in a ditch. Undeterred, his friends rescued the car, told him to sit in the back and go to sleep and continued on their journey. On arrival at Saratoga Springs, Aitken, as ever, wanted to combine holiday with business. He met William Price, the controlling shareholder in Price's Pulp and Paper Company, to sign an agreement for an issue of the company's securities to be marketed in London when he got there. That done, the party went on to New York and embarked on the *Lusitania* to sail to Liverpool. The plan was to take a two-month holiday in Britain. In the event, and unexpectedly, the holiday in one way or another turned into the beginning of a new career.

HMS Lusitania *in dock, New York, 1907. She is met by a crowd on her starboard side.*

Max Aitken was now thirty-one years old. From the ragamuffin of his childhood, from the drifter of his adolescence, he had turned himself into one of the most skilful deal makers of the Canadian financial world. To be sure, he had learnt from his mentors, particularly John Stairs, but he had by himself developed a power of concentration, an all-embracing memory, a quicksilver ability to sift through detail and pick out the one crucial element that others had missed, a driving ambition in the pursuit of money and, last but by no means least, a degree of deviousness in dealing both with his competitors and, on occasions, with his allies. In personal terms, he had some obvious assets, and some equally obvious liabilities. A photograph taken at the time in a formal pose shows him to be good looking, clean shaven with a dimple in his chin and a smile which could easily charm, smartly dressed in a high collar, tie and three-piece grey suit with a carnation in his buttonhole, and altogether well presented as a socially acceptable, if rather brash, young man. His marriage to Gladys had, as he had intended, brought with it social cachet in Nova Scotia which seemed to rub off into Montreal. If his attitude towards her was by today's standards domineering, it was by no means the only example at the time of a driven husband and a gentle wife.

What the photograph does not show is a fierce temper, a sense of mischief and occasional arrogance. How far Gladys was able to smooth over these characteristics in their social life is hard to say since there is almost no surviving evidence. Indeed, with his constant travelling and Gladys's young children, social activity can hardly have been very intense. Besides, he disliked small talk, wanting only to discuss serious business or his favourite hobby horse, the glory of the British Empire. Nor was he interested in music, painting or the theatre, and he disliked any sport other than riding and golf. Moreover, the life in Montreal's elegant social clubs, even if he were acceptable, held little attraction. Above all, from time to time the whole balance of his life was thrown into confusion by the asthma attacks which occurred seemingly at random but in truth were almost certainly sparked by moments of greatest stress.

Success had come to him early in life. He had made pots of money, as he himself put it. But it had come at a price. Among those who worked for him he inspired admiration and dislike in equal measure. Almost all of them, at one time or another, fell out with him. Although they were well paid, their morale was brought down by constant harassment and interference in the job they were supposed to be doing on their own initiative. But what was worse than the grumbling of his subordinates was the attack on his reputation in public. His role in the acquisition of Montreal Rolling Mills was 'violently denounced' as fraud.[16] The affair of the Canada Cement Company was leaving behind it a dreadful taste. Sir Sandford Fleming was not a man to be crossed and once he had put his complaints into the public domain they were seized upon by the popular press. The campaign gained momentum when the company demonstrated its monopoly power in aggressive pricing. Farmers in the prairie belt, outraged, took up the baton. They were clear that there was only one target. Aitken himself was held to be personally responsible for what many of them saw simply as a swindle. He should be called to account.

Aitken was no fool. Nor was he wholly insensitive. In the face of the hostile barrage he decided that his best plan was to leave Canada to allow everything and everybody to calm down. Allied to this plan was another. 'My success in making mergers in Canada', he later wrote, 'had turned out so wonderfully well. Why not exercise the same talent in making a worthy contribution to the effort of bringing all the Empire units into one commercial combine?'[17] Imperialism was still, as it had been throughout his youth, the paramount theme in his yet unformed political philosophy. Of course, put simply, the idea of an imperial commercial combine was absurd, but at least it gave him something to think about during the long, and rough, crossing on the *Lusitania*. As for the enemies he left behind him, he knew that 'they would never forgive [him]'.[18] He was right. They never did.

CHAPTER 6

ENGLAND 1910

'I am now a Lancashire man ... from Canada'[1]

No expense, it seems, was to be spared. When the Aitkens embarked in New York on the *Lusitania* for the Atlantic crossing, they found suites no. B 87 and 85 awaiting them. (Gladys's maid had to make do with a berth on a lower deck.)[2] Each suite, as a matter of course, had a sitting room and private bath. 'Panelled in mahogany', runs one description,

> satinwood and veneered walnut, and furnished with inlaid desks, wardrobes and dressing tables ... Their private marble-walled bathrooms included white-enamelled, cast-iron claw foot tubs fitted with shower cages and silver-plated fixtures ... washbasins ornamented with onyx – as well as toilets – were rimmed in gilt ... The suites came with a personal steward to cater to the needs and whims of their travellers.[3]

There were banks of flowers waiting to greet the fortunate passengers. (Aitken thought that they had come from Canadian well-wishers.) During the crossing, for those few who managed to avoid seasickness, there was dancing to a string orchestra, cocktail parties hosted by the ship's captain, and dinners of sumptuous variety. It was a taste, and more than just a taste, of the rewards of money. If it could buy this, it could buy other things as well.

The journey from Liverpool, where the *Lusitania* docked, to London was made by car. There is no record of the make of car or cars chosen but it would not be surprising if it was a Rolls-Royce. Always interested in motor cars (he had been one of the first to own a car in Halifax), before departing New York, Aitken had heard that Charles Rolls, one of the co-founders of the Rolls-Royce motor company, had been killed in an aircraft accident. Never one to miss a business opportunity, Aitken soon found out that Rolls had died leaving his elder brother, Lord Llangattock, as his heir and that Llangattock had no great interest in motor cars. Moreover, Henry Royce, Rolls's partner, was on leave of absence owing to overwork. The board of Rolls-Royce duly looked for an outside investor. 'Capital should not be idle,' Aitken declared, and negotiations for the purchase of the Rolls shares were soon under way.[4]

The couple (presumably with Gladys's maid, although she does not rate a mention in any of the records) arrived in London at the end of July 1910. Rather than staying in a hotel, Aitken had arranged to rent a flat in Cavendish Square, just north of Oxford Street and west of Regent Street, thus conveniently placed for access to the City to the east and the medical practices of Harley Street to the north. Laid out for the Earl of Oxford in the early part of the eighteenth century, and named after his wife, the square quickly become fashionable. True, the buildings even at the time were not quite up to the standard of convenience of the newer developments in Belgravia and Kensington, but they had, and still have, in spite of the bombs of the Second World War and subsequent reconstruction, a certain dilapidated elegance. That suited the Aitkens well. Their new home was to be a spacious apartment on the eighth floor of No. 19.

Their arrival in England had coincided with the end of the London social season. The gentry and their wives had left for their country estates. In fact, apart from completing the purchase of the holding in Rolls-Royce and the occasional foray into the City to sell Price Company or Stelco securities, there was not much for him to do. To occupy the time, Aitken decided to take Gladys to Scotland to show her, and indeed to find for himself, the home of his ancestors. They visited Torphichen, looked piously at a number of gravestones in the churchyard and triumphantly identified the nearby Silvermine, where his grandfather had been the tenant. Yet apart from some rather perplexing conversations with an old man who turned out to be a distant cousin they found little to interest them and after no more than a few days they drove back to London.

It was to be a holiday of only two months. Nevertheless, although it was meant to be a holiday, there was much going on in Canada, and Aitken kept himself informed in detail about the major issues of the day. As always, there was much to keep him occupied. Apart from the persistent attacks on his conduct of the Canada Cement amalgamation he was concerned about the way the whole affair had blown up into a general assault on the Laurier government and their supposed reluctance to deal with trusts, be they good or bad. Initially, the government response earlier in the year had been to introduce a bill, to be known as the Combines Investigation Act, whose purpose was to allow investigations into 'combines, monopolies, trusts and mergers which may enhance prices or restrict competition to the detriment of consumers'.[5] The bill was the brainchild of the young Minister of Labour, William Lyon Mackenzie King. However, Mackenzie King had run into immediate trouble when he conceded that he himself was a supporter of large industrial organisations. It was clear even then that the bill would have a rough ride. Nothing could be more detrimental to the successful placement of Cement and Stelco securities, as Aitken was well aware, than a continued and acrimonious public debate about their legitimacy.

At the same time, in the spring of 1910, there had been a movement in Washington towards mutual reduction of tariffs between Canada and the United States. By the end of the summer President William Taft was proposing an all-encompassing free trade agreement. Nothing could be more threatening to the campaign for imperial preference. Canadian Conservatives, under their leader Robert Borden, mobilised for the battle. Aitken, too, responded to the call to arms. Sensing that there would at some stage be a battle to be fought, whether in defence of trusts or against 'reciprocity' with the United States, in January 1910 he had launched a weekly magazine known as the *Canadian Century*. Its purpose was proclaimed (in language that would become familiar many years later) to the sound of verbal trumpets. 'It is the mission of *THE CANADIAN CENTURY* to succeed where others have failed and then speed onward and outward.'[6] Although the content of the magazine varied, its main message, in its editorials, was to denounce the wickedness of reciprocity and highlight the unsurpassed virtues of the British Empire, at the same time proclaiming the virtues of industrial amalgamations.

By the autumn of 1910 Aitken had to be content with firing his bullets from London via the *Century*'s office in Montreal. In September, Gladys had decided to go home, her holiday over and her children waiting to see her. She left London on 27 September, sailed from Liverpool on the *Megantic* on 1 October and arrived home on 9 October 'feeling fine', she cabled him. 'Bad trip children delighted splendid many thanks flowers best love how are you'.[7] Not getting any reply, Gladys sent a further, slightly tetchy, cable: 'How are you and where are you?'[8]

Gladys Aitken photographed c. 1910.

Aitken had not been idle. He had been cautious. He had decided to stay in London, realising that those who were after his blood in Canada were far from calming down. But the Cavendish Square flat without Gladys (and her maid) was much too large. He therefore moved west to a smaller flat in Parkside Mansions in Knightsbridge. Now on his own, it was time to make a further attempt to 'take the plunge into [British] public life'.[9] So far, his plan for an entry onto the London stage had not worked. Nobody was taking any notice. London, as he was coming to realise, was not Halifax or Montreal. It was a much bigger world.

As it turned out, there were three exceptions to the general London indifference, each of which was in its own way to become crucial to Aitken's advancement. Alfred Harmsworth had started as a free-lance journalist but, together with his younger brother Harold, had gradually built up a magazine empire, with titles such as *Comic Cuts* ('Amusing without Being Vulgar')[10] and *Forget-Me-Not* aimed prin-cipally at women and children. From there they went into tabloid journalism, buying the *Evening News* in 1894 and starting the *Daily Mirror* in 1903 and the *Daily Mail* in 1896. Moving upmarket, they bought *The Observer* and *The Times* in 1905 and 1908 respectively. Along the way Alfred had collected a baronetcy in 1904 and a peerage, as Baron Northcliffe, in 1905, while Harold, at that point very much the junior partner, had to be content with a baronetcy in 1910.

In these days of radio, television and the internet it is sometimes difficult to appreciate the power of the printed word in the years before 1914. Editorials in *The Times* were universally read and discussed by politicians, civil servants, businessmen and even royalty, while the polemics in the *Daily Mail* and the *Daily Mirror* stirred the spirits of nationalism. Northcliffe was without a doubt one of the most powerful men in Britain. He also had a passion for hot-air balloons, an enthusiasm which was shared by Charles Rolls. Northcliffe saw them as a way of promoting the *Daily Mail*. When Rolls had a tender fitted to his Silver Ghost Rolls-Royce so that it could be attached to a balloon which then lifted car and driver into the sky, the *Daily Mail* featured the event as an unparalleled example of English derring-do. The passion for balloons was transferred in due course to aeroplanes, so much so that when Rolls made a non-stop flight to France and back in ninety minutes the *Daily Mail* proclaimed him a national hero. His death on 12 July was presented as a glorious sacrifice in a noble cause. 'The cause', as one commentator has put it, 'was Britain's future leadership of the world's most exciting innovation – and the increased circulation of the *Daily Mail*.'[11]

Newspaper proprietor Lord Northcliffe, pictured in 1908, was a motoring enthusiast who imported a number of Mercedes cars from Germany in the 1900s and owned the first Mercedes in the country.

It is little wonder that Northcliffe took an intense interest in the ownership of the Rolls-Royce company, particularly when a large part of it went to an unknown Canadian adventurer. His enquiries into Aitken's affairs were detailed and not entirely happy. He apparently said then, and continued to say, that Aitken 'only just got away from the arm of the law'.[12] Nevertheless, Northcliffe was content to help Aitken with the affairs of Rolls-Royce. At the time, of course, he had no idea that Aitken would become a press rival. Nor, for that matter, had Aitken himself.

There was one appointment which Aitken made, with Northcliffe's approval, to the board of Rolls-Royce which turned out to be important for his subsequent move into British politics. Edward ('Paddy') Goulding, the Unionist MP for Worcester, was a prominent figure in the City, a friend of fellow City figure Ion Hamilton Benn, and a participant in the investor syndicates which Aitken had been quick to identify. By the time he met Aitken in the summer of 1910, Goulding was in his late forties, unmarried, undeniably rich and with a bluff Anglo-Irish charm. Like many well-off politicians of the age, he had a large and architecturally undistinguished country establishment, Wargrave Hall, on the banks of the river Thames between Henley-on-Thames and Twyford. It was there that he entertained his guests on spring weekends to admire the cascading wisteria and early roses or in summer to picnics on the long grass verge leading down to the river, his sister dutifully acting as hostess. Invitations, once given, were generally not refused. It was a place where politicians and journalists were able to meet and discuss, or plot as the case may be, without interference. It was to Wargrave Hall that Aitken went for the first time on the day Gladys left London, 27 September.

Goulding was not only a dedicated Unionist but one of the most enthusiastic followers of Joseph Chamberlain and his programme of imperial protectionism, or tariff reform as it was generally known. As such, he was able to give Aitken all the information he needed to engage in the British politics of the day. But it was an easy task. Aitken was familiar with the tariff reform programme which Joseph Chamberlain had proclaimed in 1903. He knew vaguely that after Chamberlain's stroke in 1906 the cause had faltered; that the Liberal landslide of 1906 had brought a government, now led by Herbert Asquith, in favour of free trade; that the Unionists, who had broken from the Liberals over William Gladstone's proposals for Irish Home Rule, were allied to the Conservatives in opposition; and that the Unionist majority in the House of Lords had taken the provocative step of throwing out Chancellor David Lloyd George's 1909 Budget on the grounds that it was too radical in its tax on land, thus triggering a general election from which the two main parties, Liberal and Conservative/Unionist, came out with almost equal numbers, leaving the Irish National Party, together with the young Labour Party, to hold the balance of power.

Yet, as Aitken himself later wrote, 'My knowledge of politics was confined to the Empire issue. The powers of the House of Lords did not interest me. Home Rule was a dangerous subject. I was not an opponent at heart. The Welsh Church meant nothing.'[13] Goulding was able at least to make a start with Aitken's political education. By the end of September, Aitken was receiving invitations to weekends at

Wargrave Hall to meet some of the more prominent tariff reform sup-porters of the day: James Garvin, the editor of *The Observer*; Howell Gwynne, the editor of the *Standard*; Frederick (F. E.) Smith, the waspishly brilliant Tory barrister; Sir Edward Carson, the formidable Ulster Unionist leader; and, above all, and once again, Andrew Bonar Law. In fact, it was at a lunch with Goulding in late September that Aitken and Bonar Law embarked on what truly became more than a mere political friendship.

It was at the same lunch that Aitken sat next to Ralph (R. D.) Blumenfeld, the American-born editor of the *Daily Express*, a daily newspaper founded in 1900 by one of the Harmsworth brothers' rivals, Arthur Pearson. Blumenfeld recorded his impressions of his young neighbour. 'A comparative youth, carelessly dressed, with tousled hair, searching eyes, alternatively hard and twinkling, and a large full lipped mouth which made him look cold and forbidding in repose, and extraordinarily attractive when it spread itself in a smile over his colourless face.'[14] Blumenfeld later recorded in his diary that 'he told me then that he proposed winning a difficult seat, and I did not believe him'.[15]

Ralph Blumenfeld, the American-born editor of the Daily Express.

Aitken was taken in hand by Bonar Law to prepare his candidature. In his gloomy house in Edwardes Square in North Kensington, Bonar

Law, sad, ascetic and teetotal (he had irritated Aitken initially by offering whisky while he himself drank lime juice), relentlessly smoking his pipe, did his best to instruct his new protégé. The controversy over the powers of the House of Lords after its rejection of Lloyd George's Budget had, he explained, dominated political discussion since the last general election. Although the Lords had waved through the Budget after the election without a division, that had not been enough for the Liberals. The upper house must be brought to heel. Attempts in the summer, Bonar Law went on, to broker a deal between Liberals and Conservative/Unionists over proposals to restrict the powers of the House of Lords had come to nothing. There would have to be another general election on the issue. Asquith was in negotiation with a reluctant King George V to create a large number of Liberal peers if he won the forthcoming general election and the Lords refused to accept the Liberal proposals. The general election, the second of 1910, was going to be a bitter affair, with the Conservative/Unionists, led by Arthur Balfour, determined to support the Lords, and the Liberals, led by Asquith, determined to force the upper house to surrender.

Bonar Law was, of course, like almost all Conservative/Unionists, opposed to the Liberal proposals for the upper house. But that was not his current problem. It was the fear that the whole controversy over Lords powers would so dominate the coming general election that the cause of tariff reform would be forgotten. Its supporters had come up with the idea that the way to get it back to where it should be, high on the political agenda, was, in Goulding's words, for 'some front bencher to take his life in his hands & fight Manchester & give a lead to the country'.[16] Manchester, of course, was the bastion of free trade. Goulding went on to say that he had discussed the idea with the Earl of Derby, the overlord of the Lancashire Unionists, and with Garvin to test the possible press reaction, and that both had expressed their strong view that he, Bonar Law, would be the appropriate sacrificial lamb for the purpose. Bonar Law had taken a month to reflect on the plan, reasonably enough since he was being invited to give up his safe seat of Dulwich in the outskirts of London. Nevertheless, he replied that he would give it a try, although he could not give a final commitment until he had talked to the Manchester Unionists to sound them out.

It was in the middle of these deliberations that Bonar Law had start-ed the process to find Aitken a winnable constituency. 'I saw Hood [Sir Alexander Acland, the Conservative/Unionist Chief Whip]', he wrote on 6 October, '& he has promised to speak to [Percival] Hughes (the nominal head of the Conservative Central Office) about any suit-able seats available.'[17] Goulding followed that up two days later with a letter saying that the constituency of Eskdale in Cumberland was well worth looking at and that 'it would be well if you could phone him [Mr J. W. Bagley of the Tariff Reform League] ... [who] would arrange for you to meet the Chairman'.[18]

Aitken quickly followed up. In fact, he leapt too fast. A series of tel-egrams sped between him and the Carlisle solicitor I. H. Mawson, the chairman of the North Cumberland Conservative Association. These became more frenetic as October went on, Mawson and his supporters being ever more enthusiastic and Aitken trying to leave the possibility open while pedalling energetically backwards. He knew that Bonar Law was vacating Dulwich, a much more attractive option, and that Bonar Law was also pressing him to fight alongside him in a Manchester seat.

On 21 October, Aitken wrote to Mawson what was meant to be a friendly holding letter. It does not make happy reading. In truth it would be thought insulting even if it had come from a seasoned and senior politician such as Bonar Law himself. After saying how flattered he was, Aitken explained that

> I have given the matter my most careful and serious attention, and I have come to the conclusion that my engagements are such that I consider myself honour bound to accept the candidature of a Manchester seat if it were offered to me. If, however, your Commit-tee would accept me as prospective candidate on the condition that I should be at liberty to accept the Manchester seat if it were offered me, I shall be pleased and proud to offer my services willingly.[19]

On top of that he had unwisely written to R. B. Bennett on 22 Octo-ber that 'I have now been selected to run in a constituency ... on my merits or on my supposed merits ... They say money does not count but I am sometimes suspicious...'[20]

The North Cumberland Conservative Association met immediately to consider Aitken's letter. Some fifty members turned up for what was a lively meeting. Surprisingly, only a small faction, led by Lord Morpeth, wanted to row back from their invitation to Aitken and appoint an alternative candidate. The majority, noting the advantage to North Cumberland generally and Eskdale particularly of the rich and dynamic Canadian as a candidate, wished to give him further breathing space. On the other hand, they thought that it would be unwise for Aitken to visit the constituency until he had made up his mind. They decided 'to further adjourn for three weeks ... It was felt that in three weeks-time you would be able to say definitely whether you would be our candidate or not.'[21]

Aitken hedged again. On 25 October he sent a telegram to Mawson: 'Have received your letter and telegram writing you in a day or two every reason to suppose will accept shortly.'[22] But both Bonar Law and, almost more important, Lord Derby were starting to get irritated. Bonar Law wrote that on Lord Morpeth's advice he did not think that North Cumberland would wait for long and that he wanted to talk to him about a Manchester seat. Lord Derby at the end of October wrote to Bonar Law to ask whether Aitken would be prepared to look at the West Salford constituency. But Aitken had not yet given up on Dulwich. In short, it was all becoming a great muddle. Sooner or later, somebody would lose his temper.

The first to do so was Aitken himself. Bonar Law was unaware at the time either that Aitken had his eye on Dulwich or that he might get help to secure Dulwich from Conservative Central Office. Bonar Law himself had received a warm welcome from Conservative/Unionist leaders on a visit to Manchester on 8 November and had been offered the candidacy of Aston-under-Lyne, on the edges of Manchester itself, but he decided that he would rather fight a constituency closer to the heart of Manchester. On 14 November he therefore wrote to Major J. B. Pownall, the chairman of the Ashton Constituency Association, declining the offer. 'As regards your constituency,' he went on, 'if you want an outside man there is a young friend of mine, who, I think, would make a very good candidate...' He then added a handwritten postscript. 'I have spoken to Sir Alexander Hood about him and I just learned that he has a seat in view for him near London. You might therefore give me your own opinion as soon as you conveniently can as to whether there is any chance of his being considered for Ashton as if I should happen to go to [North West] Manchester I should prefer to have him in Lancashire.'²³ Bonar Law made a somewhat half-hearted effort to help his friend with Dulwich, but it soon became evident that the constituency was a plum which Central Office had reserved for a more experienced candidate. Now that Pownall had offered to meet Aitken in Nottingham, where Unionist leaders were in a prolonged process of agreeing a common platform on which to fight the election, it seemed clear that Ashton was the best option.

The meeting took place on the morning of Thursday 17 November. It was cordial enough, but by that time Conservative Central Office had started to meddle in Ashton's affairs. When he heard about this, Aitken exploded. He sat down and wrote a furious letter to Bonar Law. The letter is undated, but its timing is clear. Angry handwriting scrawls untidily across the page.

> The facts are that Hughes offered the seat to Gwynne and Goulding Thursday evening (presumably after receiving your message [about North West Manchester]) for a Labour Candidate. Gwynne and Goulding will ring & anxious to make me the Candidate. I will positively refuse to accept under such conditions. The Central Office has ignored my offer to [secure?] the party in the interests of tariff reform & … [illegible] … from the period of my first visit … I am deeply grateful to you for the interest you have taken in my ambitions and only regret the incidents which make it impossible for me to offer further service to the party … I cannot accept further humiliation at the hands of a body which cannot accept proffered services in the spirit in which I approached the subject.²⁴

So that was that. But it was not long before Aitken had to retract. It says much for Bonar Law's patience, and its own kind of paternal friendship, that he allowed what now seemed to his Unionist colleagues to be little more than a self-important and vain young man to recover ground. Other politicians of Bonar Law's seniority would without a doubt have thrown him overboard. It was not the way for juniors, however ambitious, to behave. But quite apart from Bonar Law's patient persuasion, the Ashton delegation were determined to pursue the matter. The fact was that it had now become extremely urgent. Prime Minister Asquith had announced on the Friday that he had requested King George V, and the King had agreed, to dissolve Parliament on 28 November and proceed to a general election over the weekend of 3–4 December. Constituency associations had been quick to close out their options and prepare for the campaign. Dulwich went early, and North West Manchester just as quickly sealed Bonar Law as their candidate. Aitken was left Ashton-under-Lyne or nothing.

On the morning of Saturday 19 November, the Ashton delegation arrived in London to meet Bonar Law and Aitken at Pembroke Lodge. Aitken was already wavering. Over lunch, at which, apart from Bonar Law, who drank his usual lime juice, they 'took to the excellent and possibly overproof Scotch whisky'.[25] Bonar Law continually pressed Aitken to accept the Ashton offer. The more he thought about it, the more difficult it was to refuse.

In fact, there were many reasons, apart from Bonar Law's pressure, why a swift retraction of his tantrum was unavoidable. Aitken had already made arrangements through Miss de Gruchy and Arthur Doble in the Montreal office of RSC to collect press cuttings about his achievements in Canada (but leaving out the trusts and financial dealings) and to get an article prepared for the *Montreal Star* which could be fed in turn to the English press. Moreover, he had arranged for Gladys to return in haste to help him in his campaign. She had dutifully changed all her plans, had set sail on 14 November and, following a tortuous route through Ireland, would land at the Welsh fishing port of Fishguard on the 21st. Finally, Gwynne had already sent a telegram to Rudyard Kipling asking him to use the one speech he had undertaken to make during the campaign to speak on Aitken's behalf in Ashton.

Aitken realised that Kipling was a potential ace. By 1910 he was the acknowledged poet and prophet of the British Empire. He had won the Nobel Prize for Literature in 1907, was tipped as the next Poet Laureate to succeed the ageing Alfred Austin and was on conversational terms with the King. True, he could hardly be called a democrat. He had refused a knighthood on the grounds that its recommendation could only have come from a political party, regarded Parliament as no more than a place where people with no knowledge of things as they were could dictate to people who did real work, and was firm in the belief, nurtured in his long years in India, that the white races had the ability to exercise benign authority in a way that others, although they may have different qualities, did not. In other words, he was authoritarian, paternalist and, above all, imperialist. He was also notably bad tempered.

Aitken's approach had been typically bold. On 14 November he had sent Kipling a copy of an issue of *Canadian Century*, pointing to an article by George Foster attacking the principle of Canadian reciprocity with the United States. He knew that Kipling had spent time in the United States and had been critical of the way the Americans managed what he called 'the white man's burden', in particular that they were failing in their moral obligation, after occupying the Philippines in 1898, to govern their 'new-caught, sullen peoples, half devil and half child' in a proper manner.[26] He also knew that Kipling was endlessly worried about money. Kipling needed only the most perfunctory research before taking Aitken's bait. Here was a bright young man, fresh from an imperial Dominion, holding all the right opinions and with plenty of money. Kipling responded to Gwynne that he would be glad to put in an appearance for the candidate for Ashton-under-Lyne and speak as asked.

Aitken was caught. The following day he sent a telegram to Goulding: 'The Major and Councillor Shaw are too persuasive ... I am ready to accept if you and F. E. Smith will guarantee to address a meeting ... on 28 November ... Unless you [and] Smith give me warranty that you will come the deal is off.'[27] Goulding immediately sent his congratulations, telling him to concentrate on his own campaign and stop worrying about outside speakers. The deal was done. On Monday 21 November, the *Ashton Reporter* was able to announce: 'A Conservative Candidate Secured' and that the adoption would take place the following evening at a meeting of the 'Executive of the Conservative Council, the Junior Imperial League and the Liberal Unionist Association. Mr and Mrs Aitken will attend.'[28]

The town of Ashton-under-Lyne, which Aitken sought to represent in the House of Commons, could not in all honesty be said to have been a place of great beauty. Situated in the foothills of the Pennines, on the north bank of the river Tame some ten kilometres east of Manchester, whose sprawl has now more or less absorbed it in the Metropolitan Borough of Tameside, it was a town whose prosperity since the late eighteenth century had risen and fallen with the fortunes of the cotton industry. Quite why it was called Ashton is unclear, although local historians claim that the name has its origins in a Saxon settlement amid ash trees. The origin of the suffix 'under-Lyne' is even less clear, opinions ranging from the Celtic word for elm to the Saxon word for hill. Whatever the history, in 1910 it was town of some 45,000 souls, a figure which has remained more or less stable to this day. There was not much to look at: the streets were straight, lined with houses which were no more than slums; the mill work-ers wore rough clothes and clogs on their feet as they trudged home from work; but all of them were proud children of Lancashire, gritty, with a dry and somewhat fatalistic sense of humour, and generous to a fault. Although those who came to Aitken's adoption meeting on 22 November could hardly understand a word that he said in his harsh Canadian accent, his speech was greeted with waves of applause and he was unanimously adopted by acclamation. The constituency had changed allegiance a number of times over the years. In February the Liberal candidate A. H. Scott, the owner of a chain of local grocery shops, had displaced the sitting Conservative, H. J. Whiteley, with a majority of 293 in a poll of just over 8,000. It was certainly winnable, and Aitken set about the task with his usual ruthless sense of purpose and with his habit of going to the edge of legality but never beyond it. 'Treating', buying votes, was clearly illegal. Anything else, however morally dubious, was permitted.

Aitken went into action. Secretaries were installed at the Midland Hotel in Manchester, where he stayed, to transact business, while the George and Dragon Hotel in Ashton was virtually taken over as Conservative campaign headquarters, fleets of cars turning up each morning with the candidate. A card index system was set up to record the names and addresses of those entitled to vote. Canvassers were sent far and wide, by taxi if necessary. Leaflets were printed almost beyond number. Crowning the campaign was a reception given on the afternoon of 30 November by the Ashton Women's Unionist Association, at which Gladys was the star performer. (Although women did not have the vote, Aitken was shrewd enough to realise the influence they could have on their husbands.) According to the *Ashton Reporter*, 'between two and three thousand women of all classes and ages … presented themselves', the crush being so great 'that many did not get beyond the reception room'.[29]

Newspaper clipping displaying photographs of 'The Candidates and Their Wives' in the Ashton Reporter, *3 December 1910.*

Aitken's election address was loyal to the Conservative/Unionist agreed positions. Scott, his opponent, mocked that it 'showed wonderfully quickly acquired knowledge of the requirements of Tory policy'.[30] Aitken then issued a personal manifesto, which ignored the pressing issue of the day, the powers of the House of Lords, and accused the Liberals of rushing the election in the hope that 'the question of paramount importance to all Britons – namely the solidarity of the Empire – may be overlooked'.[31] Scott again mocked. '[My] opponent is new to political life. He has not yet perhaps had sufficient facts pumped into him. The inoculation was still proceeding – and he was paying a stiff price to his professional advisers.'[32] Scott's punches, telling as they undoubtedly were, had little effect. On polling day Aitken installed a magic lantern in the market square to project a portrait of himself onto a white screen hung outside the George and Dragon. Armies of canvassers and fleets of taxis were sent to bring out the vote, with Aitken himself chasing them if they looked like taking a break. The electors of Ashton had never seen anything like it. But, on balance, they went for it.

The result was declared at 9.15 p.m. Aitken had won by 196 votes in a poll of 7,652. Major Pownall was almost delirious with excitement. The winner himself was, according to onlookers, in tears, shouting, 'I am now a Lancashire man – a Lancashire man from Canada.'[33] Forgetting to make an acceptance speech, he made a celebratory tour of Conservative and Unionist clubs, at the end of which he called for three cheers for his defeated opponent. There were to be two more celebrations, one in Ashton and one in London, at which Aitken's speech received only a guarded welcome from senior Conservatives. It was said to be too bumptious. There were the usual complaints about the conduct of the Ashton election, accusations of corruption, prostitution and other sins freely aired in the local press. More important, however, was the state of Aitken's health. As on many occasions of great excitement, his asthma attacks became more frequent and he became listless. In Canada it was reported that he had had a nervous breakdown.

It was time for him to go away to a climate gentler to his asthma than the damp smog of Manchester, and he and Gladys set out for the south of France to arrive in time for Christmas. It was also time for Gladys to see her children again. On 30 December she cabled Elizabeth de Gruchy from Cannes: 'Would you bring children to me immediately if necessary: Gladys', a rather puzzling way of asking but to which Miss de Gruchy tersely replied 'Yes'.[34] The whole family was to be reunited for the year to come. 1910 had certainly been exciting. It almost goes without saying that they knew 1911 would be at least its equal.

CHAPTER 7

CHERKLEY

'...his Canadian record is of the shadiest...'[1]

Don't mind if you find the House, at first, about as stimulating as a
Fundy fog-bank and as easy to handle as a mud-fence in thaw. *All* the
chaps, except the abject fools, feel that at the first go. Then they get
their second wind. Of course, the whole secret of Government is to
prevent that damned House doing anything at all: but in these days
alas! that is not possible so one tries to minimise the harm it does.[2]

Such was the advice Rudyard Kipling gave to his friend Max Aitken
at the outset of his career as a member of the British House of
Commons. In fact, as it turned out, Kipling had read his man well.
In some excitement, Aitken had expected on arrival at the Palace of
Westminster to find a hive of activity, a constantly full Chamber and
the continued cut and thrust of informed and penetrating debate.
Instead, he was as bemused as everybody else by the flummery of King
George V's first State Opening of Parliament, at which the King read
out in a monotone and without conviction a speech written for him
by somebody else and after which followed hours of weary listening to
overlong speeches, waiting and doing nothing very much. In short, he
quickly saw that parliamentary life was not to his taste at all.

The Aitkens had returned to London from Cannes well in time
for the start of the parliamentary session on 6 February 1911. Given
that they now had the two children with them, together with nannies and Gladys's maid, the Parkside flat was no longer big enough.
Besides, Aitken soon realised that the House of Commons, boring as
its formal proceedings might be, gave ample opportunity for what he

was supremely good at: making important and useful acquaintances. Once made, these needed nurturing, and the best form of nurturing was to imitate his aristocratic English colleagues and find a country establishment within easy reach of London where he could entertain and, if necessary, plot. Furthermore, London was not a place for young children used to the bracing Canadian air. Nor was it at all good for Aitken's asthma, which had been helped, as had his general health, by the balmy early spring of the Riviera. In short, there had to be a place in the country, and Gladys, perhaps rather surprisingly, was handed the task of finding one.

In the meanwhile, there was much to be done, and many people to meet. Aitken spent much of February either in Ashton on constituency duties or in London cultivating new political friends. To help him, Gladys, by then a popular figure in Ashton, seemed happy to take on responsibilities there while her husband was in London. For instance, one of the high points of her February constituency month was the organisation of an 'At Home' event held at the town hall on the 28th. The event was a triumph for Gladys. Over 5,000 Ashtonians crowded the doors to get in. The *Ashton Reporter* gave the event a gushing two-page spread, noting in particular that

> Mrs Aitken captivated everyone present by her sweet and graceful manner; she was exquisitely dressed in brown chiffon, over blue satin embroidered in passementerie, with a blue and brown picture hat to match, trimmed with ostrich feathers, and she wore a lovely diamond pendant ... The decorations of the hall were never prettier ... The concert was in every way excellent ... Madame Gillespie's songs included such favourites as 'Beauty Sleep', 'The Nightingale' and 'Good-Bye' ... [She] was in capital voice and was repeatedly encored...[3]

Aitken managed to attend the reception (incidentally, to be told that he looked perfectly well) but even by the second week of February he was complaining that he 'must devote a great deal of time to [Ashton] myself ... [but it] is almost impossible at present on account of my business interests which I am not prepared to sacrifice'.[4] But by way of compensation, he had attracted favourable publicity in London. The March edition of the *London Magazine*, for instance, ran a long piece about him, and *The Commentator* chimed in, both of them highly complimentary although it was noted that he was no orator and that 'he was so little acquainted with English money that he had to do a mental sum to see what it was worth in dollars and cents'.[5]

Aitken's next move came as a surprise to everybody. Restless as always, and already disenchanted with his political life in England, he suddenly decided to resign Ashton and return to Canada to fight in the general election due to take place there later in the year. It was already known as the reciprocity election since the main bone of contention between the Liberals and Conservatives was the proposal for an overarching trade agreement with the United States. The issue was potent enough, it seems, to stir even the most somnolent imperialist hearts, and on this issue Aitken's heart was far from somnolent. The deal with the United States should be opposed and imperial preference promoted.

On 4 March, Aitken wrote firmly to R. B. Bennett in Calgary. They should form, he said,

> an Imperial Preference party, determined to oppose all American negotiations ... I want you to understand that this letter is written in all seriousness, and is a solemn proposal. My own choice is Montreal West or Northumberland County ... [Robert] Borden would have to agree that Conservative candidates would not run as well in our respective constituencies...[6]

In an equal fit of enthusiasm he wrote on the same day to George Foster and Allan Davidson, his old friend from Newcastle. To Foster he did raise the problem of his business reputation but to Davidson he claimed that he 'had really intended to wait for three or four years until all that Trust business died out but the situation is too interesting...'[7]

Aitken's scheme, of course, was both romantic and hare-brained. His Canadian correspondents knew perfectly well that the formation of a new, single-issue party was difficult enough, and much more so when stage managed from London, let alone with the encumbrance of

Aitken's personal history. His campaigning success in Ashton had obviously gone to his head. They knew, as did everybody else involved,
that the secret of success in their common anti-American endeavour
lay with the Conservative leader, Robert Borden.

During March, Aitken fretted. The House of Commons was boring,
Ashton was too far away, Gladys was looking for the country home
for the family without, apparently, being aware that her husband was
thinking of abandoning England in pursuit of glory elsewhere, and
his new political friends were starting to sniff that there might be
bad news soon to come from Canada. Always hating idleness, while
waiting for news about his scheme he started to sift through other
matters: begging letters, to be treated with care, given the publicity
which might result, and the occasional largesse; the queue of owners
of newspapers or magazines anxious to unload to a rich foreigner who
did not know better; improbable business propositions. Most of all
that could be brushed aside, but Aitken was at least tempted, encouraged by Kipling, to flirt with the owner of the *Evening Standard*,
Davison Dalziel, who 'evidently has no brains'.[8] Brains or not, Dalziel
was not yet ready to deal, and the flirtation came to nothing.

These diversions were put aside quickly at the end of the month.
There had been developments in Canada. On 3 April, Aitken wrote to
his friend Gordon McDougall that he had been asked by Borden 'to
lead the party in New Brunswick and to accept office in the Conservative Administration if the Party is successful in the polls' and that he
had 'practically decided to accede to this request'.[9] This was confirmed
two days later by Borden himself, who pleaded with Aitken with some
force that his duty to Canada ranked higher than his duty to his English
constituents. The die was almost cast. Yet it was at that point that Sir
Sandford Fleming had launched his missile about Aitken's supposedly
nefarious dealings over Canada Cement. A memorandum had been
submitted to Laurier, who had initially hedged in his response but soon
realised that a public inquiry into the affair could be to his political
advantage in blackening Aitken's reputation. Laurier, always cautious,
left the suggestion hanging in the air while Fleming continued to fume.

By then, word of Fleming's allegations had trickled through to
London. Nervous politicians started to look again, and askance, at

the highly praised young Canadian who had achieved one of the few Unionist victories of the December 1910 general election. Winston Churchill, for instance, had been planning a trip to Canada and had been seeking Aitken's advice in setting the trip up. Aitken had written a long letter to Churchill offering to arrange a visit and to make the necessary introductions (he was, however, careful to explain that he was not free from controversy in Canada and that Churchill should take care to avoid the question of trusts). On 5 May, however, Churchill wrote abruptly that unfortunately his trip to Canada had to be postponed. No reason was given, but the inference was clear.

Not to be seen to be too hostile, as a sop Churchill invited Aitken to dinner to meet important guests, including Louis Botha, the South African Prime Minister. Aitken was anxious to maintain whatever good relations he could under the circumstances and eagerly accepted. His subsequent letter thanking Churchill for the occasion was more than usually oleaginous. 'I want to tell you', he wrote,

> how much I appreciated the dinner party. You said that evening you would pay £10 to dine with Balfour any night and I said to myself I would pay £20 to dine with you. Then you seated me next to [David] Lloyd George. He did not arrive but that does not change things. Every other person wanted that place since Botha sat next to you.[10]

No reason was given for why Lloyd George failed to show up at Churchill's dinner party, but it does seem that political support seemed to be growing dangerously thin. Goulding wrote to him a sympathetic letter to encourage him, and F. E. Smith stood by as a frequent dinner companion. Kipling, not altogether helpfully, was urging him to meet his cousin, Stanley Baldwin, describing him as a delightful fellow as well as a man of business. The one senior politician who steadfastly remained by his side was his mentor and fellow New Brunswicker, Andrew Bonar Law, who had lost North West Manchester at the general election but had been returned to the House of Commons in a by-election at Bootle. Law was in daily contact with Aitken to reassure him of his support.

Gladys had in the meantime found a country home for him and the two children. Since the prevailing, and healthier, wind lay in the west to south-west, her search had led her, as so many others, to what has now become London's southern green belt. Deputed to find a suitable property, it had in fact taken no more than a quick search to fix on what was then the pleasant country village of Worplesdon, which, then as now, had access to a fast train service on the Portsmouth–London line. There Gladys found 'a long white rambling house' on the main road running through the village, in those days mercifully free of traffic, known as Worplesdon Place.[11] It was a good place to park the children and their nannies, and particularly suitable for Janet's new-found interest in ponies. Accordingly, a six-month lease of the house, furnished and fully equipped, including stabling and the right to graze horses (or donkeys) in the neighbouring field, was signed, with occupation commencing on 25 April 1911 'for the clear rent of Six hundred pounds (£600)'.[12]

Yet there was to be no time for peace and quiet. On 21 April, Aitken wrote to Borden that

> Sir Alexander Acland-Hood, Chief Whip of the Unionist Party, called last evening and offered me a Coronation Knighthood. I told him that I would like to consult you as it was possible I might desert my seat and go to Canada. Sir Alexander replied that the Knighthood was being offered for the purpose of rewarding me for services to come and to the Unionist Party and not to the Canadian Party.[13]

There is little doubt that Bonar Law was behind the proposal, although Acland-Hood insisted that the honour was in his own gift. Aitken asked Borden whether a knighthood would be of help in Canada, since

> it does not add to my position in England in the least … I would very much like to refuse it, because none of the persons who expect to get Front Bench rank in England will accept Knighthoods or Baronetcies, and I must modestly admit that I am generally regarded as a Front Bench probable.[14]

Aitken asked Acland-Hood to treat his acceptance as provisional and dependent on Borden's response.

In fact, Borden's response was not much help. As far as Canada was concerned, he wrote, a knighthood was neither here nor there. What was important, he emphasised, was that

> [the reciprocity election] will assuredly determine whether Canada's future path must lie within or without the Empire. Any public man in Great Britain whose vision extends beyond the three-mile limit must realise this truth … It is the plain duty of the Unionist Party to release you from any obligation which would prevent you from joining us at the first signal.[15]

There matters stood at the beginning of May. But after five weeks of fuming Fleming had had enough. He presented his allegations to the parliamentary committee which was debating a bill to improve Canada Cement's financial position. On 11 May the committee chairman read out Fleming's allegations in public. This put them into the parliamentary record under privilege, so that anybody outside could quote from them without fear of prosecution. There was then, as Fleming had hoped, a media storm. The *Montreal Star*, for instance, on the following day reported the 'rather startling charges' and pointed out that it was clear 'from a circular letter addressed to the [Canada Cement] shareholders … that Mr W. M. Aitken MP is the party against whom Sir Sandford Fleming makes the charge of benefiting in the transaction'.[16] Thereupon, the Laurier government announced that it would hold an inquiry.

Aitken was badly shaken. Some of his friends in Canada tried to reassure him that the political damage could be contained, but he was not convinced. 'I am under very heavy fire', he wrote in response to a friendly letter from Goulding, 'and must forego everything for the moment … Don't let anybody know I am taking the slightest notice of it, because I must keep an undisturbed exterior.'[17] He was keeping his options open but, significantly, he had not withdrawn his acceptance of the coronation knighthood.

On 11 July 1911, the *London Gazette* published a long list of coronation knights without citations. Near the top of the list came 'William Maxwell

Aitken, Esq., M.P.'. The announcement provoked another bout of Canadian press fury: that he had 'got rich out of … evil' (*Ottawa Journal*) or that he was 'an archmergerer, a wholesale stock waterer' (*Montreal Witness*) were two of the politer comments. Even the Governor General, Earl Grey, reported that the appointment had evoked 'a howl of indignation and disgust throughout the Dominion'.[18] Both Borden and Bennett took note. They were by then coming to believe that Aitken had crossed the boundary between being a political asset to being a political liability.

Aitken made up his mind. On 3 July he wrote to Davidson in Newcastle, New Brunswick. 'I have finally decided', his letter runs, 'to remain in British politics, and I will not be mixed up with a Canadian contest as I am determined to remain neutral as all British members must.'[19] This 'neutrality' was, of course, little more than a pretence. In the same letter he agreed to pay all the legitimate expenses of the candidate for Northumberland County provided he was acceptable to Davidson (in other words to Aitken himself). Furthermore, he helped finance other Conservative candidates, including Bennett in Calgary, and put more money into *Canadian Century* with instructions that it ramp up its anti-American campaign.

Aitken's withdrawal from openly contesting the Canadian general election was enough to allow a deal to be struck over the inquiry into the Canada Cement affair. The company's directors sent a senior journalist on the *Montreal Star* to Ottawa to assure Laurier and his Cabinet that Aitken would agree not to return to Canada 'to take charge of New Brunswick and Nova Scotia on behalf of the Conservative party' if the government would reverse its decision.[20] That was enough for Laurier, who had been pushed into the decision in the first place against his better judgement. The inquiry was quietly shelved.

In England, there were many fences to be mended. The British press, even in Ashton, had picked up and repeated the insults that had been hurled at Aitken in Canada. He now had to convince his constituents that he had absolutely no intention of leaving them to pursue a political career in Canada. The first step was to make his maiden speech in the House of Commons. He had only once, and fleetingly, intervened on a question in April. It was now time to make a proper speech which would be listed as a 'maiden' and heard by the House with the usual respect. This was done, in a rather dull speech, on 20 July. He then persuaded his predecessor as Member for Ashton-under-Lyne, A. H. Scott, to make a speech in Ashton itself on 22 July, praising his successor's work and explaining (perhaps rather defensively) that possession of great wealth was not a sin. He then cabled Bonar Law on 1 August asking him to 'write me a letter early tomorrow morning that my obligations to my constituents and to yourself politically are such that will not justify resigning from parliament at this time to join conservatives in Canada...'[21] This Bonar Law did, in the sternest possible tones.

By coincidence, that first day of August, the hottest of the year as it happened, saw what was without a doubt the most important political event of 1911: the passage in the House of Lords of the Parliament Bill. It had been tabled by Prime Minister Asquith in the Commons almost immediately after the February general election. Its purpose was to prevent the Lords from voting on finance bills and to introduce a mechanism for enacting other laws without the Lords' approval after a two-year delay. The legislation had a rowdy passage in the Commons, had been delayed by the suspension of political activity during the period of the coronation of King George V, had been passed by the Liberals with the support of the Irish National Party and had reached the Lords towards the end of July. Aitken had taken almost no part in the debates in the Commons. He was far too occupied with affairs in Canada and, as he had explained to the electors of Ashton, he was not particularly interested in the issue. In fact, it was Kipling, now full of righteous disgust at a proposal which he considered tantamount to subverting the monarchy, who urged him to be more active in the resistance offered by Conservatives and Unionists.

When Aitken did start to take an interest, he found Bonar Law equally detached and more occupied with the promotion of tariff reform. Nevertheless, Law did take the trouble to set out his views in a letter to *The Times* of 27 July. He had no time for the passionate opposition of the Tory diehards, arguing that 'if Lord Lansdowne [the Tory leader in the Lords] had allowed the House of Lords to be swamped [by Liberal peers] ... the Unionists in the country would be cursing the folly of their leaders'.[22] Goulding, on the other hand, told Aitken that the Unionists in the Lords would go against their instructions from Balfour and the shadow Cabinet and throw the bill out. Aitken passed this on to Kipling. They were both quite wrong. Enough Unionists followed the official line to approve the Second Reading by 131 to 114. Balfour hardly waited for the vote before retiring to his customary holiday retreat in Bad Gastein.

Aitken had not quite finished with the Canadian general election. As a last throw, he urged the London correspondent of the *Montreal Star* to get in touch with Kipling and invite the great imperialist to write something about the perils of reciprocity for publication before the event. This was duly done and on 6 September, Kipling sat down to answer the request. It was in the form of an open letter and, by any standards, was heady stuff. 'It is her own soul', the letter ran, 'that Canada risks today. Once that is pawned, for any consideration, Canada must inevitably conform to the commercial, legal, financial, ethical and social standards which will be imposed on her by the sheer admitted weight of the United States.' As though this were not enough, Kipling then threw in a stick of political dynamite. 'She might, for example, be compelled later on to admit reciprocity in the murder-rate of the United States which at present, I believe, is something over one hundred and fifty per million per annum.'[23]

Kipling's letter was published just two weeks before polling day. It was, of course, in the worst possible taste. Aitken, however, was delighted with it and the effect it had on Laurier's Liberals. For years afterwards, he would recall how the threat of innocent Canadians being slaughtered in their beds by brutish Yanks had swung the election. That may not have been altogether true, but it was the kind of provocative gesture which was already an Aitken characteristic and of which there were to be many in his political future. That aside, however, and whatever the true effect of the Kipling letter, Borden's Conservatives cruised to victory on 21 September. Reciprocity was finally pronounced dead.

Not only was reciprocity dead but Aitken's attempt at a Canadian political career had been buried with it. Borden was appreciative but distant. Bennett was now a Member of the Canadian House of Commons with his own political agenda. Aitken's friends were either part of the new Conservative administration or were content to pursue their business lives. Aitken finally recognised the truth. He could not lead a double political life. That said, and given the continued hostility in Canada, his only serious option was to pursue his business interests with greater concentration and devote more attention to what had been, up to then, his stuttering British political career.

There is no clearer evidence of what was in Aitken's mind at the time than his purchase of Cherkley. On their way back from a visit to Kipling in Sussex the Aitkens made a detour to visit a property near Leatherhead which was up for sale. If he was to make a serious career in British politics, he would need a country establishment. Worplesdon had been a convenient temporary base, but now that he had decided to remain in Britain, he required a permanent residence. It was with this in mind that he and Gladys went to inspect the property, known at the time by the name of Chirkley Court. On 26 September Aitken instructed his lawyers, Francis and Crookenden, 'to offer Twentyfive [*sic*] thousand pounds for the Chirkley Court Estate, Stock lock, and barrel'.[24] The offer was transmitted to the trustees who were in charge of the sale and immediately accepted, subject to contract. Negotiations proceeded smoothly and the final payment on the property was made by Gladys, in whose name the estate was registered. By that time it had been re-named Cherkley Court and ever thereafter referred to as 'Cherkley'.

The view from the garden at Cherkley Court, c. 1900.

Cherkley was, and is, a house with no more than infinitesimal architectural merit. It was built in the late nineteenth century for a Birmingham industrialist, but it seems to have been used only rarely since it had no electricity, no central heating and only spasmodically running water. Aitken spent a further £10,000 on improvements and delegated the task of decoration to Gladys (with the help of Mrs Kipling) while making a substantial order for prints of famous statesmen to hang on the wall. Bonar Law contributed a lorry-load of books which 'bulk large but are not of much value'.[25] Friends described the result as an overgrown suburban villa. Aitken's aristocratic Unionist colleagues sneered behind their hands. Later visitors were even harsher in their judgements. 'The house', wrote one, 'is of remarkable hideousness both outside and inside. It is an imitation of a French château, and the décor of the rooms in those days reminded one of the worst taste of the 1920s.' But the writer admitted that 'the house had beautiful gardens and a splendid view'.[26] Yet it suited Aitken. In fact, it suited him well for the rest of his life.

While Cherkley was being made ready, Aitken decided that it was time for him to go back to Canada on a tour to congratulate Borden and his allies on the victory. Nevertheless, in order to protect himself from continuing, and still virulent, press hostility he invited Goulding to go with him. The two embarked on the *Lusitania* on 7 October. Almost immediately they had a row. It was nothing to do with Canada but all to do with the makings of a political upset in Britain. Throughout 1911, Conservatives and Unionists, now more closely bound together than ever, had been muttering about Balfour's leadership. He was readily acknowledged to have an outstanding mind, a brilliant debating style and a cool ability to ride above the pressure of current events. But the thoughts of many of his party were expressed by one of his backbenchers in July: 'He does not lead – he is like a sleepy lion who has to be poked up to roar occasionally.'[27] After his insouciance over the Lords vote on the Parliament Bill, his position – not that he cared very much – was in obvious jeopardy.

The row between Aitken and Goulding was about who should be supported as Balfour's successor if, or more plausibly when, Balfour resigned. Two candidates were frontrunners: Austen Chamberlain, Joseph Chamberlain's eldest son and Chancellor of the Exchequer in

Balfour's government, and Walter Long, a landowner of almost measureless acres in Wiltshire, formerly Balfour's Secretary for Ireland and, as such, leader of the Irish Unionists. Goulding favoured Chamberlain. Aitken, loyal to his friend and mentor, persuaded him that Bonar Law was the right man. That achieved, the voyage proceeded harmoniously.

As it turned out, the timing of their trip could hardly have been worse. In fact, Balfour had made up his mind several weeks before, but the secret had been well kept. The rumours became ever more persistent towards the end of October. Aitken and Goulding realised that they were in danger of being left out of things. They scrambled back on to the *Lusitania* yet again but could only get back to London on 7 November. To their dismay, Balfour's resignation was formally announced the following day. For the two travellers, and indeed for Bonar Law, the train, such as it was, had almost left the station.

In fact, nobody knew what to do next. There was no agreed procedure for appointing a successor. The only point on which all could agree was that the responsibility for organising the event lay with the Unionist Chief Whip, David Lindsay, the 10th Earl of Balcarres, known to his friends as 'Bal'. Balcarres, as it turned out, was up to his responsibilities. He made meticulous soundings of Conservative and Unionist opinion. It was generally agreed that there should a ballot, that the electorate would be Conservative and Unionist Members of the House of Commons and that the whole thing should be done as soon as possible. Balcarres then made his decision. There would be a meeting at the Carlton Club on Monday 13 November at which the matter would be settled once and for all.

By Thursday 9 November, the electoral mist had started to clear. On that morning, Chamberlain told Balcarres that in order to prevent the danger of the contest slipping into deadlock, he would be prepared to withdraw in favour of Bonar Law, providing that Long did the same. Balcarres immediately chased after Long and asked him to consider following suit. Long replied that he was reluctant to let down his supporters, but the unity of the party made this course necessary. Early in the afternoon Balcarres found Bonar Law and put the proposition to him. 'B. L. said that the proposal took him rather by surprise, and that he could not answer offhand. He was very frank. Said that he had definitely

determined to stand, even though it would involve his defeat.'[28] Law
said that 'he was being pressed by his friends' (Aitken among others) but
'he did not feel himself fitted for the post from inexperience'.[29]

Balcarres started to have doubts, wondering whether Bonar Law
had sufficient backbone. Furthermore, by the time he arrived back
at the House of Commons the same evening, the news had filtered
through. Tension was high. There were objections: Law was no more
than the 'third best man'; what was wanted was a 'country gentleman';
Law could not entertain and 'he occupies no great social position'; he
lacked experience; finally, 'B. Law would not be the free selection of
the party, that his choice is "arranged", undemocratic etc. etc…' Later
that afternoon there came another objection: 'the influence of Max
Aitken on Bonar Law is not good, and … the way in which the *Daily
Express* is promoting that candidature is American – and sinister'. By
the evening it was known that 'Lady Londonderry is fulminating because B. Law isn't a country magnate'.[30]

These voices could not simply be ignored. Balcarres wondered
whether the Chamberlain–Long deal could hold. At the same time,
Bonar Law himself was starting to waver. He had been asked by James
Garvin, on a personal visit, not to let his name go forward. Goulding,
too, was reporting that others were joining what seemed to be a growing body of objectors. James Hope, for instance, MP for Sheffield
Central and a strong Chamberlainite, claimed that his standing 'may
gravely prejudice Austen's chances and in any case cannot fail to leave
a nasty taste'.[31] Garvin was a journalist and could be ignored. Hope,
on the other hand, represented a respected body of Unionist opinion
and his intervention required a considered answer.

On the Saturday morning, Bonar Law drafted a long and conciliatory letter to Hope, saying that he was not seeking the leadership but if it
was offered, he could not in all honour refuse it. He added that he did
not think that his position affected the chances either of Chamberlain
or of Long. When he showed his draft to Aitken it was met with dismay.
It looked as though he was preparing to pull out of the race. Aitken
later wrote that he 'had read the letter and thrown it on the fire'.[32] That
may be no more than another example of Aitken's flair for narrative
embroidery. The truth is that Aitken was unable to dent Bonar Law's

determination to sit firmly on the fence, however uncomfortable it may turn out to be. His final version to Hope read that 'friends of mine have asked me whether I would accept the position, if it were offered to me, and I have said that I would. I do not see what else I could do.'[33]

Bonar Law then spoke to both Chamberlain and Long. It seemed that they were both prepared to stick to their agreement, although in the nervousness of the moment any outcome was possible. The party leaders might decide what they wanted but the decision would be made by the backbenchers. All would depend on their mood. On the Monday, at midday, 232 Conservative and Unionist Members filed into the smoking room of the Carlton Club. The veteran ex-minister Henry Chaplin took the chair and immediately invited Long to speak, which he did, finishing by nominating Bonar Law. Austen Chamberlain then followed, seconding the nomination. The reception was so warm that Chaplin, instead of calling for a ballot, called for voices. There was no doubt about it. The noise was loud and unanimous. Bonar Law had become leader. Sir Edward Carson was then asked to escort him into the meeting. 'By this time all doubts and hesitations had vanished. On entering Bonar Law had an ovation – all stood and cheered, with one exception, namely Banbury who remained seated in the front row. This caused comment afterwards.'[34]

Andrew Bonar Law with his two sons, New Brunswick, 1911.

The question now was whether Aitken would be rewarded for his role in supporting Bonar Law to the leadership. At first, Aitken seemed interested in becoming Bonar Law's Parliamentary Secretary. On 18 November he cabled Douglas Hazen, the Conservative leader in New Brunswick, asking him to get Borden to send a message to Bonar Law recommending him for the post. This was duly done. On second thoughts, however, Aitken rowed back. On 23 November he wired Hazen again that he 'was grateful to you. Was offered appointment but declined account of uncertainty regarding Fleming.'[35] Bonar Law confirmed this in a subsequent letter to Borden. 'As regards Sir Max Aitken,' he wrote,

> he is the most intimate personal friend I have in the House of Commons (in spite of the comparatively short time I have known him) and not only because of his remarkable force and agility I should have preferred him as my Secretary to anyone else ... but he desires to continue to help me without any public announcement.[36]

For Aitken, 1911 had been a momentous year. Moreover, apart from the persistent shadow of Fleming, it was ending to his undoubted satisfaction. Christmas was spent at Cherkley, which Aitken, for the first time, was able to show off. The Kiplings with their two children and Bonar Law with those of his six children who had not been parked elsewhere were able to join with the young Aitkens for plays, food and fireworks. No fewer than twenty-two people sat down to dinner. Gladys was by then six months pregnant with her third child. In metaphorically patting himself on the back, Aitken could claim that he had used his money wisely to buy himself what money could buy. What money could not buy, of course, was his reputation in Canada or, in his new country, access to the high reaches of the English upper class. In fact, it was not to be long before he would again be pilloried in Canada and, to cap that, described by one of the haughtiest English ladies as 'a vulgar Canadian of the lowest reputation'.[37]

CHAPTER 8

IRELAND

'He's a jolly good fellow!'

By the end of 1911, Max Aitken was in danger of losing allies on both sides of the Atlantic. In Canada he was of course the object of persistent media attack. Irritating as it was, and at times distressing, there was nothing new about it and nothing much he could do about it; but to add to it he had in Britain managed to provoke irritation both in the small world of Westminster politics and in the wider world of London society. Worst of all, since he nurtured hopes of political preferment under Bonar Law in a future Unionist government, he had made the ultimate mistake of offending the Unionist Chief Whip.

In his analysis of those he called Bonar Law's 'intimate friends', Balcarres was not far short of venomous. He noted that

> Goulding is a wirepuller – but we are on good terms, and I can combat any ill-chosen advice he offers – and the man is under some obligations to myself. Sir Max Aitken however is much more seri-ous. He at any rate is a whisperer. He may be a dangerous element – I don't know. I have scarcely ever spoken to him – his attendance here is to say the least desultory; his interest in our domestic politics is nil. Few even know him by sight. His manner is clumsy to a rare degree – his gesture uncouth, his conversation a series of grunts, his face too old for his years.[1]

As if that were not enough, Balcarres went on to weigh the odds if it came to a showdown. 'He may be a source of strength to B. L.,' his diary goes on,

or he may not. If he tries to influence him too far, or takes opportunities to undermine my influence, I shall have to fight him.
My machine is strong, and it can grind pretty close. It would be a
long battle extending over twelve months – and I am by no means
certain who would emerge victorious. But if he beats me, he will
not long survive his victory.[2]

Balcarres had at least half a point. In domestic politics Aitken had
shown almost no interest in the protracted battle to curb the powers
of the House of Lords until prodded to do so by Rudyard Kipling. On
the proposed disestablishment of the Welsh church his mind was an
apparent blank. The minutiae of Treasury business were of no interest,
defence policy passed him by and the maintenance of law and order
in a fractious Britain was of only occasional concern. Furthermore,
Balcarres had noted Aitken's reluctance, which he himself admitted, to
perform the menial tasks expected of a Member of Parliament in his
constituency. In this case, however, Balcarres had rather less than half
a point. In fact, Aitken's attendance in Ashton, however inconvenient,
had increased in frequency by the beginning of 1912 for a very simple
reason: Gladys was in the sixth month of her third pregnancy and had
been obliged to reduce the number of times she could represent her
husband in his more boring constituency duties.

Nevertheless, leaving aside the reason, as his attendance increased
so did his tetchiness in doing what he had hitherto assumed to be her
job. For instance, he flatly refused to attend the annual social event of
1912 of the Ashton Conservative and Unionist Women's Association,
prompting its chairwoman, Mrs Neild, to protest to the chairman of
the main association, Councillor G. H. Coop. Coop passed on the
message. 'I am afraid you are making a very great mistake in not being
present because they have got it into their minds that you don't fully
appreciate the work they do...'[3] Aitken's reply was unpleasantly bad
tempered: 'I am amazed at the suggestion ... If they are dissatisfied
with their Member I will be the first to give them an opportunity
of selecting another.'[4] Three weeks later he followed it with another
salvo. 'I am quite prepared', he wrote to another constituent, 'for the
ordeal of opening the Ashton Stall at the Bazaar on the 9th May. For

your private information I may say that there is nothing I dislike so much as opening Bazaars.'[5]

Constituency duties aside, there were two broader political issues which could not be ignored: tariff reform and Irish Home Rule. To be sure, tariff reform, or imperial preference as it came to be known, was, as it had been ever since he started to take an interest in public life, first on the list. It was a matter of unbreakable conviction. On the other hand, his interest in the second was not so much out of conviction, in spite of Kipling's continual and vocal insistence that Ireland was inextricably part of Britain itself, but out of loyalty to Bonar Law (and almost as a living reminder of his Canadian Presbyterianism) in the protection of the predominantly Protestant population of Ulster. Furthermore, in the spring of 1912 the matter of Irish Home Rule was the only political game in town.

Initially, Aitken showed at least some enthusiasm for the Unionist campaign against the whole construct. Just before Christmas 1911, he had written to R. B. Bennett, by then a Canadian MP sitting for the Calgary constituency, that he 'expected to make an arrangement with you by which you would abandon the Canadian House of Commons and go into politics here, campaigning against Home Rule. Here we are all Protestants and no man is at a disadvantage on account of his anti-Roman views.'[6] He had followed that up the following January asking whether the Orangemen of Ontario were prepared to demonstrate in support of Ulster. Bonar Law noted all this with approval. 'Max Aitken', he wrote to Sir Edward Carson,

Member for Ashton and a great personal friend of mine wrote to Sam Hughes a member of Borden's Cabinet asking him to try and get an agitation in Canada against Home Rule. Aitken has a cable from Hughes this morning saying that he has set the heather on fire on the subject in Ontario and Rodgers, another member of Borden's Cabinet, is doing the same in Manitoba.[7]

Yet in spite of all these efforts nothing much resulted. Borden, as the newly elected Canadian Prime Minister, was understandably reluctant to strike an attitude against the sitting British government, not least, in practical terms, because the majority of Canada's Roman Catholics openly supported Irish nationalism. Equally, although he was privately sympathetic to Bonar Law, there was a limit to the extent to which he could publicly side with the Unionists, who were, after all, in opposition. Borden knew perfectly well that the Commons parliamentary arithmetic favoured Prime Minister Asquith. True, the Unionists were strengthened by a formal merger with the Conservatives (all of them now referring to themselves simply as 'Unionists'), but they still faced a Commons majority of Liberals, Labour and the Irish National Party on Irish Home Rule. Oppositions may shout but governments decide, and by the time Asquith introduced the Home Rule Bill into the House of Commons on 11 April 1912 there seemed to be little that the Unionists could do other than shout.

Shout they certainly did. On 9 April, Bonar Law addressed no fewer than 100,000 Ulstermen outside Belfast standing under what was said to be the largest Union flag ever made. On the same day, Kipling, now the Unionists' chief rabble-rouser, published his poem 'Ulster' in the *Morning Post* (by then under Howell Gwynne's editorship). It was, as might be expected, inflammatory. 'Rebellion, rapine, hate / Oppression, wrong and greed / Are loosed to rule our fate / by England's act and deed … Before an Empire's eyes / The traitor claims his price / What need of further lies? / We are the sacrifice…'[8]

Kipling's poem had a mixed reaction. Even some Unionist MPs found it too much to stomach. Aitken, on the other hand, was delighted. 'Must publish in Canada. Have stirred up much agitation there … Don't leave us out.'[9] Aitken went on quickly to establish copyright and to pass the text on to the Canadian press. Given its content, however, it is not surprising that there is no record of publication.

As the debate moved from the outside world onto the floor of the House of Commons, the Unionist shouting became more muted. Kipling's advice to Unionist Members, relayed to Aitken when the bill was published, was suitably provocative. On Second Reading,

in the event of a member of the Government rising to appeal for order the simple statement 'What need of further lies / We are the sacrifice', clearly and continuously delivered would do much good.

Similarly, if [John] Redmond [the Irish National Party leader] is drawn into the riot: 'Before an Empire's eyes / The traitor claims his price' is obviously the proper remark.[10]

Fortunately for parliamentary order, Kipling's advice was largely ignored.

Nevertheless, Aitken, as an elected Member of Parliament, was under some pressure, not least from his constituents, to explain his views on the matter, such as they were. This he did in a speech to the Old Trafford Conservative Association on 22 April and in a follow-up article in the *Ashton Herald* of 22 June. Both show signs of careful coaching from Bonar Law. His argument, as so often, related the British issue to the situation in Canada. The parallel that had been drawn between the granting of self-government to the colonies and the establishment of a separate Parliament for Ireland, he wrote, was a false one. Ireland had her own representatives at Westminster while the colonies were governed directly from Downing Street.

Furthermore, forty-two Irish Members would remain in the British Parliament after Home Rule. There would still be a subsidy of £2 million a year to Ireland, or ten shillings a year from every English man, woman and child, over which Westminster would have no control. Finally, the principal safeguard in the Home Rule Bill, the power of the British Parliament to veto any measure passed by the Irish Parliament, was worthless. There was a similar provision for legislation passed by colonial governments. 'It is an accepted fact, however,' Aitken went on,

> that in the case of the self-governing Dominions the Imperial Government dare not exercise their veto, even if they thought it advisable, for fear of arousing ill feeling. The danger undoubtedly exists, but how much greater would it be in the case of Ireland, where there is displayed a spirit of intolerance and violence unknown in any Colony.[11]

Having delivered his opinion (unsurprisingly, in fact, the straight Unionist line), Aitken took little further part in the debates over Irish Home Rule. In part this was because the subject no longer interested him. But it was also because one of the few friends he had made in the House of Commons was the Member for North East Cork, Timothy ('Tim') Healy, and Aitken so enjoyed his company that he would do almost anything to avoid outbursts of Healy's notoriously ferocious temper.

Healy was, in truth, a man after Aitken's own heart. Born in Bantry, County Cork, in May 1855, he was the second son of Maurice Healy, clerk of the Bantry Poor Law Union. In the years leading to the split in the Irish Party he had been an active supporter of Charles Stewart Parnell and had become Parnell's secretary. Short in stature, flaming red haired, with a square forehead and staring eyes, a devout Catholic, gifted with a sparkling intelligence, a fearsome power of invective and a sense of mischief, he had made a name for himself first as a polemical journalist in support of Parnell, then as a lawyer defending cases of perceived injustice in the Irish, and later in the English, courts and after that as a Member of the House of Commons for a succession of Irish constituencies.

*Tim Healy, the veteran Home Rule MP who became the first
Governor General of the Irish Free State in the 1920s.*

In the folk memory of Irish politics, Healy is known for his striking contribution to the debate over Parnell's leadership of the Irish Party in December 1890. At a meeting in the House of Commons,

John Redmond tried to confirm Parnell as 'the master of the party'. Healy shouted, in an obvious reference to Parnell's adulterous affair with Katharine O'Shea, 'Who is to be the mistress of the party?' (A record of the meeting notes that the intervention was met by 'cries of "shame", noise, several members calling out remarks which could not be distinguished in the uproar'.) Parnell replied in kind, calling Healy 'that cowardly little scoundrel there [noise] that in an assembly of Irishmen dares to insult a woman [loud cheers and counter cheers]'.[12] Healy, it was reported, crossed his arms and remained unmoved.

Healy had not stopped there. He continued his onslaught on Parnell and after Parnell's death in 1891 joined the Irish National League under John Redmond. Not content with the Anglophile Redmond's attempt to assume Parnell's mantle, he dismissed him as a 'finished elocutionist … Mr Parnell at any rate was a man and not a music box.'[13] Expelled from the League, Healy then joined the Irish National Federation under John Dillon. That went no better, and from then on Healy jumped from one movement to another and from one reconciliation to another angry split.

By the time Aitken made friends with him in 1910, Healy cut a lonely figure in the House of Commons. Yet he was still a politician of skill and, when he wished to deploy it, great charm. For Aitken, there were two things above all to Healy's credit. First of all, they were of the same height and could talk to one another as physical equals. Secondly, Aitken recognised in Healy a fellow mischief-maker. Healy was no respecter of persons and enjoyed poking fun and, on many occasions, launching verbal thunderbolts as required. Aitken loved that almost above all else in both politics and, of course, journalism.

Part of Healy's attraction for Aitken was his way with children. Aitken's third child, and second son, named Peter Rudyard, had been born in March 1912. Kipling had agreed to be the baby's godfather and took a great, if somewhat gloomy, interest in the boy. The arrival of the baby and the attention he attracted had naturally left the elder children feeling neglected. The situation was rescued at Cherkley by Healy, 'a small Irishman with twinkling eyes, white hair and a beard … immaculately dressed and smelling of sweet lavender'. Janet was entranced. 'He helped me make my tree house bigger … told me about leprechauns and the "little people" who lived in his country.'[14] With Gladys preoccupied with her new baby and Aitken unpredictable in mood ('I never knew where I was with him'[15]) it was a relief to have a friend who could be relied on to keep the children happy.

Aitken's mood in the early summer of 1912 was certainly unpredictable and, on occasions, irritated. He was having more trouble with his constituents. His response to begging letters, which at first had been sympathetic, became more and more terse. His initial enthusiasm in sending Ashtonians to seek their fortune in Canada was noticeably waning. One prospective emigrant received a brusque letter from his secretary: 'Sir Max wishes me to say that he holds very strong views regarding supplying people with letters of recommendation in Canada … has been subjected to constant worry … The recipients apparently laboured under the idea that the letters carried obligations to find them sinecures.'[16] Another act of kindness that threatened to cause unwanted trouble was his plan to provide the children of Ashton with one hot meal a day during the national coal strike of 1912. The programme proved so popular that it threatened to evolve into a permanent institution even as the miners returned to work. Aitken finally agreed that it would continue until the workers had received their first post-strike wages and should culminate in a final feast before closing down.

He was also losing patience with his agent, J. C. Buckley, almost to breaking point when he found that he was obliged to pay, of all things, for Buckley's summer holiday. That was on top of what he saw as Buckley's general sloppiness. Of particular irritation was Buckley's tardy response to a peremptory request, via a letter from a secretary, that one of Aitken's rare speeches in the House of Commons should be

> printed verbatim in both the Herald and the Reporter … Mr Healy's remarks concerning Sir Max he wants given special prominence. Mr Healy is considered one of the very best Parliamentarians and as you may imagine it is a great 'boost' for Sir Max to have him talk in such flattering terms.[17]

Needless to say, Aitken's interest in publicising himself in the press was not confined to the Ashton provincials. He had already stepped into the turbulent waters of the London press with his loan to the *Daily Express* following his meeting with R. D. Blumenfeld at the beginning of 1911. In March he followed this up by taking effective control of one of London's seven evening papers, *The Globe*. He was soon to be called on further. It turned out that his loan, and drips of further support during the year, had not been enough to save the *Express* from failure. By the end of May 1912, it was public knowledge that the paper was in deep trouble and was likely to fold at any moment. Blumenfeld appealed to Bonar Law, who in turn drew in Arthur Steel-Maitland, the chairman of the Conservative and Unionist Party. Steel-Maitland was well aware of the value of the *Express* to the Unionist cause and set about, together with another MP, Oliver Locker-Lampson, forming a syndicate of wealthy backers to buy the newspaper outright.

This was not at all what Blumenfeld was after. Although he realised that he was not much of a business manager, he prided himself on his independence as an editor. The Locker-Lampson proposal would put him at the editorial mercy of a group of unknown financiers. He then went back again to Bonar Law for help. Bonar Law, not knowing what to do, in his turn asked Aitken to work out a plan that Blumenfeld could accept. Aitken's response was simple and direct. He and one of his American banking friends, Otto Kahn, would also offer to buy the paper outright but, in doing so, they would guarantee Blumenfeld's editorial independence. When he heard of this, Locker-Lampson wrote a furious letter to Blumenfeld complaining that

> although you gave me your solemn word that you would not com-
> municate again with Aitken you have seen him constantly since
> his interference in our affairs; that you have gone to him for advice
> against me and that you have shown him our correspondence ... It
> releases me from any further obligation to consider your feelings in
> the matter.[18]

It was left to Steel-Maitland to sort the mess out. Locker-Lampson was out of the game. Instead, he managed to bully the Duke of Westminster, Lord Howard de Walden and the chairman of the Great Central Railway, Sir Alexander Henderson, to dig into their pockets. Extra money came, no doubt, from party funds, as was customary at the time. The shareholding of the paper was duly reconstructed. Aitken remained with a small but, as time would show, significant stake.

Certainly, in the middle of 1912 the Unionists needed all the favourable publicity they could get. Things were not going well for them. Lloyd George's welfare reforms were proving popular, the country was at peace and there seemed to be a general air of confidence in the Asquith administration. Opposition was even harder work than usual. Added to that were the internal difficulties over the Unionist programme for tariff reform. To be sure, the difficulties were nothing new. They had bedevilled the party (and its antecedents) not just for years but for decades. In fact, they had been the origin of the original split in the Conservative Party over the repeal of the Corn Laws in the 1840s; they had been the cause of Winston Churchill's defection from the Unionists to the Liberals in 1904; and they had provoked a similar defection, in the opposite direction, of Lord Lansdowne in 1903. At times, the difficulties could be contained within the normal confines of party discipline. At other times, however, the volcano which was thought to be dormant would suddenly erupt. 1912 was one such event.

There were three problems, all of them interlinked. The first was with tariff reform itself, the programme to charge tariffs on imports to Britain from sources outside the Empire to protect imperial trade. There was undoubtedly much support for the programme from manufacturers in the Midlands, who had been among the first to push Joseph Chamberlain forward in 1906. Lancashire, however, was a different story. Lord Derby and his cohorts were far from convinced, not least because imports of cotton for the area's textile firms would be penalised. The second problem was that the tariff reform programme was in some minds, but not in others, linked to the imposition of similar tariffs on foodstuffs imported from outside the Empire. Proponents and opponents formed factions. The 'Free Fooders', as they were known, were implacably opposed to the rise in domestic food prices that 'food taxes' would entail. Their opponents, the 'Whole Hoggers', maintained that the main tariff reform programme could not succeed unless foodstuffs were part of it.

So far, so difficult. In an effort to keep the peace between the two factions, the then Unionist leader Arthur Balfour had, in a major speech in the Albert Hall on 29 November 1910, at the height of the general election campaign, pledged that a future Unionist government would submit the policy of 'food taxes', or 'stomach taxes' as the Harmsworth press called them, to a plebiscite. The rider, which he was careful to spell out, was that Asquith and the Liberals should undertake to do the same for Irish Home Rule.

Bonar Law was a Whole Hogger. Levies on industrial goods and on foodstuffs were inextricably linked. The party had to row back from Balfour's pledge. Accordingly, on 20 February 1912 Bonar Law convened a meeting with Lansdowne and others for a discussion on the matter. Lansdowne claimed that 'the conditions under which the original offer was made have become obsolete ... [Balfour] himself does not consider that as a party we are bound by the Albert Hall declaration.'[19] That was enough. On 29 February he summoned the shadow Cabinet to a meeting in Lansdowne House. The general view, expressed by everybody with only Lord Londonderry in opposition, was that although food taxes were an electoral albatross, 'we must carry our handicap honourably and boldly'.[20] Balfour's pledge was at that point proclaimed dead. The only proviso was that the new policy should not for the time being be announced so as not to embarrass Balfour. What none of them seems to have more than dimly realised was that they were throwing a grenade into the crater of the volcano, risking a full-scale eruption which would threaten to blow the whole party to bits.

It was against this background that the visit to Britain in early summer by Borden assumed such importance. The truth was that Canada held the key to unlock the solution to their problem. If Canada, as the largest economy in the Empire, came out in favour of imperial protection not only for industrial goods but also for foodstuffs, it would go a long way towards persuading the Free Fooders that unity of the Empire was paramount. Their objection to reneging on Balfour's pledge would be muted, thus removing, in the words of one, the albatross from the Unionists' collective neck.

Up till that point Aitken had taken little part in the controversy. He was not a member of Bonar Law's shadow Cabinet and was regarded by Lansdowne as something of an intruder. But he did have Bonar Law's ear, he knew about Canada and Borden's strengths and weaknesses, and, above all, he had a country home where the two men could meet in private. Accordingly, Borden was duly invited to a meeting with Bonar Law at Cherkley Court soon after his arrival, Aitken, as always, playing the facilitator. It was all, it seems, very friendly. Borden listened carefully to what Bonar Law had to say. Having listened and reflected, he replied politely that although he had the greatest sympathy for what he had heard, he felt unable to make any public declaration of support.

Yet all was not entirely lost. As Aitken later told Kipling:

Borden agreed with Bonar Law at my house that in the next Budget he would refer to the offer emanating not only from the United States but from Germany for preferential trade relations with Canada and that he would indicate that the present policy of the present administration in Canada is to patiently wait for the present for a policy of preferential trade relations with Gr. Britain.[21]

Rudyard Kipling (left), Sir Max Aitken (right) and Mr Schofield Heap (centre) at a mass meeting, under the auspices of the Junior Imperial and Constitutional League, held at Ashton-under-Lyne, where Kipling was a speaker. Pictured in the Manchester Dispatch, *19 October 1912.*

To follow this up, Bonar Law asked Aitken to go to Canada to see Borden and others who might be of help to argue the case again for a strong statement from Canada as soon as possible. Aitken agreed to go, along with Walter Long and his family (and 'a retinue of servants'), who were visiting Canada on holiday, and R. B. Bennett, who had been spending time in England 'in the busy whirl where political opinion and gossip is rife'.[22] To add to the fun, Aitken asked F. E. Smith to join him when he arrived in Calgary, where he was to meet up again with Bennett to close two major business deals on which Bennett had been working. In the middle of August, with a suitable entourage of secretaries and servants, they all set sail in the *Lusitania* for New York.

Politically, the visit was not a success. Try as he might, Aitken could not persuade Borden to change his mind. On the other hand, in terms of business, the visit was a spectacular triumph. After travelling west in a private railway car with his old friends Frank Jones of Canada Cement and W. D. Ross of the Metropolitan Bank of Toronto, Aitken met up with Bennett and F. E. Smith in Calgary. There they sealed contracts to buy all the grain terminals in the province of Alberta along with two flour mills and 135 grain elevators. If there were to be food taxes favouring Canadian wheat imports to Britain, Aitken, Bennett and Smith were making sure that they would profit from the increase in trade which would inevitably follow. Electric power would be needed too, so they also concluded arrangements for the immediate development of a new hydroelectric plant at Kananaskis Falls, some 100 kilometres from Calgary. There would be money to be made there as well.

On his return to Montreal, Aitken, almost as a sideshow, joined in a syndicate to buy at auction the Montreal High School for $1,370,000, considered to be the record for a real estate deal in the city. He also went to a meeting of the Royal Securities Corporation to signal his resignation from the position of president of the company and approve the appointment of Arthur Doble as his successor.

Amid this flurry of business activity there was just room for one family moment. Aitken's parents had asked him to come to see them in Newcastle, but he found that he could not find the time. Instead, he commissioned a special railway car to ferry them and his brother Allan (and the family doctor) to Montreal. The visit was apparently short, since waiting for Aitken were the president of the Ashton Association, James Dolphin, and the secretary, Thomas Reade. After that, on 9 September, Aitken and his party left Montreal for New York to embark on the *Mauretania* bound for Liverpool.

As it happened, it was good timing. After the resignation of Sir Edward Clouston from the Bank of Montreal in November 1911, the bank had decided to sue Sir Sandford Fleming and Joe Irvin on their personal guarantees. Fleming by then was suffering from advanced dementia but Irvin was quite prepared to renew the public attack on Aitken and others implicated in the Canada Cement affair. Although there was no longer a threat of a government inquiry, the lawsuit, if it came to trial, would certainly command a high profile. During the first nine months of 1912 the two sides prepared for battle. It was not until the end of October that the case proceeded to examination for discovery. The lawyers for the two sides had agreed that the principal actors in the drama should be interviewed. But by that time Aitken was safely out of the country.

On his return to England, Aitken found the Unionist Party in a state of anxious expectation. At a meeting in early October, Lansdowne had suggested that the right moment to announce the party's repudiation of Balfour's referendum pledge would be at the party conference in the Albert Hall on 14 November. Furthermore, Lansdowne himself volunteered to make the speech setting out the new policy. Bonar Law was mightily relieved that the leader in the upper house had made the gesture. Since he was to follow Lansdowne, he would be able to tailor his speech to the audience reaction.

When the day came, the Albert Hall was full. The political temperature was verging on acute. The House of Commons had been adjourned by the Speaker to allow tempers to cool after 'an infuriated Unionist MP, Ronald McNeill, inappropriately but with stunning accuracy hurled the Speaker's own copy of the *Standing Orders of the House* at Churchill's head'.[23] The excitement had hardly died down before 'the diminutive Lansdowne, raising himself to his full height', stood up to announce that the next Unionist government would consider themselves free to introduce tariffs 'as they saw fit'.[24] The only qualification was that the new tariff on foodstuffs would be modest and would not thereafter be raised without consultation with the electorate in a subsequent general election.

The announcement was received with wild enthusiasm. When Bonar Law rose to speak, he was greeted with such cheering that it took several minutes before he could make himself heard. There was more cheering when he said simply that he agreed with everything Lord Lansdowne had said. At the end of the conference the Unionist leadership were congratulating themselves on what appeared to be a masterstroke.

They had, however, an unpleasant shock when the news made its way to the rest of the country. Opposition to food taxes across the nation was widespread and resolute. The price of food would go up: that was the message in the country, and the country did not like it. The strongest opposition came from Lancashire, where Lord Derby was having difficulty in preventing a motion to reject the Lansdowne proposal being passed overwhelmingly at a meeting of all Lancashire associations due to be held on 21 December.

It was clear that Bonar Law had to make a big speech, if only to calm the spirits. Aitken then took a hand. He persuaded Bonar Law to make his address at Ashton-under-Lyne. It was, after all, a Lancashire constituency and there was no better place for Bonar Law to set out once for all the new Unionist policy on tariff reform. But it was to be no ordinary speech. It was going to be another Aitken spectacular. Bonar Law agreed, and the date was duly fixed for 16 December. Immediately, Aitken threw himself (and a substantial staff) into the organisation. There would be musical entertainment before the event in the Ashton Theatre Royal and a torchlit procession after the event led by Councillor Coop's motor car, which was to be commandeered for the purpose and fitted with special headlamps, ending at the Central Conservative Club in Stamford Street.

It all happened as advertised. Over three thousand men turned up an hour before the show started ('on account of the limited accommodation ladies were precluded from attending') and by the time Bonar Law and Aitken arrived, having dined together at the Midland Hotel,

Manchester, 'there was a most animated scene ... prolonged cheering and the singing of "He's a jolly good fellow"'. Aitken himself led with a rather ponderous attempt at humour about the government's legislative programme before introducing Bonar Law. As it turned out, it was not one of Law's best efforts. He spent a long, and rather weary, time attacking Lloyd George, the Labour Members who were trade unionists, and Lord Crewe for his speech on India before coming to the meat of what he had to say. When he came to it, the result was startling. 'What we intend to do', runs the account in the local press,

> is to call a conference of the colonies to consider the whole question of preferential trade, and the question whether or not food duties will be imposed won't arise until those negotiations are completed ... then ... the food duties will not be imposed ... All we ask is that our countrymen should give us authority to enter into that negotiation, with power to impose certain low duties on foodstuffs and with strict limits which will never be increased.[25]

Torchlit procession or no, Bonar Law had introduced yet another caveat to the Lansdowne formula: that not even low food duties would be imposed if the colonies said that they did not want them. In spite of the national Unionist papers claiming that he had set out the policy clearly and beyond doubt, Bonar Law had done no more than further muddy the already dirty waters. It was a gloomy Christmas at Cherkley when Bonar Law and his family arrived for what should have been a celebration only to find that both wings of the party, the Whole Hoggers and the Free Fooders, were up in arms preparing for civil war. On 29 December, Balcarres noted in his diary that 'unquestionably we are in a parlous state'.[26]

Early in the New Year of 1913, help was at hand. Sir Edward Carson, the Irish Unionist leader, could not, as he said, give a fig for tariff reform, food taxes, referendum pledges and the rest of it. What concerned him was Irish Home Rule and the future of Ulster. If the Unionist Party were to split, his hopes for an honourable future for Ireland and Ulster would come to nothing. But if Balfour's referendum pledge were restored, it had quickly become clear that both

Bonar Law and Lansdowne would resign and the party would lose all hope of unity and possible consequent electoral victory, in which case the result for Ulster would be the same. Carson, whose mind was as fertile as it was aggressive (he had destroyed Oscar Wilde in his libel case against the Marquess of Queensberry), worked on a solution. On 6 January he got in touch with his confidant Captain James Craig, MP for East Down. That evening, Craig, with Carson's solution in his head, saw Aitken to ask him to arrange a meeting with Bonar Law.

Edward Carson, Baron Carson, leader of the Irish Unionists from 1910 to 1921, speaks out against Home Rule at a meeting in Belfast, 1913.

The meeting duly took place in Aitken's Knightsbridge flat. Carson's formula was subtle. Picking up on Bonar Law's Ashton speech, it was a compromise which would allow the Unionist leadership both to slide away from the Albert Hall speech and to unite the party. Carefully drafted, it went as follows: '…as a result of such a [colonial] conference [the British government] finding it desirable to impose duties upon foodstuffs … the proposals formulated should be forthwith brought before Parliament or first submitted to the electors for their decision'.[27] The formula was to be set out in a document, oddly named a 'memorial', to be signed by as many Unionist Members as possible. After some hesitation Bonar Law agreed with the idea but stipulated that he would only continue in office if the memorial were signed by a convincing majority of his parliamentary colleagues.

It was during the final drafting of the memorial that Aitken received news that Gladys's father, Major-General Drury, had been taken seriously ill and was near to death. There was only one thing to do: the Aitkens had to leave for Canada immediately. As it happened, although the news was distressing, it came as some political convenience to Aitken himself. As a Whole Hogger he did not like the new formula at all. But it would save Bonar Law and Lansdowne as leaders of the party. In the event, he was saved from signing the memorial by being abroad. (Nevertheless, when the memorial was finally published a year later Aitken had made sure that his name was there as a signatory.)

Two hundred and thirty-one out of two hundred and eighty backbench Unionist members signed the memorial. That was enough for Bonar Law and Lansdowne. They accepted the formula (although quite what it would mean in practice was anybody's guess). The Whole Hoggers in the Unionist press were duly furious. Aitken was widely, and quite unfairly, blamed for Bonar Law's change of heart. J. L. Garvin of *The Observer* was apoplectic:

We have been played with ... Aitken is our leader ... There is no Bonar Law but only a receptacle which must always be inhabited by another personality. The Hermit Crab in this case is Aitken, always putting himself into the other man's ear and swaying in his sinister, insistent way as he likes that strange enfeebled mass of timidity and ambition.[28]

CHAPTER 9

ODD MAN OUT

'In my opinion no war…'[1]

By February 1913, when the Aitkens returned to London after the burial of Gladys's father, the political landscape had changed. True, hostilities between the Unionist opposition and the Asquith government continued without remission, but with the passing of the tariff reform crisis in the Unionist Party the battleground had shifted back to Irish Home Rule. Here, too, there had been changes. What had been an Irish question had developed into an Ulster question. On 28 September 1912, Carson had launched a 'Solemn League and Covenant'. The language reflected the equally dramatic Scottish Remonstrance of the seventeenth century. In its first few days the covenant was signed by no fewer than a quarter of a million Ulstermen, some, it was reported, in their own blood. The message was simple: 'in the event of [a Home Rule Parliament in Ireland] being forced upon us we … solemnly and mutually pledge ourselves to refuse to recognise its authority'.[2] From then on Carson started to take point position in the opposition's assault on the government's bill.

In truth, apart from his abiding wish to support his fellow Canadian, Bonar Law, Aitken's interest in Ulster affairs had lost its initial enthusiasm. Moreover, he had started to worry, not for the first time and certainly not for the last, about his health. Gladys, too, on return from Canada, had succumbed to one of her periodic bouts of what was euphemistically described as nervous disorder. As for Aitken himself, the symptoms of his illness were both uncomfortable and embarrassing. At the beginning of March 1913 he wrote to Goulding that 'I go to hospital tomorrow. I have had some unfortunate trouble which I fear means a rather serious operation. I think stone in the bladder but the doctors haven't decided yet.'[3] In fact, his doctors, after an invasive examination of his bladder when he reported passing a stream of blood rather than urine, opined mysteriously that it was not a stone but 'phosphates in ... urine', which could be dealt with by medication.

Politician Max Aitken looking deflated in 1910, at a time when his health issues became more widely known.

At the same time, Aitken was starting to realise that all was not well with his Canadian business interests. The 1912 accounts of the Toronto branch of RSC proved on his examination to be in unacceptable disarray. The Halifax branch accounts as well were in a condition on which an early report was a matter of urgency. Even more seriously, he was losing control of the West Indies utilities. A warning shot of what looked dangerously like a rebellion was fired in late April 1913 by the board of Porto Rico Railways. They complained that his residence in England meant that he could not properly participate in the board's proceedings. Accordingly, they decided that he be removed as president and elected honorary president (without any powers). In a furious letter Aitken rejected 'the honour the Board of Directors wishes to confer on me', demanded that he be given an opportunity to appeal to shareholders and, as evidence of his plan for revenge, requested 'a full report of the proceedings of the Board meeting in question and the names of the Directors present and the division, if any, on this question'.[4] In the face of what threatened to be their impending decimation the Porto Rico board called for a truce, but then made their case so persuasively that Aitken agreed, in the following August, to resign the presidency but to remain a director. By then Aitken was convinced that he should travel again to Canada to take the whole of his business portfolio in hand. Moreover, there was work to do with his Canadian lawyer, A. M. Stewart, on the evidence he would give when the Bank of Montreal case against Joe Irvin and Sir Sandford Fleming came to trial.

As so often happened, when faced with what threatened to turn into a crisis, Aitken's health magically improved (prompted, too, no doubt, by the fee his doctor was quoting to accompany him to Canada). So too, perhaps out of relief, did Gladys's indisposition. But before they could leave for Canada there was business to be done at Ashton. On Thursday 29 May 1913, Sir Max Aitken MP and Lady Aitken were 'at home' at the Ashton Town Hall from 3 p.m. to 5 p.m. and from 7 p.m. to 9 p.m. 'The function', reported one of the local newspapers, 'was one of the most successful social gatherings ever held in the borough … During the afternoon three thousand guests paid their respects to the host and hostess … Many expressions of gratitude at [their] restoration to health … Appetising refreshments were liberally provided.'[5] The evening was an even greater success. Over four thousand guests turned up, to the point where the Aitkens could no longer man the receiving line since the queues outside had become too long and people were becoming impatient. Shortly before nine o'clock the Aitkens took their places on the platform while the band played, and the audience sang 'He's a jolly good fellow'.

After some polite preliminaries, Aitken came to the point. The newspaper report records his words carefully:

> I have been a failure as a Member of Parliament. (Cries of 'Oh no, not at all.') … shadowed by illness … unable to attend to my duties … Not very long ago I spoke to the Chairman of the Conservative Party and told him that the borough of Ashton might seek another representative in Parliament if the people so wished. ('No.') I stand in that position today. ('We don't wish it.') … The nature of my illness is such that for a long time to come, for months and months to come, I cannot hope to sit in Parliament … I am ready to make way for another man. ('No.') … To make this speech is a very great effort for me. ('Hear, hear.') I have the deepest regret in not having been able to perform the political services which I thought I could render to the borough…[6]

It is very hard to believe that this bout of verbal self-flagellation was entirely sincere. Aitken had made it clear that he was getting tired of Ashton and the demands on his time. As always, Canada and Canadian affairs were his priority. It is more probable that his May speech at Ashton was a ploy. It was designed to allow him a dignified exit, should he so wish, at any time in the future. As a ploy, of course, it was well executed. He perhaps exaggerated a bit when he claimed 'a bond of sympathy … attachments which we value much more highly than possibly you appreciate'; then, carried away by the occasion, when he paid a rare public tribute to Gladys:

> She has been very much to me in the last three or four months. I greatly regret that I should for one moment discuss my personal affairs, but I feel that she occupies a position in this borough superior to my own. ('Hear, hear' and laughter.) May I just pay one compliment to her, one acknowledgement of all that she has meant to me, not only in my Parliamentary life but in my personal, everyday life. (Salvo of cheers.)

Gladys then made a short, dignified speech (without referring to Aitken's compliment), and the meeting ended with 'the huge audience [joining] in the singing of "God Save the King" and ringing cheers'.[7]

Aitken's trip to Canada in June did not last long, but it was enough to complete the text of his evidence in the Bank of Montreal case and to start the process of shaking up the management of the RSC offices in Toronto and Halifax. He instructed the company secretary, H. G. Boyle, to make a complete report as quickly as convenient. That was as much as he could manage. Stewart and the Bank of Montreal would have to wait. By then feeling unwell again and with the distressing symptoms returning, he and Gladys took ship back to England. There were more consultations with his London doctor, Dr Thomas Horder. The result was that he was advised to put himself under the care of a certain Professor von Müller at his clinic in Germany. Müller (the 'von' was not an aristocratic title but an honour granted by the King of Bavaria) was one of Europe's leading experts in disorders of the blood which affected, among other organs, kidneys and the liver. His clinic, the II Medizinischen Klinik, lay in an attractive open site on the left bank of the river Isar in Munich. Müller had the advantage of fluency in English (he had lectured in Oxford in 1911) as well as a fully equipped laboratory for advanced research and a highly qualified staff. There was no doubt that he was the right man to find a solution to Aitken's problem.

The difficulty, of course, lay in finding out what the problem really was. On the train journey to Munich, Gladys reported, Aitken had a 'severe setback although every precaution was taken'.[8] Admitted to Müller's clinic as an in-patient, Aitken underwent a series of tests to establish a diagnosis. It was not easy. At first, Müller suspected Bright's disease, a condition of the kidney which would nowadays be called acute nephritis. Tests for that showed negative. After twenty-two days in Müller's clinic, the professor had found nothing more serious than an excess of uric acid in the blood as well as the urine. The diagnosis was clear. The pain he was experiencing was due to gout. For this Müller prescribed three doses of *Sachsäure* a day (a formulation of hydrochloric acid from rock salt, not recognised, it should perhaps be noted, in today's medicine) and rest at high altitude.

Towards the end of July, Aitken and Gladys left Munich and, following Müller's advice, took up residence in the Swiss Alps at the Grand Hotel in St Moritz under the care of Müller's good friend Dr Strübli.

The stay, and the attentions of Dr Strübli, certainly did him good. His health improved markedly, and by mid-August he was bored enough to want to return to England. Müller thought that his return was premature (although he was mollified by a most generous donation of £10,000 from Aitken to his charity). He wrote on 19 August that

> I do not know anything so helpful for overstrained nerves than a longer stay in the high altitudes. But of course a sojourn of a short time will not be able to mend a wrong which has been done to the nervous system through many years. There can be no doubt that the mental and nervous overstrain of many years is the real origin of most of your troubles and that you will return to normal health only if you will go back to a more quiet life. You must give up some of your ambitions and your plans and live more after the fashions of the English country gentry more than that of an American railroad king. You and Lady Aitkin [sic] will be by far more happy if you will follow this my advise [sic] and I feel compelled to give you this advise as a good friend of yours.[9]

In fact, Müller's advice was no different to the advice which George Stairs had given Aitken all those years ago and which had most recently been reiterated by Bonar Law himself. They had all noted that Aitken was by character highly strung. So he was, but he did not like being told so, and their opinions, however politely expressed, had little effect. But Aitken did accept that after his stay in St Moritz he was in much better health than he had been for some time. As proof of this, he now felt ready to address the problem of the Bank of Montreal's suit against Irvin and Fleming. Stewart reported that there had been another complication. Sir Edward Clouston had died in November 1912. As a result, Irvin apparently felt free to disclose, on examination, that he and Aitken had offered, and Clouston had accepted on behalf of something described as the Bank of Montreal syndicate, a payment of $1 million in Canada Cement common stock if the bank supported the amalgamation.

Aitken did not deny that the offer had been made. In fact, he saw nothing wrong with it and volunteered to appear in court for the trial, which was due to start in the Ontario Superior Court in Toronto on

17 November. Irvin's revelation, however, was enough to frighten the Bank of Montreal that there would be further damage to its reputation, inevitable in a long drawn-out trial with detailed cross-examination. The olive branch was duly extended, and the case was settled in early November. The defendants paid over half of their debt to the bank and the remaining loss was split between the bank itself and Aitken. Aitken's contribution of $17,500 was for him a worthwhile price to pay to bring the legal fallout of the Canada Cement affair to an end. Besides, as he learnt later from Frank Jones, Canada Cement would pay his legal expenses.

As it happened, it was on the day the Bank of Montreal case was settled, 6 November, that a second meeting had taken place at Cherkley between Asquith and Bonar Law to try to find agreement on the issue which had been the source of bitter verbal blows between the two: Irish Home Rule. By the time of Aitken's return from Germany the debate had become so emotionally charged that King George V had decided to intervene. 'He is … haunted', Lord Crewe wrote to Asquith in September from Balmoral,

> by the feeling that if he does not take off his coat and work for a settlement of some kind, and there is a serious loss of life after the Bill passes, he will not only be held responsible by Opposition partisans but will actually be so to some extent.[10]

The King had invited Bonar Law in the third week of September to Balmoral, where Churchill, then First Lord of the Admiralty, was minister in attendance. The two had a long talk, which Churchill reported to Asquith, and Bonar Law reported to Lansdowne and Carson. The result had been a guarded approach by Asquith to Bonar Law suggesting talks on neutral territory. Bonar Law agreed and suggested Cherkley as the venue. Accordingly, on 14 October, after lunch, Asquith motored to Cherkley for their first meeting. 'He arrived to find Bonar Law, characteristically, engaged in a game of double dummy with his host – the need for secrecy precluding a four.'[11]

In the end, nothing came of the three Cherkley discussions of 14 October, 6 November and 9 December 1913. Pressed by Bonar Law and F. E. Smith on the one side and by Tim Healy on the other, Aitken himself took no part other than ensuring that the participants had all that they required (Bonar Law habitually abstaining, Asquith very much the opposite). Besides, he himself resolutely maintained that he had no firm opinion on the matter.

There was also another worry. Reports from Newcastle, New Brunswick, were full of bad news about his father's own health. In fact, Aitken had been receiving regular bulletins from his old Newcastle friend Allan Davidson during 1912 and 1913. Kipling had even sent the old man a copy of his book *Rewards and Fairies* in July 1912, with which he had been delighted. Yet his sight was feeble, he had difficulty walking and seemed to be going steadily downhill. By the end of the year he had made a slight recovery, writing to his son that 'with my walking stick in hand I can now hobble hither and thither all over the house' and that 'it is even possible I might once more see old Scotland … to sit once more "'mong the bonnie bloomin' heather" – to wander around its shadowy woods and rugged hills and deep secluded glens'.[12]

He never did manage to make it back to Scotland. During 1913 there was a steady deterioration. At the end of November, Davidson was sending warning signs to Aitken. On 2 December, Aitken cabled Davidson asking whether he should take a ship immediately. The reply was that there had been a decided improvement and that Aitken should stay put. 'Will cable daily,' Davidson assured him. On 6 December, the recovery appeared ongoing and Aitken *père* was 'all right now'. Then the blow fell. On 13 December, Davidson cabled 'Mr Aitken died suddenly this morning.'[13] There was nothing more that could be done. Aitken asked Davidson whether he should return, sought assurances about his mother and asked for details about his father's death. After an initial cable advising Aitken that there was no need for him to return (and hinting that it might upset his mother) since Jean and Allan were already there, Davidson wrote a long letter about what had happened (a sudden cardiac arrest) and explained that the other brothers and sisters were on their way.

There is no record of Aitken's reaction to his father's death. They had been respectful and affectionate rather than particularly close, and Aitken's periodic visits to Canada after 1910 had been too occupied with his business dealings to leave much time for family affairs. True, he had taken a filial interest in his father's well-being in the later years, but then only from a distance and mainly through Davidson's inter-mediation. Yet a father's death, whatever the relationship, is always a milestone, and it was a rather subdued son who presided over another generously populated Cherkley Christmas and the New Year of 1914.

Up till the late summer of 1914, the political agenda was dominated by Irish Home Rule. The Cherkley talks to find a compromise over the bill had come to nothing. Time was now short. A new parliamentary session was to start in early February and the government would be entitled in April, if the bill was passed unchanged by the Commons, to invoke the provisions of the Parliament Act and send it straight to Royal Assent. In March, a group of Unionists, led by the redoubtable Viscount Milner, announced yet another covenant. 'We do solemnly declare', it read, 'that if the Bill is so passed, we shall hold ourselves justified in taking or supporting any action that may be effective to prevent it being put into operation...'[14] Carson, Lord Milner, Austen Chamberlain and Walter Long launched what became known as the British Covenant on 4 April. It soon collected no fewer than two million signatures. Emboldened by this support, the brigadier commanding the Third Cavalry Brigade stationed at the Curragh camp in County Kil-dare, along with fifty-seven out of seventy of his officers, declared that if the choice was taking military action against Ulstermen or dismissal, they would choose dismissal. Bonar Law even thought of moving an amendment to the Army Act to prevent British troops from being used to enforce the implementation of the law in Ulster. The King himself was worried enough to seek advice about the refusal of Royal Assent for the first time since the reign of Queen Anne. Undeterred, Asquith reiterated his commitment to send the bill to Royal Assent if it passed its Third Reading unamended in the Commons on 26 May.

The House of Commons was at its rowdiest. Some said that it was little more than a noisy zoo. The Army was bordering on mutiny. There were widespread demonstrations, frequently leading to violence in the streets. In short, Britain looked to be perilously close to the edge of civil war. In all this turmoil Aitken was unsure which way to turn or, indeed, to whom he should listen. Pulled by Tim Healy one way and by F. E. Smith and Kipling the other way, he could not make up his mind in which direction he should jump if, indeed, he should jump at all. Nevertheless, for the first time in his life he started to sense the intense, and at times all-consuming, drama of parliamentary politics. Up till then, public life for him had been the pursuit of strategic objectives such as tariff reform, even if the mechanism to achieve them involved complicated, and sometimes devious, manoeuvres. Parliamentary politics had been no more than a kind of incomprehensible game in which ambitious people vied for personal advancement. Now the journalist in him saw it for what it was: political red meat.

Much later in his life, Aitken responded to a letter which had come to him unexpectedly. It was about Irish Home Rule. 'I have thought for some time', he replied, 'that I ought to do a story on the negotiations leading up to the Irish Treaty. The years of 1913 and 1914 were exceedingly interesting, with immense efforts to reach a settlement.'[15] In other words, he was still looking at the events as he did earlier when the lightning was flashing at its brightest, not as a participant but as a journalist from the boundary.

Yet just as his interest in parliamentary politics was sparked by the experience of the cauldron of Anglo-Irish disputes, so, almost as a mirror image, did his interest in his Canadian ventures start to wane. Canada, for all his family ties, was looking provincial and, dare it be said, a trifle dull. Nevertheless, there was still work to be done. He had accepted that his hold on the West Indian utilities had been weakened by his inability, try as he might, to follow day-to-day events from London. Montreal Engineering was performing badly. The investigation of RSC's offices by Boyle in 1913 had revealed shocking sloppiness amounting to negligence. True, RSC had come through the sharp stock market fall of 1913 without damage, but Aitken believed that the whole company had become too complacent, and complacency was never acceptable under any circumstances.

In January 1914, Aitken launched what would turn out to be his last offensive to reassert control in Canada. Carl Giles, who had been president of Montreal Engineering at its beginning in 1907 but had moved in 1911 to join Charles Cahan and Almon Lovett in establishing a new investment bank, was persuaded to return to his old job. His first task was to organise the transfer of the management of three West Indian utilities, Trinidad Electric, Demerara Electric and Camaguey, from Halifax to Montreal, where they could more easily be controlled. Hard as he tried, however, by April, Giles had become convinced that this was simply too difficult. 'W. B. Ross [by then a Senator] was in Montreal last Saturday,' Giles reported to Aitken. 'He expressed the opinion that there would be a very strong opposition to having the management ... transferred to Montreal.'[16] So it proved.

Things were not much better at RSC. Aitken had sent Izaak Killam to sort the company out. He had recruited a young and aggressive assistant, Ward Pitfield, to help him. The two immediately started work. Such was their enthusiasm that they managed to upset most of the staff. 'Do you know any way of getting Killam to show a little tact and discretion?' Doble wrote to Aitken on 4 July. 'He is rampaging around like a young bull.' Then, a few days later, came a long letter of complaint, noting that '[his] dealing with the staff has resulted in upsetting everybody and everything to the point of disintegration'.[17] This, of course, was exactly what Aitken had asked Killam to do. But such drastic treatment left many scars and it was not until the end of 1914, when Doble left and Killam took over, that the business started to recover.

In July 1914, the disputes over Irish Home Rule reached a somewhat bizarre climax. King George V had become so worried that he had asked Asquith to convene a conference of all interested parties, to be held in Buckingham Palace. The conference duly opened, in the intense heat of a London July, on the 21st: Asquith and Lloyd George led for the government, Bonar Law and Lansdowne for the Unionist opposition, John Redmond and John Dillon for the Irish Nationalists and Carson and Craig for the Ulstermen. In truth, the only serious issue dividing the parties was whether or not County Tyrone should be excluded from, or included in, the jurisdiction of the proposed Irish Parliament; in other words whether it should be officially deemed to be part of 'Ulster', the counties already agreed as excluded. The argument went to and fro. Carson and Craig persisted in the exclusion of County Tyrone. Redmond and Dillon insisted on its inclusion. Division of the county was rejected by both sides. The argument went on for two full days.

Herbert Asquith, Liberal Prime Minister 1908–16. Asquith's government
was at odds with the Unionist opposition. He and Lloyd George led
for the government over the Irish Home Rule debate, July 1914.

The Buckingham Palace Conference then broke up without a conclusion, since it was clear that none could be reached. When it did
so, the main protagonists, Redmond and Dillon, Carson and Craig,
having wrangled in notably bad temper for three suffocatingly hot
days, parted with warm handshakes and generous words. Asquith
summed up his feelings: 'Aren't they a remarkable people? And the
folly of thinking that we can ever understand, let alone govern them.'[18]

Yet even then the disputes over Ireland were starting to take second
place to the threats of conflict on the European continent. An Austrian archduke had been assassinated at Sarajevo in late June; Austria
had demanded reparation from Serbia, followed by declaration of
war; two days later Russia had ordered partial mobilisation. Germany
claimed that Russia was actively preparing for war and mobilised in
return, threatening France. The skies were darkening by the hour.

On 27 July, a worried R. B. Bennett had sent an encrypted telegram
to Aitken: 'Cable your opinion war situation … grain company hold
considerable wheat.' Aitken's reply was also in code. 'In my opinion no
war best authority thinks otherwise if war breaks out must be universal.'[19]

There is little doubt that the 'best authority' was the British Foreign Secretary, Sir Edward Grey. Bonar Law, as Leader of the Opposition, was being briefed daily by him. Furthermore, there is some evidence that Aitken asked Healy for Grey's view and received the same message.

Aitken was to learn more the following weekend. On Friday 31 July, Bonar Law, F. E. Smith and Carson had arrived to stay with Edward Goulding at Wargrave. Aitken arrived later than the others, only to find that they were still talking about Ireland. Smith managed to turn their attention to current reality when he relayed a query from his friend Churchill. Since the Cabinet was divided on whether to go to war, would the Unionists be prepared to fill the Cabinet places of any Liberal ministers who resigned? Bonar Law dismissed the idea out of hand, partly out of dislike for Churchill and partly out of pique that the idea had not come from Asquith himself.

On the Saturday morning, there being no more news, the party decided to stay at Wargrave. Carson and Smith took a boat on the Thames and Bonar Law started a game of tennis with Goulding. Halfway through the morning, two Unionist MPs, George Lloyd and Lord Charles Beresford, arrived with news from the French Embassy that the whole situation had deteriorated overnight and that they should return to London. Although Bonar Law was determined to finish the set (he was winning), they all recognised when they settled down that Wargrave was no place for them to be. Aitken quickly arranged the motor cars and they all set off back to London. Once there, they went to Lansdowne House for a hurried meeting with two other senior Unionists who had stayed in London over the bank holiday weekend, Lansdowne himself and Arthur Balfour. All agreed that Bonar Law and Lansdowne should without delay get in touch with Asquith and place themselves at his disposal.

That done, the party, all but Aitken and Smith, adjourned to Pembroke Lodge for dinner and to await Asquith's response. Smith had persuaded Aitken to go with him to the Admiralty to get from his friend Winston Churchill directly the most up-to-date news. Aitken had been reluctant, not because he minded going behind Bonar Law's back but because he shared Bonar Law's distrust of Churchill. Once there, a message came through that a threatened German ultimatum to Russia had not been sent. It seemed, at least for the moment, that the crisis was over. Somebody then suggested a rubber of bridge. As there were five men there, they cut to see who would be odd man out. Aitken lost the cut and sat to watch the game as Churchill sat down and dealt. But it was not long before the game was interrupted by the arrival of 'an immense despatch box ... Churchill produced his skeleton key, opened the box and took out a single sheet of paper ... On that sheet was written "Germany has declared war against Russia".' Churchill immediately informed his guests and got ready to leave. 'He asked me', Aitken's own account goes on, 'to take over his partly-played bridge hand, leaving me, I must add, in an extremely unfavourable tactical situation.'[20] The game of bridge continued nervously as Smith and Aitken waited for Churchill to return with further news. He did not come back. It was nearly morning before they left for their homes.

By that time, early on the Sunday morning, Austen Chamberlain had arrived back in London. He went straight to see Lansdowne and, while Lansdowne was breakfasting, drafted two letters for Bonar Law to send to Asquith, the first urging unconditional support for France and promising Unionist support and the second calling for immediate mobilisation and a demand for an absolute German commitment to respect Belgian neutrality. Armed with these drafts, Lansdowne and Chamberlain went to Pembroke Lodge. At first, Bonar Law was no more than lukewarm. He and Lansdowne had already offered to be of assistance if required. It was now up to Asquith to respond. As the argument became more heated, Bonar Law saw the merit in pressing further. Using parts of Chamberlain's drafts he agreed to send a letter to Asquith affirming that

> it would be fatal to the honour and security of the United Kingdom to hesitate in supporting France and Russia at the present juncture; and we offer to His Majesty's Government the assurance of the united support of the Opposition in all measures required by England's [sic] intervention in the war.[21]

The letter was duly despatched to Downing Street.[22]

Asquith's response was muted. He replied that the government would take into account the points which Bonar Law had made about

France and Belgium. This was not good enough for Bonar Law. He immediately took Asquith's letter round to Brooks's club, where Lansdowne and Chamberlain were waiting. All agreed that Bonar Law and Lansdowne should go and see Asquith as soon as possible. In fact, it was not until the morning of Monday, 3 August, that they were able to do so. By that time, it was clear that Germany had every intention of violating Belgian neutrality and marching her army through Belgium to attack northern France. Immediately after the meeting with Bonar Law and Lansdowne, Asquith went back to the Cabinet, the position now beyond recall. Later in the afternoon Grey made a famous speech to the House of Commons. 'I would like the House to approach this crisis in which we are now', he said in the most solemn voice but with obvious emotion, 'from the point of view of British interests, British honour and British obligations, free from all passion as to why peace has not been preserved.'[23] Bonar Law followed immediately afterwards, pledging Unionist support. The House also gave its support convincingly, and on that very evening an ultimatum was sent to Germany to respect Belgian neutrality. It was rejected. From 11 p.m. on Tuesday 4 August 1914, Britain was officially at war.

The Daily Mail *reports the story that Britain declares war on Germany, 5 August 1914.*

In his accounts of the drama leading to the outbreak of war, both written and retold verbally to his first biographer, Aitken makes out that he played a starring role in bringing the Unionist leadership round to supporting the war party in the Liberal Cabinet and hence the government's final decision to defend Britain's honour. As with many of Aitken's accounts, it is right to be cautious. True, he was at most of the meetings of the Unionist leadership when they were debating what they should do, but it was very much as a fringe player. The decisive influence was undoubtedly Austen Chamberlain, who first persuaded Lansdowne to a robust line and then, with his support, led the attack on Bonar Law's hesitancy.

Nevertheless, credit must be given where credit is due. Aitken perceived at a very early stage that the prospects for Canadian heavy industry, if it converted to the production of armaments for the mother country, were almost unlimited. For instance, the demand for steel would be enormous and Stelco would accordingly benefit. Aitken knew that he had the ability and the connections to be the driving force in a prosperous Canadian armaments industry. Another personal fortune was awaiting him. He nevertheless decided to stay away from the temptation and to contribute what he could to the British cause. Others could, and did, particularly in the United States, make their fortunes. Aitken's loyalty was now, quite firmly, elsewhere – to his new home.

CHAPTER 10

THE EMPIRE AT WAR

'In glory will they sleep, and endless sanctity.'[1]

When war broke out in August 1914, Max Aitken was thirty-five years old, in his prime, small in stature but full of bounce and ambition. The world too was, if not quite his oyster, at least one of almost endless opportunity. Had he at the time even thought of pausing to take stock, he would certainly have been able to point to many positives in his life to date: emergence from a dreary childhood; the discovery of an ability, some said amounting to genius, in financial manoeuvres; the committed friendship of one of the great figures in British politics; what passed for a country home suitable to his status in society; a wife and family apparently in harmony, at least to the outside world; and, above all, the financial cushion which his stellar performance in his Canadian youth had secured.

On the other hand, of course, he might have been compelled to admit some negatives: his reputation was far from what he would have wished either in Britain or, more particularly, in Canada; he was clearly not suited to the muddy and endless debates characteristic of representative democracy; his health was subject to the temper and rhythm of his working life – when bored or distracted he was inclined to hypochondria, when stimulated he was prone to overwork leading to exhaustion and illness; family life, as the world knew it, was not altogether to his taste; in spite of a wide circle of acquaintance in both Canada and Britain he had few that he could call real friends; and his one clear political belief, the greatness of the British Empire, was far from the absolute priority that he sought in Britain's international relations. In short, if he had made a personal balance sheet in August

1914, he could easily have said to himself: so far, so good, but some things need attention.

That was in August 1914. But the world then changed, and was to change for ever, with the onset of the First World War. Oddly enough, as it happened, the first result was a jump-start in precisely the way he could have wished. The reaction to the declaration of war, at least in the white Dominions, was an outburst of support for the mother country. In Canada, for instance, with the irritating exception of Quebec, the response was immediate. The Governor General, the Duke of Connaught, was moved to cut short his family holiday to lead the appeal for Canadians to enlist. In Ottawa, in spite of a pall of black smoke from neighbouring bush fires, there were parades by the Governor General's Foot Guards, their band booming out 'Rule Britannia' and 'The British Grenadier'. Women gathered in groups to learn how to knit Balaclava helmets and 'cholera belts'. (There was even a piece of verse published in all the newspapers, entitled 'Grey Knitting': 'All through the country, in the autumn stillness, / a web of grey spreads strangely, rim to rim…')[2] An enterprising businessman founded, and funded, a new regiment, to be named after the Duke of Connaught's daughter, Princess Patricia, six feet tall and inspirationally beautiful, who graciously agreed to be its patron and, as a sign of her commitment, designed and embroidered a regimental colour, soon nicknamed, for no apparent reason, the 'Ric-a-Dam-Doo'. The cap badge, also designed by Princess Patricia, was perhaps not as heroic as its wearers might have wished, as it turned out to be a daisy. Finally, the government of Prime Minister Robert Borden summoned a five-day war parliament to debate and pass an Emergency War Measures Bill which would confer on the government powers to suspend *habeas corpus* if need be and to impose a tax on coffee, sugar, spirits and tobacco.

On the surface, therefore, the sleeping imperial lion was waking up just as Aitken would have wished. Nevertheless, as is usual in such matters, below the surface all was not entirely well. For a start, the Duke of Connaught was hardly ideal as Governor General. True, he was a prince of the blood, Queen Victoria's third son, godson of the Duke of Wellington, and was tall and distinguished in presence, but his only intellectual resource was his intimate knowledge of all the detailed insignia of every regiment in the British Army. Besides, he was a careless shot (on one shoot he had almost decapitated the Queen of Italy). In short, he had become something of an embarrassment to his brother King Edward and Edward's successor King George. It had become a matter of course that he should be parked as soon as possible in a safe environment where he could do no harm. The next one available, as it turned out, was Canada's Government House. There, in 1912, he had arrived in great splendour with his wife, Louise Margaret, daughter of Prince Friedrich Karl of Prussia, together with a substantial retinue. In truth, it was not a happy appointment. Nor was it a happy house. The duke was pining for his long-term mistress he had left behind in Ireland and the duchess soon became known for her liking of whisky and her extended conversations, in German, with that most charming agent for the very best champagnes, Herr Joachim von Ribbentrop. Nevertheless, by the accident of events, their Royal Highnesses were the beacons around which the Dominion was summoned to gather to go to war.

Nor was the recruiting drive as successful as was proclaimed. Certainly, the numbers were impressive, but the quality of the new soldiers was far from certain. The reason is not far to seek. Mackenzie King, who had stayed close to the leader of the Liberal opposition, Wilfrid Laurier, even after losing his parliamentary seat in 1911, was quick to notice. Far from being the flower of Canadian youth, they 'looked as though they were unemployed', as he recorded after watching an early parade, 'and had taken the work as an act of despair. They were poor in physique and badly drilled.'[3] Moreover, two thirds were apparently recent British immigrants who had come to make their fortune, had failed and were now living in poverty. Furthermore, officers had been hard to find since although there were a few idealists, many reservists, or 'summer soldiers' as they were called, thought it better to stay at home rather than get involved in real fighting.

It was against this background that Aitken was giving thought to where his future lay. There were opportunities, of course, for financial advantage. The lead-up to the war had seen a measure of panic in the markets and Aitken was able to take a long and profitable position in gold. He made a further purchase of gold to the value of £100 for Kipling, later also advising him also to invest in Canada and the United

States, where 'there are great bargains in Canadian Municipal Bonds ... New York bonds are very cheap.'[4] He guaranteed an overdraft of £7,000 for F. E. Smith, who had left his lucrative practice at the Bar to become, at Lord Kitchener's request, director of the press bureau, in other words the official censor. There were also his Canadian businesses to attend to, slipping away from him as they were as war started to throw up difficulties in even the simplest means of commercial communication.

Nevertheless, all this was far from constituting a full menu. Nor did the immediate political agenda, where he found himself very much on the fringe of events. Almost in self-justification, on 19 August 1914 he wrote to Arthur Doble with an exaggerated account of the role he had played in the previous two weeks:

> I happen to have been the medium through which the Conservative Party agreed to support the Prime Minister in his War policy. I was also present at the Admiralty on Saturday night when the Fleet was mobilised ... On Thursday night I dined with the new War Minister [Kitchener] and he has promised me a job which has not yet materialised.[5]

And so it went on. Not much of it was more than half truth. The Doble letter betrays his frustration in those early weeks of the war. There was simply not enough to do.

Aitken's solution to the problem of his frustrated inactivity was, as it turned out, characteristically inventive. He had noted that there were hardly any war correspondents at the Front. This, as it turned out, was a matter of deliberate policy. Earl Kitchener thought all reporters were 'drunken swabs', and he was supported by Winston Churchill, in spite of his previous career combining active service and reporting for the *Morning Post* in the Boer War. 'The war', Churchill said firmly, 'is going to be fought in a fog.' In fact, the only printed reports of the early months of the war were written by a British staff officer and released to the press under the byline 'Eyewitness'. As these reports mostly confined themselves to descriptions of the local weather, the byline, according to one editor, should have been 'Eyewash'.[6]

Aitken saw an opening. If the British were not prepared to sanction the role of accredited war reporters, there was no reason why the

Canadians should follow suit. Furthermore, he could think of no better candidate for the task than himself. Encouraged both by Bonar Law and F. E. Smith, on 23 September he sent a telegram to Sam Hughes, the Canadian Minister of Militia and Defence, asking him, as he told his friend Allan Davidson, 'to gazette me as lieutenant Newcastle Field Battery or other regiment as I can be selected for Secretarial position with Staff Officer to Indian Army ... Please reply immediately.'[7] Optimistic as always, Aitken assumed that his request would soon be granted. He had, after all, contributed to Hughes's campaign in the general election of 1911. But it was not to be as easy as that. Hughes was not easily persuaded. In truth, Hughes himself had a dubious reputation. He had served competently in the Boer War but had somewhat blotted his record by claiming that he should have had a Victoria Cross had he not been denied it by unscrupulous and unnamed opponents. He was a strong Orangeman, had been elected for Lindsay, Ontario, and had lobbied tirelessly when in opposition to become Minister for Militia, finally in tears promising Robert Borden, on his becoming Prime Minister, 'to be on his best behaviour'.[8] The deal had been done. Borden duly appointed him to the Ministry for Militia, a place in which in peacetime it was thought he could do no harm. As luck would have it, however, he, and Canada, found himself in August 1914 unexpectedly in charge of the whole of Canada's war effort. Fired up for the task, he certainly showed the required energy and drive. But even at the age of sixty-one he was given to intemperate shouting. Some even questioned his mental health. 'His features', runs one description, 'suggest the Roman Caesars ... His attitudes are ungainly and heavy; clapped into a black gown and tonsured, he might pass for a coarse but resolute Irish priest of the Middle Ages.'[9]

Hughes himself had two problems with Aitken's request. The first was Aitken's reputation in Canada. Although the hostility towards him had calmed down, it had not disappeared. The second was the unavoidable fact that he was still an elected Member of the British House of Commons. To try to clear these two hurdles Aitken decided to sail to Canada, with Tim Healy as a somewhat unlikely companion, to lobby Hughes in person and, if possible, Prime Minister Borden. Unfortunately, the convoy containing the first Canadian contingent, of around thirty-six ships carrying 32,000 men, 105 nursing sisters and thirty-four chaplains, was just at that moment lumbering in the opposite direction towards Portsmouth. In a fit of enthusiasm, Hughes had at the last moment decided to take a faster ship to be there when they arrived. Borden in turn had taken the opportunity to go on a golfing holiday in Virginia. As a result, Aitken found that there was nobody of influence in Ottawa to talk to. In fact, his only achievement on this short visit was to reorganise the Royal Securities Corporation and hand over the presidency to Izaak Walton Killam. But at least he could claim that by reducing his involvement in Canadian business he was showing good faith in his application for the new job.

Back in England, throughout November and December, Aitken fretted. On 5 December, Bonar Law wrote to Borden, yet again, recommending him. But in telling Bonar Law, and F. E. Smith, about the prospect, Aitken had given the impression that the decision had been made. This was duly published as fact in, of all places, Ashton-under-Lyne. This was already embarrassing, although in the Lancashire winter of 1914 nobody was taking much notice. To avoid further embarrassment, Bonar Law, F. E. Smith and Kipling discussed the whole matter again at Cherkley over Christmas and advised Aitken to force the issue. Accordingly, on 28 December, Aitken cabled Hughes, telling him that the 'most important section of London Press agrees to give me the opportunity to describe Canadian mobilisation in series of illustrated articles ... May I have the appointment now.'[10] He also had support from Nathaniel Curry, a Canadian businessman living in London and Hughes's friend.

There remained, however, the stumbling block of Aitken's membership of the British House of Commons. In the end, he decided to take the problem head on. In a typical Aitken manoeuvre, carefully calculated as they all had been (and would be) to skate on the edge of sharp practice, he sent a telegram to Douglas Hazen, the Conservative Premier of the provincial New Brunswick government, that he had asked General Hughes 'of appointment of which he can inform you. If appointment is given at once I will definitely engage to stand against Loggie [the sitting Liberal] at next election providing intention secret...'[11] Needless to say, Aitken did not inform the electors of Ashton of his proposal to Hazen. The reason was simple: he had no intention whatsoever of honouring it.

The bait was taken. The attraction of Aitken's money to the

Conservative cause in Canada was too strong to resist. The following day Aitken was able to cable Hughes, 'Have received telegram from Hazen who will telegraph you that I will be candidate in New Brunswick next election will this be sufficient...'[12] It clearly was. On 6 January, a Committee of the Privy Council, on the recommendation of the Minister of Militia and Defence, advised

> that Sir William Maxwell Aitken ... be appointed to take charge of the work connected with records generally appertaining to the Canadian Overseas Expeditionary Forces, and particularly the reporting of all casualties occurring therein from the time of the arrival of the said forces in England ... that Sir W. M. Aitken be granted the honorary rank of Lieutenant-Colonel in the Militia.[13]

Newspaper clipping showing a photograph of Sir Max Aitken on his appointment as 'Eyewitness with the Canadians' from the Manchester Courier, *19 January 1915.*

It was a very strange brief. If Aitken had been inclined to interpret it in its broadest possible sense, he would have found himself reporting on the unruly behaviour, and subsequent casualties in street fights, of the

Canadians once they had arrived in England. For instance, Hughes, a convinced teetotaller, had ordered that the troopships should be alcohol-free in the three days before their arrival. On arrival in Plymouth there had apparently been a rush for the pubs, with the customary results. Furthermore, over the winter they had been camped in dreadful conditions for training on Salisbury Plain, but from time to time they had broken out to get drunk in the pubs of Salisbury. The officers were apparently no better than the men. 'A picket goes around every night dragging drunken Canadians out of pubs,' one rather frightened lady reported. 'The night I was there, there were 100 arrests, including 22 officers.'[14] London had many attractions, not least with the increase early in the war in the number of prostitutes lining up along Piccadilly, with a consequent increase in the incidence of venereal disease. Officers generally did better, being steered to the comforts of the Cavendish Hotel in Jermyn Street, where the madame, Rosa Lewis, did her patriotic duty by giving them all they wanted, 'including a "nice clean tart" and a parcel of luxuries when they left'.[15]

Troops of the 1st Infantry Battalion, Canadian Overseas Expeditionary Force, Valcartier, Canada, 1914. The Canadian Forces Base, Valcartier, was erected as a military training camp in August 1914, as part of the mobilisation of the Canadian Expeditionary Force at the onset of World War I.

None of this, of course, was reported by the new lieutenant-colonel, who styled himself 'Canada's Eye Witness'. Encouraged, and helped, by Kipling (but discouraged by Healy, who worried about his health), Aitken was keen to get on with the job of covering Canadian heroics at the Front. According to one press report he was anxious to join in active service (his three brothers, Allan, Mauns and Arthur, as well as Gladys's brother, had already joined up) but his asthma had stopped him. If that was not possible, he would do his best to show the Canadian public the reality of the battles their boys were fighting. For the purpose, he set himself up in a large suite of eight rooms on the fifth floor of the Hyde Park Hotel, recruited a sizeable staff, bought himself a uniform with his rank clearly marked and prepared his first visit to the Front. So as not to be disappointed, he made sure of his comfort by buying a sizeable shareholding in the hotel. (But he was not so fortunate with his tailor, as his uniform turned out to be singularly ill-fitting.) Similarly, he rented a large house in St Omer near the general headquarters of the British Expeditionary Force, being careful to stock it with enough excellent food and wine to entertain officers from the Front and any distinguished guests who turned up from London.

Newspaper clipping with photographs of the four Aitken brothers (Max, Arthur, Traven and Allan) involved in World War I, entitled 'Five in the Army: Ashton M.P. and Four Brothers Serving', from the Manchester Dispatch, *1 July 1916.*

Aitken's first tour of Canadian positions in the Ypres Salient, the section of the Flanders Front where the Canadian Division had arrived in mid-February 1915, had to some eyes its moments of comedy. A fleet of Rolls-Royces would turn up unexpectedly at a Canadian regimental headquarters; out of one would jump a small figure in a jacket that was too long, a cap that was too small for his head and boots that were so large that they made his legs look ludicrously short. He would immediately accost the nearest soldier and start firing off a string of questions. Since his knowledge of military matters was almost non-existent, his questions were frequently wide of the mark and were treated at times with derision. 'I hear Max Aitken has been around again', wrote one officer to his girlfriend at home, 'pestering to be shown what a sap is.'[16] Yet he knew that what mattered was that his questions were precisely those which his Canadian public would have asked. Furthermore, as a Canadian he escaped the British censorship. He could tell the truth without fear or favour. (He could also mention names of men serving, something Kitchener had expressly forbidden to British reporters.)

Aitken's first despatch as 'Eye Witness' appeared in newspapers across the whole of Canada on 27 March 1915. Its style is dramatic as well as colourful, the first of many writings that illustrate his ability as a journalist. 'Picture to yourself a narrow street, the centre paved, the sides of tenacious mud. Line it on each side with houses, rather squalid, and with a few unimportant stores…'[17] This despatch was soon followed by others, describing in detail the first Canadian engagements at St Eloi and Neuve-Chapelle in defence of the Ypres Salient. But the most striking account of all was the description of the heroic stand of the 1st Canadian Division in the Second Battle of Ypres. On 22 April, the Germans had launched the first substantial gas attack of the war against the French positions on the left flank of the Canadian line. 'The French troops, largely made up of Turcos and Zouaves, surged wildly back',[18] leaving a gap through which four German divisions were about to launch an attack once the gas had dispersed. To cover their left flank until British reserves could arrive, the Canadians swung back in retreat so that they ended up forming a V-shaped line protecting the village of St Julien and, behind it, the town of Ypres. Although severely outnumbered, the Canadians held their line against wave after wave of German attack, met by equal waves of counter-attack, for five terrible but memorable days.

The account of Second Ypres, as it became known, was published on 1 May 1915, not just in Canadian newspapers but in the press throughout the English-speaking world. It made Aitken's name as a journalist of verve and courage. It even went some way to silence those in Canada who were still sniping at him. Strangely, however, there is some doubt as to whether Aitken wrote it all himself or whether Kipling had a hand, or perhaps more than a hand, in its drafting. Certainly, the language is ultra-Kiplingesque ('As long as brave deeds retain the power to fire the blood of Anglo-Saxons, the stand made by the Canadians in those desperate days will be told by fathers to their sons.')[19] Moreover, it was reported in a Canadian newspaper that Aitken had been ferried back to London on 24 April suffering from pneumonia, thus missing most of the battle. That was certainly not true, since Aitken himself records that his illness was over by 21 April and that he was returning to France. Yet it is perfectly possible that Aitken himself – not, others have noted, endowed with great physical courage – subsequently decided that he, an asthmatic, should keep well away from gas attacks and that he and Kipling put the piece together in London. If so, it would have been no more than journalistic licence to give the piece the dateline of 'Canadian Divisional Headquarters in Flanders, April 30, via London'.

The despatch about Second Ypres certainly improved Aitken's reputation in Canada. As a corollary, of course, it made him a more attractive candidate for the Newcastle constituency of Northumberland County, New Brunswick, which in turn made it more difficult for him to wriggle out of his initial offer. Hazen had written to him in January explaining that until the offer had arrived the best candidate seemed to be a certain William Park but that Aitken would be very much better. He had gone on to suggest that quiet preliminary soundings be made with various Newcastle friends. Aitken had seized on this and on 26 February had written back to Hazen that 'I take it from your letter that your plans will be as well suited if Mr Park stands for

Northumberland instead of myself. Consequently, I enclose an order
... [for] $10,000 ... and when the election takes place I will subscribe
$10,000 towards Park's election fund.'[20]

But Hazen would not let go. During March and April, he pestered Aitken. On 17 April he wrote asking Aitken to let him know
the position. Aitken replied on the 21st that he had been ill and was
about to leave for France. Nevertheless, in another twist, he did say,
'If Park selected I will pay expenses up to $20,000 but think $10,000
sufficient ... if necessary for me to stand think best [plan] would be
for me to place $25,000 under your direction now and stay at war
during election arriving a few days before the poll.'[21] He reaffirmed
this on 6 May: 'Replying letter 17th I am prepared to stand or support
Park.'[22] His friend Allan Davidson also weighed in, writing on 15 May
that the nomination was his for the taking if he wanted it. At that
point, however, Aitken had a stroke of luck. A proposal to extend the
term of the Canadian Parliament beyond its natural limit of five years
(which was eventually sanctioned by the British North America Act,
1916) on account of the war prompted Hazen to write that he had
anticipated the next election would be held in June 1916 but 'I do not
think so now and believe that they will not be held until a later date'.[23]
The heat was off. The correspondence, and the project itself, went
no further.

By coincidence, at the same time the first political crisis of the war
erupted in London. Aitken was in France at the time, but he had noted
that throughout the spring dissatisfaction at the stalemate in the war
was fraying political nerves. Lord Northcliffe launched a campaign in
his newspapers against Kitchener, asserting with some ferocity that he
was responsible for the shortage of ammunition for the British guns
and that a separate ministry, removed from the War Office, should be
set up to deal with the matter. The government response was to set up
a committee, under the chairmanship of Lloyd George, to study the
matter. A much more potent political bomb exploded, however, with
the resignation of the First Sea Lord, Lord Fisher, on 15 May. Fisher,
who had been called out of retirement by Churchill in October 1914,
was the darling of the Unionists, as Churchill himself had become
something of a hate figure for them. Fisher and Churchill had fallen

out over the expedition to the Dardanelles, undertaken in response to Russian appeals for help in diverting the Turkish forces from attacking them in the Caucasus.

Kitchener had initially refused to send ground troops and had suggested naval action instead. This had put Churchill, as First Lord of the Admiralty, firmly in charge. Fisher was resolutely opposed to the whole adventure and was not slow in saying so. During February, when the operation started, through March and April, the battle inside the Admiralty became more and more venomous. At that point it had become clear that the naval operation was unsuccessful. Kitchener duly reversed his opposition to the use of ground troops, and on 25 April the first Allied units landed on the Gallipoli peninsula. On 14 May, Churchill asked the War Council, over Fisher's objections, for authority to send naval reinforcements in support. This was agreed. But it was too much for Fisher. 'After further anxious reflection,' he wrote to Churchill, 'I have come to the regretted [sic] conclusion I am unable any longer to remain your colleague … I am off to Scotland at once so as to avoid all questionings.'[24]

As it happened, Fisher did not go to Scotland but to the Charing Cross Hotel, where he was easily tracked down by emissaries of the furious Asquith. Fisher, however, was not persuaded to change his mind, leaving Asquith with no option but to support Churchill in finding a replacement. Bonar Law and his Unionist colleagues decided to support Fisher and to vote against any replacement. Asquith was faced with the prospect of an acrimonious debate in the House of Commons and the withdrawal of Unionist support for his administration. That, in turn, would in all probability lead to a general election. Reluctantly, at Bonar Law's suggestion, Asquith agreed to form a government in coalition with the Unionists. The price was to be Churchill's head.

By the time Aitken arrived back in London on 18 May, the new government had been agreed and was to be announced the following day in the Commons. Bonar Law, much to Aitken's irritation, had accepted the post of Colonial Secretary, in wartime a job of little significance. Yet what affected Aitken most was the treatment meted out to Churchill. Armed with his proposals for membership of a new

Admiralty Board, he had gone down to the House of Commons to seek Asquith's approval, only to be told bluntly by the Prime Minister in his office in the Commons that he no longer had a job.

That same evening, Aitken, at dinner with F. E. Smith, heard the full story. Afterwards they went to the Admiralty, in sympathy, to find Churchill 'at the bottom of an intense depression'. 'Looking back on that long night that we spent in the big silent Admiralty room till day broke,' Aitken's own account runs,

> I cannot help reflecting on that extreme duality of mind which marks Churchill above all other men – the charm, the imaginative sympathy of his hours of defeat, the self-confidence, the arrogance of his hours of power and prosperity. That night he was a lost soul, yet full of flashes of wit and humour.[25]

Aitken was caught, as others before and since, in admiration. On his side it is not too much to say that the night vigil in the Admiralty was the beginning of a true, if from time to time unsteady, lifelong friendship.

With Bonar Law in government, Aitken expected to follow into office on his coat-tails. At least, he assumed, he would be a junior minister. Bonar Law turned out either unable or unwilling to oblige. Nevertheless, he suggested to the Duke of Connaught that Aitken might be included in the Colonial Office section of the June honours list, on the grounds that his account of Second Ypres 'had done more than anything else to make the British public realise what splendid work had been done by the Canadians'. Connaught, however, would have none of it. Bonar Law quite understood 'the objections to that, and on receipt of the reply from the Governor-General I offered him in the name of the Prime Minister a baronetcy'.[26] This, too, turned out to be a mistake. Embarrassingly, Asquith was reluctant to refuse outright but was clearly less than pleased. The upshot was that Bonar Law withdrew. 'I am very much obliged to you for your message about Aitken,' he wrote to Asquith on 2 June. 'I wished to be in a position to say that he could have a baronetcy but I had not consulted him, and in answer to my communication I have just received the enclosed letter from him.'[27] Aitken's letter was short and to the point: 'I need not say how much obliged I am to you for the proposal made in your letter today but as I feel certain that the honour would be criticised on the ground that it was given to me on account of personal friendship I must definitely decline it...'[28]

There is no reason to believe that Aitken's reason for his refusal was anything other than genuine. He of all people knew that there would be another bruising row if he accepted, like the row over his knighthood and even the simmering discontent over his appointment as 'Eye Witness'. Besides, he did not want to fall out with Prime Minister Borden, and guessed, rightly, that Borden was not at all enthusiastic about the idea. In fact, he went so far as to write to Sir George Perley, the Canadian High Commissioner, asking him to write to Borden that 'Mr Asquith offered me a baronetcy and that I had the good judgement to refuse'.[29] Perley duly obliged.

In his letter to Borden of 5 June, Bonar Law had suggested that Borden visit the United Kingdom to discuss the progress, or rather the lack of progress, in the war. Borden was quick to accept. He sailed from New York on 30 June on the *Adriatic* (the *Lusitania* had been torpedoed off the coast of Ireland the previous month, causing such outrage that the German submarines held off their attacks) and motored from Liverpool to London. Officially he was the guest of the British government, but a subsidiary task was to appoint Aitken as Canada's Military Representative. His job as 'Eye Witness' was to end; he would have an office at the general headquarters of the British Expeditionary Force in St Omer, a room in the War Office and a staff to back him up. In addition, the work that he had previously undertaken, and financed, privately in the collection of Canadian war records was to be made official.

Aitken's 'Eye Witness' reports had attracted much attention, perhaps, as he himself noted, more in Britain than in Canada, as a result of the piece on Second Ypres. From May onwards he had devoted himself 'entirely to the work of collecting information on and the writing of official reports and "Eye Witness" articles on the progress of our arms, for the Canadian and British Press'.[30] That role changed with his new appointment on 1 September. As a result of some protracted negotiation, assisted by F. E. Smith, British censorship had been relaxed. This in turn allowed Aiken to start issuing a weekly communiqué for the Canadian government to release to the press. (In fact, this was largely the work of Aitken's subordinates led by a British officer, Lieutenant-Colonel Manley Sims.)

Aitken had enjoyed the whole 'Eye Witness' venture, not least because of the attention it attracted and the consequent plaudits. On 14 September, for instance, Prime Minister Borden himself had written to him in the most effusive terms:

> I know that you in common with most Canadians are intensely proud of the magnificent valour and heroism which have distinguished the Canadian forces at the Front. Much of that splendid story would have been lost or would have existed in fragmentary form if it had not been told in the record which you have [given] to the world as Eye Witness. Will you permit me to say that the clearness, the dignity and the impresiveness [*sic*] with which the story was told were worthy of the great achievements which it recorded.[31]

There would be no such encomia in his new job. He was to report directly to the erratic Sam Hughes, the Minister of Militia. He would be much more involved in the conduct of the war and consequently less in the limelight of publicity. That, and the feeling that the war was going badly, led him to write to Kipling's wife asking when Kipling would be back from France, where he had been sent as a roving reporter. 'I want to see him,' he told her. 'I must talk to him about the position. I am desperately downhearted.'[32] Downhearted or not, Aitken set about organising a centre for the collection of Canadian war records. He made available the RSC offices in Lombard Street, eight rooms with fire-proof vaults, which were soon turned into what looked like a military base. Almost overnight the staff of five were recruited to service, one made a sergeant and one a corporal, and all were provided with uniforms. Further recruitment was to come from the pool of Canadian soldiers wounded and repatriated from France.

Newspaper clipping with photograph of Sir Max Aitken in a Rolls-Royce, seated beside the chauffeur, together with Sir Sam Hughes (centre back seat) and David Lloyd George (on right hand side), from the Montreal Star, *18 August 1916.*

The task took up much of Aitken's time during the autumn of 1915. Fortunately, his duties as Canadian Representative at the Front were comparatively light. Some, of course, were melancholy. That September, at the Battle of Loos, Kipling's only son, John, had been posted as 'wounded and missing', although his family retained the hope that he might have been taken prisoner behind enemy lines. Aitken offered help in the search, but it soon became clear that John was lost for ever (his grave was eventually identified as lying in St Mary's ADS Cemetery in Haisnes). Others were more cheerful. On one of his visits to France in December he discovered that Churchill was in St Omer. Having taken most of the blame for the Gallipoli disaster, Churchill had resigned from the government in November and had decided to serve an expiatory term in the trenches. He had been expecting to be gazetted as brigadier-general to command a brigade but at the last moment there was a change of command in the BEF and Asquith had put a stop to the idea to allow the new commander, Sir Douglas Haig, full freedom of action. As a result, Churchill was kept waiting with nothing much to do until Haig made up his mind. Aitken was happy to issue an invitation, and Churchill was equally happy to write to his wife on 20 December, 'I have now moved into Max Aitken's house – a sort of Canadian war office – where I am very comfortable and well looked after.'[33]

That apart, 1915 ended on a sour and depressing note. The visitors' book at Cherkley records no guests for Christmas; the Kiplings said that they wished to be by themselves to mourn for John. Reports from the Front continued their litany of tragic waste, and there was a growing feeling in London that the Asquith administration had lost its way. None of that boded well. For Aitken, however, there was at least one beacon for the future. As Churchill's biographer puts it:

It was the beginning of a lifelong intimacy between the two men. At St Omer, Aitken gave Churchill renewed hope in his future … It was a time when Churchill desperately needed such encouragement. He never forgot how at that moment, when almost everyone else seemed against him, Aitken held out the hand of hospitality and hope.[34]

CHAPTER 11

1916

'I fear Sir Max isn't quite a gentleman'[1]

1915 may have ended on a sour note, but the New Year of 1916 promised no better. The winter was cold and bleak. Cherkley without
the Kiplings at Christmas had lacked its usual magic, and the news
from the Front was little more than a daily recital of fallen brothers,
husbands, sons or lovers, seemingly with no end in sight. Furthermore, now that Bonar Law was in government Aitken was no more
than holding on to the edge of London political life. To cap it all, his
asthma was reacting badly to the weather. Both at Cherkley and in
his rooms in the Hyde Park Hotel, the elaborate equipment to deal
with it was in use more frequently than usual. As a result, he had taken
to having breakfast in bed, both at Cherkley, with the unexpected
company of his daughter Janet, who had taken to climbing into his
bed when she woke in the morning, and in London, when the morning papers stirred him to activity on his bedside telephone.

Breakfast in bed was all very well but, in spite of the asthma, Janet's
cuddles and the flatness of his political life, there was still serious work
to be done. The priority was the organisation of the Lombard Street
office. During January it had assumed the name of the Canadian War
Records Office (CWRO). Initially, its function, as Aitken put it, was
to act as a depository for war records of Canadian units in the field as
they came in, to be properly retained for sorting, indexing and filing.
Yet Aitken's plan had been, and still was, more ambitious than simply
to establish and retain an archive of record. The CWRO was to take
on, no more and no less, the role of publicist for Canada's war effort.
To make a start, using his rank as lieutenant-colonel, Aitken gave out

junior ranks as he thought fit. The head clerk became a sergeant-major, the book-keeper a sergeant and there was a scattering of corporals and lance-corporals, all of them in military uniform with appropriate badges of rank. From the initial five the total complement had by the end of January risen to seventeen. Moreover, a British journalist, now captain, Wilfred Holt-White, was in charge of the staff, and an official photographer, Captain H. E. Knobel, had been appointed. There were plans to engage a cinematographer to take films of the troops in the trenches, and one section of the staff were engaged in producing a broadsheet, the *Canadian Daily Record*, including news from home, for circulation to the Canadians on the Front.

Mobile cinema equipment being loaded into the back of military vehicles.
Sir Max Aitken is shown the equipment by military officials, c. 1916–18.

To finance the whole operation, Aitken sought approval both from Sir Sam Hughes, to whom he was nominally responsible, and from Borden. Writing to the latter on 1 January, he applied 'for an estimate for expenditure not exceeding $25,000 for year 1916 … I already act without salary and pay my own personal expenses.' He went on to explain that 'material will be compiled by trained civilian compilators drawn from the British Museum or other experienced staffs'.[2] Needless to say, the directors of the British Museum had no idea that their staff was to be raided; nor indeed did those in charge at the Public Records Office in Chancery Lane, or at the Historical Section of the Imperial Defence Committee, or at the office of the Canadian Dominion Archivist. Sooner or later, one by one, they were all in their turn to be upset by the demands of the bustling amateur.

Borden immediately agreed to Aitken's request for funds, but Hughes, forever relentlessly interfering (the more so after receiving a knighthood the previous August), on his own initiative recruited an assistant designed to support the management of Aitken's project. However well meant, Hughes's choice fell on a candidate who from the outset was quite plainly unsuitable to do what was required, which was to introduce a professional discipline into what was something of a ramshackle affair.

Hughes's choice, Henry Beckles Willson, was ten years older than Aitken, a wandering journalist who, born in Montreal, had migrated to Britain in 1892. With good looks and a suave, if from time to time obsequious, manner he had managed to ingratiate himself in and around the London drawing rooms. Yet in spite of his undoubted social skills, 'all the latent defects in his character began to overtake all his energy and ability'.[3] Fatally, he fell out with the great Lord Northcliffe and returned to Canada in the spring of 1913 to what he hoped would be a new life in Nova Scotia. Even that was far from a success. By 1915 he was on the verge of bankruptcy. There was nothing for it but to go to Ottawa, to establish himself in society (among other tasks helping the Duchess of Connaught to her 'whisky at lunch')[4] and write a stream of letters to ministers seeking employment.

The only minister to respond, early in January 1916 and for no obviously identifiable reason, was Sir Sam Hughes. Hughes, once he had adopted Willson, would brook no argument. Willson was to become an officer in the militia with immediate effect at a salary of $4,000 per annum. He was to go forthwith to London as second in command of the CWRO. He was to present himself to Sir Max Aitken and follow his instructions. Accordingly, on 12 February 1916, Willson, in a new major's uniform, presented himself by appointment at 10 a.m. at the Hyde Park Hotel. There he found Aitken 'breakfasting in bed. He greeted me cordially, a bullet-headed, dull-skinned little man;

his laughter and manner very boyish…'⁵ Willson duly fell victim to the Aitken charm. Although he was quickly disabused of the idea that he would be second in command of the CWRO, let alone take over from Aitken himself, he considered it a privilege to take on a subordinate role.

It so happened that Aitken, in spite of his asthma, was in a particularly good mood. The first volume of his book *Canada in Flanders* had been published in January. It had been a startling success. Based on the despatches of 'Eye Witness', it described the heroics of the Canadians at Second Ypres and elsewhere. To be sure, the language to the modern reader is rather ponderous, but in its day it served its purpose. Certainly Kipling, for one, could find no fault with it and the London press tumbled over themselves in praising it: 'a book to thrill and inspire', sang the *Sunday Times*; 'an epic of Canadian manhood', proclaimed the *Sunday Pictorial*; 'their courage makes us tingle with pride', trilled *Reynolds News*.⁶ Aitken, understandably, was delighted and, as she reported, was quick to show the reviews to his daughter Janet.

Less pleasing, however, were the problems the fledgling CWRO were meeting. Canadian commanders in the field were starting to resent the imperious demands for documents coming out of Lombard Street. 'The same audacity and arrogance which made Sam Hughes supreme and omnipotent in military affairs in Canada', Willson observed, 'was exercised here by his representative and lieutenant in London.'⁷ It would have been easier if the minister himself had commanded the undying loyalty of his troops. Disturbingly for Aitken, Hughes himself was becoming increasingly unpopular both with the commanders in the field and with the soldiers under their command. There were many complaints against him, too, in both Ottawa and London. He had a running feud with the Duke of Connaught (like many others, Connaught thought Hughes 'a conceited lunatic')⁸ and he made insistent and intemperate demands for his son to be promoted and for other of his cronies to be given high commands. Moreover, he was said to have been involved in some way in fraudulent munitions contracts early in the war. All that, at least for the moment, could be ignored. What could not be ignored, however, was his determination that the Canadian Expeditionary Force (CEF) should use the Ross rifle.

The Ross rifle was in Hughes's eyes in every sense Canadian. True, it had been designed by a Scottish entrepreneur, Sir Charles Ross, but it was manufactured in a factory placed defiantly on the Plains of Abraham in Quebec City, which the British had stormed in 1759. Hughes had followed its development from the outset of its introduction towards the end of the Boer War, through the disputes which followed, to the point where, in 1908, as chairman of the Small Arms Committee of the Canadian House of Commons, he had routed all opposition in his defence of the rifle's qualities. These, he claimed, were the long barrel, imitating the barrel used by the Boer long-range snipers, the speed of its straight-pull action and its accuracy at a distance. Hughes, even after many had challenged his judgement, never wavered in his view that the Ross rifle was the proper weapon for the Canadian infantry as they went into battle in Flanders. Above all, it was Canadian.

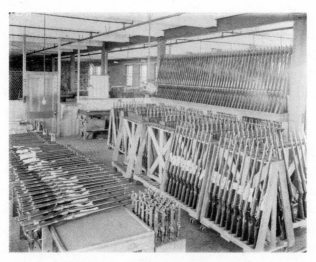

Interior of the Ross Rifle factory, Quebec, c. 1900–05.

That was certainly not the view of the British general appointed to command the Canadian First Contingent in the autumn of 1914 and who was still commanding what became the Canadian Expeditionary

Force in 1915. The British Lieutenant-General Edwin Alderson had taken command of the Canadians when they arrived in England. Contrary to the information given by Hughes, rather than a fully trained army he found a raw, ill-disciplined and inexperienced bunch of ruffians. He set to work to produce what in the end, at Second Ypres, was fast becoming a hardened and courageous fighting force. Yet even on the training ground of Salisbury Plain the Canadians found that the Ross rifle had a habit of jamming. This was made worse by the lack of suitable ammunition from Canada. Alderson pressed for the Canadians to be re-equipped with the British Lee-Enfield rifle, but Hughes would have none of it. By the time of Second Ypres, Canadian soldiers were seen openly throwing away their Ross rifles and searching for Lee-Enfield replacements where they could; some, it was said, picking them up from British corpses.

By February 1916, Alderson had had enough. Not only had Hughes ignored all the tests showing the superiority of the Lee-Enfield over the Ross rifle but he had taken to bombarding Aitken with cables demanding that his chosen favourite, Brigadier-General Richard Turner, be given the command of a second Canadian division and that his son Garnet be appointed to lead its Fourth Brigade. Alderson at first seemed to agree but almost immediately backtracked. Aitken, in support of his minister, had leaked the story of Garnet's new appointment but then he too had to row back. To cover himself, he blamed Alderson. 'Unfortunately General Alderson was most inconsistent', he wrote to Borden, 'and afterwards talked most indiscreetly.'9 The two issues, of Turner and the Ross rifle, became inextricably linked.

To clear the air, Alderson commissioned another series of tests of the two rifles. There was no doubt about the result. The Lee-Enfield fired from 100 to 125 rounds as rapidly as possible. The Ross jammed from the twenty-fifth to the fiftieth round. Alderson sent the report to General Willoughby Gwatkin, the Canadian Chief of Staff, with an accompanying letter. The report, he claimed, actually flattered the Ross. 'It does not state,' he went on, 'as was the case, that the hands of men using the Ross were cut and bleeding owing to the difficulty they had in knocking back the bolt.'10 Hughes duly exploded. Bypassing Gwatkin, he sent an abusive letter to Alderson accusing him of ignorance and incompetence. He then told the Canadian House of Commons that Alderson did not 'know the butt from the muzzle'.[11] Not content with that, Hughes sent a copy of his letter to Alderson to 281 of Alderson's subordinate commanders in the field. He then took ship to London to settle the matter with Alderson once and for all.

Aitken was at that point uncertain where to turn. He had allowed himself, without any idea of the relative merits of the two rifles, to side with Hughes's claim that it was all part of a British conspiracy to play down the Canadian contribution to the war effort. Following the success of the 'Eye Witness' reports and of *Canada in Flanders*, he had been irritated by the reaction of the London press and of those in the War Office, who complained that it looked as though the Canadians were the only people fighting the war.

Apart from the dispute over the rifles, the other point of friction, the Turner problem, was reaching red heat. Alderson now insisted not only that he would not promote Turner but that he should be sacked. After Second Ypres there had been recriminations over the high Canadian casualty rate during the battle (some units had suffered up to 50 per cent casualties). Accusations went back and forth. Alderson blamed Turner for the mistakes made which put Canadian lives unnecessarily at risk. Hughes insisted that Alderson himself was to blame. Whatever the truth, and the probability is that both generals made tactical errors, the dispute quickly moved into the political arena. Hughes, when he heard what Alderson intended, blustered that the British were determined to remove competent Canadian generals and replace them with incompetent cronies. Aitken, while supporting his minister, took a rather more muted line. As he later pointed out, there were two authorities involved in the appointments of senior Canadian military posts: the War Office in London and the Canadian government. There was bound at times to be disagreement between the two.

Aitken's more balanced view did not help. On 20 March, Hughes arrived in London, stormed into the Ritz Hotel and settled down with his aides, Colonel John Carson and Captain John Bassett, and '2 or 3 extremely plain females, including the celebrated Miss Ena MacAdam, who apparently compose his travelling harem'. But Alderson refused to call upon him unless he was summoned and 'Sir Sam says he is damned if he will'.[12] Aitken did his best by organising a dinner in the Marlborough Club, but Alderson refused to attend. Instead he asked to see Aitken privately to explain his case. It was a mistake. At the end of a stormy interview Aitken said bleakly, 'I am sorry, General, but please understand that I am first, last, and all the time with the minister.' After the meeting Aitken said to Willson, 'I fear Alderson must lose his command.'[13]

On 31 March, Hughes received an urgent telegram from Borden ordering him to return to Canada to defend himself against allegations in the Commons over the munitions contracts. There was only time for a quick consultation over the weekend at Cherkley. There was no doubt in their minds that Alderson had to be replaced but neither of them could devise a suitable tactic to achieve his dismissal. Hughes, 'very pale and worried', left Aitken to find a way.[14] This was not going to be easy, not least because Alderson had only recently received the accolade of a knighthood. In the course of the weekend, however, Aitken had mentioned the name of a possible successor, Major-General Sir Julian Byng. Hughes brushed the suggestion aside.

As luck would have it, the 2nd Canadian Division, commanded by Turner, went into action at St Eloi on 27 March. It was little short of a disaster. After a fortnight of heavy fighting, the division lost 1,400 men and achieved nothing. Alderson, acting on the advice of his superior commander Sir Herbert Plumer, who also wrote to Haig in support, formally wrote to Hughes and Haig that he wished, with immediate effect, to relieve Turner and one of his brigadiers of their commands. Haig had already been warned by Plumer, who had mentioned 'some feeling against the Canadians'. Haig was by then fully aware of the problem even before Alderson's strike. Furthermore, he noted in his diary that 'the main point is whether the danger of a serious feud between the Canadians and British is greater than the retention of a couple of incompetent commanders ... After careful thought I have decided not to concur with Plumer as regards Turner but to keep him on.'[15]

Knowing about Alderson's threat to remove him from his command but unaware of Haig's decision, Turner appealed to Aitken in London. Seeing an opening, Aitken immediately went to France to put Turner's case to Haig in person. After presenting his case to Haig's Chief of Staff, Aitken saw Haig himself at his headquarters in Montreuil on

23 April, unaware that the decision had already been taken to keep Turner in place. According to Haig's diary for that day, Aitken said that he was 'representing the Canadian Government'.[16] This was, of course, quite untrue. Only a few weeks before, he had told Willson that 'his status in the military hierarchy had not been very clearly defined ... We counted on the arrival of the Minister [Hughes] to secure a public confirmation that he [Aitken] was the Minister's chief, and indeed exclusive representative...'[17] That confirmation had not been given, either in public or in private.

According to Haig's diary, Aitken

> took up a very reasonable attitude. The Prime Minister of Canada makes a personal request that General Turner should not be removed; on the other hand, if I considered that Turner is not sufficiently competent to be entrusted with the command of a division in the field, with due regard to the great interests at stake, then the Canadian Government would loyally accept my decision.[18]

Haig was not to know that it was so much nonsense. Borden had not even been told that Aitken was meeting Haig and even Hughes had not given any instruction about the outcome. Nevertheless, Aitken's meeting with Haig proceeded. 'We then discussed', Haig's diary continues,

> the organisation of Canadian forces in Europe ... It was agreed that an Inspector General ... be appointed with HQ in England ... General Alderson is to be asked by the Canadian Government to become Inspector General ... and General Byng would be most acceptable to Canadians as successor to Alderson in the field.[19]

At the time, neither Borden nor Hughes had any idea what was going on. With the agreement with Haig secured, whatever the embarrassment of not knowing that Turner had already been reprieved before he even got to see Haig, Aitken needed authorisation for what he had agreed to as soon as possible. Of course, he knew perfectly well that it would be impossible for Borden to disavow him without exposing the confusion at the heart of his government. Accordingly,

Borden explained the matter to his bemused Cabinet, which duly gave their consent. On 27 April, Aitken cabled Haig, 'Have received telegram from Sir Robert Borden advising me cabinet has approved of my proposal ... [he] also asks for information about Major-General Byng', adding disingenuously, 'I hope you will not find it necessary to take action in this connection until I communicate Sir Roberts [*sic*] views to you.'[20] Again, Borden was put in an impossible situation and immediately conceded. 'The Canadian Government', Aitken triumphantly cabled Haig the following day, 'leave to you the nomination of General Alderson's successor'.[21]

It had been a classic Aitken manoeuvre. By cheek or misrepresentation, however it is interpreted, by holding his cards close and not allowing them to be revealed until he chose the moment, by playing on the weaknesses, one by one, of all his interlocutors, he had changed the command structure of the Canadian Expeditionary Force. It was, of course, quite shocking. Nevertheless, like his earlier financial manoeuvres, it turned out to be a startling success. Byng, Aitken's nominee, was not only more attuned than Alderson to the Canadian military mindset and the influence of emerging nationalism but also more tactically astute in the field. By the end of May he had taken over, sorted out the difficulties with Turner and subsequently led the Canadians to their greatest moment at Vimy Ridge in 1917.

Canadian Byng Boys returning after defeating the Germans at Vimy Ridge, France, May 1917.

While all that was happening, on 24 April there had been a violent nationalist uprising in Dublin. Known later as the Easter Rising, and brutally suppressed by the British authorities, it had in turn brought the Irish problem back to the centre stage in Westminster. In an attempt to contain a potentially explosive issue, Asquith had asked Lloyd George, Minister of Munitions, to mediate between the Irish Nationalists and the Ulster Unionists to devise an agreement on how to achieve Home Rule without provoking sectarian violence. In the event, the initiative failed, but a side effect was not only that the Home Rule Bill was taken out of storage and put on the statute book pending commencement, much to Unionist fury, but that Lloyd George took a liking to Edward Carson, the Ulster Unionist leader. In fact, it was not just a liking. Both agreed that Asquith's conduct of the war was failing. Moreover, both believed that some reorganisation at the higher reaches of government was necessary to achieve a much greater sense of purpose.

· Nothing as yet, however, could move Asquith to alter course. He had managed to ride above the disputes over conscription and in May had persuaded Parliament to legislate to introduce it with immediate effect. Furthermore, the summer promised what was hoped would be the decisive moment of the war. The French fortress city of Verdun was under heavy German attack. The French Army on the ground, under General Pétain, seemed resolute in resisting the German onslaught in spite of appalling casualties but needed a diversion. The British War Council, under pressure from the French, had agreed to launch a major offensive on the German lines to the north-west of Verdun to relieve what was turning into a protracted and bloody siege. It was agreed that the British attack was to be in maximum force on a broad front along the line of the river Somme. By the end of May, preparations were already well advanced. Whatever Lloyd George and Carson may have felt, it was certainly not the moment for political ructions.

On a more mundane level, there was a problem at the CWRO. The Canadian Dominion Archivist, Arthur Doughty, had been one of those irritated by Aitken's raid of the staff of his London office. Twelve female stenographers had been lured away, apparently on the grounds that the toilet facilities in Lombard Street were superior to those in Doughty's office. But it was more than that. Doughty himself was a scholar in his own right and could not be ignored. He had the authority, both as a scholar and as Dominion Archivist, to request, and receive, from Borden an honorary commission with the rank of major of the militia to go to London, as he put it, 'to save the material from which a true account of the share of Canada in the war could be written … so that we shall not depend on men such as Sir Max Aitken'.[22]

Doughty claimed, in his first visit to Lombard Street on 1 May, that all Canadian records, civil, naval and military, belonged by law to the Dominion Archives. It was a claim that Aitken could not possibly resist. Willson thought it was some sort of bluff and rushed round to the Hyde Park Hotel the following morning before Aitken had fully woken up to tell him that Doughty was intent on undermining him and the whole record office. It was not a good move. Aitken was far too shrewd to fall for that line. It took only an hour's conversation for Aitken and Doughty to become seemingly the best of friends. Aitken assured Doughty that after the war all records in the CWRO would be passed to the Dominion Public Record Office, naturally without charge. Doughty was converted. 'He is the right man in the right place,' he recorded in his diary. 'It is surprising how keenly he looks after the detail of the war records office.'[23] Willson's days were over. Aitken passed him on to the *Daily Express*, for Blumenfeld to find him suitable employment. The amateur ways of the CWRO, excellent in many ways as was Aitken's original initiative, gave place under Doughty's supervision to a new professionalism.

Yet the war could never be ignored, and in the late spring there were two hammer blows for the British. On 31 May, the British Grand Fleet of 149 warships, including twenty-eight dreadnoughts, engaged the German High Seas Fleet of 100 warships, containing sixteen dreadnoughts, which had left its northern German ports and was attempting to reach the open Atlantic. The battle, of epic proportions, took place in the North Sea off the coast of Jutland. Much to the surprise, and shock, of the British, they found themselves outgunned by the Germans and lost three battle cruisers and eight destroyers to the German losses of two battleships, four cruisers and eight destroyers. In terms of casualties the toll was nearly 7,000 British against 3,000 Germans.

All in all, the result was little more than a draw, although the British claimed at least a partial victory in that it was the Germans who broke off the engagement and retired to the safety of their ports. But the pride of the Royal Navy had been badly hurt.

The second blow came five days later on 5 June. HMS *Hampshire*, bound for Murmansk with Lord Kitchener and his staff on board, struck a mine off Orkney and went down with all hands. Kitchener's body was never found. The loss was not simply a blow to the British war effort. Kitchener was still a respected figurehead, although his powers as Secretary of State for War had been much reduced with the formation of the Ministry of Munitions. Worse than that, however, in political terms it left a large gap in the Cabinet.

The problem, of course, was how to stop Kitchener's job going to Lloyd George. The generals, led by the Chief of the Imperial General Staff, Field Marshal William Robertson, declared for Walter Long, but that was mainly because they thought he would do what they said. Aitken went to see Bonar Law to try to push him into demanding the job, but Law was reluctant to put himself forward. Aitken then arranged for Law and Lloyd George to meet at Cherkley over the Whit weekend of 10–11 June. At that meeting, over lunch and well into the afternoon, Bonar Law and Lloyd George, mutually suspicious, nearly fell out. In the end, however, after a 'prolonged discussion',[24] Bonar Law promised to back Lloyd George's claim to the War Office.

The following day, Aitken accompanied Bonar Law to see Asquith at his country house, The Wharf, in Sutton Courtenay. Asquith, in a last attempt to block Lloyd George, offered the job to Law. It was too late. Law had committed himself. With a sigh of resignation, the Prime Minister gave way. Lloyd George was to become Secretary of State for War. Asquith's wife, Margot, reflected the view of those around him. 'I look upon this', she wrote in her diary on the eve of the announcement to the Commons, 'as the greatest political blunder of Henry's life.'[25] Be that as it may, Lloyd George at that point became at least joint favourite to Bonar Law in the succession should Asquith stumble. For Aitken, as it happened, there was an unexpected bonus. As Canadian Representative he had a perch in the War Office a few doors down from the Secretary of State. While Kitchener was there, it did not hold much advantage for him. With Lloyd George in place, however, life would become very much more interesting.

Equally interesting was the prospect of a baronetcy in the birthday honours list. Bonar Law had written to Borden in early May asking him to put Aitken on the Canada list. This time Borden was entirely in favour and in turn wrote to the Duke of Connaught that 'my [fa-vourable] view is expressed in a telegram [to Bonar Law of 16 May] to the Colonial Secretary and I have the honour to leave the matter for the determination of Your Royal Highness'.[26] His Royal Highness was not at all pleased. He regarded Aitken as a creature of his enemy Sam Hughes. Accordingly, while submitting Borden's request formally, he wrote a private letter to his nephew King George V saying that Borden personally was unhappy about the recommendation given Aitken's reputation in Canada. The King shook his head, leaving Bonar Law no option but to put the recommendation on the Prime Minister's list. The King continued to object but even he could not veto a rec-ommendation from his Prime Minister and the appointment to the baronetcy duly went forward.

The newly ennobled Sir Max Aitken in uniform,
the Nottingham Guardian, *19 December 1916.*

On 1 July 1916, fourteen British and Allied divisions launched the much-advertised attack on a 20,000-yard front along the line of the river Somme. Their assault followed a massive artillery barrage which, it was assumed, would crush the German defences. Far from being crushed, the defences were deep enough to withstand the barrage and to meet the infantry assault the German troops emerged to manage their intact machine guns. That day on the Somme turned into one of the worst days in the history of the British Army. Of the 120,000 soldiers who took part, 19,000 were killed outright and a further 38,000 were either wounded or missing.

The Somme battle soon became yet another stalemate. As the weeks and months went by there were more heavy casualties with little or no gains in territory. The lists grew longer, the stream of crippled men coming home became more tragic (among others, Asquith's son Raymond was killed in the battle) and the political fallout more bitter. Added to that was the effect of constant German submarine attacks in the Atlantic and the realisation that the financial burden of the war was crippling the British economy. By the autumn of 1916, morale, both in London and at the Front, had reached a new low.

In Canada, too, there was frustration and anger. In October the Duke of Connaught, after one indiscretion too many, had been levered out by Borden. 'I am chased out of the country,' he is said to have told Wilfrid Laurier. 'Your Minister [of Militia] is the embodiment of impertinence and your Premier is the personification of weakness.'[27] Hughes himself, having been cleared of improper, even corrupt, behaviour over the munitions contracts, promptly insisted, with the support of Aitken and Bonar Law, on being promoted to lieutenant-general. He then set off for England to organise an Active Sub-Militia Council in London, with Sir Edward Carson as president, to assume control of all Canadian forces in Europe. Furthermore, he announced that he proposed to appoint Aitken as High Commissioner. A furious Borden only found out about this from the Canadian newspapers. On being questioned about the Sub-Militia Council, Hughes denied setting anything up. Borden responded by hinting that the Canadian High Commissioner, Sir George Perley, would be made a minister with military command. 'Borden proposed ... place

Perley Minister in charge of all Militia matters in Britain,' Hughes cabled Aitken in panic. 'You and I both to be out … If Borden passes Order I purpose resigning … Friend suggests Borden be placed now as Judicial Committee or Supreme Court Chief. Minister Militia form Cabinet recognising certain Liberals. When could you come. Please advise on whole matter.'[28]

Ignoring the hint of a possible militia *coup d'état*, Aitken advised Hughes to keep calm and abandon thoughts of resigning. But the damage had been done. On 1 November, Hughes sent another insulting letter to Borden. After consulting his Cabinet and other senior Conservatives, on 9 November, Borden wrote to Hughes demanding his resignation. When he heard the news, Aitken was quick to retreat. He had already known of Hughes's unpopularity with the troops in the field, but even he might have been surprised at some of the reactions. 'The mad mullah of Canada has been deposed' was one. 'Joy, oh Joy … I do not like to kick a man when he is down but I am willing to break nine toes in kicking Sam in the stomach or in the face or anywhere else.'[29]

Aitken moved quickly. First, fearful about what Hughes might say which could be interpreted as complicity in a constitutional plot, he advised him to 'weigh carefully your public statement'.[30] Then, in a more considered cable, he asked Hughes to make the position clear. 'It is necessary on account of my position in my constituency and elsewhere to make a statement regarding the proposal that I should accept the post of High Commissioner and Overseas Minister … I have always been against it and have stated so on every occasion.'[31] Not content with that, he followed up on the same day: 'You would please me greatly if you would make a statement on your own account to say that I had declined to serve on Overseas Militia Council as I insisted on devoting all my time to Canadian War Records work … I propose to send letter to *Times* tonight.'[32] Furthermore, as an inevitable consequence of Hughes's resignation, Aitken no longer kept his position of Representative at the Front. Conveniently, this allowed him to distance himself publicly from Hughes (although in private he maintained the friendship).

By early November the political temperature in London was rising. Lord Northcliffe was running a strident campaign in his newspapers demanding Asquith's head. Asquith himself was drinking too much, living up to his nickname 'Squiffy'. He was still able to dominate the House of Commons but was irresolute and vague at morning Cabinet meetings. 'Of course,' remarked a colleague, 'the two hours before lunch are those in which his spirits and his stock of spirit are at their lowest measurement.'[33] Lloyd George was telling anybody who would listen that he thought the Somme was a 'ghastly failure' and that 'everything was in a muddle'.[34] Bonar Law was badly shaken on 8 November when Carson launched an attack on the government in a debate about who should be allowed to acquire assets which had been confiscated in Nigeria and led a substantial minority of Unionists into the opposition lobby. Law had always said that he would resign if he lost control of his party. Aitken, unwisely, advised him to do so straight away but Bonar Law knew that the consequence would be an immediate collapse of the government. Caution prevailed.

Aitken, in turn, was using his office, near to that of Lloyd George, to make overtures to the Secretary of State along the corridor. As it happened, the timing was right, and the overtures were welcome. At a meeting on 13 November, Lloyd George gave Aitken an account of his grievances. 'These he explained to me', Aitken later recalled,

> with great vigour, fullness and frankness ... I came away from the interview with an entirely new conviction in my mind – that the Coalition Government was in essence defective and that we should go down in the War if the defect was not remedied ... I came away determined to help him to the best of my ability...[35]

Lloyd George went on to explain that he was in favour of a War Cabinet of no more than three people: himself, Bonar Law and Carson; and he was quite open in describing the project. Of course, it was all done with a purpose and he had been supremely skilful in making this new convert. He knew that Aitken held the key to the door that led to the man he had to win over, in spite of their mutual mistrust; and he had persuaded Aitken to use it.

The spark that finally lit the political fire came from an unlikely source. Lord Lansdowne had been thinking of leaving the Cabinet in

August, after a painful operation on his hand, but he had stayed on even though he had no portfolio. He had now come to the conclusion that the strategy of 'breakthrough' which lay behind the 1916 campaigns had failed. Taken together with the damage caused by German submarines and the financial constraints, he believed that it was time to listen to any offer of peace or mediation that could end the war. On the same day as Aitken was hearing Lloyd George's laments, Monday 13 November, Lansdowne submitted a Cabinet paper setting out his views.

Lansdowne's paper was due to be discussed in Cabinet on Wednesday 22 November. On the previous Saturday, Aitken briefed Bonar Law on his meeting with Lloyd George and suggested that he should talk with Lloyd George and Carson as soon as possible. Law agreed. The meeting duly took place over dinner at the Hyde Park Hotel on 20 November. 'We discussed there the question of a smaller council with a division of responsibility,' Bonar Law subsequently wrote,

> so that in some way or other the practical conduct of the war should be placed in the hands of Lloyd George ... in such a way as not to inflict any humiliation at all on [the Prime Minister] or, indeed, in any way to destroy the dignity of his office.[36]

They then agreed to meet again on the following Saturday for lunch at Bonar Law's house in Edwardes Square.

When the Cabinet met on the 22nd, the Lansdowne paper was discussed, but in a somewhat cursory manner. Lloyd George said that there should be a special Cabinet meeting to review it as it was clearly an important document. He went on to praise Lansdowne's courage in writing it. At the same time, he 'differed from it as he thought a knock-out blow was possible'.[37] Nevertheless, the mere existence of the paper, and its general pessimism, spurred Bonar Law and his colleagues to action. Before Lloyd George and Carson came to lunch, Bonar Law recalled, 'I had written out ... a suggestion to the Prime Minister as to the way he could make the announcement to the Cabinet...'[38] (The original of the document may or may not have been drafted by Aitken, as he claimed.) The 'suggestion' set out the elements of Lloyd

George's formula. There was to be a three-man War Committee in charge of the direction of the war, chaired by Lloyd George with two other members whose names were left blank. The Prime Minister was to be president of the committee but with a strictly non-executive role. Agreement on these principles was reached over lunch and Bonar Law was deputed to present them to Asquith that afternoon.

It was not the easiest of tasks, but Bonar Law did his duty. Asquith's reply was not entirely negative but that he needed time to think about it. Needless to say, having thought about it, Asquith wrote to Law rejecting the whole plan. Law went back to see him to explain his view that

> after all the one thing which seemed to me essential was that he and Lloyd George should work together with the close co-operation which existed at the time the Coalition was formed ... The two of them [should] have a frank talk together and see to what extent they could come to an agreement.[39]

Asquith agreed, and a meeting was fixed for Friday, 1 December.

During the following five days Aitken busied himself in organising a press campaign in favour of Lloyd George. Almost by accident, and certainly without any fanfare, he had just acquired control of the *Daily Express* in a transaction which was to be completed on 2 December. In fact, financial control was not at present of great importance since his relationship with Blumenfeld was close enough already for him to be able to get whatever he wanted into the newspaper. Accordingly, a series of articles appeared in the *Daily Express* and the *Daily Chronicle* lavishing praise on Lloyd George as the man to bring the country out of the crisis. At the same time, Aitken achieved an unexpected success: he managed to arrange a reconciliation between Lloyd George and Lord Northcliffe. As Cecil Harmsworth, Northcliffe's brother, noted on 3 December, 'Alfred has been actively at work with Ll.G. with a view to bringing about a change.'[40]

At their Friday meeting, Asquith and Lloyd George discussed in some detail a paper prepared by Lloyd George with the position of the Prime Minister defined as 'not a member of the War Council but to exercise from outside the right both of initiative and of veto'.[41] Bonar Law had thought that this was more favourable to Asquith than the previous version. That was true, but Asquith still found it unacceptable, insisting that he must retain the chairmanship, and the meeting ended without agreement.

The following day the main newspapers were full of stories about the imminent resignation of Lloyd George. Suspicions about the source varied but it was widely believed that Lloyd George himself had planted them. In fact, it was Walter Long who had it right. 'These Ll.G. intrigues', he said, 'have been largely conducted by Max Aitken – at luncheon rooms in hotels – where there have been eavesdroppers.'[42] Aitken himself confessed to Bonar Law, who 'had no idea of the extent to which I had carried on the Press campaign. He was much startled and perturbed by the news.'[43]

Feeling that events were moving too fast for comfort, Bonar Law decided to call a meeting of Unionist members of the Cabinet at his house for Sunday 3 December. The Unionist ministers duly assembled as requested, apart from Lansdowne, who was in the country, and without the steadying presence of Balfour, who had contracted a bad dose of influenza three days earlier. They were more than usually irritable, thinking that they were not being told what was going on and that they were in danger of being bounced into a crisis by Lloyd George. For instance, that morning's *Reynolds News*, 'with which Ll.G. is intimately connected', as Balcarres reported, 'gives the fullest exposition of his mind, his grievances and his decision to resign, this afternoon'.[44] When the meeting started Bonar Law explained the situation as he saw it, and pointed to Asquith's dilatoriness in agreeing to any reform. He referred to what he perceived as his loss of authority in the Nigeria debate and said that 'he now thought he must resign'. Rather than allowing him to do so unaccompanied, his colleagues insisted, after an hour's discussion, that 'the best chance of forming a stable administration would be for Asquith himself to resign and ask the King to consider the matter ... We decided that we should tender our eight resignations in the event of Asquith declining to do so for the Government en bloc...'[45] A statement was drafted quickly for Bonar Law to present to Asquith when he arrived back from the country in the afternoon. For Aitken, sitting impatiently in another room, the wording was unfortunate. It said that 'in our opinion the publicity given to the intention of Mr Lloyd George makes reconstruction from within no longer possible'.[46] Worried that his management of the press campaign would come to light, Aitken tried to persuade Bonar Law to leave out the words 'the publicity given to'. Bonar Law refused, pointing out, rightly, that it was a document with collective authorship and that he could not alter it without the approval of his colleagues.

The day wore on. At two o'clock Bonar Law saw Asquith and presented the Unionist case, although he forgot, so he later said, to give Asquith the document. Asquith professed himself surprised and shocked, said he was due to see Lloyd George later on and asked Bonar Law to put the Unionist resignations on hold as he was minded to reconstruct his government, in which case they would all be asked to resign. After waiting for most of the afternoon, at half past five the Unionists decided to move nearer to Downing Street and encamped in F. E. Smith's house in Wilton Street, with Aitken tagging along. At a little before eight o'clock Bonar Law turned up to report on his latest meeting with Asquith, at which the Prime Minister had told him 'that he had come to a complete understanding with Lloyd George as to the status and function of the Committee, but that they were not entirely agreed as to the personnel'.[47] Asquith had insisted that he would be remodelling his government the next day. The meeting ended in the belief that a concordat had indeed been reached and that the war would be directed by a small committee headed by Lloyd George. On that note of harmony, Bonar Law and Aitken then went back to Edwardes Square for dinner, Aitken finally making his way back to the Hyde Park Hotel at 1 a.m.

The next day was spent waiting for news. There were desultory gatherings of Unionists, at the India Office at lunchtime and in Bonar Law's room at the Colonial Office in the afternoon, but they were so frustrated that they sent out for an evening paper to see whether they had missed something. Bonar Law arrived to tell them that he had seen Asquith again and 'was disturbed to find that as it seemed to me he was not quite as decided ... as he had been the previous evening'.[48]

The meeting then broke up in an atmosphere of renewed gloom. Later that evening Aitken dined again with Bonar Law and gave his opinion that Asquith would have to resign. What they did not know was that late that night Asquith was to write to Lloyd George that 'after full consideration of the matter in all aspects, I have come decidedly to the conclusion that it is not possible that such a Committee could be made workable and effective without the Prime Minister as its Chairman...'[49] In other words the concordat, such as it was, had very quickly, and finally, expired.

Tuesday 5 December 1916 was the decisive day. It was at this point that Balfour joined the debate. He had heard that Lloyd George had expressed the view that there should be a change at the Admiralty. Accordingly, he wrote to Asquith from his sickbed that

> one thing seems clear: that there is to be a new War Council of which Lloyd George is to be the working Chairman and that, according to his views, this Council would work more satisfactorily if the Admiralty were not represented by me. In these circumstances, I cannot consent to retain my office, and must ask you to accept my resignation ... I am quite clear that the new system should have a trial in the most favourable possible circumstances.[50]

Asquith simply replied to Balfour with one line: he thought he could best answer by asking him to read the copy of last night's letter to Lloyd George, which was attached. No sooner had the reply been sent than Asquith agreed to a deputation from three senior Unionist ministers, Austen Chamberlain, Lord Robert Cecil and Lord Curzon. They found him in conversation 'firm and vigorous, quite different from his own comatose and indolent self'.[51] He had obviously been incensed by a leader in *The Times* the day before telling him to resign and give way to Lloyd George. He had also received support from his Liberal colleagues in the Cabinet and from Allied diplomats. Apparently, Asquith 'swept aside all suggestions of concession or compromise with a gesture of finality and scorn'.[52] Even Lloyd George's vigorous response attacking the whole conduct of the war had failed to move him.

Balfour's reply came soon thereafter. 'I am very grateful,' it runs:

> ... I do not, however, feel much inclined to change my views. I still think (a) that the break-up of the government by the retirement of Lloyd George would be a misfortune, (b) that the experiment of giving him a free hand with the day-to-day work of the War Committee is well worth trying, and (c) that there is no use trying it except on terms which enable him to work under conditions which, in his own opinion, promise the best results. We cannot, I think, go on in the old way ... I am still of opinion [*sic*] that my resignation should be accepted and that a fair trial should be given to the new War Council *à la* George.[53]

For Asquith, that was the last straw. For a former Prime Minister, now First Lord of the Admiralty, to resign from his government as well as the Secretary of State for War would be a fatal blow. Even if he could persuade Bonar Law and his Unionist colleagues not to jump ship, the ship itself would be so badly holed that it would inevitably sink. 'That afternoon', Bonar Law recalled,

> there was again a meeting with my Unionist colleagues during which we asked Lord Curzon to go to the Prime Minister and ascertain from him whether or not he was going to resign on behalf of the Government, as, if not, all our resignations would be handed in. Lord Curzon on returning informed us that the Prime Minister had decided to resign, and therefore no action was taken by us.[54]

There was then the matter of who would form a new government. Since Asquith believed that he might still be called, it was clear that there could be an orderly succession. It was therefore agreed later that night that King George V should be asked to convene a meeting in Buckingham Palace to discuss the options and arrive at a conclusion. The King agreed and set the time: 3 p.m., on 6 December. Invited to the meeting were Asquith, Bonar Law, Lloyd George, Arthur Henderson (the Labour leader) and Balfour. Seeking advice, the King asked Balfour to come half an hour early. At the King's command, Balfour rose from his sickbed and presented himself punctually at the Palace. The King then not only asked Balfour for his advice on what should happen but asked him to lead the discussion.

The discussion took its course, 'very moderate in form but, so far as Asquith and Ll.G were concerned, with a sub-acid flavour'.[55] In the end, it was agreed that Bonar Law should try to form a government which, if possible, should include Asquith, and that Asquith should consult his colleagues on whether that was practicable. At the end of the meeting Balfour invited Bonar Law back to his house for a further discussion. He persuaded Bonar Law to have a final shot at trying to convince Asquith to join his government. It turned out to be a hopeless task. Two hours later, Asquith wrote to Bonar Law that he had consulted his colleagues and that 'they are unanimously of the opinion that I ought not to join your Government'.[56] Since without Asquith Bonar Law could not rely on wholehearted Liberal support, and since 'he himself was most reluctant to be the head of the new government because, by whatever name it might be described, Ll.G. would undoubtedly be its most powerful member and he would much prefer that the forms of power and the substance should go together',[57] Bonar Law handed the task over to Lloyd George. Yet Balfour's part was not finished. At half past nine the same evening, Bonar Law returned accompanied by Edmund Talbot, the Unionist Chief Whip. They brought a formal request from Lloyd George that Balfour serve in his government as Foreign Minister, not least because 'it would greatly help with the rest of our Unionist colleagues'.[58] Without hesitation Balfour agreed. He had played the final, decisive card. The Lloyd George government was duly formed.

Aitken's role in the crisis of December 1916 has been much discussed, not least by Aitken himself. One of his biographers has devoted a whole chapter to it under the title of 'The Kingmaker'. That is stretching the evidence too far. The kingmaker, if indeed there was one, was undoubtedly Balfour. It was he, after all, who had fired the missile which had fatally wounded Asquith and it was he who had ensured the formation of Lloyd George's government by agreeing to take the Foreign Office. In the most dramatic moments of the crisis, Aitken had been little more than a bystander; sitting, as it were, permanently in another room. Nevertheless, there were times when his particular talents were brought to bear with success: hosting events in the Hyde Park Hotel with diplomatic skill; manoeuvring the reconciliation of Lloyd George and Northcliffe; and organising the press campaign. Perhaps above all, however, was his unwavering support for Bonar Law. The mere fact of his presence, and readiness to listen, was a comfort to his fellow countryman. To borrow a phrase, there was a corner of west London which was forever New Brunswick.

The question then in Aitken's mind was what would be his reward? 'I expected the Board of Trade', he later wrote, 'and had good ground for my expectation.'[59] Whatever the truth (Lloyd George later said that the idea had never crossed his mind), nothing happened. From Lloyd George came a quite different offer. 'There are two or three important business Departments', went his letter of 9 December, 'which have no representatives in the House of Lords and therefore no spokesmen. Would you allow me to recommend your name to the King for a Peerage? You could then answer for these Departments in the H. L.'[60] Aitken replied immediately. 'I am grateful to you for your offer and I shall be glad if I can be of any help to you in the way you indicate.'[61] The offer was made and accepted. But neither Lloyd George nor Aitken expected the storms it was to set off both in London and in Canada.

CHAPTER 12

THE LORD BEAVER

'Max's devotion to Bonar had a very feminine aspect'[1]

A quietude like death settled on the Hyde Park Hotel. There were no more calls from politicians – no more agitated interviews. No special messengers arrived with notes. Even the telephone bell ceased to ring. The reaction was tremendous. It is said that people in a balloon do not feel any sensation of motion, but simply think the earth is drifting past them. There came to me this same curious sense of detachment – passing by degrees into boredom and then into anxiety, and finally into a kind of desperation. I had been in the centre of affairs and now I found myself translated to the extreme circumference.[2]

Thus did the newly ennobled Baron Beaverbrook, formerly Sir Max Aitken MP, describe in later life his transition to the ranks of the hereditary aristocracy. It had been an inauspicious start. For one thing, he had told his Ashton constituency that he was to become a minister and that they should prepare themselves for the by-election, as was the requirement at the time, only to be told casually by a senior civil servant that one Albert Stanley had been given his job. Then Bonar Law, in another fit of indecision, had first advised him against accepting a peerage, after a warning from Leopold Maxse, the editor of the *National Review*, about Aitken's suitability, only to change his mind and hope 'you will accept L. G.'s offer … It would be a delight to me if I felt that this would give you pleasure.'[3]

There had also been a wrangle with the College of Heralds over the name he was to take. His suggestion of 'Baron Miramichi' was regarded as much too frivolous and anyway difficult to pronounce. Only after negotiation did he agree to 'Beaverbrook', a small New Brunswick community. (At least Kipling was delighted with the name, as he was able to design a coat of arms featuring two beavers and to endow the new lord with his nickname of 'Beaver'.) Even that was only acceptable if 'Cherkley' was added to the subsidiary title. At least the College of Heralds knew where it was.

The reaction in Canada to the news was at first muffled. It only burst into flames a year later in a debate in the Canadian House of Commons on a resolution presented by the Conservative MP William Folger Nickle to submit an Address to the King 'praying that Your Majesty hereafter may be graciously pleased to refrain from conferring any hereditary titles upon your subjects domiciled here in Canada...'[4] The debate spilled over into 1919, with many uncomplimentary references to Beaverbrook – not, of course, by name but, for instance, as someone undeserving of a title since he was 'more famous for his cement merger than his accomplishments on behalf of the Empire'.[5]

Most damaging of all, however, was the reaction in London. King George V was, as frequently happened after a good lunch, not in a good temper. He had already made his opinion clear over the baronetcy. He regarded the peerage as little less than a slap in the royal face. Lord Stamfordham, the King's private secretary, was commanded to write to Bonar Law in the most robust language. 'I cannot conceal from you', his letter runs, 'that His Majesty was surprised and hurt that this offer should have been offered without his consent ... The King does not consider that the public services rendered by Sir Max Aitken from last June, when a Baronetcy was conferred upon him, justify this further higher distinction...'

He went on to note that the King had reluctantly agreed since the news was already in the public domain and concluded with a polite warning: 'But in thus signifying his acquiescence, His Majesty commands me to say that he feels that the Sovereign's Prerogative in this respect should not be disregarded and he trusts in future no honours whatever will be offered to any Minister until his approval has been informally obtained.'[6]

It was in these inauspicious circumstances that Beaverbrook was introduced into the House of Lords on Wednesday 14 February 1917. News of the King's displeasure had spread widely to those, already many, in the know. The attendance in the House on that day was noticeably thin. Of the grandees, only Curzon and Balcarres turned up (obliged as Leader of the House and Lord Privy Seal to attend), no doubt with teeth firmly gritted. There was one bishop but, beyond that, there were no more than fifteen peers present. Nevertheless, the deed had to be done, and Beaverbrook, now 'Baron Beaverbrook of Beaverbrook in the Province of New Brunswick in the Dominion of Canada and of Cherkley in the county of Surrey', accompanied by his two supporters, Lord St Audries, formerly Sir Alex Acland-Hood and Unionist Chief Whip, and Lord Rothermere, with the Gentleman Usher of the Black Rod and Garter King of Arms 'preceding', all in the pomp of their formal dress, processed into the Chamber. Beaverbrook, 'on his knee' (only one knee was the required protocol), then presented his Patent to the Lord Chancellor on the Woolsack.[7] The Patent was then smoothly transferred to the Reading Clerk at the Table who read it all out in full. Beaverbrook then took the oath of allegiance in a loud voice (and, it was noted, in his unadorned New Brunswick accent). That done, the new peer and his supporters processed round the Chamber, doffed their cocked hats three times, as required, to the Lord Chancellor before making a dignified exit, shaking hands with the Lord Chancellor on the way out.

Beaverbrook himself never revealed what he thought of the ceremony. It is true, however, that he didn't attend the House for the remainder of the year. In fact, the whole affair illustrated some uncomfortable truths. The thin attendance in the Lords on that day was no accident. The fact was that there was no particular enthusiasm for Beaverbrook among his Unionist colleagues or, for that matter, in the *beau monde*, such as it was, of London aristocratic society. It was not just that his Canadian history, however distorted in perception, made him seem untrustworthy at best and crooked at worst. It was not even his conspicuous display of wealth, his lavish lifestyle, the Rolls-Royces, the champagne, the cigars, the pretentiousness of Cherkley, or his habit of making fun of people, or even his infuriating grin. He just did not fit in with the tribe, and the tribe, as all tribes do with those who do not fit in, resented him to the point of rejection.

Nevertheless, a peerage of the United Kingdom gave Beaverbrook a status that was denied to a mere baronet, and more doors, even if they were not at the most coveted addresses, were open to him. Furthermore, he was, in his balloon, free from the pressures of the past two years. Gladys was, after all, safely tucked away at Cherkley, her hands full with looking after Janet, Max and Peter. His brothers and sisters were all satisfactorily involved in the war effort. All four of his sisters were nurses, either in the Red Cross or in American hospitals. His four brothers, too, were in the right places, one in Calgary in charge of recruitment, one in active service in the Canadian infantry, one in the Royal Army Medical Corps and the youngest, Allan, with Haig's staff in France.

Lady Beaverbrook (Gladys) and her children: Janet Aitken on the left, John (known as Max) on the right, and Peter below. The Herald, 10 June 1916.

On the domestic political front, however, there were no more than meagre pickings. The Lloyd George administration was in place.

Bonar Law, as Chancellor of the Exchequer and Leader of the House of Commons, had moved to 11 Downing Street, next door to the Prime Minister and convenient for their daily morning meetings. He had brought with him his private secretary from the Colonial Office, a conscientious if rather solemn Aberdonian by the name of John Colin Campbell (always known as J. C. C.) Davidson. By way of parliamentary back-up he had as parliamentary private secretary the Member of Parliament for Bewdley in Worcestershire, Stanley Baldwin. Beaverbrook's access to his old friend and mentor was now no longer a matter of his own choosing.

As for Davidson, he and Beaverbrook never really got on. The relationship in those early days was summarised neatly by Davidson himself. 'I was a Scotsman', he wrote,

> with an independent turn of character, which was one of the reasons why, although I often accompanied my chief [Bonar Law] down to Cherkley, I never slept a night under Lord Beaverbrook's roof. I dined, I lunched there, but I never slept there. I didn't like the house or the way it was run. Perhaps I was puritanical, but I wanted to be independent and not beholden to his lordship in any way.

Yet he recognised Beaverbrook's qualities:

> It was always my view that Beaverbrook – politically – was amoral, but there was absolutely no corruption in his relationship with Bonar Law, to whom he had an extraordinary devotion ... Max was a very quick mover and he had a very bright attractive mind; there was no doubt at all about that, and Bonar was very much amused by Max, and Max's devotion to Bonar had a very feminine aspect.[8]

Baldwin, of course, was another matter. He had already served nearly ten years in the House of Commons after inheriting, as it were, his father's constituency of Bewdley, but his performance to date had been rather less than shining. He had been parliamentary private secretary to Bonar Law at the Colonial Office and had migrated with him and Davidson to the Treasury. In order to seal off any further accusations that he was stealing his acolytes from the Colonial Office, Bonar Law, as was his right as Chancellor, in June 1917 secured Baldwin's appointment to the senior non-Cabinet ministerial post of Joint Financial Secretary to the Treasury. At first, Beaverbrook welcomed, albeit guardedly, his arrival. As he later wrote, '[Baldwin] is very amiable and popular in a colourless kind of way,' qualities which he thought would recommend themselves to Bonar Law's habitually morose temperament. 'Mildness, amiability, caution, lack of self-assertion and ambition, such were, in fact, his qualities in this first phase. He was written down as a good neighbour, a trustworthy friend, a man of all the domestic virtues – but for all his public capacities no one cared a whit.'[9]

With no seat in the House of Commons and being no longer Canadian Representative at the Front, Beaverbrook in 1917 was at something of a loose end. As he wrote himself, 'My position in public life was that of a frustrated and disappointed seeker after employment.'[10] True, there were jobs which could be done on the periphery of the main action. He was, for instance, useful to Bonar Law in the war loan issue of February 1917. The Treasury, the Bank of England and the most important banks in the City insisted that the bonds should carry a coupon of 6 per cent as a minimum. Beaverbrook was able to persuade Bonar Law that the issue could be successful with 5 per cent and undertook to convince the Governor of the Bank of England, Lord Cunliffe, of the case. This he failed to do but his argument was strong enough for Law to stand his ground with the Treasury team. As they came out of the decisive meeting, Davidson was able to ask John Maynard Keynes, the junior member of the team, 'Well, Maynard, have you persuaded the Chancellor?' Back came the answer: 'No – we have had no effect, and, quite frankly, his argument was beneath contempt, but I have a feeling that the old man is right.'[11]

Beaverbrook then set about organising the publicity for the issue, enlisting the support of Lords Northcliffe and Rothermere as well, of course, as Blumenfeld. Rothermere agreed to second George Sutton, the manager of the *Daily Mail*, to head the campaign with Beaverbrook advising him. True to form, they produced ideas of brilliance but startling vulgarity. For instance, they wanted 'green illuminated eyes in the lions of Trafalgar Square so that you could see the lions at night looking at you ... a tank set up in Trafalgar Square and Cabinet Ministers to give half an hour each, selling War Bonds...'[12] In the event the issue was a resounding success, raising £1,000 million by the end of February.

There was also the matter of Lloyd George's determination to remove Sir William Robertson as Chief of the Imperial General Staff. It had long been his view that the generals wielded too much political power and should be brought to heel. The difficulty was that the Unionists, Bonar Law in particular, allied to the Northcliffe and Rothermere newspapers, were resolute in support of the generals. It was to be a protracted campaign before Lloyd George achieved his objective towards the end of 1917. Yet again, Beaverbrook proved to be the emollient. As a reward to his supporter in his introduction to the House of Lords, he suggested to Lloyd George that Lord Rothermere might make a good Secretary of State at the new Air Ministry. Whatever the merits of the candidate, Lloyd George took the point and the deed was done. As a result, the attacks on Lloyd George from the Northcliffe and Rothermere newspapers (the brothers, as it were, seemingly in harness) suddenly ceased.

Whatever the ins and outs of political events, throughout 1917 Beaverbrook was careful to keep his friendship with Bonar Law intact. He was happy to act as intermediary for Lloyd George when the Prime Minister wished to bring Winston Churchill into his government as Minister of Munitions, knowing that Law was unremitting in his dislike of Churchill. F. E. Smith, too, now famous as Attorney General after the prosecution of the Irish revolutionary Sir Roger Casement for high treason, sought his help in obtaining a baronetcy. In both cases, Beaverbrook's advocacy was successful.

Yet the friendship went deeper than that. Bonar Law, like so many others, was worried about his two sons, Charlie and James, who had enlisted. With no wife, ascetic in his tastes and at times lonely, working almost as a recluse, he had invested what emotional energy he had in his children. The first shock was devastating. Charlie, at the age of nineteen an officer in the King's Own Scottish Borderers, had been posted to Palestine. On 11 April 1917 the telegram that all families dreaded arrived in 11 Downing Street. Charlie was reported missing after the Battle of Gaza. 'When I heard of it', Bonar Law said later, 'I felt at first that I must give up everything...'[13] As it was, he mourned in solitude for a full week before he could return to work.

Yet a week had not been enough. Beaverbrook, who had remained close to provide moral support, never stopped worrying. In the middle of June, the Apostolic Delegate in Constantinople reported the news that Charlie might be a prisoner of war. 'He is a different man since the news came,' wrote a colleague.[14] The news proved false, and Bonar Law went back into depression. Even before then, on 10 July, Beaverbrook was worried enough to write to Lloyd George: 'Could you manage to send Bonar Law on a mission to Paris for a few days in order to distract his mind ... I feel quite certain that if something of this kind is not done at once he will have a very bad breakdown...'[15] Lloyd George duly organised a trip and, at least for a time, the cure seemed to have worked. At least Beaverbrook was able to report that Bonar Law was afterwards 'in a good state of mind'.[16]

The second blow fell in September. Law's eldest son, James, was a pilot in the Royal Flying Corps, assigned to 60th Squadron and posted to France on the 17th. Three days later his aircraft was shot down. He was posted as missing but there was little hope that he had survived. (In fact, his body was never found.) Bonar Law fell again into deep depression, and again Beaverbrook came to the rescue. He persuaded Law to go to France to meet Jim's fellow officers. Law asked to see an aircraft of the type his son had flown. When he saw it, he levered himself into the small cockpit and sat there in silence for over two hours. When he emerged, he seemed more composed, at least enough to return to London and bury himself in his work. When his subsequent diligence drew comment, he simply replied, 'My sons would have wished it.'[17]

If Beaverbrook's relationship with Bonar Law had, as Davidson remarked, a touch of the feminine, the opposite was true in his dealings with the editorial staff of the *Daily Express*. He was back to his old ways of running the Royal Securities Corporation, hectoring and interfering, even making mischief. On 7 September, Blumenfeld wrote an exasperated letter accusing him of being deliberately mischievous:

> [J. B.] Wilson [news editor of the *Express*] tells me that you say I have been dodging you … This situation has become both impossible and intolerable and you, being possessed of more than usual intelligence must understand the mischief that is worked by the sending of the sort of messages I have received through subordinates … I can't in the least understand your sudden attitude of hostility.[18]

Beaverbrook was undeterred. Soon afterwards he wrote another furious letter to Blumenfeld, complaining about the positioning of the small advertisements, the items on the front page, the By-the-Way column, the editorials and the general presentation. Blumenfeld felt, like many of Beaverbrook's editors since, that he could do no more than sit and listen.

Yet the *Daily Express* occupied only part of his time, as did his directorship of the Colonial Bank in the City, and there was more to be done on the home front of the war effort. By the end of 1917, Beaverbrook had become head of the Pictorial Propaganda Committee, at the time under the direction of the Department of Information. He had set up the Canadian War Memorial Fund, to be chaired by Lord Rothermere, an independent fund administered through the Canadian War Records Office, whose aim was 'to secure the services of the most brilliant artists … in order that the episodes and general character of this colossal struggle and the personalities and figures of those who took part in it may be rescued from oblivion',[19] and recruited already established names such as Augustus John and Wyndham Lewis. In addition, he took the chair of the War Office Cinematographic Committee. 'In the world of publicity', he wrote,

> the cinematograph stands alone. It creates its own audiences without effort, because men are naturally drawn to what they wish to see … The film … possesses all those qualities which make it not only an art in itself but the most powerful instrument for appealing to the mass of the people.[20]

For the time, these views were little short of revolutionary.

There is no doubt that in all these many activities Beaverbrook's peerage acted to his advantage. So too did it help in London's social life, leaving aside the seemingly implacable opposition of the high aristocracy. As 1917 moved on, and the war ground yet again to a stalemate, the frenetic excesses of the earlier months of the war, when London was full of drink- and drug-related partying, gave way to more modest entertainment. The daily lists of young men killed or wounded had taken their toll on the young women who had been left behind. There were still parties, but they were parties not to celebrate military adventures but to disguise the empty feeling of mourning. There was hardly a female, young, middle-aged or old, who had not lost a son, lover, brother, husband, father, uncle or cousin. Put brutally, there was a dearth of young, or youngish, men available. A 38-year-old Canadian peer, millionaire to boot, was a good catch, and Beaverbrook, with Gladys and the children safely at a distance in Cherkley, was not slow to take advantage.

It was not all high life with fashionable young ladies. In November 1917, Beaverbrook met the journalist and novelist Arnold Bennett. In a newspaper tribute, published in the *Sunday Express* two days after Bennett's death in 1931, he recounted how he had instigated their first meeting: 'He came to lunch with me at my house at my urgent solicitation. I wanted to meet him because I admired his books so much.'[21] Bennett was some twelve years older than Beaverbrook, the son of a pawnbroker turned solicitor in Stoke-on-Trent who had made his way in journalism before branching out with a series of very successful novels. Physically he was unattractive, with a prognathous jaw and receding chin. But he had great charm, and in his years spent in Paris before the war he had acquired a certain sophistication as well as a rather difficult French wife. His writings brought in a satisfactory income, which he was happy to spend, staying frequently in London's most expensive hotels. (He is one of the few celebrities to have a dish named after him. 'Omelette Arnold Bennett' was a confection of eggs, Parmesan cheese, cream and smoked haddock. It was devised by the chef of the Savoy and Bennett liked it so much that he insisted on having it wherever he stayed.)'

*Lord Beaverbrook's friend Arnold Bennett, versatile
British writer, novelist, critic and playwright.*

Before long the two men were regularly lunching and dining together. Bennett fell for Beaverbrook's charm and Beaverbrook fell for Bennett's slightly quirky sense of honesty. 'With the exception of Bonar Law, he was practically the only man I have ever met who would not tell a lie of any sort – not even the ordinary harmless social lies that we all tell every day.'²² Apart from the attraction to Bennett's character, Beaverbrook learnt much from him about painting, and was instrumental in getting him appointed to the Imperial War Memorial Committee with the possibility of securing commissions for young painters. But Bennett would come to be most useful in 1918 when Beaverbrook was given a new job.

Before that happened, however, there occurred a strange, and alarming, incident. As always, there were madmen about, and it was one of those, Robertson Lawson, a seemingly reputable Scottish businessman known to Beaverbrook, who some time before the end of 1917 cornered him in his office in Lombard Street. '"God charged me"', runs Beaverbrook's account of Lawson's opening remarks, 'to put the matter to the test. If you are good you will be exalted. But if I find that you are a power for evil you are to be destroyed...' He was wearing a raincoat and a gesture towards his pocket convinced me that Lawson carried a revolver ... The test was to be that 'The Holy Ghost will descend in the form of a dove...' As no dove appeared I suggested we should seek Heavenly Grace ... Together we sang ... the twenty-third Psalm ... at the end of the prayers there was still no sign of the dove ... Then I had an idea. 'There are so many wicked men in this building that the Holy Ghost cannot enter it ... let us go to the House of God...'

Beaverbrook had talked his way out of danger. The traffic in Lombard Street allowed him to escape. Lawson was subsequently arrested and 'a day or two later he died in a padded cell'. Whether or not Lawson's revolver was loaded is not recorded. F. E. Smith, when Beaverbrook told him about the incident, thought the whole thing to be a huge joke.[23]

On 23 January 1918, Frederick Guest, the Liberal Chief Whip, wrote to Lloyd George. 'Dear Prime Minister,' his letter runs, 'I do hope you will consider Max for Controller of Propaganda. He is bitten with it and I want him anchored.'[24] Guest knew that Lloyd George had been tinkering with the idea of bringing Beaverbrook into his government but had not found the right slot. Offers of the directorship of finance at the Ministry of Munitions and of the post of Paymaster General had been batted away by Beaverbrook, although he had added pointedly, 'I hope however that should circumstances alter and my health permits I might yet be able to serve the Government in some suitable capacity.'[25]

Guest had another, sharper point. It was a matter of urgency to fill the post, since there was danger of a bureaucratic nervous breakdown. At the outbreak of war in 1914, the Asquith government had created a War Propaganda Bureau under the management of the then Chancellor of the Duchy of Lancaster, the Liberal MP and journalist Charles Masterman. Masterman was a Christian Socialist and intellectual (with a double first from Cambridge among his prizes) who developed a careless habit of losing elections: on his appointment to the Cabinet he had lost his Bethnal Green South West seat in a by-election and subsequently failed to be endorsed by the voters of Ipswich three months later. He eventually resigned from the Cabinet in February 1915. He was, however, valuable for his literary connections and was allowed to continue with war propaganda, recruiting a number of writers, Rudyard Kipling, Arnold Bennett, H. G. Wells, Sir Arthur Conan Doyle and John Buchan among them, and several painters of equal distinction. Running parallel to Masterman's bureau was another bureau, at first in the Home Office but transferred to the Foreign Office early in 1916. To add to the confusion, a new Department of Information had been set up in December 1916 under the supervision of Sir Edward Carson but with John Buchan as director-in-charge and an advisory committee consisting of Lord Northcliffe, Lord Burnham (proprietor of the *Daily Telegraph*), Robert Donald (editor of the *Daily Chronicle*) and C. P. Scott (editor of the *Manchester Guardian*). Reasonably enough, early in 1918 Lloyd George had decided to merge these three bodies into one Ministry of Information; and, as Guest pointed out, a new ministry needed a new minister.

It was not to be an easy process. Lloyd George knew that to snare Guest's favoured candidate he would have to offer a post which carried with it membership of the Cabinet. The Chancellorship of the Duchy of Lancaster was the only one immediately vacant. Yet it was not a happy choice. The Duchy itself was, and still is, the private estate of the Sovereign in his or her capacity as Duke of Lancaster. As such, it administers a large property portfolio mainly in the north of England and has rights to appoint to various offices in its area such as Lords Lieutenants and High Sheriffs and to Church of England offices where the Duchy is patron. Although the Chancellor has little to do with the day-to-day management of the estate, he is answerable to Parliament for its performance. Altogether, the Duchy was hardly a suitable appointment for a Presbyterian from New Brunswick.

When the news leaked out there was a chorus of disapproval from the London press. *The Globe* thought it 'a rather bad joke'; the *Evening Standard* opined that 'one can hardly conceive a more unsuitable appointment'; the *Westminster Gazette* concluded that Beaverbrook 'lacked the necessary skills for the position'; and *The Times* criticised the powers that he would be given.[26] The *Daily Chronicle* was one of the few newspapers offering support.

King George V, as might be imagined, was not at all pleased. Lord Stamfordham wrote a sharp letter to Frederick Guest:

> The King expressed much surprise that, considering past circumstances, he should now be asked to agree to Lord Beaverbrook's presiding over the Duchy, which, as it were, is the personal property of the Sovereign and entailing closer relations between the King and the Chancellor than with many of his Ministers. His Majesty asks whether some other arrangement could not be made to meet the case.[27]

Lloyd George wrote a terse reply. 'I cannot get him without offering him Ministerial rank. He is a first-rate business man and will administer the Duchy well. I wish to assure His Majesty that I attach great importance to the appointment of Lord Beaverbrook to this post…'[28] The King was obliged to swallow hard and accept his Prime Minister's request. It was all the more galling that Beaverbrook would become a Cabinet minister and as such would become a Privy Counsellor (kissing the King's hand after taking the oath). As for Beaverbrook himself, he was badly upset by the press attacks and was busy drafting letters of resignation, never delivered but threatened right up to the moment he entered No. 10 and was won over by the Lloyd George charm.

Lord Beaverbrook, the Minister of Information, 1918.

On 10 February the announcement was made, but the political reaction was as hostile as that of the press. Matters were made worse by the further appointment of Northcliffe as head of enemy propaganda with direct access to the Prime Minister. When Bonar Law on 18 February answered a question in the House of Commons from a Liberal MP on whether Beaverbrook would receive confidential information, he was able to brush it aside. But the following day there was uproar. The attack was led by Austen Chamberlain, out of office but angling for a return, on the floor of the House. Lloyd George's appointments, he maintained, had meant that the government had

surrounded themselves with an atmosphere of suspicion and distrust because they have allowed themselves to become intimately associated with these great newspaper proprietors ... You cannot escape trouble of this kind as long as you try to combine in the same person the functions of a director of a Press which asserts its independence and a member of a Government who owes loyalty to the Government.[29]

Others were quick to follow suit. That same day, the Unionist War Committee passed a resolution that in their opinion, 'no one who controls a newspaper should be allowed to be a member of the Government or to hold a responsible post under it so long as he retains control of that newspaper'.[30] The resolution was put forward by the committee's chairman, Lord Salisbury, who described Beaverbrook as a very wicked man and, when asked to justify his comment, simply remarked, 'Oh, ask anybody in Canada.'[31] But, as Guest pointed out to Lloyd George, accepting the resolution would mean sacking not just Beaverbrook and Northcliffe but Rothermere (Secretary of State for Air) as well, which would be read, rightly, as a sign of prime ministerial panic. Lord Milner was next in line, writing to Lloyd George on 27 February to declare that

there is more stir about this than I have yet known in any of these purely domestic rows ... So many of our real friends are disgruntled ... The less people hear or see of Northcliffe, Beaverbrook (certainly the most unpopular name of all) etc. for the next few weeks the better.[32]

Austen Chamberlain renewed his attack in the Commons on 11 March. This provoked Lloyd George into a robust defence of his appointments, particularly that of Beaverbrook. Lord Hugh Cecil joined in the row, demanding to know whether Beaverbrook was fit to be a peer and Chancellor of the Duchy in view of its role as ecclesiastical patron. Tim Healy leapt to Beaverbrook's defence with an attack on Cecil's High Church leanings. At that point Bonar Law was acutely aware of an uncomfortable dilemma. He could not support Beaverbrook without supporting Northcliffe, which he could not in all honesty do. He wavered. The simplest way out was to advise his friend, in the face of all the political criticism, to resign. He even drafted a letter of resignation for him. Beaverbrook consulted his friend Healy. 'Don't resign,' Healy replied. 'Wait until you are sacked.'[33]

The parliamentary assault soon died down, not least because on 21 March the German Army, reinforced by fifty-five divisions released from the Eastern Front by the Russian collapse, launched what was to be its final offensive on the Western Front. General Gough's Fifth Army was routed. A German breakthrough to the Channel was almost inevitable. All attention was focused on the danger, and the birth pangs of the Ministry of Information were of little consequence. Nevertheless, Beaverbrook was determined to get on with the job. His problems, as he was quick to realise, were, first, that the responsibilities of the new ministry had never been properly defined and, second, that the finances of the three constituent bodies were in a state of chaos.

To be sure, the second problem was the easier for him to deal with. Applying the same methods as had served him well in his Canadian days at the Royal Securities Corporation, he proceeded to march over individual susceptibilities with his usual mixture of compulsive energy and indifference to its effect. Directors from the business world were brought in. A private firm of accountants was commissioned to report on the state of the finances and to recommend remedial action (without reference to the Treasury). Staff were pushed around, reallocated and shouted at if they bleated in protest. The headquarters were moved from Wellington House to the more modest Howard Hotel. At the same time, an overseas press centre was set up for foreign journalists, with particular attention, as might be guessed, to friendly Canadian reporters. (Contributions to the ministry's expenses were welcomed.) All in all, Beaverbrook was able to report to a committee of the House of Commons that matters had improved. The committee accepted the conclusion but noted that the practice of ignoring Treasury recommendations on the size of directors recruited from the private sector should stop. Furthermore, they added rather mournfully, 'Considerable entertaining would appear to be done by the Ministry of Information.'[34]

The qualities that made Beaverbrook so successful in the internal organisation of his ministry were precisely opposite to the qualities needed to negotiate with his colleagues running other departments. In short, if there were political toes to be trodden on, Beaverbrook was there stamping hard. On 20 February, he sent to the War Cabinet a memorandum setting out his plan for an Intelligence Department of the Ministry of Information. 'The arrangement [to transfer the Intelligence Branch of the former Department to the Foreign Office]', he declared loftily,

> should be cancelled ... All items of political information collected by the Admiralty and War Office Intelligence branches should be transmitted to my Intelligence Department ... A liaison officer of this Ministry should be attached to the staff of the Secret Service, and ... it should be his business to arrange for the forwarding of all political information to this Ministry.[35]

At a stroke, Beaverbrook offended Sir Eric Geddes at the Admiralty, Lord Derby at the War Office and, last but by no means least, the Foreign Secretary, Arthur Balfour. Not content with that, Beaverbrook sent a further missive to the War Cabinet two days later. 'Assuming that Home Propaganda is part of my province,' it ran, '...various Government Departments, such as the Ministry of Food and the Ministry of National Service, have their own Propaganda bureau ... Money would be saved and efficiency increased if these were brought under the Ministry of Information.'[36]

The circle of ministerial colleagues he had offended was widening almost by the day.

It was Balfour who led the counter-attack. Beaverbrook's proposals, he wrote to the War Cabinet, were 'not only indefensible from the point of view of organisation but would render secrecy more difficult to maintain than it is at present'. The proposal to amalgamate propaganda and intelligence was 'based on a fundamental fallacy … The former depends on the latter for inspiration but in their inherent nature and method of operation they have nothing in common.' Balfour was prepared to support the idea of a liaison officer to co-ordinate activity but insisted that he be based in the Foreign Office and that the Foreign Office be the intermediary through which the information be collected, sifted and analysed before being passed on. 'In a word', he concluded witheringly, 'Lord Beaverbrook's scheme seems inferior in all respects to that recently sanctioned by the War Cabinet.'[37]

The War Cabinet met to consider the matter on 5 March in a fractious mood. Wrangles between government departments always resulted in bad-tempered argument and the tense balance of the war added to the nervousness around the table. Unable to resolve the dispute, and impatient to move on, Lloyd George asked Lieutenant-General Jan Smuts, a fellow member of the War Cabinet, to call a meeting of all concerned to try to resolve the issue. Smuts duly performed his task as best he could and reported back to the War Cabinet on 15 March. 'Various expedients tried by me to overcome the difficulty have failed', his report states, 'and I can only report to the Cabinet for a definite decision on the point.'[38] Beaverbrook then sent another memorandum to the War Cabinet restating his demands. In obvious irritation, the War Cabinet requested Lord Robert Cecil, Balfour's junior minister, to try to settle the matter in direct negotiation.

At the end of March 1918, more bad news arrived from France. The German offensive had indeed broken through. It looked as though Amiens might fall and the rest of the British Army to the north would be pinned in with its back to the Channel. In the days following, there was in London a sense of acute danger, bordering on panic, and fear that Britain might after all lose the war. Ministers were desperately seeking answers. More men were needed, so conscription was to be extended to Ireland, with the palliative to the Nationalists that the Home Rule Bill was to be revived, provoking yet another parliamentary row. In the panic, interdepartmental disputes over territory had to be stopped immediately. Accordingly, Cecil wrote to Beaverbrook an emollient letter, saying that the Foreign Office undertook 'to do all it can to help the Ministry of Information in its work'.[39] It was, of course, insincere, as Cecil himself admitted in a letter to Geddes at the Admiralty only three weeks later. But there was an urgent need to get Beaverbrook, to put it crudely, to shut up.

Beaverbrook would not remain silent. Seemingly oblivious to the danger to the nation, he persisted in his private Whitehall battle. Believing that the Foreign Office had caved in, he switched his attack to the Admiralty. There, the First Lord, Geddes, proved to be a formidable opponent. At a meeting on 12 April, Geddes refused to give ground. 'The Foreign Office', he declared, 'was an old established office which had been accustomed to dealing with [intelligence] information of this kind … It was essential that the Foreign Office should be the medium through which political information reached the Department of Education.'[40] Beaverbrook also fell into further disfavour with King George V. On 18 April the *Daily Express* published the news that Lord Derby had been moved from the War Office to become Ambassador in Paris and that he was to be replaced by Lord Milner. The newspaper was correct, but it had published before the appointments had been officially made public. J. T. Davies, Lloyd George's principal private secretary, fielded a telephone call from Stamfordham, who rang to say that 'His Majesty is most indignant that the appointments of Lord Derby and Lord Milner should have appeared in this morning's 'Daily Express', and that His Majesty hopes you will endeavour to find out how this leakage came about'.[41] Beaverbrook protested his innocence to Lloyd George. He may well have been right. Blumenfeld may well have discovered the news from his own sources, as Beaverbrook said. The problem was that nobody was inclined to believe him.

There was another collision with Balfour over a proposed mission to Japan to present a Field Marshal's baton to Emperor Yoshihito. The mission had been in the planning stage in the Foreign Office for some time, although Beaverbrook only learnt about it in the middle of

March. He quickly sent a memorandum to the War Cabinet proposing to expand the mission to include 'one or more men versed in the difficult work of propaganda'. His memorandum had been considered at the War Cabinet meeting of 18 March. Lord Robert Cecil, with Balfour beside him, argued that it would be a good idea to send someone of distinction to present the general case for Britain to 'raise our prestige in Japan'. It was agreed to invite the Duke of Connaught to head the mission. In addition, 'the Minister of Information should consider the names of minor officials who might be suitable as members'.[42]

Beaverbrook, of course, had no intention of sending minor officials on the mission. He had already recruited Lord Charles Beresford, a retired admiral, to be his front man and was feverishly trying to contact other equally distinguished businessmen. Balfour then was obliged to put his foot down. In an angry exchange of letters with Beaverbrook in April he pointed out there could only be one Foreign Office and he was running it. Recognising the weakness of his position, Beaverbrook wrote yet another memorandum to the War Cabinet saying that if he was not to be involved in the current mission he would like permission to send his own mission to Japan 'for propaganda pure and simple'.[43]

By that time the War Cabinet were getting tired of what most of them thought of as Beaverbrook's childish games. Furthermore, there had been another incident with Buckingham Palace. On 28 May the *Daily Express* had published a story about the Prince of Wales visiting the Vatican for an audience with Pope. The long-suffering J. T. Davies was again at the end of a furious Stamfordham telephone call. The King apparently regarded the article 'as a direct attack on the Crown and as it appears in a paper owned by a Member of the Government he is very much annoyed'.[44] The matter, Stamfordham went on, should be raised in Cabinet. (In fact, it was not even mentioned once it became known that it was Balfour himself who had advised the Prince that he could not possibly visit Rome without seeking an audience with the Pope.)

On 13 June, Beaverbrook sent Lloyd George a long memorandum complaining about all the difficulties and frustrations he had suffered over the past few months. In an accompanying letter he told the Prime

Minister that he did 'not wish to roll the Apple of Discord among the various Departments concerned' and was therefore appealing to him personally rather than to the War Cabinet.

> I fear that if I sent it to the War Cabinet the discord would be serious because my case, contained in the Memorandum, is so ir- refutable that it is bound to win. Such a victory based purely on the logic of the situation would produce infinite soreness among the defeated parties and serious trouble for the Government ... I am nearly worn out with my effort to put this Ministry on its legs...[45]

He had chosen the wrong moment. The tide in the war had turned. The German offensive had ground to a halt. American troopships, with the flower of the nation's youth, were docking almost every day in the Channel ports. Lloyd George could at last scent the prospect of victory. When Beaverbrook wrote to him on 18 June offering to resign, he did not even bother to answer. On 24 June, Beaverbrook wrote yet again. The dispute with the Foreign Office had left him exhausted. He concluded that his only option was to resign. 'Since I cannot make my view prevail, I must with sincere regret place my resignation in your hands and ask you to act on it immediately.'[46] Even now, Lloyd George was not yet ready to give up. During the first half of July he made efforts to heal the breach between the two departments. But Balfour would not be moved. As he wrote to Lloyd George on 12 July, '[Compromise] would not only result in increased friction but might seriously affect the constitutional position of the Secretary of State for Foreign Affairs. We should end by having two Ministers responsible to Cabinet for Foreign Policy, each having its own officers.'[47] In terms of personal politics, it was no less than game, set and match to Bal- four. Beaverbrook was forced to acknowledge defeat. A further appeal to Lloyd George was running up against the Prime Minister's driving determination to bring the war to a victorious conclusion. Nothing else mattered.

It was not until the end of August that Lloyd George finally lost patience. The *Daily Express* published a leading article stating that the paper would not be prepared to endorse the Lloyd George coalition in a future general election unless the Prime Minister gave specific pledges on tariff reform and imperial preference. Lloyd George immediately assumed that the leader was at Beaverbrook's dictation. 'Have you seen the leader in today's Express?' he wrote to Bonar Law. 'That is Max. Having regard to the risks I ran for him and the way I stood up for him when he was attacked by his own party I regard this as a mean piece of treachery. It explains why no man in any party trusts Max.'[48]

From that point on, Lloyd George would no longer be prepared to refuse Beaverbrook's resignation should it be offered. In fact, it was not to be long delayed. By the middle of September, Beaverbrook was starting to notice a succession of painful abscesses in his mouth. He was no longer able to give his full attention to his ministry. By October he felt that he could no longer go on. On 21 October he wrote to Lloyd George, 'I have spent my strength in the organisation of the Ministry and it is with deep regret that I find myself unable to continue my work.'[49] Lloyd George was effusive in his reply while accepting Beaverbrook's resignation. The press, too, was more generous than it had been on his appointment. All in all, it was a dignified exit, even if Beaverbrook's dream of establishing a fully fledged and powerful ministry alongside the more traditional Foreign Office had fallen foul of Balfour and the Whitehall political firewall.

Beaverbrook's illness, unlike others of which he complained from time to time, was not imagined. He had contracted an infectious disease known as actinomycosis. The origin of the disease varies but, in his case, it seems most likely that it was the result of incompetent dentistry leading to bacterial infection. Nowadays, of course, the condition is easily treated with antibiotics, but in the days before the discovery of penicillin, treatment was, to some extent, hit and miss. But it was painful and unpleasant. It also marked the end of Beaverbrook's war. The November celebrations almost passed him by. To be sure, Cherkley was a haven to which he could retreat, but the difficulty there was that the war had so concentrated his mind that his wife and family had been neglected. In fact, London gossip had it that he had already embarked on a career of serial marital infidelity.

CHAPTER 13

ALL CHANGE

'Bring Bonar Back'[1]

Beaverbrook's illness, first detected in August 1918, made the closing months of the year and the early months of 1919, give or take short periods of recovery, never less than uncomfortable and from time to time quite miserable. After successive visits to expensive dentists and a throat specialist, a tentative diagnosis of his condition was reached. It seemed to be more than a simple infection of the mouth and larynx. The probability now was cancer. Understandably very depressed, he arranged to see Sir Wilfred Trotter, the leading cancer specialist of the day. Trotter advised an exploratory operation. This took place in October. The conclusion was that his condition was not of cancer but of the equally dangerous actinomycosis. So far, so bad.

During the period of recovery from the exploratory operation, once the bandages and stitches had been removed, Beaverbrook grew a beard to cover the remaining scars. The beard, to put it mildly, was not a cosmetic success and, perhaps fortunately, it was soon time to operate again, this time more substantively in order to remove the underlying fungus. On 15 February 1919, the second operation took place. Trotter managed to take out the growth and pronounced his patient clear. But this was soon proved wrong. A new fungus appeared. Almost in desperation, on the recommendation of a friend who had himself been cured of the disease, Beaverbrook turned to a previously unknown Portuguese doctor. The treatment he recommended was, to say the least, unorthodox. Four hundred drops of iodine were poured down the patient's throat every day. 'I lay in bed most of the time,' Beaverbrook recorded, 'with my heart pounding, my head bursting, my eyes rolling out tears.'² Astonishingly, the treatment worked. A subsequent small operation was enough to finish what had originally looked to be a life-threatening illness.

A bearded Lord Beaverbrook recovering from actinomycosis, walking in the park with his nurse, 1919.

As might be imagined, Beaverbrook was not a good patient. Gladys's ministrations at Cherkley were constant and kind, but in the Hyde Park Hotel nurses came and went, arriving charmed by his flirtatious wit and leaving alarmed by his bouts of rage. When there, he could hear the celebrations marking the end of the war in November 1918 but was explosively angry at being unable to take part. In the event, his enforced idleness was alleviated by a visit from Winston Churchill in late November 1918. Much to his relief, it turned out to be no ordinary visit. Churchill had been sent by Prime Minister Lloyd George to canvass Beaverbrook's support, and by extension that of his newspapers, for the coalition in the general election which had been called for the following month. Dinner, Churchill said, was proposed at his temporary home, a comfortable house in South Kensington opposite the Natural History Museum, at the time, as it happened and perhaps in anticipation of future events, showing a collection of recently discovered dinosaur skeletons. The proposal was accepted, and Beaverbrook 'appeared', as he later wrote, 'with my head grotesquely swathed in white bandages, which must indeed have given me a strange appearance'.[3] Undeterred by the appearance, Lloyd George not only asked for support but also asked Beaverbrook to rally Lord Rothermere of the *Daily Mail* and Sir Edward Hulton of the *Daily Sketch* to the cause and orchestrate the press campaign. Glad to be back in harness, this Beaverbrook did, with his usual bouncing energy and, ultimately, with resounding success.

Although he was prepared to act as intermediary for the event, Churchill had not been entirely happy with the political attitude previously adopted by the *Daily Express*. He had gone so far as to complain to Lloyd George, who murmured Churchill's complaints to Beaverbrook. Beaverbrook was robust in defence. 'I take an independent attitude,' he wrote to Churchill on 26 November:

> I claim the right to criticise the Coalition leaders in their public capacity in the columns of a daily paper ... You are a close friend of mine. But surely you would not expect that fact to make a vital difference in any public comment I made on your policy in affairs of state.[4]

In fact, Beaverbrook put this principle into practice the following year when he roundly condemned Churchill's efforts to give military assistance to the White Russians in the Russian civil war. Churchill was, as always, outspoken in his irritation, but Beaverbrook insisted that he was still 'a personality very congenial to me ... I had supported him in his days of adversity and was to tender him the same support again when the bad time came round ... I found him infinitely agreeable and my company was pleasing to him.'[5] That was certainly true, but their disagreement about Russia was not the easiest time for their friendship.

Smiling portrait photograph of Max Beaverbrook
in a suit with a rose in his buttonhole, 1916–19.

Another interlude in Beaverbrook's struggle with his illness was a visit
to Paris in January 1919 for the opening of the Peace Conference. For
the event, of course, the whole political world was assembled. It was
an occasion not to be missed, and Beaverbrook, by then without his
beard and his bandages, was certainly not prepared to be an absentee.
There was an added advantage. Edwin Montagu, in his role as Secretary of State for India, was part of the large British delegation lodged
at the Hotel Majestic. There was no place there for wives and Venetia
Montagu had to look elsewhere. Beaverbrook provided the solution.
On 14 January, Diana Manners was writing to her fiancé Duff Cooper:

> [Beaverbrook] and Venetia turned up just as we were turning out.
> It's a disgusting case – her face lights up when that animated little
> deformity so much as turns to her. They are living in open sin at the
> Ritz in a tall silk suite with a common bath, and unlocked doors
> between while poor Ted is sardined into the Majestic, unknown and
> uncared for.[6]

However barbed Diana Manners's description of the living arrangements, Beaverbrook had found a devoted observer of the comings
and goings in Paris when he was back in London for the final stages

of his treatment. There was a succession of gossipy letters charting the social progress of the Peace Conference, what was thought of President Woodrow Wilson's endless 'Sermon on the Mount' and of the French Premier Georges Clemenceau's remark that Wilson should go quietly to sleep. Yet it was not all gossip, and Venetia certainly acted as a fruitful mole, charting for 'my dearest Max' the progress of the negotiations. Furthermore, when she was back in England, seemingly bored by Edwin's dedication to the whole business, she was not only looking through, at Beaverbrook's request, the draft of the book he was writing about the events of 1914 to 1916, later to be published as *Politicians and the War*, but volunteering copies of Asquith's letters to her about Churchill's conduct in the early years of the war, adding, 'I [would] send you the Cabinet papers for your archives'. By Christmas 1919, Venetia was signing herself 'Yrs always'.[7]

For the whole of 1919, political attention was focused almost entirely on the negotiations in Paris. Ministers went back and forth across the Channel, apart from Lloyd George, who took up almost permanent residence in the capital. Bonar Law, on the other hand, disliked Paris and was always anxious to get back to his desk at the Treasury. The one minister who enjoyed all that Paris had to offer was F. E. Smith, now Lord Chancellor with the title of Lord Birkenhead, whose appetite for French women, not to mention French champagne and French brandy, was duly noted. Venetia's letters also recounted the dinner parties, the quarrels, the universal dislike of the United States President Woodrow Wilson and the cattiness of the women. Beaverbrook read all her letters avidly (while securing her husband's complaisance by guaranteeing a large overdraft for him at Barclays Bank).

As his involvement in domestic politics waned, so did Beaverbrook's enthusiasm for journalism increase. Just after Christmas 1918 he launched the *Sunday Express*, the printing presses set in motion by Diana Manners, whom he had also commissioned to write a series of articles. At first, he thought that it would simply be a Sunday version of the daily, edited by Blumenfeld, written by the same journalists and produced by the same operatives working overtime. That turned out to be a bad mistake. In January 1919 the circulation suffered 'a very heavy drop'. 'The principal criticism', Beaverbrook was told, 'is that the paper is too much like the D. E. I think we shall have to make the paper more of a Sunday paper and not a 7th day D. E.'[8] This was confirmed by the circulation manager of the daily. 'One and all', he reported after talking to agents,

> declare there is nothing in the paper to appeal to the Sunday Reader. It is too much like the 'Daily Express' without being up to the standard of the daily. The make-up of the paper is not considered attractive enough; more illustrations are needed; our special articles are of a poor quality; the Diana Manners contributions are everywhere condemned as the veriest twaddle...[9]

They were right. In fact, it took two years, any number of editors and half a million pounds to turn the paper around.

By contrast, the daily was doing well. Blumenfeld was recruiting young talented journalists, including Maurice Woods as political leader writer and a young Canadian, E. J. ('Robbie') Robertson, hired to sharpen the management. At the end of 1918, the daily circulation was touching 350,000. By the end of 1919 it had risen to nearly 500,000. The rate of improvement, of course, was not enough for Beaverbrook, and he continued his hectoring of Blumenfeld. In a memorandum sent to Blumenfeld by his secretary in April 1919 he demanded that the financial page be brightened up, that more attention be given to sports coverage, that a particular reporter should take advice from a senior and, for good measure, that the paper should

> work up a campaign against the present organisation and the Charter of the Bank of England ... and oppose its renewal and urge for Government control of the institution ... I wish you would write some stories on the changed condition of the Stock Exchange since the end of the War ... I understand the House has assumed quite a different appearance from the War days.[10]

The suggestion that Blumenfeld should 'work up a campaign' was typical of Beaverbrook at a time when he felt that he had not enough to do. Furthermore, some of his proposals were surprisingly radical.

He was adamant in his opposition to Churchill over military intervention in Russia, arguing instead for making peace with the Bolsheviks. Then in October 1919, in one of his rare speeches in the House of Lords, he questioned the established view that direct taxation should only be levied on income. Fortunes had been made in the war and remained untaxed. Beaverbrook proposed a 'Capital Increases Tax ... as an act of fiscal justice and a relief sorely needed for the strained finances of this kingdom'.[11] The idea even went as far as a Cabinet committee until it was killed off by an irritated Bonar Law.

With the ending of the Paris Peace Conference in January 1920, domestic politics returned to somewhere near normality. By then Beaverbrook had decided that his living arrangements, the Hyde Park Hotel, Cherkley at weekends, entertaining at the Savoy and a pied-à-terre in the Temple, needed change. Besides, although he kept his Canadian domicile, his residence was now firmly in London. He had also had to concede to Gladys first that her visits to London, now that the dangers of a Zeppelin attack had passed, were less than pleasant in the confines of the Hyde Park Hotel and second that his two sons would not be sent to New Brunswick for their education, as he had wished, but would go to school in London. There was a price to be paid, as he recognised, for her goodwill.

The answer was to look for a property which could serve as a London home for Gladys and the children on their visits and also as an operational base. It took little time for Beaverbrook's agent to find a convenient solution. A decaying house in the western suburb of Fulham, in Hurlingham Road in the near neighbourhood of the Hurlingham Club, was ideal for the purpose. It was called the Vineyard. Originally of seventeenth-century construction, it had eight bedrooms on the two upper floors, and, according to the surveyor's report, on the ground floor a 'small Lounge Hall, Drawing room, Dining room, Pantry, Kitchen, Scullery, Larders ... There is good cellarage.'[12] In addition, there was a large garage, an open space large enough for a covered tennis court if required and a sizeable garden. In short, it was a large property, although Beaverbrook liked to pretend that it was no more than a suburban cottage. Yet, taken all in all, it was ideal for quiet meetings and dinners with no pursuit from hungry journalists, with friendly games of tennis and, it need hardly be said, with suitable camouflage for discreet extra-marital assignations. Once it had been repaired and redecorated, Beaverbrook would be ready to move out of the Hyde Park Hotel.

The Vineyard, Hurlingham Road, Fulham, exterior view of rear elevation, 1968.

Even before the work was under way, however, he found himself embroiled in another controversy, largely, it must be admitted, of his own making. Since the end of the Peace Conference the coalition had moved into politically choppy waters. The British economy was in near recession; the 'Homes for Heroes' which had been promised in December 1918 were not being built; and, above all, the problem of Irish Home Rule, shuffled aside for so long, had placed itself firmly back on the Westminster agenda. Beaverbrook's foray into the controversy of the Excess Profits Duty, where he insisted that the *Daily Express* support a rise proposed by the Chancellor, Austen Chamberlain, from 40 per cent to 60 per cent against all Unionist and business cries of anguish, was, for a start, quite unnecessary. Not only that, but the paper went on to claim that the main attack on Chamberlain had come from the *News of the World*, whose proprietor, Lord Riddell, was at the time staying with Lloyd George. The implication was clear: the Prime Minister himself had briefed against his own Chancellor. Lloyd

George was, reasonably enough, almost beside himself with anger. Beaverbrook soon discreetly retracted.

While the Vineyard was little more than a building site there was time to take a break from London and what others thought, with some justification, to be using his newspapers for no more than making political mischief. There was, in addition, another reason. Leaving Gladys and his family behind, Beaverbrook went to Canada in July, intending to go from there to a meeting in New York. His Canadian visit went smoothly enough, but in his discussions with friends and family there he came to realise the damage done to Britain's reputation in the New World by the conduct of the coalition government, and the consequent violent reactions in Ireland, in their continued blunders over Irish Home Rule.

In the general election of 1918 the relatively moderate Irish National Party had surrendered its seemingly impregnable lead to the much less accommodating Sinn Féin. While the Peace Conference was in process the sporadic violence which broke out in 1919 could safely be ignored in London. Beaverbrook himself was unconcerned about the stories from Dublin which appeared from time to time in the *Daily Express*. This in turn drove Tim Healy to angry reproach. 'I read with regret the stuff in the Express about Ireland,' he wrote in December 1919. 'It is all warped and untrue ... When I spoke about my country ... you truly say it does not interest you. Why then interest yourself against us? Can't you leave us alone?'[13]

During 1920 the violence in Ireland had escalated. The British government took the view that negotiation with Sinn Féin was impossible, that they were no better than thugs or terrorists and that order must be restored by military force. Against that, the Irish associations in Canada and the United States were running a massive and successful campaign against Britain. Suddenly, Beaverbrook realised, the unity of the Empire, the one political imperative from which he never wavered, was looking more fragile than ever. It was time for him to focus on Ireland.

Back in London in October 1920, Beaverbrook was subjected to more salvoes from Healy. 'Put us down you never will, except in coffins.'[14] 'Now mark my forecast ... The ministers who made the unhappy boast that they would "put down the murder-gang" will soon be mocked at by their supporters, and for every lad they torture or hang a dozen will come forward to take his place.'[15] The salvoes continued almost in proportion to the brutality of the 'Black and Tans ... these creatures are mere thieves & cutthroats commissioned to rob & slay in the King's name'.[16] As 1920 gave way to 1921, Healy's attacks became more direct. 'Why is every step taken in Ireland by the Government a false step?', he asked. 'Can they do nothing right?'[17]

It was a fair question, to which there was little answer. The truth is that the coalition government was entering the long process that would eventually lead to its disintegration in the autumn of 1922. The beginning of the process was the removal of one of the coalition's building blocks in March 1921 when Bonar Law wrote to Lloyd George to submit his resignation. 'I very much regret to have to inform you', his letter of 17 March runs, 'that I am no longer able to continue my political work ... I am quite worn out and my medical advisers have warned me that my physical condition is such that unless I have an immediate and long rest an early and complete breakdown is inevitable.'[18] Bonar Law, the leader of the Conservatives and to all intents and purposes Lloyd George's Deputy Prime Minister, had given up the battle.

On Saturday 19 March, a cold and windy day with only the occasional burst of wintry sun, a small group stood on the platform at Charing Cross Station to see him on his journey to his retirement in the warmer climate of the south of France. 'The little knot of friends surrounding the traveller at the railway station', as Beaverbrook later wrote, 'was undistinguished. Three secretaries about to transfer their allegiance to other ministers, several members of the family, and I – that was the company.'[19] Bonar Law was touched by Beaverbrook's gesture, so much so that on his arrival at Dover he wrote to Lloyd George asking him 'to send for Max just to have a talk with him ... The feeling he has had that I prevented him from having a free hand ... perhaps made him more difficult than if I had been out of it altogether.'[20]

Lloyd George did issue a tentative invitation to Beaverbrook for a meeting at the London house of Bonar Law's parliamentary private secretary, Sir Philip Sassoon, but it was no more than tentative and was easily side-tracked. In fact, Lloyd George was still simmering with anger at an incident earlier in March. It concerned, strangely enough, the matter of the import into Britain of Canadian cattle. For reasons of protection for British farming there had been a wartime embargo, but with the assurance that this would be lifted after the war. Nothing had happened. In February 1921, Lloyd George had appointed Sir Arthur Griffith-Boscawen, the Unionist MP for Dudley, to be Minister of Agriculture. On his seeking re-election, the *Daily Express*, in alliance with the Meat Traders Association, demanded an assurance that the embargo would be lifted. Griffith-Boscawen refused. The *Daily Express* thereupon published a series of articles attacking him personally and Dudley was lost. In order to save face, Lloyd George agreed to set up a Royal Commission to determine the matter. The commission met and in due course recommended, to Beaverbrook's satisfaction, that the embargo be lifted. This was done by the elaborate procedure of a free vote in both Houses of Parliament. It comes as no surprise that Beaverbrook was not Lloyd George's favourite of the moment.

Their relationship deteriorated further over the reconstruction of the government as a result of Bonar Law's resignation in March. Austen Chamberlain took Law's place as leader of the Unionists and of the House of Commons, leaving the Treasury vacant. Churchill considered, reasonably enough in Beaverbrook's view, that he himself should be appointed Chancellor. Lloyd George took a different view and appointed Sir Robert Horne, leaving Churchill with the Colonial Office. 'Mr Churchill', Beaverbrook noted, 'returned from holiday in Egypt a disappointed man. I was also of the opinion that he had not been treated well. Under these circumstances we renewed a friendship tentatively – for the scar of the Russian disagreement still remained.'[21]

It was not long before Churchill became a frequent visitor to the Vineyard, often for dinner with Birkenhead, whose relationship with Lloyd George was at the time particularly cool, and Edwin Montagu. Needless to say, dinners where three senior ministers sat down with the proprietor of a daily newspaper with a circulation of 500,000 (and rising rapidly thanks to the success of its racing tips) could not fail to attract attention. Rumours started to circulate that there was a plot being hatched to dislodge Lloyd George. In fact, this was not altogether far from the truth. Beaverbrook was already urging Bonar Law to return. 'Come home now ... I offer you my little house until you find your new home ... Winston is very-very-very-very angry. F. E. is as bitter as Winston is angry.'[22] Bonar Law politely refused. 'I will not go back to England for while,' he replied.[23] Undeterred, Beaverbrook tried again in May. 'Please do come home for Whitsuntide,' he cabled Bonar Law in Paris. 'You can arrive in disguise stay at Vineyard and go away again before holidays if you wish ... please do come. Max'.[24] He even went to Paris with Edmund Goulding to argue with Law in person, but the result was the same.

There was no doubt that at that point the Lloyd George government, as Beaverbrook wrote to Sir Robert Borden, was running into difficulties. Yet, as so often when in near crisis, Lloyd George acted decisively. On his return to London, Beaverbrook cabled Law again. 'My plans smashed. Little man [Lloyd George] made terms with Colonial [Churchill] and made Smith a Viscount. The Jew [Montagu] will probably get an OBE. I get vicious denunciations scattered broadcast. Won't you come over for week end.'[25] Bonar Law did in fact come over for the weekend on 15 June but did no more than reiterate his refusal to take any part in any political manoeuvre. But his mere presence in London was enough to spark suspicion. Lloyd George confided to his secretary and mistress Frances Stevenson that 'Beaverbrook is clearly engineering for a coup ... Bonar Law came home for the weekend not for any ostensible reason, but ... it looks suspicious he is so entirely in Beaverbrook's hands.'[26] The immediate result was an article which appeared in Rothermere's *Daily Mirror* of 22 June revealing a 'plot' organised by the diners at the Vineyard. The following day the *Manchester Guardian* took up the story, specifically singling out Birkenhead and Beaverbrook as plotters. This in turn, of course, provoked a flurry of embarrassed denials.

Lloyd George's tactic had worked. There was no more talk of plots and no more hints of resignation. Lloyd George had also succeeded in digging himself out of another nasty hole, the result of a bungled attempt to remove his housing minister, Christopher Addison. All in all, the government seemed to be sailing towards smoother waters. That being so, it seemed a good time for the Prime Minister to engage in another typical Lloyd George manoeuvre. Having undermined Beaverbrook by clever press briefing, he was now going to make friends again. After all, the proprietor of an increasingly powerful daily newspaper could not be allowed to remain an enemy for long, and there was one policy shift Lloyd George was considering for which he needed all the support he could get.

The problem, of course, was Ireland. In December 1920 the coalition government had finally met what they thought had been their wartime obligations. Parliament passed legislation to divide Ireland into two autonomous regions within the United Kingdom with bicameral parliaments. As in Canada and Australia, the British Crown would retain the ultimate executive power, retaining control over defence, foreign affairs and the currency, but it was expected that some sort of prime ministerial arrangement would emerge. Yet none of this was good enough for Sinn Féin. They had won 73 out of 105 seats in the United Kingdom general election of 1918 and considered themselves entitled to declare independence as the Irish Republic and form their own Parliament, the Dáil Éireann. Unsurprisingly, this was pronounced illegal by the Lord Lieutenant on behalf of the Crown in September 1919.

The result was that even before the Royal Assent of the 1920 Act, Sinn Féin, through its military arm, the Irish Republican Army, was waging its war of independence. Healy was reporting all this to Beaverbrook in terms of boiling anger. 'British statesmanship is bankrupt in Ireland and quite unteachable,' he wrote on 9 May 1921. 'All talk of peace is eye-wash to tide over a difficulty.'[27] The situation moved from bad to critical with the elections in May 1921 for the new Southern Ireland Parliament. Of the 128 new members of the House of Commons of Southern Ireland, 124 were Sinn Féin. They promptly declared themselves to be the Second Dáil of the Irish Republic. By 28 May, Healy was writing to Beaverbrook excoriating the behaviour of Sir Hamar Greenwood, the Chief Secretary for Ireland:

> Greenwood's brag has had more disastrous consequences than even I anticipated. Instead of cowing the Shins [Sinn Féin] he has nerved

them to daring which I did not believe them capable of … Out of Bedlam no such councillor of the King such as Greenwood could have been selected. His lies alone would set the hearts of this people ablaze. They make no account of the loss deaths & wounds he has inflicted on them & they will take a vengeance more fearful than any he can decree.[28]

At the same time, improbable as it may seem, there were discussions in Cabinet on whether membership of Dáil Éireann ought to be treated as treason to be followed by death.[29]

Healy's bombardments were having their effect. Beaverbrook was provoked, somewhat against his own will, to take an interest. It so happened that his sudden interest came at a time when the English electorate seemed to be getting tired of Ireland. Even the Archbishop of Canterbury, Randall Davidson, had spoken from his pulpit, calling on all sides to renounce violence and to engage in peaceful negotiation. Much more potent, however, was the speech delivered by King George V at the opening of the Ulster Parliament in Belfast on 22 June carrying the same message. This in turn, on the King's prompting, was followed by a letter from Lloyd George to Éamon De Valera, the Sinn Féin leader, and James Craig, the Ulster Unionist leader, inviting them to London for discussions. Nothing was easy, but after some delicate dancing the invitation was accepted. The result of the meeting was that a truce was agreed and implemented on 11 July. For good measure, an agreement was reached to call a conference to settle the matter once and for all.

Few had any doubts about the historic nature of the event and what was at stake. In that atmosphere, precisely three months later the conference on Ireland held its first session at 10 Downing Street. Beaverbrook was by then fully committed to helping Healy both in his role as adviser to Sinn Féin, as a moderating influence to calm the wilder spirits, and in his unofficial role as fully involved observer of the conference itself. When he was in London, Healy stayed at the Vineyard, with the result that not only were the supportive articles in the *Daily Express* remarkably well informed, but ministers continued to be struck by 'the amount of information he [Beaverbrook] already possessed'.[30] Inevitably, as the conference wore on there were leaks for which Beaverbrook was blamed (as were Churchill and Birkenhead). Undeterred, he continued to instruct his editors with great care as to what they should write. Healy was duly appreciative. 'I am indeed grateful', he wrote on 17 November, 'for all you are doing for Ireland. You have more than kept your word to me. The articles are splendid and much cleverer than anything I could have suggested because they have such an English appeal. They are copied extensively here and carry the greatest weight.'[31] He even praised his Cherkley hostess. 'Tell Gladys I asked about her (who stood by me against Bonar for Ireland) that you helped the good old cause in dire straits.'[32]

After two months of tortuous and occasionally bad-tempered ne-gotiation, on 6 December 1921 the Anglo-Irish Treaty was signed. The Irish Free State was to be created and, as a reward for his labours, Beaverbrook's friend Tim Healy was to become the first Governor General. Yet if one Beaverbrook friendship was cemented, another fell away. Rudyard Kipling was disgusted with the result of the Irish negotiations and was quick to show his anger to anyone who had come out in support. In fact, the relationship with Beaverbrook had been cooling for some time; the last time Kipling's name appeared in the Cherkley guest book was in December 1920, although Gladys had remained in friendly contact with Kipling's wife. Beaverbrook tried from time to time to restore the relationship but without success. 'I tried to re-establish myself,' he wrote much later to Kipling's biogra-pher, 'but I didn't succeed. I tried again on another occasion. Failure.'[33]

The success of the Irish negotiation, and the burst of congratulation which followed, encouraged Lloyd George to consider calling an im-mediate general election. At a dinner in Birkenhead's London home in Grosvenor Gardens, senior coalition ministers were invited to dis-cuss the possibility. Beaverbrook had also been invited on the grounds that he would again be asked to orchestrate the press campaign. Despite Lloyd George's efforts to persuade them, the Conservatives, as they were now calling themselves with greater frequency, were un-convinced. Sir Archibald Salvidge, the Liverpool Conservative who was also present, pointed out the one weak spot in the coalition front: the absence of Bonar Law. 'I said that "Bring Bonar back" was the best watchword I could give them,' Salvidge recorded in his diary.[34] Beaverbrook, it need hardly be said, was delighted with the slogan.

Yet Bonar was not coming back. Nor was there to be a general election. For a time in January 1922, Beaverbrook continued to press Lloyd George, promising support from his newspapers if he would put the 'Empire banner in the forefront of the battle line'[35]. Lloyd George, however, was far too wary of the menace spelt out by Sir George Younger, the chairman of the Conservative Party, that many Tories would abandon the coalition and stand in their own right. As for Bonar Law, when Lloyd George met him in the Carlton Hotel at Cannes and tried to tempt him with the post of Foreign Secretary the response was a polite but firm refusal. Beaverbrook continued to believe, however, that the Prime Minister would seek to test the popularity of the coalition at the polls, writing to a Canadian friend in April, 'We will have an election over here shortly. George has lost his opportunity. He did not take his tide at the flood during last January ... he may get another chance.'[36]

All thoughts of a general election vanished during the summer of 1922 with the outbreak of another crisis in the Near East. Yet again, it was part of the fallout from the war. In the Treaty of Sèvres, signed in August 1920, Greece had been awarded the European territory of Thrace and the city of Smyrna on the coast of Asia Minor, while Constantinople remained under Allied occupation with a demilitarised area around the Dardanelles. The Turks, organised by the victor of Gallipoli, Mustafa Kemal, were determined to retake what they regarded as their territory. The Greek government appealed to Britain for help, only to find the British government split between those who supported them, notably Lloyd George and Lord Curzon, and the rest of the Cabinet, who looked with horror at the prospect of yet another British military adventure.

Beaverbrook, up until then only dimly aware of the detail of the problem, became involved during a visit to Deauville in August 1922. Crossing the Channel with Churchill, Gladys and his daughter Janet, he left his wife and daughter at Le Touquet and went on to Deauville with Churchill. The attractions were obvious. Not only was there an exceptionally active casino but the Dolly Sisters were there to entertain the punters (and to gamble large sums of money). Churchill spotted the Shah of Persia 'parting with his subjects' cash, handed to him packet by packet by his Prime Minister'.[37] It also happened that another distinguished Muslim, the Aga Khan, was staying, in some splendour, at the Hotel Royal, where both Beaverbrook and Churchill had pitched their camp.

The flamboyant Dolly Sisters, Jenny and Rosie, on stage, 1920s.

The weather at Deauville was windy and wet. Beaverbrook made the mistake of going for a swim in the cold sea. As a result, he caught a bad chill. Churchill cabled Gladys in Le Touquet to come and look after him since he himself had to leave for an appointment in Paris. While he was lying in bed feeling sorry for himself, Beaverbrook was visited by the Aga Khan. 'He was most emphatic', Beaverbrook wrote later, 'in urging me to go to Turkey and informed me of a safe conduct … and a friendly reception by Mustapha Kemal.'[38] Unwilling to go without some sort of official mandate, Beaverbrook, now recovered, made his way back, with Gladys and Janet, to Le Touquet and thence to England. Once there, he wrote to Lloyd George, Churchill and Birkenhead to discuss the crisis and the terms under which he might be allowed to negotiate. After an unsatisfactory three days with them at Cherkley, Lloyd George being particularly evasive, it was no clearer on what basis he might negotiate, if at all, with Mustafa Kemal. He therefore decided that he would go, as he put it, at the request of the *Sunday Express*.

Lord and Lady Beaverbrook, with Miss Helen Drury (sister of Gladys Beaverbrook on left), Deauville, August 1922.

On 27 August he set off, taking, as Janet later reported, herself and her brother Max, 'as part of our education … his valet and a clutch of secretaries'.[39] The journey, railway to Brindisi and ferry across to Greece to catch a ship from Athens, was tedious and unpleasant. It was also too long, since by the time he arrived in Constantinople the Turks had sacked Smyrna in the most brutal fashion and moved their armies into the Dardanelles zone at Chanak (modern Çanakkale) threatening to cross the Straits and march on Constantinople. Mustafa Kemal, when Beaverbrook finally met him, was in no mood to negotiate. There was nothing for it but to go home empty handed.

By the time Beaverbrook arrived back in England on 20 September, Lloyd George, Churchill and Birkenhead had joined forces in deciding that there was no alternative to war with Turkey. Successive lunches at the Vineyard over the following three days failed to change their minds. Fortunately, the general commanding the British forces in Constantinople refused to deliver an ultimatum to Mustafa Kemal as instructed and Curzon, the Foreign Secretary, was starting actively to lead a Cabinet rebellion. Finally, Beaverbrook appealed to Bonar Law, now back in London in his new home in Onslow Gardens. On the evening of 6 October, Bonar Law dined at the Vineyard and told Beaverbrook that he had written a letter to *The Times*. Its message was clear. Britain should not intervene without the support of the French. (Law knew perfectly well that the French were supplying arms to the Turks.) In the *Sunday Express* of 8 October, under the heading 'The British Empire First', Beaverbrook delightedly wrote that Bonar Law's pronouncement was 'of vital importance'. 'We cannot', he says, 'act alone as the policeman of the world … [We] should leave Europe alone and concentrate on the home front and the British Empire.'[40]

Bonar Law's letter was decisive. Those Cabinet ministers who argued for war, above all Lloyd George, Churchill and Birkenhead, realised that if they pursued their campaign, they were facing the defection of a large group of Conservative MPs and the almost certain collapse of the coalition. Worse than that, Bonar Law had in practice, and almost without realising it, declared himself in opposition to the coalition and presented himself as an alternative candidate for Prime Minister leading an all-Conservative administration. During the following days he was bombarded by letters urging him to come out and resume the leadership of the party. A group of peers, led by Salisbury, Long and Derby, were actively canvassing for him. Yet these were members of the upper house. A champion was needed in the House of Commons. In fact, it was not long before one appeared, in the unlikely form of Stanley Baldwin, then president of the Board of Trade. As supporting chorus, Beaverbrook's newspapers 'thundered that Bonar was the Saviour of the Nation, that the Coalition was dead, and that he should take over the Government'.[41]

On 11 October, Lloyd George and his allies, who by then included Austen Chamberlain, Horne and Balfour, decided that the only way out for the coalition was to call a general election. Before making their decision public they had decided that Lloyd George would make a speech attacking the Turks in bellicose and provocative terms. This he did in

Manchester on 14 October. The tactic was clear: to unite the coalition behind the perceived threat from the east. But it was an error. It only served to cause Curzon to submit his resignation as he was in the process of starting a dialogue with Kemal to explore the possibility of a truce and had grown tired of Lloyd George's ceaseless interfering. The next tactic was to shore up Conservative support for the coalition. Austen Chamberlain, as leader, accordingly convened a meeting of Conservative MPs and peers holding government office for Thursday 19 October.

Inevitably, the decision to call a general election leaked. Beaverbrook, with Bonar Law's approval, immediately started 'a campaign of propaganda against Lloyd George and his Conservative colleagues'. 'There was to be no end', he later wrote,

> for many a long day. Old friendships were severed. Alliances were broken down. Companionships were sundered, and relationships were strangely altered ... Between Sunday the 15th and Thursday the 19th the struggle became less like a battle than a series of single duels. Every man's political soul was required of him. Promises and promotions were sprinkled from Downing Street on the green benches with a hose. The orthodox Tories appealed to the age-long traditions of a Party now caught fast in the house of semi-Liberal bondage. But all eyes turned to a single figure.[42]

The single figure, of course, was Bonar Law, and the question was whether or not he would turn up on the Thursday morning in the smoking room of the Carlton Club. If he did, it meant only one thing: the coalition was finished. If he did not, the matter was in doubt. On the Monday afternoon Conservative junior ministers clubbed together at a lunch and agreed that the party should leave the coalition and form a separate government after a general election. They presented their case to Austen Chamberlain, who told them firmly to shut up and go back to work. They had, however, been noticed. On the Tuesday, at a lunch to discuss tactics, Sir Samuel Hoare suggested to Baldwin and J. C. C. Davidson that they canvass Conservative backbench opinion. Invitations to a meeting were then busily issued to some eighty carefully selected MPs. Baldwin then went again to see Bonar Law to tell him about the latest developments. Law replied that he had consulted his doctor, who had advised against any return to active political life. Possibly, as Beaverbrook surmised, Bonar Law 'was convinced that [Sir Thomas] Horder would solve all his difficulties and relieve all his doubts by advising him against any return to active life at all'.[43] Law, in fact, had been far from frank with Baldwin. Horder had advised, as Law's sister Mary told Davidson on a subsequent visit, that he could indeed resume work. The rebel leaders, Baldwin, Hoare and Davidson, renewed their attack.

On Wednesday 18 October the first visitor to Onslow Gardens was Curzon, announcing that his letter of resignation was in the hands of the Prime Minister. This was not enough to encourage Bonar Law, who told Curzon gloomily that he had decided that he was not up to shouldering further responsibility and that he was going to resign from the House of Commons. The news was relayed to the rebel leaders, who rushed round to convince him to change his mind. 'We lunched with Bonar and pressed him hard,' wrote Davidson.

> After some three hours of arguments [Baldwin] left with the words: 'You are leaving all the white men on the beach. They can't get on without you to lead and it means that we shall all sink out of politics and leave them to those people who are not as honest.'[44]

Davidson returned to Onslow Gardens in the early evening. The arguments were continuing, not least between Bonar Law and his sister, daughter and son-in-law. They soon heard that the meeting of the backbenchers had been held and had decided unanimously to support a break from the coalition at the next general election. Seeking another opinion, Bonar Law at about seven-thirty called Beaverbrook at the Vineyard, where he was suffering from a heavy cold. In spite of his illness, Beaverbrook made the journey to South Kensington, where he found the argument in full spate. Bonar Law set out the case for and against his attendance. Beaverbrook reiterated the arguments in favour. Bonar Law listened hard and finally agreed that he would go. Beaverbrook immediately asked whether he could release the news to the press and was given leave to do so. 'I fled,' wrote Beaverbrook. 'Not a moment did I waste in reaching a telephone.'[45]

The morning of Thursday 19 October was cold and windy. A crowd had assembled outside the Carlton Club in Pall Mall, with Beaverbrook, well wrapped up, among them. Both Austen Chamberlain and Birkenhead were heckled as they arrived and when Bonar Law arrived with Derby and Davidson a cheer went up. Once inside the club they were told the result of a by-election at Newport: the Conservative candidate had won comfortably over the coalition candidate. It was a pointer to what was to come. In the event, the meeting was surprisingly good tempered. Some wag even arranged for large tumblers of brandy and soda to be placed in front of Chamberlain and Birkenhead in honour of their drinking habits. That raised a laugh, but it soon subsided when the business began in earnest.

The motion before the meeting was that the party would fight the next election independently. Chamberlain opened by speaking against the motion, defending the government's record and appealing for loyalty. Baldwin spoke next, in favour of the motion and attacking Lloyd George for having destroyed the Liberal Party and being in the process of destroying the Conservatives. The mover and seconder of the motion, as well as a handful of backbenchers, made their contributions. Then it was time for Bonar Law. It was noted that he did not look well, his face worn with distress. His voice was so weak that people quite close to him had to strain to hear. But there was no doubt about his message: the coalition must be put to rest. Balfour made a final speech supporting Chamberlain, 'delightful, so mellow and genial', according to Balcarres, 'but too subtle to count'.[46]

The meeting then voted. The motion was carried by 185 to 88, with one abstention. Events then moved at speed. The King hurried back to London from Sandringham. The Cabinet met early in the afternoon, without the rebel ministers, for the last time. Lloyd George then went to Buckingham Palace to submit his resignation. He advised the King to send for Bonar Law. It took an earnest request from Stamfordham for Law to agree to see the King, as he wished to secure a vote of confidence from his party before accepting the King's Commission. This was duly done. On Monday 23 October, Bonar Law kissed hands as Prime Minister and First Lord of the Treasury.

CHAPTER 14

FROM BONAR
TO BALDWIN

'A certain glory has departed'[1]

Bonar Law's arrival in 10 Downing Street on 23 October 1922 was anything but triumphant. In fact, as Beaverbrook later wrote, Law was 'plunged in gloom … there was neither confidence nor joy at future prospects'.[2] As it happened, the gloom was amply justified. For a start, the big guns of the outgoing coalition, Birkenhead, Balfour, Austen Chamberlain and Horne, had all made plain their refusal to serve in the new government, Birkenhead with typical asperity. Nor was there any question of making an offer to Churchill, a maverick Liberal who was deeply disliked by most Conservatives. As if that were not enough, Bonar Law's attempt to recruit Reginald McKenna to the Exchequer was met with a rebuff on the grounds that the government could be no more than a temporary arrangement. In fact, McKenna had a point. It was widely known that there would be a general election once the Anglo-Irish Treaty had passed through Parliament, and he did not think that Bonar Law would win it. As a result, and almost by default, the job fell to Stanley Baldwin. In short, it was little wonder that the new administration was greeted with public derision as no more than a team made up of the second eleven.

Beaverbrook was not offered a post in the new government. Nor did he want one. He had already excluded himself, writing to Bonar Law on 21 October that 'I think it would be better if I remained outside, doing everything in my power to secure your election through the columns of the "Express" only'.[3] In other words, although he would never say so publicly, he was starting to enjoy his role as a newspaper proprietor (or 'press baron' as the disgruntled Conservatives dubbed him). He could campaign on issues which caught his eye, even in opposition to the government, while protesting unswerving loyalty.

Andrew Bonar Law, Conservative Prime Minister,
in his office at 10 Downing Street, c. 1922.

One such issue, in fact, appeared when the Bonar Law government was still in its early days. In the *Sunday Express* of 5 November, the editorial declared that 'the most urgent issue of the General Election is that we should evacuate Mesopotamia and Palestine bag and baggage *and at once*'.[4] The declaration must have come as something of a surprise to those who thought that the level of unemployment of the day far outweighed in importance the presence of British troops in the Middle East, but Beaverbrook's eye had been well and truly caught. Not only was he going to run a campaign in his newspapers on the issue of British withdrawal 'bag and baggage' but, as he warned Bonar Law, he was going to try to bring public pressure on Conservative candidates to support his policy. The threat was obvious. If they did not rally to his cause they would be pilloried in his newspapers.

He was as good as his word. Nor did he only bring pressure on candidates over his policy, but, by way of a bonus, he decided to interfere in the mechanics of the general election itself. When a deal was struck between the Conservatives and coalition Liberals to allow candidates to withdraw one from another to allow a free run against Labour, Beaverbrook stood out against it. Not only that, but he funded a number of independent Conservative candidates to stand against co-alition Liberals, in clear violation of the agreement. The most notable case was the constituency of East Dorset, where Frederick Guest, the former Liberal Chief Whip and Secretary for Air, was standing as a coalition Liberal. Beaverbrook put up an independent Conservative against him. Guest's reaction was splenetic. 'The world has said', he wrote furiously,

> that you were an adventurer from a closed past, that you were subtle, ambitious, unscrupulous and unreliable and that the word friendship was an unknown word to you. Can it be the world was right in its diagnosis…? It is not too late to reassure me. Otherwise it is goodbye.[5]

Beaverbrook was quick to retaliate. 'I am utterly opposed', he wrote back, 'to the continuance of the Alliance between followers of Lloyd George and Conservatives either in the constituencies or at Westmin-ster … I cannot put you in a category apart in response to an appeal based on friendship.'[6] He then visited Poole to speak for his candidate, Ralph Hall Caine. The intervention was spectacularly successful. In the election of 16 November, Hall Caine turned a traditionally Liberal seat into a Conservative majority of 5,000. Overall, Bonar Law's Con-servatives were returned with a Commons majority of seventy-seven. One of the chief casualties was Churchill, who lost his seat in Dundee.

Beaverbrook's intervention for the Conservative cause against a renewal of the coalition, apart from its success, brought a surprising result. Impressed by Beaverbrook's exercise of media power allied to money, Lord Rothermere proposed that they should become partners. Rothermere's brother, Lord Northcliffe, had died in August and his estate was in the process of liquidation. *The Times* was sold to Jacob Astor and Rothermere acquired the *Daily Mail*, transferring its own-ership to the newly incorporated Daily Mail Trust. The deal proposed by Rothermere was that the trust should acquire a minority sharehold-ing in London Express Newspapers, Beaverbrook's holding company.

Lord Faringdon and Sir John Ellerman, survivors from the days when the Express papers were mouthpieces for the Unionist Party, would be bought out, leaving Beaverbrook's holding company in control of both titles. In return, Beaverbrook would acquire a minority interest in the Daily Mail Trust. The arrangement, when concluded, left Beaverbrook with his controlling interest in London Express Newspapers intact, a large minority position in the Daily Mail Trust and £200,000 in cash.

It could hardly be said to have been a match made in heaven. The two men did not much like one another. Rothermere was wary of the brash Canadian newcomer and Beaverbrook was contemptuous of his new partner's business acumen. Yet the arrangement made a degree of sense for both of them. Together, they could drive down the cost of newsprint and rationalise printing facilities and back offices. Where it made no sense at all for Rothermere was that it allowed Beaverbrook to use the steady income stream from the stolid *Daily Mail* to finance the cash-hungry expansion of its thrusting competitor. It took some time before Rothermere woke up to the trick that Beaverbrook had played. In terms of the exercise of power, however, Rothermere had no doubt who was the senior partner in the alliance. In late April 1923 he was writing to Beaverbrook in the language of no less than patrician arrogance. 'Sometime in early June', his letter went,

> I propose that you, Bonar and myself have a discussion as to how his administration can be made one of the most successful of modern times ... If Bonar places himself in my hands I will hand him down to posterity at the end of three years as one of the most successful Prime Ministers in history, and if there is a General Election I will get him returned again. This may sound boastful but I know exactly how it can be done.[7]

As it turned out, Rothermere's claim to be able to swing a general election was never put to the test. Political troubles and the precarious nature of his health overtook the new Prime Minister. At the end of January, Bonar Law had found himself one of a minority of three in his Cabinet over the settlement of British war debt to the United

States. In truth, the story had been one of confusion and unforced error. Baldwin had been sent earlier in the month to Washington to open discussions but to make no commitment. Once in Washington, however, Baldwin had come under heavy pressure from both the British Embassy and J. P. Morgan, at whose house he stayed. Beaverbrook later recorded, 'Suddenly Baldwin sent a cable to Bonar Law asking for authorisation to settle … He cabled back to his Chancellor of the Exchequer "Come home".'[8]

Baldwin did indeed come home. But on arrival at Southampton, thinking that he was speaking off the record, he told the waiting journalists of the terms, a staged repayment and a running interest rate of 5 per cent, and claimed that they were the best that could be obtained. His words, or a version of them, promptly appeared in almost every national newspaper. Beaverbrook immediately denounced the deal in the *Sunday Express*, much to Bonar Law's irritation, since the Cabinet had not yet had a chance to discuss it. But there was worse to come. In spite of his irritation, Bonar Law agreed with Beaverbrook that it would be possible to get a better deal if the government played for time. In a strange turn of events, on the morning of the crucial Cabinet meeting, 30 January, a letter appeared in *The Times* signed by 'Colonial' setting out all the objections to the deal which Baldwin had agreed. It soon became clear that 'Colonial' was none other than Bonar Law himself. Yet in spite of this bizarre manoeuvre, or perhaps because of it, the Cabinet was almost unanimous for acceptance. Bonar Law considered resignation but on the following day, in a display of general bad temper, he was persuaded against it by his senior colleagues' appeal on the by then somewhat slender grounds of party loyalty.

As with many government crises, almost everybody came out badly. Beaverbrook was in no doubt that the chief sufferer was Bonar Law himself. 'It appeared to me', he later wrote, 'that the declension of his spirits and general well-being began with the issue of the British debt to America.'[9] Others felt the same. By the middle of February, he was said to have a 'relaxed throat' and, while he continued to faithfully attend the House of Commons, he was unable to respond to the debate on the Address in late February in anything other than a whisper. March brought further bad news. While Beaverbrook was re-suming his by then futile campaign for military withdrawal from the Middle East (now baptised as 'Bring back the Bayonets') there were three by-elections. The results turned out to be a cumulative disaster for the government: on 3 March, the seats of Mitcham and Willesden East were lost to Labour and the Liberals respectively; three days later, on 6 March, Labour claimed another victory in Liverpool Edge Hill. By the end of the month, when Parliament rose for the Easter recess, it was clear that Bonar Law's government was in electoral trouble. Furthermore, Law himself was still having difficulty with his voice. A fortnight at Torquay brought a modest improvement, but when the House of Commons resumed on 10 April, he still struggled to make himself heard.

Nevertheless, Baldwin's Budget of 16 April was well received, and the clouds seemed to be starting to lift. Curzon had finished a suc-cessful conference in Lausanne. Neville Chamberlain was proving an energetic and effective Minister for Health. There was general agree-ment that the winter storms seemed to have receded, and it was at this point that Rothermere wrote his letter of support. Yet the moment of relief, and confidence in the future, did not last long. Rumours about Bonar Law's health started to appear in the press with accom-panying speculation about his future. To muddy the political waters further, a strange story emerged that Bonar Law had sent a message on 10 April through Beaverbrook and Rothermere to Austen Chamber-lain inviting him, as Chamberlain wrote to his sister, to 'join Bonar's Govt ... with Bonar's verbal understanding that he will resign on August 1st in my favour...'[10] It seems certain that some sort of offer was made to Austen Chamberlain and that Beaverbrook and Rother-mere had hatched it up. Chamberlain was sensible enough to consult his younger half-brother Neville, who immediately went to see Bonar Law. Law denied having sent any message to Austen through any agent and described the suggestion that the Conservatives would qui-etly accept Austen as 'grotesque'.[11] The two press lords had perhaps taken a step too far.

By the last week in April, Bonar Law's doctor, Sir Thomas Horder, was advising a complete rest. Beaverbrook joined in but was finding the patient intractable. 'The whole of this business of inducing the Premier to hand over command and go abroad for a time was an absolute death grapple with his unwillingness to do anything of the kind and cost hours of time,' he later wrote.[12] Finally, Law gave in and on 1 May sailed from Southampton on board the Dutch liner *Princess Juliana* bound for the sunshine of the Mediterranean.

The cruise did not go well. Nor was Bonar Law to be left alone. On 5 May, Davidson travelled overland by train to meet him at Genoa. Davidson was accompanied by John Berry, a Treasury messenger, as an assurance of security since he was carrying a new cipher code for delivery to the Prime Minister. On 8 May, after a short stop in Algiers, the liner arrived in Genoa. 'When the Laws came ashore at Genoa', Davidson recalled, 'it was quite clear that Bonar was no better and Dick Law reported this very definitely to me. Those of us who were close to him feared, but never mentioned, that his disease might be incurable and his fate sealed.'[13] The party then decided to abandon the cruise and to travel by sleeping car to Aix-les-Bains. There, they met Rudyard Kipling and his wife. Kipling in turn was so shocked by Bonar Law's appearance that he immediately cabled Beaverbrook to hurry out to Aix. Bonar Law had, in fact, already sent a 'de profundis' letter, 'begging him to come out or he would throw himself under a train'.[14]

For all the urgency of the messages from Aix, Beaverbrook delayed. The truth was that he was held up in London in negotiating yet another business deal. It was not until 11 May that Davidson cabled Beaverbrook yet again. 'Voice very little better. He is longing to see you.'[15] That was enough. Beaverbrook cabled Davidson that he was summoning Horder to Paris for a re-examination and that the whole Law party should move from Aix to Paris, where rooms were booked for them at the Hotel Crillon. Beaverbrook himself would be staying at the nearby Ritz. On 16 May they arrived. Thinking that it would cheer Bonar Law up, Beaverbrook persuaded him to go to a dinner party organised by the eccentric Earl of Granard, then a member of the Senate of the Irish Free State and, for good measure, a director of Arsenal Football Club. But it was not a success. Law spent the whole evening in pain and silence.

The next day Horder conducted his examination. Without telling Law the full result he simply said that the condition was worse than he had feared. He then telephoned Beaverbrook at the Ritz and invited him to a walk along the Champs-Elysées. He told Beaverbrook that the position was serious. 'He much hoped that the patient did not have cancer – but ... he was not comfortable in his own mind on the point.'[16] With due caution, he offered his preliminary diagnosis: the Prime Minister had cancer of the throat. The two of them then went back to the Crillon and told Bonar Law that he had little option. He should resign.

As it happened, Bonar Law accepted the verdict with a sense of relief. A burden had been lifted from his shoulders. On 19 May an announcement was made, signed by two doctors, that 'the state of the Prime Minister's health is not good'. On 20 May, Bonar Law wrote his resignation letter to the King, to be delivered to the Sovereign in Aldershot, where he was staying at the time, by the Prime Minister's son-in-law, General Frederick Sykes, and his principal private secretary, Colonel Ronald Waterhouse.

The news of Bonar Law's resignation sparked off the usual explosion of speculation about his advice to the King on his successor. Curzon was an obvious choice, but he had the disadvantage of a seat in the House of Lords. He had also irritated Bonar Law by writing a series of bombastic letters staking his claim to the succession. Baldwin, on the other hand, who was the only obvious alternative, had little experience of high office. Bonar Law was determined to keep out of the whole battle and was reassured by voices that there was precedent for a resigning Prime Minister unable or unwilling to recommend a successor to the Sovereign. Yet unknown to him, and apparently without his authority, Davidson, a known Baldwin supporter, had already written a memorandum which Waterhouse duly delivered to Stamfordham, stating that it 'expressed the views of Mr Bonar Law'.[17] It was undoubtedly murky, but the trick worked. Curzon travelled up to London believing he was about to be awarded the prize, only to find that Baldwin had been summoned by the King and invited to form a government.

Bonar Law's last five months of life were of sad tragedy. Beaverbrook did what he could to make their passing easier, arranging visits to Brighton for fresh air, to Le Touquet for golf, to the Vineyard for lunch with old colleagues and games of cards or chess. It was even said that he propped up Bonar Law's portfolio by buying up any stock which was in danger of falling in price and proclaiming the success of the investment. By the autumn, however, nothing more could be done. On 30 October 1923, in his house in Onslow Gardens, Bonar Law died. The funeral took place on a cold 5 November in Westminster Abbey. 'At the Abbey', recalled one onlooker,

> we sat immediately behind members of the Cabinet. All these prayers and hymn singing very alien to the B. L. known to me. He once remarked to me that L. G. still had some sort of belief in a future life and clearly implied that he, B. L., had none whatever.[18]

Beaverbrook was near to tears throughout the ceremony. He had certainly felt nothing like this since the death, all those years ago, of his first mentor, John F. Stairs.

Beaverbrook was not just deeply and personally affected by Bonar Law's death. It also marked a break in his involvement with the inner workings of British politics. 'Something was severed for ever in my political associations,' he wrote soon afterwards.[19] In fact, he had one last throw. In November, Baldwin decided on a general election. His platform, as he told Beaverbrook, would be a measure of protection for British manufacturing industries. Beaverbrook advised against an immediate appeal to the electorate and followed that up with a firm statement that his newspapers would only support the Conservatives if Baldwin came out with a full programme of imperial preference. Baldwin refused. 'The grandeur of an all-embracing association between the Empire peoples,' Beaverbrook wrote later, 'of fiscal union giving benefit to all and harming none, was something he did not understand.'[20]

Beaverbrook in turn refused a request for funds for the Conservatives. Instead, he told Sir George Younger that he would pay in full the expenses of two candidates who were prepared to support a policy of imperial preference. He then invited the old lions of the coalition to

Cherkley to discuss what might be done to rescue what was looking increasingly like a catastrophic mistake. As he reported by telegram to Rothermere, 'George, Churchill, Chamberlain, Birkenhead spent week end [12 November] with me. Conclusion of conference was unanimous advice to Chamberlain and Birkenhead to join Baldwin's government...'[21] The plan was that they would join the government and then speak against Baldwin's policy of protection. The plan backfired when Arnold Bennett, who had been at the Cherkley meeting, leaked the whole story to a journalist on the *Daily News*. Baldwin had indeed made a tentative offer to Chamberlain and Birkenhead but this was now rapidly withdrawn. In a letter to the former Canadian Prime Minister Sir Robert Borden, Beaverbrook revealed that when Baldwin had tried to persuade Birkenhead to speak in support of the Conservatives without more than a vague promise of office if they won, the latter had remarked, 'My stock of oratory for sale. It is at the top of the market just now. You can buy now in cash, or you can't buy at all.'[22]

In the same letter to Borden, Beaverbrook predicted that at the forthcoming general election, due on 6 December, the Conservatives would be returned 'with a small, but hardly a working majority' of between ten and fifteen seats, anticipating that they might be expected to lose in the region of thirty to forty seats overall.'[23] Unfortunately, even such a modest forecast proved overly optimistic. Once the votes had been counted it was clear that the Conservatives had lost their overall majority; the Liberals, with Lloyd George playing no more than second violin to Asquith, came in a bad third. Labour, under Ramsay MacDonald, came in as the second largest party. When Parliament re-assembled, Baldwin tried to hold on but neither Asquith nor MacDonald were prepared to keep him in power and the government was defeated in the House of Commons on the Address. After Baldwin's resignation there was some loose talk of a revived Conservative–Liberal coalition under Balfour but Asquith put an end to it swiftly and the first Labour government was sworn in.

For Beaverbrook, there were two immediate consequences. First, he no longer had any personal connection to anyone near the seat of power. Lloyd George was now only one member of an Asquithian Liberal rump. Churchill was in the wilderness. The two Chamberlains were merely part of a shadow team in opposition and Birkenhead was fulminating to himself. Secondly, the Labour Party had no press mouthpiece apart from the small-circulation *Daily Herald*. There were no more urgent calls from Downing Street begging for support for this or that policy, no more consultations with senior ministers about the direction of government or the virtues and vices of individual ministers. The lines were silent.

Relations with Baldwin, already at a low ebb after the disagreement on election policy and the attempted infiltration of Austen Chamberlain and Birkenhead into the government, deteriorated steadily. Baldwin proved ineffective in opposition and Beaverbrook was openly contemptuous of his efforts. 'Now that [Baldwin] is stripped of power and patronage,' he wrote in the *Sunday Express* in February 1924, 'he must rely on his own capabilities as a parliamentarian … [These] are suited to a minor post, adequate for an Under-Secretaryship, but far below the level of Prime Minister or Leader of the Opposition.'[24]

Not content with public abuse, Beaverbrook threw the weight of his newspapers against the official Conservative candidate for the Abbey Division of Westminster in a by-election held the following month. It also allowed him to campaign for a familiar figure, as Winston Churchill sought an opportunity to return to the Commons, this time openly as a Conservative. Churchill had applied to be selected by the local association but was rejected in favour of the nephew of the previous incumbent. Undeterred, he decided to stand as an independent under the label 'Constitutionalist'. Beaverbrook immediately decided to back him. When Baldwin wrote a letter of support to the official candidate, Beaverbrook fired another broadside. Claiming that Churchill had been the preferred candidate of Conservative Central Office, he argued that in backing his friend,

> I was doing my best to put myself in line with them and help the Tory Party to an invaluable recruit … Yet I am left opposing the official Conservative candidate in the Abbey Division! Why?

Simply because when it came to the point of conflict I stood to my guns while Mr Baldwin ran away ... He has mistaken his natural position in the Conservative hierarchy. In the secondary rank he was a marked success – in the primary position he has proved a terrible failure.[25]

The result was a disappointment for both Beaverbrook and Churchill as the latter fell short by forty-three votes.

It was not long before Baldwin retaliated. He had never been happy with the close, indeed near incestuous, network of press and ministers under the coalition and was now quite prepared to go into battle to tear it apart. In May 1924, *The People* published what it claimed to be an exclusive interview under the headline 'Baldwin Turns and Rends His Critics'. It was heady stuff. The first attack was on the 'sinister and cynical combination of the chief three of the Coalition – Mr Lloyd George, Mr Churchill and Lord Birkenhead'. The assault went on to Rothermere, who escaped relatively lightly, and then on to Beaverbrook:

> The last time I spoke to Lord Beaverbrook was at Bonar's funeral. He had contracted a curious friendship with Bonar and had got his finger into the pie, where it had no business to be. He got hold of much information, which he used in ways in which it was not intended. When I came in, that stopped. I know I could get his support if I were to send for him and talk things over with him. But I prefer not. That sort of thing does not appeal to me ... What do the intriguers want? Simply to go back to the old dirty kind of politics! Not while I am leader of the Party.[26]

On the article's publication, Baldwin made no more than a feeble effort to recover ground. Using the politician's customary formula of blaming the journalist, he wrote to Beaverbrook the following day that 'I am deeply distressed that I should have been so grossly represented'.[27] Beaverbrook publicly accepted Baldwin's claim of misrepresentation, writing the following year that as a result of the 'celebrated "interview" episode' he had 'met Mr Baldwin afterwards at his request and accepted completely his repudiation of the words placed in his mouth with reference to me. In fact they were … incredible and absurd.'[28] *The People* stood by its story. The lines for future battles with Baldwin had been drawn. There could be no quarter.

That done, there was no virtue in sitting back and doing nothing. In fact, there was much more to be done in the world of the press. Beaverbrook's deal with Rothermere had given him, among all the rest, a controlling interest in the *Evening Standard*. With that had come an opportunity to acquire the long-coveted premises which sat next to the *Express* offices and production sheds. With the daily paper reaching a circulation of over 900,000, with a sixteen-page edition, the extra space was quickly filled and the plant rebuilt. At the same time, it was attracting advertisers. A particular success was the arrival of the Barker Group of department stores, including John Barker itself, Derry & Toms and Pontings, all major names in the retailing of women's clothes. The number of women readers grew almost exponentially.

Quick to capitalise on this development, Beaverbrook introduced new features to the newspapers to keep a firm hold on his growing female audience. Racing tips were given less prominence, fashion was openly discussed and society gossip found its way into the middle pages of the *Daily Express*. Beaverbrook himself wrote for the *Sunday Express* under his own name while expecting editorial writers on the daily to follow his line. In fact, the less time he spent on politics, the more he interfered in the running of the papers. He was constantly on the telephone to his editors, bursting with ideas or barking out reprimands. Gradually all this was becoming too much for Blumenfeld. He saw his job as editor of the daily to keep it focused on politics. He was out of sympathy with advertising or gossip columns. Furthermore, he was still recovering from a prostate operation in 1922 which had gone wrong. To cap it all, his friendship with Baldwin was cooling and there were no longer any political titbits coming out of the Conservative opposition.

Beaverbrook later used Blumenfeld as the leading specimen in supporting his belief that after such an operation, 'a man was no good either mentally or physically'.[29] Whatever the truth of this wholly unqualified medical observation, by the autumn of 1924 he had decided to replace Blumenfeld. He moved a young Canadian, Beverley Baxter, from the *Sunday Express* to the bigger job of editing the daily, promoting, if that is the right word, Blumenfeld to the position of 'editor-in-chief', where he could be safely ignored. Baxter was a good-humoured popular journalist who was much more comfortable with the new style. With another Canadian, E. J. Robertson, managing the daily's business side, Beaverbrook had the team he wanted.

With the new management in place, Beaverbrook could turn his attention to recruiting writers. Chief among the talent spotters was Arnold Bennett. Bennett, in fact, was at this time much more than a recruiting sergeant. He was a partner, and opponent, at tennis; companion to the theatre to performances which Beaverbrook from time to time financed; adviser on music, in which Beaverbrook took a passing interest; travelling companion (although unsuccessful in persuading Beaverbrook to spend time on his yacht, since boredom set in quickly); and, above all, friendly critic of Beaverbrook's own writings at the time. The literary circle, too, was widening thanks to Bennett. H. G. Wells, D. H. Lawrence, William Gerhardie, Michael Arlen, all in turn fell for the Beaverbrook charm. Gerhardie describes it well in his account of their first meeting in October 1925. 'Lord Beaverbrook', he wrote, 'like Mr Lloyd George has the air of being enormously privileged in meeting someone whom no one else has ever met, or even heard of. He made me feel as if I had indeed heard of myself.'[30]

Such charm was put to good effect during the heady days of 1920s social life. There were, of course, women, most of them casual affairs. There was dancing, there were nightclubs, there were wild dinner parties, there were trips across the Channel to gamble at Deauville or Le Touquet, or further afield to Paris, Biarritz, Cannes or Monte Carlo. On occasions Beaverbrook took with him Gladys and one or other of his children, Janet being a particular favourite, but more often he went with his favoured companion of the moment, Valentine, Viscount Castlerosse.

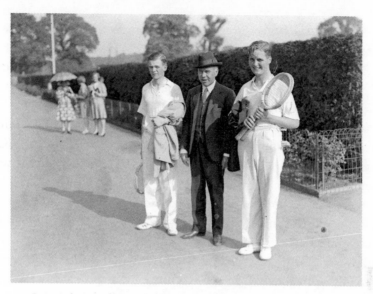

Peter Aitken, Lord Beaverbrook and John Nuthall at Junior Wimbledon, where Peter was a competitor.

Castlerosse was on the surface an unlikely companion. Heir to the Irish earldom of Kenmare, with its sprawling family seat in County Kerry, he was, according to one account, 'fat, nasty and unattractive'.[31] Yet he had had a good war, although a serious wound had put him out of action in 1918. During his recovery he became obsessed with a Parisian prostitute who went by the name of Forsanne and on his return to London floated about both looking for a job and trying to get Forsanne to London as a hospital nurse. Beaverbrook ran across him and, almost casually, offered him a job in the Ministry of Information. Needless to say, Castlerosse accepted. It so happened, almost immediately, that a party of Baptist ministers arrived to see the British war effort. Castlerosse was deputed to take them to France. When they arrived in Paris they were royally entertained, presumably by Forsanne and her friends. Beaverbrook reported that the visit had been a tremendous success as the Baptists had been delighted with both Paris and Castlerosse. This bonhomie did not extend to Castlerosse's parents, Lord and Lady Kenmare, who begged him not to send their son on any more trips to the French capital.[32]

After the war Beaverbrook found Castlerosse a succession of jobs, first with the stockbrokers Rowe & Pitman, then with a finance house in New York. Neither lasted long, and Castlerosse asked his mother's brother, Lord Revelstoke, for a job in the family merchant bank, Baring Brothers. This, too, was a failure. Impertinent wit was Castlerosse's stock in trade but that did not play well at Barings. For instance, when Revelstoke upbraided him for coming in to work late, he is said to have replied, 'But think how early I leave.'[33] Castlerosse then drifted around London, falling into debt with London's leading tailors, wine merchants and tobacconists and becoming ever fatter. Beaverbrook, however, was fascinated rather than shocked by Castlerosse and his grotesque eccentricities, and he paid the bills to keep his friend financially afloat. Castlerosse also had one quality that Beaverbrook prized: he was a well-connected member of the same British aristocracy that had spurned, and was still spurning, the Canadian interloper.

By the late summer of 1924, Beaverbrook's interest in active politics (as opposed to shouting from the touchline in the columns of the *Sunday Express*) was returning. The Labour government was no more than limping along and was finally brought down by the Liberals withdrawing their support. The ensuing general election, called for 29 October, was dominated by disputes about the Labour government's contacts with Soviet Russia, culminating in the publication in Rothermere's *Daily Mail*, on the weekend before the election, of a forged letter purporting to come from the president of the Communist International, Grigory Zinoviev, and addressed to the British Communists, with instructions for various acts of seditious violence. The result, according to the Labour minister J. H. Thomas, was a slump in Labour support: 'The people lost confidence in us; the women were frightened; speakers felt paralysed.'[34] In the event, the Conservatives won 412 seats, Labour 151 seats, and the Liberals, much to the disappointment of Beaverbrook, who had been hoping for a revival, were down to 40. The day after the election he wrote bitterly to Rothermere, 'I congratulate you most heartily on your magnificent victory. You have made the new Baldwin ministry; now control it if you can.'[35]

One of the winners had been Winston Churchill. Baldwin had offered him the safe Conservative seat of Epping on the understanding that he would stand as a 'Constitutionalist' and that there would be no official Conservative candidate against him. Churchill duly won the seat with a large majority. In putting together his new administration, Baldwin invited the old coalitionists, Austen Chamberlain and Birkenhead, to join the government as Foreign Secretary and Secretary for India respectively. Having failed to convince Neville Chamberlain to take over at the Treasury, he then offered the Chancellorship of the Exchequer to Churchill. Elated, Churchill went to dinner at the Vineyard. Birkenhead was there as well, asking Churchill, 'What have you got?' Churchill refused to say. Birkenhead shouted at him, 'You have been consulting with Max for weeks past in the most intimate way – you've been taking his help and advice and support. You were ready enough to appeal to him in your despair and now you neglect him in your hour of triumph.' Finally, during dinner Churchill revealed that he had been appointed Chancellor of the Exchequer. Gleefully sensing an opportunity for some mischief, Beaverbrook threatened to publish the news if he heard it from another source. A telephone call, almost certainly from Samuel Hoare, provided him with the confirmation. Primed with the evidence, he declared that the *Daily Express* would lead with the announcement and only relented when Churchill beseeched him not to spoil his hour of triumph. At the conclusion of the evening, Birkenhead resumed his criticism of Churchill's behaviour, but Beaverbrook had guessed the reason for their friend's unfamiliar reticence. Churchill confirmed his suspicions; he had promised his wife Clementine, who had acted as chauffeur that evening, that he would not reveal the secret that Beaverbrook had finally drawn out of him.[36]

Churchill's tenure of office at the Treasury was enlivened, as with all things Churchill did, by an air of unpredictability. 'The trouble with Winston', Beaverbrook wrote in May 1925, 'is that he will take no advice when he is "up". When he is "down" it is another matter – and his judgement being fundamentally bad he is, when he is in the "up" frame of mind, sure to land himself and his party in difficulties.'[37]

Although their relations remained cordial, Beaverbrook's censure of Treasury policies irritated Churchill. In his book *Politicians and the Press*, Beaverbrook observed the nature of his friend's sensitivity to criticism: 'Mr Churchill likes praise and dislikes blame more than Mr Lloyd George. And he differs from the latter in this respect: he resents an assault on his public policy as much as Mr Lloyd George does an attack on his private life.'[38] Particularly irritating was Beaverbrook's decision to commission a series of articles from John Maynard Keynes attacking the government's whole economic policy. The return of sterling to a fixed parity with gold was an obvious target (although Keynes was, unlike Beaverbrook, not against the whole construct but was critical of the rate at which parity was set).

Throughout 1925, Beaverbrook kept up his attack on Baldwin, although he recognised a certain solidity of purpose:

> It is only fair to say that, although he is often so confused in his mind that he hardly knows what he really does mean, once he has cleared his decision up he adheres to it through thick and thin, and no threats of pains or penalties either from the Press or from his own supporters will deflect him from his course.[39]

The truth was, of course, that the Baldwin administration was proving surprisingly stable and Baldwin himself was giving the impression of quiet competence.

Since he was at a distance from the political centre and nobody of consequence seemed to be paying much attention to what he was saying or writing, Beaverbrook turned his main attention yet again back to his newspapers. When Rothermere sold the *Daily Sketch*, formerly a Hulton title bought in 1923, to the Berry brothers in the middle of 1926, Beaverbrook took advantage, by means of cancelling part of his holding in Daily Mail Trust in return for the cancellation of the trust's holding in London Express Newspapers, to become the sole owner of his group of titles. He now had a daily paper (*Daily Express*), a Sunday (*Sunday Express*) and a London evening paper (the *Evening Standard*). To these he would soon add the *Scottish Daily Express*.

The daily and the Sunday were both by now doing well and in profit. The *Evening Standard*, on the other hand, was far from healthy. Yet it had, in Beaverbrook's mind, one important feature: the Londoner's Diary, a gossip column, admittedly rather refined, describing the comings and goings of London society. The formula was enticing, and Beaverbrook soon incorporated it into the *Sunday Express* as 'Londoner's Log'. This became a much more salacious, much more intrusive and much more successful version, not least due to the skills, and connections, of its master and chief gossiper Viscount Castlerosse.

By this time Beaverbrook had acquired from the Crown Estate the lease on Stornoway House. Placed strategically in Cleveland Row at the southern end of St James's Street, it was a much more substantial property than the Vineyard. There were fourteen bedrooms, six reception rooms, a ballroom (convenient for Janet's 'coming out') and a library. Apart from providing space for Gladys, Janet and the two boys (now at Westminster School), it housed Beaverbrook's substantial secretarial staff: a chief secretary, a financial secretary (perhaps not a job to be envied), a social secretary, political and literary secretaries. In fact, the house, once a residence of considerable grandeur, soon took on the atmosphere of an office block.

By the end of 1925, the skies were darkening. Domestically, the family was going through a bad phase. Gladys was unhappy at her exclusion from so much of her husband's life. To be sure, there were frequent expeditions to the European playgrounds, but nobody quite knew who would be included. The only constant in the company was Valentine Castlerosse, whose mores, if that is the right word, were far from the taste of the Canadian general's daughter. For instance, even if Gladys and the boys, Max and Peter, were dragged along to Le Touquet, Deauville or Monte Carlo, their father instructed his sons to stay with their mother and be in bed by no later than ten o'clock. Beaverbrook and Castlerosse would then adjourn to the local casino for the rest of what was usually a long night. Not only that, but Beaverbrook's open infidelity was becoming a matter of constant humiliation to his wife. It came as no surprise to anybody when in 1926 Gladys decided to decamp with her daughter Janet on a long transatlantic trip.

Lord Beaverbrook and Lord Castlerosse in the Cote d'Azur,
France, 1925. Photographed in The Tatler, *14 January 1925.*

As it happened, the skies were also darkening over the British economy. As Keynes had predicted, the return to the gold standard at an
unrealistic parity had led to a fall in exports and an increase in imports. In order to defend the parity from the consequent depreciation,
interest rates were raised, subjecting the whole economy to deflation-
ary attack. Worst hit of all was the coal mining industry, still suffering
from the effects of the war. The Dawes Plan of 1924 for reparations
from Germany to the Allies had allowed Germany to export coal to
France and Italy as part of the liquidation of its debt. The United
States had also vigorously entered the international coal market. The
overall result was that British coal production was in steady decline,
and the mines were moving from a handsome wartime profit to a
peacetime loss. The response of mine owners was to propose a cut
in miners' wages. The reaction of the Miners' Federation of Great
Britain was uncompromisingly negative. Faced with this problem,
the government announced a Royal Commission to study the matter,
together with a subsidy to maintain miners' wages for nine months
while the commission deliberated.

The commission reported in the middle of March 1926. Apart from
recommending a sweeping reorganisation of the industry, they recommended a reduction of 13.5 per cent in miners' wages and withdrawal

of the subsidy. The government accepted the report's recommendations provided the two sides in the dispute agreed. The miners rejected them outright and the mine owners produced their own proposals for a reduction in wages and an extension of the working day. Perfunctory negotiations began in April but by the end of the month it was obvious that there was no conceivable middle ground of agreement. On 1 May the miners appealed to the Trades Union Congress (TUC) for support. The reaction was immediate. A general strike in support of the miners was to begin at one minute to midnight on Monday 3 May.

'I think everybody enjoyed the strike,' Beaverbrook wrote to his old friend Tim Healy after it was all over, 'volunteers and strikers alike. It was treated in a holiday spirit; and the pickets outside the "Daily Express" office were quite as amused as the amateurs working the mechanical side within.'[40] The frivolity was certainly not shared by the families of the miners, who had to get by in conditions of poverty unthinkable today. Nor was it shared by the government, which had been laying plans for several months to mobilise young men from the middle class as volunteer 'special constables' and which was more determined than ever to defeat the strike in spite of the sporadic violence they provoked. In fact, Beaverbrook's main concern was 'the sudden incursion of Churchill, in the old Gallipoli spirit, into Fleet Street'.[41]

Beverley Baxter, Lord Beaverbrook and Karl Ketchum working on the Daily Express *during the general strike, 1926.*

Churchill had taken upon himself the task of producing the *British Gazette*, a daily pamphlet designed to be published by the government until the strike-bound commercial newspapers could resume normal production. Beaverbrook and Rothermere, both enthusiastic strike breakers, lent staff for Churchill's project, three from Beaverbrook and seven from Rothermere. So far, so good, but the apparent harmony broke down when Churchill tried to requisition their supply of newsprint. Beaverbrook was convinced that Churchill 'had one of his fits of vainglory and excessive excitement and wanted to put the whole Press out of commission in order to run the circulation of the "British Gazette" up to millions'. He complained to other Cabinet ministers, who duly 'showed a disposition to come out and put a stopper on Churchill's proceedings'.[42]

Beaverbrook had been too suspicious. Churchill made it clear to the Cabinet on 11 May, when the general strike was in its seventh day (and had only a further two days to run before being called off), that he intended to bring an end to the publication of the *Gazette* 'as soon as the daily newspapers were in a position to resume normal publication … [but] resumption must be carried out on terms fair to all'.[43] On the very same day there followed an exchange of correspondence between Churchill and Beaverbrook in which Beaverbrook finally, and most reluctantly, agreed to transfer 200 tons of newsprint to the *Gazette* on the grounds that 'our only anxiety is to break the general strike'.[44] In the event that proved unnecessary since on 12 May Baldwin was able to tell the Cabinet that the TUC were withdrawing the general strike notices.

In all this, and much to Beaverbrook's fury, Baldwin came out as the clear winner.

The vitriol was unrestrained. 'The laudations which are being poured upon Baldwin', Beaverbrook wrote to his friend Arthur Brisbane, 'are pure hysteria. I have worked with him intimately at one time for ten years at a stretch and he is a man without a mind or a capacity to make one up.'[45] He even made a somewhat half-hearted attempt to get Churchill to resign and challenge Baldwin but Churchill, wisely, refused the bait. Nevertheless, in spite of the clashes over the general strike and Churchill's continued loyalty to Baldwin throughout 1926, the two men remained friends. Beaverbrook sent Churchill a box of cigars for Christmas and Churchill, in sending his thanks, summed up their relationship with characteristic generosity:

> I have a vy deep regard for you and feel the full attraction of yr vivid, genial, loyal & dominating personality. I always enjoy myself in yr company & look forward to all our meetings. The difficulty of my being in the centre of a govt to wh you have every right to be opposed has, I rejoice to think, ceased to be an obstacle to our personal intimacy. Whatever differences we may have on public matters ... we ought to keep our friendship clear & intact ... It is vital to preserve and cherish those associations wh are mellowed by time & by common experiences & adventures. Some day the wheel may turn it surely will – & political action may superimpose itself on bright companionship. In the main & on the greatest issues I expect we shd be together.[46]

The political door had shut again, leaving Beaverbrook outside the circle. Furthermore, he let it be known that he was becoming bored with newspapers and that he meant to let his staff take over. (Of course, it never happened but it amused him to keep them all guessing.) Instead, Beaverbrook sought to banish tedium with a variety of diversions available to the extremely wealthy. His preferred recourse was travelling to his favourite places on the Continent, where the gambling was good and the women beautiful and willing. The pleasure was heightened by groups of his closest friends, male and female, led by the indefatigable Castlerosse. 'It is a splendid sight', wrote one visitor to Cannes, 'to see Lord Castlerosse emerging from the Carlton Hotel in the morning, his large expanse of white waistcoat enhanced by a broad dark cherry-coloured tie, buttonhole, cigar, malacca cane. He's off to lunch at Nice, of course, escorting the two most lovely girls in Cannes.'[47]

Something of a brake was put on proceedings by Gladys's return to Britain in April 1927. In truth, it was the beginning of a sad period of a few months up to her death. Her departure with Janet for Canada had been provoked finally by Beaverbrook's open admiration of a competitor. Yet her stay there brought no comfort. She had felt unwell for much of the time and spent several weeks in hospital in Montreal, apparently with nervous exhaustion, as it was called then, which might nowadays properly be called a breakdown, requiring a further long period of convalescence. Yet the diagnosis was far from certain. None of the doctors, for instance, could explain her frequent headaches.

Gladys and Janet were at first lodged, apparently uncomplaining, in a hotel in Le Touquet while Beaverbrook and his friends continued cruising on chartered yachts along the French north coast, calling in at the fashionable resorts from time to time. (Little notice was taken of the death of Beaverbrook's mother during the summer on her way to see her daughter Laura in Scotland.) In early September, the party went on to Berlin to discuss a possible film, to be scripted by Arnold Bennett and to feature Diana Cooper. But it was there that they heard that Gladys had suffered a relapse and had gone back to London and Stornoway House. Sir Thomas Horder had been summoned. He in turn declared Gladys to be physically fit and that her troubles were emotional.

What happened next is not altogether clear. According to Janet's account, Horder called for a second opinion from his colleague Charles Wilson. 'His opinion was unequivocal; mother had a tumour on the brain and death was imminent.'[48] Beaverbrook was tracked down in Biarritz and flew back just in time, in Janet's version, to say an emotional farewell. (Others have cast doubt on this account, claiming that throughout Horder was telling Beaverbrook that she would recover.) There is, however, no doubt about the outcome. In the early hours of 1 December 1927, aged thirty-nine, Gladys Beaverbrook died.

CHAPTER 15

GLADYS AND
OTHER WOMEN

'The mighty little gnome'[1]

Gladys Henderson Drury was just eighteen years old when she married William Maxwell Aitken. Aitken, as Beaverbrook then was, had been clear in his mind about the purpose of the marriage. In fact, even in later life he was prepared to acknowledge explicitly that it was for his own social advancement. Why Gladys agreed to marry him was largely a matter of family circumstance. Not to put too fine a point on it, the Drurys were short of cash. Although Gladys's father held the high post of Halifax garrison commander his salary had been fixed by his moneyed English aristocratic predecessors and was far from enough even to cover the outgoings of the official residence.

The classic response to the problem, soon adopted by General Drury, was to marry off daughters as soon as convenient. When a brash but ambitious 26-year-old laid siege to the first in line, the general was content to ignore the difference in both age and social class. Gladys would do what she was told, subject, of course, to the final point of stamping her foot in invincible refusal. As it happened, Max played his hand well. Some twenty years later Gladys's sister, Arabella, remembered 'those happy days in Halifax at the dreadful hotel – when we used to giggle and tickle you!'[2] The young man had obviously learnt at an early age one of the male's most successful weapons in seduction: carefully directed flirtatious humour. It was a weapon he was later to hone to perfection.

The wedding completed with military efficiency (and least cost), Gladys turned out to have little to laugh about. The principal lines of engagement for the newly-weds were clearly established in their Cuban honeymoon, during which the bridegroom spent his time travelling the length of the island pursuing business deals, leaving the bride presumably staring at the sea. Gladys, of course, made no complaint. She had been far too well brought up. As F. E. Smith, Lord Birkenhead, wrote in a relentlessly enthusiastic appreciation after her death, reproduced in the *Daily Express* on the following day, 'She was essentially womanly, and being womanly she was incredibly under-standing. She made allowances easily and generously.'³

Birkenhead's 'appreciation', which 'reached the *"Daily Express"* office last night' (as the night editor was quick to point out), was typical of the tributes paid to Gladys over the years. However effusive they are, they all seem to strike a suspiciously false note. Birkenhead himself gave the game away by asserting that the 'position she acquired in English society … [did not depend] … even upon the extraordinary talents of her distinguished husband'.⁴ This was not normal Birkenhead language. But he, and others, knew full well that, whatever the truth, any false move in writing about Lady Beaverbrook would bring down a media hailstorm of biblical intensity from her distinguished husband.

This makes it difficult to define with precision a profile of the real Gladys Beaverbrook, either in her physique or in her character. The task is made more difficult by Beaverbrook's destruction of almost all correspondence between the two and, perhaps, although nothing is for certain, many valuable photographs. Those that remain show a shy, even slightly disapproving, face with one eyebrow raised some-what higher than its twin, hair (said to be auburn, titian or fair de-pending on the observer but probably simply brown) parted in the middle and falling in a classical style, in curls to cover her ears and a nose fractionally too long for her thin lips. Her figure was stocky rather than refined but she was (an important asset) even shorter than Beaverbrook himself. In one photograph, however, the whole, rather nondescript appearance is enlivened and enlightened by her smile. It seems to start with her lips but rises to a twinkle in her eyes and dimples in both cheeks. Somehow it becomes possible to believe what was said, that Beaverbrook's brother, Allan, was more than a little in love with her.

Gladys, Lady Beaverbrook, photographed in the early 1920s.

In character, Gladys seems the model of a military daughter. The public records and the accounts of others show that she responded to any request to support her husband in his ambitions with dutiful alacrity, although perhaps without total enthusiasm, speaking at women's meetings and visiting wounded Canadian servicemen in hospital. Moreover, as a mother she could hardly be faulted. She brought up her three children with affection and concern, with a special relationship to her daughter Janet. As a hostess at Cherkley and Stornoway House she was quiet but efficient, even with her husband's boisterous companions, but reserving a particular place for the charm of Tim Healy. She was unostentatiously religious, courteous to all comers and, perhaps surprisingly, very good at tennis, a talent inherited by her youngest son. In short, and taken all in all, she would have made a perfect wife for a career soldier like her father.

Aitken, of course, did not fit that bill at all. He was almost the opposite to a career soldier following a path of dedication and discipline. Politically ambitious, he had a large streak of mischief in his character which told him that life was there to be enjoyed with at least a large dose of fun. Marrying the two was not easy but Aitken, soon to become Beaverbrook, devised a solution. He bought Cherkley, in 1911, in Gladys's name, as a house for the family and for social activity at weekends. The fun was to be had in London, particularly after he bought the Vineyard in 1922.

It is far from clear when fun changed into infidelity. There was limited scope for fun during the war, and infidelity, if it took place, was presumably of a casual nature common in the stress of wartime. As the war drew to its close, more serious opportunities started to present themselves. In 1917, for instance, Sarah Shaughnessy makes an appearance. In her late twenties, she was a woman of dazzling beauty, with large, dark eyes and hair as black as a raven's, a true belle from Nashville, Tennessee. In 1912 she had married the son of the Canadian railway magnate Lord Shaughnessy, only to be widowed in 1916. Since her husband's death she had decided 'to spend the duration of the War living for pleasure – with the Duke of Connaught, Beaverbrook and, later, the Prince of Wales among her many admirers'.[5] A letter to her from the Canadian lieutenant Talbot Papineau, just before he left for Passchendaele, where he died, confirms that 'Lord Beaverbrook was much attracted to you and I fumed and stormed quite naturally and sincerely.'[6] In July 1918, Sarah noted that she went over to Cherkley 'to lunch with Gladys Beaverbrook and stayed on to dinner. That menage is not going well. Lord B. came down in the afternoon and we played tennis together after tea. There is a lot I might say but perhaps it is wiser not to.'[7] This was followed by her note of the next day: 'Lord Beaverbrook asked me to go over for dinner, so I did and he motored me home.'[8]

Sarah Shaughnessy, in truth, was at the time something of a social butterfly. Talbot Papineau had been smitten almost to distraction and Sarah had never shown much sympathy. Beaverbrook was another matter. Yet, whatever her feelings towards him, the response, although unrecorded, does not appear to have been more than tepid enthusiasm. Sarah, by all accounts, was not very bright and Beaverbrook was easily bored. In 1920, she married Piers 'Joey' Legh, an equerry to the Prince of Wales and later Master of the Household to King George VI.

In 1919 a much more serious challenge to the 'menage' and to Gladys's own position appeared. This was no lightweight. It was no less than H. G. Wells's mistress, the fiery and fiercely intelligent novelist Rebecca West. West was born Cicily Isabel Fairfield in London in 1892. After her father had deserted the family her mother had taken her and her two sisters to grow up in Scotland. She later moved to London to train as an actress but soon moved into radical journalism using her new pseudonym. She joined the suffragettes and wrote for the left-wing journal *Clarion* and the feminist periodical *The Freewoman*. It was while working on the latter that she had occasion to review Wells's novel *Marriage*. Her piece was sufficiently provocative to entice the author into suggesting a meeting. Wells regarded his marriage (and for that matter all extra-marital relationships as well) as something of an open house and it was not long before West became his mistress, bearing him a son named Anthony in 1914. As her reputation grew so did Wells's jealousy, quite apart from the number of double infidelities about which he consistently lied. As a couple, they were later depicted by Anthony, who also became a successful writer, as two 'high-powered, world famous and unmarried parents' in his 1955 *roman à clef* novel *Heritage*, leading to a permanent estrangement between mother and son.[9]

Cicily Isabel Fairfield, known by her pen name Rebecca West (later, Dame Rebecca West), was a renowned English author, journalist, literary critic and travel writer.

In September 1918, Rebecca wrote to Beaverbrook, then Minister of Information, asking whether she could write some articles for his ministry. In her letter she added that she had already received an offer from the *Express* 'which I haven't accepted, but I have given them some very useful information about running a paper for which I haven't charged'.[10] Beaverbrook, who was always taken with a touch of playful cheek, wrote back promising to find her some work. It was not long afterwards that she and Wells were invited to dinner at the Vineyard. Beaverbrook found her a match for him; dark, thin featured, startlingly intelligent, contemptuous of convention and waspish in humour. He was not going to forget her. But for the time being there were other women catching his roving eye.

Venetia Montagu, Herbert Asquith's long-standing pen friend, may have been 'living in sin' with Beaverbrook during the Versailles negotiations of 1919, or she may just have been sharing his suite as there was no room for her with the official British delegation. (Given Beaverbrook's reputation it was perhaps a risky thing to do, although Venetia, tall and stockily built as she was, 'had the reputation of rendering even the most virile man impotent'.)[11]

Diana Manners, who acquired the surname Cooper on her marriage to Duff Cooper in 1919, was, both in character and in looks, quite different. The illegitimate daughter, so it was said, of the Duchess of Rutland, she had been accepted as a full member of the Manners family and brought up accordingly. In spite of a long and debilitating childhood illness which left her with recurring bouts of severe depression, she became, almost effortlessly, the symbol of the vivacity of post-war London high society. Wherever there was a party she was the shining centrepiece with her lustrous beauty and sharp wit. Beaverbrook, of course, was duly smitten and entertained her royally (he was seen to be in tears at her wedding, after presenting the couple with a motor car). She, on the other hand, according to her biographer, fell equally hard for his money.

There were, it need hardly be said, others at the same time. Those were boom years for Hollywood and the theatre. Beaverbrook, as the owner of a chain of cinemas and a newspaper with a widely read gossip column, not to mention his wealth and what has been described as his 'daemonic charm', had key cards to attract aspiring starlets and was never shy about using them. Furthermore, the same cards could be used in reverse if a relationship turned sour and engaged Beaverbrook's particular streak of malice. Reputations previously favoured were suddenly rubbished in print, or candidates for coveted roles were abruptly made aware that their services were no longer required.

There was apparently no shortage of glamour in those who took the Beaverbrook bait. It was the time for dinners at the Savoy, musical revues, dancing all night in the Embassy or the Kit-Cat Club, late evening theatres or even, be it said, of quiet assignations at the Vineyard. Nevertheless, much of what was eagerly noted as sexual passion turns out on less salacious study to be not much more than the froth of fashionable flirtation. Tallulah Bankhead, for instance, the undoubted star of the day and suspected by Beaverbrook's daughter Janet of much more than friendship with him, was indeed shown around London's *vie mondaine* and featured prominently in *Express* gossip columns. Yet, on her own account, 'his interest in me, I may say, was purely paternal', so much so, in fact, that 'Max introduced me to Michael Wardell ... We were soon engaged.'[12] She was, nevertheless, fascinated. 'Dinner over,' she later wrote,

> Max took the floor. A magnum of champagne in his hand, he circled about the room, talking constantly and entertainingly on an amazing variety of subjects. One minute he'd be deep in the Old Testament, the next in a recital of the flight of Sweden's Charles XII after his defeat at Poltava by Peter the Great. Max was smallish, built like a brownie, but he kept us fascinated until daylight, uninterrupted.[13]

Jose Collins, another star of the cinema of the 1920s, was apparently, again according to Janet, caught in bed with Beaverbrook one morning in the Hyde Park Hotel. Yet Janet's nephew is clear that 'Aunt Janet would never let the facts stand in the way of a good story'.[14] Rebecca West was certain that Beaverbrook was carrying on an affair with the beautiful young actress Gwen Ffrangçon-Davies. The theory was plausible enough but for the fact that Ffrangçon-Davies was a lesbian. The 22-year-old Barbara Cartland apparently believed that Beaverbrook was in love with her. At least, in later life she claimed that Beaverbrook had said to her that 'I can't ask you to marry me, but I'll make you the most important journalist in the world ... Of course, there was an "if" to that. I said "No".'[15]

Tallulah Bankhead, American actress and bonne vivante, pictured at the time she had been cast to play Iris Storm, the lead role in the dramatised version of The Green Hat, *based on the sensational novel by Michael Arlen. Photographed in* The Tatler, *September 1925.*

Jose Collins, Ziegfeld Follies singer and actress, 1923.

they came out a little while later and a few days later she told me that she had a contract at MGM and she did go to MGM and she did very well, and I say hooray for Lord Beaverbrook![18]

Brooks refused at the time to disclose the identity of the 'darling girl' on the same grounds as she used to refuse to describe the sexual experiences that would explain who she was and what she had done. In one sentence, memorable for its double entendre, she explained, 'I cannot unbuckle the Bible Belt.'[19] It was not long before Beaverbrook's conquest, if it can be called that, was revealed as a 21-year-old from Alabama, the daughter of a clergyman and with a failed marriage behind her, by then known as Dorothy Sebastian.

Dorothy was as honest as Louise Brooks. 'So I was a Scandals girl for a while,' she reported when interviewed.

I met butter-and-egg men, hobohemians who threw red ink parties, Middle Western bankers whose wives misunderstood 'em, and college boys from Princeton, Dartmouth, Harvard, New York, New Haven and Hartford. It took me two months to realise that all this wining and dining was the bunk. But chorus served my purpose. It brought me publicity in the Sunday roto sections and in a few magazines. Cheney Johnson took my picture and that helped too. I figured it all added to my chance of getting into pictures.[20]

Dorothy Sebastian and Buster Keaton, appearing in Spite Marriage, *1929.*

As it happened, Dorothy struck lucky. After a stuttering start, Dorothy co-starred with Buster Keaton in *Spite Marriage* and almost immediately became Keaton's mistress. Some years later, Louise spoke openly of Sebastian but kept Beaverbrook anonymous, referring to him only as 'a diminutive newspaper publisher'. Off the record, she described Beaverbrook as 'an ugly little grey man who went directly to his object with no finesse'.[21]

Dorothy was by no means alone. 'There was a group of hand-picked girls', Brooks later wrote,

> who were invited to parties given for great men in finance and government … We had to be fairly well bred and of absolute integrity – never endangering the great men with threats of publicity or blackmail. At these parties we were not required, like common whores, to go to bed with any man who asked us, but if we did the profits were great. Money, jewels, mink coats, a film job – name it.[22]

As it happened, the Ritz in New York had been the scene of another of Beaverbrook's amatory adventures only a few months before his encounter with Dorothy Sebastian. During the spring and early summer of 1923, Rebecca West was finally disengaging from her long-standing lover and the father of her son, H. G. Wells. Beaverbrook presented an immediately attractive alternative. As she wrote to her friend Sally Melville, 'I had dinner with Beaverbrook and his wife last Thursday – it was so funny. I must tell you all about it.'[23] What she told Melville has not been recorded, but in later life she produced an unlikely story that an unnamed lover's wife (presumably Gladys) had told her of her husband's intention to seek a divorce and propose to Rebecca. At all events, during the summer Beaverbrook and West met frequently, finally culminating in Beaverbrook's invitation to her to become his mistress.[24] She later recalled that she awoke 'entirely happy and only distressed by what I was to tell H. G., how I was to protect Max from H. G.'s vindictiveness'.[25]

The immediate problem was solved by Beaverbrook failing to turn up for their next assignation, pleading a business meeting abroad called inconveniently for the same time. 'Perplexed,' records one of Rebecca's biographers, 'Rebecca was forced to admit that she was in fact in love with Beaverbrook.'[26] At the same time, Wells embarked on a bizarre affair with a young Austrian widow which ended up with her appearing in his apartment naked, shouting, 'You must love me or I kill myself' before slashing her armpits and wrists.[27] Wells made the whole matter worse by telling Rebecca a series of lies about the incident. It was enough to reassure her that she was doing the right thing by breaking off her relationship. Accordingly, for the rest of the summer and autumn she planned her American tour lecturing on feminism and on the modern novel. Disregarding Wells's attempts to make it up, she left for New York at the end of October 1923.

It was almost to the day that the *Mauretania* slipped out of Liverpool on its transatlantic run that Bonar Law died. Five days later he was buried in Westminster Abbey. Whether as a break from what had been a distressing few months, or from irritation that Rebecca had sailed for New York without telling him, or simply for the chase (or possibly a mixture of all three), Beaverbrook himself soon decided to follow her. After a strenuous first leg of her lecture tour, speaking at colleges and women's clubs in the Mid-West, she had returned exhausted to New York for a Christmas break. Beaverbrook's office tracked her down at the Town House Hotel on Central Park West and, apparently, arranged for a happy transfer to the Ritz.

As Rebecca said some fifty years later, 'it was on the understanding that they were in love'. As their supposedly idyllic fortnight went on, however, it became clear that they 'were completely unsuited to be husband and wife'.[28] By that time Rebecca had convinced herself that Beaverbrook's failure at their sexual relations had been his and his only. A near contemporary version, however, written to her American friend Fannie Hurst, tells a slightly different story. At a lunch at the Vineyard during the summer of 1924,

> he talked quite lightly of our past infatuation as if it were a tremendous joke. I suddenly realised that he was physically quite indifferent to me. Fannie, I'm not telling you the truth. I'm leaving out the point. He casually implied in a phrase that when he had made love to me in London first he was drunk, and that it had been very awkward for him when he found I took it seriously.[29]

After a fortnight Beaverbrook announced that he was leaving her to return to London. The statutory mountain of red roses was duly delivered and there the affair, such as it was, ended. But if for Beaverbrook it had been little more than yet another casual fling, for Rebecca it had been a second time that she felt she had been in love. She fell ill, took refuge with Fannie Hurst (and her secret refuge from the alcohol ban of the days of Prohibition) and postponed the remainder of her lecture tour. Back in London the two continued to meet, and Rebecca was able to write to Beaverbrook as 'pet lamb' and 'heart of my heart (without prejudice)'.[30] Little remains of the rest of their correspondence, since Beaverbrook, meticulous in the preservation of other documents, destroyed all copies. Rebecca, on the other hand, started to try to achieve a kind of catharsis in 1925 by writing a lurid fictionalised account of her affair with Beaverbrook, to be entitled *Sunflower*. But in 1926 she came across William Gerhardie and made the mistake of telling Gerhardie about it. Word quickly got back to Beaverbrook, who quickly warned her off with threats of legal challenge. The novel remained unpublished. In 1927 she went into psychoanalysis, but, as her biographer reports, 'since her analysis focused on the same problems as her novel in progress, the two got rather mixed up'.[31]

It is not easy to guess at the atmosphere at Cherkley Court for the Christmas festivities of 1923. The master of the house was not present, for the first time since the end of the war, and many of the usual jollities must for that reason have fallen rather flat. Equally, it is impossible to believe that there was no whispered gossip about where Beaverbrook was. The company invited by Gladys had a strong Canadian content, with the new recruit to the *Sunday Express*, Beverley Baxter, leading a cast which, compared with previous years, can only be described as no more than politically second eleven. But Baxter must have known where his proprietor was (although perhaps not what he was doing), and H. G. Wells, who was not invited to Cherkley, was still pursuing Rebecca but would stay at home over Christmas 'because R. is having the time of her life in America and I don't want to interrupt it'.[32] What H. G. Wells knew, of course, anybody within reach of a telephone knew soon enough.

By the time Beaverbrook returned to London it was clear that all was not well. Gladys was hinting to Janet that she wanted to buy her own house in London and had to be talked out of the idea by Beaverbrook with a promise of Stornoway House in exchange. Nevertheless, the evenings at the Vineyard continued, gatherings which had started to include a new name, the brilliant young classical pianist Harriet Cohen. To that extent, not much had changed.

It was not until the middle of 1925 that Gladys's forbearance was put to the most severe test, a test which in the end broke her marriage, her health and, finally, her life. Jean Norton, twenty-seven years old, married with two children by her husband Richard Norton, was strikingly beautiful. Scottish, with the brightest of blue eyes and golden hair, clear in complexion and slender of figure, with a sharp wit and a dancing mind, she was quite clearly marked down as a target by Beaverbrook almost from the time they met. He quickly arranged for her to run a cinema he owned in London and by the end of the year was inviting her to Cherkley. In May 1926 she and her friend Edwina Mountbatten were operating the *Express* switchboard while Gladys ran the canteen. There were trips with Castlerosse and Michael Wardell to Deauville and Le Touquet, and, most humiliating for Gladys, an almost permanent residence in a cottage in the estate at Cherkley. There was no mistaking the signs; the torch had clearly passed.

Jean Norton (the Hon. Mrs Richard Norton), 1929.

CHAPTER 16

TILTING AT WINDMILLS

'Who is for the Empire?'[1]

On 3 December 1927, Gladys Beaverbrook was buried in the parish churchyard of Mickleham, the village just below Cherkley. The weather on the day, like the attending company, was miserable, damp and cold to the marrow. The service was no more and no less than what was required by the canon law of the Church of England and, as was customary, finished with handfuls of earth erratically scattered on the coffin after it had been lowered into its resting place. 'These funeral rites in an English winter', Arnold Bennett wrote in his diary, 'are absolutely barbaric ... Max was leaning on young Max's arm and looked quite old.'[2] Nevertheless, the ceremony was completed in due form and a small group of invited mourners, which included, as a matter of course, the Vicar of Mickleham, but also Beaverbrook's old banking friend James Dunn and his partner in frivolity Valentine Castlerosse (but did not include Jean Norton), were ferried back to Cherkley for a short and melancholy wake. It was, in truth, a sad end to what had been, in its final stages, a sad life.

But it became clear that it could not just be left at that. Beaverbrook himself went on to mark the event by having a large cross erected in the grounds below the house, glaringly illuminated by night. When asked about it by a visitor, his reply was succinct: 'It's to remind me that I am a Christian.'[3] The symbol, and the explanation, was clear. He had been more affected than he would have liked to admit both by the fact of Gladys's death and by the circumstances surrounding it. In fact, guilt, and accompanying grief, made him over the next months, and even years, tetchy and, at the same time, uncharacteristically listless.

A spotlight illuminating a cross, erected at Cherkley Court to remind Lord Beaverbrook of his Christian faith. Photograph taken August 1940.

For a start, he was annoyed that Janet insisted on going through with her marriage to Ian Douglas Campbell, the 11th Duke of Argyll, only nine days after her mother's funeral. He went on to order his staff to move his entire office from his rooms at the *Daily Express* to Stornoway House, muttering that, at the age of forty-eight, he was growing old and was thinking of retirement. When E. J. Robertson tried to cheer him up by suggesting that he might visit Russia to reopen trade relations, he did no more than consult Churchill, who duly advised against the idea, claiming that 'nearly everyone who has had anything to do with the Bolsheviks ... has come off soiled or disillusioned or poorer'.[4] Three months later, in May 1928, he was writing to Davidson that his aim was 'to move ... more and more in the direction of an old age devoted to contemplation and repose'[5] and to Frank Wise that 'the real truth is that I am no longer of any use in the world'.[6] Finally, he was furious with his court jester, Castlerosse, who in May secretly married a notorious *poule de luxe* by the name of Doris Delevingne, whose motto, apparently, was 'an Englishwoman's bed is her castle'.[7]

Of course, none of this self-deprecation was taken too seriously, either by his close friends or, more important, by the employees on his newspapers, who were bombarded with ever greater frequency with missiles about the paper's content. It was, after all, they said to themselves, only a passing phase in the aftermath of Gladys's death. Yet there is no doubt that throughout 1928 he was unusually subdued, even to the point where some of his friends were losing patience. 'Where are you going and what are you going to do next?' demanded H. G. Wells.

> Why the hell don't you set about doing something new & big enough to kill you with it unfinished? It's a damned sight worse not to take yourself seriously enough than to take yourself too seriously & your energy, capacity & decision – & the big bit of time you still have left to live ought to be spent in something better than peddling horses.[8]

Beaverbrook replied tamely that 'I don't know at the moment what I mean to do'.[9] It was no good. The downbeat mood continued. Hospitality at Stornoway House was reduced to two parties in the year and two guests at his daily lunch. Weekends at Cherkley were severely reduced except for Christmas and his birthday, and he rarely went out to the theatre or cinema or restaurants, and if invited out he was apt to be moody. (As always, he was a much better host than guest.)

The consolation, if it can be called that, was that his relationship with Jean Norton had become more open, and very much more intense. She had become, to tell the truth, a replacement for Gladys, a surrogate wife. She on her side had deepened her friendship with his children, particularly Janet, and he in turn had reciprocated, with shows of predictable generosity, with her children. Jean also helped him to buy furniture for and decorate a new house at Newmarket to satisfy what turned out to be a short-lived and expensive interest in owning racehorses. In fact, after one success at Epsom in the Great Metropolitan Stakes in 1928 (Alacrity, which romped home at 25–1) and a fruitless visit to Ireland in search of promising colts, he soon realised that the sport was not quite as honest as he had naïvely first believed. Moreover, he was obviously not enjoying himself and, as soon became a matter of comment, he was becoming a figure of fun at race meetings. According to one gossip columnist, he was frequently to be seen at meetings 'wearing a soft black hat which makes him look like an artist, and sadly watching his horses come in last'.[10] By August he had decided that the game was not worth the rather expensive candle. The project was abandoned, the house and the horses sold.

Lord Beaverbrook at Lingfield Park races, June 1928.

Beaverbrook was, as always, much more astute in his financial dealings. In November he sold all his cinema interests at a large profit and disposed of his holdings in the Daily Mail Trust and Canada Cement. From then on he steadily moved his whole portfolio out of equities and into fixed interest bonds, mostly government securities. It turned out to be another brilliant move ahead of the game. Equity prices were at an all-time high and government stocks attractively low. By selling equities and buying fixed interest government stock, in other words by moving defensively at just the right time, he survived financially unscathed the crash which was to come in October 1929.

Financially secure he may have been, but he came suddenly and alarmingly close to death in a serious road accident. After the celebrations at Cherkley at Christmas 1928 in which the main theme had been the birth a fortnight earlier of Beaverbrook's first grandchild, Jeannie, the car in which he was travelling back to London with Maurice Woods was hit by a lorry while driving through Surbiton.

Beaverbrook himself was badly bruised and deeply shaken, but Woods had to be extricated from the car with multiple injuries, including two badly fractured ribs, and rushed to hospital. After six painful weeks in hospital he died of pneumonia. For Beaverbrook, it was both a personal and a professional loss. Woods had researched and drafted his early books (the first volume of *Politicians and the War* had just been published) and had left drafts of chapters of others which were to be published later. In fact, there was no one to replace him.

Beaverbrook had, however, found, and had subsequently employed, two younger men who were also to become close companions, particularly while Castlerosse was out of favour: Robert Bruce Lockhart and Michael Wardell. Lockhart was something of a brilliant oddity. The son of a Lowland father and a Highland mother, he claimed to have inherited characteristics in equal measure from both: from the Lowlander a capacity for sustained hard work; from the Highlander a romantic impetuosity as well as a degree of introspection; and from both an affection for alcohol. Dark, squat, with a big head and a chubby face, he had a beguiling charm he would deploy if intent on seduction, as frequently happened. His career had been peripatetic: educated in Scotland, Berlin and Paris to prepare him for the Civil Service, he decided on a whim to go with one of his uncles to Malaya to start a new rubber estate. There he fell violently in love with a Malayan princess who broke all convention by agreeing to live with him in his bungalow.

The scandal drove him out of Malaya, but on his return to England he landed safely on his feet by joining the Consular Service. Posted to Moscow, he picked up a wife *en passant* but was serially unfaithful and was sent home, only to be sent back again after the revolution to negotiate with the Bolsheviks – who promptly put him in prison. Released after a month, he was posted to Prague, took a job in a bank which brought him back to London, acquired a mistress in the form of the third wife of the Earl of Rosslyn and spent the years from 1922 to 1928 travelling in central Europe. By the time Beaverbrook offered him the job on the Londoner's Diary, he was heavily in debt and drinking too much. But he made Beaverbrook laugh. Besides, he played golf with the Prince of Wales and his then mistress, Freda Dudley Ward (noting, however, that 'the Prince does not like Beaverbrook, says he wants to get everyone under his wing and, if he cannot get them, he tries to down them').[11]

Mike Wardell was another friend of the Prince of Wales. A former captain in the cavalry regiment the 10th Hussars, he had lost an eye in a riding accident and wore a black patch which gave him a piratical look, apparently lethally attractive to women. Like Robert Bruce Lockhart, he was married and serially unfaithful to his wife, Harriet, who finally divorced him in 1929. Among other attachments he was one of Edwina Mountbatten's lovers and, as such, came to know her great friend Jean Norton. It was through that connection that he was offered a job on the *Evening Standard* by Beaverbrook himself and in almost record time was made a director. Some, not least Lockhart, said that his conversation was a trifle boring, but although he might not have made Beaverbrook laugh, he was a faithful acolyte for thirty years.

To speed his recovery from the motor accident, Beaverbrook decided in January 1929 to take a party of friends (as might be imagined, mostly female) on a cruise to the West Indies. Before he left, however, he had announced, with something of a fanfare, that in gratitude for his 'good fortune' he was proposing to 'distribute £25,000 to various persons and objects'. Moreover, surprisingly, he asked the Prime Minister to allocate the gift.[12] Equally surprisingly to the outside world, Baldwin accepted the task. In fact, the motives on both sides are not difficult for political cynics to detect. A general election was due in 1929. Whatever the circumstances, Beaverbrook never lost interest in politics and Baldwin was, as ever, anxious to secure the support of his newspapers in what was clearly going to be a difficult electoral battle.

In fact, it proved to be more difficult than Baldwin had expected. With the election due to take place on 30 May, the Conservatives campaigned under the slogan of Safety First, a rallying cry Beaverbrook thought utterly uninspiring. His newspapers offered instinctive but tepid support and he blamed the Prime Minister for the public's apathy, as he saw it, towards the party and its programme. In late March, he wrote to an American friend that Baldwin had 'frittered his heritage away again. He cannot help it. He sits down in the garden with his arms folded and talks about the beauty of it, while the weeds grow all around him.'[13] Two days later he was writing to Sir Robert Borden praising Lloyd George and telling him that 'Churchill was more defeatist than ever. I dined with him last night and I judge he is certain the Government is going out. The Conservative faith in Baldwin has evaporated.'[14] Finally, in response to a desperate plea from Lord Daryngton he declared that 'I have done all that I can in personal contact with him [Baldwin] and in discussions with Churchill and with Davidson to get any sort of programme that would enable me to support the Conservative Party. I have failed completely.'[15]

The result of the general election was the defeat of Baldwin's Conservatives. Labour emerged as the largest party without an overall majority. Contrary to Beaverbrook's own prediction, Lloyd George's Liberals decided to support a minority Labour government, and Ramsay MacDonald duly formed his second administration. A chorus of blame was directed at Beaverbrook, as well as Rothermere, for displaying insufficient enthusiasm for the Conservative cause through their newspapers. Birkenhead in particular made a caustic reference to it at a Derby Eve dinner, reportedly saying that Beaverbrook 'had contributed as much as Lord Rothermere to the destruction of the Conservative Government'.[16] Beaverbrook responded by comparing Birkenhead to Jemmy Twitcher, a character in *The Beggar's Opera*. This further goaded Birkenhead to a furious response. 'I have received your telegram,' he wrote back immediately, 'which I think was not intended to be agreeable ... Editors are as much in public life as politicians. The only thing that friends are entitled to claim from one another is that they shall not say things which are inconsistent with friendship and with loyalty.' Warming to his task, he went on to complain about the *Evening Standard*'s cartoonist, David Low, who 'over a long period of time published filthy and disgusting cartoons of me which were intended and calculated to do me deep injury'. Finally, thinking that he had perhaps gone too far, he concluded that 'I should profoundly regret it if you decided to take any real or permanent offence at what I said...'[17]

Beaverbrook was certainly not going to lie down. 'I am staggered by your letter,' he replied. After asserting that Birkenhead agreed with him that Baldwin deserved defeat, he went on to refer to David Low. 'You are out of touch with the times, and I am too old at fifty. The new generation like the Low caricatures. Ask Eleanor [Birkenhead's daughter].' Lastly, 'the Conservatives are trying to blame everybody but the right persons for their failure at the polls. They had better concentrate on their jockey. Yours ever…'[18] Birkenhead was only partially mollified. 'If you are friendly,' he wrote back, 'so am I. As to your filthy cartoonist I care nothing about him now. But I know all about modern caricature and I never had cause for grievance until you, a friend, allowed a filthy little Socialist to present me as a crapulous and corpulent buffoon.'[19]

Such pleasantries aside, Beaverbrook's main complaint was addressed to all three political parties. In the *Daily Express* of 26 June, he wrote that 'we have just come through a General Election in which the Empire was hardly mentioned by any of the three contending Parties. Or, if mentioned, it was merely mumbled.' This was taken up and challenged the following day by the *Morning Post*:

> Who aided and abetted them in that neglect more than Lord Beaverbrook himself? … If Canada and other Dominions feel slighted by the narrow parochialism of home politics, they know [who to blame] … We do not doubt that today he feels his position acutely [but what is] difficult to endure patiently is his presuming to rebuke those whom he not only led into temptation, but positively forced into sin. That, if we may use a colloquialism, is 'a bit thick'.[20]

Beaverbrook's response came three days later in an article under his own name in the *Sunday Express*. Entitled 'Who is for the Empire?', it set out a proposal for an imperial fiscal union, to include Great Britain, the Dominions and the Dependencies in a customs union similar to that of the United States. He acknowledged that he himself had been diverted from pursuing the cause of Empire by paying too much attention to the affairs of his newspapers, a lapse for which he now declared himself penitent. In evangelical language he went on to proclaim:

> We have let slip so many opportunities in this direction – the last and greatest at the time of the War. Why? Because we are like the

Muck-rakers in the 'Pilgrim's Progress'. We are so busy raking in trifles out of the dirt at our feet that we cannot look up and see the Golden Crown suspended above.[21]

Initially, Beaverbrook hoped that the cause would be taken up by the Conservative Party, and he went on to badger senior ex-ministers for support. But the memory of the general election and the betrayal, as they saw it, of Beaverbrook and Rothermere was too raw. 'I have now exhausted my efforts', ran a letter of 3 July, 'and I am bound to say that there is a list of "Untouchables". Both you [Rothermere] and I are on it.'[22] The next step was to announce that the 'Crusade', as it had now become, should be independent of political parties but should take advantage of any offer of support regardless of where it came from. Furthermore, it was not simply a re-run of Joseph Chamberlain's tariff reform programme, nor was it mere imperial preference with tariff barriers erected against the rest of the world. It was to be a full fiscal union.

As a slogan, 'Empire free trade' had immediate appeal. The first real test of the Crusade was at a by-election in Twickenham. Beaverbrook managed to convince the Conservative candidate, Sir John Ferguson, to support Empire free trade by the simple tactic of threatening to run an independent candidate against him unless he agreed. Ferguson was immediately disowned by Conservative Central Office, and MPs who wished to speak for him were told that they did so in their personal capacity and in any event, they should not deviate from settled party policy. This compromise was ridiculed by the *Daily Express*, which then ratcheted up the pressure by announcing, on the basis of one leading article in the *Alberta Farmer*, that 'Canada joins the Great Empire Crusade'.[23] When it came, on 8 August, the result at Twickenham was a near disaster for the Conservatives. Ferguson won, but the majority was cut from 6,000 in the May general election to 500. The *Daily Express*, needless to say, announced it as a triumph for the Empire Crusade and blamed Baldwin for the reduced majority. Beaverbrook sent a message to Ferguson congratulating him on his 'splendid victory against overwhelming forces for evil'.[24]

Two days later, Beaverbrook set off on a trip to Russia. Originally, as suggested by Robertson, the purpose was to promote trade, but the Labour government had pre-empted that objective by opening direct discussions with the Soviets. Nevertheless, he had decided that he would still go ahead with the visit, but this time without an official purpose or, indeed, any purpose other than curiosity. He had been in touch in June with Frank Wise, a left-wing Labour MP with Soviet connections, requesting him to cable the Soviet authorities to ask whether he could charter a special train, whether they would provide hotel accommodation in Moscow (for 'about six people and one or two servants'[25]) and whether his party could dispense with visas.

The request fell upon stony ground. There was then a rush for visas and an appeal to the Foreign Office for help with accommodation. This proved successful and Beaverbrook, his brother Allan and a group of courtiers including Arnold Bennett, Wardell, Venetia Montagu, Edwina Mountbatten and Jean Norton duly set off from Immingham on board the *Arcadia*, destination Leningrad. The journey passed peacefully enough, the passengers reading on deck or playing cards, with Beaverbrook playing table tennis with Wardell. The ship called at Oslo and Danzig before arriving in Leningrad on 18 August. After an afternoon visit to the Hermitage and dinner at the Hotel Europa, the party took the night train to Moscow in the two special cars which had been reserved for them.

Once in Moscow, they found that they were being housed as guests 'at a house overlooking the Kremlin which once belonged to a sugar king – sumptuous breakfast and vast rooms'.[26] There was a full programme of sightseeing, they were entertained by Foreign Minister Litvinov and his English wife, Ivy, and on their second day called on Litvinov in the Kremlin. (Beaverbrook claimed later that he also saw Stalin, although there is no record of the event in the Soviet archives, either in Stalin's personal collection or in the official list of visitors to his office in 1929.)[27] The night train took them back to Leningrad and, for Arnold Bennett and the women, a day trip to see the Amber Room at the royal palace at Tsarskoye Selo while Beaverbrook, feeling ill, stayed in their hotel. He was no better when the *Arcadia* left Leningrad for home on 22 August. Five days later, Jean was noting that 'M not speaking to me all day. Fancy dress ball after dinner. M refused to play Baccarat and went to bed and Edwina, Venetia and I played rummy.'[28]

Lord Beaverbrook, one of the strongest opponents to England's breaking off diplomatic relations with Russia, visiting Moscow in 1929 to acquaint himself with the Russian capital. Beaverbrook is shown second left, with Lady Louis Mountbatten (left), Arnold Bennett and the Hon. Mrs Richard Norton (right).

Beaverbrook was in better health, but no better mood, on his return. After the *Arcadia* docked at Southampton on 31 August, he went straight to Cherkley. Robert Bruce Lockhart found him the following day and recorded in his diary that 'he has returned from Russia with no good impressions. The whole thing seems to have depressed him. Mike Wardell says it is because the Bolsheviks did not make enough of him, but he saw Stalin and Litvinov lived in his pocket and he was given special cars...'[29]

By the end of October 1929, Beaverbrook was back in campaigning mode. Yet he was less bullish about the prospects for Empire free trade than he had been in the summer, admitting that it was unlikely that the policy could be applied immediately. Public opinion had to be won over but the use of his newspapers for the purpose had to be rationed. With unexpected, and untypical, caution he wrote to a friend that 'the balance must be maintained day by day, measured by the reaction of our readers'.[30] He was even prepared to meet Baldwin again to listen to a lecture on the importance of campaigning in Parliament rather than in the press. It left him unmoved.

In fact, the meeting with Baldwin had, perversely, persuaded Beaverbrook to abandon his caution and revert to wholehearted use of his newspapers in shouting his message as loudly as possible. Anybody who complained about lack of objectivity was told that space was limited, and every inch was needed for putting forward the views of supporters. Even Beverley Baxter was reprimanded for suggesting that the concentration that he, as editor of the daily, had been forced to give to Crusade matters had injured his paper.

At the same time, in the dying weeks of 1929 the Crusade was organising itself. Headquarters were set up in Trafalgar Square under the control of Frederick Doidge, an executive on the *Daily Express* from New Zealand. A committee was assembled, consisting of three peers, two knights, one Liberal and one Conservative MP, with Beaverbrook in the chair. Robert Bruce Lockhart and Mike Wardell became Beaverbrook's two lieutenants, Lockhart assigned to writing speeches and articles after persuading his friend Harold Nicolson to take on the Londoner's Diary. Staff were moved from the *Express* office to provide administrative back-up. By the end of January 1930, the motor was running at full throttle.

Yet it was far from clear where it was heading. In fact, throughout the early weeks of 1930 Beaverbrook hoped, against Rothermere's advice, to persuade Baldwin to move from his stated position of mild protectionism to full-blown support for Empire free trade. Baldwin appeared to make a move in a speech on 5 February, advocating greater co-operation across the Empire, but it was not enough for the Crusaders. One week later Beaverbrook met Baldwin and asked him three questions:

> First. I said would he object if we put up Empire Free Trade Conservative candidates in constituencies. He replied that of course it would be 'disastrous'. I expected no other reply. Second. Would he object if we tried to get Empire Free Trade candidates before the selection committees ... Would the candidates receive the Conservative Leader's approval ... He showed plainly that he would not countenance such a course. Third. Would we be entitled to push over the brink into a declaration for Empire Free Trade members of the House of Commons sitting on the Front Bench, and others. He made it quite clear that he could not tolerate an Empire Free Trade declaration from his colleagues in the last Government.[31]

Beaverbrook decided that it was not possible to win Baldwin over. The major obstacle was the same as the one which had brought tariff reform to a halt twenty years earlier: the proposal to impose taxes on foodstuffs imported from outside the Empire (still derided by opponents as 'stomach taxes'). Baldwin was quite clear that it was not a policy which could be sold either to the Conservative Party or to the country. Beaverbrook concluded that the only course available was to form a new party. Baldwin in turn indicated that it would be the least damaging course for the Conservatives. On 17 February, with much trumpeting, the United Empire Party was born. Much to Beaverbrook's satisfaction, Rothermere immediately pledged his support.

It was a bad mistake, as Baldwin, a very much cleverer politician than Beaverbrook, knew perfectly well. The editor of the *Morning Post*, Howell Gwynne, was quick to point out why:

> You have made the huge mistake of changing a wonderful movement into a party ... Rothermere will kill you [although] not wittingly by his appalling personality ... You have risked all [your] advantages by forming a party because it is bound to turn the whole thing into a personal issue Rothermere cum Beaverbrook v. Baldwin, and the public sympathy will be with Baldwin.[32]

Gwynne was joined by the senior Conservative MP Leo Amery, also sympathetic to the Empire Crusade, in urging a compromise with Baldwin. Gwynne even offered to act as intermediary.

Privately, Beaverbrook agreed with them. But the new party had only just been launched. He could not possibly climb down yet. A fighting fund of £100,000 was set up. On 27 February, Beaverbrook spoke at the inaugural meeting of the party in the Shire Hall at Gloucester. According to the *Daily Express* it was

> the greatest meeting the city has ever witnessed. Great crowds of people assembled hours before the advertised time and long queues stood waiting. Hundreds were unable to obtain an entry. They flowed into corridors and adjoining rooms, where loudspeakers conveyed the speech to them. Many more listened to loudspeakers in

the streets. It was a tremendously enthusiastic gathering, and Lord Beaverbrook's speech was cheered again and again.[33]

Even allowing for the inevitable hyperbole in the *Express* reporting it does seem that the meeting was a success, although the text of Beaverbrook's speech is rather flat and lurches from time to time into irrelevant byways, such as the failures of the Labour government or the voting intentions of the newly enfranchised female voters. Nevertheless, in spite of the success, on his return to London Beaverbrook was ready to receive another message, this time from Sir Robert Horne, a former Chancellor of the Exchequer, urging him to make one more effort of reconciliation with Baldwin. Coming from that source, the request could hardly be refused, and through Gwynne's intermediation a meeting was arranged for the morning of 3 March at Baldwin's home in Upper Brook Street.

Baldwin had obviously taken note of the success of the Gloucester meeting and realised that the United Empire Party needed to be stopped, or at least hijacked, before it reached the point of damaging the Conservatives. On the only contentious issue, food taxes, Baldwin suggested a compromise. He proposed two general elections, at the first of which there would be no mention of food taxes, but, if the Conservatives were returned, they would negotiate with the Dominions to devise a plan for food taxes which could be presented at the second. Beaverbrook countered with a proposal that popular consent should be sought not in a second general election but in a referendum. Having set out his stall, Beaverbrook left to seek Rothermere's advice.

At half past nine in the evening Baldwin and Beaverbrook met again in the house of the Conservative Party chairman, J. C. C. Davidson. This time Baldwin brought with him Sir Bolton Eyres-Monsell, his Chief Whip. He told Beaverbrook that they accepted his proposal provided it was not presented as a victory for the United Empire Party. Beaverbrook called again on Rothermere, brought him round during an uneasy discussion in which Rothermere reiterated his distrust of Baldwin and, on the following morning, sent Baldwin a message of agreement. That evening Baldwin announced the new policy at a meeting of the Council of the National Union of Conservative and

Unionist Associations. The *Daily Express* called it 'the path of true statesmanship' and noted with satisfaction that Baldwin had 'made many generous tributes to the valuable educational work done by the Crusade'. Beaverbrook was for once more cautious. He welcomed the fact that they would no longer be running candidates against the Conservatives but noted that 'the country has yet to be persuaded' and 'we must work harder than ever'.[34] But he still had doubts. 'I pointed out the bridge to Baldwin,' he wrote on 11 March. 'He built it. Now it remains to be seen if the piles will hold the structure. Many signs point to weakness which will destroy the bridge...'[35] The Conservatives were more effusive. Baldwin was back on first-name terms with 'Max' and Davidson attributed the compromise to a higher authority. 'Thank God!' he wrote to Beaverbrook. 'The ranks are closed.'[36]

The main casualty of the whole affair was the United Empire Party. Once the deal had been done and the possibility of competing candidacies removed, there was no point in a separate political organisation. Beaverbrook was in favour of closing the whole thing down. Rothermere, on the other hand, wanted it kept as a useful campaigning vehicle on issues unrelated to the Empire Crusade: 'ruthless economy in social expenditure, no more surrenders in India, no diplomatic relations with Moscow'. This, as Beaverbrook pointed out, was 'a complete departure from the original [single-issue] aims for which the United Empire Party was formed'. In a cautious exchange of statements on 8 March ('our close personal relations remain unaltered'), it was announced by both that the party would be taken under the umbrella of the *Daily Mail*, that Beaverbrook would sever his ties with it and that contributions to the fighting fund would be reimbursed.[37]

It was not long before the structure started to collapse in the way that Beaverbrook had feared. First, Lord Salisbury entered the fray, announcing in a weighty letter to *The Times* that while he applauded Empire free trade as 'an ultimate aspiration ... the fruits of this policy do not belong to the immediate future and unless this be fully grasped it may not merely be useless, but dangerous'.[38] Almost immediately, Conservative Central Office published a leaflet with assurances that food taxes would not be unilaterally imposed, and the Conservative candidate in the Nottingham Central by-election, Terence O'Connor, appeared to speak against them. When Beaverbrook complained in a letter to O'Connor which the Conservatives took to be an attack on Baldwin, both Davidson and Neville Chamberlain tried to cool him down, but Beaverbrook would have none of it. Encouraged by Rothermere's repeated warnings of Baldwin's betrayal, he went to Nottingham to set out yet again that the Empire Crusade was not a unit of the Conservative Party and would accept support from other parties if it was offered. He then complained about the Central Office leaflet, provoking an angry retort from Chamberlain: 'You spend all your time pointing out to the public how entirely unreliable and un-trustworthy is the only instrument available to carry [your policy] out ... Stop stabbing at those who are trying to help.'[39] Beaverbrook replied simply that he thought Baldwin was 'determined to shelve the policy. I am as anxious to make it impossible for him to do so.'[40] In the event, O'Connor won with an increased majority. David-son in turn felt bruised by the whole affair and gave way as party chairman to Neville Chamberlain. As he later wrote, 'Let Neville take the responsibility for trying to get an agreement with Beaver-brook, which will start all right but which will end by Beaverbrook running out.'[41]

Relations were only partially restored at the time of the next by-election, at West Fulham on 6 May. The Conservative candidate, Sir Cyril Cobb, fighting to recapture the seat he had lost to Labour in 1929, was a strong supporter of Empire free trade. Beaverbrook conse-quently gave him all the resources he needed, stayed at the Vineyard in the heart of the constituency and spoke several times on his behalf. It was enough, but only just enough, to win the seat by a thin majority but more than enough for the *Daily Express* to present the result as a triumph for the Crusade. Even Baldwin was moved to congratulate him. 'My dear Max,' he wrote the day after the declaration, 'you must be nearly dead – and I congratulate you on your gallant conduct in the arena once more – it must have brought back happy days at Ashton once again.'[42] Beaverbrook was unimpressed. One week later he was writing to a friend, 'I will make no progress in co-operation with

Stanley Baldwin. He is a useless fellow and I hope he will have to walk the plank, or get the black spot, or anything else you like to call it.'[43]

During May and June there was continued skirmishing between Beaverbrook and Conservative leaders to no particular effect. In fact, there were signs that Beaverbrook was getting tired of it all. Since the inaugural meeting of the Crusade at Gloucester he had made over thirty major public speeches and was the centre of a whirlpool of constant activity. He had tried, and failed, to entice a leading Conservative figure to take over the leadership of the Crusade and now felt that he was trapped in a life like 'that of a bell boy in a hotel who has to jump up and run every time the bell rings'.[44]

Towards the end of June 1930 there was one success at least. Rothermere had always been doubtful about the electoral wisdom of taxing foreign foodstuffs. But the *Daily Mail* had carried out 'a very careful inquiry to be made all over the country and among all classes of voters'. The conclusion was that food taxes were 'not only economically desirable but electorally possible'. 'Lord Rothermere's Bombshell' was the banner headline in the *Daily Express* of 24 June. The two most powerful newspaper proprietors were united in support for the Crusade.

Beaverbrook, it need hardly be said, was delighted. Yet he would have paused had he realised Rothermere's change of mind, and his new allegiance to the Crusade, signalled the beginning of what was to become a war between the two of them and Baldwin. It started during the by-election in early July in North Norfolk. The Conservative candidate, Thomas Cook, was a convinced Empire free trader, and Beaverbrook soon descended on the constituency accompanied by Castlerosse, two secretaries and three motor cars. Once there, he made no fewer than eleven speeches, but the most striking feature of his campaign was a large black box which gave out a loud buzz every minute. When it did so, Beaverbrook announced that another thousand pounds had just been spent on imported food. The voters of North Norfolk, however, were not impressed, and the seat went to Labour. Beaverbrook was disappointed but not downcast. As he wrote to Leo Amery, he hoped that in the future the Crusade would have the chance 'of contesting a seat against a Conservative Central Office candidate' in an industrial centre.[45]

Lord Beaverbrook is seen addressing railwaymen at Melton Constable during his fight for Empire free trade in the North Norfolk by-election, 8 July 1930.

Before that could happen, however, Neville Chamberlain made an effort to mend bridges. As there are two different, and incompatible, versions of what Chamberlain proposed in a meeting on 18 July (one recorded by Chamberlain and the other by Beaverbrook), it is impossible to reconstruct what precisely was on the table other than that it concerned procedures for the selection of candidates for by-elections. Not that it matters very much since negotiations quickly broke down.

Hostilities were resumed in earnest when Rothermere's son, Esmond Harmsworth, was put forward as a possible candidate in another by-election, this time at Bromley. In the event the local association selected another Crusader, but on the understanding, as Beaverbrook put it, 'that he would declare for Baldwin's support and that he would not make the contest a Beaverbrook election ... There is never to be peace again. We are to be hounded out of the Conservative Party.'[46] As if that were not enough, a further row exploded, this time in Canada. Beaverbrook had given an interview to the *Toronto Globe* in which he appeared to lend his support to the Liberal Prime Minister, Mackenzie King, against his opponent, Beaverbrook's long-standing friend and now Conservative leader, Richard Bedford Bennett. His justification was that Mackenzie King seemed to be flirting with Empire free trade and that any help was welcome. Unfortunately, the paper held the publication of the interview until the eve of the general election, which took place on 28 July and which Bennett's Conservatives duly won. Bennett, never one to overlook a slight, remained silent for the moment but stored up his reply for a later and more suitable occasion.

Bennett's opportunity duly arrived at the Imperial Conference, held in London in early October. He duly announced curtly that for Canada, Empire free trade was neither 'desirable nor possible'. He did, however, as a palliative, suggest that Canada would consider arrangements with Britain on preferential tariffs. Baldwin's response was ambiguous, accepting the principle of imperial preference and seeking a free hand on how to achieve it. This in turn provoked a series of broadsides from Beaverbrook. On 11 October, 13 October and 15 October the *Daily Express* carried articles whose language became increasingly hysterical and personal to Baldwin. On 16 October the *Evening Standard* picked up the tune. '[Mr Baldwin's] successive attempts to find a policy remind me of the chorus of a third-rate review. His evasions reappear in different scenes and in new dresses and every time they dance with renewed and despairing vigour. But it is the same old jig.'[47] Beaverbrook even appealed to Bennett to take the lead, but the ground there had become impenetrably stony. Bennett merely advised him to make peace with Baldwin. Beaverbrook refused.

Beaverbrook was given another chance to throw mud at Baldwin at yet another by-election, due to be held on 30 October, this time in Paddington South. The local Conservatives had played for safety in adopting the incumbent chairman, Sir Herbert Lidiard, as candidate. Rothermere in turn put up a United Empire candidate, Mrs Stewart-Richardson, but Beaverbrook so disliked her that he refused to support her, going instead to see Lidiard and persuading him to sail under the Crusade flag. Rothermere accordingly withdrew his endorsement of Mrs Stewart-Richardson, only to learn that she refused to stand down. At that point Neville Chamberlain wrote to Lidiard withdrawing Central Office support. Lidiard, prompted by his association, quickly reversed his position by a public pledge of loyalty to the Conservative Party. Beaverbrook was so incensed that he organised a meeting of Crusaders at which Vice-Admiral Ernest

Taylor was adopted as their candidate. The result of all this confusion was startling: after a bad-tempered and occasionally violent campaign Taylor won the seat with a majority of 941. 'The Empire wins South Paddington', screamed the *Daily Express*.[48]

If Baldwin was dismayed by the result, he was also reasonably encouraged by a vote of confidence in his leadership passed by a majority at a meeting of Conservative MPs, candidates and peers at Caxton Hall on the morning of the Paddington South poll, in spite of a substantial minority voting against him. He was much more cheered by their approval of his policy of a 'free hand' in negotiations over food taxes. He may also have been secretly pleased by the demonstration of hostility towards Beaverbrook when he rose to speak. Certainly Beaverbrook himself took careful note. It was obviously not going to be easy to dislodge Baldwin. He had to rethink his strategy. After failing to persuade the Conservative candidate at another by-election to adopt Crusade policy, Beaverbrook seemed ready to accept a conciliatory proposal from Chamberlain to lower the temperature. It was only when Chamberlain admitted that Baldwin was not prepared to change his mind on food taxes that negotiations stalled.

In the New Year of 1931, Beaverbrook wrote to Borden setting out the problem:

> Baldwin is trying to get the best of both worlds. In the South he is a food taxer; but in the North he dare not go quite as far as this. So he says that he will not support food taxes unless he can get a first-rate bargain with the Dominions in return. To this we answer that we want duties on foreign foodstuffs unconditionally and we want a definite mandate from the electorate to impose them.[49]

To Arthur Brisbane, he set out his new strategy: 'I am going out entirely for by-elections this year, and shall exclude all other forms of propaganda. I shall make the by-elections the occasions for my propaganda. It then becomes more human and far less boring to the people.'[50]

An opportunity to test the new strategy presented itself almost immediately at Islington East, where the sitting Labour Member had died. The date of the by-election was set for 19 February. The Conservative candidate, Thelma Cazalet, straight away declared herself sympathetic to Empire economic unity, prompting the withdrawal of the Crusader nominee, the barrister Paul Springman, who wrote to her pledging his support. Beaverbrook followed this up with a draft statement for Cazalet to sign spelling out the policy of Empire free trade, including food taxes. Cazalet refused the bait, later claiming in a public statement that 'Lord Beaverbrook's ... primary object and interest lies no longer in Empire matters but rather – as he has told us in two of his recent speeches – "in smashing up the Conservative Party"'.[51]

Egged on by Rothermere, writing from the comfort of the Italian resort of San Remo that 'if you, with my assistance, can overthrow the Central Conservative organisation, the Conservative Party is ours',[52] Beaverbrook quickly produced another Crusader candidate, Brigadier-General Alfred Critchley. In fact, Critchley was a good choice. By the end of the war he had left the Royal Flying Corps as the youngest brigadier-general in the British Imperial Forces, and had then founded the Greyhound Racing Association and introduced greyhound racing first to Manchester and then to the White City and the Haringey Arena in London. With his war record to appeal to the middle-class vote and his devotion to greyhound racing to appeal to the working-class vote, Critchley looked a winner.

There was, however, a complication. Critchley was tabled as standing for the Empire Crusade and the United Empire Party, adding to the confusion as Thelma Cazalet styled herself the Conservative and Empire candidate. As Lockhart pointed out, 'I fear the shilly-shallying will do Max harm, will strengthen the public's belief in Baldwin as an honest man and in Max as a twister. The whole episode gives the impression that Max is more intent on doing Baldwin down than on getting his policy through.'[53] Lockhart was, of course, right. That was Beaverbrook's aim, and the campaign waged by the *Daily Express*, amply supported by the *Daily Mail*, reflected it.

As it reached its climax, the noise, both real and in print, grew louder. Every time Beaverbrook himself appeared he was greeted with 'a storm of cheering and applause'. At a rally held in Islington Town Hall, 'the fire of his attack, the relentless logic of his case and his smashing blow against dead party politics wound up a great day!' On the eve of poll the *Daily Express* was adamant: 'It is a decision ... between action and lethargy ... between the candidates of the old party failures and the enterprising policy represented by Brig-General Critchley, the Empire Crusade candidate.'[54] Having considered the decision, the voters took the opposite view and split the Conservative vote, leaving the Labour candidate the winner with an increased majority in a seat he had expected to lose.

No sooner had the Islington East result been announced and analysed than another by-election was declared in the constituency of Westminster St George's, with polling due on 19 March. Baldwin was by then in difficulty. The minority which had voted against him the previous October had swollen in size. The official policy of giving a measure of self-government to a federal India was proving unpopular with the rank and file of the party and provoking ill feeling in the leadership, with Churchill the leader of the malcontents. On 28 February the prospective Conservative candidate for Westminster St George's, John Moore-Brabazon, declared that he could not any longer support the leadership and withdrew. On the same day, the West Country industrialist Sir Ernest Willoughby Petter announced that he would stand as an Independent Conservative on a specifically anti-Baldwin ticket and that he would pay his own expenses. Both Labour and the Liberals declined to contest what was for them a hopeless seat.

At that point the Conservative leadership cracked. Led by Neville Chamberlain, they endorsed a report by Sir Robert Topping, the party's principal agent, on the extent of the discontent and, on 1 March, sent it to Baldwin with a strong hint that he should resign. At first, Baldwin agreed to go, but he soon changed his mind and told Chamberlain that he would wait for the result of the Westminster St George's by-election before making up his mind. None of this was known to Beaverbrook at the time. But there was no doubt in either his or Rothermere's minds that the decisive battle had now been joined. 'The primary issue of the by-election', Beaverbrook wrote to Brisbane on 3 March,

> will be the leadership of the Conservative Party ... Petter is a hard-shelled Tory, and without any taint of the adventurer – the charge

which they are always trying to fasten on to me … If he is defeated we shall not be seriously discredited. If he wins, Baldwin must go, and Empire Free Trade must become the accepted policy of the Conservative Party.[55]

Both the *Daily Express* and the *Daily Mail* endorsed Petter as a matter of course, although it was admitted that 'it was not until recently that the public generally recognised in him a new and challenging force, and that here was a man with wide business knowledge and deep experience allied to firm convictions and unflinching determination'.[56] (In other words, nobody had any idea who he was and Beaverbrook was worried that Petter, like Springman at Islington East, would fall victim to Chamberlain's blandishments.)

On the morning of 5 March, the *Daily Telegraph* reported that Alfred Duff Cooper, the husband of Diana Cooper, had been nominated as Conservative candidate for the by-election. Beaverbrook immediately tried to contact Diana, but she had already left London. Writing to Duff, he explained what he wanted to say to her by quoting what Bonar Law had once said to Churchill: 'I shake your hand tonight because I may not be on speaking terms with you when I read the newspapers in the morning.'[57] There followed a series of attacks on Duff Cooper in both the *Daily Express* and the *Daily Mail*, all of them, as might be expected, in the worst of taste. He was, among other things, 'Mr Cooper', a 'softy' or, alternatively, 'Mickey Mouse'.

At first, Petter was doing well. Baldwin's unpopularity, and doubts about the Conservatives' Indian policy, played in his favour. But on 16 March, helped by a pact between the Viceroy, Lord Irwin, and Mahatma Gandhi which ended the Indian nationalist campaign of civil disobedience, Baldwin made a fine speech to his backbenchers which defeated Churchill's attack and earned him a standing ovation. The following evening, he turned his fire on Rothermere and Beaverbrook. Their newspapers, he said,

are not newspapers in the ordinary acceptance of the term. They are engines of propaganda for the constantly changing policies, personal wishes, personal likes and dislikes of two men. What are their methods? Their methods are direct falsehood, misrepresentation, half-truths, the alteration of the speaker's meaning by putting sentences apart from the context, suppression, and editorial criticism of speeches which are not reported in the paper … What the proprietorship of these papers is aiming at is power, and power without responsibility – the prerogative of the harlot throughout the ages.[58]

Baldwin's speech was played down by the *Express* and the *Mail*, but other papers carried it prominently. Word was also spread by the cohort of Mayfair ladies, led by Diana Cooper in full fig, sporting an early flowering white camellia in her hat, with her sister-in-law the Duchess of Rutland. The domestic servants, who formed a sizeable section of the electorate, were theirs to the last butler and between maid; upstairs, the readers of carefully ironed copies of *The Times* were told in thunderous tones how they should vote; and vote they all did.

The result, when declared, was a decisive victory for Duff Cooper by 17,242 votes to Petter's 11,532. It was a triumph, too, for Baldwin, whose leadership was secured. Chamberlain, taking advantage of Beaverbrook's obvious disappointment, was quick to suggest a reconciliation. 'There is now a lull in the storm,' he wrote on 23 March. 'Is this not a good opportunity to make contact again?'[59] Beaverbrook was in no mood to refuse, or, indeed, to bargain hard. After a series of meetings, a truce was agreed. The terms were all in Baldwin's favour. 'I have discussed [your] terms with Mr Baldwin', runs Chamberlain's concluding letter,

and he authorises me to say that you have correctly stated the present Conservative policy in regard to agriculture. It is his intention to employ for the development of agricultural production all or any of the methods you enumerate [quotas, prohibition of or duties on foreign foodstuffs] as they may best effect the object aimed at, and to ask the electors for a mandate for that purpose.

Beaverbrook in turn gave his guarantee that if that was the case, 'I for my part will do everything I can to help to carry the programme to fulfilment.'[60] The Stornoway Pact, as Beaverbrook liked to call the exchange, was sealed. In fact, it was more a document of surrender. Two last-minute manuscript amendments to Chamberlain's final letter make the point: 'present' had been inserted, and 'free hand' in the original text had been changed tactfully to 'mandate'. But Beaverbrook knew perfectly well that 'mandate' meant in practice 'free hand'. The clever Mr Baldwin had won.

The Empire Crusade had effectively come to an end. In fact, it had come to a halt well before the Westminster St George's by-election. Like all populist movements, it had started with great appeal. Everybody could approve of the Empire. But the more serious analysis was applied, the more Empire free trade turned into series of windmills with no substance. There was lofty talk about 'the Dominions' but Australia had been largely ignored and nobody seems to have been aware of the existence of South Africa. Canada, which Beaverbrook relied on for support, was taken out of the equation by its own Prime Minister and Beaverbrook's friend Richard Bedford Bennett. There was no serious thought given by Crusaders to India or the West Indies. In the end, apart from a few empty slogans about 'fiscal union' (whatever that was meant to mean), the whole enterprise had descended into a civil war in the Conservative Party, the *casus belli* being the state of English agriculture.

It had all been a huge effort, with much expense and in the end to no great purpose. Churchill for his part could not understand why Beaverbrook had started it in the first place. Lockhart made a note of a conversation between Churchill and Harold Nicolson in November 1930:

> They discussed Max. Winston thinks he is a neurotic; said it was a thousand pities that, when there are so many second-rate people in politics, this man, who with his wonderful dynamic force, his boundless vitality and energy could do so much for the country in its hour of need, was spending all his strength in disruptive enterprises merely out of vanity or boredom.[61]

Beaverbrook may or may not have been neurotic. He was not physically vain, but he was certainly self-important. His friend William

Gerhardie thought that the invention of the Crusade was a reaction against tedium and listlessness. 'Here is a man', he wrote, 'in need of a vocation to complete his personality, and so Empire Free Trade had, like Voltaire's god, to be invented.'[62] That may be true. But it should not be forgotten that his wife and the mother of his children had not so long ago been consigned to her grave in the churchyard of Mickleham. The grief, and the guilt of how it happened, needed to be allowed to work themselves out. Ghosts often have a powerful effect. Frenetic activity is one way to exorcise them.

CHAPTER 17

NO MORE WAR

'Are you for peace?'[1]

It is never easy to admit defeat, and certainly it was not an experience Beaverbrook ever relished. Yet, in spite of some brave words in letters to well-wishers and in carefully planted articles, he was forced privately to acknowledge that the Empire Crusade, as such, had come to its effective finale in the electoral crucible of Westminster St George's. Of course, this was never openly admitted. In public, the word was one of defiance verging on bluster. 'The Empire Crusade', the *Daily Express* announced on 30 March 1931, 'will not lose its identity but will remain a fighting force working alongside the Conservative Party.'[2] The bold assumption was that the Stornoway Pact would hold, that the Conservatives would include the taxation of foreign foodstuffs in their manifesto for the next general election and that all their candidates would support it. As it turned out, it was Rothermere who took a sharp pin to this balloon by asking what Beaverbrook would do if a Conservative candidate, when asked, said that he was not in favour of food taxes. In that case, replied Beaverbrook, unashamed, 'I shall oppose [the] candidate.'[3]

Beaverbrook's snappy mood after the failure of the Empire Crusade was compounded by the mournful news of the death of two of his closest friends, Tim Healy and Arnold Bennett. It was only a week after the St George's by-election that the news came through of Healy's death at his Irish home. Beaverbrook had been kept informed by Healy's sister Elizabeth of her brother's illness and had thought about a visit but was told that it would not be a good idea. Healy himself had told his sister firmly that the last thing he wanted was to drag Beaverbrook over to Ireland and away from London politics.

There is no doubt that Beaverbrook was deeply moved by the loss of his old Irish friend. 'I never think of him unhappily or mournfully,' he later wrote to Elizabeth in asking whether the family needed money. 'I always talk of him and usually with laughter and high spirits. That is the attitude he took to life. And his philosophy is now my own.'[4] This was followed up with a letter to another of Healy's sisters: 'He was the strongest and best character I have known in my life. None of us need to be ashamed of falling short of the standard he set. None of us should fail to emulate his example so far as possible. I really try to do so.'[5] Coming from a Scottish Presbyterian to a dedicated Irish Catholic it was no mean tribute, not least in its recognition of what bound them together: a (frequently malicious) sense of fun.

Arnold Bennett was a different matter. His death, coincidentally a day after Healy's, was unexpected. He had contracted typhoid during a visit to Paris the previous January but seemed to be coming through the worst until a relapse in March led to a sudden decline and a quick end. Bennett's doctor had forbidden him to receive visitors during the last stages of his illness, much to both Bennett's and Beaverbrook's annoyance. As with Tim Healy, Beaverbrook's own encomium, this time made public in a piece he wrote for the *Sunday Express*, concentrated on Bennett's character rather than his literary achievements. 'Arnold Bennett', his piece runs,

> was extraordinarily lovable and supremely honest ... His conversation was so engaging as almost to defy praise or comment. Indeed, the pleasantness of his company outstrips description. He was at once shrewd, witty and cynical, and yet simple – and above all an immensely human fellow who had seen much of life from many standpoints, and looked on them all at once with sympathy and what is sometimes the enemy of sympathy – understanding.[6]

Towards the end of April 1931, Beaverbrook was happy to get away from London, spending a few days with Jean in Paris before going on to Munich and from there to Berlin. But, all in all, he was in a bad mood. H. G. Wells thought that he was showing the first symptoms of 'hardening of the brain', evidenced by 'a dislike of contradiction and an avoidance of all people who are likely to contest anything he says'. Wells had been down to Cherkley and 'had returned with the determination never to visit Cherkley again, since one came away with a vague sense of humiliation and an acute sense of disquiet'.[7] Beaverbrook was also having sporadic but fierce rows with Jean, accusing her, quite unfairly, of wanting to spend too much time with her children and not enough with him. There were, too, flashes of spite, one in particular directed at Harold Nicolson, who had announced his affiliation to Oswald Mosley's New Party. Beaverbrook did not like his acolytes drifting away.

Not only was Beaverbrook morose and bad tempered but he took to worrying, yet again, about his health. This time it was to do with kidney stones. Two German doctors were consulted, Professors von Müller in Munich and Thannhauser in Freiburg. Both recommended drinking large quantities of water and taking plenty of exercise, perfectly sensible prescriptions but impossible to follow while travelling abroad. Back in London at the end of the second week in May the regime was followed almost obsessively, along with an intense and detailed interest in individual kidney stones as they appeared. 'On Thursday last, late at night,' Beaverbrook wrote to von Müller on 12 May, I passed a small calcium oxelate stone weighing 20 milligrammes. Yesterday I went to be X-rayed, and another stone was located in the pelvis of my kidney.'[8]

On 2 June he reported to Professor Thannhauser:

I would very much like to go over to see you, but I think it is better for me to stay here in the country, riding every day and drinking large quantities of water in the hope of moving my stone ... I think I wrote to you that the stone is about the size of a millet seed ... [It] may have been in the pelvis of my kidney for an indefinite time.

Yet he could not help blaming someone else and laughing at himself at the same time. 'It is [Wilson's] fault that I was ever X-rayed. If I had not been exposed to that enquiry I would never have known of the presence of the stone. If I had not known about it I would have been a comfortable and happy man.'[9] Robert Bruce Lockhart was also dragged in. Beaverbrook told him to seek out a Harley Street specialist who had been recommended, pretend that he had a stone in his kidney, fake Beaverbrook's symptoms (although it was not at all clear what they were) and ask for an opinion. The ruse was designed to see whether the specialist seemed any good. In the event, 'he struck me as a gas-bag and a liar', Lockhart reported. Nevertheless, Beaverbrook was inclined to give him a try. Later, over dinner, 'we discussed doctors most of the evening. He is worried about his stone and is in rather low spirits.'[10]

There was little let-up in his low spirits throughout June and August 1931. By-elections in the spring had come and gone, lacklustre affairs with unsensational results. Neville Chamberlain periodically tried to cheer Beaverbrook up, but to little effect. 'Neville will never be Prime Minister,' wrote Lockhart. 'He is as cold and clammy as a dead trout.'[11] On 24 June, Beaverbrook and Lockhart travelled to London together, with Lockhart recording in his diary that his employer's melancholy seemed to have deepened to the point where he was 'pessimistic about himself, says his life's work is done and wants to pull out of England altogether'.[12] Sensibly, Lockhart advised him to take a holiday before making any decision. Beaverbrook agreed. It was time for another visit to Canada.

The difficulty was to decide, apart from his trail of secretaries and personal servants, who was to accompany him. Jean was determined to go to the south of France with her children and said so in her most tempestuous voice. Castlerosse was in disgrace after setting a trap in the middle of the night to catch his wife's lover and beating him half to death in the street. The incident may have amused London society, but it only aroused Beaverbrook's Presbyterian indignation. As a result of his public indiscretion, Castlerosse was curtly told that his reputation had put him off Beaverbrook's travelling list; Lockhart recalled how Castlerosse had 'begged to be taken and in the end [he] had cried

… Max … could not resist the tears. Doris [Castlerosse's wife] apparently also rang Max up and promised to divorce Valentine if only Max would take him to Canada.'[13]

Reasonably enough, Beaverbrook had expected his summer visit to Canada to follow the pattern of previous summers. There would be business to be done and friends to catch up with. But two days out into the Atlantic, all that changed. On 31 July the British government published a report by the Committee on National Expenditure, under the chairmanship of Sir George May, recommending extensive public sector cuts and increased taxation as a response to the economic depression which had culminated in a run on the Bank of England's gold reserves. At first, the government's response was leisurely, not least because the Prime Minister, Ramsay MacDonald, was on holiday. The holiday was soon interrupted by urgent messages from the Bank that sterling was under renewed and heavy pressure to the point where the reserves were dwindling near to danger levels. Once assembled, from 20 August to 24 August the Cabinet argued about what to do but ended irreconcilably split. Finally, at their meeting of 24 August, the acting Liberal leader, Herbert Samuel, suggested a National Government headed by MacDonald. Baldwin and the Conservative colleagues quickly agreed.

It was the first major British political crisis that Beaverbrook had missed since his arrival in London in 1910. There was no doubt in his mind about what he should do. He had to return without delay. Passages for his party were immediately booked on the first available liner out of New York, the Norddeutsche Lloyd *Europa*. As it happened, it was quite a relief to head back, as his holiday had been far from pleasant. For instance, he had visited, as was customary, his first home town of Newcastle, New Brunswick. There, far from being welcomed, he found that he was pursued by men who had known him when he was a boy, or who had been at school with him, begging for help in their distress. Unable to go into the town, he had stayed in a private railway car in a siding eight kilometres out. But it was not just in Newcastle. The scene was repeated wherever he went. The summer visit was turning into a nightmare.

Lord Beaverbrook during a return trip from Canada, on board the Europa, *1931.*

To make matters worse, during the return crossing Beaverbrook suffered a painful attack of shingles. It was enough, and more than enough, to put him in a bad temper. Baldwin was a fool, he told anybody who would listen. He should have told the King that he would form a government, declare that he would shore up the national finances by calling a general election on tariffs and 'he would have come back with 350–400 Conservatives'.[14] Back in London at the end of August, and only partially recovered in health, he immediately mobilised the *Express* heavy artillery. Convinced that the National Government could not survive for long, his tactic was to set the tone for a general election by a series of journalistic broadsides. The rallying cry, however, was familiar: there must be a 'wide-flung tariff wall round the Empire. It would mean the greatest area of Free Trade you can obtain in this wicked world of tariffs. Therefore give up all this truck with Europe. Turn your hearts and minds to the Empire.'[15] The (by then somewhat ragged) army of Empire Crusaders was summoned to the colours. 'One more struggle and the victory is ours ... Everyone is clamouring for tariffs.'[16] Brushing aside Baldwin's leadership claims, he even went so far as to trumpet Ramsay MacDonald as the 'man of destiny ... He has won the complete confidence of the nation ... The Conservative Party will follow him loyally once he declares for home and Imperial tariffs.'[17]

Beaverbrook was right in believing that the National Government was unstable. After a fierce Budget and the abandonment of the gold standard on 24 September 1931, the Conservatives demanded, and were granted, a general election. That was all very well, except for the fact that the electorate was left wholly unclear about what it was supposed to vote for or against. On the one hand, all parties agreed to campaign for what became known as a 'Doctor's Mandate', a vague commitment to consider all remedies for the current economic malaise. On the other hand, each party was free to campaign for its own manifesto. On this uncertain note the electorate was invited to pronounce on 27 October.

'Now is the hour of trial, the test of strength, the time of decision.'[18] So ran the first of the *Express* rallying calls. Others in a similar vein followed almost daily. Needless to say, the theme of all of them, repeated over and over again, was the absolute necessity for Empire free trade as the only viable policy for success. Yet in spite of the ever-increasing volume of his efforts, Beaverbrook was unable to convince the Conservatives of the merits of his case for food taxes. The best Baldwin could do was to 'continue to press upon the electors that in my view the [general] tariff is the ... most effective weapon ... to reduce excessive imports' and to assert that there should be 'assistance to cereal farmers ... by means of a quota and guaranteed price for wheat'.[19] It was far distant from Beaverbrook's requirements but just enough to ensure the support of his newspapers in the campaign (which, it need hardly be said, was Baldwin's sole objective).

In fact, the result was never in doubt. It was only the size of the National Government's majority which was uncertain. As it turned out, it was crushing. Labour was routed, and the independent Liberals reduced to a rump. Nevertheless, celebrations in the *Express* camp were muted. Any analysis of the new House of Commons (and Beaverbrook was quick to make his own) would show that although there were enough new members who supported Empire tariffs, the Conservative leadership was divided and a backbench revolt was unlikely to succeed. By December, Beaverbrook was losing heart. As always, Baldwin was singled out as the leader of the procrastinators. 'I do not know at this moment', Beaverbrook wrote mournfully to a friend, 'where he [Baldwin] stands on agricultural protection.'[20]

All now depended on the Imperial Conference to be held in Ottawa in July and August 1932. Beaverbrook had hoped to be summoned by R. B. Bennett, to be his adviser, but he had overestimated Bennett's enthusiasm for Empire free trade and underestimated Bennett's political sense. The call, wisely, was never made. It was not just the potentially ominous effect of Beaverbrook's presence on the conference. The whole thing was made impossible once it became known that the British delegation would be led by none other than Stanley Baldwin.

'We had forgotten', Beaverbrook later wrote, 'the cunning of Stanley Baldwin.'[21] Admittedly, the conference affirmed the principle of imperial preference, broadly defined as 'home producers first, empire producers second, foreign producers last', but this was far distant from Empire economic unity and had only served as a framework for a series of bilateral agreements which had excluded anything remotely resembling food taxes. Baldwin had marshalled the British delegation in stubborn resistance and, apart from a concession on quotas for wheat imports, that had been the end of the matter.

The truth was, as Beaverbrook reluctantly acknowledged, that in the prevailing economic climate there was little popular interest in the Empire, let alone in the arcane arithmetic of international trade in foodstuffs. When Beaverbrook put up a candidate on a platform of meat taxes and, bizarrely, Scottish nationalism, in the East Fife by-election in February 1933, he found himself frequently arriving at a village hall to speak only to discover it empty and in darkness. The remaining supporters of the Empire Crusade, too, were drifting away. Empire economic unity had finally been consigned to the dustbin of lost causes.

None of this meant that Beaverbrook had lost his appetite for political campaigning. He had, however, lost his taste for party politics and for politicians, who, as he wrote to his friend Arthur Brisbane, 'have no compassion, no pity, no consideration for each other'.[22] Since the National Government was proving unable to resolve its divisions on economic policy between those, led by Neville Chamberlain, who argued for lower public expenditure and lower taxes, and those, led by Labour ministers in the government, who argued for the opposite, Beaverbrook felt free to strike out on his own. The answer to the nation's problems, he and his newspapers proclaimed, was 'higher wages'.

It was not just a matter of higher wages, although that was the catching headline. It was no less than an ambitious programme of public works, such as 'reclamation of land and re-equipment of the railways';[23] 'a million new houses, new docks, improved port facilities and railway electrification'.[24] All in all, 'My plan for prosperity', as he called it,

> is a dual one ... 1. I want to bring to an end any further movements in the direction of wage reductions ... 2. I want to put more money into the pockets of the spending classes in the interest of trade and industry. More purchasing power will benefit us all.[25]

The plan was much in line with ideas put forward by radical economists in the United States and Britain and, like them, was systematically derided by the majority, including, surprisingly, the trade unions. Yet although the campaign, such as it was, never caught fire, it did attract some of the younger spirits on the political left. Jennie Lee, Aneurin Bevan, Frank Owen, Tom Driberg, Michael Foot, all were drawn into his net, all of them, in this unlikely alliance, sharing Beaverbrook's instinctive dislike of the English upper class. There was ample opportunity for them to poke fun at Cabinet ministers in the columns of the *Express* or the *Evening Standard* (Beaverbrook finally bought out the Daily Mail Trust's shareholding in May 1933) and nobody enjoyed their sallies more that the proprietor.

Of all these young socialists, Bevan was Beaverbrook's favoured conversationalist of the day. Never happier than when he was proclaiming, in his squeaky Welsh voice, the evils of capitalism, he was the perfect foil to Beaverbrook's other favourite, the wayward, red-haired and unfailingly charming Irish MP for North Paddington, Brendan Bracken. Although nominally a Conservative, Bracken shared with the others their dislike of the English upper class. He could also match Bevan in repartee. Of course, much champagne was drunk at their regular dinners, Beaverbrook holding the ring in the fast-moving verbal bouts (Bracken used to call Bevan a 'Bollinger Bolshevik'). It was all good fun.

In fact, in the period between 1932 and 1935 Beaverbrook lost much of his interest in serious domestic politics. He was gloomy about the current leadership. 'MacDonald does not count a great deal,' he wrote to his former headmaster in Canada, Philip Cox, at the end of 1933. 'Baldwin pretends to be stupid ... Lloyd George does not have any following in the country ... Winston Churchill is now almost out of public life.'[26] Even the commercial success of his newspapers, particularly the *Express* under the new, thirty-year-old editor from Liverpool, Arthur Christiansen, was no more than what he would have expected, and the usual forays abroad, to the casinos of Le Touquet or Deauville, or even further afield, were no more than amusing diversions.

As it happened, the vacuum, such as it was, was soon filled. During 1932 and early 1933 in Germany the political scenery had started to shift. By a series of manoeuvres, including the use of street riots, bribery, corruption and brazen threats, the National Socialist (Nazi) Party had forced the weak Weimar presidency to accept Adolf Hitler as Chancellor. Hitler immediately called a general election for a new Reichstag on 5 March 1933. The ensuing campaign was both violent and fraudulent and culminated in the torching of the Reichstag building on 27 February, allowing Hitler to blame the Communists and immediately arrest 4,000 of them before dawn the following day. Even so, in spite of all their efforts, the Nazis did no more than achieve a simple majority in the new Reichstag. Undeterred, they bullied the cowed Centre Party delegates to assent on 23 March to the Enabling Act, which gave Hitler all-embracing dictatorial powers.

The reaction in London was muted. Many were relieved that a strong hand was taking control of a palpably failed regime. Some thought that the provisions of the Versailles agreement, concluded at the end of the war, were, in spite of the modifications which had been subsequently agreed, still too harsh. Finally, for those who wished to turn a blind eye, there was comfort in the international arrangements which had been made in the previous decade to prevent future wars: the League of Nations, the Locarno Treaties of 1925 and the so-called Kellogg–Briand Pact of 1928. Baldwin, for instance, went out of his way to reaffirm the Locarno principles of border guarantees in his speech to the Conservative Party conference in early October 1933.

Beaverbrook felt differently. For a start, he was opposed to any

British military involvement on the European continent. In June he had announced the policy of isolationism. 'By that policy,' he had explained, 'we mean the development of the British Empire as a self-sufficient ... unity ... relying for defence on its own strength and for peace on its freedom from external entanglements ... The League of Nations is, I consider, the enemy of Isolationist policy.'[27] Then, in response to Baldwin, he told his readers that 'we must get out of this terrible incubus of Locarno if we are going to save ourselves and our children from a catastrophe in Europe'.[28]

At first, Beaverbrook was sympathetic to Hitler's new government. He had, after all, regularly visited Germany and had maintained contacts there. In fact, Germany's declared intention to leave the League of Nations, taken together with a pacifist Labour candidate's defeat of the National Government candidate in a by-election in Fulham East in October, lent support to his policy. However, the brutal murders of Hitler's rival Ernst Röhm and many of his followers during the Night of the Long Knives in the summer of 1934, combined with the hysterical theatre of the Nuremberg Rally held that September (later immortalised in Leni Riefenstahl's *Triumph des Willens*), gave him and others pause. Lockhart recorded that once Röhm's fate had become known, Beaverbrook 'now turned solidly, fanatically, anti-Hitler' and began to compare the German leader to Al Capone and to refer to the Nazis as 'gangsters'.[29] He was also quick to deny that he had any love for Fascism. 'The Fascists attack Parliament ... I am a Parliament man. An alliance with Fascism would be an unholy alliance.'[30] In passing, he noted that the Röhm massacres finished Oswald Mosley and his movement as a serious political force.

Whatever Beaverbrook thought of Hitler, nothing stopped the flow of rhetoric coming out of the *Express* newspapers throughout 1934 and into 1935. When supporters of the League of Nations launched a massive 'Peace Ballot' to test support for the League and collective security, dubbed by the *Express* as the 'Ballot of Blood', Beaverbrook stepped up his campaign, even volunteering a broadcast appeal to voters to tear up their ballot paper. Not even a winter trip to South America with Jean and Diana Cooper, intended as a leisurely search for winter sun, reduced the quantity or the volume of his attacks.

The problem was that nobody was really listening. The result of the Peace Ballot was a decisive vote in favour of the League. Undeterred, Beaverbrook announced his own ballot of professional men, clergymen, solicitors and doctors. (As it turned out, the result mirrored that of the Peace Ballot.) Nevertheless, it was time for him to get to know rather more about the politics, as opposed to the scenery or the facilities for diversion, of the countries he had been writing about. Conveniently for the purpose, he had discovered the aeroplane as a way to shorten continental visits. By chartering privately, he could fly, with the usual accompaniment of secretary and valet, to any Western European capital and be back in London within two days. Admittedly, he was not a good flyer. Apart from recurrent air sickness and breath shortage, both of which were normal in the bumpy flights of those days, he was, not to put too fine a point on it, frightened. (His staff were often dismayed to hear him singing the twenty-third Psalm in a loud voice during take-off or landing.)

Of course, however brief in terms of time spent, there was no point in going without careful preparation in advance. Beaverbrook had not much cared for the formalities of diplomacy, or for the company of diplomats, but that was soon remedied. Even the grandees of the Foreign Office were keen to open its doors to the proprietor of influential national newspapers and it was not long before an invitation to dinner was extended by the grandest of them all, Sir Robert Vansittart, the Permanent Under Secretary. The occasion bore fruit when Vansittart introduced him to Count Dino Grandi, the Italian Ambassador. Beaverbrook soon found out that Grandi shared his view about the League of Nations. It was not far from there, and a liberal dose of the Beaverbrook charm, to an invitation to visit Rome and meet the Italian dictator Benito Mussolini.

As it happened, Vansittart was not the only source of ambassadorial introductions. Beaverbrook's young socialist friends had been trumpeting the supposed virtues of the Soviet system. In fact, it had been one of the continuing themes of the raucous but friendly disputes between Bevan and Bracken. In listening to them, Beaverbrook's curiosity was aroused, and he soon invited Bevan to introduce him to the relatively new, and undoubtedly charming, Soviet Ambassador, Ivan Maisky.

Ivan Mikhailovich Maisky had been appointed Soviet Ambassador to Britain in October 1932. The appointment, in truth, had come as a surprise both to him and to those who were familiar with the workings of the Kremlin. A product of imperial St Petersburg, he had joined the Social Democrats when at university, had been exiled to Siberia and then, partially reprieved, had travelled to Western Europe, settling in London in 1912. Back in Russia at the time of the October Revolution he had wavered in his allegiance, finally settling with the Bolsheviks in 1922 and joining the diplomatic service. There followed a series of appointments, culminating in 1929 with the Soviet Embassy in Helsinki.

Russian diplomat Maxim Litvinov (left), with Ivan Mikhailovich Maisky (right), the Soviet Ambassador to Britain, accompanied by a government official, c. 1935.

By the time he arrived in London, Maisky spoke good English and had assembled a group of friends from the political left wing. His brief from his superior in Moscow, Maxim Litvinov, had been clear: 'Develop as many contacts as possible, in all strata and circles! Be *au fait* with everything that happens in England and keep us informed.' Using his considerable charm and waspish sense of humour, Maisky followed the instruction, and, as he himself put it, not without success.[31] But it was not altogether straightforward. By the middle of 1934, the Soviets had changed the emphasis of their diplomacy. Until then, the objective had been to cultivate left-wing sympathisers in the West who would be helpful in promoting revolution when the time came. With the resurgence of a militaristic Germany, priorities changed. The objective now was to cultivate opponents of Nazism. For this purpose, Maisky found Beaverbrook a useful contact. Not only did the *Daily Express* write complimentary pieces about Stalin (rewarded by a regular supply of Russian vodka) but Beaverbrook himself introduced Maisky to those senior Conservatives who were still in favour. This included Churchill, of whom he wrote that 'he was without a rival in British politics ... I know all about his prejudices. But a man of character who tells the truth is worth much to the nation.' The commendation bore fruit, as Churchill told Maisky that 'in view of the rise of Nazism ... which threatened to reduce England "to a toy in the hands of German imperialism" ... he was abandoning his protracted struggle against the Soviet Union'.[32]

Beaverbrook's new friendship with Ambassador Grandi was perhaps of less moment but at least it secured his interview with Mussolini. After brief sweeps in his private plane (now conveniently parked at Cherkley) first to the south of France and then, by way of holiday, to Spain, he was received in July at the dictator's summer quarters. The meeting, it appears, was jovial, Mussolini reminding Beaverbrook that he had started his career as a journalist and showing unsuspected interest in newspaper management. But nothing of substance was said, and Beaverbrook did not even bother to record it.

In truth, his meeting with Mussolini was pointless. But that pointlessness was no more than a reflection of the whole pattern of Beaverbrook's life in the early years of the 1930s. His undoubted energy, and occasional brilliance, had been spent on fruitless campaigns, such as the Empire Crusade or higher wages, or in pursuing vendettas against cleverer politicians such as Stanley Baldwin. When these failed, he was no longer anywhere near the centre of gravity of British, or international, politics. Moreover, although he spent time dictating newspaper articles, writing letters and scribbling notes, serious writing came to an end with the publication of the second volume of *Politicians and the War* in 1932. Lastly, although Beaverbrook was loath to admit it, the radio was challenging the printed word for the dissemination of news. The press barons, so powerful in the 1920s, were losing their stranglehold on public opinion.

To be sure, it was not such a bad time to be on the periphery of politics. As Churchill wrote to his wife in March 1935,

> The Government stock is very low. They are like a great iceberg which has drifted into warm seas and whose base is being swiftly melted away, so that it must topple over. They are a really bad government in spite of their able members. The reason is there is no head and commanding mind ranging over the whole field of public affairs ... The wretched Ramsay [MacDonald] is almost a mental case – 'he'd be far better off in a Home'. Baldwin is crafty, patient and also amazingly lazy, sterile and inefficient where public business is concerned. Almost wherever they put their foot they blunder.[33]

Yet by the middle of 1935 the political climate was starting to change, and not for the better. Hitler was becoming ever more strident with the reintroduction of compulsory military service, Mussolini was dreaming of a new Roman Empire in Africa, King George V's health was failing, the National Government was looking as tired and ill as Prime Minister MacDonald himself, and Churchill had caught out Baldwin in his underestimate of German air strength. It was not to be long before the iceberg toppled over into a general election. It was time for Beaverbrook to re-engage with the tangled world of British domestic politics.

CHAPTER 18

'GOD SAVE OUR KING FROM BALDWIN'

'Our cock won't fight'[1]

He was not going to stay on the margin of British politics for ever. There was too much of interest, too much fun to be had and, if the truth be told, from time to time too much mischief to be made. As it happened, events, as always, played their part. In June 1935, Ramsay MacDonald finally gave way to Baldwin as Prime Minister, and in the ensuing government reconstruction Beaverbrook's old friend Sir Samuel Hoare had become Foreign Secretary. Hoare had spent much energy at the India Office piloting the India Independence Bill through the House of Commons, and the Foreign Office was his reward. With Baldwin now firmly, if regrettably, in charge, and with his reliable friend at the Foreign Office, it seemed a good moment for Beaverbrook to re-enter the arena.

In some ways, Hoare is one of the sadder figures of twentieth-century British politics. With a fine mind educated at Harrow and Oxford, where he took a double first, he had the further advantages of a background of banking wealth, of inheriting a baronetcy at the age of twenty-five and of marrying Lady Maud Lygon, the youngest daughter of the 6th Earl Beauchamp. Thus armed, he had moved almost effortlessly up the ranks of Conservative politics, first as Member of Parliament for Chelsea and then, after the First World War, as a minister in all the Conservative and National governments from 1921 to 1940. There were, of course, disadvantages. Physically, he was small and unattractive, with a head too large for his body, eyes which had a tendency to bulge and lips too thin for uninhibited laughter. Moreover, his colleagues did not much care for him. R. A. Butler, who served as his junior minister on the India Bill, later wrote of him that 'I was amazed by his ambition; I admired his imagination; I shared his ideals; I stood in awe of his intellectual capacity; but I was never touched by his humanity. He was the coldest fish with whom I ever had to deal.'² Birkenhead, typically more colourful, was heard to remark that Hoare was 'descended from a long line of maiden aunts'.³

British Foreign Secretary Sir Samuel Hoare (left) and Prime Minister Stanley Baldwin (right), December 1935.

Yet Hoare was one of the few among the English upper class that Beaverbrook could call a real friend. Hoare had supported, albeit from something of a distance, Beaverbrook's Empire Crusade. Beaverbrook, in turn, had supported Hoare when he was short of funds and, more generously, had supported Lady Maud's economic extravaganzas. When Hoare became Foreign Secretary, Beaverbrook wrote him a letter of congratulation which was more than usually effusive. Little did either of them suspect that Hoare's tenure would last only a few months and would founder, as would his political reputation to posterity, on the rock of a small and hitherto barely noticed African country.

On 3 October, Italian troops invaded Abyssinia (as the Kingdom of Ethiopia was then called beyond its own borders). Almost immediately after Hoare's appointment in June, Mussolini had made demands for territorial concessions as part of his programme to restore, after a lapse of centuries, imperial Rome's domination of North Africa. Here was an issue on which Beaverbrook could find again his political voice. In truth it was the same voice that Bonar Law had employed over the Chanak crisis. 'We Cannot, We Will Not, We Must Not Police the World Alone' and 'Let Us Seek Peace' was the message from the *Daily Express*.[4] That was all very well. But a plan concocted by a junior minister for League of Nations affairs, Anthony Eden, designed precisely to seek peace but, fatally, by offering territorial concessions to Mussolini, was deemed 'A Monstrous and Shameful Transaction'.[5] When Eden's plan was rejected by Mussolini, the way was open for Baldwin, on 25 October, to call a general election, using as a platform not only a call for continued domestic stability but also the persuasive formula for the Abyssinian crisis: 'all sanctions short of war'.

'I am not going on a platform,' Beaverbrook wrote to a friend in early November:

I am not in sympathy with the National Government. I hate the elements in it, drafted from the Socialists and the Liberals. I am against the policy of 'collective security' and the League of Nations. I am entirely in favour of Isolation. I am opposed to the Government's fiscal policy. I want Empire Free Trade and cannot get it. I can only get bits of it – just enough to swindle me out of the promises they made me in 1931.[6]

The *Daily Express* invited voters to ask their candidates where they stood on isolationism and vote accordingly. Furthermore, 'ask your candidate, then, if he will favour withdrawal of Britain from her European commitments and denunciation of all our obligations to go to war on that continent'.[7]

It was all to no avail. On 14 November, Baldwin's National Government was returned with a decisive (if reduced) overall Commons majority of 242. Beaverbrook bemoaned the result but claimed that 'we have not finished with Isolationism … The international situation must now get steadily worse … and as the sky darkens the hopes of Isolationists must rise.'[8] He had a point. The Abyssinian crisis was no nearer resolution. In fact, the League of Nations, in some desperation, authorised Britain and France to devise an acceptable compromise between Italian claims for territorial expansion in Africa and the dignity of the Abyssinian kingdom.

The baton then passed to Hoare and his Permanent Secretary, Sir Robert Vansittart, one of the authors of the earlier Eden plan. Hoare arranged an immediate visit to Paris for discussions with his French counterpart, Pierre Laval. Vansittart also travelled to Paris, but on a different train and accompanied by none other than Lord Beaverbrook. On 7 December, while Hoare and Vansittart were in meetings with Laval, Beaverbrook had dinner with a long-standing acquaintance, Jean Prouvost, the owner of the newspaper *Paris-Soir*. The following day the Hoare–Laval Pact was agreed. The proposal was to allow Abyssinia access to the sea through a corridor in British Somaliland while conceding to Italy some of the territory she had occupied, but, more important, in addition Italy was to have a monopoly on economic development, under League of Nations supervision, of a large zone in the east and south-east of Abyssinia. That done, Hoare and Vansittart left for London to prepare a paper for the British Cabinet. On 9 December, the Cabinet met and approved Hoare's paper with two minor amendments. Much relieved, Hoare then left for a holiday in Switzerland.

Almost everything then went wrong. The leaks started in Paris, notably with *Paris-Soir*. By the time news of the proposals reached the British press, the Emperor of Ethiopia, a small figure but with a fearsome black beard, had already been hailed as the Lion of Judah, whose lineage, so it was claimed, could be traced directly to King Solomon and the Queen of Sheba. Ras Tafari, or Haile Selassie as he was known (among his many names), was the hero of the hour. Ignoring his otherwise dubious reputation, the British public adopted him as their perennially favourite character: the little man fighting heroically against the big bully.

It was no contest. Baldwin realised quickly that he would have to go into reverse. Hoare was immediately summoned to return without delay. The order fell on ears which were deaf following a nasty skating fall resulting in multiple bruises and a broken nose. Encouraged by Beaverbrook, who promised (perhaps rather cheerlessly) 'to stand unswervingly in support of you in this crisis'[9] and who volunteered to help him write his Commons speech, Hoare, broken nose and all, returned determined to fight his corner. As it happened, the speech, when made, was well received. Nevertheless, at a Cabinet meeting on 18 December Lord Halifax, the Lord Privy Seal, urged that Hoare should resign in order to 'protect the whole moral position of the Government before the world', fearing that if 'the Prime Minister were to lose his personal position, one of our national anchors would have dragged'.[10] Amid much muttering, the Cabinet agreed.

Neville Chamberlain was deputed to deliver the Cabinet's verdict. That done, the following day Hoare delivered his resignation speech to the House of Commons. The *Daily Express* of 20 December lavishly reported the event. Hoare had 'triumphed in defeat by talking such stark common sense with such courage conquering ill health that the great ovation he received meant plainer than words "Why is he out and the Government in?"' Baldwin's solemn tribute, by contrast, 'cringed to an expectant House ... Mr Baldwin must go ... The rest of the Cabinet who are tarred with the same brush should follow him.'[11] Baldwin, in an attempt to make it up, wrote to Hoare promising him an early return to government. Hoare showed the letter to Beaverbrook but, in doing so, suggested somewhat ungraciously that even though they were both to spend their Christmas in Switzerland it would be better if they did not meet, to avoid any publicity. Beaverbrook readily agreed (no doubt also because Hoare was not the most entertaining lunchtime companion).

All in all, it was a shabby affair. The only person who came out of it at all well was Beaverbrook, not because he approved of the policy but because he again showed one of his most attractive traits of steady loyalty to a friend in difficulties. The policy, as he saw with clarity as well, would never have worked. Neither Mussolini nor Haile Selassie could possibly have accepted it. The result was that on 7 May 1936 Italy officially annexed Abyssinia/Ethiopia and on 1 June Mussolini proclaimed the creation of Italian East Africa, merging Ethiopia with Eritrea and Italian Somaliland. As Beaverbrook recorded, Baldwin had presented two victims for sacrifice in order to preserve his premiership: 'The Emperor of Abyssinia sacrificed by Baldwin to the Italians' and Sir Samuel Hoare 'sacrificed by Baldwin to the anti-Italians'.[12]

On 20 January 1936, King George V died. Beaverbrook, like other Privy Counsellors, was summoned to the Accession Council, called, as tradition had it, immediately after the death of a Sovereign to swear allegiance to his or her successor. The dress code was formal: levée (formal court) dress for civilians and full dress for the military with, for both, a black crepe armband. Beaverbrook unsurprisingly found difficulty in getting into his outfit, which dated back to his initial swearing to the Privy Council in 1916. As he later wrote, 'It was not my habit to attend official functions ... but on this occasion I was eager to pay homage to King Edward. A new reign, with a young and independent-minded sovereign, excited my imagination.'[13] That may be so, but there were two further matters to be thought about. First, Beaverbrook's sustained political position was always to be in support, in whatever context, of the British Empire. The English Crown was the root of the imperial tree. The Privy Council oath is a direct assertion of loyalty, not just to the institution, but to the Sovereign in person. Beaverbrook, whatever his later doubts about the King, was bound to respond to a royal request.

But there was another reason, more mundane, for Beaverbrook to show interest in the new King. As Prince of Wales, Edward had attracted a large popular following. Good-looking, charming, seemingly intensely interested in other people's lives, he had come to the throne buoyed by widespread and enthusiastic support, particularly of those who had fought in the war. Few outside a limited circle, however, were aware that he had a darker *alter ego*. As one historian puts it:

[Edward] was by any standards a monster of egocentricity and breathtakingly stubborn … He moved from one dominating enthusiasm to another, pursuing them with blind and total devotion while they lasted. These included, variously, horse riding, golf, gardening, drink, casual sex and, finally, something that would change his life for ever: an unreasoning obsession with one woman.[14]

Beaverbrook was the proprietor of the largest-selling daily newspaper, by then with a circulation of nearly 2.5 million. He was aware of both sides of the King's career as Prince of Wales. He was also aware that the *Express* would have to tread with the greatest caution. Nothing could destroy a tabloid newspaper quicker than finding itself on the wrong side of the Sovereign without proper cause.

In fact, the first months of the new reign were dominated by the worsening international situation. No sooner had Abyssinia shown the Locarno Treaties to be little more than waste paper than the paper itself was shredded by the German remilitarisation of the Rhineland on 7 March. It was a clear case under Locarno: the signatories to the treaty had an obligation to intervene in force to send the German Army back home. Yet the event, with all its pointers to the future, was brushed off by Eden, who had succeeded Hoare as Foreign Secretary, and by Beaverbrook himself. 'No war', he wrote, 'and no sanctions against Germany.'[15] Eden then suggested a new League of Nations mandate to replace Locarno. This was too much for Beaverbrook. 'The bond to fight for France which we gave at Locarno was bad,' he declared, 'but the new bond would be worse.'[16] The volume was turned up when the British and French governments reached an agreement which appeared to suggest that Britain might find itself compelled to resist a German act of aggression against any of the nations inside what became known as the *cordon sanitaire*. 'If we make this alliance we must fight to maintain Czechoslovakia … We must fight for Poland … If we make this alliance we commit ourselves to a war.'[17]

During March, Beaverbrook suffered his first really serious attack of asthma. He had had episodes of breathlessness before, like others in his family, which had been built up in his chronic worry about his health into alarms, but there had never been anything of such magnitude. 'I am at present suffering', he wrote to a friend, 'from an attack of bronchial asthma. I have never had it in my life before. And it is as difficult to get rid of as the Treaty of Locarno.'[18] In fact, Locarno had already died, as Eden had recognised. Hitler had abrogated the treaty on the grounds that it had been violated by the Franco-Soviet defence pact of 27 February and, failing any reaction from other parties, was therefore null. It was his justification for moving his troops into the Rhineland and, much to the enthusiasm of the Rhinelanders, after a referendum, whose result was never in doubt, to incorporate the territory into the Reich. Under the circumstances it is hardly surprising that neither in France nor in Britain was there any stomach for a fight. But it did not stop there. Ambassador Maisky noted that

> the Sunday Press is appalling. In the Observer, Garvin chides Hitler mildly for his bad manners, then insists on the need to pay due attention to 'the Führer's brilliant and timely proposals' and 'to do so in a spirit of sympathy and good will' … I haven't met with any influential people about this (the 'weekend!'), but I sense a new and very dangerous turn towards Germanophilia in British policy.[19]

Germanophilia seemed even to have spread to Cherkley. It so happened that the latest visitor there was none other than the former champagne salesman of Montreal and friend of the Duchess of Connaught, Joachim von Ribbentrop. Ribbentrop had come a long way since then. As one of the few Nazis with knowledge of the world outside Germany, let alone his connection with the British royal family, he had been one of the senior figures to be used by Hitler to cultivate and then influence 'the broadest possible range of British public opinion in a pro-German direction'.[20] He had set up his own organisation, financed by Berlin, to develop a network of British and French connections who might be induced to support Hitler's Germany. If the truth be told, he was astonishingly successful. Together with Carl Eduard, Queen Victoria's grandson and Duke of Saxe-Coburg and Gotha, who spearheaded the attack on the English aristocracy from the Prince of Wales downwards, he had even by the middle of

1936 assembled a group of sympathisers. One of the most influential of these, given his ownership of the *Daily Mail*, was Lord Rothermere. It was only natural that, sooner or later, Ribbentrop would contrive to land on the doorstep of Rothermere's fellow press baron Lord Beaverbrook.

Joachim von Ribbentrop, German Ambassador in Britain and later German Foreign Minister, featured in The Bystander *magazine and described as having a 'clever, humorous face', 1935.*

On 4 June 1936, Ribbentrop and his wife dined at Cherkley. The evening passed quietly, not least because Beaverbrook was worried about asthma attacks and because Ribbentrop took pains not to reveal the real import of his mission. Ribbentrop then wrote his letter of thanks, referring to 'the little party at your charming country house', which, he went on, presented a view from the terrace 'over the woods and valleys, which I shall not forget'.[21] What was not forgotten, of course, was Ribbentrop's next move: an invitation to the Berlin Olympic Games in August. Beaverbrook immediately saw this as a possible family trip. In replying to Ribbentrop he proposed taking his daughter Janet and her husband Drogo Montagu as well as his son Max. A few days later he added Mike Wardell and Brendan Bracken. It was all grist to Ribbentrop's mill. 'Of course all your friends are welcome to me' was the response.[22] The party duly set off for Germany on 31 July.

Ribbentrop and Coburg had done their work well. The list of people who attended the opening ceremony on 1 August, as one German historian has described it, 'reads like an extract from *Burke's Peerage* combined with the *Almanach de Gotha*: Lord and Lady Aberdare, Lord Barnby, Lord Camrose, Lord Douglas Hamilton, Lord Hollenden, Lord Rennell Rodd, the Duke of Coburg, the Prince of Wied, the Hesse princes, the Duke of Braunschweig, the Hohenzollern-Sigmaringens'.[23]

Beaverbrook was not impressed. According to Janet he was in a sour mood and claimed that his room at the Hotel Adlon was bugged. In the event he only went to the opening ceremony before he told his party to pack up ready to catch the next train home.

Courtesy demanded an unctuous letter of thanks to Ribbentrop and this was duly sent. He was equally fulsome in his congratulations to Ribbentrop on his appointment as German Ambassador to the Court of St James. 'Never, never, never was any appointment to an Ambassadorial post in London as well received as your own,' he wrote on 12 August. 'You have praise from the press and from the people. You may save the peace of Europe, I truly believe, by your conduct here.'[24] His true feelings, however, were contained in a letter to Lloyd George, who had written favourably about an interview he had had with Hitler.

> I have been very interested in your German experience, and the viewpoints you brought back from that country. I went there too. But I hated so much the regimentation of opinion that I could not bear it. I was in Berlin at the opening of the Olympic Games. On that occasion privilege and class had a run the like of which has not existed in this country since the aristocracy began to marry chorus girls.

'However,' he added as an emollient to Lloyd George's enthusiasm, 'this is only my point of view. I do not present it to you as an argument. On subjects of this kind there is no use arguing. Men's opinions are bound to differ.'[25]

By the autumn of 1936, Beaverbrook was preparing for his winter abroad. In spite of the gruesome development of the Spanish Civil War he believed that the threat of an all-embracing European war had receded. Abyssinia had been sacrificed to Mussolini's ambition, Germany had absorbed the Rhineland without serious opposition and the League of Nations was falling to bits. 'The path is now clear,' he declared in the *Daily Express* of 6 November. 'Collective security has been smashed and broken. Locarno is at an end. All our engagements in Europe have come to nothing. And the commitments that involved us so deeply have passed away.' Earlier in the same article he had written about his own future.

> The British race will walk in the paths of peace. We will reject alliances and pacts with the quarrelling European races. We will walk these paths in Isolation ... But if we are to impose the policy of Isolation, we must have a standard-bearer ... I must plead for another and younger man to carry through the campaign for peace and Isolation ... The opportunity is big, very big. And the triumph is certain.[26]

On 14 November he sailed for New York aboard the *Bremen*, announcing, 'I am going away. I am going away for a long time ... back again to see once more the forests and rivers of that province of New Brunswick.'[27]

It did not quite work out like that. A few weeks before, on Tuesday 13 October, he had received a telephone call from Buckingham Palace. The King himself was on the line. He would be grateful if Beaverbrook would come to see him and mentioned that the subject for discussion was the divorce case of Mrs Wallis Simpson, due to be heard at Ipswich Assizes on the 27th. Beaverbrook had heard about it through the *Evening Standard*, whose editor had asked permission to publish the story. Initially, he had agreed, but thought it wise to consult Mrs Simpson's solicitor, Theodore Goddard. Goddard had asked for privacy for his client, but Beaverbrook found his request unconvincing and refused it.

*Twice-divorced Mrs Wallis Simpson, who became the Duchess of Windsor on her marriage
to Prince Edward, Duke of Windsor (ex-King Edward VIII), pictured in 1936.*

This in turn brought the intervention from the King. At their meeting
on 16 October, Beaverbrook, now fully briefed about the background
as far as anybody outside a small circle in the Palace and the Cabinet
could be, prepared to listen to what the King had to say. He knew that
Mrs Simpson was openly acknowledged as the King's mistress, that Mr
Ernest Simpson, her second husband after her first divorce, had obligingly provided the evidence of adultery necessary for the case to be
marked as uncontested. What he almost certainly did not know was
that Edward, in one of his high-octane phases, was, as Hoare reported
after a shooting party at Sandringham, 'contemplating a morganatic
marriage if the lady is free'.[28] Nor did the King refer at all to the possibility of marriage, morganatic or otherwise. He referred to the divorce
case and said that

> he wanted mention of the case to be kept out of the newspapers
> until the action was heard, when he hoped to secure from the press
> a limitation of the publicity … She was ill, unhappy, and distressed

by the fear of publicity. And, as the publicity was due to her association with him, he, for his part, felt that he should protect her.[29]

Beaverbrook was suitably impressed by the King's argument and
agreed to his request. His first port of call was Walter Monckton, the
Attorney General of the Duchy of Cornwall, who seemed at least to
be trusted by the King, and the King's solicitor, George Allen. The
programme was mapped out. Beaverbrook would see those proprietors with whom he had most influence: Esmond Harmsworth,
Lord Rothermere's son, who was now running the *Daily Mail*; Sir
Walter Layton, director of the *News Chronicle*; Alexander Ewing,
director of the principal Scottish newspapers; and James Henderson
and Lombard Murphy of the Irish newspapers north and south of
the border.

To be sure, it was not the most impressive list. The major broadsheets
were outside Beaverbrook's influence. Yet the fact that Beaverbrook
was masterminding the campaign for silence was enough to ensure
some sort of calm both in Britain and in Canada. When the event
finally took place, the Ipswich court was besieged by reporters but the
coverage on the following day was no more than a deadpan recital of
the facts. *The Times*, for instance, headlined its account 'Undefend-
ed Divorce Suit ... Case at Ipswich Assizes' and gave the petitioner's
name as 'Mrs Wallis Simpson ... of Beech House, Felixstowe'.[30] The
American press, on the other hand, was outside anybody's control.
The front pages were dominated by accounts of the event. The French
press was more muted; Jean Prouvost promised to let Beaverbrook
know before publication if he wanted to mention it again.

In the days after the event the King continued to pester Beaverbrook about the American press coverage. But the more he pestered
the more it seemed that it was not just about Mrs Simpson's divorce.
Marriage was not mentioned, only rumoured, and Beaverbrook had
no wish to be involved in anything more than dealing with the press.
Nevertheless, he accepted an invitation from Lord Brownlow, one of
the King's lords-in-waiting, for dinner on 5 November to meet the
King in person and Mrs Simpson herself. Apart from a fleeting acquaintance at a party given by Diana Cooper, it was the first time he

had met the lady. He had not been particularly impressed on the first occasion and was decidedly less so on the second.

> She appeared to me to be a simple woman. She was plainly dressed. She had a mole on her face which I believed to be unattractive. I did not like her hairdressing and thought that she shaved the back of her neck, which did not appeal to me at all. Her smile was too affable, and her conversation interspersed with protestations of ignorance and declarations of simplicity of character and outlook.[31]

At the end of dinner, the King took Beaverbrook away for a private talk, but it was little more than a series of complaints about the American press.

There was no further contact between the two before Beaverbrook's departure for New York on 14 November. In fact, King Edward spent the following weeks doing what he did best. There was a house party at his residence of Fort Belvedere in Windsor Great Park, an official reception at Buckingham Palace for the Polish Foreign Minister and the ceremony of wreath laying at the Cenotaph on Armistice Day. Later the same day he left to conduct a review of the Royal Navy's Home Fleet at Portland. The review, in the worst possible weather, turned out to be an outstanding success. Hoare, now First Lord of the Admiralty and the minister in attendance, could hardly contain his excitement. 'Here, indeed, was the Prince Charming', he later wrote, 'who could win the hearts of all sorts and conditions of men and women and send a thrill through great crowds.'[32]

The *Bremen* was only two days sailing into the Atlantic when the first cable from Walter Monckton arrived. The situation had changed. Monckton wanted to tell Beaverbrook, or somebody in his stead, all about it. It was the first of a series of telegrams, either from Monckton directly or routed through Beaverbrook's secretary, each more hysterical than the last, imploring him, on the King's behalf, to turn round and come straight back home 'to control the publicity likely to arise from a situation now developing. You alone could do it.'[33] When Beaverbrook enquired what it was all about, Monckton replied that 'Friend has now declared to authorities definite decision as soon as absolute coast is clear'.[34] It did not need a trained spy to decipher Monckton's juvenile code. The King had told Baldwin that he was determined to marry Mrs Simpson as soon as the divorce decree was absolute.

It was on 13 November, the day before Beaverbrook's departure, that what had been no more than a scandal had exploded into a constitutional crisis. The fuse had been lit by the King's much-disliked private secretary, Major Alexander Hardinge. In a pompous and ill-judged letter of that date Hardinge had told the King, on his return from Portland, that

> the silence of the British Press on the subject of Your Majesty's friendship with Mrs Simpson is not going to be maintained. It is probably only a matter of days before the outburst begins ... the effect will be calamitous ... There is one step [to avoid the situation] ... for Mrs Simpson to go abroad *without further delay* ... PS I am by way of going after dinner tonight to High Wycombe to shoot there tomorrow, but the Post Office will have my telephone number.[35]

The King, on receipt of the letter and in something near to nervous collapse, had immediately consulted Monckton, brushed aside his counsel of patience, and in a car journey back to Fort Belvedere after tea with his brother the Duke of Kent had poured out his whole heart to his mistress. The Duchess later recalled how he had taken her hand, 'with the calm of a man whose mind is made up', and told her: 'I'm going to send for Mr Baldwin to see me at the Palace tomorrow. I'm going to tell him that if the country won't approve our marrying, I'm ready to go,' whereupon she burst into tears.[36]

By the time Beaverbrook arrived in New York on 20 November and checked in at the Waldorf Astoria, he was more or less up to date. The King had seen Baldwin on the 16th and had told the Prime Minister of his decision. The King had then left for a long-planned visit to South Wales, where he had been greeted with almost overwhelming rapture. What Beaverbrook did not know, and what Monckton had not told him, was that Esmond Harmsworth had entertained his apparently dear friend Wallis Simpson to lunch at Claridge's on 19 November and had set out to her the opportunity offered by a morganatic marriage.

This, Harmsworth had explained, was an arrangement whereby neither the wife nor her children would share the dignities or the possessions of her husband in spite of being properly married in all other aspects. The result would be, Harmsworth argued, to allow the King to marry her without her becoming Queen, thus satisfying all parties. She in turn had been much taken with the idea and had promised to try to persuade the King of its merits.

In New York, Beaverbrook, under hourly pressure by telegrams from Monckton and George Allen, decided to catch the *Bremen* on its return trip. On arrival at Southampton on Thursday 26 November, he drove straight to Fort Belvedere for lunch, to be greeted by the King himself on the doorstep. During lunch the King brought Beaverbrook up to date. The previous day, he said, he had asked Baldwin for official ministerial advice on the suggestion of morganatic marriage. Beaverbrook, dismayed, urged the King to withdraw the request without delay since it conceded the initiative to Baldwin. Furthermore, he advised finding a sympathetic ally who could put his case to Cabinet and gauge the strength of opinion for and against him within Cabinet. The King agreed, and Beaverbrook hurried on to London to see Monckton, to call Churchill to suggest that they join forces in their efforts to save the Sovereign and, finally, to see Samuel Hoare at the Admiralty and ask him to take on the role of the King's spokesman in Cabinet. At their meeting, he argued that Hoare need not approve of the course of action which the monarch proposed to take, rather that 'he would simply be an advocate representing the King's point of view'.[37]

The rest of the evening was spent in Stornoway House on the telephone to potential supporters. His line was simple: given enough time, the King would get over his infatuation and all would return to normality. When he thought he had done enough for one day he went to bed. His slumbers, however, such as they were, were disturbed by yet another telephone call from the King wanting to know where Hoare stood. Beaverbrook replied that he was to see Hoare the following morning to find out. As the conversation continued it became obvious that the King was not going to withdraw the morganatic marriage proposal as it was clearly Mrs Simpson's favoured solution. At all events, the moment had passed, since Baldwin had called an emergency Cabinet meeting for the following morning to discuss the proposal.

The Cabinet duly met at 11.30 a.m. on the Friday. There was little discussion. Baldwin gave a full account of the story to date, after which all present seemed to agree that a morganatic marriage was out of the question. Hoare said nothing. Only Duff Cooper spoke up for the King, not because he supported the proposal but to urge 'the desirability of gaining time'.[38] The Cabinet, however, did decide that there was an obligation under the Statute of Westminster 1931 to seek the opinions of Dominion Prime Ministers on the matter, including the possibility of legislation to give effect to a morganatic marriage.

Baldwin knew perfectly well that the response of the Dominions would be uniformly unfavourable. So, for that matter, did Beaverbrook. When he heard of the Dominion involvement at lunch with Hoare, during which Hoare also told him of his refusal to act for the King in Cabinet, Beaverbrook asked for an immediate audience at the Palace. This granted, he arrived later that afternoon in a state of unusual agitation. 'Sir, you have put your head on the execution block,' he exclaimed. 'All Baldwin has to do now is to wield the axe.'[39] In some desperation, he did his best to persuade the King to send his own messages to the Dominions. But the King's response was at best lukewarm and it seems that nothing was done. This is hardly surprising, since the King was at that moment worrying about Wallis Simpson's safety and preparing to whisk her out of London to the relative calm of Fort Belvedere.

On Sunday 29 November, Hoare dined yet again at Stornoway House. According to Beaverbrook's account, his guest brought two further pieces of news. First, there was no doubt that 'the Cabinet was unanimous, that there would be no breach in the front and that there was no light or leaning in the direction of the King'. Secondly, 'most momentous of all, he told me that publicity was about to break forth'.[40] The following evening Beaverbrook had his third and, as it turned out, final face-to-face interview with the King. He passed on Hoare's news and argued at great length that the King should withdraw completely his request for ministerial advice. The King was unmoved until, obviously tired, he appeared to acquiesce, although precisely what he agreed on remains uncertain. Beaverbrook thought that his plan had been accepted. Yet in the event, much as usual, nothing happened. Beaverbrook then went on to warn that the publicity could no longer be contained, that Hoare had conveyed to him Baldwin's hope that the press would be united in support of the government and that he had sent back a message to Baldwin that he was 'a King's man'.

Recognising his failure so far to influence the King, Beaverbrook devised a new strategy. On the evening of the Monday he invited to dinner at Stornoway House a group of those whom he felt to be personally closest to Edward: Monckton, Allen, Harmsworth and Brownlow. News of the dinner was leaked by Brownlow and was recorded the following day.

> They were all in agreement that the marriage cannot be allowed to take place, and the only avenue of approach to the demented lovesick sovereign was Wallis Simpson herself. And they bullied Perry Brownlow into promising to see Wallis today, and warn her confidentially that the country will not accept the marriage, and that she must go away for a few weeks and allow the talk to simmer down, and put all thoughts of marriage out of the King's mind.[41]

Brownlow duly made an attempt but was told at Fort Belvedere that Mrs Simpson was unwell and could not see him.

On Wednesday 2 December, the long-predicted publicity storm started to break. The previous day the Bishop of Bradford, the aptly named Dr Blunt, had spoken to his annual diocesan conference about the Coronation oath and a King's need of God's grace. In doing so, he had almost casually gone on to hope that the Sovereign was aware of this need. 'Some of us wish that he gave more positive signs of his awareness.'[42] This was picked up by the *Yorkshire Post*, whose editor wrote a somewhat starchy leader fearing that 'the King may not yet have perceived how complete in our day must be that self-dedication of which Dr Blunt spoke if the Coronation is to bring a blessing to all the peoples of the Empire, and is not, on the contrary, to prove a stumbling block'.[43] He then sent his text to the Press Association for open circulation.

Beaverbrook picked it up immediately and straight away called the King. It was too late for more than cursory treatment in the nationals the following day, he said, but the King must expect the full blast on the Thursday. He followed up by recommending a full-blooded campaign in support. But the King refused to give his consent. 'Max', Edward later wrote, 'urged me forcefully to allow his newspapers to strike back vigorously. "Many others hold with me that there is nothing wrong in the King's marrying a woman who has divorced her husband…" But I could not see it that way.'[44] The King went on to say that he was to see Baldwin that evening and wanted Beaverbrook to be available afterwards.

At ten o'clock that evening Monckton arrived at Stornoway House to say that Baldwin had offered the King three alternatives: '1. Give up Mrs Simpson. 2. Marry in the face of advice to the contrary from his Ministers. 3. Abdicate.' Baldwin had recommended the first. If the King found it impossible, the second course was equally impossible if the King were to remain on the throne (after the resignation of his whole government). In that event there was nothing left but abdication. 'While we were still at Stornoway House the King came on by telephone and indicated clearly that he was proposing to abdicate and retire into private life. The conversation was very long and one-sided. I made no attempt to argue.'[45]

After his meeting with Baldwin, the King returned to Fort Belvedere to report to Wallis that he had finally decided to abdicate. Horrified, she asked him to stay his hand, told him that she had decided (independently, as it happened, of Beaverbrook and Brownlow) to leave him and go abroad. Furthermore, she urged him to set out his case in a radio broadcast to the nation. The King, with some reluctance on the former, accepted both her suggestions. He was sensible enough to realise that with hostile publicity would come the threat of violence and that she would be an obvious target.

As it happened, the morning press on the matter struck an uncertain note. Nobody knew quite what to say and readers were suitably mystified. It was the *Daily Mirror* which proved to be the exception. In its later editions it splashed a full-page portrait of Wallis and on the inside pages carried lurid accounts of her history and of the royal romance. By the evening, just as the King and Wallis were saying their sad goodbyes, every evening paper in the land was running the story. In the House of Commons, Clement Attlee had put down a Private Notice Question to the Prime Minister, which Churchill followed by demanding that Parliament be consulted before any irrevocable step was taken. In private, Churchill was 'completely on the rampage, saying that he was for the King and was not going to have him strangled in the dark by ministers and bumped off without a chance of saying a word to Parliament or the country in his own defence'.[46] Outside Parliament there were demonstrations in support of the King (one placard read GOD SAVE OUR KING FROM BALDWIN). In short, the megaphones were taking over the debate.

Of the two, Beaverbrook and Churchill, Churchill, of course, had the larger megaphone as a Member of the House of Commons and as a master, when required, of invective. Moreover, Beaverbrook's megaphone, the *Daily Express*, was muted by the King himself. Finally, during the morning of 4 December, Beaverbrook received a message from Lord Brownlow that

> he is now to give up seeing me ... [since] ... he wants to negotiate the terms of the King's abdication ... although he still wants to avert the abdication ... he should sever himself sufficiently from those opposing the government's views to escape the danger of any impediments in the financial arrangements.[47]

Churchill now took the lead in championing the King's cause. Although he and Beaverbrook had had any number of discussions on the matter and had jointly edited the King's draft of the broadcast which was never made, their tactics had been different almost from the beginning. Churchill was for outright, and if necessary, public opposition to the government, where Beaverbrook, as always, preferred to work behind the scenes. Still hoping to persuade the King to postpone a final decision in the belief that Mrs Simpson might yet be induced to end their relationship, he wrote to Edward asking for an audience and requesting permission to discuss the matter with

Churchill, who was due to dine with the King at Fort Belvedere on the evening of 4 December. According to his account, when no reply arrived it was a sign

> that the King could not discuss the matter with me any longer. The situation was emerging from the point where abdication was the issue. It had reached the stage where discussion turned on the terms of the abdication. And in these discussions I was no use. I was rather a hindrance.[48]

Following his meeting with the King, Churchill visited Beaverbrook at Stornoway House to inform him of their discussion. Churchill reported that he had advised the King to ask for a delay and said that he intended to write to Baldwin to convince him of the need to proceed slowly and not invite a sudden rupture in relations between the monarch and Parliament. Beaverbrook again pressed his plan to persuade Wallis to withdraw, but Churchill argued that his course of action stood the greater chance of success. The following morning the two met again without resolving their differences.

> So I left Churchill's house, without coming into conflict with him, but making it plain that we were taking different paths and that I was not a party to the attempt to stand against the Government. I went to Cherkley. I considered myself out of it. It was all over as far as I was concerned.[49]

It was the truth. Although when he arrived at Cherkley he found a coded message from Brownlow that Wallis Simpson was prepared to withdraw from the marriage, it was all too late. At Churchill's request, the King called him that evening. 'We had a long talk. The meaning of it was abdication … There was nothing more until the King's abdication was announced [on 10 December], when he called me on the telephone. He told me that he wanted to say goodbye and that we would soon meet again.'[50] And that was the final word. For Beaverbrook, the abdication crisis was truly over.

The Daily Express *front page reporting the abdication of King Edward VIII,*
12 December 1936.

CHAPTER 19

JEAN AND OTHER WOMEN

'You are such a queer, odd thing'[1]

Max Beaverbrook's love life (if it can be called that) after Gladys's
death in 1927 is not easy to disentangle. The background scenery, of course, is set by his long relationship with Jean Norton, who
had arrived like a cuckoo in the Cherkley nest while Gladys was still
alive. Beaverbrook's daughter Janet, who had whisked her mother off
to Canada when Jean was moving in, was convinced that her father
was deeply in love with the newcomer. That is as may be, but, whatever the vagaries of their relationship, there can be no questioning Jean's
credentials for the role of *maîtresse en titre*. She was an acknowledged
beauty, with a sparkling sense of the ridiculous, was part of the set
around the Prince of Wales through her cousin Piers Legh, and, together with her great friend Edwina Mountbatten, was to be seen at
all the best parties in London.

In addition, for those who cared about such things, her provenance
was impeccable. As Jean Mary Kinloch, daughter of Brigadier-General
Sir David Kinloch of Gilmerton (11th Baronet), on 3 April 1919 she
had married the 27-year-old Honourable Richard Henry Brinsley
Norton, son of the 5th Lord Grantley. As it happened, Norton himself already had a colourful history. Blown up by a shell in 1915 and,
by his own account, falling on 'the only bit of dry land in Flanders',
he was left with a hunched back which gave rise to the nickname of
'Wicked Uncle'. Nevertheless, he was, according to a friend, 'one of
the most quintessentially aristocratic men I have ever known. He had
dark bright eyes, long, thin-boned ankles and an eye glass that was
not in the least comical.'[2] As befitted a descendant of the playwright

Sheridan, he was full of outlandish tricks, many of them involving high-speed motor cars, and besieged by creditors. By the time Beaverbrook managed to seduce his wife, it was said that Norton had run up debts of £40,000 and was certainly not in a position to object to any arrangement which would be of benefit to his shaky finances.

It would be easy to take a cynical view that Jean was no more than a convenient and attractive target for a middle-aged man with a substantial bank account, but it would be wrong. There is no doubt that Beaverbrook, for his part, felt protective, in fact possessive, in what became a quasi-marriage lasting many years, and that Jean, for her part, felt cherished and even, perhaps, loved. Money, of course, was freely available, as was plenty of cheer. Beaverbrook knew how to make women laugh and, in times of domestic relaxation, was a mine of absorbing information about anything from the fall of Babylon to the constitution of the United States. If dinners at Cherkley were suddenly terminated by the host calling for adjournment to the cinema room to watch, yet again, a performance of his favourite, *Destry Rides Again*, that was no more than an easy price to pay. If there were flies in an otherwise benign ointment, they came in the form of Jean's two children. She, for her part, did her best, with some success, to befriend Beaverbrook's children. Beaverbrook himself made little effort with hers. In fact, it is much to her credit that she insisted on putting her foot down in favour of her children when their interests collided with those of her lover.

It would be equally wrong to take the innocent view that the relationship was forever monogamous or that there were never moments of separation. The destruction of most of Jean's diary and almost all their correspondence (Beaverbrook was as thorough in the destruction as he was in keeping records of his public life) makes it impossible to chart these with any accuracy or identify decisively what relationships were formed outside the bond that kept them together. What can easily be said is that to the outside world that particular bond, with its flaunting in public, must have seemed distinctly unusual, and that it was not only Mrs Churchill who found it profoundly distasteful (as she frequently reminded her husband). After all, for a married lady of the highest social class to desert her husband and two young children for long periods on trips to, for instance, South America with her lover, a brash Canadian multimillionaire of dubious reputation, and to allow herself to be housed for long weekends in a cottage on his vulgar estate, all this was enough to keep the gossips' tongues wagging energetically. Of course, when the tongues wag, what passes for a brain behind them gives out additional fodder. If two people can behave like that, the narrative goes, it is obvious that what is on view represents only the tip of an exciting iceberg.

Jean Norton (the Hon. Mrs Richard Norton) pictured in Paris, 1931.

As it happened, there was no limit for those who wished to explore the iceberg. There were plenty of opportunities for Beaverbrook to stray if he was so minded, and plenty of candidates have been put forward with varying degrees of plausibility. Gladys's sister, 'the delightful, soft-voiced Helen Fitzgerald', a later hostile reviewer reports many years later, was one. 'He had, of course, seduced [her] and kept [her] financially dependent on him most of her life.'[3] Edwina Mountbatten,

Jean's best friend, whom Beaverbrook had rescued from publicity when she was threatened by being cited as a co-respondent in a divorce case, was another. She certainly had an established reputation for relentless promiscuity which even her daughter had noticed. '[Our home] was large,' she wrote,

> but even it could not provide enough rooms to ensure that no young man was aware of the others. When my mother returned from shopping one day she was met with 'Mr Larry Gray is in the drawing room, Mr Sandford is in the library, Mr Ted Philips is in the boudoir, Señor Portago is in the anteroom and I don't know what to do with Mr Molyneux.'[4]

Lady Louis Mountbatten

Lady Louis Mountbatten, formerly Edwina Ashley (Countess Mountbatten of Burma and Vicereine of India 1901–60). Photographed by Madame Yevonde in The Bystander, *3 March 1937.*

Doris Delevingne, before, during and after her marriage to Valentine Castlerosse, was reputedly free with her favours. Bridget Paget, between her marriage in 1922 and her divorce in 1932, is reported as saying that 'no one wanted to marry me, darling. I give in too quickly. For instance, the Duke of Westminster proposed to me on a Tuesday. I went to bed with him that night and never saw him again.'[5] Daphne Weymouth, married to the son of the Marquess of Bath, was for a time among the first on the list to be invited on Beaverbrook's travels. Sibell Lygon was another rumoured *inamorata* who was said to have persuaded Beaverbrook both to suppress the scandal of her father's homosexuality (the 7th Earl Beauchamp was forced into peripatetic exile to avoid the threat of a trial) and to induce the Home Secretary, Lord Simon, to rescind the arrest warrant issued against him to allow the Earl to attend the funeral of his son Hugh in 1936.[6]

There were, of course, others in what was, after all, a period of social relationships best described as turbulent. Yet it would be wise to stand aside from the gossip and rely on hard evidence before running to judgement. Beaverbrook may well, in the early stage of his relationship with Jean (who was not by any means beyond jealousy), have behaved as shamelessly to her as he had to Gladys in the later years of their marriage. But there is no evidence to support the charge, and for good reason. Helen, flighty as she may have been, was his sister-in-law; Edwina was too rich to be bought and she enjoyed, as a regular lover, Mike Wardell, Beaverbrook's employee; Doris was too tied up with the absurd Castlerosse; and Bridget was terminally indiscreet. Of course, Beaverbrook may have slept with any or all of them, and there is no shortage of both friends and enemies to claim that the room was full of smoke (which indeed it was) and that therefore there was a roaring fire. Yet there are no discernible ashes for the diligent to sift through. On the contrary, many of the apparent candidates seem to have formed a joyful coterie: witness their collective attendance at Beaverbrook's fiftieth birthday lunch in May 1929, when the guests received cheques for £250 and Edwina Mountbatten was awarded an emerald and diamond brooch.

One candidate of the time, however, passes at least one test. Of a different order from Beaverbrook's society flirts was the dark, spirited and beautiful concert pianist Harriet Cohen. Born in December 1895 in London of Russo-Jewish parentage, she studied at the Royal Academy of Music and went on to immediate success, in spite of her small hands, as performer of the keyboard music of J. S. Bach. Pablo Casals invited her to play with his orchestra in Barcelona and Wilhelm Furtwängler, after hearing her play in Switzerland, tried to entice her to Berlin. At the age of twenty-nine she gave the first 'all-Bach' recital at London's Queen's Hall.

Harriet Cohen, accomplished British musician, playing the piano, c. 1930.

Her spectacular musical career had accompanied an equally spectacular private life. At the age of nineteen, in 1914, she had started an affair with the 31-year-old composer Arnold Bax. There was no doubt about the passion. 'My mouth longs for your soft mouth and the pink petals of your beautiful breasts,'[7] Bax wrote to her in March 1919, inventing also her nickname 'Tania'. In 1918, Bax had left his wife and children, apparently for Harriet, but he was refused a divorce and told her that their relationship had to remain secret in spite of her miscarriage in 1919. In fact, the truth was that Bax was starting to become weary of Harriet's explosions and was soon, unbeknown to her, to seek comfort with a second and less turbulent mistress, Mary Gleaves.

It was Arnold Bennett who first introduced Harriet to Beaverbrook in 1923. There were dinners at the Vineyard and weekends at Cherkley, but it was not until 1928, during one of Harriet's periods of distance from Bax, that a whimsical flirtation turned into something more serious. By the end of August, the temperature had risen. After a weekend at Cherkley it was 'Darling Max, This is my "bread and butter" letter … I felt strangely protected and cared for beneath your roof last night – in more ways than one !!!!! … I always feel when I am with you that we just adore each other…' Thereafter came a string of effusive and, from time to time, eccentric letters (she addressed Beaverbrook once as the prophet Isaiah and on another occasion, somewhat improbably, as 'Angel Face') until he seemed to tire of her and sent her the customary shower of red roses.[8]

As though to get some relief from Harriet, at the end of August 1931 Beaverbrook made another move. He was on board the *Bremen* sailing from New York across the Atlantic to Liverpool. On the first night at sea he was dining with Castlerosse in the first-class Ritz restaurant when he noticed a slender, fine-boned, beautiful lady, elegantly dressed in a black lace dress over a satin slip, dining at a nearby table. The temptation was too much, and Castlerosse was told to move into action. It turned out that the lady in question was Mrs Dorothy Hall, returning to Europe with her two children after the funeral of her father. In fact, Dorothy, better known by her maiden name of Schiff, had herself already spotted 'two unusual-looking men – one a big fat man with a red complexion and the other … a little man with a huge head'.[9] Of course, she knew perfectly well who they were. She was, after all, the granddaughter of the banker Jacob Schiff and her brother was a partner of Kuhn, Loeb. At the age of twenty-eight she had already made her impact in New York society and was far too shrewd not to recognise money when she met it.

Castlerosse's approach was crude, to say the least. He wandered over to Dorothy's table and said simply that 'the big boss over there wants to meet you'. Dorothy's hostess, Mrs Gordon Douglas, snapped back. 'Bring him over here, if he wants to meet her.' 'Well, he won't do that. Just join him for a coffee and a liqueur; then I'll come and bring you back. He's very easily bored.' Dorothy decided to accept the challenge and went over to Beaverbrook's table. After some desultory conversation he asked her whether she knew how to set up a backgammon board, as he had forgotten. On being told that she did, Beaverbrook said to Castlerosse, 'Valentine, you may go back and join those people [the Douglases]. Mrs Hall is going to show me how to set up the backgammon board.'[10]

The following morning three dozen roses arrived at Dorothy's cabin with a note saying that she was to sit at his table for the rest of the voyage and Castlerosse would sit with the Douglases. The arrangement held until towards the end of the voyage when Beaverbrook insisted that she come with him to London and stay in Stornoway House. She refused on the grounds that she had to settle her children in Paris. Beaverbrook promptly moved into his suite at the Ritz in Paris. As Schiff's biographer delicately put it, 'There wasn't time for much backgammon in Beaverbrook's Ritz suite, the hours being taken up by other games.'[11]

Their stay in Paris was short, but not without incident. Dorothy's father's stable manager, Vicomte Sebastien Foy, nicknamed 'Bastien', was a competitor for her attention. 'He was charming and divine,' Dorothy recorded, 'a good ten years older than I, and really lovely. Also he was very fat; in fact, quite ludicrous looking. He had pink cheeks, terribly white skin, poppy pale blue eyes, and, with all that weight, he looked silly on the golf course.'[12] Not that Dorothy was impressed by Beaverbrook's looks, which she described as 'having lost a lot of hair on top of that huge head but having gained a potbelly and with it a wart on his face'. 'He really did resemble a bull frog', she went on, 'and in spite of the little valet he was rather unkempt – almost seedy. He would wear brown shoes with a blue suit. He was not what we used to call an Arrow collar type.'[13]

Needless to say, the two competitors had little time for one another. Bastien called Beaverbrook 'a terrible man – dangerous and evil'. Beaverbrook declined to engage in insults. Instead, he persuaded Dorothy (who rather agreed with Bastien but thought it part of her lover's attraction) to move with him to London. Jean was away with her children; Janet's room in Stornoway House, on the fourth floor overlooking Green Park, was unoccupied and the governess and the children could be parked at the Hyde Park Hotel. Dorothy, still under the spell, accepted.

Once installed, she found herself employed as Beaverbrook's hostess during September 1931, when the future of the National Government was at stake. Since the ladies of society were still away from London, Beaverbrook's evening salons consisted almost entirely of men, none of whom, however distinguished they were, caught Dorothy's attention. By the end of the month, Dorothy had had enough. Not only that, but Jean Norton had come home. There was a showdown. 'Hell of a row,' Jean recorded. 'Decided to leave tomorrow.'[14] Leave she did, for Paris and the comforts of shopping at Schiaparelli and tea at the Ritz. When she got back to London, uncertain of her status, she was relieved to find that Janet's room was again empty. Dorothy Hall had left.

There were no broken hearts. Nor were there any roses. Beaverbrook had made an effort to soften what he thought would be a blow by palming Dorothy off to another admirer, his Tory friend Leslie Hore-Belisha. Nevertheless, she was reluctant to let go, and did her best to keep the flame alive. But, as with Jean, her children were too much of an alternative attraction. It was a situation which Beaverbrook found too uncomfortable. But Jean could not be discarded at will. Dorothy had to go.

It was in 1933 that a successor appeared, almost the opposite to the society elegance of her predecessor. Catharina Koopman had been born in 1908 on the Indonesian island of Java. Her father was a colonel in the Army of the Dutch East Indies, as it then was, with particular responsibility for the purchase of horses from Australia for the Army's cavalry. Such was his love of one of his charges that he named his baby daughter 'Toto' after it. The name was rejected by the official registrar and she became officially 'Catharina'. The official view was soon ignored, and she remained 'Toto' from then onwards. Toto's father was of pure Dutch extraction. Her mother, on the other hand, was half Javanese with a strain of Chinese in her ancestry. The taint of mixed race was much noticed, and despised, by Dutch society on the island and Toto's upbringing, together with that of her brother, was not easy. Accordingly, she was sent to Holland at the age of eleven to a boarding school and from there to a finishing school in London. Yet her birth and upbringing were not without their advantages. First, she developed into an acknowledged beauty, tall, slim, with high cheekbones, green eyes and black hair which had heads turning wherever she went; and, secondly, her response to her family's treatment by Dutch Indonesian high society was both a rebellious and feisty character which defied anybody to drag her down and also a cheerful disregard for conventional morality.

Catharina 'Toto' Koopman, the Dutch-Javanese actress who appeared in The Private Life of Don Juan, *June 1934.*

In 1928, Toto arrived in Paris. With her looks, she was an immediate success in the café society of the Left Bank. Her obvious career path was fashion modelling and she duly applied to some of the famous names active at the time. She was taken on, in a humble role, by Coco Chanel. After six months she walked out, protesting that she did not like 'the way Coco touched her during the fittings'.[15] This demonstration of prudishness was short-lived, and she proceeded to use all her available assets to advance her career, letting it be known on the way that she was bisexual. Within two years she became a lead model (known as 'jockeys', since the designers employed them to wear their latest confections to the grand parties almost every evening); had formed an open relationship with a bogus Russian prince, Alexis Mdivani, helping him spend the money of his wife, the Woolworth heiress Barbara Hutton; had announced that she was of noble Belgian blood and should henceforward be called Baroness van Halmaëll; and, most important of all, had been taken up by the fashionable photographer George Hoyningen-Huene, who had featured her lavishly in the magazine *Vogue*.

It was the ambition of most successful fashion models to progress to making movies, and Toto was no exception. Her opportunity came in 1932 when she met the Austrian actor Conrad Veidt, who was passing through Paris on his way to London to make a film with the young Hungarian director Alexander Korda. Veidt persuaded Toto to follow him and take a screen test. Korda was, of course, enthralled and Toto was engaged to play one of the ladies in his production *The Private Life of Don Juan*, featuring the ageing and overweight Douglas Fairbanks and Korda's current mistress, Merle Oberon. Toto did her (modest) bit, but her entire contribution ended on the cutting-room floor. The movie was a disaster.

Undeterred, Toto began a torrid relationship with the lesbian queen of the moment, the flame-haired Tallulah Bankhead. In September 1934 they went together to the première of *Don Juan*. Their appearance together caused something of a sensation, not least because Tallulah had recently cut her hair in the short style favoured by Toto, prompting her devoted admirers to do the same and cast their locks at her feet as they emerged from the cinema. The affair was too intense to last, and when Toto decided that she'd had enough of film making and walked off Korda's set, the whole thing came to an end, though not before Tallulah had shown her off to her powerful friend, Lord Beaverbrook.

Toto was immediately captured by the sense not just of money but of power. She was soon shown the life of those at the centre of events: dinners at the Savoy or Stornoway House, weekends at Cherkley, talk of momentous doings. At the age of twenty-six Toto had discovered a new world, peopled by men seemingly with wit, wisdom and generosity. At the age of fifty-six, for his part, Beaverbrook had discovered another living doll, and one with the temerity to contradict him when she felt like it to prevent him lapsing into boredom. True, 'like many others, he found her beauty and sexual energy disconcerting', and it can hardly be said to have been a match made in heaven, but 'Toto became his mistress with her head held high, believing theirs was an even exchange'.[16]

During the remainder of 1934 and the first months of 1935 all seemed to go well. Toto knew how to spend her lover's money. She also knew that to keep him interested the secret was to leave him alone without her (for short periods). A sudden enthusiasm for opera meant short trips to opera houses on the Continent (she knew perfectly well that Beaverbrook could not abide opera and was happy to let her go). That was all very well, but by the late summer of 1935 the absences were becoming rather more frequent and the returns apparently less exhilarating. Something, Beaverbrook realised, was going on. In fact, Toto had taken her duties as a mistress lightly. Castlerosse was forever knocking at her door until Doris threatened to divorce him, citing Toto as co-respondent. She had a brief passage with Winston Churchill's ill-mannered son Randolph before settling on a lover much more to her taste. The difficulty was that the new lover was none other than Beaverbrook's elder son, the elegantly attractive, good-looking and virile Max Aitken.

Beaverbrook was understandably furious. But his behaviour was worse than anger. It was a mixture of jealousy and unreasoning spite. His newspapers were forbidden to mention her name. He spread rumours about her, referring to her as 'that negress' and hinting at all sorts of depravity.[17] He then turned his fire on his son, offering him a motor car, a better job, as much money as he wanted if he would give Toto up. None of that worked. Max and Toto had decided to get married and escaped to Spain for a while to avoid what was becoming a full-blown social scandal. It was only a temporary respite. On their return, Beaverbrook told Max, 'I'll give you a lot of money if you promise not to marry that girl.' Toto told Max to take it. Beaverbrook then offered Toto a lifetime annuity on condition that she would never become his daughter-in-law. Toto took that as well, and a contract was duly drawn up and signed. For the next four years Max and Toto lived in a luxurious penthouse in Portman Square.

It would be reassuring to believe that Beaverbrook had learnt his lesson from this sordid affair, but this is far from the case. In the spring of 1937, Beaverbrook, with the customary group of boisterous men friends, decided on a short visit to Cannes. Once there, they decided one evening to eschew the casinos of the Riviera and, unlikely as it may seem, to attend a performance of a Viennese ballet company. 'There were all these pretty girls,' one of Beaverbrook's companions recalled. 'Beaverbrook took a fancy to them and sent [Mike] Wardell off to invite four of them to dinner at the Carlton Hotel.'[18] The invitation was accepted and dinner for eight was duly ordered. Since only one of the Viennese ballerinas spoke even fractured English, she was placed next to Beaverbrook.

Lily Ernst had been born in Hungary before moving to Vienna with her family when she was a child. Dark-haired and possessing a spirited, gamine figure which betrayed her training as a classical ballerina, she was well-educated, which meant that in spite of the language barrier she was no fool when it came to the intentions of wealthy older men. When Beaverbrook asked her over dinner what was her programme for the next day she said that she wanted to shop for a dress. Beaverbrook could not contain himself. 'I'll go with you,' he said, 'and, if you like it, I will buy it for you.' Lily's response was sharp and to the point. 'Does that mean I will have to sleep with you?' she asked. Beaverbrook was put in his (unaccustomed) place.[19]

Lily Ernst, oil on canvas portrait painting, by Colin Colahan, 1952.

After a few days driving her around Cannes and receiving another sharp rebuke for shouting 'bloody old Jew' at an old beggar who was in the way, Beaverbrook returned to London. Lily had waited in vain for his telephone call to say goodbye before her train left for Vienna, but she was not going to let go. She wrote to him thanking him 'for a real good time for me' and asking 'whether you miss me a little. And when do you come to Vienna?'[20] Just to make sure he got the hint, she added her address and telephone number at the bottom of her letter.

Beaverbrook returned to England on 10 May; a month later, on 9 June, he decided on a whim that the same group of companions should return to the Continent to seek out Lily and her friends in Vienna. The hastily assembled party departed on his private plane, but the trip did not prove to be a success. When he got there, he found, to his disappointment, that in the interim Lily had acquired a fiancé in the form of a young, and extremely suitable, Jewish doctor. Accepting that he had travelled in vain, Beaverbrook assured Lily, it need hardly be said, of his undying friendship and promptly boarded his plane for the return journey.

Lily reminded him of this in a letter of 1 May 1938. Six weeks earlier the German Army, with Hitler at its head, had marched through the streets of Vienna. Lily, like all Jews in the city, was fearful. She recalled that he had told her that he would 'always be a good friend of me. If you are still of this opinion you could make me happy in giving me a few kind words.'[21] Beaverbrook responded immediately with his usual concern for those of his friends who were in trouble. He called Lily and asked what he could do to help. Lily wrote after the call, 'I cannot tell you what it meant to me yesterday that you were still interested in my life.' She told him that there was no immediate danger but 'every chance you could offer me would be a great help and make me deeply thankful'.[22]

On 18 May, Beaverbrook cabled the British Consulate in Vienna asking for assistance in arranging a visa for Lily to enter the United Kingdom. On 25 May a letter was sent to the chief immigration officer at Dover stating that Lily was leaving Vienna that same day for a visit to Britain at Beaverbrook's invitation, that she was travelling on a Yugoslav passport, would stay no longer than six months and would have sufficient funds.

What happened then is something of a mystery. Lily duly arrived in London a few days later, but it was late in the evening. She managed to find her way in darkness to Stornoway House, but the staff had not been told about her and had no idea what they should do. In the end, she was let in, but Beaverbrook seemed to want to keep her at a distance. She, on the other hand, was only too anxious to show him her gratitude for his help and generosity in getting her safely out of Austria. The problem was that Jean had already smelled what appeared to be another unpleasant rat and made a fuss. Beaverbrook's rather lame explanation was that Lily was in London to help in translating Hitler's broadcasts. The upshot was that Lily during the balance of 1938 lived a strange half-life, parked, according to Beaverbrook's daughter Janet, in London at the Vineyard, looking after the growing number of German and Austrian refugees, but with regular visits to Cherkley. In fact, it was at one of those visits, in September 1938, that Michael Foot fell 'really in love with her'.[23] But she did not respond. Her attention was elsewhere.

It is not entirely clear when Lily Ernst finally supplanted Jean Norton as Beaverbrook's preferred mistress. Throughout the early months of 1939, Beaverbrook did his best to keep their relationship quiet, to the point where one of Lily's friends who came from Vienna thought that he was treating her 'very shabbily'.[24] With the onset of war Jean decided immediately to volunteer for war work. She had realised, or if she had not, Janet had told her, in the same comforting fashion as she had nursed Gladys's feelings all those years previously, that Lily was taking her place. The Women's Volunteer Service was a welcoming haven, and it was noted, as befitted the wartime spirit, that she was less attentive to her appearance.

Lily had one great advantage: her mother language of German. In order to keep up to date, Beaverbrook installed at Cherkley a large radio receiver to pick up German broadcasts. He needed a translator, and Lily was to hand. She spent more and more time at Cherkley and, according to Janet, 'was soon to move into Jean's cottage … Their [Lily and Beaverbrook's] relationship was deeper than I thought and was to last several years.'[25] Whether it was in Jean's cottage or in another cottage on the Cherkley estate, as others have assumed, by May 1940 Lily was properly installed. Her relationship with her lover was indeed to last several years but, like those of Gladys and Jean, would in due course end in disappointments, betrayals and, ultimately, tears.

CHAPTER 20

FROM ISOLATION TO TREASON AND BACK

'Beaverbrook himself opposes the war'[1]

Those who suffer from acute asthma are quick to claim, not without reason, that their more serious attacks evoke the fear of immediate death in a particularly frightening way. As the sufferer's airways, already inflamed, narrow further to reduce the airflow into and out of the lungs, panic sets in, exacerbating the condition to the point where the feeling is one of imminent and speedy strangulation. Nor does the latent fear end there. Attacks can be triggered by any number of conditions, from physical exercise to dust mites, and can arrive suddenly, frequently without warning. Modern medicine, and, in particular, the development of corticosteroids, has provided a measure of relief, but no cure.

When Beaverbrook became seriously affected by the condition in 1936 not only was there no cure but the only effective treatment was the slow and deliberate inhalation, through a mask, of gulps of pure oxygen. Needless to say, this raised a number of problems. Although Beaverbrook was known for his continued, frequently unnecessary, preoccupation with his health, his concern on this occasion was fully justified. Cherkley and Stornoway House had to be equipped with the most up-to-date apparatus, in Cherkley almost filling one room, and wherever he travelled warnings were sent out to be prepared for an event. Not only that, but he decided that the English winter was an enemy to be avoided. Certainly, he had been accustomed to spending the odd winter week at the Carlton Hotel in Cannes, where he felt better. Now he started to look for a more permanent perch on the French Riviera where he could overwinter while, of course, remaining in contact with his affairs in London.

That, however, was for the future. What was needed now was warm and dry air. The abdication crisis over, he left again for New York with his customary entourage of secretaries and valets. This time, instead of heading north to New Brunswick, he decided on Arizona. To get there from New York, to solve the problem of allergen-free transport he bought, and had suitably equipped, a medium-sized Lockheed aircraft. Once that was ready he flew to Tucson ready to spend the winter breathing the pure Arizona desert air. It was not a success. Instead of the pure desert air there were constant dust storms mingled, in the towns of Tucson and Phoenix, with the pervading smell, when the wind was in the wrong direction, of the stockyards where the cattle were slaughtered. In short, it was not long before the decision was reversed, and the caravan headed for the more salubrious seaside climate of Florida and the charms, such as they were, of the best hotel in Miami.

Miami was more congenial, but not congenial enough. From there he went back to the south of France, 'where the climate is not so agreeable as in Arizona but where there is more to entertain a man passing from middle age to old age'. From there came a short stay in Paris, with lunch with the French socialist Prime Minister, Léon Blum, but it was not until the end of April 1937 that he decided that it was safe to return to the murky climate of London. In fact, he was just in time to boycott the coronation of King George VI on 12 May. 'There are seven hundred and forty-seven peers', he wrote to his new friend the editor of the *Arizona Daily Star*, 'and seven hundred and forty-six of them were at the Abbey on Wednesday. One was absent. It was your friend.' Nevertheless, he kept a beady eye on the event, noting in particular the appearance of Prime Minister Baldwin in the coronation procession. 'He had a great reception from the crowds. He had been given a closed carriage to ride in, but he leaned out of the window and generally conducted himself so as to win the public applause. And this he got in immense measure...'[2]

Irritating as was Baldwin's popularity with the London crowd, Beaverbrook was already looking forward to the Prime Minister's imminent retirement. It duly happened in suitably theatrical fashion. As one of his last acts, Baldwin announced an increase of £200 per annum in the salary of Members of the House of Commons, their first raise since 1911. Unsurprisingly, when he announced his resignation on the same day, 27 May, he 'made his last statement amid loud applause ... No man has ever left in such a blaze of affection.'[3] The gratitude of Buckingham Palace apparently knew no bounds. At his audience with the King the following morning, Baldwin was made an Earl and a Knight of the Garter, while Mrs Baldwin, for reasons no one could quite explain, was made a Dame of the British Empire.

The send-off from the *Daily Express* was very much less enthusiastic. In a signed article on 29 May entitled 'Mr Baldwin is always right', Beaverbrook let loose his invective:

> Mr Baldwin makes his bow ... The turn has lasted for just fourteen years ... And in those fourteen years the chief actor has given us our money's worth – not in statesmanship, not in solid gain to the public welfare, but in variety, in interest and in bewilderment ... What an extraordinary record it is! A record of paradoxes, reversals of judgement, recoveries after deep disaster, sudden changes from ill-fortune to good ... The biggest paradox about Mr Baldwin is that he claims to be right when he does a thing, and claims also to be right when he undoes it. The truth is that Mr Baldwin is always right when he contradicts himself ... What will the historian make of a record as baffling as Mr Baldwin's? He will look for a man embarrassed by the inconsistencies of his policy and the contradiction of his statements. But he will not find that man. For Mr Baldwin has been, all through, remarkable for the calm sense of rectitude with which he has pursued its opposite...[4]

It was heady stuff. Yet behind it all it is not difficult to detect a grudging respect, even admiration, for a long-standing political opponent who, Beaverbrook was forced to recognise, had won all their battles. What is certain is that once Baldwin had migrated to the Valhalla of the House of Lords and Neville Chamberlain had kissed hands as the new Prime Minister, Beaverbrook found himself, to change metaphors, without a fox to hunt. To be sure, he had been disappointed in Chamberlain's lukewarm support for Empire free trade but he liked him well enough personally and was not going to pick an unnecessary fight. Nor, for that matter, was he going to serve in a Chamberlain government. When an impudent editor of a rival newspaper suggested that Chamberlain would appoint him Colonial Secretary, he received a stinging rebuke from Beaverbrook's secretary: 'Lord Beaverbrook is done with governments. He will never be in any governments anymore.'[5]

Whether Beaverbrook really meant it or whether it was just another gesture of frustration, there were at the time few opportunities for political stunts. Chamberlain's government needed, and deserved, a fair wind. The international theatre was unusually quiet: Italy had achieved her aim in Africa, Germany had absorbed the Rhineland without protest, France was learning to cope with a left-wing government and the Spanish Civil War was digging itself into a gruesome self-defeating mess. True, Beaverbrook's socialist friends were making a good deal of noise about it, and some of them were volunteering to join the International Brigade, but isolationism demanded that Britain stay far away from the dispute, and all efforts to engage the interest of Beaverbrook's newspapers were met with a resolute silence.

It was now time to devote energy to the three newspapers. Beaverbrook was well aware of the power of radio in conveying a message to a wide public. He was also aware of the potential of the relatively new medium of television. Instead of diversifying into these as others had done, and were to do, his whole effort was directed to building up his newspapers as tools for propaganda. This required both an emphasis on a marketing strategy to increase circulation and a clear message to go with it. With Christiansen proving a more than competent editor of the *Daily Express*, revolutionising the presentation of the front page, Beaverbrook was able to concentrate on policy. 'The progress of the British people', he wrote to the general manager on 20 August 1937, 'must be the story of the rise of our newspaper. If it is not the story of the rise of our newspaper, then we may become big but we will never become great.'[6]

The drive to increase circulation was hardly a stunning success. In September 1937 the net daily sale of the *Daily Express* was recorded as 2,407,780. Beaverbrook set a target of three million for the following year. But in July 1938 the audited figure was 2,479,922, a creditable rise but nowhere near his target. Nevertheless, it was comfortably above the equivalent figure for the *Daily Mail* and allowed Beaverbrook to claim that his newspaper was 'the first ... to serve every class in the community, rich and poor, high and low, barbarian, Scythian, bond and free'.[7]

The language became even less restrained as 1937 drifted into 1938. On 7 January the headline in the *Daily Express* announced that it was 'The World's Greatest Newspaper', with the copy underneath listing the figures for its competitors (the *Daily Mail* was selling 800,000 fewer copies), explaining its advantages over its main competitors and its ambitions 'to reach the entire newspaper reading public of the country. Our desire is to be everywhere. In all households...'[8] By March it was near hysteria:

> The purpose of the Daily Express is to secure for each boy and girl equal educational facilities, the same opportunities, and a fair start for all together. And the joy of living must not be restrained, limited or confined by any measure whatsoever. The Express is allied to the group of human beings who like to have a good time.[9]

It did not take the cynics long to laugh at Beaverbrook's pretensions to support social equality, and it certainly did not take long for the wags to link defence of 'the joy of living' to his colourful lifestyle of the time.

Of greater interest was the divergence of views between his three newspapers on the issue of Germany. While Beaverbrook was overwintering in Miami and dictating bombastic articles about the splendours of the *Daily Express* and the virtues of isolationism, the editor of the *Sunday Express*, John Gordon, a patriot almost from a former age, was advocating active resistance to Hitler and all his works, and Frank Owen, the outspoken left-winger whom Beaverbrook had made editor of the *Evening Standard*, was relentless in his support for a popular front and even in his personal attacks on Ribbentrop. All this, of course, did no more than reflect the sharp differences of the time. When Beaverbrook returned from Miami in early March, he found a new Foreign Secretary, Lord Halifax, succeeding Eden, who could no longer stomach Chamberlain's efforts to make friends with Mussolini. As for Halifax, one supporter saw his appointment as a triumph: 'A saner, more intelligent, happier appointment has never been made.'[10] Beaverbrook, however, saw it differently. 'A considerable improvement,' he wrote, 'but I do not think that he has the respect of Hitler, who calls him "Christ's brother".'[11] 'The great new factor in British politics', he wrote to another friend, 'is ... the rise of Chamberlain ... his decisions are honest and his conclusions are wise.'[12]

On 12 March 1938, German troops crossed the Austrian frontier and entered Vienna unopposed. Austria was forthwith annexed into the Reich and Hitler was received rapturously on his visit to Vienna two days later, the day on which Chamberlain told the House of Commons that only the combined forces of Europe could have stopped Germany. Not everybody was convinced. 'Chamberlain (who has the mind and manner of a clothes-brush)', wrote one critic, 'aims only at assuring temporary peace at the price of ultimate defeat ... If we assuage the German alligator with fish from other ponds she will wax so fat that she will demand fish from our own ponds.'[13]

Even Beaverbrook was starting to have some as yet glimmering doubts. Using as his platform the more hard-line *Sunday Express*, he began by agreeing with Chamberlain that nothing could have been done about the German annexation of Austria. 'So that story is ended,' was his verdict,

> but our conduct in future must be determined by the new situation. And the big decision ... is quite simply this: will we disturb the existing industrial situation in this country to implement the building of aircraft for national defence? ... We must consent to the imposition of a new Defence of the Realm Act ... will we approve? ... Yes. We should do so ... Liberty will in some degree be sacrificed. But fortunately, if we are compelled to cede some of our rights we shall be ceding them to a democracy and not to a dictatorship. [This] merely emphasise[s] and strengthen[s] ... the need for the policy of Isolation ... With the policy of Isolation there comes the need for adequate defences ... It imposes a duty on all of us. A readiness to make sacrifices. A willingness to bear heavy burdens for the sake of our national security ... The price of our safety will be high. We should be prepared to pay it.[14]

The policy of isolation was in direct contrast to the pursuit by Winston Churchill of support for Czechoslovakia, the next country, with its sizeable minority of Sudeten Germans, to be an obvious target of

Hitler's expansionism. Invited by the editor of the *News Chronicle* to give his backing to Churchill, Beaverbrook was ready to admit their differences:

> Churchill ... unhappily ... would bring pressure on the Government forthwith to give a guarantee to Czecho-Slovakia [*sic*] that we too will fight in defence of that artificial nation brought into existence by Messrs. George Clemenceau and Wilson ... I want the soldiers to stay at home and guard the frontiers of Britain, and protect the Empire, and keep watch on our outposts.[15]

Throughout the spring and summer of 1938, Beaverbrook continued to defend the policy of isolation, even as the Sudeten German Party demanded the creation of a partially autonomous state and, soon after, on 20 May, the Czech government ordered partial mobilisation of reservists in what he called 'a mild attack of hysteria ... some people still think we have had a narrow escape from war. But there is not a shred of evidence that Germany contemplated anything of the kind.'[16] When criticised by Halifax, who claimed that the policy of isolation was unrealistic if Britain was to pursue the role of mediator in European conflicts, Beaverbrook retorted that isolationism was 'compatible with such a role provided it was not accompanied by a pledge of armed intervention in order to uphold the provisions of any convention or treaty. Supporters of isolationism ... have nothing to say against the mediator who appeals to the quarrelling nations in the name of peace.'[17]

On 1 September 1938 the *Daily Express* published a long article by Beaverbrook, entitled 'There will be no war', in which he argued that

> Hitler has shown himself throughout his career to be a man of exceptional astuteness ... If the Czechs fail to make the necessary concessions ... the French and the Russians will not come to their aid and in that case the danger of war is over. And if the Czechs (after making the necessary concessions) are supported by the French and the Russians ... the coalition is much too strong and the Germans would be destroyed ... I predict, therefore, a peaceful solution of the present troubles in Central Europe.[18]

There is no doubt that Beaverbrook, apart from the odd moment of hesitation, was as convinced in private as he was in public. 'The threat [of war]', he wrote to a friend, 'has been exaggerated. The omens have been misunderstood. The preparations which have been going on are not, in my judgement, preparations for war, but preparations for negotiation. That is the way things are done in Europe, with the loaded gun on the table.'[19] Furthermore, Chamberlain was in the prime position to act as mediator, and when he flew to Berchtesgaden on 15 September for the first of his three face-to-face meetings with Hitler, Beaverbrook wrote to him to ask that a 'Minister be appointed to deal with the newspaper proprietors. They are all anxious to follow you … It is not information we need. It is guidance.' He suggested that his friend Samuel Hoare be given the job as he had 'the necessary balance, judgement and prestige'.[20] Support came from the Foreign Office. The British Ambassador to Berlin, Sir Nevile Henderson, urged that the press should be encouraged 'to write up Hitler as an apostle of Peace'.[21]

Chamberlain's report of his meeting, that Hitler's objectives were limited to the inclusion of Sudetenland into the Reich, and the subsequent agreement with the French government to accept, were duly endorsed by the *Daily Express*. On 22 September, the day on which Chamberlain flew to Cologne for his second meeting with Hitler at Bad Godesberg in order to settle the matter, it pronounced, yet again in an article signed by Beaverbrook, that 'Britain never gave any pledge to protect the frontiers of Czecho-Slovakia. Britain was twice asked and twice refused. There is no duty or responsibility whatsoever on this country to defend that Central European Power.'[22] Not that it mattered very much, since by the time Chamberlain arrived at Cologne for a meeting at Bad Godesberg, to be greeted by some ragged strains of 'God Save the King', the Franco-British proposal was out of date. The Polish and Hungarian minorities in Czechoslovakia were demanding the same treatment as the Sudeten Germans, and Hitler used their demands as an excuse for an ultimatum. In a memorandum of 24 September, the German government set a date, 28 September, by which Sudetenland would be ceded to the Reich. Otherwise, it would be occupied by force.

There was a further flurry in the chancelleries of Europe, verging on panic. Chamberlain instructed Lord Perth, the British Ambassador to Italy, urgently to see Mussolini and to ask his intervention to put the deadline back by a day to allow spirits to calm. This Mussolini did, with the side effect that there would be an immediate four-power conference (including him) at Munich to settle the Sudeten problem once and for all. As Chamberlain flew off to Munich at 8.30 a.m. on 29 September, the *Daily Express* was already on the stands shouting its enthusiasm. 'It's All Right!' was the headline, echoing Chamberlain's exclamation to the crowd outside Downing Street the previous evening. When the message from Hitler agreeing to the meeting was handed to him as he stood at the Despatch Box just beginning his peroration

> the House of Commons swept aside all the rules, and public, diplomats, peers and commoners cheered and clapped in a scene of wild enthusiasm. Mr Chamberlain, himself openly weeping, wound up his speech in a few moments and, with the 'God Speed' of Government and Opposition alike ringing in his ears, hurried over to Downing Street to prepare for his third trip to Germany.[23]

The agreement signed at Munich by Chamberlain, the French Prime Minister Édouard Daladier, Hitler and Mussolini at about 1.30 a.m. in the morning of 30 September had been formally introduced by Mussolini, although it had been drafted by the German Foreign Office. Unsurprisingly, it was almost identical to the Godersberg memorandum: German armed forces would complete the occupation of Sudetenland by 10 October and an international commission would decide the future of other disputed minority areas. Later in the morning, Chamberlain called on Hitler to invite him to sign a peace treaty between Germany and the United Kingdom. Hitler cheerfully agreed. Chamberlain returned to London amid scenes of wild enthusiasm. He appeared on the balcony of Buckingham Palace with King George VI and Queen Elizabeth. From there, he went back to Downing Street to lean out of a window to acknowledge the cheers of the crowd. The *Daily Express* duly reported his assurance in its headline: 'You may sleep quietly – It is peace for our time.'[24]

The Daily Express *front page reporting the signing of the Munich peace agreement and Prime Minister Neville Chamberlain's declaration, 'It is peace for our time', 1 October 1938.*

Yet beneath the surface all was not entirely well. Halifax, already unhappy with the result at Bad Godersberg, had been taken to task by his pugnacious Permanent Secretary, Sir Alexander Cadogan, over the Munich agreement and was starting to believe that Hitler could not be trusted. Beaverbrook himself, whatever his newspapers might say in public, was equally critical in private. 'Mr Chamberlain and his Government', he wrote, 'interfered in foreign affairs at a moment when the country was not adequately prepared ... It is against this policy of foreign interference ... that I cry out so strongly and protest so frequently.'[25] As 1938 came to an end he became even more pessimistic, and even tetchy. He was irritated by the outrage in Britain over the pogrom in Germany known as *Kristallnacht* (after the amount of shattered glass from the Jewish shops which had been attacked by Nazi thugs). 'The German savagery has come as a shock to opinion', ran one letter, '... but that in itself could not entirely account for the bitterness of feeling over here over the German pogrom.' He put this down to the 'big position in the press here'. He went even further.

'The Jews may drive us into war ... They do not mean to do it ... [but] their political influence is moving us in that direction.'[26]

It was time, and perhaps more than time, yet again to avoid the harshness of an English winter. The choice was between Miami and the French Riviera, but Miami was too far away for quick return if the European volcano unexpectedly erupted, and the decision was for the Riviera. As it happened, it was a choice Beaverbrook never had cause to regret. His stay was short, since war seemed still to be an ever-present threat, but he did spot a villa, called La Capponcina, which he quickly realised would provide the kind of asthma-free winter home that he needed. Owned by Captain Edward Molyneux, a dress designer with a fashionable reputation, the villa stood on the promontory of Cap-d'Ail, some three kilometres west of Monte Carlo. Protected from intruders by a high wall, the villa's main feature was a large drawing room with

> a row of French windows on one side and a great stone fireplace at the far end over which the arms of some long-forgotten nobleman are carved, together with the motto '*Ne derelictas me Domine*' ('Do not forsake me O Lord') ... The room opens onto a wide verandah and garden, with a colonnade that frames a matchless view over the Mediterranean.[27]

The sale was duly negotiated and work begun to get the villa into shape for the winter of 1939–40.

La Capponcina, Cap-d'Ail, south of France, view from above looking towards the sea, undated.

Beaverbrook was still in a mood of optimism throughout January and February 1939. Chamberlain's popularity was high, and his policy of appeasement seemed likely, as Beaverbrook wrote to an American friend, 'to carry the country with him. His Government is very strong now.'[28] But by early March the mood had changed, suddenly and dramatically. On 9 March, Maisky reported in his diary that

> Beaverbrook told me that Chamberlain had a talk with Churchill the other day and was forced to admit that the policy of appeasement had failed. Chamberlain will, of course, make every effort to deter conflict and alleviate the tension through various manoeuvres, but the PM can see now that lasting peace and genuine friendship between Britain and Germany are impossible.[29]

The ambassador was also the recipient of a bounty of 'rather heavy compliments' from his guest, who prophesised that if he stayed in his post for another couple of years, he stood 'to reap a rich harvest in the sphere of Anglo-Soviet relations which your work will have prepared over preceding years'.[30]

Chamberlain's policy shift back towards a version of collective security found expression in a new agreement with France for mutual defence and co-operation in military planning provoked by Germany's total disregard of the Munich agreements. A series of political upheavals in Czechoslovakia, carefully orchestrated from Berlin, had led, on 15 March, to occupation by the German Army and the subsequent dismemberment of the country under German control. Beaverbrook refused to be fazed. 'The Czech-Slovak partition', he wrote to the Canadian politician Edward Mortimer Macdonald, '...was sure to come ... The structure was bound to fail as soon as the weight of reality was imposed upon it.'[31]

Beaverbrook must have been one of the few people left in London who kept, almost obsessively, to the view that the risk or war was negligible. In fact, he even thought of making one of his usual springtime holiday trips to Paris and onward, perhaps to Berlin. On the day that German tanks rumbled into Prague he received a letter from his old acquaintance, now German Foreign Minister, Joachim von Ribbentrop. 'My dear Lord Beaverbrook,' it ran:

I heard that your health, which had troubled you in former years, was now quite restored ... I am writing to you from Prag, where I arrived with the Führer this evening, and I hope the Führer will settle the future relations between the German and the Czech peoples once and for ever and to the benefit of all. If you have the intention of coming to the Continent some time during spring, I would be delighted to see you in Berlin and have a talk with you again after this interval of about two years since I last saw you. Hoping to see you in Berlin before long as my guest ... With kindest regards...[32]

Beaverbrook's reply was equally friendly, if somewhat guarded. 'I am very happy to have your letter,' it went:

It was indeed in my mind to make a brief holiday on the Continent sometime in the near future. And when sunny days come, I shall certainly contemplate a visit to Berlin. In going there, one of my desires would in any case have been the prospect of seeing you again and having a talk. Now that I have your charming invitation, the desire is all the stronger...[33]

But even Beaverbrook could not ignore the worsening international weather. When, on 31 March, the British and French governments signed a pledge to guarantee Poland's frontiers against any future German aggression, the protest from the *Sunday Express* was unusually muted:

We must expect alarms to continue, anxieties to persist, and uncertainties to multiply ... There will be no war ... [but] those who share our beliefs must realise, as we do, that the nation has now embarked on an undertaking and an excursion which implies a denial and rejection of the teachings of this newspaper.[34]

Along with a change in the international climate came a change in Beaverbrook's own personal weather. On 25 May 1939 he was sixty. All his birthdays were marked by one celebration or another (and the ritual largesse to his lady friends) but the end of each decade required a more introspective balance sheet. The reckoning in the spring of 1939, when totted up, was unhappy. True, the newspapers were going well, but beyond that nothing seemed to have worked in his favour. Politically, he was a figure who was regarded with wariness at best, distrust for the most part and downright hatred by those whom he had insulted over the years in his newspapers. He was unmarried, with grown-up children with whom he had relationships of varying warmth; with Janet of affection in spite of her waywardness, with Max of alternate bursts of pride at his talents and fury at his indolence, and with Peter of total, almost non-speaking, distance. Cherkley was boring and Stornoway House suffocating. Finally, his asthma was getting no better. In short, there was only one possible conclusion. It was time to retire.

At that point Beaverbrook decided to make no more pronouncements about the likelihood or otherwise of war. On a visit to Paris in July, with Castlerosse who was then convalescing from a serious illness, he made a feeble effort to canvass French and German opinion by sending Geoffrey Cox, the Paris correspondent, to Berlin and Castlerosse to the Parisian streets to ask the question 'Will your country fight for Danzig?' After three days, meeting at the Ritz, Cox reported to Beaverbrook that the Berliners were firmly behind Hitler. Castlerosse, on the other hand, said with customary flippancy, 'I haven't got much further than the bar at Fouquet's. No one at the bar at Fouquet's is going to fight for Danzig.'[35]

More seriously, but equally ill-conceived, was Beaverbrook's scheme to sell his financial interest in his newspapers to their employees. It was, as his official biographer ruefully concluded, 'an appalling project'.[36] The price for a package of shares with limited voting rights in the holding company London Express Newspaper Limited was to be £3 million. The shares could be sold on to the public in carefully controlled tranches. Since none of the journalists could afford the £200,000 required, they were obliged to sign notes detailing their debt and redeemable when they managed to sell their shares, thus locking themselves in to a loyalty penalty in the event of their leaving. On the other hand, it would have been a bold journalist who told Wardell, the scheme's orchestrator, that he refused to join in. Nor was there any doubt where control of the newspapers would continue to lie.

On 5 August, Beaverbrook sailed for Canada, in his usual opulent style, on board the *Empress of Britain*. By 31 August, he was back in

London with his retirement indefinitely postponed. E. J. Robertson had told him of the Molotov–Ribbentrop pact of nonaggression between Germany and the Soviet Union and had advised him to return as soon as possible before war broke out. Yet for all the haste of his return he found on arrival that there was little for him to do. On the following day German armies invaded Poland. The British and French governments issued an ultimatum, which Hitler ignored. On 3 September the sad voice of a depressed Chamberlain announced on the radio that as a result Britain was at war with Germany.

Almost immediately, Chamberlain reconstructed his government. A War Cabinet of nine ministers was set up, and Churchill was brought back into government as First Lord of the Admiralty. A Ministry of Information was formed headed by a Scottish peer, Lord Macmillan. Beaverbrook, much to his and others' surprise, was not offered the post. 'I would have been the best man for the job at the outset,' he later wrote to his old friend Sam Hoare. 'I have the experience in journalism and propaganda. And in character I am just the type to have made a success and a real success at that.'[37] Needless to say, he then embarked on a detailed critique of the ministry and how it was run.

By then, Beaverbrook's absurd scheme for selling shares to his staff had collapsed, and with nothing better to do, after a few days of inactivity he decided on his own diplomatic mission: he was going to find out what the Americans thought about the war. On 20 September he sailed on the SS *Manhattan* to New York. His objective was not only to speak to as many formers of American opinion as he could in the month he was going to stay there but to seek an interview with President Franklin Roosevelt himself. He prepared carefully, in the knowledge that Roosevelt was an enthusiastic collector of first editions and historical records. When the meeting did take place, much of their discussion was about history. In fact, there is no doubt that the two men got on exceptionally well, Roosevelt deploying his famous charm and Beaverbrook his spiky and irreverent sense of humour. Beaverbrook, in an effort to add cement to the foundations of a genuine friendship, followed up by sending Roosevelt a colour print of 'The New Brunswick Fashionables' and an engraving of General Wolfe. Roosevelt responded that he was 'delighted to have the Wolfe print because I have made a special study of the relative strategy between the

Wolfe attack on Quebec and the later attack by General Montgomery, who married a cousin of mine from Dutchess County'.[38] Whether or not Roosevelt was telling the truth (he was apt from time to time to exaggerate the extent of his historical studies), it was enough to stimulate a flow of books and historical documents from Cherkley to the White House lasting until Roosevelt's death in 1945. As a reward, Beaverbrook received the ultimate accolade: he became firmly known as 'Max'.

On his return to London, Beaverbrook duly reported to Halifax on his conversation with Roosevelt and, as though to follow up, wrote a long letter to Roosevelt with his views on the current state of the conflict. Much more revealing, however, was his account of his American visit to Ambassador Maisky at lunch on 15 November. 'His most interesting revelation', Maisky noted in his diary, 'was that ... Roosevelt is quite definite in his support for the war and the participation of the USA in the war on the side of the Allies because he believes that fascism must be crushed once and for all'.

No doubt that was interesting to Maisky, but what followed was more revealing about Beaverbrook. 'Beaverbrook himself', Maisky's diary note goes on,

opposes the war. 'I am an isolationist', he fretted. 'What concerns me is the fate of the British Empire! I want the Empire to remain intact, but I don't understand why for the sake of this we must wage a three-year war to crush "Hitlerism". To hell with that man Hitler! If the Germans want him, I happily concede them this treasure and make my bow. Poland? Czechoslovakia? What are they to do with us? Cursed be the day when Chamberlain gave our guarantees to Poland! A peace conference must be convened immediately, without any preliminary conditions. Were this to be done, I'd support the move with all the means at my disposal, even if I had to *ruin my papers* to do so.'

By then Beaverbrook was obviously in full flow. He is

sure that Chamberlain will retire soon for reasons of ill-health. He thinks that either Hoare or Halifax will succeed him. Churchill, apparently, has no chance at all. Even Eden is more likely to become

prime minister. We shall see, however, whether Beaverbrook's forecast proves correct, particularly as far as Churchill is concerned. I've
noticed that Beaverbrook's attitude to Churchill is very changea-
ble: one day he might praise him as Britain's greatest statesman,
on another he might call him a 'swindler', 'turncoat' or 'political
prostitute'. Today he is madly annoyed with Churchill...[39]

Having thus declared himself to Maisky, Beaverbrook went quiet. His
newspapers continued sniping at the incompetence of the Ministry
of Information, but by then asthma was on the march again and it
was time to leave for the Riviera. He would have preferred Miami, of
course, but the journey was too hazardous. In fact, he was lucky, since
the work of refurbishing La Capponcina to his taste required personal
supervision and he arrived at the right time to make sure there were
to be no mistakes. It was only when the Soviets invaded Finland on
30 November that he realised that it would be safer, and more interesting, to be in England.

Christmas 1939 was spent at Cherkley. But it was not as it used to be.
Some twenty evacuees from London, all around twelve or thirteen, had
been billeted there, apparently for the duration of the war. Although
they were at first welcomed, Beaverbrook became progressively more irritated until he announced that he was shutting the whole place down.
He himself, he went on, would live in a small cottage on the estate. The
evacuees, rather to their relief, were shunted back to London.

Beaverbrook was as good as his word to Maisky. During the first
months of 1940 he flirted with almost anybody who had anything
like a credible plan for an immediate negotiated peace. There was no
shortage of candidates, some of which were considered with care by
the British government as they purported to originate in Berlin. But
Beaverbrook was after something much more spectacular, and his first
opportunity came towards the end of January. The Duke of Windsor,
who had been given the rank of major-general and attached to the
British Military Mission in Paris, was on a visit to London (carefully
tracked, as always, by operatives of MI5).

In the early evening of 22 January, Beaverbrook met the Duke at the
home of his loyal adviser Walter Monckton. So alarmed was Monckton

at what followed that he reported the conversation to his friend Charles Peake, head of the Foreign Office News Department. Peake in turn wrote to Oliver Harvey, a senior Foreign Office official at the time serving as Envoy Extraordinary and Minister Plenipotentiary to France. Copies went to 'Alec' (possibly Sir Alexander Cadogan, Permanent Under Secretary of State at the Foreign Office) and 'Ronald in Paris' (presumably Sir Ronald Campbell, the British Ambassador to France).

'W. M. tells me', Peake's letter ran,

> that he was present at a frightful interview between the D. of W. and the Beaver two days ago. Both found themselves in agreement that the war ought to be ended at once by a peace offer to Germany. The Beaver suggested that the Duke should get out of uniform, come home and, after enlisting powerful City support, stump the country in which case he predicted that the Duke would have a tremendous success. The support of the Beaver press was pledged to him. W. M. contented himself with reminding the Duke that if he did he would be liable to UK Income Tax. This made the little man blench and he declared with great determination that the whole thing was off. This shows you what a menace the Beaver is.[40]

Of course, the story reached Downing Street almost immediately. On 27 January, Chamberlain wrote one of his discursive letters on public affairs to his sister Ida: 'I have … learnt on *unimpeachable* authority [presumably MI5] that while the Duke of Windsor was here this week Beaverbrook tried to induce him to head a peace campaign in this country promising him the full support of his papers. Fortunately the Duke has wiser & more patriotic advisers.'[41] He had heard that Monckton had warned the Duke, after Beaverbrook had left, of the danger of incurring a charge of mutiny at best, given his military commission, and of high treason at worst. What was left hanging in the air, of course, was whether Beaverbrook was running a similar risk as a conspirator.

It was not long before Beaverbrook meddled again in a peace movement. Writing to the editor of the *Philadelphia Record* in early March, he noted that the various peace initiatives were having little effect. 'Only in Glasgow and Clydeside generally', he went on, 'have they any real hold. There is the stronghold of the Independent Labour Party, whose leaders [John] McGovern, [Jimmy] Maxton and Campbell Stephen are men of force and integrity as well as being pacifists.'[42] Beaverbrook followed up by inviting the three men to dinner at Stornoway House on 5 March. As might be expected, it turned out to be a confused affair of which no contemporary record exists. Later accounts differ on how much was drunk (all participants claimed at various times to have abstained the whole evening, leaving open the question of what happened to the two bottles of champagne which went missing), on who was present (Beaverbrook's butler, Albert, later recalled that Campbell Stephen was absent) and on what might happen next. McGovern later claimed that Beaverbrook had offered to fund the party '£500 for every seat you fight',[43] but if the promise was made, there was no follow-up.

Hard on the heels of one came yet another initiative which Beaverbrook was quick to latch onto. Captain Basil Liddell Hart, a military historian who had been advising the government at the same time as writing for the *Daily Express*, had heard about peace feelers apparently coming via Dublin from Berlin and communicated through the pacifist Lord Tavistock to Richard Stokes, a Labour MP known to be on the left of the party. On the same day as the ill-fated dinner with McGovern and company, Stokes had written to Beaverbrook at Liddell Hart's suggestion to request a meeting. It so happened that on the evening of 7 March, Liddell Hart was in discussion with Beaverbrook about his own role when, just as he was leaving, Stokes turned up. 'He referred to the peace terms which Tavistock had published,' Liddell Hart recorded,

> whereat Beaverbrook showed scepticism of anything that came from that source. Stokes admitted that Tavistock himself might not amount to much but insisted that the terms themselves were genuine. He went on to say that he was making a speech at Barrow on Monday, whereupon Beaverbrook jumped up, strode to the dictaphone and dictated that it was to be promptly reported.[44]

It all came to nothing, and for a simple reason. In the early hours of 9 April, Germany launched Operation *Weserübung*, the invasion of Denmark and Norway. It had been well prepared and was a triumphant success. At long last Beaverbrook was forced to accept that all peace initiatives were now irrelevant. As for his own role, 'I am too old a man to take more than a small part in this war.'[45] By the beginning of May it had become clear that the British effort of intervention to halt the German occupation of Norway had failed dismally and was leading to an ignominious evacuation of the Norwegian ports. Chamberlain's survival suddenly became an immediate political issue. When urged to lead a move to dislodge him, Beaverbrook refused. 'You will note', he wrote in response, 'that in every case the revolt that broke the Government came from within. The same applies this time. Those who try to do it from without are simply wasting their ammunition.'[46]

In the event, it was the House of Commons which decided the issue. Beaverbrook had written, in the *Daily Express*, his final acceptance that a negotiated peace was no longer an option, that

> the whole nation is now fixed and settled in its purpose to fight the war to its conclusion … All hopes of an early peace have now been vanquished … All men … are now at one in urging counsels of resolution, of decision, of violence to the point of exhaustion.[47]

Chamberlain had taken due note. 'Splendid article in the Express this morning,' he wrote. 'When so many are sounding the defeatist note over a minor setback it is a relief to read such a courageous and inspiring summons to a saner view.'[48] Beaverbrook replied in kind with a letter recounting Bonar Law's experience in 1916 when he defied a 'truculent House'.[49]

The Commons debate on 7 and 8 May was certainly lively. It started calmly as a debate on the adjournment but gathered pace when the Labour leadership moved it to become a vote of censure, in other words a matter of confidence. Harold Nicolson recorded that, in the final twenty minutes or so,

> passions rose, and when the Division came there was great tensity [*sic*] in the air. Some 44 of us, including many of the young Service Members, vote against the Government and some 30 abstain.

This leaves the Government with a majority of only 81 instead of a possible 213, and the figures are greeted with a tremendous demonstration … [Chamberlain] walks out looking pale and angry.[50]

Beaverbrook later claimed to have seen Churchill on the morning of 9 May, but his pencilled note is undated and contains factual inaccuracies, and there is no record of such a meeting either in his or Churchill's appointments diaries. In fact, he was very much on the outside during that crucial day. Chamberlain had decided that there should be a National Government. The question then was whether Labour would serve under him or would demand an alternative. By the evening, the two Labour leaders, Clement Attlee and Arthur Greenwood, after consulting their colleagues in the National Executive Committee in Bournemouth, had told Chamberlain that they would not serve under him at any price. Halifax, one of two possible candidates, had already told Chamberlain in the afternoon that 'if I was not in charge of the war (operations) and if I didn't lead in the House, I should be cypher'.[51] By the late evening of 9 May, Churchill was confident enough to tell his son Randolph, 'I think I shall be Prime Minister tomorrow.'[52] The *Daily Express* political correspondent, Guy Eden, had also sniffed out the story. 'Churchill expected to be new Premier' ran his headline in the morning edition of 10 May. 'Chamberlain to resign.'[53]

Yet there was to be another twist to the story. At dawn on 10 May, the German Army launched a massive attack along a wide front from the Netherlands in the north to Belgium and Luxembourg in the centre to the French Meuse at Sedan in the south. A shocked Chamberlain, in response, reversed his previous intention to resign.

I had fully made up my mind as to the course I should pursue and had fully agreed it with Winston and Halifax. But as I expected Hitler has seized the occasion of our divisions to strike the great blow and we cannot consider changes in the Government while we are in the throes of battle. The next two or three days will probably decide the fate of mankind for a hundred years.[54]

His change of heart, however, did not survive the arguments put forward at the War Cabinet in favour of a National Government and the Labour insistence that he should not lead it.

Chamberlain submitted his resignation to the King late in the afternoon of 10 May. The King went out of his way to be sympathetic. He 'told him how grossly unfairly I thought he had been treated & that I was terribly sorry that all this controversy had happened'.[55] Churchill was then summoned to Buckingham Palace and invited to form a government. In fact, it would not be too long before he was able to provide a list to the King of his new ministers. But much to the King's surprise, and, indeed, to his dismay, one of those who figured on Churchill's list was somebody who had claimed that he was too old to play an active part in the war: Churchill's on-and-off friend of twenty-five years' standing and arch supporter of the King's brother, the Duke of Windsor. Lord Beaverbrook, it appeared, was to be invited to join His Majesty's government.

British statesman Winston Churchill (left), who became Prime Minister on 10 May 1940, with Neville Chamberlain (right) at an outdoor ceremony, 1940.

CHAPTER 21

DIE LUFTSCHLACHT
UM ENGLAND

'Your old and faithful friend'[1]

'**M**y dear Prime Minister,' began King George VI's first letter, dated 10 May 1940, to his newly appointed head of government.

> I have been thinking over the names you suggested to me this evening in forming your Government, which I think are very good, but I would like to warn you of the repercussions, which I am sure will occur, especially in Canada, at the inclusion of the name of Lord Beaverbrook for aircraft production in the Air Ministry. You are no doubt aware that the Canadians do not appreciate him, & I feel that as the Air Training Scheme for pilots & aircraft is in Canada, I must tell you this fact. I wonder if you would not reconsider your intention of selecting Lord Beaverbrook for this post. I am sending this round to you at once, as I fear that this appointment might be misconstrued.[2]

Such was the apparent urgency of the message that the King's letter, written in his own hand, was hastened down the Mall to Admiralty House, where Churchill was working on Cabinet appointments. The letter was duly read and, for the moment, put aside. But just after nine o'clock that evening, when Neville Chamberlain had broadcast his resignation, Churchill sent to the King his list of five senior ministers: the Conservatives were represented by Lord Halifax at the Foreign Office and Anthony Eden at the War Office, with Chamberlain remaining in government as Lord President of the Council; Labour's

A. V. Alexander was to become First Lord of the Admiralty; while the leader of the Liberal Party, Sir Archibald Sinclair, was handed the role of Secretary of State for Air. There was no mention of Lord Beaverbrook.

Churchill was in difficulty. He and his old friend had had a congratulatory lunch by themselves at Admiralty House that very day. The matter of aircraft production was undoubtedly high on the agenda and a possible ministerial job was in the offing. Beaverbrook was interested but cautious. He knew perfectly well that he had enemies in Westminster across the political spectrum who resented his use of his newspapers to criticise and, at times, to undermine them. Baldwin's political ghost was still stalking the corridors. The King's letter was an open invitation to Churchill to play on Beaverbrook's caution and drop both his friend and, almost by accident, one of his pet projects.

Nevertheless, the letter itself, on further reading, turned out to be distinctly odd. First of all, it was not at all clear why the King, who had obviously not objected to Beaverbrook's name at the earlier meeting with Churchill, should then, immediately afterwards, have felt moved to write. As for the content of the letter, his objections to Beaverbrook's appointment were no better than flimsy. Beaverbrook's reputation in Canada had been bandied around for years and Churchill, of all people, did not need to be told about it. Moreover, to suggest that the Canadian government might refuse to implement a training scheme at a time of such peril was not far short of ludicrous. All in all, the more the text of the letter and the surrounding circumstances are examined, the more likely it seems that the King had reported to others the content of his meeting with Churchill and had been told to row back. It is tempting, and perhaps more than tempting, to see the hand of Queen Elizabeth guiding the King's pen. She had been uncompromising in her hostility to Wallis Simpson and, by extension, to the Duke of Windsor. To have both the Duke's most vocal supporters at the head of government must have been bitter gall.

Be all that as it may, Churchill decided to ignore the King's warning. He urged Beaverbrook to overcome his doubts and accept the job. Having played hard to get wholly to his satisfaction, Beaverbrook acquiesced, and on 14 May formally agreed to serve as minister at the new Ministry of Aircraft Production (MAP), reporting directly to the War Cabinet. The decision taken, Beaverbrook wasted no time in seeing Sir Charles Craven, the chairman of Vickers-Armstrong, who had been appointed as Civil Member for Development and Production at the Air Ministry in April, as well as other officials from the Air Staff to discuss priorities. He also met with Air Chief Marshal Sir Wilfrid Freeman, the Air Member for Development and Production and the senior Air Force officer at the ministry. The Beaverbrook machine was moving into action.

Lord Beaverbrook, Minister of Aircraft Production, in Whitehall, 15 May 1940.

Thus began the year, from 14 May 1940 to 1 May 1941, which his official biographer has claimed entitled him to be numbered 'among the immortal few who won the Battle of Britain ... At the moment of unparalleled danger, it was Beaverbrook who made survival and victory possible.'[3] The verdict is supported by no less an authority than Churchill himself. After the war, in his memoirs, he wrote that 'during these weeks of intense struggle and ceaseless anxiety Lord Beaverbrook rendered signal service ... This was his hour. His personal force and genius ... swept aside many obstacles. New or repaired aeroplanes [*sic*] streamed to the delighted squadrons in numbers they had never known before.'[4] Further corroboration is provided by Air Chief Marshal Sir Hugh Dowding, commander of RAF Fighter Command in the summer and autumn of 1940. 'The effect of Lord Beaverbrook's appointment', his official despatch runs, 'can only be described as magical.'[5]

Prime Minister Winston Churchill is pictured in discussion with Lord Beaverbrook in the garden of 10 Downing Street, 1940.

There were, as might be expected, dissenting voices, which have become louder as time has passed. Air Vice-Marshal Arthur Tedder, who worked at MAP until November 1940, wrote to the Air Minister Sir Archibald Sinclair in a valedictory appraisal of his time at the ministry:

> It is essential in the interests of the Service and the country that a drastic change be made with a view to return to a rational and responsible organisation based on the principles of co-operation, loyalty and honesty without which such a Ministry cannot perform its sole function, which is to meet the requirements of the fighting Services.[6]

Air Commodore John Slessor, at the time Air Officer Commanding No. 5 (Bomber) Group, later wrote that the real hero was Wilfrid Freeman, who 'had laid the essential foundation and built up the structure of a working organisation ... until the new Minister lost no time in producing a new production programme ... [which] ... bore little or no relation to strategic requirements'.[7]

On one point, Beaverbrook's supporters and his critics can agree. There was a new production programme, the result of the discussions with Craven on 15 May but quite clearly of Beaverbrook's authorship, to give until the end of September 'special and exceptional priority to some types [of aircraft] and suspending development of others'.[8] Wellingtons, Whitley Vs, Blenheims, Hurricanes and Spitfires were to be favoured. The reasons were simple: they were the aircraft which could make the greatest impact in resisting the expected German assault.

There can be no doubt that the decision to adopt the new programme was 'one of the most important single incidents in the history of war production' in that it enabled the provision of the equipment to fight, later on in the year, what was to become known as the Battle of Britain.[9] Not only did it safeguard the supply of materials already marked for the five types of aircraft but it paved the way for the diversion of materials and manpower in their favour. Taken together with the decision to cannibalise damaged aircraft for working parts rather than repair them and to expropriate any supplies held up in the supply chain wherever they were, the Beaverbrook initiative, for which he should be given due credit, created the framework for the surge in fighter production in the early months of 1941.

Yet it would be wholly wrong to credit Beaverbrook, as many have done (including, naturally, Beaverbrook himself) with the earlier surge in fighter production which took place in the spring of 1940. This was largely due to increases in capacity which had been long planned. Deliveries of fighters to operational squadrons, as well as overall productive activity, 'began to rise fairly steeply in the months immediately preceding the establishment of MAP ... reached a peak in June 1940, very early in the Beaverbrook period, and was already falling quite steeply as the Battle of Britain arrived at its climax'.[10] It may well be that the infusion of energy that Beaverbrook brought to the task hastened the delivery of aircraft from factories to squadrons, but the evidence is slim. In fact, the monthly deliveries of fighters declined from a peak in July to a low point in December, when 'aircraft deliveries were some way *below* the level that had been achieved in the month of Beaverbrook's appointment'.[11] Yet here, too, caution is necessary. The German air assault which began in earnest towards the end of June 1940 was directed first at ports and shipyards but was soon extended to airfields and aircraft factories. Whether as a result or not, the index of aircraft production started to fall in August and dropped quite sharply in September before picking up later in the year when the German targets had shifted to London and other major cities.

The transfer of the existing machinery for aircraft production to the new ministry was not in itself a drastic administrative step. Situated in the Yorkshire spa town of Harrogate, the department was a 'highly structured organisation – dominated by senior air force personnel and professional civil servants – within which committees flourished, set procedures existed for carrying out the work, and the functions of staff were clearly defined'.[12] In fact, Freeman had built up the capacity and performance of the unit to the point where it had become a rival to the Ministry of Supply. It was a perfectly logical step, even desirable if it injected new energy, to hive it off as a ministry in its own right. Moreover, there was no denying that Beaverbrook was the man to provide the impetus.

The difficulty was that Beaverbrook had no time for the stately rhythms of Harrogate. He set up his headquarters in Stornoway House. The bedroom on the top floor was a private office, with two private secretaries drafted in from the *Express*. Every room in the building below was turned into an office, to accommodate officials brought in from other departments; Sir Archibald Rowlands from the Treasury was to become Permanent Under Secretary, with John Eaton Griffiths and Edmund Compton to run the private office. There were also appointments from industry: Patrick Hennessy from Ford UK, Trevor Westbrook from Vickers, William Lawrence Stephenson from Woolworths, A. J. Newman from Newman Industries and G. C. Usher from International Combustion. As with his newspapers, Beaverbrook was a good picker of men. All of them brought their knowledge of how factories worked as well as a goodly ration of public sector drive. It is little wonder that the 'air marshals', as Beaverbrook contemptuously called them, were upset. As for supporting staff, they were transferred in bulk from the *Express* offices to Stornoway House but stayed on the paper's payroll (Beaverbrook himself took no salary). In fact, the machinery of the ministry itself soon became too unwieldy for Stornoway House, and the whole circus, including the staff from Harrogate, found a new home in an ICI building near Lambeth Bridge.

'It may be said', reports an official history, 'that, broadly speaking, there was no central planning in MAP for the first six months of its existence.'[13] The decision to change production priorities had upset the careful modules set up by the Air Ministry. Furthermore, Beaverbrook announced, by posting a notice in his office, that 'organisation is the enemy of improvisation'. There were no longer to be committees (another notice read 'Committees take the punch out of war'). The only concession to structure was a ministerial council, meeting somewhat randomly with no fixed membership in the evenings, at which Beaverbrook would listen to reports from his senior staff (the membership fluctuated with his moods), review the daily output reports from the assembly plants, storage depots and engine factories and bark his orders down the telephone. By two o'clock in the morning everybody was more than ready for bed, knowing that they had to start work again six hours later. On Saturday afternoon the reports of emissaries who had been sent to evaluate the performance of the factories charged with meeting the requirements of the Air Ministry, together with lists of suggested improvements, would arrive for inspection. Staff were allowed to take every other Sunday off. All in all, life was one of 'informality, spontaneity and improvisation'.[14] To officials in or from Whitehall, it was perilously close to chaos.

Immediately after MAP was formed on 17 May, Beaverbrook set about enlarging it. At the first War Cabinet meeting he attended on the following day, he asked to be given the authority to take over the aircraft storage units and the Royal Air Force repair depots from the Air Ministry, and to withhold delivery of aircraft to Canada and raw material to Australia. The next target was the takeover of the 'ferry pools' whose function was to fly aircraft from factories to storage before transfer to operational squadrons. This involved another bruising row with Sir Archibald Sinclair and threats to appeal to Churchill.

There was then one near cataclysmic event which, as it turned out, acted in Beaverbrook's favour. The final days of May 1940 saw the evacuation of what remained of the British Expeditionary Force from the beaches of Dunkirk. Beaverbrook, like everybody else in Britain, followed developments with a mixture of despair at the military defeat and pride at the intensity of the rescue effort. By 31 May more than three hundred thousand British and Allied men had been brought home. But it was not just the heroism of the event. Dunkirk signalled the true end of the 'Phoney War'. For Beaverbrook, this meant the end of talk of isolationism, of finding a settlement with the Germans, of belief that a deal could be done. What was now at stake was the survival of Britain and the British Empire. For him, and for the rest of the country, nothing else mattered.

This change of mood was illustrated by the publication on 5 July of 'the most influential wartime tract Britain had known for over two hundred years, and the best-selling ever'.[15] Entitled *Guilty Men*, it had been written in four days, from 1 to 4 June, by three of the staff of the *Evening Standard*, Michael Foot, Frank Owen and Peter Howard, mostly on the roof of the newspaper's office when they were not engaged in producing the paper itself. Their purpose was clear at the outset. It was 'to pillory and to condemn the National Government', and Neville Chamberlain in particular, with 'uninhibited venom'.[16] Of course, there was no attempt at scholarly analysis of the facts. It was a polemic, and, as such, it was an outstanding success. To give the flavour of the language, Howard in one of his chapters targets Sir Thomas Inskip, the pre-war Defence Minister, 'speared for all time as "Caligula's horse", depicted as a complacent, stupid, "bum-faced evangelical"'.[17]

Guilty Men certainly caught the public mood. It was reprinted seven times during July by its publisher, Gollancz, and by the end of 1940 had sold over 200,000 copies. Needless to say, since the authors had wished to remain anonymous by adopting the name of the ancient Roman 'Cato', there was immediate speculation about who was behind it. Duff Cooper was put forward but rejected on the grounds that he could not possibly have written in such a vulgar manner. Randolph Churchill was another, more plausible, runner, not least because Churchill himself came out of it lightly. A few even suggested Beaverbrook, but without much conviction and he was able to make a joke about it. Michael Foot cleverly ruled himself out by reviewing the book critically in the *Evening Standard*.

One of the consequences of the change in Beaverbrook's mood was a subtle but noticeable change in his relationship with Churchill. Now that they were both playing for the same side, as it were, without reservation about the ultimate objective, Churchill, as he later wrote, 'was glad to be able sometimes to lean on him'.[18] Beaverbrook had the knack of cheering him up when he felt depressed, partly by blunt words of encouragement, as at St Omer in 1915, and partly by scabrous (and frequently malicious) gossip. In the dark moments of June 1940, Beaverbrook saw Churchill almost every day, particularly at dinner at Admiralty House or later in the evening at Stornoway House. Along with Brendan Bracken and Churchill's other old friend Frederick Lindemann (universally known as 'the Prof'), he was one of a small and trusted group to whom Churchill could unburden himself when his depression threatened to take hold.

Yet it was not only a matter of personal friendship. Churchill valued Beaverbrook's political advice even though, as Attlee pointed out after the war, he did not always take it. When he did, it was decisive. On 13 June, Churchill led an almost desperate mission to the French town of Tours to meet the French Cabinet and bolster their resistance to the German advance. Beaverbrook, almost by accident since he happened to be in Admiralty House when the decision was made, was swept into the eight-man mission. Never an intrepid flyer, he endured a truly dangerous flight in appalling weather before landing in a thunderstorm at an airport pitted with craters from the previous night's bombing. Nobody greeted them or, indeed, knew who they were. In pouring rain, they found their way to the Préfecture, where in due course a bedraggled French Premier, Paul Reynaud, turned up. The British were immediately told that unless there was an immediate pledge of support from President Roosevelt, the game was over and French resistance would collapse. A message to Roosevelt along those lines was already in draft.

Churchill asked for an adjournment of the meeting and led his colleagues out into the garden of the Préfecture. Pacing up and down amid the puddles underfoot and without any idea what they should do next, they debated among themselves for a good twenty minutes without conclusion before Beaverbrook spoke out. As one of the participants put it, 'his dynamism was immediately felt'. 'There is nothing to do but to repeat what you have already said, Winston,' runs the report. 'Tell Reynaud that we have nothing to say or discuss until Roosevelt's answer is received. Don't commit yourself to anything ... We are doing no good here ... Let's get along home.'[19]

It was good advice, and Churchill duly delivered the message. The meeting might then have ended with at least a degree of cordiality. Unfortunately, Reynaud, for reasons which have never been fully explained, had failed to tell Churchill that the remainder of the French Cabinet were assembled at the nearby Château de Cangey waiting for the British to engage with them. But having delivered Beaverbrook's message, Churchill led his colleagues back to Tours Airport. They had no choice. They had to take off before darkness. But none of them were under any illusions. The French ministers in turn thought that their departure signalled a brush-off. All in all, it was an unhappy ending to an unhappy meeting.

Once back in London, Churchill summoned the War Cabinet to meet that very evening at 10.15 p.m. While in session they were told of Roosevelt's reply to an earlier message from Reynaud. The United States government, they were assured, was doing 'everything in its power to make available to the Allied governments the material they so urgently require'. Roosevelt was particularly impressed by Reynaud's declaration that 'France will continue to fight on behalf of democracy, even if it means slow withdrawal, even to North Africa and the Atlantic'.[20] Churchill told the War Cabinet that Roosevelt's message was as far as the President could go without consulting Congress. Beaverbrook chimed in, saying that 'it was now inevitable that the United States of America would declare war'.[21] In their late-night euphoria, the War Cabinet agreed that Roosevelt should be requested to allow publication of his message. In itself it would bolster French morale and encourage them to fight on.

The bad news came early on the following day, 14 June. Cordell Hull, the American Secretary of State, had come down firmly against publication. Furthermore, almost immediately on the refusal a further message arrived from Roosevelt to Reynaud. His previous message, he stated, 'was in no sense intended to commit and did not commit the Government to military participation in support of Allied gov-ernments', his previous message should not be published and the best he could do was 'immediately to furnish food and clothing to civilian refugees in France'.[22]

It was a depressed and deflated Churchill who during the day of 14 June moved, with his family and household, at long last from Admiralty House to 10 Downing Street. But Churchill 'thought it best' not to spend what remained of the night there. Instead, he asked Beaverbrook if he could stay at Stornoway House. On arrival there, he and his friend took time to reflect on all that had happened in the past two days. In the hope that Roosevelt might be open to persua-sion, Churchill drafted a further message, warning of the dangers to America of a German victory. 'If we go down you may have a United States of Europe under the Nazi command far more numerous, far stronger, far better armed than the New World.'[23] But Washington ears were now deaf. On 16 June, France sued for an armistice. What Churchill called the Battle for France was over. The Battle of Britain was about to begin.

On the same day, Beaverbrook, impervious to the general cloud of gloom, drafted the first of his letters to Churchill complaining that he did not have the authority to run his ministry in the way he wished. The letter was never sent, but it was followed on 19 June by a memo-randum to the War Cabinet on the progress. In its final version, again, it did not include a carefully drafted closing paragraph proposing that somebody else should take over his ministry and manage it 'on lines more satisfactory from the viewpoint of the Air Ministry'.[24] But by the end of the month Beaverbrook had had enough. The constant battles with the Air Ministry and the knowledge that senior Air Force officers in his own ministry such as Wilfrid Freeman were openly voicing their disquiet was affecting his health. The asthma attacks were becoming more frequent.

On 30 June he wrote to Churchill. 'It is imperative', his letter runs,

that the Ministry of Aircraft Production should pass into the keeping of a man in touch and sympathy with the Air Ministry and the Air Marshals ... My decision to retire is based on my firm conviction that I am not suited to working with the Air Ministry or the Air Marshals ... I am convinced that my work is finished and my task is over.[25]

Interestingly enough, his letter nowhere comes out clearly submitting his resignation. It reads more like a proposal for a change in management. Churchill, however, took it as a resignation, and proceeded to swat it aside. 'I have received your letter of June 30', he wrote back,

> and hasten to say that at a moment like this when an invasion is reported to be imminent there can be no question of any Ministerial resignations being accepted. I require you therefore to dismiss this matter from your mind and to continue the magnificent work you are doing on which to a large extent our safety depends.[26]

Beaverbrook acquiesced, somewhat grudgingly, insisting that he could 'not get the information which I require ... The breach which has ... been made between the Air Ministry and myself cannot be healed ... It is obvious that another man must be called upon who can work with the Air Ministry and the Air Marshals.'[27] In fact, there was a good deal of play-acting in all this. After its heavy losses in France, the Luftwaffe had taken time to reorganise and set up bases along the coast. It was not until the middle of June that the German High Command felt able to sanction what were called *Störangriffe* ('nuisance raids'), widespread attacks by a few aircraft. Yet nobody in London was under any illusion. The raids were a prelude to what was to come. As Churchill pointed out, the resignation of a senior minister at this point was simply unacceptable.

Nevertheless, Churchill clearly felt that he needed to keep Beaverbrook from issuing any more damaging threats. The warfare, too, with the Air Ministry had to be stopped. As the nuisance raids grew in number throughout July, accompanied by daylight attacks by Stuka dive bombers on British Channel shipping, ports and coastal airfields and by night raids on aircraft repair and assembly facilities, it became more and more apparent that Beaverbrook's ministry was, as Churchill had foreseen, central to the task of winning the air battle.

Churchill's solution to his friend's grumbles was simple. At the end of July, he invited him to enter the War Cabinet with increased powers of supervision over the chain of aircraft production and delivery. But Churchill's gesture was not simply one to placate an unsettled minister. British intelligence reported that the main Luftwaffe assault on radar installations and airfields, codenamed *Adlerangriff* ('Eagle Attack'), was due to be launched on 6 August. The aim was to destroy Britain's fighter strength in the south of England in four days, then move to bombing military and economic targets up to the Midlands until daylight attacks could be resumed over the whole of Britain. The final act would be a mass bombing attack on London. Beaverbrook's ministry, as Churchill had told him yet again, would be central to Britain's survival.

Even in these tense moments there was room for some more play-acting. In his reply to Churchill's invitation Beaverbrook alluded to their previous exchange and the implication that he was not wedded to his task. 'Having reflected on it,' he wrote on 29 July,

> I am convinced that no change should take place at this Ministry ...
> I cannot lay the job down without doing real damage to the project.
> I am only too willing to serve in the War Cabinet if obliged to do so,
> but not at the expense of abandoning my plans here.[28]

Churchill's reaction is not recorded, but he certainly could be forgiven a wry smile at Beaverbrook's cheek.

On 2 August, Beaverbrook became a member of the War Cabinet. On 12 August, *Adlerangriff*, held up for a few days by bad weather, was launched. From then until the end of the month and into September, wave after wave of bombers, escorted by fighters, attacked airfields and the radar chain which was so effective giving the British fighter groups early warning. The attacks were intense. In the two weeks from 24 August to 6 September, 295 Spitfires and Hurricanes were lost and 171 badly damaged against a total output of 269 new or repaired aircraft. If that haemorrhage was not staunched, it was clear that the Battle of Britain would be lost.

That it was not lost was due at least in some part to the Luftwaffe's assessment of the damage inflicted on Fighter Command. German intelligence had apparently concluded that the Royal Air Force was no longer capable of providing an impregnable fighter shield. The way was open for more intensive bombing of industrial targets throughout England and Wales. Furthermore, the Luftwaffe's pride had been pricked on 25 August by a raid by British bombers on Berlin. Their targets had been industrial and commercial, but the cloud cover was so low that accurate identification was impossible. The result had been that the British bombs fell randomly across the city. The German response was immediate. On 7 September a series of raids, with nearly 400 bombers and 600 fighters, targeted the area of the London docks. It was the opening move in the campaign of mass bombing of London which was to last into 1941 and earn itself the nickname 'the Blitz'.

It was bad enough, and frightening enough, being subjected to almost round-the-clock air raids, particularly for someone susceptible at any time to asthma attacks. It was just at this point that Beaverbrook realised that he had a serious problem in the organisation of his own ministry. The hectic improvisation of the summer months had to be replaced by a more structured system. This was not something that he liked or, in truth, that he was much good at. He had therefore asked Patrick Hennessy to devise a method that would provide greater operational coherence. Hennessy duly produced a system based on carefully worked out coefficients of floor space and machining capacity available. Targets for output would be set on that basis, with the additional heroic assumption that capacity would be used to the full at all times. It was a mathematically elegant formula but in real life turned out to be wholly unrealistic. The targets were accordingly set at too high a level. This, of course, was much to Beaverbrook's liking. He was used to setting unrealistic targets for his newspapers, believing that they provided a stimulus to the greatest possible effort. (In practice they seem to have been largely ignored.)

Nevertheless, by the end of September, production figures were moving upwards. The problem was that the fighters that had won the

Battle of Britain in the summer were ill suited to night operations. For the purpose, aircraft had to carry, and deploy, a system of airborne intercept radar. The aircraft of choice turned out to be the Bristol Beaufighter, which was at an early stage in its operational development. Given the inadequate nature of London's anti-aircraft protection, the Beaufighters in service carried a heavy load and on many nights were too few in number to counter the mass of German bombers.

There were problems on the ground as well. Arguments in the War Cabinet were sharp and at times noisy. The debate on the use of labour was one such. Beaverbrook argued that the sole aim was maximum output. (When he found out that valuable time was lost when workers took cover at the sounding of the warning alarm, he suggested that the alarms be switched off.) The Minister of Labour, the trade union leader Ernest Bevin, took an opposite view, saying that workers needed proper protection and welfare provision if they were to give of their best. To make matters worse, Bevin was given to shouting, and Beaverbrook was not used to being shouted at. Bevin was chalked up as another enemy. But the list was becoming alarmingly long.

With the service chiefs, the atmosphere was little better. One exception was Charles Portal, Commander in Chief of Bomber Command and newly promoted to Chief of the Air Staff. Portal had been a bomber pilot in the First World War and learnt thereafter to keep quiet on the major political issues of the day. Always charming and well mannered, he took it upon himself to engage politely with ministers whoever they be. General Alan Brooke, however, was another matter. As Commander in Chief, UK Land Forces, it was his job to organise as best he could the national military defence against a German invasion. His diary records:

> To make matters worse ... Beaverbrook ... began to form an army of his own to protect aircraft factories in the event of invasion. He acquired large proportions of armour plating for the production of small armoured cars called 'Beaverettes', with which he equipped Home Guard personnel of factories for their protection.[29]

Standard Beaverette reconnaissance car of the British 4th/7th Royal Dragoon Guards, Royal Armoured Corps, 25 July 1940.

Brooke's hostility soon became personal. At Chequers in mid-August, he noted:

> Beaverbrook was present; after dinner he sat at the writing table, pouring himself out one strong whisky after another, and I was revolted by his having monkey-like hands as they stretched out to grab ice cubes out of the bowl. The more I saw of him throughout the war, the more I disliked and mistrusted him.[30]

RAF Squadron Leader Max Aitken with his sister Janet (Mrs Drogo Montagu) at their father's country home, Cherkley Court, August 1940.

By the autumn of 1940, Beaverbrook had offended most of the War Cabinet and a substantial group of service chiefs. Yet their hostility was tempered by the knowledge that his relationship with Churchill was unbreakable (and by the acknowledgement of his son Max's bravery as fighter pilot). There was also the matter of the support of Beaverbrook's newspapers. Churchill, for his part, knew that, whatever the mutterings of colleagues, he could not sack Beaverbrook after promoting and then defending him without losing authority himself. So the play-acting continued. By early December, Beaverbrook was pleading ill health and his inability to get on with other ministers.

> A bold policy is now needed. This bold policy means much inter-ference with other Ministries ... I am not now the man for the job. I will not get the necessary support. In fact, when the reservoir was empty, I was a genius. Now that the reservoir has some water in it, I am an inspired brigand. If ever the water slops over, I will be a bloody anarchist.[31]

Churchill's response, yet again, was decisive. 'There is no question', he replied,

> of my accepting your resignation. As I told you, you are in the gal-leys and will have to row on to the end. If you wish for a month's rest, that I have no doubt could be arranged ... I am so sorry your asthma returned yesterday, because it always brings great depression in its train. You know how often you have advised me not to let trifles vex and distract me. Now let me repay the service by begging you to remember only the greatness of the work you have achieved, the vital needs of its continuance and the good will of your old and faithful friend.[32]

Two weeks later there was more oil for troubled waters. 'Minor diffi-culties ... no relation to the vast issues with which we have to deal ... Let us keep plodding on together and see how things look in another year. I think they will look much better.'[33]

Christmas at Cherkley was, by pre-war standards, a sombre affair.

Since it was in range of German bombers, black-out was strictly enforced and guests were given clear instructions about where they should take shelter in the event of a raid. Beaverbrook himself had acquired an armoured car and had provided his secretary, his valet and his Air Force driver with sub-machine guns with a duty to protect him if he was threatened by attackers, although it was never specified who they might be. Nevertheless, the house party had its moments. With Randolph Churchill, his wife Pamela and Roosevelt's newly appointed special envoy to Europe Averell Harriman as guests, and Beaverbrook's young secretary Betty Bower in attendance (throughout the feast diligently pursued by the First Lord of the Admiralty, A. V. Alexander, and finally forced to take refuge in the asthma room), life was anything but dull.

Christmas over and, back in London, the scenery in the Ministry for Aircraft Production had shifted. Sir Hugh Dowding had been removed from office, Wilfrid Freeman had been appointed Vice-Chief of the Air Staff (he would have got the top job had he not been divorced, thus incurring a veto from Buckingham Palace) and Charles Portal had become Chief of the Air Staff. Production figures were encouraging. There were new faces and new ideas. The main effect of the changes was to firm up the view of Beaverbrook and Hennessy that the days of improvisation were over, and the ministry should settle down to a more orderly working method. Finally, it had become apparent to all the belligerents that the Blitz had failed in its objective to destroy British morale. In fact, Hitler had on 18 December formally called off the German invasion plan (such as it was).

As a consequence, Beaverbrook's previously erratic gestures of resignation became much more serious. Early in the New Year, Churchill suggested that he should, in addition to the Ministry of Aircraft Production, take on the chairmanship of the Import Executive. The reply was immediate and, in truth, verging on impertinence. 'It is with deep regret', Beaverbrook wrote,

> that I am compelled to refuse to undertake the Chairmanship of the Import Executive ... The reason for my refusal is that I will make a failure under the conditions you are compelled to impose. I am not

a committee man. I am the cat that walks alone. For some time I have been most uncomfortable and I have asked for my release on that account. It is now imperative that I should go out ... I have had the joy of serving you through the dark days. Now I will watch with praise and exultation as you go forward to the final triumph.'[34]

Churchill immediately returned fire. 'Your resignation', he wrote back the same day, 'would be quite unjustified and would be regarded as desertion. It would in one day destroy all the reputation you have gained and turn the gratitude and goodwill of millions of people to anger. It is a step you would regret all your life.'[35] Undeterred, Beaverbrook simply repeated his arguments, adding, for good measure, 'I did not want to join the Government. The place in the Cabinet was undesired and was, indeed, resisted by me.'[36] Churchill yet again thought it wise to call a truce. 'My dear Max,' he wrote soothingly. 'You must not forget in the face of petty vexations the vast scale of events & the brightly-lighted stage of history upon wh we stand. I understand all you have done for us; & perhaps I shall live to tell the tale.'[37] The tactic worked. Beaverbrook's resignation was, at least temporarily, off the table.

The truce was not to last long. Beaverbrook was bored with his ministry and the way it was being organised by officials. On 15 April he wrote again to Churchill. 'It is with deep regret and a complete sense of failure that I write my resignation. I have been unable to attend to my duties efficiently for more than two months ... The office of Aircraft Production requires fierce & even violent control. I cannot serve it any more.'[38] Churchill by then was losing patience with his old friend. He needed Beaverbrook's support, and reassurance in the dark hours, but there was a limit to the number of times he could juggle with ministerial offices. Towards the end of April, he offered Beaverbrook a job as supervisor of all units of production, injecting a sense of greater urgency even though the danger of invasion was past. He even invented a new title: Minister of State. Finally, he appointed him deputy chairman of the Cabinet Defence Committee (Supply) with an office in No. 12 Downing Street. It was never going to work. True, Beaverbrook had been released from the Ministry of Aircraft

Production, but only to find himself in a ministerial vacuum. 'There is no use', he wrote to Churchill, 'adding my name to the list of "Ministers without Portfolio". You will just have to let me go. On retiring from the Government, I am ready to take a journey for you to Egypt or any war zone. The only request I make is "real authority".'[39] It was not an unreasonable request and, as it happened, was to be met sooner than either he or Churchill had expected. On 22 June 1941 the kaleidoscope of war was shaken yet again. The full might of the German war machine had been turned to the east. Germany had invaded the Soviet Union. There was more, much more, to be done, and Churchill turned yet again to his old friend for help in doing it.

CHAPTER 22

ENTER THE BEAR

'A Christmas-tree party'[1]

Early in the morning of Sunday 22 June 1941, Jock Colville, Churchill's duty private secretary for the weekend at Chequers, woke to the strident ring of the official telephone at his bedside. The matter, he was told, was of the highest importance. Not only that, but the caller from the Prime Minister's office in London insisted that all the guests at Chequers, including Churchill himself, should be informed immediately. The message was simple: the German Army had crossed the frontier with Russia. Germany was at war with the Soviet Union. Colville, by then fully awake (but perhaps not as fully dressed as he might have wished), immediately went the round of the bedrooms to break the news. The reaction of most of the guests was one of surprise and even shock, but 'it produced', Colville recorded, 'a smile of satisfaction on the faces of the P. M., Eden and [John] Winant [the US Ambassador]'.[2]

In fact, Churchill had predicted the event at dinner the previous evening (adding that he thought that Russia would be defeated). He was on firm ground. Others were not to know it, but what appeared to be a prediction was in fact based on Enigma intercepts, only recently available again after a break in decryption, bringing him daily up-to-date information on German troop movements. Nor was he the only one to make use of this intelligence goldmine. The previous Sunday, Eden had gone further with Ambassador Maisky. With Churchill's blessing, he had shown Maisky excerpts from the intercepts which depicted in minute detail the deployment of German forces along the border with Russia. Maisky was duly impressed but was unable to shake off the current Moscow view that the whole thing was little more than fabrication. Yet, as Maisky noted, 'the atmosphere in London [was] thick with anticipation of a German attack on the Soviet Union. The press writes about it; it is discussed in the corridors of Parliament; Churchill has spoken about it in public more than once, offering us the British Government's assistance...'[3]

Maisky himself admitted that he was confused. But it was nothing compared with the bewilderment of his masters in the Kremlin. Although warned by many in the West about the German military build-up, Stalin persisted in the belief that Hitler would only attack if he had reached a prior agreement with Britain. 'When war broke out,' recalled Maxim Litvinov, the People's Commissar of Foreign Affairs, 'all believed that the British fleet was steaming up the North Sea for a joint attack with Hitler on Leningrad and Kronstadt.'[4]

Chequers on the morning of 22 June was all hustle and bustle. Churchill, on hearing the news, had immediately decided to broadcast to the nation. He stayed in bed, as he often did, working on a text until mid-morning before coming downstairs to sharpen it up. Earlier, he had sent for Stafford Cripps, Britain's Ambassador to Moscow, at the moment on leave in England, and Lord Beaverbrook. Cripps and his wife motored over from their country home and arrived well in time for lunch. Beaverbrook took rather longer. Untypically, he had overslept and had only learnt the news from his secretary, David Farrer, at about ten o'clock. The summons from Churchill soon arrived and he was on his way from Cherkley with all speed. During the journey he reflected on what was happening. 'We were alone no more,' he later wrote. 'A vast new prospect opened up before us. If Russia could hold out, there was victory at the end of the road.'[5]

Eden and Winant had left Chequers for London, Eden uneasy because he had not been able to read through Churchill's draft. The next shift, as it were, had taken over: Beaverbrook, ever the optimist, and Cripps, on the other hand, at least on this occasion, a confirmed pessimist. Yet both were agreed with Churchill that the twin purposes of the broadcast were to rally the British public to support their new co-belligerent and to reassure the Soviets that Britain, in spite of Churchill's personal history, was firmly on their side.

Churchill went on air at 9 p.m. The broadcast was a triumph. 'A forceful speech!' was Maisky's first comment. 'A fine performance! … Bellicose and resolute: no compromises or agreements! War to the bitter end! Precisely what was needed!'[6] At the same time, a message came through from the Kremlin that the Soviets accepted a suggestion from Cripps that a mission be despatched as soon as possible to learn what help was needed and how far Britain could meet it.

For the moment, at least, it seemed that the Soviet mistrust of British motives was outweighed by the prospect of a quick defeat unless the immediate German thrust could be contained. Cripps, for one, believed that Russia would easily succumb to a repetition of the blitzkrieg that had brought France to her knees. Beaverbrook was, as always, less gloomy, but they were at one with Churchill in his conviction that 'Russia should be given all the aid in Britain's power'.[7] Furthermore, Churchill had made up his mind that the programme required the leadership of a senior minister with the energy and ability to brush aside all the obstacles in his path.

He did not have to look far. Beaverbrook had been in a fractious mood ever since leaving Aircraft Production. The job of overseeing three supply ministries without any executive power to intervene turned out, as he had foreseen, to be deeply frustrating. He let off steam by writing long complaining letters to anybody he thought would read them. When Churchill suggested in early June that he should become Minister for Food, he had replied in the rudest possible terms. 'Dear Winston,' he wrote, 'I do not know anything about food, and cannot grasp the problem in a short time. Experience is needed. I have none. It is not even a production job. I have energy and a sense of urgency. These are at your disposal if you can use them.'[8] This letter was followed by another, running to several pages, setting out all his grievances, real or imagined. At the same time, at lunch with Maisky,

[he] launched a splenetic attack on the English: they are carefree and sluggish, underestimate the severity of the situation, do not look ahead, are always late, have grown accustomed to the quiet life and don't want to give up their comforts. They are capable of doing so many stupid things![9]

It is a mark of Churchill's patience that, in the middle of running a war, he was prepared to tolerate what other Prime Ministers would have shut down in terminal irritation. True, there were moments when he let his feelings be known in gusts of anger, but they passed soon enough. In fact, although it seems strange, it was something of a relaxation for Churchill to respond, usually in dictation late at night, to Beaverbrook's long and self-pitying missives. Yet it was a sign of a deeper relationship between the two men that for all the moments of uproar they remained steadfast in their friendship. Not only that, but Churchill held to the view that however difficult his Canadian friend was, and however much Mrs Churchill disapproved of him, Britain in her time of trial needed him.

Churchill finally found the right slot: the Ministry of Supply. As a ministry, Supply was rather a ramshackle affair. It had been set up in 1939 to co-ordinate the supply of equipment to all three armed forces, but such was the guerrilla warfare between the three that aircraft production lay outside its remit and the Admiralty refused to give up its responsibility for supplying the Royal Navy. This left the Royal Ordnance factories, producing ammunition, heavy guns and small arms, and various army research establishments. Even so, it was something of a managerial muddle, since many of the ordnance factories were run on an agency basis and there was an ill-defined demarcation line between Supply, the Ministry of Works and private building contractors. Supply was, as well, nominally responsible for the design and production of tanks and armoured cars, but in practice these were mostly designed and built by private engineering companies.

The organisation chart of the Ministry of Supply may have looked awkward enough, but the ministry ran itself surprisingly well. Since October the minister had been Sir Andrew Duncan, a genial Lowland Scot who had been successful in the shipbuilding industry before moving south to take a place on the court of the Bank of England and to become at the same time Conservative Member of Parliament for the City of London. As his junior minister, Harold Macmillan was enjoying his first taste of ministerial office and was showing his ability in standing in at times for Duncan in the House of Commons.

Churchill may have hoped that Beaverbrook would accept his offer of Supply with alacrity. He was to be disappointed yet again. At first, Beaverbrook refused 'to lift it out of Sir Andrew Duncan's hands unless he is a party to my doing so'.[10] A copy of this letter to Churchill was sent to Duncan himself, who, sensibly, replied that 'I deem it a clear duty to accept the Prime Minister's ... decision, and I do it without the slightest reservation. I am therefore indeed a willing party.' Beaverbrook, still dissatisfied, wrote again to Churchill asking him, among other things, to agree to limit his period of office to five months and to allow him to keep his present office. Churchill, for once, let his temper show. 'No one', he reminded Beaverbrook, 'has ever taken more trouble to meet the wishes and suit the bent of a colleague more than I have with you on account of my admiration for your qualities and our personal friendship.'[11] Beaverbrook, wisely, beat a retreat. On 29 June, Beaverbrook's Rolls-Royce arrived at the main entrance to Shell-Mex House, the headquarters of the Ministry of Supply. (He had, however, secured agreement to keep his office in No. 12 Downing Street. Churchill was certainly not going to let go of their evenings together.)

It was not long before Beaverbrook discovered, as he had expected, that the injection of energy he was supposed to provide had little effect on the well-oiled machine that Duncan had bequeathed to him. By the middle of July, he was reporting to Churchill that 'the sense of urgency must be in all that we do ... We thrive on unrest. And I want to take advantage of it for the production programme during the months that lie ahead.'[12] In short, the Ministry of Supply was turning out to be hard going. Fortunately, Beaverbrook's true role, in Churchill's mind, was not in energising the Ministry of Supply but in assuming the role of lead minister in negotiating with the Soviets about their military requirements.

In early July, Roosevelt had sent his most trusted adviser (sometimes so obviously trusted that he became known as 'Deputy President'), Harry Hopkins, to Moscow to assess the strengths and weaknesses of the Soviets against the German onslaught. Hopkins duly went about his task and came to the conclusion, at first even to him surprising, that after surviving the first initial shock (Stalin was said to have spent the first seven days in his dacha in a sea of alcohol), the Soviets were robust in their conviction that in the end, if it could get that far, the Russian winter would treat Hitler in the same way as it had treated Napoleon. The only problem was to make sure that they had enough help to grind the German offensive down to a halt to allow the winter to do its worst. This, as Stalin pointed out to Hopkins, meant tanks, guns, aircraft. Hopkins was duly impressed and reported as much to Roosevelt and, more personally, to Churchill on his way back through London.

In late July, Hopkins hitched a lift on the British battleship HMS *Prince of Wales*, which carried Churchill, together with a retinue of Chiefs of Staff and senior officials from the Foreign Office, as well as a clutch of escort vessels, to a meeting with President Roosevelt, himself with an equivalent show of naval power, at Placentia Bay on the coast of the Canadian province of Newfoundland. Their meeting, oddly enough the first time the two men had met since 1919, was billed as an opportunity for the two leaders to get to know one another and, if possible, define a common policy against Japan. It was also their first opportunity to show the world their joint commitment, even though the United States was not a belligerent, to the fight against totalitarianism. This was spelt out in what became known as the Atlantic Charter.

Averell Harriman and Lord Beaverbrook on board HMS Prince of Wales *during the Atlantic Charter Conference, August 1941.*

Beaverbrook arrived in Newfoundland by air on 12 August, the second day of the formal meeting, in time to join in the discussion of the charter and to learn that he and Averell Harriman were to lead the mission to Russia (Hopkins was ruled out on grounds of health). Beaverbrook later claimed, wrongly, that he had managed to secure a change in the wording of the charter to protect imperial preference, but the important message for him was that he was acceptable to the Americans as a negotiator in the Anglo-American effort to satisfy Soviet requirements: 'a welcome guest', as Churchill put it to the War Cabinet, 'at a hungry table ... [The] President welcomes Beaverbrook's arrival in Washington and I am convinced this is a needful practical step.'[13]

At last, Beaverbrook felt that he had a job worth doing. In Washington he had discussions with American executives in the major engineering companies to persuade them to raise their production targets. At the same time, he was constantly on the telephone to his newspapers telling their editors to bang all the drums for Russia. 'Tanks for Russia' was to become the theme, urging the workers in Britain to increase output as a gesture of solidarity with their Russian comrades.

Yet everybody recognised that timing was of the essence. In his report to the War Cabinet on 28 August, Beaverbrook, now back in London, said that the Americans would not be ready before the middle of October. Churchill replied that this was too late. Eden added his voice, writing to Churchill that delay beyond the end of September 'will only give the Russians the impression that we are not confident of their ability to hold and are waiting and watching to see their fate'.[14] Beaverbrook complained that without the Americans he would have little to sell. Even Churchill in reply agreed that

> the long term supply of the Russian armies ... can only be achieved almost entirely from American resources ... Your function will be not only to aid in the forming of a plan to help Russia but to make sure we are not bled white in the process and even if you find yourself affected by the Russian atmosphere I shall be quite stiff about it here.[15]

On 3 September, Winant moved the pace of events up by telling Churchill that the Americans, for their part, were ready to announce the composition of their team for the mission to Moscow and were ready to send a posse of Army and Navy staff officers to London for a conference to discuss the overall production needs and the distribution of current production. Churchill immediately minuted Beaverbrook, Sir Alexander Cadogan and General Ismay that they should, as a matter of urgency, 'prepare our side of the Mission' (now developing a capital M) 'and also to arrange for the previous conference in London'.[16]

Almost immediately, all preparations were disrupted. The next morning, Maisky requested an urgent meeting with Churchill to convey a personal message from Stalin which he had just received. The text, Maisky noted, was a model of clarity, 'firm, clear and ruthless words; no illusions, no sweeteners; the facts as they stand; the threats as they loom; a remarkable document'.[17] The message was one of unrelieved gloom. Maisky recalled how he arrived at Downing Street late in the evening to deliver the message, where he was met by the Prime Minister, 'wearing a dinner jacket and with the habitual cigar between his teeth ... Churchill looked at me distrustfully, puffed at his cigar and growled like a bulldog: "bearing good news?" "I fear not," I replied, handing the Prime Minister the envelope with Stalin's message.'[18]

The message, presented to the War Cabinet the following morning, was indeed bleak. The recent stabilisation of the Russian front was not sustainable. 'The Germans believe', it went on,

> that they can beat all their adversaries one by one; first the Russians and then the British. As a result we have lost the greater part of the Ukraine and the enemy is now at the gates of Leningrad ... The only way out was to establish all ready [sic] a second front somewhere in the Balkans or in France ... as well as secure at the same time for the Soviet Union 30,000 tons of aluminium at the beginning of October and a minimum monthly delivery of some 400 airplanes and 500 tanks.[19]

Churchill told his colleagues of his immediate response to Maisky: that there was nothing effective that could be done before the end of

1941, that it was physically impossible for a second front to be built up in the Balkans unless Turkey came into the war. As for a second front in France, 'the Channel', he had said, 'which prevents Germany from jumping over into England, likewise prevents England from jumping over into occupied France'.[20]

In the discussion that followed, Churchill reiterated his belief that 'Stalin was worthy of being told the truth' that Britain could not possibly offer the level of assistance that the Soviet leader urgently sought, concluding that 'we should ... [not] ... make promises which we could not possibly fulfil'. He did, however, confirm that he would invite the Chiefs of Staff to meet Maisky and brief him on the reasons for this decision. Beaverbrook then protested that this was too 'harsh and depressing' and suggested that for the tanks and aircraft they should make 'an immediate promise that from the time when navigation would reopen, we would provide the Russians with half of this demand from our own resources. We would then press the Americans to supply the other half from their own resources without diminishing our appropriations.' Ernest Bevin, unusually, lent his support on the grounds that 'workers would respond to a call to give help to Russia without lessening the fulfilment of our own needs'. Churchill concluded the discussion by agreeing that he would 'look further into the possibility of making a definite promise to fulfil half the Russian demands from our resources', a course which he 'was inclined to favour'.[21] The final terms of the reply, including Beaverbrook's halfway house, a scaled-down agreement to despatch a small amount of aluminium in October, and an assurance that there was no question of cash payment, were agreed at a further meeting on 8 September.

The way was now open to accelerate preparations for the Moscow Mission. For the moment, however, Beaverbrook had other ideas. Earlier in the year, on 10 May to be exact, Hitler's deputy, Rudolf Hess, had flown in a specially prepared Messerschmitt Bf 110 on a circuitous route from the airfield of Augsburg-Haunstetten with the intention of ending up at Dungavel House, the spacious home of the Duke of Hamilton. His intention was to contact the Duke, who had been reported (wrongly) to be a Nazi sympathiser, and present proposals for an end to the war. Unfortunately for him, he was picked up by radar near Newcastle, was chased by three Spitfires in turn (who lost him) before he was spotted by a Boulton Paul Defiant out of Ayr. Hess, nearly out of fuel and aware that he was being chased down, took his Messerschmitt up to 6,000 feet and bailed out. Still struggling with his parachute when landed, and with an injured foot, he was discovered by a local farmer and ended his journey in the robust hands of the East Renfrewshire Home Guard. Hess gave his name as 'Alfred Horn'.

The wreckage of Rudolph Hess's World War II Messerschmitt aircraft, which he crashed in Scotland, May 1941.

Despite the somewhat *opera buffa* nature of Hess's arrival, his visit almost certainly had a serious purpose. If, as he claimed, he was Hitler's emissary, it was a matter of the highest possible importance not only to the British government but to Britain's co-belligerents and, tangentially, the United States. Beaverbrook certainly believed that Hess had been sent by Hitler. As he told Maisky soon after Hess had landed, 'There are many proofs ... the most convincing: an additional fuel tank was attached to Hess's plane, and he flew from Germany to Scotland assisted by a Perlongator [radio direction finder].'[22] (In fact this was no proof at all. Hess was obsessed by flying and already owned three Messerschmitts. Furthermore, as Deputy Führer he could within reason order what equipment he liked.)

Recent research has lent support to Beaverbrook's view, and suggests that Hess had brought with him a written proposal from Hitler that Britain should allow Germany her liberty in Europe and that in return she would face no threat to her Empire. Unfortunately for the credibility of his mission, Hess had told his British interrogator that the German leader was not prepared to negotiate the terms of the deal with Churchill's government, as its members had been consistently hostile to the Nazi regime; the Führer would prefer, he implied, a more accommodating cast of peacemakers.[23]

That, and a sense of journalistic curiosity, was enough for Beaverbrook. On 1 September he wrote to Hess reminding him of a previous meeting in Berlin and suggesting that they meet again. Hess agreed, provided that the meet was 'of an unofficial character without any witnesses'.[24] Beaverbrook then set about getting the necessary military permit for a visit to Mytchett Place in Surrey, where Hess was held in custody (and being extensively debriefed).

Such was the security surrounding Hess that visitors, and Hess himself, were given pseudonyms. Beaverbrook's permit records him as 'Dr Livingstone' while Hess was recorded in the log book as 'Jonathan'. Accordingly, 'Dr Livingstone' and 'Jonathan' met at 7.30 p.m., on 9 September, for some bizarre reason in Hess's bedroom. Their discussion was long and rambling. Apart from Hess's attacks on Russia and 'Bolshevists' generally, there was little substance. For instance, Hess's claim that Germany had invaded Russia to prevent Russia invading Germany, which she was bound to do in due course, was rightly greeted by Beaverbrook with comic disbelief. Finally, the duty officer, apparently tired of waiting outside, interrupted to announce dinner. Beaverbrook made his escape, promising to return. Needless to say, the promise was never kept. Nor was Beaverbrook's promise to ensure the meeting and its content remained private. He had made sure it was fully recorded.

On 11 September the War Cabinet agreed a timetable for discussions with the Americans prior to the joint delegation leaving for Moscow. The discussions were expected to last four to five days and there would be no pause before the delegation left London by train on the first leg of the long and circuitous route by sea to stay out of range of German aircraft based in Norway. Almost immediately there was a dispute about who was to do what. Within two hours of the Americans' arrival at Hendon Airport after their long transatlantic flight they were bundled into a meeting with 'a roomful of British officers and officials from all the armed services, the Ministry of Supply and the Ministry of Aircraft Production'.[25]

Beaverbrook, who had started in a mood of friendly optimism when he met Harriman (his former Christmas guest) and his colleagues at Hendon, seemed at the meeting to relapse into a mood of tetchy bullying. He demanded a declaration of 'what quantities of munitions and raw materials the United States was prepared to offer the Russians'.[26] Only when that was known could the extent of Britain's contribution be decided, and even that would have to wait until the Soviets' requirements were finalised at meetings in Moscow. Harriman's riposte was sarcastic. If what the US had offered was already on the table, 'this would relieve the Americans of the necessity of going to Moscow'.[27] Beaverbrook quickly protested that the two nations must go together. But it had not been an entirely happy beginning.

It was the first, and most serious, spat in an otherwise harmonious relationship between the two. But Churchill, when told by Lindemann of the episode, was alarmed enough to invite Harriman to dinner to soothe any hurt feelings. 'I know how difficult he [Beaverbrook] can be. But it's a vital matter. I depend on you.' Beaverbrook invited Harriman to dinner the following evening. But it was not a success. Kathleen Harriman, in a letter to her sister, summed it up. 'Lord Beaverbrook', she wrote, 'doesn't like to be contradicted and he's inclined to be set in his ways and views about people ... Dinner tonight was in rather sharp contrast to last night – with the PM. One's a gentleman and the other is a ruffian. Ave, luckily, can talk both languages.'[28]

The debate, such as it was, about what should be offered to the Russians passed back and forth between Downing Street and Whitehall and from there on to Washington and back. By 18 September, at a meeting of the full War Cabinet, Beaverbrook reported that the American position had been 'stiff and even harsh'. On the following day, in his report to the Cabinet's Defence Committee, he went further. 'There is a general retardation [*sic*] in the American production programme

... The figures now supplied to us ... are much lower than anything we have had before.'[29] The committee then addressed the problem of how much Britain could afford without weakening its own defence. It was far from easy. Harold Balfour, the Parliamentary Under Secretary of State, who was in attendance, recalled that the meeting

> started at 6 o'clock, went through three cigars – Mr Churchill's – until 9 p.m., adjourned, resumed at 10 for a two cigar session ... and only finished officially at about midnight and less officially in Lord Beaverbrook's room at No 12 ... I regret to say this session lasted till after 2 a.m.[30]

Lord Beaverbrook with members of the War Cabinet, 1941. From top left: Arthur Greenwood, Ernest Bevin, Lord Beaverbrook, Sir Kingsley Wood. Seated: Sir John Anderson, Winston Churchill, Clement Attlee, Anthony Eden.

In fact, the meeting had, finally, been productive. At dinner tête-à-tête, Churchill and Beaverbrook, as so often, made good progress, and the result was a detailed list of items that Beaverbrook would be authorised to offer to the Russians. Subsequently approved by the Defence Committee as the 'Guide for Lord Beaverbrook', it recognised that Britain was promising the maximum possible but that the United States 'is believed to be willing to accept a large responsibility for further expansions effective in 1943'.[31] The document, at Beaverbrook's insistence, was not printed or circulated to the War Cabinet for fear of leaks, which, he pointed out, would prejudice his whole position in Moscow.

Churchill also took the opportunity to write a letter to be delivered personally by Beaverbrook to Stalin. 'Lord Beaverbrook', he wrote, 'has the fullest confidence of the Cabinet, and is one of my oldest and most intimate friends. He has established the closest relations with Mr Harriman, who is a remarkable American wholeheartedly devoted to the victory of the common cause.'[32] Finally, as security cover, Beaverbrook and Harriman were advised to let it be known that they were travelling by air. Beaverbrook, of course, did this in his own style, publishing in the *Daily Express* of 20 September a message he was sending to workers in the tank-building factories as part of the 'Tanks for Russia' campaign: 'I am on my way to Moscow'.[33]

On the afternoon of Sunday 21 September, members of the joint Mission assembled on the platform of Euston Station, where a special train was waiting to take them north to Thurso, to arrive the following day at 8.50 a.m. From there, after a leisurely breakfast, they were to transfer to Scapa Flow to board the cruiser HMS *London* for the journey to the north Russian port of Archangel, where they expected to arrive the following Saturday, 27 September. They were advised to travel light, with personal baggage limited to 50lbs. Service personnel were to carry personal weapons, gas masks and steel helmets, civilians to carry gas masks and steel helmets if they had them. (Beaverbrook, of course, delegated these tiresome details to his apparently ever faithful valet, Albert, who accompanied him.)

Among the twenty-three members of the British party were Harold Balfour, Conservative Member of Parliament for the Isle of Thanet, who had served with distinction in the Royal Air Corps in the First World War and was now Parliamentary Under Secretary of State for Air; Major-General Sir Hastings ('Pug') Ismay, Deputy Secretary to the War Cabinet and Churchill's most trusted military adviser; Sir Gordon Macready, the Assistant Chief of the Imperial General Staff;

and, strangely, Sir Charles Wilson, Churchill's personal doctor, whose task, apparently, was 'to advise on medical supplies' (and, presumably, to cope with Beaverbrook's asthma).[34] There were officials from the Cabinet Office and the Ministry of Supply as well as clerks, cypherers, interpreters and, of course, Albert.

HMS *London*, it need hardly be said, was a warship built for war not for comfort. Passengers were at best something of a nuisance and were treated as such. All but admirals and the ship's captain had to sleep on the floor in passageways and, of course, were required to move quickly from there if the ship was called to action stations. Beaverbrook and Harriman were allotted, respectively, the admiral's and captain's day cabins, but these were below deck and the atmosphere was dry and polluted. Beaverbrook opted for a smaller deck cabin instead.

The journey itself was uneventful. The weather was calm and the sea kind. Beaverbrook was at his most entertaining, teasing the British and Americans alike, full of anecdote, reminiscence and gossip, with the occasional flash of poetry. He even found time to write a fierce letter (on Ministry of Supply writing paper) to Robertson at the *Daily Express* telling him that the paper was not shaping up to the times and that he must do better. But uppermost in his mind was the business to come in Moscow, and during the journey he set out his plan. It was, to use a phrase adopted by David Farrer in his unpublished account of the Second Front campaign, 'to be a Christmas-tree party', and there was to be 'no excuse for the Russians thinking they were not getting a fair share of the gifts on the tree'.[35] His object was clear; it was to shut out those like Cripps who thought of the Mission as a bargaining process in which Britain supplied arms and in return the Russians supplied information about the true, as opposed to the published, state of their armed forces.

In fact, both Beaverbrook and Harriman had quietly decided to exclude their respective Ambassadors from the party. Beaverbrook had gone so far as to send one of his staff in advance to arrange for comfortable accommodation in the Hotel National, avoiding the company in the British Embassy of the vegetarian and teetotal Ambassador. Harriman, too, had come to the conclusion that 'Stalin would be franker with us if we did not take the ambassadors along'.[36] To be fair,

Cripps had never expected to play more than a walk-on part. Even before the Mission left Scapa Flow he was confiding to his diary that

> HMG have appointed all the leaders of the military Mission to be part of the conference under Beaverbrook, but I shall not, of course, be in it nor do I want to be. I would rather stay outside and give any help that is wanted as I think that on the whole that will be the best thing from the point of view of efficiency.[37]

The arrival of the Mission in Russia did not bode well for its future success. At the mouth of the river Dvina they transferred to a Russian destroyer for the short journey to Archangel. Waiting for them on board the destroyer was Vyacheslav Mikhailovich Skryabin (known by his adopted name, as was the custom for Soviet leaders, as 'Molotov', the Hammer), whom Cripps's military attaché, General Mason-Macfarlane, described as 'one of the most unpleasant creatures I have ever met'.[38] There were speeches, toasts and much vodka. Once through that, and safely in Archangel, the Mission embarked on four large Russian transport aircraft to fly to Moscow. Four hours later, on their approach to Moscow, 'Soviet anti-aircraft guns opened fire and the Soviet pilots had to dive low into a wood before landing'.[39] The episode left Beaverbrook, for one, badly shaken and bitterly complaining about Russian incompetence. Furthermore, anti-aircraft guns were immediately relegated to a precarious existence on the Christmas tree.

Nevertheless, on the same evening, 28 September, almost before they had time to settle down in their respective lodgings, Beaverbrook and Harriman were invited to meet Stalin without delay. Driving through Moscow in total black-out was an 'eerie experience', as Harriman recalled.

> The Kremlin ... had been camouflaged to deceive the German bombers. A gigantic stage canvas had been hoisted in place over the high wall overlooking the Moscow River. From the far bank of the river the solid wall looked like a row of houses with gabled roofs. A wooden house had been placed over Lenin's tomb in Red Square, and Lenin himself spirited away to a secret location.[40]

Furthermore, the security at the entrance to the Kremlin was daunting. Once they were admitted, however, the atmosphere lightened up. Stalin, flanked by Molotov, stood to meet them. As interpreter, shabbily dressed they noted, was Molotov's predecessor, Litvinov. He had been quickly summoned for the task by Molotov at Cripps's request. Cripps had heard that the Russians wanted one of their own, Konstantin Umansky, but '[t]his would have bedevilled the whole thing', Cripps wrote in his diary, 'since Oumanski [*sic*] is an intriguer and most unreliable ... I got Dunlop to ring up Molotov's very nice Secretary and ask him to arrange for the translation to be done by Litvinov.'[41] Molotov agreed, but his staff failed to provide Litvinov with proper clothes. 'He was a pathetic figure. Shabby, worn, with holes in his shoes.'[42]

Their first meeting with Stalin went very much better than Beaverbrook and Harriman had expected. Stalin did most of the talking, brushing Molotov into silence when he tried to intervene. Put simply, the military situation was near to desperate. Although the Russian infantry was a match, and more, for the Germans, German superiority in tanks and aircraft put in doubt the main Russian objective to hold Moscow at all costs. The monthly requirement of tanks required from Britain and America was 1,100, to which could be added the 1,400 to be produced in Russia. When his visitors offered only 500 tanks a month, Stalin moved smoothly on to his other requirements: 300 fighters and 100 bombers, reconnaissance planes and, of course, large quantities of barbed wire.

The meeting lasted three hours, fuelled by refreshments, surprisingly not of vodka but of tea and cakes. When it broke up the visitors agreed to meet Molotov the following morning to set up six tripartite committees to discuss aircraft, army, navy, transport, raw materials and medical supplies, the committees to report in time for an evening meeting with Stalin. Both Beaverbrook and Harriman 'considered the meeting to have been extremely friendly and were more than pleased with ... [their] reception'.[43] Beaverbrook was apparently so pleased 'that he talked of settling the whole complicated negotiation in just one more session and going home'.[44] Harriman, rightly as it turned out, was more cautious.

That evening Cripps invited a cheerful Beaverbrook to dinner at the British Embassy. Perhaps surprisingly, given their respective backgrounds, the two had taken to one another. 'He is a very amusing and exasperating person,' Cripps confided to his diary,

> though not to me ... B[eaverbrook] told me that he and Anthony [Eden] were the only Crippsites in the cabinet! And that the only real supporters of out and out help for Russia were the Tories ... He mentioned to me the need for me to join the Government, but I told him that I thought I should find it very hard to work with him as our ideas were so very different ... He was a little upset I think the other evening when I told him he was thick skinned and a little later that I was sure he would lie like a trooper for his country. He explained in a pained voice that he didn't regard it as being a bad thing to be like that and that he would do anything, however dishonest, if he thought it would serve his country. And I believe him. He must be a very difficult person to work with though alright to work under.[45]

Dinner finally ended at a quarter to one in the morning.

The next meeting with Stalin on the following evening was, in dispiriting contrast to their first, 'very rough going'. According to Harriman, Stalin gave the impression that he was 'much dissatisfied with what we were offering ... He appeared to question our good faith.'[46] Beaverbrook noted that the Russian leader was restless, walking about and smoking continuously, 'and appeared to both of us to be under an intense strain'.[47] He was also discourteous, barely offering to open the letter from Churchill which Beaverbrook handed him and leaving it on a table unread. Finally, he was contemptuous. 'The paucity of your offers', he said dismissively, 'clearly shows that you want to see the Soviet Union defeated.'[48] Nevertheless, much to the relief of his visitors, he agreed that they should meet again the next day.

Beaverbrook left the meeting angry and depressed. 'Max was rattled,' recalled Harriman.

[He] was constantly thinking of his own reputation with his colleagues in the British Government. It was for this reason, I suppose, that he asked me to present at the third meeting with the combined list of weapons and materials that the British and American governments were prepared to supply. Then, if things did not go well, the fire would be directed at me.[49]

Not only was Beaverbrook angry but he was in one of his worst moods. Cripps's friend and fellow politician Hugh Dalton later recorded in his diary what Cripps had told him.

Incredible stories of the behaviour of the Beaver in Moscow. He took possession of Cripps's office in the Embassy and turned him out of the room. When he wanted him, he opened the door and bellowed 'Cripps!' When dining out, he demanded that an orchestra should be produced, and two rather decayed musicians were discovered. He demanded that they should play the Volga Boat Song but was told they couldn't; they were 'only a Caucasian band'. He then ordered that they should go away and learn it and come back again and play later in the evening. Once he tried to take them with him in another car behind his own, but when they reached their destination they had disappeared. They had been arrested by the police.[50]

The third meeting with Stalin went very much better. Truculence and hostility had turned into unexpected cordiality. Harriman duly followed the plan as agreed. 'We developed our tactics in the form of a cumulative effect,' Beaverbrook recorded. 'We built up the concessions that we could make from time to time and followed up with lists of articles that could not be conceded. Then a long list of materials with which we were in agreement.'[51] Stalin sat smoking his pipe and nodding from time to time. When Harriman had finished the list (of some seventy items), Beaverbrook, sensing the moment, 'asked with a laugh "are you pleased?" Stalin smiled and nodded, indicating satisfaction.'[52] At that point, apparently, Litvinov jumped out of his chair shouting, 'Now we will win the war.'

*Lord Beaverbrook, Vyacheslav Molotov and Averell Harriman signing
the Supply Agreement at the Moscow Conference, October 1941.*

The following day, 1 October, was spent reviewing the work of the
tripartite committees, who were having difficulty in translating the
decisions of the previous day into workable documents. Cripps's staff
were starting to complain. 'I hear plenty of Beaverbrook's rudeness,'
wrote one,

> which is commonly mistaken for efficiency. I imagine that he is
> very good at getting things done quickly for a short time, but he
> does them at such a speed and in such a slap-dash way that any
> kind of organisation is quite impossible, and heaven help the people
> who have to clear up the mess after he has done his bit. This time
> most of the cleaning up will fall to us and we don't look forward
> to it much.[53]

Nevertheless, between the main players there was nothing but sweet-
ness and, perhaps to a lesser extent, light. Harriman's report concluded
that the conference had broken up 'in the most friendly fashion possible ... Stalin made no effort to conceal his enthusiasm ... Beaverbrook
has been a great salesman. His personal sincerity was convincing. His

genius never worked more effectively.'[54] The new alliance was celebrated at a gala dinner that evening in Catherine the Great Hall in the Kremlin. It 'was an extremely good show', Cripps noted,

> and I really think that everyone enjoyed it. The atmosphere was so
> genuinely friendly and Stalin and Molotov were both in very good
> form ... Of course the food was excellent and much too much of it
> ... All the two hours or so that we were at dinner (there must have
> been 120 of us) we had endless toasts of every sort and kind.[55]

At the end of dinner the guests were ushered into another room for coffee, fruit and Russian brandy. About an hour later, they were all invited to Stalin's private cinema to watch films and drink champagne. After two indifferent films, both unintelligible to his guests, and with the threat of a third, Beaverbrook and Harriman summoned up the courage to ask to take their leave. Before he sat down to watch the third film, Stalin, holding yet another glass of champagne, waved them out. It was 1.30 a.m.

In the midst of all this apparent bonhomie, in a pause between toasts, Stalin had slipped in a question. 'What', he asked, 'is the point of having an army if it doesn't fight? An army which does not fight will lose its spirit.'[56] Harriman thought that it was a tactless intervention given that Stalin had signed an agreement with Hitler which left Britain on her own in the fight against Fascism. Ismay did his best to explain that the British Army was fighting in the Middle East and that an early invasion of Continental Europe was out of the question. Stalin was not persuaded. Harriman later recalled how the Soviet leader had declared that the British had to realise 'that they could no longer depend on their sea power. They would have to build their army and learn to fight on the ground, or they would be defeated.'[57] Beaverbrook sat on the sidelines of the argument, but the more he heard the more he became convinced that a British cross-Channel invasion of France was the quickest way to bind in the Russians and to put an end to the war. If it was to be called 'the second front', then so be it. On his return to London, he resolved to take up the cause, as usual when he had decided on a crusade, in the manner he knew best:

through his newspapers. Before he could do so, however, another page in the story of the war had been turned, since on 7 December 1941 the Imperial Japanese Navy Air Service had launched a crippling attack on the United States naval base at Pearl Harbor. The war was no longer a European affair. It had become global.

CHAPTER 23

THE YANKS ARE COMING

'Stalin is my friend. I'll do anything for him'[1]

'**H**eartiest Congratulations to you and all … No one could have done it but you.'[2] Churchill's plaudits were echoed by others. 'No doubt of Max's personal triumph with Stalin,' wrote Robert Bruce Lockhart. 'Everyone agrees … Stalin and Max did everything two lovers can do except sleep together, and that only because too busy.'[3] To be sure, there were dissenters. The Chiefs of Staff muttered that too much was being given away to the Soviets at the expense of Britain's perilous position in the Middle East. Stafford Cripps, whose staff were busy restoring diplomatic links in Moscow which the Mission had swept aside, was heard complaining about being left on the margin of the Beaverbrook/Harriman circus. But they were only a minority, however important, and the popular mood was against them. In fact, throughout Britain there were celebrations in lavish measure. 'Everything Russian', Ambassador Maisky noted with something near to smug satisfaction,

> is in vogue today; Russian songs, Russian music, Russian films, and books about the USSR; 75,000 copies of a booklet of Stalin's and Molotov's speeches on the war … sold out instantly … The Russian Tank Week, organised by Beaverbrook prior to his departure for Moscow, was a brilliant success … The Athenaeum and the St James Club have elected me their honorary member.[4]

On 13 October, just two days after his return to London, Beaverbrook was invited by Churchill to broadcast to the nation about the Mission and its results. Naturally, he accepted, but the text when it came to be broadcast must have surprised at least some of his colleagues and many in the Kremlin. After explaining, as his listeners would have expected, the agreements reached, and earnestly urging them to play their part in implementing them, he launched into a different mode. It was no less than a hymn of praise to Stalin. 'He was', they were told, 'an exacting man ... He is short of stature – well dressed, very well dressed ... always quick to laugh, quick to see a joke and willing to make one. His eyes are alert. His face quickly reflects his emotions. Gloom and joy are marked therein.'[5] It must have been unpalatable for those listeners who were aware of the criminal brutalities of Stalin's regime to hear him praised in such audacious terms by a government minister. But for Beaverbrook (and, for that matter, Churchill) this was not the moment to point to the ugly blotches on the face of the new ally.

Russian Ambassador to Great Britain, Ivan Maisky, thanks workers as he receives the first tank – christened 'Stalin' – produced by the factory in 'Tanks for Russia' week in September 1941. He was visiting British factories in the Midlands which were donating their entire tank production during the week to Russia, forming part of Britain's aid.

Beaverbrook now had the beginnings of a crusade: to support the Russian war effort. (In the rhetoric of the time, the expression 'Russia' meant the brave and patriotic people. The expression 'Soviet Union' was rarely used since it represented the Communist bogey.) He built on his broadcast throughout the autumn of 1941 and the first weeks of 1942 by arguing for some dramatic initiative to follow up the Mission's success. His first effort was an intervention at the meeting of 17 October of the Defence Committee of the Cabinet, followed by a memorandum.[6] It was a broad-sweep approach with a hint of the scattergun. First, he proposed the despatch of a large force to Murmansk. Then, in his memorandum, he launched an assault on the Chiefs of Staff and, at the same time, in the subsequent discussion he supported an attack on German positions in occupied Norway. None of this got him very far. His memorandum fell on particularly stony ground. Sir Alexander Cadogan, the Permanent Under Secretary for Foreign Affairs, who was present at the meeting which considered it, wrote that the memorandum 'read like a Daily Express leader' and showed that Beaverbrook was

> playing some game. I couldn't make out what it was, but it gradually dawned on me that it was this: by waving his arms and barking that he disagreed fundamentally with the Government he put a certain amount of wind up Winston. Then he switched over to particular controversies he has had with W.O. [War Office] and A.M. [Air Ministry] about supplies to Russia, and got Winston – in order to avoid worse difficulties – to back him over those! What a monkey![7]

'Rush Aid to Russia' poster, with the heads of Lord Beaverbrook and Averell Harriman stating: 'We have pledged your faith, the faith of the men and women of Britain. You must do the deed... STALIN MUST BE SUSTAINED', 1940s.

Churchill soon ended the discussion by pointing out that there was little virtue in going to Murmansk at a time when it was winter darkness and everywhere would be frozen.[8] Beaverbrook, thus rebuffed, on 25 October wrote to Churchill explaining his impatience that he was 'a victim of the Furies. On the rockbound coast of New Brunswick the waves beat incessantly. Every now and then there comes a particularly dangerous wave that breaks viciously on the rocks. It is called the "Rage". That's me.'[9] He followed by asking to be allowed to resign from the Defence Committee, pleading 'continuing and violent attacks of asthma'.[10] In fact, this was far from another Beaverbrook bluff. Bruce Lockhart had noted on 19 October that 'Max ... looks old and ill and is killing himself with overwork. Cannot relax, cannot sleep.' On the following day he recorded:

> Max still in bed. His asthma was bad last night, and he looks very ill. I have doubts he will last the war. At any rate, he cannot keep up the pace. He works entirely on his nervous energy which is tremendous, but he has aged terribly in the last year.[11]

Worse still, news of his health was seeping out. *The Times* of 29 October carried a Press Association report that he had been suffering severely from asthma for several days and that while he would certainly do his utmost to continue his work, 'it would not be surprising if the tremendous strain which Lord Beaverbrook has imposed on himself in the last 18 months had not necessitated a brief spell of rest'.[12]

The news quickly reached Washington. Lord Halifax, the British Ambassador, cabled Churchill: 'Averill [*sic*] [Harriman] has just telephoned that the reports of Max's contemplated resignation are being used to make mischief here. If, as he trusted and supposed, they are not true, he hoped they could be publicly denied.'[13] That was too much to ask, but Churchill once again went out of his way to address Beaverbrook's current source of discontent. It turned out that this was not the relatively mundane, if never-ending, job of spurring on those, from chief executives to shop stewards, responsible for the ultimate task of raising production of the armaments and materials needed for Russia. The real problem was that the supervision and co-ordination of the various ministries involved was a shambles – so much so that, on his instruction, his junior minister, Harold Macmillan, had been working on a plan to construct a super-ministry embracing the Ministries of Supply, Aircraft Production, Shipbuilding, Works and Buildings and (perhaps) Labour.

Representatives of employers and employees hear proposals from Ernest Bevin for the reorganisation of vital war production. Pictured from left to right are: Captain Oliver Lyttelton, Sir Andrew Duncan, Ernest Bevin (standing, centre), Lord Beaverbrook and Ralph Assheton (standing, right), 29 January 1941.

It was Beaverbrook's second effort to give greater help to the Russians. But this one too looked perilously like running into an early sand. The plan, for a new overarching ministry, started well. It took the customary time wending its way through the Whitehall thicket, but by the second week in November, Beaverbrook was able to write to Churchill suggesting that Bevin be put in charge of the new ministry since 'my health makes it impossible for me to undertake added labours. I could not be a candidate for the Production Ministry.'[14] Churchill, who was far from convinced that the super-ministry was necessary, thought that if it happened Beaverbrook would be the obvious choice as minister. This became more obvious when Beaverbrook and Bevin, in an exchange of letters of barely veiled hostility (Beaverbrook attempting flattery but sounding hypocritical, Bevin grumpily suspicious), failed to find any common ground. In some desperation, Beaverbrook was near giving up. By early December, Beaverbrook was writing to another colleague, 'It is my intention ... to give up my Office on January 1st according to my plan.'[15]

As with everything else, the pace and direction of the war changed with the Japanese assault on the American naval base of Pearl Harbor. The United States declared war on Japan on 8 December. On 11 December, Germany and Italy declared war on the United States, which straight away responded in kind. In London, Churchill decided on an immediate trip to Washington. He was undeterred by the loss, just before he left, of the battleships *Prince of Wales* and *Repulse* to Japanese assault aircraft in the South Pacific. Nevertheless, the visit would go ahead, although, in keeping with the mood of the time, his party was much reduced. Beaverbrook and Churchill's doctor, Sir Charles Wilson, were the only civilians apart from Churchill himself, and the military presence was similarly pared down.

The agenda was simple. Churchill was to discuss strategy with the President and his advisers, while Beaverbrook was to discuss supply with American captains of industry. Following that agenda, neither of them was to lose any time, even if it was the Christmas holiday. In fact, only five days after their arrival on 22 December, Beaverbrook had found out enough to present a paper to Roosevelt which began, 'The production of weapons in the United States, Britain and Canada is entirely inadequate. The deficits are so considerable that immediate steps must be taken to increase the production period in all directions.'[16] He followed this up two days later by another memorandum emphasising again the need for immediate action. Official Washington, hitherto still in a peacetime rhythm, was stung into frenetic activity. Vice-Admiral Dorling, the British Admiralty Supply Representative in America, was quick to note the change, and reported to Beaverbrook that the US Navy had 'raised their sights very considerably as a result of your letter and have already taken energetic action'.[17] Other services had followed suit and Roosevelt had submitted a war budget to Congress requesting a large increase in expenditure on the war effort. Beaverbrook was pleased enough with the results of his efforts to christen his report on his mission 'Raising the Sights'.

Lord Beaverbrook, Eleanor Roosevelt, Winston Churchill, Franklin D. Roosevelt and
General Edwin Watson about to leave the White House for Christmas Day service
at the Foundry Methodist Church, Washington, 25 December 1941.

There is no doubt about Beaverbrook's success in Washington. Equally, there is no doubt that he was starting to get on Churchill's nerves.
They had a fierce row in early January when Beaverbrook claimed that
the supply of aircraft to Russia was not living up to the promises made
in Moscow and agreed to cuts in US deliveries to Britain to make
good the deficit. Churchill, when he heard of it, was understandably
furious. When stories of the row leaked out, Beaverbrook yet again
threatened resignation. In what was by then becoming a familiar but
tiresome ritual, Churchill refused to accept it, adding, rather sorrow-
fully, that 'I had hoped that you would share our homeward voyage
and resume your duties at the Ministry of Supply, which were never
more urgent and onerous than now'.[18]

A fragile peace was restored when they chose to return to London
in a 'flying boat', an amphibious aircraft by then in service with the
British Overseas Aircraft Corporation. Service, in this case, was of
a luxury that had not been known since the outbreak of war. The
dinner menu was carefully laid out: cold consommé, shrimp cocktail,
filet mignon, dessert, all with accompanying champagne and liqueurs,
with coffee to finish. By the time they had recovered from the dinner
they were, apart from Beaverbrook, who stayed up most of the night
reading, safely in bed. Churchill was up early, insisting on occupying

the co-pilot's seat and doing his best to persuade the pilot (unsuccess-fully) to let him take over.

The party returned to London on 18 January 1942 to a sense of crisis. Hong Kong had capitulated to the Japanese on Christmas Day. Singapore would certainly be the next to go (and soon did so under humiliating circumstances on 15 February). The Army in the Middle East had been defeated and was in full retreat. It was the third winter of the war and national morale had reached a nadir. Churchill was coming under heavy criticism, to the point where there were mut-tered plots to replace him. Nor could Beaverbrook escape censure. What now appeared to be an obsession with Russia was leading him to divert supplies badly needed by the British Army to Russia and to advocate a post-war settlement which would allow the Soviet Union to annex the Baltic states, a large part of eastern Poland and pieces of Romania and Finland. That was far from an agenda, to put it simply, acceptable to most of the Cabinet or the Conservatives in the House of Commons.

Churchill badly needed to regain the political initiative. Success in a House of Commons vote of confidence on 29 January was a start, but more had to be done: he needed both to refresh his government and, at the same time, to launch the new Ministry of Production. At first sight, it seemed that Beaverbrook was coming to the rescue. On 2 February he produced a document, much of it written by Macmil-lan, which outlined the shape of the new ministry. To other members of the Cabinet it came as an unpleasant shock. It proposed almost dictatorial powers for the newcomer over its constituent ministries. The plan was immediately met with furious objections from those ministers whose powers would be swept away from under their feet: Ernest Bevin at Labour, Sir Andrew Duncan at Supply and A. V. Al-exander at the Admiralty. All threatened resignation. Churchill was forced to withdraw Beaverbrook's document and redraft it himself as a government White Paper. Yet to get it through he had to accept the objections and deprive the new ministry of almost all power over the constituent ministries. This in turn infuriated Beaverbrook, who at first refused to accept the new format and only did so at Churchill's angry insistence.

Worse was to come. Beaverbrook had tried to enlist Harriman in a campaign to agree Stalin's plan for a post-war settlement, in spite of blanket resistance from Attlee, Bevin and Herbert Morrison. But even Harriman was losing patience. 'Beaverbrook has quibbled and quarrelled with the PM', he wrote to Roosevelt,

> to the point where the PM will not tolerate it any longer. He feels Beaverbrook has been unjust and disloyal to seize this moment of all moments to make an issue. I believe Beaverbrook over-emphasises the adverse effect on the government of his resignation. The PM is confident it will not be serious, and, even if it were, there is nothing he can do about it.[19]

In this unhappy atmosphere, on 12 February, Churchill and Beaverbrook presented the White Paper to the House of Commons and House of Lords respectively. Churchill was enthusiastic, Beaverbrook less so. For him, the scheme's only attraction was that it was closely linked to the promised aid to Russia and its implementation. Writing to Samuel Hoare five days later, he was particularly downbeat: 'The public have got used to the ugly duckling and think it will grow up to be a swan. The ugly duckling does not think this at all.'[20]

In the same letter Beaverbrook told Hoare of Churchill's manoeuvres in refreshing the government. Cripps had returned from Moscow, riding a wave of popularity as the architect of the Russian alliance. Both Churchill and Beaverbrook thought that he should be found a ministerial position. On the evening of 18 February, Churchill summoned Beaverbrook to a meeting in his annexe in the War Rooms under the Treasury. He showed Beaverbrook two lists of possible members of a new War Cabinet, one with seven members and the other with five. Cripps's name was on both lists as Leader of the House of Commons, and Attlee was on both as Deputy Prime Minister. Beaverbrook and Bevin were on the list of seven but below the line on the list of five (in other words excluded from the War Cabinet).[21] Beaverbrook's reaction was immediate. 'Take the five and leave me out,' he said. 'I want to retire.'[22] He went on to attack Attlee: 'His contribution towards fighting the war has been nothing ... We need tougher fellows at a time like this. Fighting men.'[23]

Churchill was by then very angry. Peremptorily, he invited Beaverbrook to go into the next room and repeat what he had said. There, obviously assembled for the purpose, was Attlee himself along with Eden, Brendan Bracken and James Stuart, the government Chief Whip. Undaunted, and by then equally angry, Beaverbrook did just that, for good measure adding that Attlee had made 'a very bad speech to the Labour Party [conference] … an additional reason why he should not be Deputy Prime Minister'. Attlee asked, 'What have I done to you that you treat me in this way?' Beaverbrook replied, 'Why should I not talk frankly? You criticise me and I make no objection.'[24] Attlee, obviously wounded, denied the charge. Finally, Churchill intervened with a harsh rebuke for Beaverbrook, who then marched out of the room, with Bracken in his wake, shouting as he went down the corridor.[25] Later that evening Beaverbrook, seeking a truce, wrote to Churchill in untypically jokey language:

> While I am your man out and out, your humble servant, your complete and absolute supporter, your unswerving friend for the duration of the war, I must say that there are certain circumstances in which I would not be prepared to sit in the Cabinet. But, outside the Cabinet, I am ready to hold office.[26]

In reply, on the following morning Churchill made his final offer, more by way of making peace than expecting acceptance: go to Washington or stay in the government as Lord Privy Seal. Beaverbrook's reply was that he would go to Washington but only as Churchill's personal representative. All that was left was to agree a face-saving formula: an announcement that he had been offered government office but that he had chosen to retire on the grounds of ill health.

A few days later Beaverbrook sent to Churchill his final letter of resignation. The language was more than fulsome, even verging on the operatic:

> All the time everything that has been done by me has been due to your holding me up. You took a great chance in putting me in and you stood to be shot at by a section of Members for keeping me here

... I owe my reputation to you ... And my courage was sustained by you ... In leaving then, I send this letter of gratitude and devotion to the leader of the nation, the saviour of our people and the symbol of resistance in the free world.[27]

Churchill's reply was equally generous:

Thank you for all you say in yr splendid letter wh is a vy gt comfort and encouragement to me. We have lived and fought side by side through terrible days, & I am sure our comradeship & public work will undergo no break. All I want is for you to do now is to recover your health and poise.[28]

Few tears were shed by Beaverbrook's colleagues at the turn of events. They had never understood the depth of the relationship of the two men, and were inclined to Bevin's cynical, but memorable, explanation: 'Well, you see it's like this; it's as if the old man had married an 'ore. He knows what she is but he loves her.'[29]

The announcement of the reshaped War Cabinet added, as had been agreed, that Beaverbrook had declined membership on grounds of health, that he would shortly go to the United States to carry on work already begun and, in a mysterious phrase, to perform 'such other special duties as may be entrusted to him from time to time by the War Cabinet'.[30] In other words, he would do whatever he and Churchill cooked up.

At the beginning of March, Churchill asked Beaverbrook to accompany him on a trip to Tehran for a meeting with Stalin. When that slipped off the agenda, Churchill made a second proposal: Beaverbrook should go immediately to Washington but, in addition, take some time off to regain his health in Miami or the Bahamas. Beaverbrook agreed to go but not simply to follow up his previous work. His real purpose was to talk to Roosevelt about Russia. In particular, he wanted support for recognition of Russia's 1941 frontiers, an issue on which the British were still divided and the Americans non-committal; an increase in shipments of tanks and aircraft to Russia; and a raid onto the European continent as a prelude to a full-scale invasion.

There was an immediate political flurry in the House of Commons when the news of his American trip leaked out. Attlee, when questioned, unwisely stated that Beaverbrook would be working under the supervision of the new Minister of Production, Oliver Lyttelton, and that he had no diplomatic duties assigned to him. It took soothing words from Brendan Bracken as Minister of Information, an official announcement and a letter from Churchill to prevent immediate cancellation. 'Max is off tomorrow', Churchill wrote to Hopkins, 'and I shall be grateful if you will impress on the President that though he is out of office at his own wish, we remain close friends and intimate political associates.'[31]

Beaverbrook's transatlantic journey turned out to be more than usually uncomfortable. It had been organised by an Australian Senator, R. D. Elliott, who had come to London to work at the Ministry of Aircraft Production and had subsequently attached himself to Beaverbrook's personal support team. The first leg was by a crowded flying boat to Lisbon, during which Beaverbrook's privacy was only secured by a curtain round his seat. Already irritated, he then, much to his further annoyance, found that he was scheduled to spend a day with the British Ambassador. The second leg took him to Bathurst, capital of The Gambia, where, to more annoyance, another day was spent with the Governor. Then it was on to Brazil and Trinidad, where Elliott had organised a reception at Government House. Finally, after a five-day journey, the party arrived in Washington on 25 March. Elliott was promptly sent back in disgrace to London.

That same evening, Beaverbrook dined at the White House with Roosevelt and Hopkins. After dinner the three settled down to a long discussion. Rather than talking about Russia's post-war frontiers or the current supply problems, Roosevelt wanted to talk about the war strategy for 1942. Much to Beaverbrook's surprise, 'The President had come to the conclusion that an Anglo-American invasion of Europe should become the strategy of 1942 and that the invasion should take place as quickly as might be.'[32] Beaverbrook was so moved that he immediately made plans to give Roosevelt public support. As luck would have it, when in Washington he received, and accepted, an invitation to be the principal speaker at the annual banquet in New

York of the Newspaper Publishers Association of America. It was the perfect platform.

The next day, Beaverbrook left the White House at one o'clock, called on Halifax to report on his talk with Roosevelt and set off for Miami. But all ideas of rest and relaxation in the health-giving Florida sun had to be shelved in favour of preparing his speech for New York. By way of a dress rehearsal, on Sunday 29 March, he made an evening broadcast on Canadian radio. In fact, it was a first draft of a speech which he was to make on various platforms over the coming months. There was certainly no doubt about the message: 'Today there is one word which stirs the heart of each hero in this company of warriors. The word is "attack". Attack by sea, attack by air, attack in the field.'[33] Moreover, just in case the Canadians had not tuned in or others had ignored it, the text of the broadcast was reproduced in its entirety by the *Daily Express* in London.

Beaverbrook was soon back in Washington following a request from Roosevelt. On 31 March he spent the morning with Halifax at the British Embassy before meeting the President in the evening. It was another long session. The White House log shows that it started at 10.45 p.m. and went on until 12.50 a.m.[34] But the message was simple: the President had decided to send Harry Hopkins and General George Marshall to London to seek agreement from the British for an invasion of France at the latest in the spring of 1943 and, if possible in the summer of 1942. Furthermore, he wanted Beaverbrook to go with them. The answer was immediate acceptance, and on that note Beaverbrook went back to Miami to await an official summons.

It never came. On 3 April he received a message from Roosevelt telling him that 'I put my foot down for the very good reason that I want you here. As you know, there is no one else I can talk to when we get word in the course of the next few days.'[35] In fact, it was Roosevelt at his most devious. He had realised his mistake: a party of Hopkins, Marshall and Beaverbrook would raise the hackles of everybody in London apart from Churchill. Beaverbrook had to be left behind, and Roosevelt, typically, used flattery to soften the blow. From then on, his messages to Churchill made no mention of his talks with Beaverbrook. In announcing the visit, he wrote to Churchill, 'I have come to certain conclusions ... The whole of it is so dependent on complete cooperation by the United Kingdom and United States that Harry and Marshall will leave for London in a few days to present first of all to you the salient points.'[36]

Beaverbrook had been, at least for the moment, left on the beaches of Miami. He spent time, obsessively, on the draft of his New York speech, lunched with Joseph Kennedy, the former US Ambassador to Britain, and his successor, John Winant, travelled the short distance to Nassau to dine with the Duke and Duchess of Windsor, went to the Sea Island resort in Georgia for a few days' relaxation before returning to Washington for lunch with Roosevelt and from there to New York.

On the evening of 23 April 1942, Beaverbrook delivered his speech to the Newspaper Publishers Association. He had been irritated to find that he was not in fact the principal speaker and thought that his audience would be tired of speeches by the time he rose to deliver his own. He need not have worried. His audience, as well as those who listened in on coast-to-coast radio, was captivated from the outset. It was no less than a soaring panegyric in praise of Stalin and Soviet communism. 'Communism under Stalin', he declared,

> has produced the most valiant fighting army in Europe. Communism under Stalin has provided us with examples of patriotism equal to the finest [in the] annals of history. Communism under Stalin has won the applause and admiration of all the Western nations. Communism under Stalin has produced the best generals in this war.

Any worry about racial, religious or political persecution was brushed aside. Acknowledging the purges and show trials of the past, he claimed that 'it is now clear that the men who were shot down would have betrayed Russia to her German enemy'.[37] The punch came at the end: 'This is a chance, an opportunity to bring the war to an end here and now ... Strike out to help Russia. Strike out violently. Strike even recklessly. But in any event such blows that really help will be our share and contribution to the Russian battlefront.'[38]

The speech was widely reported on both sides of the Atlantic. Halifax recalled meeting Beaverbrook in his suite in the Waldorf Astoria where he was 'chuckling over the effect of his speech as reported from London where people did not know whether this was a speech made with authority or against the Cabinet, or kite flying! He is a puckish person.'[39]

Back in London on 5 May, Beaverbrook set about launching his campaign for what was now openly called the 'Second Front'. There was to be a poll to test public opinion and a large public meeting at the London Hippodrome on 24 May. Before that could happen, however, he had to square some uncomfortable circles with Churchill. On 11 May they dined together. Churchill told Beaverbrook that the Hopkins–Marshall mission had not been a success. General Sir Alan Brooke, although sympathetic to the theory of a Second Front, had formed a low opinion of Marshall's strategic ability. His plan, Brooke confided to his diary, 'does not go beyond just landing on the far coast! Whether we are to play baccarat or chemin de fer at Le Touquet or possibly bathe at Paris Plage is not stipulated!'[40] Churchill himself was opposed to the whole project, yet he still needed Beaverbrook as a counsellor and friend. Equally important, he wanted at all costs to strangle the campaign for a Second Front at birth.

Churchill's first offer was to put Beaverbrook in charge of all the British wartime missions in Washington. That did not go down well. Churchill then raised his offer: the Washington Embassy. Beaverbrook was tempted at first, so much so that Churchill, without consulting Eden or Cadogan, let alone Halifax, asked Hopkins to sound out Roosevelt, who responded with enthusiasm. By that time Beaverbrook had spotted Churchill's real intention and realised that as Ambassador he would be barred from campaigning for anything other than government policy. The offer was politely refused.

Free from any official restraint, Beaverbrook launched a campaign 'of remarkable intensity and range, designed to force the Government into an invasion of Western Europe'.[41] He took advantage of the range of committees and societies dedicated to friendship and solidarity with the Soviet Union that had mushroomed across the entire country in the wake of the Russian resistance to the German onslaught. Beaverbrook himself was inundated with requests to give speeches or send messages of support, which he was quite prepared to agree to provided

there was no party affiliation. Needless to say, the campaign was en-
thusiastically supported by the Express newspapers and the *Evening
Standard*. The *Daily Express* formed a 'Centre for Public Opinion' to
publish a succession of favourable polls and dubbed the day of its first
public meeting 'Second Front Sunday'.

During the late spring and early summer of 1942, the campaign
went according to plan. It had clearly caught a rising tide. The tide
flowed even more strongly after the signature on 23 May of a Treaty
of Alliance between Britain and the Soviet Union and the subsequent
agreement between Roosevelt and Molotov in Washington on 11 June
announcing that 'full understanding was reached between the two
parties with regard to the urgent tasks of creating a second front in
Europe in 1942'.[42] It was in a mood of optimism that Beaverbrook
planned his speech for the grand rally which was to take place in
Birmingham on 21 June, the first anniversary of the 1941 German
invasion of Russia.

As might be expected, Beaverbrook had prepared a stirring address
suitable for the occasion. But just as he was getting ready to mount
the platform to deliver it, he was told by a journalist that Tobruk,
which had held out under siege so heroically the previous year, had
surrendered to General Erwin Rommel's Afrika Korps, with hardly a
fight and with some 30,000 mainly Empire troops laying down their
arms and marching into captivity. Hitler raised Rommel to the rank
of Field Marshal. Rommel, in thanking his Führer, announced that he
was now heading for Suez.

Beaverbrook immediately understood what the news meant.
Rommel was on the march. His army was only a short distance from
the Egyptian frontier and from there to Alexandria and the Suez Canal
was a matter of a few days for his armour. In the inevitable scramble to
protect the canal and Britain's oil supplies, the Second Front would be
relegated to the back of the strategic queue. 'On the morning of June
21st', Beaverbrook later wrote, 'the Second Front was a near certainty;
by the evening the odds were 100–1 against.'[43]

The surrender of Tobruk was the first of several damaging blows to
Beaverbrook's campaign. On 18 July, Hopkins, Marshall and Admiral
Ernest King, Chief of US Naval Operations, arrived in London for

further discussions of future strategy. The choice was between 'Sledge-hammer', a cross-Channel invasion of the European near continent, and 'Torch', an invasion of North Africa. Marshall still insisted on Sledgehammer until Roosevelt used his authority as Commander in Chief to order him to agree with the British and opt for Torch. Last, but by no means least, on 19 August, Allied troops staged an amphibious raid on the French coastal town of Dieppe. It was a disaster. Almost everything that could go wrong did go wrong. The result was heavy casualties. Out of 6,000 men who made it ashore, some 3,600 were killed, wounded or captured, the majority of them Canadian. The Royal Air Force lost 106 aircraft to the Luftwaffe's 48. In sum, the Dieppe raid showed more clearly than anything else the difficulties of cross-Channel adventures, let alone a mass invasion.

The campaign for a Second Front stuttered, and then came to a virtual halt. On 8 November the Allied invasion of North Africa was successfully launched. In January 1943, Churchill and Roosevelt met at Casablanca to determine Allied strategy for the next phase of the war. They decided that the next step, once North Africa was clear, would be to take Sicily and then move on north up the Italian peninsula. Beaverbrook was not invited to the conference. 'I see Churchill seldom,' he wrote to Sam Hoare on 2 February.

> I say that it is Churchill's fault, but Bracken says it is my fault. For my part I don't feel it is good for me to be in close contact with him at present. It seems better that I should look on him as the peasants of Savoy look on Mont Blanc, with astonishment and admiration.[44]

In conversation he took to referring to the Prime Minister as 'that fellow Churchill'.

That was not all. He was, as ever, not above making mischief. Although the date is not secure (1943 is the most plausible estimation – though certainly in the period of his estrangement from the Prime Minister), Beaverbrook, according to James Stuart, 'conceived the astonishing idea that our national interests might be in better hands' and had concocted a plan to form a leadership triumvirate 'consisting of Eden, Bevin and himself.'[45] He appears to have approached both Bevin and Eden for their reaction. Eden's is not recorded but Bevin's was forthright: not only was it negative but he would immediately report the matter to Churchill. What happened next is not known, except that the idea of a triumvirate died a quick death, much to the relief of Stuart, who witnessed the whole bizarre affair and seemed even to take it seriously. One moment's thought should have been enough to show that it was not only astonishing but also ludicrous. Even if Churchill had been minded to step down, after having recently won a decisive confidence vote in the Commons, the obstacles to getting any such arrangement approved by the King, the Cabinet, both Houses of Parliament and the electorate at a time of high national peril made a nonsense of the whole idea.

Mischief-making apart, Beaverbrook did his best to revive the Second Front campaign by celebrating the surrender of the German Fifth Army at Stalingrad in early February 1943. Two speeches in the House of Lords, on 3 and 23 February, repeated his admiration for Stalin, who would 'go down in the long list of Russian heroes as Stalin the Great',[46] and called for an immediate invasion of north-west Europe. That was enough to provoke what passes in the House of Lords for a row. Lord Simon dismissed the Second Front as a 'catchpenny phrase' and advised his colleagues 'to do all in your power to help get rid of what are mere slogans based really on ill-informed clamour'. Beaverbrook retorted that Simon was a 'master of distortion', who had held him up to 'ridicule or contempt'.[47]

In truth, it was all so much froth. The new-found affection for the House of Lords was no more than an effort to fill the vacuum of a declining public campaign. Oddly enough, it was Roosevelt who came to the rescue. On 24 March he wrote to Beaverbrook that he had 'a hunch that you are due for another holiday over here. I hope you may find it possible to come over this spring and, incidentally, to talk with me about many things.'[48] When he heard of this, Churchill made another attempt to persuade Beaverbrook to stay in America with a view to taking over from Halifax. But by then the word had spread to the Foreign Office. 'The worst of all possible worlds,' Eden complained. 'What can the President want by inviting the Beaver? Does he like him? Does he want him as ambassador? ... There must be no question of letting H[alifax] go in these circumstances.'[49]

Churchill knew perfectly well that Beaverbrook would use the Roosevelt invitation to press the case for an immediate Second Front. He had already tabled a motion on 20 April in the House of Lords calling for action and had only withdrawn it on Churchill's assurance that it was a matter of urgent consideration. Churchill, obviously determined to keep his man on a short rein, also slipped in an invitation to rejoin the government as Lord Privy Seal and Leader of the Lords. By then it was time to seek a meeting with Roosevelt to plan Allied strategy for Sicily and beyond. When Roosevelt agreed, Churchill pressed Beaverbrook to join him and the two sailed from Greenock on 4 May (on the *Queen Mary*, which, as it happened, was also carrying 5,000 German prisoners of war).

Although Beaverbrook claimed that the atmosphere on the voyage showed the abiding cordiality of their friendship, Harriman, who was also with them, thought that Beaverbrook was rather sulky and ill at ease. On their arrival in Washington he was quick to go to a hotel, thus emphasising that he was not an official visitor. Once there, however, he was immediately summoned to lunch at the White House.[50] During lunch Roosevelt repeatedly asked Beaverbrook for his advice, much to his embarrassment as he continued to claim that he was not part of Churchill's mission. In fact, his mere presence in Washington was causing confusion both there and in London. Halifax was kept in the dark and Churchill had to tell Attlee how he should reply to questions in the Commons. 'Lord Beaverbrook', ran the text,

> received a personal invitation some weeks ago from the President to visit him and it had been arranged that he should go by air during the present week. However, as the Prime Minister was going over by sea, he offered Lord Beaverbrook the courtesy of a passage with his party. Lord Beaverbrook has no mission from the Government and is travelling purely as a private person.[51]

It was a good try, but it did nothing to stop the muttering, and a good deal of cynical laughter, in London.

What started as embarrassment soon developed into yet another quarrel. Roosevelt invited Beaverbrook to spend the weekend with him and Churchill at Shangri-La, the presidential summer retreat. When consulted, Churchill said that he had no objection provided Beaverbrook refrained from all discussion of military strategy with the President. But it was far from clear what he was meant to do if Roosevelt himself asked for his opinion. He could hardly remain silent. Sensing that it was all getting too difficult, Beaverbrook sent a message via his secretary David Farrer to Harry Hopkins with apologies to the President but he would prefer to be excused. Hopkins's reply, Farrer wrote later, was 'sharp and instant. "Tell Lord Beaverbrook", he snapped at me down the telephone, "that the President is not accustomed to having his invitations refused."'52 That was that. Inevitably there was indeed a discussion about the Second Front. Roosevelt was still inclined to an early date, and Beaverbrook duly supported him. Later that evening Churchill stormed at Beaverbrook, claiming that he was taking the side of the Americans. Beaverbrook countered that the American general's demand for an early invasion was in Britain's interest. Churchill replied that Beaverbrook had no business involving himself in strategic projects. The two men parted in anger.

Beaverbrook decided that it would be wise to keep a distance from Churchill and left for New York the following day, remaining there until Churchill had returned to London. There was then a much more relaxed weekend with Roosevelt at Shangri-La. Farrer was quick to explain: 'The President had the greatest admiration for Churchill as a great war leader, but on occasions found him an unconscionable bore; the fellow would never for an instant stop talking, pontificating, about the war. Not even at meal times, not even over brandy and cigars.'53 With Beaverbrook he was able to talk about his stamp collection in what, as he subsequently wrote, was 'another grand weekend and ... the kind of real relaxation and fun which comes so rarely these days'.54

Back in London, the mood between Churchill and Beaverbrook was still far from sunny. An attempt at reconciliation by Churchill by offering dinner in Downing Street failed miserably. Harriman was there as well, noting that 'Max was tired and would have preferred to go to bed ... The dinner, which included Mrs Churchill and Kathleen [Harriman], was argumentative and some of the fundamental disagreements between the two men came out. This type of argument with Max always upsets the Prime Minister.'[55]

The stand-off with Churchill continued throughout the summer. Beaverbrook had taken a liking to the House of Lords, unworried that it was not reciprocated by their lordships. He made speeches in debates on the United Nations Food Conference, post-war employment prospects and milk marketing. He also offered Churchill some unsolicited advice on sending Brendan Bracken as Ambassador to Washington, which Churchill ignored. The invasion of Sicily in July had gone to plan, and the Allies had moved on into southern Italy.

On 21 September 1943, the Chancellor of the Exchequer, Sir Kingsley Wood, died suddenly. An immediate Cabinet reshuffle was necessary. That same afternoon Churchill addressed the House of Commons on the progress of the war. After rehearsing the facts as they stood, he went on to speak about the future. 'The Second Front', he told the House,

> which already exists potentially and which is rapidly gathering weight, has not yet been engaged but it is here, holding forces on its line. No one can tell – and certainly I am not going to hint at – the moment when it will be engaged. But the Second Front exists … It has not yet been opened, or been thrown into play, but the time will come.[56]

By coincidence, Beaverbrook had at the same time tabled a motion in the House of Lords calling for urgency in bringing a Second Front forward and had composed a fiery speech in support. The speech was never delivered and the motion was withdrawn. The reason was simple and dramatic. Churchill had sent for Beaverbrook to tell him that an attack across the Channel would take place at the latest in the spring of 1944. Beaverbrook would have his Second Front. In return, Churchill offered him yet again a place in the government. Beaverbrook could hardly refuse. He was satisfied that he could 'give again, without reservations, the full support he had always wanted to give to the Prime Minister who was also the object of his abiding affection and admiration. Thus it remained until the end.'[57]

CHAPTER 24

KEEPER OF THE SEAL

'I have lost my moorings'[1]

Beaverbrook was, on the face of it, an unlikely candidate for the office of Keeper of the Privy Seal. He did not much take to the flummery which accompanies the eccentricities of the (unwritten) constitution of the United Kingdom and by which, as one of the Great Offices of State, his office was surrounded. Furthermore, the Privy Seal of which he was meant to be the guardian had, to use the technical expression, fallen into desuetude. Altogether he was much in sympathy with the MP who, when appointed, complained that he was not a lord, nor was he a privy, and he was certainly not a seal.

Nevertheless, as it has turned out, even in the modern political world the office has come to have its uses. Its holder is ex officio a member of the monarch's Privy Council and is entitled to sit in Cabinet. Furthermore, the appointment carries with it a salary, officially recognised in the consolidating Ministerial and Other Salaries Act 1975. It was therefore doubly convenient to attach the appointment to an active portfolio which otherwise carried with it no salary and no seat in Cabinet. Over the years the obvious candidates had emerged: Leader of the House of Lords and Leader of the House of Commons.

Beaverbrook managed to avoid such complications, not least because he would have been unacceptable to his noble colleagues as their leader. The current incumbent as Leader of the Lords, Viscount Cranborne, duly agreed to vacate the office of the Privy Seal, and the title, and move to Dominion Affairs, another post which carried a salary. Thus, on 26 September 1943, Beaverbrook and an unusually small staff, headed by his two private secretaries, David Farrer and George

Thompson, moved into the appointed offices in the elegance of Gwydyr House, an eighteenth-century mansion on the eastern side of Whitehall which had miraculously survived the Blitz. There they were met and welcomed by the formidable Miss Elizabeth Hogg, styling herself APS (Assistant Privy Seal) and, according to one member of Beaverbrook's team, 'Scot[tish] … very blonde, very precise, and very much in complete command'.[2] Most notable of all was the room allocated to the Lord Privy Seal himself. It was enormous, stretching from the Whitehall frontage right through the building to overlook the gardens behind. The internal decoration was sumptuous to match, overlooked by the beautifully moulded pattern of the ceiling.

Beaverbrook was now back in the world where he believed he belonged, on the inside looking outwards rather than on the outside looking in. In truth, he had been rather bored over the previous few months and the pattern of boredom had been familiar. As before, when he was out of office and had no political cause to occupy his energy, he invested in projects which in other times he would have thought frivolous. Once it had been racehorses. This time it was dairy farming. A number of farms in Somerset had come on the market and Beaverbrook was there as a buyer. One of them, at Cricket Malherbie, came with an old manor house, where friends could be offered hospitality while Cherkley was on a war footing against the threat of German bombers. It also produced excellent honey which could be, and was, distributed to friends.

Nor could boredom be relieved by parties and pranks. It was still, after all, wartime. Certainly, in the spring of 1943, there was a renewed feeling of cautious optimism but nothing that could justify exuberant celebration. In fact, in September 1943 any thought of celebration was ruled out by the death of the main party cheerleader, Valentine Castlerosse. The two had hardly met since the death in 1941 of the Earl of Kenmare, which led to Castlerosse's succession to the Kenmare title and the Irish property at Killarney. True, debts continued to be paid off and shelter was offered at Cherkley after Castlerosse's ex-wife Doris committed suicide in December 1942. Beaverbrook also sponsored his marriage six weeks later to the three-times widowed Enid Furness. But he refused to get involved when Enid, in a bid to claim inheritance to the Killarney property, declared (at the age of fifty-one) that she was pregnant. Enough was enough. As Beaverbrook himself acknowledged, his relationship with Castlerosse was out of the ordinary, perhaps of the master and his court jester who kept him entertained, but nonetheless entirely genuine. As he wrote to Castlerosse's uncle, Maurice Baring, his death 'leaves a feeling of futility with those who are left behind, and for my art a void that can never be filled'.[3]

Lord Beaverbrook (right) talking to his friend and adviser Brendan Bracken, 1945.

Once sworn into office, and installed in Gwydyr House, Beaverbrook set about rebuilding his political networks. His closest political friend at the time was Brendan Bracken, Minister of Information, who shared both Beaverbrook's dislike of the traditional English upper class and his sense of (frequently malicious) fun. The two met regularly for dinner after Cabinet meetings to dissect what had been said and by whom. To be sure, their open contempt for traditionalist Tories provoked corresponding hostility. Bracken, for instance, was considered by one such a 'kind-hearted, garrulous, red headed gargoyle, whom I have always considered a fraud'.[4] The animus against Beaverbrook ran deeper, not least because of his continued close friendship with Churchill. But the animus was not confined to the Tories. For instance, when the rumour began to circulate that Churchill wanted in July 1942 to bring Beaverbrook back into government, Bevin told Halifax that he would 'certainly [in that case] resign'; Attlee 'spoke in strong terms', as did Cripps. Furthermore, James Stuart wrote to Churchill that the rumour was having 'a disturbing effect' on 'a very large section of opinion in the House'.[5]

Perhaps strangely, given their obvious political differences, Beaverbrook then fixed on the Home Secretary, Herbert Morrison, as a third participant at his post-Cabinet dinners. In fact, Beaverbrook had been making overtures to Morrison for some months. In November 1942, Morrison had been promoted to the War Cabinet. Beaverbrook wrote to him that

> it is a personal delight to me that you have received this promotion ... and I send you my warmest congratulations ... For certain it is that, Churchill apart, you are today by far the biggest figure in the country. And I look forward with the most complete confidence to the leadership you will give. I hope to live under you as Prime Minister.[6]

(It helped, of course, that Morrison was intensely disliked by both Attlee and Bevin.)

It needs no profound political analysis to understand why Churchill was so determined to have Beaverbrook back in government. The job of Prime Minister is lonely at the best of times, but with the burden of running a war it sometimes was near to becoming too much for Churchill and as a consequence leading dangerously close to one of his sporadic fits of severe depression. One of Lloyd George's disciples summed it up: 'Winston is undoubtedly a very lonely man.'[7] Beaverbrook had the magic touch. He could make Churchill laugh, join him in evenings of brandy and cigars, poke fun at pompous ministerial colleagues and, generally, bring his share of devilry to match Churchill's own. Yet Churchill knew perfectly well that there could be no true intimacy such as he wished unless Beaverbrook was brought into the government, sharing the secrets and helping with the burdens. Come what may, the Beaver had to be brought back into the circle.

Once brought back in, the difficulty was to find something for him to do other than be Churchill's jack of all trades. Fortunately, there was one clear task that Beaverbrook could take on: the planning for the construction of a worldwide system of civil aviation to come into effect when the war was over. To be sure, by his own admission Beaverbrook knew next to nothing about civil aviation, but as there was no question of turning the job down, he recognised the necessity of bringing in an expert to guide him. Quick as ever when speed was needed, he decided on the one candidate whom he knew personally as he had edited an official aircraft recognition journal for the Ministry of Aircraft Production.

Peter Masefield had been born in 1914, into a family of doctors. There was enough money there to send the boy to Westminster School (where, by coincidence, he was fag to Beaverbrook's son Max), Chillon College in Switzerland and Jesus College, Cambridge. At the age of thirteen he had been captivated by the notion of powered flying and thereafter took every opportunity either to fly himself or to work in aircraft maintenance at the Imperial Airways workshops in Croydon. At the outbreak of war in September 1939 he decided on aviation journalism as air correspondent of the *Sunday Times* and war correspondent with the RAF. When the United States entered the war, he was seconded to accompany the Eighth Air Force on daylight B-17 sorties. Although still formally a journalist, he frequently acted as co-pilot or rear gunner.

Peter Masefield, who joined Lord Beaverbrook's staff as personal adviser on civil aviation to the Lord Privy Seal.

At the request of the United States government, in September 1943 Masefield embarked on an educational lecture tour of US Air Force training bases and industrial plants. It was at one of these, the Republic P-47 plant on Long Island, that he received a peremptory telegram from Gwydyr House telling him to drop everything and come back to London. Only four days later, on 27 September, Masefield was ushered by Miss Hogg into Beaverbrook's huge office. 'Rising from his desk, [Beaverbrook] said "Peter, how are you? The Lord God (pronounced Gaad) moves in mysterious ways ... now you must come to work for me here."'[8] There was no argument, but, much to Beaverbrook's annoyance, it took the best part of three weeks before Masefield was able to free himself from all his commitments and join Beaverbrook's staff full time as personal adviser on civil aviation to the Lord Privy Seal.

On his first day in Gwydyr House, Masefield sat down to study what was by then a mountain of files. Apart from documents setting up the newly created War Cabinet Committee on Post-War Civil Air Transport, of which he was to be the secretary, there were the minutes of the three-day Commonwealth Conference held the previous week and a minute dated 10 June 1943 from Churchill to Lord Cherwell (the ennobled Professor Lindemann) proposing a 'global plan for civil air transport with all airports open to through traffic of all nations (except the guilty)'.[9] This had been debated at the conference but without conclusion other than a vague proposal for an Empire-wide network and a British-built aircraft to fly it.

Masefield soon realised the difficulties. The Americans had, or were developing, at great cost, civil versions of their military aircraft capable of flying a worldwide network. Led by the giant Pan-American, they believed they could knock out all competition. But the British, with the Dominions and the colonies, controlled the underpinning terrestrial structure of any plausible network and could use this as a lever to secure flying rights. There was certain to be a tough negotiation to marry the ambitions of both. Masefield nervously wondered what sort of negotiator Beaverbrook would turn out to be. He was already, in the first few weeks, discovering the many sides of Beaverbrook's character, and later wrote his assessment in his own autobiography:

He was unlike any other man I ever knew. For all his foibles and tough exterior, he was at heart deeply sensitive and often lonely. Critical, thrusting, demanding, self-centred and intolerant, he could be kind and even generous, just as he could be hasty and vindictive. He could reverse passionate feelings within hours. He perpetually maintained a hard front, even when the man inside had softened. I often thought of the frightened little boy in Canada, whose Presbyterian father had drunk away the family's slender funds. Some have said he was evil, he was not, though that depends on how the word is defined. Some have said that he was ruthless, he was not, but he was unpredictable. He was fascinated with power and politics. He was sometimes unfair, yet often magnanimous. He was mesmerised with the written word, yet impatient. His character was kaleidoscopic.

So far, so gently positive. But Masefield could not help adding at the end, 'The better I came to know him the more wary I became.'[10]

Masefield immediately set about the task, as instructed by Beaverbrook, of writing a policy. He asked for a little time, which Beaverbrook was not altogether happy to allow him, to rework an article he had written for the *Atlantic Monthly*, to be published in January 1944, as a position paper for future policy. In his paper, Masefield argued in favour of a number of airlines of all nations with the capability, operating free as far as possible on an internationally agreed network with the minimum of bureaucratic restrictions. This was the formula he repeated in his policy paper. Beaverbrook was delighted, not least because Masefield's proposal ran directly counter to the proposal of the Air Ministry for a single flag British airline with tight control over landing and traffic rights. Beaverbrook was quite happy, and perhaps more than happy, to have another battle with the Air Ministry on his agenda. By the end of November, he had already won the battle with them over the priority to be given to the conversion of the Lancaster IV Bomber to a civil airliner to be known as the Tudor, and he was ready for more.

Nevertheless, there was little point in launching a new policy in the run-up to a Christmas at which many were trying to forget that they were in the fourth year of a relentless war. In any case, the launch had to be carefully prepared so as to avoid the predictably hostile volleys from both Washington and Whitehall. After reflecting at, for him, unusual length, Beaverbrook decided that the most politically astute step would be for him to set out the policy in a speech in the House of Lords, where he would speak as a minister from the Despatch Box. Such a statement would be taken, then as now, as a statement of settled government policy.

The timetable was in place and the speech had been drafted when news came through which threatened to bring to a halt not just Beaverbrook's project but the whole of the Allied war plan. On 11 December 1943, on his way back from the conference with Roosevelt and Stalin at Tehran, Churchill broke his journey to stay a few days at General Eisenhower's villa at Carthage on the outskirts of Tunis. In the middle of the night he woke with a painful sore throat. In the morning he was running a high temperature and his doctor, Charles Wilson, decided that the Cabinet and Mrs Churchill should both be immediately and fully briefed. Furthermore, Jock Colville, back in Churchill's private office, was deputed to escort Mrs Churchill on her journey to Tunis to be at her husband's side.

It took time, and the arrival in Tunis from Cairo of a pathologist and two nurses, together with a radiographer with a portable X-ray apparatus, to fix on a diagnosis. The X-ray was decisive. It showed a patch of congestion at the base of Churchill's left lung. On 14 December the diagnosis was firm enough for a bulletin to be issued. 'The Prime Minister, who is on his way back to London from the Middle East, has contracted pneumonia and is confined to bed.'[11] This blunt account of the patient's health greeted Mrs Churchill when she arrived on the following day.

In fact, Churchill recovered remarkably quickly. By 18 December his temperature was back to normal and he was shouting at his doctors, who were insisting that he stay in bed for at least another fortnight. As a compromise he finally agreed to sit by his bed for a few days, but he was determined to preside over the Christmas celebrations. In return the staff produced 'a magnificent Christmas dinner ... [Churchill] clothed in a padded silk Chinese dressing-gown decorated with blue and red dragons – a most extraordinary sight'.[12] By 27 December he was well enough for the whole party to leave Tunis and fly to Marrakesh, where he was due to convalesce in comfort in 'the spacious and luxurious, if slightly vulgar' Villa Taylor.[13] It was arranged that Churchill, Mrs Churchill, Wilson, Colville and senior staff stayed in the villa, while the secretaries and junior staff stayed in the luxury of the best hotel in Marrakesh, La Mamounia. Once everybody was settled down, Mrs Churchill sent a message to Beaverbrook inviting him to Marrakesh to try to revive her husband's spirits. 'She used', remarked Charles Wilson, 'to dread his influence on Winston, but when Winston became Prime Minister she resolved to bury the past. It was a wise choice for a difficult task.'[14]

On 28 December, Beaverbrook, with his valet, Nockels, and his secretaries, George Thompson and David Farrer, sulkily in tow given the short notice, arrived at the Villa Taylor. Beaverbrook had also brought with him his elder son Max, who was on his way to take up a regional RAF command in Cairo. With their arrival and Churchill's speed of recovery, the party became more cheerful. Nevertheless, there was one piece of business to be done. On the first evening after dinner, it was time for official duty: the Prime Minister decorated 'Little Max', already a holder of the DSO and DFC, with the 1939–43 Star. Churchill made an elegant speech, full of praise for Aitken's heroism during the Battle of Britain. That done to everybody's satisfaction, they settled down to play poker. (Colville made the mistake of repeatedly calling Beaverbrook's bluff. He lost heavily.)

Churchill convalescing in the sunshine of Marrakesh, Morocco,
after a bout of pneumonia, 31 December 1943.

The days followed a predictable pattern. In the mornings and evenings when he was not seeing French or Moroccan officials, Churchill would concentrate on his painting. Just before lunch a fleet of cars would draw up to take the party on an expedition. The most popular destinations turned out to be the mountains of the High Atlas or the old city of Medina. In either case there would be a picnic lunch, perhaps better described, given the richness of the fare, as a luncheon out of doors. After they had eaten, Churchill, slumped in contentment beneath an enormous sombrero, talked of old campaigns and controversies to an increasingly sleepy audience.[15] Beaverbrook told Farrer that he suffered 'agonies of boredom' watching Churchill sketching, alleviated only by taking time out to lead a shopping expedition or teasing General Bernard Montgomery. But the days went by smoothly without Beaverbrook making any effort to leave for home. Luckily, just in case the routine might be verging on *accidie*, on 10 January the party was livened up by the arrival of the Duff Coopers. He was to take over from Harold Macmillan as Minister Resident and she, of course, was determined to revive the social life in Algiers which Macmillan, having left his wife in England, had allowed to decline.

It was time for Churchill and his entourage to go home. On 14 January 1944 the main party left Marrakesh to fly, in four aircraft, to Gibraltar. From there they sailed in the battleship HMS *King George V* out into the Atlantic before making a half-circle and heading to Plymouth. There they took the sleeper train, arriving in the morning of the 18th to be met by the Churchill family and the Cabinet. Churchill was given a hero's welcome, but for Beaverbrook the holiday, for that was what it was, had come to an end. He and his party had left the others at Gibraltar to fly back to England.

The reason was simple. He was due at last to make his speech on 19 January. Masefield had drafted the speech but it needed final attention before delivery. Much to his surprise, however, when the time came, Beaverbrook left the script to one side and delivered the speech from memory. It was, according to Masefield, an 'astonishing performance'.[16] It was also, unlike many of his political speeches, a masterpiece of clarity. 'Our first concern', he stated, 'will be to gain general acceptance of certain broad principles whereby civil aviation can be made into a benign influence for welding the nations of the world together into a closer co-operation.'[17] In other words, civil aviation was to be an agreed template for a new world order.

It was on the face of it, like many of Beaverbrook's grand visions, potentially inspiring. Similarly, like those, it led back to his constant theme, the British Empire. A victorious post-war Britain, he declared, would be in possession of an Empire 'in every respect suited to the use of this new means of transport ... All our Empire problems can be made to yield to the new science, the science of transportation.'[18] Yet once again the vision, inspiring though it might be, was some distance away from reality. As before, his 'Empire' consisted of the developed English-speaking countries, as though the Indian subcontinent and sub-Saharan Africa did not exist. Furthermore, the language of Empire would hardly appeal to the anti-imperialist Roosevelt administration. Nevertheless, in spite of the sour reception in Washington for Beaverbrook's rhetoric, it was agreed on both sides that negotiations should start in early spring to resolve differences and arrive at a joint policy.

In the meantime, Beaverbrook took the opportunity to lecture Churchill on the future electoral chances of the Conservative Party. '[It] has ... an excellent programme,' he wrote to Churchill on the day after his speech in the House of Lords:

> ... The case is in our hands. Where we are in default is the exposition ... It may be said that this is something I can rectify so far as the principal newspaper is concerned ... but it is necessary that this campaign should be conducted effectively, not only in the columns of newspapers but on the platforms of candidates.[19]

There was also the matter of post-war reconstruction, where Beaverbrook thought that Labour had grasped the initiative. It was high time to grasp it back.

On 3 April 1944 formal discussions on civil aviation started in London. The American delegation was led by one of Roosevelt's inner circle of advisers, Adolf Berle. Berle, however, carried with him one great disadvantage, in that almost everybody seemed to dislike him. Born in 1895 in Boston, physically short in stature but an intellectual heavyweight with seemingly irrepressible energy, he had passed the Harvard entrance exams at the age of twelve, taking up his place two years later and achieving stellar results: bachelor's degree in 1913, master's in 1914, then the Harvard Law School, where, at the age of twenty-one, he became the youngest graduate in the school's history. He then moved steadily up the ladder of Democrat politics to become in 1938 Assistant Secretary of State for Latin American Affairs. There was no doubt about his ability or his drive, but he was abrasive and supercilious. One senior diplomat remarked in 1971 on Berle's death that 'he had an academic career at Harvard of such distinction that he has never quite recovered from it'.[20] Beaverbrook took an immediate dislike to him.

Lord Beaverbrook (centre), Adolf A. Berle (left) and Dr Edward Warner (right) at a press conference on the problem of post-war civil aviation, January 1944.

Backing Berle up was another, and more approachable, Harvard graduate, Edward Warner. Warner was known to be something of a pioneer in American civil aviation and was at the time vice-chairman of the Civil Aeronautics Board. In short, he provided the technical expertise to Berle's legal dynamics. At the very least, he and Masefield could speak the same language. Certainly, thanks to that, the talks got off to a promising start. The need for agreed technical standards and measures to ban enemy nations from post-war air transport were passed without substantive comment. The problem came over who could fly where and at what cost. The Americans wanted 'the greatest possible expansion of US aviation by free enterprise without any government ownership or any form of internationalisation of operations', while the British wished to protect the rights of their airlines to fly to British bases.[21] The negotiations did not go further, both sides agreeing to reflect on how the two positions could be reconciled. The meeting broke up with an undertaking to meet again in Washington in July.

By late spring the coming invasion of the European mainland was the prime topic of conversation. At the same time, with open encouragement from the *Daily Express*, public debate was becoming increasingly politicised as commentators turned their attention to the Britain that would emerge from victory in the war. But it was all too much for Michael Foot. He had taken over the editorship of the *Evening Standard* from Frank Owen in 1942, but by late 1943 what had started as 'a filial relationship' was beginning to look frayed. Foot was selected as Labour candidate for the constituency of Plymouth Devonport and the leaders he was writing for his paper sat uneasily with the opinions he was expressing on the platform. Beaverbrook tried to find a role for Foot, but D-Day in June 1944, bringing with it the scent of victory, crystallised the difficulty. 'The business of maintaining allegiance to my own political ideas', Foot wrote, 'and to a newspaper which fundamentally must be opposed to them is too difficult.'[22] Separation was the only possible outcome, much, as Beaverbrook made clear, to his employer's regret.

On 20 July the British negotiating party left Northolt Airport, as planned, bound for Washington and further discussions with Berle and his team. Yet again their aircraft was a Liberator whose bomb bay had been equipped with four seats on either side with mattresses and sleeping bags on the floor. Beaverbrook tried to cheer everybody up by singing the music hall song 'Abdul Abulbul Amir' in his loudest voice to be heard above the engine noise. As it turned out, he might just as well have saved his breath. The talks, in Washington and New York, lasted three weeks, but were as unproductive as the previous session in London. To try to introduce an informal note, Beaverbrook invited Berle and Clarence Howe, the Canadian Minister of Munition and

Supply, for a weekend of walks, fishing and dining in New Brunswick. It was no good. As Howe put it, their fishing proved 'about as productive as our talks on aviation'.[23] After more fruitless disagreement, it was decided to hold yet another conference in London in the autumn.

By then Beaverbrook had had enough. Privately he told Masefield that he had no intention of taking part in any future international conference. 'I prefer a "knock-down and drag out meeting". I haven't got the patience for long wrestling matches.'[24] Once back in London he asked Churchill to form a new department to deal specifically with civil aviation and suggested Viscount (Philip) Swinton, currently Minister Resident in West Africa, to run it. Churchill agreed, and Beaverbrook was able on 12 October to tell the House of Lords that Swinton's 'whole-time duty will be to carry forward at once the work of planning in the field of civil aviation'.[25] Beaverbrook himself would remain as chairman of the Civil Air Transport Cabinet Sub-Committee.

At this point Roosevelt intervened. To cut through the argument in a stroke he instructed officials to call together the fifty-five countries with an interest in the matter to a conference to find solutions to all outstanding problems once and for all. It was to meet in Chicago on 1 November. Swinton was told to scramble back to London, to be briefed in two long meetings with Beaverbrook and to set off as head of the UK delegation to Chicago. In London, a new Cabinet committee was set up, with Beaverbrook as chairman, 'to consider from day to day questions arising out of the Chicago Conference'.[26] In other words, Beaverbrook was going to pull all the strings from London.

The conference opened on 1 November and was scheduled to last until 7 December. On the first day, Berle and Swinton had lunch together and formed an intense mutual dislike which lasted throughout the conference and proved to be a major obstacle to any agreement. Beaverbrook and Masefield sat nervously in London in a 'period of hectic activity … Max's compulsive telephoning, always with a high sense of urgency, reached a level not seen since the early days at the MAP.'[27] (Perhaps, Masefield thought, that in itself was another obstacle to agreement.)

The main point of controversy was what became known as the 'Fifth Freedom'. This would allow airlines to pick up passengers at intermediate stops. For example, an aircraft on a New York to Paris service with a stop in London would be allowed to pick up passengers for the London–Paris leg only. The economic advantages of a British airline operating along this truncated route were obvious. Needless to say, the Americans regarded the Fifth Freedom as inherently free market while the British, realising that it would destroy their airlines, argued for protection.

On 21 November, Roosevelt cabled Churchill to complain that the conference was at an 'impasse' and that the British insistence on limiting Fifth Freedom traffic was 'a form of strangulation'.[28] The British response, at Beaverbrook's insistence, was robust: 'We cannot see our way to accept these new suggestions put forward, which would gravely jeopardise our own position.'[29] Roosevelt then switched to a harder line. In a letter crafted by Harry Hopkins but authorised by Roosevelt and delivered personally by Ambassador Winant, the language was clear: 'I am afraid you do not yet fully appreciate the importance of reaching a satisfactory agreement.' At that point came the blackmail. 'We are doing our best to meet your lend-lease needs. We will face Congress on that subject in a few weeks and it will not be in a generous mood if it and the people feel that the United Kingdom has not agreed to a generally beneficial air agreement.'[30] In other words, Roosevelt seemed prepared to put the wartime supply arrangements in jeopardy if American commercial interests were not satisfied with the post-war arrangements.

In reply, the British offered to accept impartial arbitration by a suitable panel of experts. But Berle and Swinton were unable to agree the mechanics. After some emollient words between Roosevelt and Churchill, the result was that the conference quietly fizzled out without conclusion. Yet for Beaverbrook there was one lasting effect. In defending their own interests, it was transparently clear that the Americans, at all levels, would negotiate all post-war matters with the hardest of heads. 'American leadership', he had written earlier in the year to John Maynard Keynes, 'is not a development we should welcome. On the contrary, we are likely to have more than our fill of it before we are finished.'[31] As an example of American leadership he trained his journalistic guns on the proposals for an international monetary system agreed at Bretton Woods in July and out for ratification by the eighty participant countries. 'This is a foolish document,' he wrote to Churchill in December. 'The folly of it lies in the defence of the Gold Standard ... That is the process which brought us to disaster after 1922 when we made a fictitious settlement of the American debt.'[32]

As a counterweight to his low opinion of American leadership, Beaverbrook's rosy view of the Soviet Union remained undimmed. Stalin had awarded him, on Churchill's recommendation, membership of the Order of Suvorov, created in memory of one of Russia's most successful military leaders of the eighteenth century. Openly pleased, as he told Churchill, he went out of his way to avoid criticism of the Soviet decision to delay their advance into Warsaw to allow the Germans to put down a Polish uprising. 'Our hope for days to come,' he wrote to Eden,

> so far as relations with the United States are concerned, depends on a close measure of friendship with Russia ... Now the issue of Poland rises before us ... Whatever the cause of the tragedy the friendship of Russia is far more important to us than the future of Anglo-Polish relations.[33]

(It was, of course, outrageous, but, if there is a defence, he had never liked the Poles and had been quite content to see Poland itself split up. Nevertheless, had he expressed such an opinion at any time other than during the Allied assault in Europe he would have been submerged in protest from those who had welcomed the bravery of Polish pilots in the Battle of Britain.)

By the turn of the year it seemed as though Beaverbrook was picking on issues on which, if the truth be told, he had imperfect knowledge and limited understanding, to make himself heard above the clamour of victorious armies. He was, as he admitted, enjoying himself as a Cabinet minister without portfolio, able to poke his nose into other people's affairs without the responsibility of executive decision. In fact, as far as his Cabinet colleagues were concerned, it was much worse than mere dabbling. After D-Day, Churchill's energy and interest were devoted above all to the battlefields of Western Europe. Although the management of domestic affairs lay by agreement squarely with Attlee, Churchill grew into the habit of passing his copy of Cabinet committee documents to Beaverbrook and Bracken with the request that they study them and, if appropriate, in his absence represent their views to Cabinet as those of the Conservative Party and, thus, of himself as leader.

The explosion came early in 1945. On 19 January, Attlee wrote a long letter to Churchill complaining about his inattention at Cabinet. 'More and more often', the letter runs,

> you have not read even the note prepared for your guidance. Often half an hour and more is wasted in explaining what could have been grasped by two or three minutes' reading of the document ... But there is something worse than this. The conclusions agreed upon by a Committee on which have sat five or six members of the Cabinet and other experienced Ministers are then submitted with great deference to the Lord Privy Seal and the Minister for Information, two Ministers without Cabinet responsibility neither of whom has given any serious attention to the subject. When they state their views it is obvious that they know nothing about it. Nevertheless, an hour is consumed in listening to their opinions. Time and again important matters are delayed or passed in accordance with the decision of the Lord Privy Seal. The excuse is given that in him you have the mind of the Conservative Party. With some knowledge of opinion in the Conservative Party in the House as expressed to me on the retirement from and re-entry into the Government of Lord Beaverbrook I suggest that this view would be indignantly repudiated by the vast majority.[34]

According to Colville, Churchill was taken aback, even thunderstruck, by the letter. He called Bracken, who said that Attlee was quite right. He then called Beaverbrook, who, surprisingly, agreed with Bracken. Not at all dismayed, he proceeded to dictate a furious reply. Later in the afternoon Mrs Churchill came into the room. Churchill told her of Attlee's letter and his reply. Mrs Churchill immediately said that she admired Attlee for having the courage to say what everyone is thinking. Colville then quietly mentioned that Churchill's letter in reply had been delayed in despatch and could be recovered. It was, and Churchill dictated a substitute: 'I have to thank you for your Private and Personal letter of January 19. You may be sure I shall always endeavour to profit by your counsels. Yours sincerely, Winston Churchill'.[35]

Just before the end of January, Jean Norton died suddenly. She had spent the latter part of the war working in a factory in Leatherhead as a lathe operator, which she continued even after her husband succeeded to the Grantley barony in 1943. She had kept the cottage at Cherkley which Beaverbrook had lent her as well as a room in the house itself. Returning to the cottage on a Sunday night in a cheerful mood after spending a relaxed evening with Beaverbrook watching a film, she went to bed. In the middle of the night, she suddenly awoke in severe pain. She immediately called out to her daughter Sarah and her sister Kitty Brownlow, who happened to be staying with her. They in turn were quick to call for emergency medical help. When this arrived, the diagnosis was swift: a massive heart attack. The following morning, specialists arrived from London. Their prognosis was gloomy: she had only a 50/50 chance of survival. Early on the Tuesday morning she lost the battle. 'And I', Beaverbrook wrote to Diana Cooper, 'have lost my moorings.'[36]

As with his wife Gladys, Beaverbrook seems only belatedly to have realised what he had lost. Jean had been his mistress for some twenty years. As with Gladys, she had to put up with any number of casual infidelities. Also, as with Gladys, she had come to the painful conclusion that history had repeated itself, that her place had been taken by a newcomer: in her case, Lily Ernst, the petite ballet dancer from Vienna. On an autumnal note, when Beaverbrook wrote to congratulate her on her children's wartime careers, she wrote back, 'I value your appreciation of my children above all others. Perhaps because of the love I have and always shall have come what may – I can say no more but that I am and always shall be your ever loving Jeannie'.[37]

CHAPTER 25

LILY AND OTHER WOMEN

'My life is just one man'[1]

Lily Ernst (she had anglicised her given name 'Lili' when she arrived in London in May 1938) brought beauty and a feisty character, both of which Beaverbrook, true to form, found sexually captivating. Nearing thirty years old and in her prime, she was, to put it bluntly, an obvious Beaverbrook target. He in turn was on familiar territory. His seduction of women was well versed in its ritual choreography. True, he was now in his sixtieth year and perhaps tending to slow up in its execution. Nevertheless, no doubt on some occasion in the spring of 1938, the choreography led to its conclusion and the deed was duly done.

But Lily also brought a problem. The problem lay, as so often in these matters, in what was to happen next. It was Lily herself who, in an effusion of gratitude for his efforts in saving her life, and in a mood of romantic adulation, introduced a degree of emotional over-load by falling spectacularly in love with him. As his protégé Michael Foot later remarked, 'The best thing I knew about Max Beaverbrook was that Lily Ernst truly loved him.'[2] Yet therein lay the problem. In short, she was not content with just casual sex. She wanted more. In particular, she wanted recognition as either his wife or his preferred mistress. That, it soon became apparent, was something Beaverbrook was not prepared to concede.

The difficulty was that Beaverbrook was a long way from recipro-cating her love with the same excited enthusiasm. He was content, and perhaps more than content, with her as a sexual partner, but he was certainly not ready to grant her the status he had granted Jean

Norton, as a clearly appointed mistress for all to see and admire. She was, in his view, too obviously unsuitable for his wider stage. She was Jewish, with black hair and dark brown eyes, delicate, fragile and exotic, with hesitant and heavily accented English. There therefore was no question of her introduction to other than a small percentage of his acquaintance. Of course, he would supply bed and board, admire her endeavours in translation, and encourage her efforts to reach out to, and to take care of, fellow refugees, but socially the best he could do was to invite her to Cherkley for a long weekend every month from May to October 1938, at which point the temperature between her, Jean Norton and Beaverbrook's daughter Janet became perhaps too hot. There is no record in the Cherkley visitors' book of her staying there in 1939. As for social life in London, she was largely left to entertaining her fellow émigrés.

Michael Foot, editor of the Evening Standard, *pictured in 1945 as a Labour candidate shortly before he became MP for Plymouth Devonport.*

A partial solution lay at hand. In the past, Beaverbrook had toyed with the idea of interesting one or other of his acolytes in taking on women he was minded to discard. While he had no intention of abandoning

Lily, he did not object to her being chaperoned by one of his protégés. Whether it was planned or not is neither here nor there, but it was during one of her weekends at Cherkley in early September 1938 that she and Michael Foot found themselves invited to a convivial dinner on the Saturday, followed by lunch on the Sunday. Foot was duly smitten. But his chances were limited. After all, he was five years her junior, shy, spotty in the face and asthmatic. Nevertheless, he had the priceless gift of speech, soaring in its power and expression in a way Lily had not heard before. She remembered this when Foot, pressed by Beaverbrook, wrote long articles for the *Daily Express* backing the Jewish cause in the maelstrom of Nazi-organised riots. But it was one article of his in the *Evening Standard* criticising the way refugees were being treated that stirred Lily. She immediately wrote to him and, just as immediately, he telephoned her.

There was thus born an unlikely and bizarre triangle. Foot was besotted with Lily. Lily, in turn, looked on him with affection as a younger brother. Beaverbrook was, as usual, a hard and demanding sexual master. All three had their role to play as long as Foot did not trespass on Beaverbrook's territory and Lily made clear her position. In fact, at one point, sensing Foot's interest to be on the edge of more than brotherly, she was quick to say, 'My life is just one man.'³ Once that was made clear, Foot, during a relationship which stretched into four years, never tried to kiss her. They would go for long walks together at Cherkley, Lily pointing out the beauties of the landscape and comparing the poetry of Heinrich Heine to Foot's hero Lord Byron. Foot would respond with eloquent analyses of British politics and the current literary scene. Together, they would drop in on Nye Bevan and Jennie Lee in London and drink the evenings away with their coterie of political friends. All in all, it was not surprising that they were seen as lovers and perhaps even secretly married. To round off the nature of the threesome, both Beaverbrook and Foot, with their shared fondness for Biblical allusion, referred to her as (and called her to her face) 'Esther', Xerxes I's Jewish queen.

The coming of war made the relationship more difficult to manage. Cherkley was put on a war footing, with staff numbers reduced from forty to fifteen. Stornoway House suffered serious bomb and blast damage on the nights of 13 October 1940, 1 November and 15 November 1940 and was rendered uninhabitable on 11 January 1941. Beaverbrook himself had left after the first attack and decamped to a makeshift flat on the first floor of the *Evening Standard* building in Farringdon Street. It was not until May 1942 that he found a more convenient perch at Brook House, 113 Park Lane. Finally, in March 1943 he became a leaseholder of Flat 95, Arlington House, which became in time his permanent London base. (Among its other advantages the property had as neighbour the Ritz Hotel.) The difficulty was finding safe accommodation for Lily. At one point she found herself sharing a Cherkley cottage with Michael Foot. In fact, it was not until September 1942 that the problem was solved. Beaverbrook took over a flat in Fursecroft, George Street, from his son Max. It had the advantage of lying to the north of Oxford Street and away from the prime targets for German bombers. Lily soon moved in.

Arlington House became Lord Beaverbrook's London base from 1943.

The threesome came to an end when Foot left the *Evening Standard* in June 1944. Lily's affection for Beaverbrook continued through the remainder of the war and for a further two years. His affection for her, on the other hand, reduced markedly once the inhibitions (and practical difficulties) of wartime had receded. After Jean Norton's death in 1945, Lily waited in vain for Beaverbrook to propose marriage.

Not only was there no proposal but she soon found out that he had resumed his previous peacetime pattern, to put it politely, of taking advantage of other opportunities as and when they occurred. By 1947, it was clear that the relationship had run its course. Then in poor health, Lily was fortunate enough two years later to meet, and soon thereafter agree to marry, a cultivated and rich English businessman, Antony Hornby, who had had the courage to ask her. Beaverbrook's reaction is not recorded but reports ranged from possessive anger to tears to attempts to bribe her to abandon her wedding. Yet one thing is certain. Lily, like Gladys and Jean before her, had been shown an unhappy, even humiliating, exit.

In October 1942, Beaverbrook agreed to rent Flat 11, 49 Grosvenor Square, initially taking the lease on behalf of the Honourable Mrs Pamela Digby Churchill. In July 1943, his secretary, George Millar, told him that Mrs Churchill wished to extend the lease for another two years. Millar wanted to know whether he was to renew the lease in her name. Beaverbrook replied that 'you may take the lease in my name of the flat, Mr M. It was an understanding between Mr ... on my part about it'.[4] The name left discreetly unfilled almost certainly was that of Beaverbrook's friend Averell Harriman.

Pamela Churchill carrying her infant son, master Winston Churchill, 23 April 1941.

Pamela Digby had been born and brought up in the customs of the English countryside's aristocracy. At the age of nineteen, however, soon after her introduction to London society and spells in Munich and Paris, she was working as a junior translator at the Foreign Office when she met Randolph Churchill at a party. That very evening Churchill proposed marriage and was accepted. The wedding, on 4 October 1939, was celebrated in style, not least by Beaverbrook, who, familiar with Randolph's erratic lifestyle, appointed himself Pamela's confidant and adviser. There were invitations to weekends at Cherkley and dinners at Stornoway House, and Beaverbrook was godfather to her son, baptised Winston. 'Following the birth of her son,' her biographer notes, 'she had lost weight, and she had become a beauty. Her hair slightly tousled, the gray streak near her part[ing] a gleaming wisp, her eyes heavy-lidded, her mouth pouty, her image seemed come-hither instead of beatifically maternal.'[5] It needs hardly to be said, but many men of a certain age in London at the time looked on her with admiration. One of those was undoubtedly the baby's godfather. Not only was Beaverbrook an attentive godfather in terms of financial support but he also arranged for baby Winston and his nanny to be parked at Cherkley.

By the spring of 1941, Pamela had found her place in the luxury of the Dorchester Hotel. Rationing was largely ignored in the private dinner parties that took place almost nightly in private suites presided over by the most distinguished of pre-war London hostesses. Pamela's name was enough to ensure an invitation to the best parties. Within those packed dining rooms, Pamela and her fellow patrons 'consumed magnums of champagne and unseemly amounts of food', the numbing scale of excess prompting Chip Channon to call it a 'modern wartime Babylon'.[6] Weekends were spent either at Chequers, where she acted as hostess at tea in the great hall, or at Cherkley, where she found amusing and more down-to-earth company. She herself admitted that it was the most exciting time in her whole life.

Randolph had left England for his posting to Cairo on 1 February 1941. He had solemnly pledged to be on his best behaviour and, above all, abstain from gambling. On the long journey round the South African Cape, however, all pledges were forgotten. By the time his ship docked at Cairo, Randolph had run up liabilities of some £100,000 in today's values. From Cairo he sent a telegram to Pamela asking her to arrange to pay off his debt 'in the best way possible' without telling his father.[7] There was only one way out: an appeal to Beaverbrook. He agreed to fund a partial settlement but in addition she was forced to sell some of her wedding presents. 'It was a lesson,' she said later. 'I suddenly realised that if there was to be any security for baby Winston and me, it was going to be on our own.'[8]

As it happened, Pamela was not entirely on her own. Averell Harriman had arrived in London as Roosevelt's emissary and had left his wife, Marie, behind in New York. It was not long before he fell for Pamela. For her, it was a special form of bonus. Harriman had his share, and more, of Wall Street money and was well able to look after her in the way she had come to expect. For Beaverbrook, there were two advantages. The first was that he was let off what had threatened to become an unpleasant hook. The second was that Pamela was quite prepared to pass on reports of her conversations with Harriman about anything of interest. Weekends at Cherkley were spent not just looking after little Winston but also in discussions of high politics. Beaverbrook benefited both from Harriman's counsel and from Pamela's insight.

It is not easy to be precise about Beaverbrook's relationship with Pamela. Certainly, when Harriman was finishing his tour of duty as Ambassador in Moscow in 1946, Beaverbrook took her with him on a week's holiday to Bermuda. Given Pamela's open decision to play the courtesan and Beaverbrook's record with women, it would be normal to conclude that what occurred during that week fell into the usual pattern, rather more than her obligingly acting as his hostess when he entertained the Governor of Bermuda. On the other hand, Beaverbrook knew perfectly well, as did almost everybody else in London and New York, that her attachment to Harriman was (at least by her standards) sincere, and that it would be unwise to make an enemy of him when he found out about the Bermuda holiday (Pamela was far from discreet in speaking about her adventures). All in all, it seems most likely that for him Pamela was in the reserve category of beautiful and high-profile women with whom he had a cheerfully flirtatious friendship but no more (Diana Cooper being a case in point).

In the years following Lily's marriage in 1949, Beaverbrook seems to have shied away from open extramarital relationships. At least in part this was due to his peripatetic lifestyle. From the end of the war onwards he never spent a winter in England. There were companions who accompanied him on his travels during the 1950s, some as secretaries, some young journalists hoping for promotion, some simply attached to one or other member of his family. What relationships developed, or in what form if they did, cannot be accurately described for lack of evidence. But Beaverbrook was seventy in 1950 and time may well have taken the same toll as it does for other less energetic brothers.

One figure stands out during this period: Marie-Edmée Escarra. Born at an uncertain date, probably 1911, she had grown up in a family of minor aristocrats before marrying the Comte Paul Champetier de Ribes in 1938. Like many of her class, she wore her marriage lightly, soon becoming the mistress of Philippe de Rothschild, a relationship which was interrupted by the Second World War but resumed after its end. 'Marie-Edmée turned up again', Philippe wrote in his autobiography, 'and that was wonderful. We went dancing and swimming, played and made love. It was my postwar honeymoon.' The honeymoon was soon over, Philippe declaring that 'life without a purpose tasted stale'.[9] He tried to avoid the staleness by taking another two mistresses, seemingly unfazed when the three disturbed his lunch when they appeared together at his table.

Marie-Edmée was introduced to Beaverbrook by one of his London friends, Lady d'Avigdor Goldsmith, ostensibly as a French teacher. But with her red hair, freckles and saucy charm she immediately made a different mark. Beaverbrook quickly saw that, apart from her sexual attraction, she was, unlike Lily Ernst, someone he could rely on as a companion into a wider world. She turned out, too, to be something of a connoisseur of classical paintings, just at the time that Beaverbrook was buying for his galleries in Canada. Nevertheless, it was never a happy relationship. 'Max was quite vile to her', wrote one of her admirers, 'and his uncouth beastliness probably contributed to [her] cancer.'[10] At all events, Marie-Edmée turned to drink and, miserable, left to live with her parents in Paris. Beaverbrook gave her a small allowance which he was always thereafter trying to reduce.

Josephine Rosenberg, Marie-Edmée's almost exact contemporary in Beaverbrook's circle, was from a different mould. Her father was a Jewish émigré from eastern Poland and her mother was from a respectable New Forest family. She had been educated at boarding schools in southern England and finished at a secretarial college, from where she went to work as a press officer first at the Conservative Central Office and then at the offices of the Central Africa Federation. In 1953, at the age of twenty-one, she started work with Beaverbrook as secretary and travel companion and stayed with him until 1960. Of Beaverbrook himself, she said, 'He was fun, amusing, nice to talk to. I looked up to him as a great man.'[11] To complete the picture of a young, attractive and intelligent girl, she made great friends with Beaverbrook's favourite granddaughter, Janet's daughter Jeannie Campbell, a friendship which Beaverbrook appeared to tolerate, even to encourage, as his own relations with Jeannie were stormy at the time.

Josephine Rosenberg with Lord Beaverbrook.

There were, of course, others. There was a plentiful supply of young journalists looking for promotion or secretaries in search of a salary rise who found it difficult to refuse an invitation from the proprietor. Yet as the 1950s drew to a close, Beaverbrook was approaching his ninth decade and it is not hard to detect a diminishing enthusiasm for the chase. One young reporter on the *Evening Standard*, for instance, remembered that he would hold her hands for hours and gaze at her, saying, 'Let me look at you. You are a woman in her prime.'[12] Another was recruited to his staff as a nurse when there was nothing wrong with him. Others were inveigled into dinner with him alone and made a quick escape. All in all, the scenery seemed to be changing. After living all those years without a wife, the great seducer was moving, for his final years, gently towards the comfortable nest of a second marriage.

CHAPTER 26

FAREWELL TO POLITICS

'The past now lives in my memory. The future has no place'[1]

It took only a few days after Germany's unconditional surrender on 7 May 1945 for the undercurrents of personal hostility within the British Cabinet to bubble to the surface. The first signs were evident as early as 18 May, when Churchill wrote to Attlee offering either an immediate dissolution or an agreement to continue the coalition until the war with Japan was won. Attlee, who was on his way to Blackpool for the Labour Party conference, replied that he would seek the opinion of the party's National Executive Committee. Churchill wrote back, irritably protesting that the decision whether or not there should be a general election should not be in the hands of a committee of a political party most of whose members had not even been elected to Parliament. Attlee in turn pointed out waspishly that Churchill had not made the objection when it was a question of joining the coalition in 1940. Besides, he went on, the committee had already made its decision to withdraw the party support from the coalition, which, it followed, must now be dissolved. He could not possibly override the decision. Accordingly, on 22 May Churchill wrote formally that he intended to dissolve the coalition and call a general election. Once the letter was sent, and without further consultation, he published the whole correspondence. The Labour ministers in Blackpool could hardly contain their anger.

From then on it went from bad to worse. Behind much of the rise in temperature, of course, was Beaverbrook, who had been, together with Brendan Bracken and the Chief Whip James Stuart, appointed to oversee Conservative preparations for the general election. Needless to say, he was urging Churchill into the fiercest possible battle.

It was no coincidence that on 23 May the *Manchester Guardian* published a cartoon by David Low (of the *Evening Standard*) showing Beaverbrook happily at the wheel of a speedboat carrying Churchill and Brendan Bracken with Attlee, Bevin and Morrison preparing to plunge overboard. As the paper commented, 'Lord Beaverbrook is at the wheel, it will be noted: he is no supernumerary.'[2] The point was taken on all sides: Beaverbrook was pushing Churchill to engage in the electoral battle with the same relentless spirit which had won the war. Furthermore, in support, his newspapers had already started on a campaign which would later be described by the US Ambassador as 'particularly violent, inaccurate and personal'.[3]

The Labour big guns were not slow to respond. Bevin, for example, in a speech at Belper on 12 June, let his temper fly: 'By heavens,' he raged,

> I have no quarrel with the Prime Minister but I have had enough these last five years of Lord Beaverbrook. He would have broken the Coalition over and over again if he had his way. I object to this country being ruled from Fleet Street however big the circulation, instead of from Parliament.[4]

By then the fat was already well and truly in the fire. True, for the outside world the formalities were properly observed. On 23 May the timetable was announced for a general election to be held on 5 July, with three weeks' delay in publishing the result to allow the service vote to be brought in. Yet even before Parliament was dissolved and the campaign proper begun, Churchill, in his first radio broadcast on 4 June, launched a ferocious attack on his opponents. 'No socialist government', he declared, 'could afford to allow free ... expression of public dissent. They would have to fall back on some form of Gestapo.'[5]

Even many of his loyal supporters thought he had gone too far. In fact, the shock waves following what became known as Churchill's 'Gestapo' speech left Attlee not one but three spectacularly open goals. Attlee was quick to score. First, he thanked Churchill for allowing the nation's voters 'to understand how great was the difference between Winston Churchill the great leader in war of a united nation and Mr Churchill the Party Leader'. Next, he played the anti-German card. His 'lurid descriptions

of life under socialism were "merely the second-hand version of the academic views" of an Austrian professor, Mr Hayek [Friedrich Hayek,
whose book, *The Road to Serfdom*, had been published in 1944]'. Finally,
he claimed to reveal the true culprit: 'The voice we heard last night was
that of Mr Churchill, but the mind was that of Lord Beaverbrook.'[6]

The next exchange of blows was not long delayed. On 14 June,
in the last sitting day of Parliament before Dissolution, Churchill
announced that he had invited Attlee to accompany him to a conference to be held at Potsdam, a suburb of Berlin, to determine the
shape of the peace. This was too much for Harold Laski, a professor
of political science at the London School of Economics and the then
chairman of the Labour Party. Laski, who according to his biographer
'wrote too much, overestimated his influence, and sometimes failed to
distinguish between analysis and polemic',[7] promptly wrote to Attlee
arguing that he should attend the Potsdam conference 'for information and consultation only' and that a future Labour government
could not be bound by any decisions taken there. Laski made the
further mistake of publishing his view in the *Daily Herald*.

This time Churchill and Attlee were on the same side. Churchill immediately wrote an open letter to Attlee declaring that his purpose was
that Attlee should accompany him as 'a friend and counsellor … merely
to come as a mute observer would, I think, be derogatory to your position
as Leader of your Party'. Attlee chimed in a statement of his own that
'there was never any suggestion [that I should go] as a mere observer…'
Laski was forced to retreat, which he did by issuing his own statement
that his intervention had been 'a personal one, made off my own bat'.[8]

That was enough for Beaverbrook and the *Daily Express* to turn
a minor squall into a full-blown thunderstorm. Under the headline
'Socialists Split: Attlee Repudiates Laski Order', it published a leading article arguing the right of voters to know 'whether in returning
Socialist MPs to Parliament … they are sending representatives of the
people … or servants of the party machine'.[9] More was to come. A
Conservative councillor wrote to the *Nottingham Guardian* that he
had been at a meeting in Newark where Laski had supported violent
revolution as a means of achieving socialism. This was taken up by
the *Daily Express* ('Socialism – even if it means violence') and even

by Beaverbrook in person. At a meeting in Streatham Town Hall, he declared that 'Laski is aiming at the destruction of the parliamentary system of Great Britain and hopes to set up in its place the dictatorship of something commonly called the National Executive'.[10]

The tone of 'mud-slinging [and] vituperation' that Ambassador Winant reported to Washington was thus set foul for the remainder of the campaign. Beaverbrook himself had a full programme.[11] He spoke at meetings, mainly in London but also in the Midlands and the north-west (on 27 June in his old constituency of Ashton-under-Lyne, a visit heralded by the *Express* as the 'Return of the Crusader').[12] The meetings were usually robust and often disorderly, Beaverbrook shouting at hecklers sent in by the local Labour Party. Not that his message was always consistent or, indeed, coherent. On 9 June, for instance, at a meeting in Fulham, he proclaimed that his 'attitude is one of complete admiration for and absolute support of Joseph Stalin'. Yet in a speech at the Memorial Hall, Farringdon, two days later he urged 'the need for a closer and more vital [British] Empire'.[13] Then, in a letter to a friend, he wrote that 'nationalisation or continued free enterprise are the alternatives between which we will have to choose – control for control's sake or its abolition at the earliest feasible moment'.[14]

Lord Beaverbrook addressing a Conservative meeting, West Fulham, 11 June 1945.

By the middle of June, no holds were barred. Michael Foot, of all people, dipped his pen in what, for his previous mentor and friend, must have been particularly venomous acid. In an article for the *Daily Herald* of 15 June, Foot ridiculed his former employer for his continued attachment to the Empire. 'He was', the article ran,

> the Old Maid of politics, perpetually rejected by the embarrassed beau on whom he had fixed his attentions. Every few years he appears at the church door, decked out in the same old dress of economic nationalism. The trousseau is getting very tattered by now ... He should give up the chase, retire from the struggle with his virtue unassailed and hand over the Daily Express to the cause of pensions for spinsters.[15]

Bevin continued the onslaught, claiming, in his gentler moments, that Beaverbrook was 'the rather flatfooted kind of Tory who often terrifies his own Party by his indiscretions'.[16]

Attlee went even further. Speaking in Solihull on 20 June, he argued, 'The power of great wealth exercised by irresponsible men through newspapers with enormous circulations is a danger to democracy and a menace in public life ... Lord Beaverbrook has a long record of political intrigue and political instability and an insatiable appetite for power.' He chided Churchill for having

> allowed the campaign to pass into the hands of Lord Beaverbrook, the man in public life who is most widely distrusted by decent men of all parties ... What Mr Baldwin said in 1931 is true today. The Conservatives, for the sake of winning the election, have allied themselves with this man. They will live to regret it, as I am sure many of them do now.[17]

Beaverbrook's reply was surprisingly muted. On 23 June he wrote to the *Manchester Guardian* pointing out that

> I have been assailed viciously by Mr Attlee and repeatedly by Mr Bevin ... I make no complaint of such incursions of personal

animosity into the election. But I do complain that you should attempt to make me the guilty man in a matter where in fact I have been the first and chief victim.[18]

The truth is that he was already preparing to leave both the caretaker government and the mainstream of British politics whatever the result of the election. Accordingly, on 4 July, the day before polling day, he wrote Churchill his final letter of resignation. It was couched in terms which were both generous and personally affectionate. After the formalities of resignation, his letter concluded:

> In parting, I want to give you my grateful thanks for so much personal kindness and understanding during the crowded and trying years in which I served under your leadership. May I express, too, the profound admiration of one who had the good fortune to watch at close quarters your immense and victorious exertions for the salvation of Britain and mankind.[19]

Equally muted was Beaverbrook's reaction to the Labour landslide victory when it was declared on 26 July. 'The truth is', he wrote to a friend, 'that the British public have been conceiving for a long time an immense dislike of the Tory Party, the Tory members of Parliament and many of the Tory ideas. They were bored and wanted a change.'[20] The reaction of many of the defeated Conservative candidates was far more vociferous. E. J. Robertson reported in early October about a meeting of some two hundred such souls who had gathered for a post-mortem where the atmosphere was decidedly hostile. 'It was a most inexplicable business', one declared, 'that he [Churchill] should be so much in the hands of Lord Beaverbrook … a man who had no standing in the Conservative Party and was the most distrusted in public life.' Another had asked, 'Why don't we expel Lord Beaverbrook from the Party?'[21] Ralph Assheton, the Conservative Party chairman, also reported complaints that his newspapers had harboured left-wing journalists who had done much damage.

Beaverbrook had never been an orthodox Conservative. His links were with individuals rather than party. That was all very well while friendly individuals were in power, but after July 1945 his friends were in opposition and his enemies in power, at least for the next five years. Criticism of his role in the election irritated him, but the real point was that he had no longer guaranteed access to the levers of government. 'I am not concerned to defend myself any further,' he wrote back to Assheton.[22] And that, at least for the foreseeable future, was that. He was saying farewell to active participation in British politics.

That decision made, the next question was how he should arrange his affairs to face an indeterminate future. To be more specific, he needed more flexible means of money transfer between currencies and jurisdictions than were possible under the wartime legislation of exchange control. In July, the European war over, he sought permission from the Bank of England to release CAN$300,000, held under the provisions of the Defence (Finance) Regulations 1939 and 1941, to allow him to fund a library for the University of New Brunswick. His request was summarily turned down. To get round the problem he decided to take up permanent residence in Canada. In April 1946 his lawyers drafted a declaration of intent designed to persuade the Inland Revenue and the Bank of England, and anybody else for that matter, of his changed status. 'Now that the war is over,' it ran, 'and with the cause of Imperial Preference lost through the course of political events, Lord Beaverbrook has decided he will go home.'[23] The document was submitted for an opinion from a senior Treasury Counsel. The response was clear. Beaverbrook would have to give up all his residences in the United Kingdom if a court were to be persuaded that his presence there could be regarded as a visit.

That was disappointing enough. Worse still, his asthma had come back in strength. At first he thought that Cornwall or the south coast would provide a solution, and a secretary was despatched to find suitable properties. This she did, but by the time she had signed them up Beaverbrook had lost interest. The focus was now on the West Indies, and late in 1946 he bought Cromarty House, a suitable property of colonial style, but of limited elegance, in Jamaica's second city, Montego Bay.

Lord Beaverbrook on holiday in Jamaica, 1955.

In fact, Cromarty House was to become a vital staging post in Beaverbrook's winter migration. At first, this was little more than a matter
of leaving London in the autumn and taking up residence in La Capponcina. Early in 1947, however, a more exciting prospect was put
in front of him. The University of New Brunswick, though small by
comparison with older European foundations, felt that it was large
enough to merit the appointment of a chancellor. Since Beaverbrook
had already funded the Lady Beaverbrook residence for men and the
Lady Beaverbrook gymnasium, as well as a number of bursaries, and
seemed minded to be even more generous, he was the obvious candidate. He was installed in May 1947.

Although the university was located in Fredericton, some distance
from his childhood home in Newcastle, Beaverbrook now had a base
in his home province and a reason for visiting rather than appearing
from time to time as a rich tourist. In fact, he took a detailed interest
in the university's affairs. The degree ceremony was moved from May
to October to suit his timetable and he was able to spend anything up

to two months each autumn interfering, as a few grumpy professors would have it, in the running of the university. He even bought more than one house as a possible home, but nothing proved suitable and he gave them to the university while he settled himself in the principal suite in the Lord Beaverbrook Hotel.

To complete his winter circuit, Beaverbrook bought a house in Nassau in the Bahamas. It was in the grand style with six bedrooms and a large dining room on the ground floor leading to a terrace where local grandees could be entertained. He quickly changed its name from Matthew House to Aitken House and declared that was to be his main winter residence for the future. No more than four months were set aside for summer in England. The path of his winter migration soon became fixed. The *Queen Mary* would take him to New York in October. From there he would go on to Fredericton for the annual convocation. That done, he would use Fredericton as a base for visits to Montreal to review his finances with his brother Allan and quick trips to Newcastle. A week in New York followed (he insisted on seeing the latest shows) before a stay, usually over Christmas, in Cromarty House. Montego Bay offered an active social life, pleasing at the beginning with West Indian notables but soon tedious to the foreign visitor, to the point where early in the New Year he moved to Nassau. The migration ended in May with the *Queen Mary* on her transatlantic liner service from New York.

The pattern, once set, was not willingly broken, but he was occasionally forced to interrupt his annual cycle by important events at home. In April 1947, the government, under pressure from journalist Labour MPs including Michael Foot, set up a Royal Commission on the press. The aim was clear and openly political: to discredit the proprietors whose newspaper coverage of politics was not to their liking. Much was made of the blacklists allegedly held of people the proprietors wished to damage. As it happened, the attack fizzled out, not least because none of the members of the commission had more than a vague notion of how a newspaper is run. Any list, as E. J. Robertson, the chairman of Express Newspapers, pointed out, was a warning list of people who had shown hostility, for instance by suing for libel.

By the time Beaverbrook was called to give evidence, on 18 March 1948 (the twenty-sixth session of the commission), the discussion had become diffuse and the members were tired (and bored). In what was for him an easy run, he described his method of control cheerfully as 'the worst kind, absentee control', claimed that he 'ran the paper purely for propaganda and with no other purpose' and finally, on the nature of profit, quoted the Shorter Catechism on which he was brought up on the 'lawful procuring and furthering the wealth and outward estate of ourselves and others'. As a parting shot, he added, 'Perhaps we will go back to it one day!'[24]

Beaverbrook was telling the truth about absentee control. On the other hand, he was not telling the truth when he said that his editors, apart from on the matter of support for the Empire, had total control of their political output. In fact, he had set up an elaborate system to ensure that he was very much in control. During his four months in England he saw all the senior staff of his newspapers and was quick to criticise any slackness. When he was in migration, there was a telephone call two or three times a week when he was in reach of a landline. When out of reach, there were written reports, ten pages every Friday from Arthur Christiansen of the *Daily Express*, and detailed letters from E. J. Robertson. Brendan Bracken contributed regular letters on the political gossip of the day.

Beaverbrook's main weapon, however, was the SoundScriber. This was a crude form of Dictaphone which produced small plastic discs (its first effort had been wax discs, which melted in the sun). These were ferried to London and deciphered by George Millar and Margaret Ince in the London office. Transcripts, consisting of strips of paper, which had been cut in order to save money, would be hurried to their destination. The advantage, of course, was that the system allowed speed of communication. The disadvantage, at least in the eyes of the recipients, was that Beaverbrook, having learnt how to work the machine, kept it beside him wherever he was, in bed, at the dinner table, at the swimming pool or in otherwise normal conversation. He could, and did, record thoughts as they occurred to him in a stream-of-consciousness fashion, whatever the time or place.

*Lord Beaverbrook holding the SoundScriber receiver in one hand while speaking
into the telephone handset held in the other, photographed
in the library at Cherkley Court, c. 1939–40.*

One of the benefits of the transatlantic liner service was the opportunity to meet, and converse at leisure with, people who might pass by unnoticed in the casual rush of urban life. For Beaverbrook, one such was Stanley Morison. Morison was self-educated, having left school after his father had abandoned his family. During his career as adviser to the Monotype Corporation he had revived or invented a number of typefaces, the most successful of which, Times New Roman, became the most used typeface of all time. He also acted as adviser to *The Times* and did a stint as the editor of the *Times Literary Supplement*. In appearance he was, as he himself admitted, like a middle-aged, somewhat bedraggled, clergyman of the Church of England. Yet he had the courage to write to his fellow passenger on the *Queen Mary*, 'If you aren't too occupied in telephoning, writing, dictating letters … would you consider answering a question regarding the circumstances of your early proprietorial connection with the Daily Express…'[25] He explained that he was writing a history of *The Times* and needed material for a chapter on London daily newspapers. Beaverbrook readily agreed, and the two sat down to what were obviously cordial chats. Once back in England, however, Beaverbrook forgot all about the chats and, indeed, Morison himself.

On 25 May 1949, Beaverbrook reached the age of seventy. Some six hundred of his employees entertained him to lunch. In his speech thanking them, he gave them his three resolutions: 'First, I will not give up my bad temper; second, I will not give up my passions [as] I have enjoyed them far too much to put them away; third, I will not give up prejudices, for these prejudices are the foundation of my strength and vigour.'[26] He also let slip that he had given up the idea of leaving London for ever. It was just too exciting where he was.

Part of the excitement, of course, was Churchill. The two had a row in February 1949 over a leader in the *Evening Standard* advocating an increase in the number of Liberal candidates for the House of Commons. Churchill was so irritated that he cancelled his acceptance of Beaverbrook's invitation to stay with him in Montego Bay. Beaverbrook at first defended the leader but subsequently retreated. As an offer of reconciliation, he invited Churchill to La Capponcina when Parliament went into its summer recess.

As it turned out, it was not a happy visit. On the night of 23 August, Churchill was playing gin rummy with Mike Wardell when, at two o'clock in the morning, according to Beaverbrook's account,

> he got up and, steadying himself with his hands on the table, bent his right leg several times as if it had gone to sleep ... He kept closing and opening his right fist ... When he woke ... the cramp was still present ... A little later he found that he could not write as well as usual.[27]

A local doctor, Dr Gibson, was summoned but, realising the seriousness of what in all probability had been a transient ischaemic attack, immediately telephoned Charles Wilson for assistance. By the time Wilson arrived, Churchill was feeling better. Yet everybody there, including Churchill himself, was aware that what had happened was a warning. At all costs, the incident must be kept out of the press. But, more than that, Beaverbrook seemed to take on a new role. He was needed to look after his old friend more closely and do his best to protect him from the 'dagger' that Churchill feared.

The following month, Morison made contact again. He would welcome, he wrote, a sight of Beaverbrook's correspondence with Lord Northcliffe. The response was generous: a four-page summary followed by an account of the sale of *The Times* which had taken place after Northcliffe's death. Morison's thanks were equally generous. He told Beaverbrook that he had been allowed by Lady Lloyd George to consult her late husband's political papers, which had been left to her in his will. Not only that, but she had told Morison that she was proposing to sell them. Beaverbrook was quick to seize the opportunity, opened negotiations for a speedy conclusion and signed an agreement to purchase on 15 June 1950.

Part of the arrangement was that Beaverbrook should commission two biographies. Bonar Law, in his will, had left his papers to Beaverbrook as his executor. It made sense for the two books to be written in tandem. He selected Frank Owen to tackle Lloyd George, although in the agreement the rather ominous words appeared: 'Lord Beaverbrook is willing to give advice to Mr Frank Owen … in the preparation of the said life story.'[28] Bonar Law was entrusted to the more reliable Oxford history tutor Robert Blake, who had edited the private papers of Lord Haig. (No similar words of warning were included in the agreement with Blake but there was no doubt that Beaverbrook would intervene whenever he wanted. But at least in Oxford Blake was not at the mercy of legions of SoundScriber messages which plagued Owen.)

Morison's *History of the Times* was duly published in April 1952. Immediately, the BBC invited Beaverbrook to review the book on television. He was due to be interviewed but refused. He insisted that it should be a one-man show straight to camera and last no more than twenty minutes. On 14 May he duly stepped up to the lectern and gave a rousing address, starting by praising Morison before moving on to a panegyric of Northcliffe. 'There is nothing in this day that rivals the extent to which Northcliffe captured the newspaper market … My own circulation is now nearest to it. I hold one fifth of the London market, Northcliffe held one half… [He was] the greatest journalist Britain has ever seen.'[29] He had been invited to repeat the performance on the Home Service, but it was only after a wrangle about being upstaged by an academic from Princeton that he finally accepted. Broadcast on his birthday, his speech describing what had happened all those years ago concluded elegiacally:

> All these events are past and gone. It is long since and this is my seventy-third birthday. Telling me I do not look it will not help me at all. Nothing helps me now except the inheritance of much strength derived from the frugal lives of my Scottish forebears, transplanted to the harsh and infertile soil of eastern Canada. The past now lives in my memory. The future has no place.[30]

There was reason for Beaverbrook's mood. Two general elections had come and gone. Churchill had asked for his advice, but this amounted to little more than listening to what he himself was saying, since the Prime Minister's increasing deafness made two-way conversation a trial of patience. The *Daily Express* attacked purchase taxes, but it was a feeble effort, and nobody paid much attention. Once the October 1951 general election was over, Beaverbrook made haste to leave England for Jamaica. Yet before leaving there was one last, futile, gesture to be made. The small red icon of the Empire Crusader had for many years appeared at the head of the *Daily Express* front page. On 15 October the Crusader was in chains and remained so for the rest of Beaverbrook's life.

It was not long before another biographer appeared. But this time it was Beaverbrook himself who was the subject, and the author was to be Tom Driberg. Driberg had formerly been a member of Beaverbrook's journalistic coterie, the first and most successful writer of the 'William Hickey' gossip column, before being elected to Parliament as an Independent MP in 1942. He had been sacked from the *Daily Express* in 1943 and subsequently continued his journalistic activities at *Reynolds News*. In 1945, he had joined the Labour Party, where he was a popular and influential backbencher. Driberg's homosexuality was an open secret, despite his marriage in 1951, and in 1935 Beaverbrook had protected his star columnist from a charge of indecent assault by hiring a leading defence counsel and using his influence to prevent the case from being reported in the press. At first the atmosphere was cordial, Driberg assuring Beaverbrook that he would 'try to make it as impartial as possible' and Beaverbrook replying that provided he 'must not be represented anywhere as having authorised the book or as having taken any part whatever in the writing of it' Driberg was to 'deal with me or my activities as you see fit'.[31]

So far, so good. But the cordiality disappeared with the deadlines Driberg missed, the meetings he failed to attend and the wrangles over serial rights. When Beaverbrook returned from his winter migration in the spring of 1953, he had to listen to Robertson, who had disliked the project from the outset, urging him to close it down. By the summer of 1954 he was telling Driberg, 'I am quite willing to drop the whole project but I am not agreeable to being pushed around.'[32] Disputes about the book's content continued to rumble on. By June 1955, Millar was writing to Driberg that 'I must inform you that Lord Beaverbrook takes no interest in your ms'.[33] By the time the book was published in early 1956, the two sides had exhausted themselves in battle and the event passed by in relative peace. In fact, Driberg was eventually invited back into the fold as though the book had never been written.

During the whole period of what turned out in the end to be a family row, Beaverbrook's attention was tuned, and was kept tuned, to the question of the moment: Churchill's health. After his first stroke at La Capponcina in 1949, Churchill did his best to measure his sometimes volcanic lifestyle. But the pressure of renewed office took its toll. In the evening of Tuesday 23 June 1953, after dinner, Churchill suffered a massive stroke. He managed to chair the Cabinet the following day, 'but his speech was slurred and his mouth drooping'.[34] Undeterred, he still wanted to stay in London to chair the next day's Cabinet and then fly to a proposed conference at Bermuda. By the morning of 25 June he was worse, 'losing the use of his left arm and left leg'.[35] There was only one solution: leave London, go to Chartwell and cancel Bermuda.

On arrival at Chartwell, Colville immediately sent manuscript messages by despatch rider to three of Churchill's 'particular friends', Beaverbrook, Brendan Bracken and Lord Camrose, the owner of the *Daily Telegraph*. The three men dropped all engagements and hurried to the scene. There, they 'paced the lawn in earnest conversation. They achieved the all but incredible, and in peacetime possibly unique, success of gagging Fleet Street, something they would have done for nobody but Churchill.'[36] In the event, an anodyne statement was issued by Lord Moran (as Sir Charles Wilson was now known following his elevation to the peerage) to the effect that Churchill needed a complete rest. It did not say why and nobody, it seems, thought to ask.

Churchill's recovery surprised everyone, not least a pessimistic Moran, by its speed. On Sunday 28 June, he was able to take the chair at lunch, with Beaverbrook as the main guest, and to dine with Bracken that same evening. By the end of July, he was well enough restored to think about resuming his duties. In particular, he set himself a target. He told Colville that 'he thought probably that this must mean his retirement, but that he would see how he went on, and if he had recovered sufficiently well to address the Tory Party at their annual meeting in October, he would continue in office'.[37] It was courageous and, as it turned out, the target was met. But nobody, least of all his old friend Beaverbrook, was under any illusion about the shadow that loomed menacingly over him.

Churchill's stroke, and his subsequent resignation as Prime Minister two years later in April 1955, drew the two closer. In September 1953, Churchill spent a month at La Capponcina in recovery. Lady Churchill had at last accepted Beaverbrook as a friend and as her husband's prime source of amusement. After the resignation, Beaverbrook sent a message through Bracken that Churchill could have La Capponcina, fully staffed, whenever he wanted between 1 December and 1 April. The long association, which had begun in St Omer in 1915 and which had survived good and bad times, was now moving into a final period of elegiac harmony.

CHAPTER 27

SUNSET

'Old age is just pills and pain. And pain and pills'[1]

Beaverbrook's autumn migrations in the late 1940s and 1950s, to
Canada and from there to the sun of the Caribbean, were in his
customary style. True, by the mid-1950s he was no longer surrounded
by the coterie of society ladies which, one way or another, had been
invited to accompany him on his travels before the Second World
War. His circle of acquaintances remained wide and varied but lacked
the intimacy of former years. The birthdays of former lovers and companions and their extended families were carefully logged in files kept
by George Millar and every anniversary brought gifts of money, jew-
ellery or flowers, and toys for the children (a ritual that was repeated
every Christmas); although those who failed to properly acknowledge
their benefactor found themselves struck off the list the following year.
Yet despite his advancing years, Beaverbrook turned his attention, as
old men tend to do, to the freshness of youth. But it was not quite
the same. There were, of course, the usual advantages in discovering
new bodies, new attitudes and new minds, yet in the company of his
youthful travellers there was never quite the fierce smell of sexuality
which had made everything so exciting in earlier years.

Nor was it quite as simple as a mere change in sexual generations.
By 1955, the migration had taken on a new purpose. It was no longer
to be an escape from the asthma peril of the north European winter
and a relief from the gout which was becoming increasingly painful.
Beaverbrook, in short, had found a new project: his fifth career, as he
called it. He was no longer going to use his time and energy in shouting from what he realised were little more than the fringes of British

political debate. He was going to make his priority the writing of history as he had lived it. More specifically, as a first effort, he was going to pick up the drafts of the personal narrative written in 1916 and 1917 as *Politicians and the War* and turn them into a more considered publication of historical substance to be published, he hoped, under the title *Men and Power*. In this new project, travelling, particularly by sea, allowed periods of concentration without other distractions and of reflection about the past he was setting out to recall.

As it happened, and as he knew full well, Beaverbrook had one supreme advantage over potential competitors: he owned three of the most important archives for his period – Bonar Law's, which he had acquired as a legacy; Lloyd George's, which he had purchased; and his own, which he had been careful to keep up to date over the years. True, they were not in much of a state for research. Fifteen tea chests of Bonar Law papers were still being packed under the supervision of a secretary at the *Daily Express*, Rosemary Brooks; another secretary, Sheila Elton, was cataloguing the Lloyd George papers, ten times as voluminous and stored in various houses sometimes far apart; and Beaverbrook's own papers, divided between Cherkley and Arlington House. Nevertheless, Beaverbrook was not one to give away such a precious advantage. Access to these archives by other historians was refused. On application they were politely told to go away and reapply after Beaverbrook's death.

Although the combination of Rosemary Brooks and Sheila Elton worked well, Beaverbrook soon realised that, at least for the first book, he needed a professional researcher. George Millar was duly instructed to conduct a detailed trawl of possible candidates on the British War Histories Register who were at the time in London. A number of names came up as suitable, but the most promising was a graduate from the University of Sydney, currently working in the Colonial Office after a spell in Chatham House, by the name of Ann Cousins. Born in 1926, the daughter of a bank teller in a Sydney suburb, Ann Hurley, to give her maiden name, turned out to be an academic of recognised brilliance, with a first-class degree from Sydney followed by a graduate scholarship to London University. Her career took a turn away from academia when she decided to abandon graduate studies and become a research assistant. She married Michael Cousins in 1951 but divorced him in 1954. Exceptionally good looking, clever and witty, just divorced, she was perfect Beaverbrook material. It was no surprise that she appeared high on Millar's list and was soon summoned to present herself at Arlington House.

Her first encounter with her future employer was to be recorded vividly in her autobiography:

> When I was shown by the valet into the large drawing room, I confronted a short figure, with a large head, earth-coloured skin, eyes of piercing blue, and a way of tilting his head for observation that ensured a thorough, though courteous, appraisal of the visitor. He looked more like a man of 50 than 75. He exuded energy. He wore a bright navy-blue suit and brown shoes – a sartorial solecism in those days.[2]

That was no more than a preview of what was to come. Ann obviously passed that first examination, as she was invited to dinner the following evening:

> delicious food at Arlington House served to each guest by the butler from a silver tray, the fillet steak perfect, the vegetables fragrant, the finest cheese and out-of-season fruits from Fortnum and Mason, the best French champagne, while a Fragonard painting of a rounded girl smiled from the wall, and the air hummed with the animated talk and gossip of a few guests from the newspaper and political world.[3]

That was enough. She was captivated – as, he soon made clear, was Beaverbrook. In August 1954 she moved out of the Colonial Office and into small and uncomfortable quarters in the *Express* building.

As Ann soon found out, Beaverbrook's methods were quite different to the normal academic routine of diligent and detailed research before composition and revision. 'It was Beaverbrook's remarkable memory of those now distant events', she later wrote, 'that provided the method and structure by which we worked. In long conversations, walking about or standing at his high, upright desk, he would recreate for me the outline and atmosphere of a political incident and illuminate it with stories and anecdotes of the personalities involved.' It was this capacity to recall events, along with his intimate knowledge of the personalities involved, that gave him 'a mastery over the documentary material that no other historian working systematically through the records could hope to achieve'.[4]

Once Beaverbrook had finished the story of what was to become a chapter, 'I would then race off to my office,' Ann goes on,

> and then I'd write it up and I would then give him the draft, and, of course, he'd read it overnight and then it would stimulate him to further recollections, and then Sheila Elton would be asked to bring up the relevant papers, and I'd redraft the chapter ... There were many stormy scenes when Mrs Elton was not able to find something he knew would be in the papers, and as one journalist said of Lord Beaverbrook, working for him 'some days it was Christmas and some days the Day of Judgment'. We would have quite a bad time, but he was always right, which is the whole point.[5]

Ann also noted Beaverbrook's constant need to travel. 'Mobility', she recalled, 'was a vital lubricant to Beaverbrook's machine. It revved his energy, calmed bouts of asthma and returned him to more vigorous work.'[6] Ann soon found herself accompanying him to his various houses abroad. Once there, she soon discovered two friends in the camp, Jeannie Campbell and Josephine Rosenberg. Jo, to give her the nickname of the time, was in Ann's own words 'a dark, highly attractive, vivacious English Jewess with exquisite taste in dress ... [who] carried her duties [as Beaverbrook's secretary] with careless ease'. As a third to the party, Jo introduced Ann to Jeannie and 'there was much chatter and laughter together'.[7] Jo herself, Ann's account goes on, 'was outgoing, innovative and daring, and mistress of many complex stratagems to counter her employer's whims'.[8] It is not hard to guess what those 'whims' might have included. Certainly, the journalists in the two *Express* newspapers, who followed Beaverbrook's amatory exploits with salacious enthusiasm, were in no doubt. 'He had a pretty healthy sexual appetite,' explained Robin Esser, the William Hickey of the time. 'He always liked to have with him a younger lady, who would attend to his needs – as you do. By that age I don't think he could actually get it up, but that didn't really matter. It was a question of what I believe the ads call "tantric massage".'[9] That, of course, may be no more than a gossip columnist's speculation. Certainly, when asked about her relationship with Beaverbrook, Jo was duly circumspect: 'He was fun, amusing, nice to talk to. I looked up to him as a great man.'[10] When pressed on detail at a second interview, she, reasonably enough, declined to be drawn. 'I went through everything with my [two] husbands and there is no more to be said.'[11]

Whatever the private 'whims' may or may not have been, Beaverbrook never lost the daily imperative of the call to work. Nor, for that matter, did he abandon the daily habit of close attention to his newspapers. If at sea, the SoundScriber was in constant use, and with landfall and the batch of copies which awaited him the telephone was in constant use, editors lining up at the London end to receive their daily quota of reproof. When in his four-month summer stay in England, he would summon his editors and columnists individually to Arlington House. Yet even in his rudest comments on their performance he never abandoned his practice of addressing all his employees, other than servants, in their surnames and proper titles. On board ship, for instance, or wherever they happened to be, other than in informal moments Jo was still 'Miss Rosenberg' and Ann 'Mrs Cousins'.

1956 turned out to be a pivotal year. *Men and Power* was published in the autumn to comfortably good reviews. To be sure, there were some grumbles about the closed primary archives, the ponderous prose style and the tendency of the author to give himself undue credit for his role in the successes of the day, but the book was well received by academics, about whose opinion Beaverbrook was most nervous. Most striking of all was a review in *The Observer* by a left-wing history tutor at Magdalen College, Oxford, A. J. P. Taylor. Normally critical to the border of acerbic, Taylor was rapturous. He praised the author's 'supreme ability as a narrator of political conflict' and asserted that 'the book is indispensable both for an understanding of Lloyd George and for an appreciation of the Great Storm'. He concluded by saying that while Beaverbrook 'may sometimes exaggerate the part that he has played in events ... No one could exaggerate his gifts in chronicling them.'[12]

Beaverbrook's reaction to Taylor's piece was equally striking. Michael Foot, who was present when Beaverbrook first read it, recalled the effect. 'A new world opened to him,' he later wrote. 'It was one of the most thrilling days of his life ... [The] review changed the whole of his outlook about the writing of books.'[13] Enthusiastic plans were laid for future works: two short biographies of his old friends R. B. Bennett (*Friends*, published in 1959) and Sir James Dunn (*Courage*, published 1961) were followed in 1962 by *The Divine Propagandist*, an idiosyncratic life of Jesus written in the 1920s but suppressed at the request of Tim Healey, and *The Decline and Fall of Lloyd George*, which arrived in 1963. Taylor was embraced into a literary relationship of mutual support which was to last up to Beaverbrook's death and beyond, to Taylor's biography and the ultimate legacy to Taylor, as executor, of Beaverbrook's own papers. At the same time, fully aware of the advantage of monopoly ownership of archives, Beaverbrook instructed Rosemary Brooks and Sheila Elton to watch for any archives of interest which might be purchased. (As it happened, the search coincided with a similar, though unrelated, pursuit of works of art to be kept in a gallery which he donated to New Brunswick.)

1956 was pivotal in other ways. The fiasco of the Anglo-French invasion of Egypt at Suez in secret collusion with Israel had blown the political world into nervous confusion. Of all the many consequential effects, the most significant for Beaverbrook personally was the breakdown of Prime Minister Eden's health and his subsequent resignation. Beaverbrook had, unsurprisingly, supported the Suez venture as a justified demonstration of Britain's imperial power and was quick to write to Eden (whom he did not particularly like) in the most fulsome terms. 'This is a letter of admiration,' his letter ran. 'You have shown courage and devotion to your duty with all the world against you save only your countrymen ... Fear nothing for the future. Time will vindicate you. And when you return to London you will be received with gratitude and affection by the citizens.'[14] Moreover, he added deeds to words. At his invitation, Eden and his wife Clarissa stayed the summer of 1957 at Cricket Malherbie, were offered winter accommodation in Nassau and found Arlington House placed at their disposal when they visited London in the winter, in each case with the customary generous maintenance.

In the ensuing contest for the leadership of the Conservative Party, Beaverbrook had little to say. Brendan Bracken kept him informed throughout the contest with a heavy bias against Harold Macmillan, to which Beaverbrook, in agreement, responded, 'I have a very poor opinion of Harold Macmillan.'[15] Bracken pursued his point, claiming that Macmillan was 'telling journalists that he intends to retire from politics and go to the morgue [House of Lords]' while manoeuvring to 'push his boss out of No. 10'.[16] When Macmillan finally became Prime Minister in January 1957, Beaverbrook wrote from Nassau, '[He] is not the choice of the people. He was selected by Churchill and Lord Salisbury. He is the wrong man. [Rab] Butler should have been taken.'[17]

1956 also saw a subtle shift in Beaverbrook's relations with Churchill. Throughout his period in office, Churchill had enjoyed the benefit of an open invitation to stay when he wanted and as long as he wanted at La Capponcina whether or not his host was there. Not only was the invitation open but all for the comfort of himself, his family and his staff was provided without question. He was assigned the best room in the house, with a majestic view of the Mediterranean, and a special place on the veranda from which he could paint at his leisure. His staff, since the house itself was not large enough to house them all, were accommodated in outlying villas, with a small working office inside the building (next, as one of the younger secretaries noted with a mixture of excitement and alarm, to a little room with shelves full of lurid pornography).

Winston Churchill painting at Lord Beaverbrook's residence La Capponcina,
Cap-d'Ail, south of France, 12 January 1949.

Late in the summer of 1955, Churchill decided to take his wife, unwell
with what had been diagnosed as neuritis, his daughter Mary and her
husband Christopher Soames to La Capponcina for an extended stay.
As it happened, the stay turned out to be even longer than originally
planned. By 18 September, Churchill was writing to Beaverbrook, 'We
are all spreading out beautifully ... There are as far as I can see no
lizards, but there are two cats with whom we have made friends, or
sort of friends. The violet heather looks lovely. Thank you so much
for lending me this beautiful place.'[18] After a few weeks Churchill was
enjoying himself so much that he was writing to Beaverbrook to ask
'whether you could keep me longer than the 31st October. I could then
fly over for my engagements in England in November and December,
and return to this sunshine world.'[19]

It was one of the happiest of Churchill's stays at La Capponcina.
Beaverbrook, in his generosity, had told Churchill to invite whomever
he wanted to a meal or drinks or any other form of hospitality. Two
of the beneficiaries of this open house were Emery Reves, a publisher
and literary agent, well known to Churchill over the years, and the

former fashion model Wendy Russell. In the course of lunch, Reves suggested a return match at his house, La Pausa, the following day. La Pausa, as Churchill immediately acknowledged, was the nearest he had yet seen to his dream house. Originally a lavender farm, at 300 metres above sea level with a panoramic view of the Mediterranean, stuffed with masterpieces from the great French artists of the second half of the nineteenth century and the first quarter of the twentieth, it captivated Churchill, who willingly accepted an invitation to stay there in 1956.

It was the first of many visits during the next three years, before Churchill fell out with Reves and transferred his enthusiasm to the patronage of the Greek shipping magnate Aristotle Onassis. According to Churchill's private secretary, visits to La Pausa substantially displaced those to La Capponcina, without ever replacing them entirely.[20] Nevertheless, all was not entirely well. There was a definite shadow. Clementine's dislike of Wendy Russell led not just to disapproval of Churchill's visits to La Pausa but insistence that their golden wedding anniversary on 12 September 1958 be celebrated not at La Pausa but at La Capponcina. Of course, this was most welcome to Beaverbrook, who wrote an effusive and moving tribute to his old friend on the occasion. Less welcome perhaps were Churchill's family, to whom the open invitation was extended (though the same invitation was not extended to Beaverbrook's own family). 'It is the family that I find rather tiresome,' he wrote after one visit, 'particularly when they charge me for cigarettes.'[21]

Finally, 1956 brought an unexpected change in Beaverbrook's personal life. On New Year's Day his lifelong friend dating back to the early days in Edmonton, Sir James Dunn, died. A fellow Brunswicker, he left a large fortune accumulated over many years of varying success and failure but ultimately based on the revived Canadian steel industry. This passed to his third wife, Marcia Anastasia Christoforides, generally known as 'Christofor'. Born in Surrey in 1909 of a Greek father and English mother, with 'a long neck, high cheekbones and hair of a slightly golden hue',[22] she had gone to work for Dunn in 1930, had nursed him through a serious illness in 1942 and had married him soon afterwards. In his biography of Dunn, Beaverbrook described not just his career as Canada's foremost industrialist and his multiple gifts to charity but also, much to the irritation of Dunn's children, his many alarming eccentricities. He insisted, for instance, on his shoes being polished until they shone like glass, discarding pair after pair until he found one to his liking and ensuring that his shoe-laces had been ironed before use. Some of his eccentricities seem to have passed down with his fortune to Christofor. (At least she showed bravado. When Dunn gave her a large packet of shares, she sold them behind his back and put the proceeds on a horse. The horse came in winner at 8–1.)

Lord Beaverbrook with his lifelong friend Sir James Dunn,
New Brunswick, Canada, undated.

Christofor took her husband's death very badly. She proclaimed herself in deep mourning and announced her intention of retiring to a convent. Beaverbrook, when alerted, decided to ride to the rescue. As he wrote to Bracken, if she did she would not like the food and would 'certainly quarrel with the Mother Superior'.[23] His answer was to revive her interest in Dunn's bequests and encourage new ventures.

One success was her agreement to help finance, and to take charge of, a new theatre in Fredericton. But it was not just a matter of new ventures. Gradually, Christofor and Beaverbrook became closer. There were long stays at Cherkley and La Capponcina, and shared visits to New Brunswick.

Lord Beaverbrook and Marcia Anastasia Christoforides, 'Christofor', at Cherkley Court.

In truth, this new friendship came as something of a blessing. By the time of his eightieth birthday in 1959, Beaverbrook was starting to feel his age. Gout and asthma were not letting up. Moreover, as he wrote to Nye Bevan,

> the friends of years ago are all departing and only two or three trees are left in the clear-felled forest. Brendan [Bracken]'s last days are dragging out in pain and agony [from oesophageal cancer]. He has the strength of his ancestors and the courage of the heroes of his race.[24]

Bracken died in August 1958. Helen Fitzgerald had died in November 1957 and Beaverbrook's brother, Allan, who had watched over his Canadian financial affairs for more than thirty-five years, was to die in 1959. Nor were the newspapers immune. In July 1955, E. J. Robertson, the chairman and managing director of Beaverbrook Newspapers, who had spent thirty-six years in calm and sagacious management, without warning suffered a stroke serious enough to prevent his continuing in office (he died in April 1960). As there was no obvious successor, Beaverbrook decided to appoint Robertson's chief assistant, Tom Blackburn, as chief executive of the company and his son Max as chairman of a reconstructed board.

Another blow fell when Arthur Christiansen, for twenty-three years editor of the *Daily Express*, had a heart attack in August 1956 while staying at La Capponcina. Part of his recovery was in the sun at Nassau. Accounts vary, but it seems that one morning he received a note from Beaverbrook requiring him to return to London without delay. Once there, he was told that owing to his ill health he was no longer to be editor of the *Express*, but he might wish to take a job at a lower level. Beaverbrook would not see him or speak to him. After another three years Christiansen asked formally to resign. Beaverbrook summoned him to Arlington House. There was an emotional meeting, after which Beaverbrook led him to the lift to say farewell. As it descended, Beaverbrook leaned forward and said, 'Well, goodbye, Chris. Sorry to see you going down.'[25] For Beaverbrook's detractors, this was the ultimate in cynical brutality. For those less passionate, it is noted that Beaverbrook called him by his nickname, probably for the first time ever, and Christiansen, on his resignation, wrote to Beaverbrook that 'at heart I will always be a Beaverbrook man. And proud to be so known.'[26]

Christiansen proved difficult to replace as editor of the *Express*. His deputy, Edward Pickering, although successful in increasing its circulation, never managed to impress Beaverbrook and was unceremoniously replaced after four years. Pickering's deputy, Robert Edwards (like Michael Foot, a former editor of *Tribune*), took over as acting editor, but lasted only a matter of months before Roger Wood was appointed in his place. Wood, in turn, enjoyed only a short period in the job before Edwards was brought back, becoming the only person to be appointed editor on two separate occasions. The sister papers were more fortunate. John Junor, acerbic and describing himself as a true Beaverbrook disciple, had taken over the editorship of the *Sunday Express* in 1954, occupying it uninterrupted for the next thirty-two years. At the *Evening Standard*, Charles Wintour, another Beaverbrook disciple, was appointed in 1959 and remained there until 1976.

None of these changes, however unsettling, altered Beaverbrook's methods in dealing with his editors and their journalists. Max may have thought that he would be able to run affairs without interference from his father, but he was soon disillusioned. If anything, the interference became worse after 1959 when Beaverbrook was persuaded by Christofor, who much disliked the West Indies, to give up the annual migration and sell the houses in Nassau and Montego Bay (and no doubt even wave an affectionate goodbye to Jo Rosenberg, who left to get married). As always, his weapons were the telephone and the SoundScriber. 'With these devices to hand,' recalled one journalist, 'he might as well have been next door.'[27] Another went further. 'His presence seemed to be everywhere. Just by picking up the telephone he sent shivers through the entire building. Even the threat that he might phone at any time from anywhere in the world was enough to keep us all on our toes.'[28] When the calls came, everybody ran to their desks. 'Who is in charge of the clattering train?' would be Beaverbrook's rasping opening. (This was the first line of a doggerel published in *Punch* in the 1930s. Fortunately, none of his editors appeared aware of its last line: 'For death is in charge of the clattering train.')[29] Perhaps the final, most authoritative, verdict was delivered by Hugh Cudlipp, who worked under Beaverbrook as managing editor of the *Sunday Express*: 'He was demanding, exacting, tyrannous, vindictive and malicious, yet all or most of the excesses of the master journalist were forgiven by the men and women who worked for him because of the success of his publishing enterprise and his impish sense of fun.'[30]

In his later years, Beaverbrook rarely visited the offices in Fleet Street. He seldom met the acknowledged stars unless they were summoned to Arlington House. On the other hand, he was unremitting in sending for the young journalists to accompany him on his morning walk in Green Park when in London or Central Park when in New York, or even accompany him on his travels. Most were eager to respond. Anne Sharpley, for instance, a reporter on the *Evening Standard*, was so smitten that she admitted that 'it was an unabashed love story', although she was careful to add that it was unconsummated and that she had her own relationships as well.[31] Another acolyte, Geoffrey Bocca, then on the staff in New York, recalled how 'being a whizz-kid for Beaverbrook meant being highly paid but the work frequently induced the feeling of being a novice on the Cresta run'.[32] Nor were his staff spared from undertaking more menial tasks: buying theatre tickets, books (preferably secondhand editions), medicines and records, all of which had to be done with the most rigorous economy.

It is not clear when precisely Beaverbrook was diagnosed with cancer. He told his secretary, Colin Vines, that he been informed by the oncologist Sir Daniel Davies that he was suffering from cancer of the bladder in July 1962. Although the verdict was not supported by a second opinion, it was enough to make him remark to Bob Edwards some months later that he was 'dying from the feet up', which Edwards took to be an admission of the illness.[33] Although he gave instructions that if anybody enquired after his health they were to be told that he was very well, visitors to Cherkley or La Capponcina could not help noticing that the brown spots on his scalp and hands were getting darker and that various forms of stairlifts were installed and a strange sort of sedan chair made ready always to take him to his car. Not only were there signs of physical decline. When *The Divine Propagandist* was published, it led to comments that he was turning his attention, as a proper Calvinist, to his place in the next world. (In fact, as he himself admitted, it was in some measure a reaction to his arguments with his father in his childhood in the manse.)

Be all that as it may, there were still issues to be fought and there was still enough energy to fight them. The proposed merger of the Church of Scotland with the Episcopal Church in Scotland provoked thunderous roars from the *Scottish Daily Express* until it was finally abandoned. Of greater consequence was Britain's application in July 1961 to join the European Common Market. Beaverbrook, of course, was vehemently opposed. It was contrary to all the principles of the Empire Crusade (he would have been in the vanguard of the Brexiteers in 2016). 'The fight may not be as lively as during the Empire Crusade before the War,' he wrote to one supporter, 'but I regret I cannot make it more so. For I am in my eighty-fourth year. It is for you young people to carry on the struggle.'[34] When reproached for the support his newspapers were giving to Prime Minister Macmillan, his riposte was clear. 'In fact,' he wrote to one of the leaders of the anti-Common Market campaign, 'we do not want to turn Macmillan out … It is the Common Market we wish to destroy, not Macmillan.'[35] Nor was he able to celebrate when, in January 1963, General Charles De Gaulle interposed his veto on the British application for all, as Beaverbrook saw it, the wrong reasons.

His health provided him with little occasion for rejoicing either; a condition that was now complicated by an unusually harsh British winter. Just after Christmas, Cherkley was almost cut off by heavy snowfall with Beaverbrook confined to bed with influenza. This soon turned into what now seems to have been recognised as pneumonia. 'For some days he lay at the point of death,' watched over by Christofor and a team of nurses, day and night.[36] It was not until February 1963 that he was well enough to make the journey to La Capponcina. But although he was mentally as alert as ever, he was severely invalided physically. Walking became in itself a trial, made all the more difficult by unremitting gout.

Once at La Capponcina, and firing his missiles as usual to his editors, he started to worry about the publication of his latest book, *The Decline and Fall of Lloyd George*, due in early March. He need not have been so concerned. Taylor, on receiving a review copy in February, had been almost embarrassingly enthusiastic. 'It is a magnificent book,' he wrote, 'written with as much verve as Men and Power, and with as much new information as Politicians and the War.'[37] When it finally came out, the book was showered with a cascade of ecstatic reviews from a raft of the literary and political élite. Only Roy Jenkins and Lady Violet Bonham Carter struck a slightly discordant note. 'A lot of incidents', Jenkins argued, 'are included … because they happened when Lord Beaverbrook was there', noting that he was also too quick to assign base motives (always excepting Bonar Law, 'the sad knight in drooping armour').[38] Bonham Carter was equally waspish. 'However dire the dangers of his enmity may be, they pale before the perils of his friendship.'[39]

In early May 1963, Beaverbrook and Christofor returned to England and to Cherkley. The surprise came when, on 7 June – as it happened, the anniversary of Christofor's marriage to Sir James Dunn – she and a gout-ridden Beaverbrook were loaded painfully into a large car. To-gether with his son Max and George Millar, they drove to Epsom Registry Office, where they took their marital vows in the civil cere-mony under English law. Apart from the odd bystander, nobody else was present. There was no announcement, and it was another week before the news leaked to the Canadian press. In truth, the marriage made, on the surface, little difference. Christofor tried to assert herself by ordering meals and enquiring in the morning what her husband was proposing to do that day and who was due to visit him, or when he intended to go to La Capponcina, but she soon gave up. Nor was he denied the pleasures of female companionship, although these en-counters were now of a more chaste and discreet nature. In short, things went on as before.

Nevertheless, his marriage was another punctuation mark. His interest in the politics of the day became more sporadic, and occasion-ally erratic. The eruption of the Profumo scandal in the summer of 1963 left him unmoved. 'Why in God's name', he asked, 'should a great political party tear itself to rags and tatters just because a minister has fucked a woman?'[40] The subsequent dogfight over the leadership of the Conservatives was a source of fun, not least because his great-nephew, Jonathan Aitken, advised him to back the ultimate winner, the Earl of Home. But he could not take Home seriously and reserved his final admiration, perhaps surprisingly, for Harold Macmillan.

In February 1964, Beaverbrook went to La Capponcina. By then he had made his final will. He was to leave no money to Christofor, on the grounds that she had ample resources of her own, but his portrait by Graham Sutherland, the bronze bust by Oscar Nemon and a vari-ety of gold and silver boxes were to be hers. Max and Janet were left nothing, again on the grounds that they had been adequately provided for during his lifetime. There were bequests to relations, staff and do-mestic employees but with special recognition for Jeannie Campbell. The balance of his estate went to the two Beaverbrook Foundations he had created: some $12.6 million to the Canadian Foundation and the balance of what had once been a fortune of some $40 million, before the substantial gifts to charity during his later years, to the English

Foundation. On a more sinister note, his personal papers were entrusted to Max and Janet for six months, during which time they were 'to examine all such papers and to destroy such as they think fit'.[41]

On his return to England, Beaverbrook found that his stay in the south of France had brought no improvement. He was in constant pain and by April 1964 could hardly walk, even with the aid of two sticks. Yet there was one grand event held in his honour which he was obliged to attend. On 25 May, his fellow Canadian Roy Thomson, his adversary and competitor over the years, ennobled as Lord Thomson of Fleet earlier that year, organised a dinner at the Dorchester Hotel to celebrate Beaverbrook's eighty-fifth birthday.

Lord and Lady Beaverbrook at the Dorchester, for a party to celebrate his eighty-fifth birthday, 25 May 1964 – the venue for Lord Beaverbrook's last speech of his life.

As it turned out, it was an event of both grand emotion and startling vulgarity. Apart from Christofor, the guests were all male (the original invitations sent to other women, such as Anne Sharpley, were woundingly withdrawn). Two sides of the Banqueting Hall were occupied by large pictures of Beaverbrook walking in his garden at Cherkley and at the Old Manse in Newcastle, New Brunswick. There were two guards of honour: one of four Canadian Mounted Police in full fig, the other of 'four Indian Chiefs resplendent in fighting feathers and traditional garb'.[42] Commonwealth flags hung from the ceiling and RAF trumpeters from Cranwell were lined up for a fanfare. The whole affair was overseen by a statuette of a beaver in precious metal, looking, to judge from the photographs, slightly out of sorts.

It was a long evening for the guest of honour, now generally known among his fellow guests, not always affectionately, as 'The Old Man'. When he finally came to speak, he managed a bravura performance. He made a rousing defence of journalism. 'No other profession is so heavily maligned', he told his audience, '[and] no other profession preached at so much.' But he also insisted that it must maintain high standards. A good journalist must show 'courage, independence and initiative … be an optimist … he has no business to be a pedlar of gloom and despondency … able to deal with highest and the lowest on the same basis'. Finally, he came to his peroration. 'It is time for me', he proclaimed in an obviously tiring voice, 'to become an apprentice once more. I am not certain in which direction, but somewhere, sometime soon.'[43] It was this that brought to the surface the wave of emotion among the normally stoical men in his audience. One of the hardest of the hard men there, John Junor, summed it up. 'I am a black-hearted Highlander', he wrote to Beaverbrook the following day, 'with too little sentiment in me. But there were tears in my eyes as you walked into that room last night – tears of pride because I was associated with you. Thank you for a night that will stay in my memory for just as long as I live.'[44]

On the return to Cherkley, Beaverbrook dictated his last letter to Churchill, thanking him for the birthday message which had been read out on BBC radio by his son Max. 'I thank you … for the signed copies of your books with which you enrich my library, and, over all else, for the friendship and companionship with which you have made my journey exciting and enjoyable.'[45] Messages and missives continued to trickle out. The final one recorded was typical Beaverbrook. 'The last time that I looked at your balance sheet', he wrote to Tom Blackburn on 5 June, 'reserves stood at £1 million but now there is only £600,000. Where did the rest go?'[46]

On 7 June he had the *Sunday Express* read out to him for the last time. But, more important, it was the anniversary of his wedding to Christofor. A few strawberries were all he could eat, but there was still time for a sip of champagne and a toast to her, 'To my beloved'. Then he, Christofor, Mike Wardell and others who were there cheered themselves up by singing the songs popular in the First World War, ending with 'Pack Up Your Troubles in Your Old Kit-Bag and Smile, Smile, Smile'. But the cheer was not to last. The following day he could eat nothing. On the morning of 9 June, 'he handed to Max Aitken his box of "secret" papers. Max and George Millar took them out on the hillside and burnt them'.[47] During the day he drifted in and out of consciousness. Finally, at 3.45 p.m., he died peacefully in Christofor's arms. The weather record shows that it was a day of fitful sunshine but that later in the evening the sun set behind the western hills in a blaze of glory.

Portrait of Lord Beaverbrook on the terrace at Cherkley Court in his final years.

EPILOGUE

Immediately after his death, on Christofor's instructions and after the necessary dressing, Beaverbrook's body was laid out on a table in the drawing room at Cherkley. It was covered up to the chin with what looked like a tablecloth, where it remained for five days while family, friends and former colleagues were invited to view it. Like many events in Beaverbrook's life, the procedure was, to put it mildly, unusual, and caused a good deal of confusion, not least because some of the invitees who had never met Christofor took her, in her severe black dress with the keys to the sanctuary dangling from her waist, for the housekeeper.

Nevertheless, the five days finally came to their unsavoury end and it was time for the cremation. The arrangements for this were equally bizarre. Guests were invited to assemble at Cherkley at midday. On arrival, they were handed sizeable drinks by a butler and, after a suitable pause, were ushered into the main dining room to enjoy a sumptuous buffet, well lubricated by a variety of German wines. Since no instructions had been issued on how to get to the crematorium, they then had to watch for a signal, jump into their cars and follow Christofor's Rolls-Royce, which set off at great speed. The whole caravan lurched forward after it at equal speed, fearful of losing the trail and missing the whole event. It was noted by one mourner that it was typical of Beaverbrook that his funeral should be conducted at breakneck pace.

Ten days later, on 24 June, there was a memorial service in London's St Paul's Cathedral. There was a large and distinguished gathering. One of Beaverbrook's few aristocratic friends, the Earl of Rosebery, gave the address. Rosebery was predictably full of praise for his subject's achievements in the Second World War, but went on to surprise the congregation by claiming that although it was written that it was easier for a camel to pass through the eye of a needle than for a rich man to enter the Kingdom of Heaven, if any man deserved to do so, that man was Max Beaverbrook. Listening to this, the congregation must have shifted uneasily in their seats (not least the member of the Astor family who, it was said, had only attended the service to make sure that Beaverbrook really was dead). But Rosebery ploughed on, pausing only to remark that Beaverbrook had had many enemies. It was no less, and certainly no more, than the truth.

The next, and final, ceremony took place on 25 September 1964 at the aptly named Beaverbrook Town Square in Newcastle, New Brunswick. All around was evidence of Beaverbrook's many benefactions: the Beaverbrook Theatre and Town Hall, a gazebo, a sundial, six Victorian street lamps, the library at the Old Manse, St James's Church with its eleven bells and pipe organ and the Sunday school. In the square was a bronze bust of Beaverbrook by Oscar Nemon standing on a plinth. It was into the base of the plinth that Christofor was to place, following instructions in Beaverbrook's will, an urn containing his ashes. This Christofor duly did, in the presence of family members and a group of awed onlookers. There followed a shaky rendition of 'Onward, Christian Soldiers'. So far, so good. But the party was somewhat spoiled by the suspicion, widely voiced, that the urn was in fact empty or, at best, contained only half of the ashes, the other half being retained by Christofor as her private memorial.

There is no doubt that Beaverbrook, had he been alive, would have hugely enjoyed all this. It was, after all, a full mixture of honesty, mystery, bombast and fun, all four of which were among his specialities. He would have particularly enjoyed Rosebery's reference to his generosity to his friends, some of whom had been unaware of his support at the time, and to his loyalty to them when their luck was out. But he would have been less than happy, perhaps even angry, about Rosebery's reference to the Kingdom of Heaven. Whatever Beaverbrook thought about Him, God was most certainly not to be mocked.

In truth, Beaverbrook's religion has always been something of a puzzle. In his childhood he had challenged his father's stern lectures in the Calvinist tradition and had never felt it necessary or right to practise with any regularity. On the other hand, he was deeply affected by the religious construct, went out of his way to defend the integrity of the Church of Scotland, memorised large tracts of the Bible and, not long before his death, had despatched one of his journalists on a private expedition to find a bust of John Knox which he had been told was buried near his family's home in West Lothian. Late in his life, too, he was apt to ask himself, and on occasions others, whether he was one of the Calvinist elect, a sign that the matter was preying on his mind, but the mood seems to have quickly passed.

The obituaries, plentiful as they were, were mixed in tone (apart, of course, from the *Daily Express*). In fact, some of those who knew Beaverbrook well had refused to put pen to paper. Clement Attlee, for instance, was reported as saying that Beaverbrook was the only evil man he ever met and that he could not find anything good to say about him. Others were more generous, but they still tended to skate over Beaverbrook's early career in Canada, where he had, in fact, shown his most fertile imagination, amounting, some had claimed, to financial genius. That territory, even more than half a century later, was still too dangerous for British readers. Instead, they concentrated on what remains his most outstanding achievement: the perception that there was a hitherto undeveloped middle-class market for well-produced newspapers and the drive to exploit it with undoubted skill and energy. Finally, his career in the Second World War was given the treatment in the bright lights which, at the time, most people thought he deserved.

Of course, what the obituaries could only hint at was Beaverbrook's private life. There was no mention of his treatment of his first wife, of his fractious relationship with his children, of his flaunting of convention in publicly parading his mistress, and his whispered record of serial infidelity. Nor were his occasional rages recorded, or his vendettas, or his malicious pranks on unsuspecting journalists, or, for that matter, his habit from time to time of conducting meetings while sitting on the lavatory or openly urinating on the Cherkley lawn. These were not things proper for public debate.

On the other hand, what does not come through in the obituaries is the sheer *joie de vivre* at Cherkley in its heyday and La Capponcina in later years. Rarely was an invitation to a Cherkley weekend refused during the interwar years, and it was rarer still to find a guest who had not enjoyed the abundant hospitality and crackling dialogue, with Beaverbrook presiding as both concert master and conductor. Nor was it a question of the lure of money. The Cherkley visitors' book is full of the names of rich and somewhat less rich, left- and right-wing, all alike. La Capponcina, too, in the post-war years was a place of laughter and sun, with the scent of Churchill in his glory.

It was generally agreed that the main driver in Beaverbrook's political life, the Empire Crusade, had, as he himself had recognised, ended in failure. Nevertheless, as failures go, it had its heroic moments, and its daughter, imperial preference, was better than nothing. Above all, Beaverbrook never wavered in his belief that true Empire free trade was the key to prosperity for millions of people not just in the United Kingdom but in the Dominions as well. Of course, his definition of Empire was selective, and it was never clear whether, on their side, the Dominions would be prepared to agree to a framework which, as his lifelong friend R. B. Bennett pointed out, would almost certainly work to their disadvantage. Equally unfortunately, the Conservative Party, with which he had a bumpy relationship over the years and which he hoped would be the main vehicle for his ambitions, could never quite accept his full programme (and was run by politicians more tactically astute).

It would be wrong to think of the Empire Crusade as a mere intellectual construct. Beaverbrook himself was a King's man, grounded in a fusion of the Loyalist tradition of eighteenth-century New England and the Scottish migration of the nineteenth century. The Crusade was born of conviction, not of the intellect. In the fervour with which he pursued the conviction, he matched the energy of another man of conviction: his old friend Winston Churchill.

Biographers are often asked, almost by way of conversation, whether they ended liking or disliking their subject. It is never an easy question to answer (unless, of course, the objective has been to demolish the subject's reputation). Months, even years, pass in the research and writing, and the writer's opinion can change in the twinkling of an eye if he or she finds something which provokes him or her. Yet there is one category of subject where the response has to be framed in a different language, where the verbs 'like' and 'dislike' no longer apply. The subject is too big a figure for the language. Nobody, for instance, uses 'like' or 'dislike' when assessing Churchill, Roosevelt or, for that matter, Hitler. The language moves up a gear into 'love', 'loathe', 'admire' or 'detest'. Beaverbrook falls, fairly and squarely, into that category.

We should, however, not leave it there. Certainly, Beaverbrook was both loved and loathed, admired and detested. When Lady Diana Cooper described him as a 'gnome with an odour of genius about him', she was near the mark. Perhaps 'genius' in the round goes too far. He was no Leonardo da Vinci. But there is no doubt about the 'gnome'. There was an unpleasant side to his character which drove him to harm people callously, as others would swat a fly. To balance that, however, there was also an undeniable magic, demonic perhaps at times, which together with his undoubted charm captivated many who came into contact with him. Above all, it captivated Churchill, and his role as Churchill's boon companion during the dark days of the Second World War should always be celebrated with proper gratitude.

When asked after Beaverbrook's death in 1964 whether he had gone to Hell or Heaven, a friend replied that it did not matter which one he had gone to as he would soon arrange a merger between the two. As an epitaph, that will serve.

SELECT BIBLIOGRAPHY

1. Beaverbrook's published writings
Canada in Flanders, vols I–II (London: Hodder & Stoughton, 1916–18).
Politicians and the Press (London: Hutchinson, 1925).
Politicians and the War, 1914–1916 (one vol. ed.) (London: Oldbourne Book Co, 1960).
Men and Power, 1917–1918 (London: Hutchinson, 1956).
Friends: Sixty Years of Intimate Personal Relations with Richard Bedford Bennett (London: Heinemann, 1959).
Courage: The Story of Sir James Dunn (London: Collins, 1962).
The Divine Propagandist (London: Heinemann, 1962).
The Decline and Fall of Lloyd George (London: Collins, 1963).
My Early Life (Fredericton: Brunswick Press, 1965).
The Abdication of King Edward VIII (New York: Atheneum, 1966).

2. Biographies and part biographies
Jonathan Aitken, *Heroes and Contemporaries* (London: Continuum, 2006).
Anne Chisholm and Michael Davie, *Beaverbrook: A Life* (London: Hutchinson, 1992).
Richard Cockett (ed.), *My Dear Max: The Letters of Brendan Bracken to Lord Beaverbrook, 1925–1928* (London: Historians' Press, 1990).
Tom Driberg, *Beaverbrook: A Study in Power and Frustration* (London: Weidenfeld & Nicolson, 1956).
Tom Driberg, *Ruling Passions: The Autobiography* (London: Jonathan Cape, 1977).
David Farrer, *The Sky's the Limit: The Story of Beaverbrook at M. A. P.* (London: Hutchinson, 1943).
David Farrer, *G – For God Almighty: A Personal Memoir of Lord Beaverbrook* (New York: Stein and Day, 1969).
Michael Foot, *Debts of Honour* (London: Davis Poynter, 1980).
Logan Gourlay (ed.), *The Beaverbrook I Knew* (London: Quartet Books, 1984).
Peter Howard, *Beaverbrook: A Study of Max the Unknown* (London: Hutchinson, 1964).
Janet Aitken Kidd, *The Beaverbrook Girl: An Autobiography* (London: Collins, 1987).
F. A. Mackenzie, *Lord Beaverbrook: An Authentic Biography of the Rt Hon. Lord Beaverbrook* (London: Jarrolds Publishers, 1931).
Gregory P. Marchildon, *Profits and Politics: Beaverbrook and the Gilded Age of Canadian Finance* (Toronto: University of Toronto Press, 1996).
Edgar Middleton, *Beaverbrook: The Statesman and the Man* (London: Stanley Paul, 1934).

A. J. P. Taylor, *Beaverbrook* (London: Hamish Hamilton, 1972).

George Malcolm Thomson, *Vote of Censure: An Eyewitness Account of the Threat to Churchill's Leadership in 1942* (London: Secker and Warburg, 1968).

Colin Vines, *A Little Nut-Brown Man: My Three Years with Lord Beaverbrook* (London: Frewin, 1969).

Alan Wood, *The True History of Lord Beaverbrook* (London: Heinemann, 1965).

Kenneth Young, *Churchill and Beaverbrook: A Study in Friendship and Politics* (London: Eyre & Spottiswoode, 1966).

3. General

R. J. Q. Adams, *Bonar Law* (London: John Murray, 1999).

R. J. Q. Adams, *Balfour: The Last Grandee* (London: Thistle Publishing, 2013).

Kingsley Amis, *Rudyard Kipling and His World* (London: Thames & Hudson, 1975).

Matthew Page Andrews, *History of Maryland: Province and State* (New York: Doubleday, 1929).

Michael Arlen, *Exiles* (New York: Pocket, 1971).

Christopher Armstrong and H. V. Nelles (eds), *Southern Exposure: Canadian Promoters in Latin America and the Caribbean, 1896–1930* (Toronto: University of Toronto Press, 1988).

Tallulah Bankhead, *Tallulah: My Autobiography* (London: Gollancz, 1952).

John Barnes and David Nicolson (eds), *The Leo Amery Diaries, vols I & II* (London: Hutchinson, 1980 and 1987).

Francis Beckett, *Clem Attlee: A Biography* (London: Richard Cohen Books, 1997).

Sally Bedell Smith, *Reflected Glory: The Life of Pamela Churchill Harriman* (London: Simon & Schuster, 1997).

P. M. H. Bell, *John Bull and the Bear: British Public Opinion, Foreign Policy and the Soviet Union, 1941–1945* (London: Edward Arnold, 1990).

Carl Berger, *The Sense of Power: Studies in the Ideas of Canadian Imperialism, 1867–1914* (Toronto: University of Toronto Press, 2013).

John Bew, *Citizen Clem: A Biography of Attlee* (London: Quercus, 2016).

Robert Blake (ed.), *The Private Papers of Douglas Haig 1914–1919* (London: Eyre & Spottiswoode, 1952).

Robert Blake, *The Unknown Prime Minister: The Life and Times of Andrew Bonar Law, 1858–1923* (London: Eyre & Spottiswoode, 1955).

Michael Bloch, *The Reign and Abdication of King Edward VIII* (London: Bantam Press, 1990).

Piers Brendon, *Winston Churchill: A Brief Life* (London: Pimlico, 2001).

Piers Brendon, *Edward VII: The Uncrowned King* (London: Allen Lane, 2016).

Michael Brock and Eleanor Brock (eds), *Margot Asquith's Great War Diary 1914–1916* (Oxford: Oxford University Press, 2014).

Alan Bullock; Peter Hennessy and Brian Brivati (eds), *Ernest Bevin: A Biography* (London: Politico's, 2002).

R. A. Butler, *The Art of the Possible: The Memoirs of Lord Butler* (London: Hamish Hamilton, 1971).

Frank Callanan, *T. M. Healy* (Cork: Cork University Press, 1996).

Jack Campbell, *A Word for Scotland* (Edinburgh: Luath Press, 1998).

John Campbell, *F. E. Smith: First Earl of Birkenhead* (London: Faber & Faber, 2013).

David Cannadine, *History in Our Time* (New Haven: Yale University Press, 1998).

Gary Chapman, *The Dolly Sisters: Icons of the Jazz Age* (Stroud: Edditt, 2013).

John Charmley, *Churchill: The End of Glory – A Political Biography* (London: Hodder & Stoughton, 1993).

Winston S. Churchill, *The Second World War, Volume II: Their Finest Hour* (London: Cassell, 1949).

Samuel Delbert Clark, *Movements of Political Protest in Canada 1640–1840* (Toronto: University of Toronto Press, 1959).

Colin Clifford, *The Asquiths* (London: John Murray, 2002).

Colin Coates (ed.), *Majesty in Canada: Essays on the Role of Royalty* (Toronto: The Dundurn Group, 2006).

John Colville, *Footprints in Time* (London: Collins, 1976).

John Colville, *The Fringes of Power: Downing Street Diaries 1939–1955* (London: Hodder & Stoughton, 1985).

Tim Cook, *Clio's Warriors: Canadian Historians and the Writing of the World Wars* (UCB Press, 2007).

Artemis Cooper (ed.), *A Durable Fire: The Letters of Duff and Diana Cooper, 1913–1950* (London: Collins, 1983).

Travis L. Crosby, *The Unknown Lloyd George: A Statesman in Conflict* (London: I. B. Tauris, 2014).

Alex Danchev and Daniel Todman (eds), *War Diaries, 1939–1945: Field Marshal Lord Alanbrooke* (London: Weidenfeld & Nicolson, 2001).

Dido Davies, *William Gerhardie: A Biography* (Oxford: Oxford University Press, 1990).

David Dilks (ed.), *The Diaries of Sir Alexander Cadogan O. M., 1938–1945* (London: Cassell, 1971).

Alan P. Dobson, *FDR and Civil Aviation: Flying Strong, Flying Free* (New York: Palgrave Macmillan, 2011).

Robert Edwards, *Goodbye Fleet Street* (London: Jonathan Cape, 1988).

Robin Esser, *Crusaders in Chains* (London: Palatino Publishing, 2015).

Newman Flower (ed.), *The Journals of Arnold Bennett, Vol. III, 1921–1928* (London: Cassell, 1933).

Adrian Fort, *Prof: The Life of Frederick Lindemann* (London: Jonathan Cape, 2003).

James D. Frost, *Merchant Princes: Halifax's First Family of Finance, Ships and Steel* (Toronto: Lorimer, 2003).

Helen Fry, *Music and Men: The Life & Loves of Harriet Cohen* (London: The History Press, 2008).

Anthony Furse, *Wilfrid Freeman: The Genius Behind Allied Survival and Air Supremacy, 1939 to 1945* (Staplehurst: Spellmount, 1999).

William Gerhardie, *Memoirs of a Polyglot: The Autobiography of William Gerhardie* (London: Duckworth, 1931).

Lorna Gibb, *West's World: The Extraordinary Life of Dame Rebecca West* (London, Macmillan, 2013).

Martin Gilbert, *Winston S. Churchill, Vol. III: The Challenge of War, 1914–1916* (London: Heinemann, 1971).

Martin Gilbert, *Winston S. Churchill: Companion Vol. III, Part 2, May 1915–December 1916* (London: Heinemann, 1972).

Martin Gilbert, *Finest Hour: Winston S. Churchill, 1939–1941* (London: Heinemann, 1983).

Martin Gilbert, *Winston S. Churchill: Never Despair, 1945–1965* (London: Heinemann, 1988).

Martin Gilbert, *Churchill: A Life* (London: Heinemann, 1991).

Martin Gilbert, *The Churchill War Papers: Vol. I, At the Admiralty, September 1939–May 1940* (New York: W. W. Norton & Co., 1993).

Martin Gilbert and Larry P. Arnn (eds), *The Churchill Documents, Vol. 18: One Continent Redeemed, January–August 1943* (Michigan: Hillsdale College Press, 2015).

David Gilmour, *Curzon* (London: John Murray, 1994).

Victoria Glendinning, *Rebecca West: A Life* (London: Weidenfeld & Nicolson, 1987).

Alfred Gollin, *The Observer and J. L. Garvin, 1908–1914* (Oxford: Oxford University Press, 1960).

Gabriel Gorodetsky (ed.), *Stafford Cripps in Moscow 1940–1942: Diaries and Papers* (London: Vallentine Mitchell, 2007).

Gabriel Gorodetsky (ed.), *The Maisky Diaries: Red Ambassador to the Court of St James's, 1932–1943* (New Haven: Yale University Press, 2015).

Sandra Gwyn, *The Tapestry of War: A Private View of Canadians in the Great War* (Toronto: Harper Collins, 1992).

W. Averell Harriman and Elie Abel, *Special Envoy to Churchill and Stalin, 1941–1946* (London: Hutchinson, 1976).

Kenneth Harris, *Attlee* (London: Weidenfeld & Nicolson, 1984).

Duff Hart-Davis (ed.), *End of an Era: Letters and Journals of Sir Alan Lascelles, 1887–1920* (London: Hamish Hamilton, 1988).

Roy Hattersley, *The Edwardians* (London: Little, Brown, 2004).

Roy Hattersley, *David Lloyd George: The Great Outsider* (London: Little, Brown, 2010).

Ronald G. Haycock, *Sam Hughes: The Public Career of a Controversial Canadian, 1885–1916* (Waterloo, Ont.: Wilfrid Laurier University Press, 1986).

Peter Hennessy, *Whitehall* (London: Pimlico, 2001).

Lady Pamela Hicks, *Daughter of Empire: Life as a Mountbatten* (London: Weidenfeld & Nicolson, 2012).

Simon Hoggart and David Leigh, *Michael Foot: A Portrait* (London: Hodder & Stoughton, 1981).

Pamela Horn, *Country House Society: The Private Lives of England's Upper Class After the First World War* (Stroud: Amberley Publishing, 2013).

Anthony Howard, *RAB: The Life of R. A. Butler* (London: Jonathan Cape, 1987).

Roy Jenkins, *Asquith* (London: Collins, 1964).

Terry Jenkins, *Sir Ernest Lemon* (Railway & Canal Historical Society, 2011).

Greg King and Penny Wilson, *Lusitania: Triumph, Tragedy, and the End of the Edwardian Age* (New York: St Martin's Press, 2015).

Maximillien de Lafayette, *Louise Brooks: Her Men, Affairs, Scandals and Persona* (New York: Times Square Press, 2011).

Jean-Noël Liaut, *The Many Lives of Miss K: Toto Koopman – Model, Muse, Spy* (New York: Rizzoli Ex Libris, 2013).

David Lough, *No More Champagne: Churchill and His Money* (London: Head of Zeus, 2015).

Charles Edward Lysaght, *Brendan Bracken* (London: Allen Lane, 1979).

Harold Macmillan, *War Diaries: The Mediterranean, 1943–1945* (London: Macmillan, 1984).

Peter G. Masefield with Bill Gunston, *Flight Path: The Autobiography of Sir Peter Masefield* (Shrewsbury: Airlife Publishing, 2002).

John McGovern, *Neither Fear nor Favour* (London: Blandford Press, 1960).

Keith Middlemas (ed.), *Thomas Jones, Whitehall Diary Vol. I: 1916–1925; Vol. II: 1926–1930* (Oxford: Oxford University Press, 1969).

Keith Middlemas (ed.), *Thomas Jones, Whitehall Diary Vol. III: Ireland, 1918–1925* (Oxford: Oxford University Press, 1971).

Anthony Montague Browne, *Long Sunset: Memoirs of Winston Churchill's Last Private Secretary* (London: Cassell, 1995).

Lord Moran, *Winston Churchill: The Struggle for Survival 1940–1965* (London: Constable, 1966).

Kenneth O. Morgan, *Michael Foot: A Life* (London: HarperCollins, 2007).

Ann Moyal, *Breakfast with Beaverbrook: Memoirs of an Independent Woman* (Sydney: Hale & Iremonger, 1995).

Michael Newman, *Harold Laski: A Political Biography* (Pontypool: Merlin Press, 2009).

Nigel Nicolson (ed.), *The Harold Nicolson Diaries: 1907–1963* (London: Weidenfeld & Nicolson, 2004).

John Julius Norwich (ed.), *The Duff Cooper Diaries: 1915–1951* (London: Weidenfeld & Nicolson, 2005).

Richard Overy, *The Battle of Britain: Myth and Reality* (London: Penguin, 2010).

Peter Padfield, *Hess, Hitler and Churchill* (London: Icon Books, 2013).

Barry Paris, *Louise Brooks: A Biography* (New York: Knopf, 1989).

John Pearson (published under the name 'Henry Cloud'), *Barbara Cartland: Crusader in Pink* (London: Weidenfeld & Nicolson, 1979).

Adrian Phillips, *The King Who Had To Go: Edward VIII, Mrs Simpson and the Hidden Politics of the Abdication Crisis* (London: Biteback Publishing, 2016).

Ben Pimlott, *Hugh Dalton* (London: Jonathan Cape, 1985).

Ben Pimlott (ed.), *The Second World War Diary of Hugh Dalton, 1940–45* (London: Jonathan Cape, 1986).

Chapman Pincher, *Dangerous to Know: A Life* (London: Biteback Publishing, 2014).

M. M. Postan, *British War Production* (London: HMSO, 1952).

Jeffrey Potter, *Men, Money & Magic: The Story of Dorothy Schiff* (New York: Coward, McCann & Geoghegan Inc., 1976).

John Ramsden (ed.), *Real Old Tory Politics: The Political Diaries of Sir Robert Sanders, Lord Bayford* (London: Historians' Press, 1984).

George Elmore Reaman, *A History of Vaughan Township: Two Centuries of Life in the Township* (Toronto: Vaughan Township Historical Society, 1993).

Robert Rhodes James (ed.), *Memoirs of a Conservative: J. C. C. Davidson's Memoirs and Papers, 1910–37* (London: Weidenfeld & Nicolson, 1969).

Robert Rhodes James (ed.), *Chips: The Diaries of Sir Henry Channon* (London: Phoenix, 1996).

W. R. Riddell, *Diary of Voyage from Scotland to Canada in 1833 and Story of St Andrew's Church, Cobourg, Ontario* (private publication, undated).

Sebastian Ritchie, *Industry and Air Power: The Expansion of British Aircraft Production, 1935–41* (London: Frank Cass, 1997).

Major Charles G. D. Roberts, *Canada in Flanders: Vol. III* (London: Hodder & Stoughton, 1918).

Stanley Salvidge, *Salvidge of Liverpool: Behind the Political Scene, 1890–1928* (London: Hodder & Stoughton, 1934).

Jonathan Schneer, *Ministers at War: Winston Churchill and His War Cabinet* (London: Oneworld Publications, 2015).

J. D. Scott and Richard Hughes, *The Administration of War Production* (London: HMSO, 1955).

Robert Self (ed.), *The Neville Chamberlain Diary Letters, Vol. IV: The Downing Street Years, 1934–1940* (Aldershot: Ashgate, 2005).

Alfred Shaughnessy (ed.), *Sarah: The Letters and Diaries of a Courtier's Wife, 1906–1936* (London: Peter Owen, 1989).

Sir John Slessor, *The Central Blue* (London: Cassell, 1956).

Donald B. Smith, *Calgary's Grand Story: The Making of a Prairie Metropolis from the Viewpoint of Two Heritage Buildings* (Calgary: University of Calgary Press, 2005).

Mary Soames, *Clementine Churchill* (London: Cassell, 1979).

Mary Soames, *A Daughter's Tale: The Memoir of Winston and Clementine Churchill's Youngest Child* (London: Doubleday, 2011).

Lyndsy Spence (ed.), *The Mitford Society, Vol. II* (CreateSpace Independent Publishing Platform, 2014).

Lyndsy Spence, *The Mistress of Mayfair: Men, Money and the Marriage of Doris Delevingne* (Stroud: The History Press, 2016).

Irwin Stelzer, *The Murdoch Method: Notes on Running a Media Empire* (London: Atlantic Books, 2018).

Hew Strachan, *The First World War: A New Illustrated History* (London: Simon & Schuster, 2003).

James Stuart, *Within the Fringe: An Autobiography* (London: The Bodley Head, 1967).

Andrew Taylor, *Bonar Law* (London: Haus Publishing, 2006).

D. J. Taylor, *Bright Young People: The Rise and Fall of a Generation, 1918–1940* (London: Chatto & Windus, 2007).

Lord Tedder, *With Prejudice: The War Memoirs of Marshal of the Royal Air Force Lord Tedder* (London: Cassell, 1966).

Ernest Sackville Turner, *Dear Old Blighty* (London: Michael Joseph, 1980).

Karina Urbach, *Go-Betweens for Hitler* (Oxford: Oxford University Press, 2015).

John Vincent (ed.), *The Crawford Papers: The Journals of David Lindsay, 27th Earl of Crawford and 10th Earl of Balcarres 1871–1940* (Manchester: Manchester University Press, 1984).

Rebecca West, *Sunflower* (London: Virago Press, 2008).

John Wheeler-Bennett, *King George VI: His Life and Reign* (London: Macmillan, 1958).

Charles Williams, *Harold Macmillan* (London: Weidenfeld & Nicolson, 2009).

Susan Williams, *The People's King: The True Story of the Abdication* (London: Allen Lane, 2003).

Philip Williamson, *Stanley Baldwin: Conservative Leadership and National Values* (New York: Cambridge University Press, 1999).

Beckles Willson, *From Quebec to Piccadilly* (London: Jonathan Cape, 1929).

Carol Wilton (ed.), *Beyond the Law: Lawyers and Business in Canada 1830 to 1930* (Toronto: The Osgoode Society, 1990).

Kenneth Young, *Churchill and Beaverbrook: A Study in Friendship and Politics* (London: Eyre & Spottiswoode, 1966).

Kenneth Young (ed.), *The Diaries of Sir Robert Bruce Lockhart: Volume I, 1915–1938* (London: Macmillan, 1973).

Kenneth Young (ed.), *The Diaries of Sir Robert Bruce Lockhart: Volume II, 1939–1965* (London: Macmillan, 1980).

Philip Ziegler, *Diana Cooper* (London: Hamish Hamilton, 1981).

Philip Ziegler, *King Edward VIII: The Official Biography* (London: Collins, 1990).

4. Selected Articles

Christopher Armstrong, 'Making a Market: Selling Securities in Atlantic Canada before World War 1', *Canadian Journal of Economics*, XIII, Vol. 13, No. 3 (1980).

Frank Callanan, 'After Parnell: The Political Consequences of Timothy Michael Healy', *An Irish Quarterly Review*, Vol. 80, No. 320 (1991).

Ann Moyal, 'The History Man', *History Today*, Vol. 61, No. 1 (2011).

John Reid, 'A Conversation with Ann Moyal, Lord Beaverbrook's Researcher', *Journal of New Brunswick Studies*, Vol. 7, No. 2 (2016).

A. J. Robertson, 'Lord Beaverbrook and the Supply of Aircraft 1940–1941', in Anthony Slaven and Derek H. Aldcroft (eds), *Business, Banking and Urban History: Essays in Honour of S. G. Checkland* (Edinburgh: John Donald, 1982).

LIST OF PICTURE CREDITS

153: Print Collector/Hulton Fine Art Collection/Getty Images
161: Parliament Archives, BBK/L/22
162: D. N. D. (Army)/Library and Archives Canada/Panoramic Camera Co. collection/ PA-066879
163: Parliament Archives, BBK/L/24
171: Parliament Archives, BBK/L/24
174: © British Pathé Ltd
177: Library and Archives Canada/Frank J. Dupuis collection/PA-107378
182: Canada Department of National Defence/Library and Archives Canada/Ministry of the Overseas Military Forces of Canada fonds/PA-001451
186: Parliament Archives, BBK/L/24
202: Parliament Archives, BBK/L/24
209: Mary Evans Picture Library/Everett Collection
212: Parliament Archives, BBK/P/1/3
222: TopFoto
224: Canada Department of National Defence/Library and Archives Canada/Ministry of the Overseas Military Forces of Canada fonds/PA-006478
228: London Metropolitan Archives, City of London
237: Roger-Viollet/TopFoto
238: Mirrorpix
244: Hulton Archive/Getty Images
257: TopFoto
262: © Illustrated London News Ltd/Mary Evans Picture Library
263: © Express Newspapers/Express Syndication
269: Parliament Archives, BBK/P/2/11
271: Granger/Shutterstock
274a: © Illustrated London News Ltd/Mary Evans Picture Library
274b: Mary Evans Picture Library/Grenville Collins Postcard Collection
276: Snap/Shutterstock
277: MGM/Kobal/Shutterstock
281: By kind permission of Lord Grantley
284: Margaret Bourke-White/The LIFE Picture Collection/Getty Images
286: Topham Picturepoint/PA Images
293: Archive Photos/Getty Images
300: Daily Mail/Shutterstock
314: © SZ Photo/Scherl/Bridgeman Images
321: Topical Press Agency/Hulton Archive/Getty Images
326: Keystone/Hulton Archive/Getty Images
333: © Illustrated London News Ltd/Mary Evans Picture Library
336: akg-images/Ullstein
346: John Frost Newspapers/Alamy Stock Photo
349: Associated Newspapers/Shutterstock
350: © Yevonde Portrait Archive/ILN/Mary Evans Picture Library
352: Sasha/Hulton Archive/Getty Images
356: Sasha/Hulton Archive/Getty Images
359: The Canterbury Auction Galleries

ENDNOTES

Prologue

1 Quoted in Philip Ziegler, *Diana Cooper* (London: Hamish Hamilton, 1981), p. 94.
2 Mary Soames, *Clementine Churchill* (London: Cassell, 1979).
3 Author interview with Miss Jane Portal, 6 June 2014.

Chapter 1: The Brunswicker

1 Motto of the Province of New Brunswick. The official (incorrect) translation is 'Hope Restored'; a better rendition would be 'He Restored Hope'.
2 Cited in Matthew Page Andrews, *History of Maryland* (New York: Doubleday, 1929), p. 284.
3 Cited in Samuel Delbert Clark, *Movements of Political Protest in Canada 1640–1840* (Toronto: University of Toronto Press, 1959), pp. 150–51.
4 Ibid.
5 Lord Beaverbrook, *My Early Life* (Fredericton: Brunswick Press, 1965), pp. 21–2, 27.
6 BBK/K/1/1.
7 National Library of Scotland, minutes of meeting of Church of Scotland Colonial Committee, 20 August 1862.
8 Ibid., minutes of meeting of Colonial Committee, 31 May 1864.
9 Ibid., minutes of meeting of Colonial Committee, 21 July 1864.
10 Extract from the records of the Presbytery of Linlithgow, meeting of 16 August 1864, BBK/K/1/1.
11 Call from the parish of Vaughan, Ontario, in the Presbytery of Toronto, 3 October 1865, ibid.
12 George Elmore Reaman, *A History of Vaughan Township* (Vaughan Township Historical Society, 1993), p. 144.
13 *My Early Life*, p. 24.
14 Ibid., p. 38.
15 Ibid., p. 24.
16 Ibid., p. 72.

Chapter 2: Mischief Maker

1 Transcript of an account given by Dr F. P. Yorston, Principal of Harkins Academy, 1892–1901, BBK/G/1/44.
2 Extract from Michael Wardell's fragment of biography (unpublished), BBK/G/1/40.
3 *My Early Life*, p. 40.
4 Ibid., p. 41.
5 Report for term ending 30 June 1885, BBK/G/1/69.
6 Yorston transcript, BBK/G/1/44.
7 Ibid.
8 Transcript of account given by Dr Philip Cox, Principal of Harkins Academy 1884–1892, ibid.
9 Yorston transcript, ibid.
10 University of Dalhousie website: 'History and Tradition', https://www.dal.ca/about-dal/history-tradition.

11 *My Early Life*, p. 75.
12 Ibid., p. 76.
13 Account of H. E. Borradaile, BBK/K/1/1.
14 Aitken to Bennett, 23 July 1896, BBK/A/218.
15 *My Early Life*, p. 80.
16 Aitken to Bennett, 11 January 1897, BBK/A/218.
17 Rev. William Aitken to Bennett, 6 July 1897, BBK/G/1/65.
18 *Dictionary of Canadian Biography, Vol. XV (1921–1930)*, Sir James Alexander Lougheed, p. 1.
19 Quoted in Donald Boyd Smith, *Calgary's Story: The Making of a Prairie Metropolis from the Viewpoint of Two Heritage Buildings* (Calgary: University of Calgary Press, 2005), p. 34.
20 A 'local resident' quoted in ibid., p. 35.
21 Aitken to Bennett, 21 June 1898, BBK/A/218.
22 *My Early Life*, p. 98.
23 Ibid., p. 104.
24 Ibid., p. 106.
25 Ibid., p. 108.

Chapter 3: From Drifter to Genius
1 *My Early Life*, p. 117.
2 J. F. Stairs to Macdonald, 6 June 1886, Macdonald Papers, quoted in James D. Frost, *Merchant Princes: Halifax's First Family of Finance, Ships and Steel* (Toronto: Lorimer, 2003), p. 156.
3 Gregory P. Marchildon, *Profits and Politics: Beaverbrook and the Gilded Age of Canadian Finance* (Toronto: University of Toronto Press, 1996), p. 28.
4 Notebook entry for 4 September 1902, BBK/G/1/4.
5 Notebook entry for 8 September 1902, ibid.
6 Notebook entry for 13 September 1902, ibid.
7 Aitken to Hal Brown, quoted but not dated, in Anne Chisholm and Michael Davie, *Beaverbrook: A Life* (London: Hutchinson, 1992), p. 37.
8 Diary entries for 14, 15 and 16 February 1903, BBK/G/1/5.
9 Extract from 'Memorandum of Association and Bylaws of Royal Securities Corporation Limited', cited in Christopher Armstrong, 'Making a Market: Selling Securities in Atlantic Canada before World War I', *Canadian Journal of Economics, Vol. XIII* (1980), p. 3.
10 Diary entry for 26 May 1903, BBK G/1/5.
11 Aitken to C. Ross Dobbin, 11 July 1903, BBK/A/2.
12 Aitken to Hayden, Stone & Co., 29 June 1903, BBK/A/3.
13 Aitken to Robb, 23 December 1903, BBK/A/7.
14 Aitken to Harris, 17 September 1904, BBK/A/12.f.
15 Harris to Aitkin [*sic*], 24 September 1904, ibid.
16 *Halifax Herald*, 27 September 1904.
17 *My Early Life*, p. 136.
18 Aitken to W. D. Ross, 30 September 1904, BBK/A/16.
19 *My Early Life*, p. 140.
20 Aitken to W. D. Ross, 14 March 1905, BBK/G/1/1.
21 Aitken to W. D. Ross, 1 February 1905, BBK A/26.
22 *My Early Life*, p. 142.
23 Ibid., p. 143.
24 Aitken to Davidson, 27 June 1905, BBK/A/19.
25 Diary entry for 23 January 1906, BBK/G/1/6.
26 Finley to Aitken, 20 January 1906, BBK/A/33.
27 Diary entry for 29 January 1906, BBK/G/1/6.

Chapter 4: Halfway There
1 *My Early Life*, p. 144.

2   Ibid., p. 128.
3   Ibid.
4   Farrell to Aitken, 18 January 1906, BBK/A/33.
5   *My Early Life*, p. 126.
6   Teele to Aitken, 12 April 1906, BBK/A/43.
7   *My Early Life*, pp. 145–6.
8   Aitken to W. D. Ross, 11 June 1906, BBK/A/41.
9   *My Early Life*, p. 146.
10   Harding to Aitken, 29 September 1906, BBK/A/34.
11   Farrell to Aitken, 6 October 1906, BBK/A/33.
12   Aitken to Burrill, 4 October 1906, BBK/A/29.
13   Aitken to George Stairs, 11 October 1906, BBK/A/42.
14   Aitken to Dr Curry, 26 November 1906, BBK/A/32.
15   Aitken to W. D. Ross, 22 November 1906, BBK/A/41.
16   Aitken to Dr Quintard, 29 December 1906, BBK/A/38.
17   Minutes of Montreal Engineering Company, 3 October 1907, quoted in Frost, *Merchant Princes*, p. 250.
18   Aitken to Wilson-Smith, 16 February 1907, BBK/A/78.
19   Aitken to Wilson-Smith, 7 March 1907, ibid.
20   *Halifax Herald*, 14 May 1907, quoted in Marchildon, *Profits and Politics*, p. 110.
21   George Stairs to Aitken, 23 May 1907, BBK/A/79.
22   De Gruchy to Traven Aitken, 15 June 1907, BBK/A/44.
23   *My Early Life*, p. 152.
24   Ibid.
25   Aitken to George Stairs, 31 October 1907, BBK/A/79.
26   Aitken to George Stairs, 24 January 1908, BBK/A/124.
27   *My Early Life*, p. 155.
28   Ibid., p. 157.
29   Nesbitt to Aitken, 18 June 1908, BBK/A/116.
30   Aitken to Nesbitt, 24 June 1908, ibid.

Chapter 5: 'Pots of Money'

1   Aitken to Churchill, undated but almost certainly April 1911, BBK/C/85.
2   Quoted in Marchildon, *Profits and Politics*, p. 181.
3   *My Early Life*, p. 158.
4   Aitken to Harris, 15 March 1909, BBK/A/151.
5   Quoted in A. J. P. Taylor, *Beaverbrook* (London: Hamish Hamilton, 1972), p. 27.
6   Jones to Aitken, 22 November 1909, BBK/A/139.
7   *My Early Life*, p. 166.
8   Ibid.
9   Fleming to Dunsford, 2 April 1910, BBK/H/313.
10   Ibid.
11   Fleming to Laurier, 5 April 1910, Laurier papers, quoted in Marchildon, *Profits and Politics*, p. 223.
12   *My Early Life*, p. 167.
13   Ibid.
14   Janet Aitken Kidd, *The Beaverbrook Girl* (London: Collins, 1987), p. 15.
15   *My Early Life*, p. 171.
16   Ibid., p. 169.
17   Ibid., pp. 171–2.
18   *My Early Life*, p. 170.

Chapter 6: England 1910

1   Bonar Law's outburst to Aitken who was thinking of looking elsewhere, quoted in *My Early Life*, p. 184.

2   De Gruchy note to Aitken, 22 June 1910, BBK/A/193.
3   Greg King and Penny Wilson, *Lusitania: Triumph, Tragedy and the End of the Edwardian Age* (New York: St Martin's Press, 2015), pp. 110–11.
4   *My Early Life*, p. 175.
5   Debate in Canadian House of Commons 18 January 1910, quoted in Marchildon, *Profits and Politics*, p. 213.
6   *Canadian Century*, 8 January 1910, quoted in ibid., p. 216.
7   Gladys Aitken to Aitken, 10 October 1910, BBK/A/180.
8   Gladys Aitken to Aitken, 11 October 1910, ibid.
9   *My Early Life*, p. 182.
10   Quoted in Roy Hattersley, *The Edwardians: Biography of the Edwardian Age* (London: Little, Brown, 2004), p. 412.
11   Ibid., p. 447.
12   Taylor, *Beaverbrook*, p. 41.
13   *My Early Life*, p. 182.
14   Quoted in Alan Wood, *The True History of Lord Beaverbrook* (London: Heinemann, 1965), p. 47.
15   Blumenfeld Diary; diary entry for 10 June 1911.
16   Goulding to Bonar Law, 4 August 1910, BL 21/3/11.
17   Bonar Law to Aitken, 6 October 1910, BBK/C/201.
18   Goulding to Aitken, 8 October 1910, BBK/C/317.
19   Aitken to Mawson, 21 October 1910, BBK/F/1.
20   Aitken to Bennett, 22 October 1910, BBK/A/219.
21   Mawson to Aitken, 22 October 1910, BBK/F/1.
22   Aitken to Mawson, 25 October 1910, ibid.
23   Bonar Law to Pownall, 14 November 1910, BL 18/8/13.
24   Aitken to Bonar Law, undated, BL 18/6/134.
25   *My Early Life*, p. 184.
26   Kipling quoted in Kingsley Amis, *Kipling and His World* (London: Thames & Hudson, 1975), p. 54.
27   Aitken to Goulding, 20 November 1910, BBK/C/317.
28   *Ashton Reporter*, 21 November 1910.
29   Ibid., 1 December 1910.
30   Ibid., 28 November 1910.
31   Quoted in Wood, *The True History of Lord Beaverbrook*, p. 51.
32   *Ashton Reporter*, 29 November 1910.
33   Ibid., 3 November 1910.
34   Gladys Aitken to De Gruchy; De Gruchy to Gladys Aitken, both 30 December 1910, BBK/A/188.

Chapter 7: Cherkley
1   Asquith to Churchill, 26 December 1911, Churchill Archives, CHAR/13/1/58.
2   Kipling to Aitken, 9 March 1911, BBK/C/197a.
3   *Ashton Reporter*, 4 March 1911.
4   Aitken to Sir Joseph Lawrence, 15 February 1911, BBK/B/4.
5   *London Magazine*, March 1911.
6   Aitken to Bennett, 4 March 1911, BBK/A/212.
7   Aitken to Foster, 4 March 1911, BBK/A/212; Aitken to Davidson, 4 March 1911, BBK/A/229.
8   Kipling to Aitken, 9 March 1911, BBK/C/197a.
9   Aitken to McDougall, 3 April 1911, BBK/G/1/55.
10   Aitken to Churchill, undated, Churchill Archives, CHAR 2/53/93.
11   Kidd, *The Beaverbrook Girl*, p. 18.
12   Memorandum of Agreement between John Robertson and Aitken, 24 April 1911, BBK/J/1.
13   Aitken to Borden, 21 April 1911, BBK/C/50.
14   Ibid.

15 Borden to Aitken, 1 May 1911, ibid.
16 *Montreal Star*, 12 May 1911.
17 Aitken to Goulding, 25 May 1911, BBK/C/317.
18 Quoted in Marchildon, *Profits and Politics*, p. 224.
19 Aitken to Davidson, 3 July 1911, BBK/A/229.
20 Marchildon, *Profits and Politics*, p. 225.
21 Aitken to Bonar Law, 1 August 1911, BBK/C/201.
22 *The Times*, 27 July 1911.
23 Kipling to *Montreal Star*, 6 September 1911, BBK/C/197a.
24 Aitken to Francis, 26 September 1911, BBK/J/11.
25 Bonar Law to Aitken, quoted in Taylor, *Beaverbrook*, p. 72.
26 Robert Blake, 'The Species Salientia', in Logan Gourlay (ed.), *The Beaverbrook I Knew* (London: Quartet Books, 1984), p. 30.
27 W. Bull diary entry for 11 July 1911, cited in R. J. Q. Adams, *Bonar Law* (London: John Murray, 1999), p. 55.
28 John Vincent (ed.), *The Crawford Papers* (Manchester: Manchester University Press, 1984), p. 245.
29 Ibid., p. 246.
30 Ibid., pp. 246–7.
31 Goulding to Bonar Law (Hope's letter was enclosed by Goulding along with his own), 9 November 1911, BLP 24/1/1.
32 Lord Beaverbrook, *The Decline and Fall of Lloyd George* (London: Collins, 1963), p. 198.
33 Bonar Law to Hope, 10 November 1911, BLP 117/1/15.
34 Vincent (ed.), *The Crawford Papers*, p. 250.
35 Aitken to Hazen, 18 November 1911; Aitken to Hazen, undated, both BBK/A/234.
36 Bonar Law to Borden, 9 December 1911, BL/33/3/32.
37 Michael Brock and Eleanor Brock (eds), *Margot Asquith's Great War Diary 1914–1916* (Oxford: Oxford University Press, 2014), p. 310.

Chapter 8: Ireland

1 Vincent (ed.), *The Crawford Papers*, p. 252.
2 Ibid.
3 Coop to Aitken, 15 February 1912, BBK/B/50.
4 Aitken to Coop, 16 February 1912, ibid.
5 Aitken to Pughe-Morgan, 5 March 1912, BBK/B/74.
6 Aitken to Bennett, 22 December 1911, BBK/A/219.
7 Bonar Law to Carson, 25 January 1912, BL/33/4/6.
8 *Morning Post*, 9 April 1912.
9 Aitken–Kipling telegrams, April 1912, BBK/C/197b.
10 Kipling to Aitken, 12 April 1912, ibid.
11 *Manchester Guardian*, 22 April 1912; *Ashton Herald*, 22 June 1912.
12 *Freeman's Journal*, 8 December 1890, quoted in Frank Callanan, 'After Parnell; The Political Consequences of Timothy Michael Healy', *An Irish Quarterly Review*, Vol. 80, No. 320 (winter 1991), pp. 371–6, published by The Irish Province of the Society of Jesus.
13 Ibid.
14 Kidd, *The Beaverbrook Girl*, pp. 21–2.
15 Ibid., p. 23.
16 Secretary to unnamed correspondent, 8 June 1912, BBK/B/7.
17 Secretary to Buckley, 27 March 1912, BBK/B/45.
18 Locker Lampson to Blumenfeld, 9 July 1912, BBK/H/2.
19 Vincent (ed.), *The Crawford Papers*, p. 261.
20 Ibid., p. 265.
21 Aitken to Kipling, 3 October 1912, BBK/C/197b.
22 *Montreal Star*, 17 August 1912.

23   Adams, *Bonar Law*, p. 82.
24   Ibid., p. 83.
25   *Ashton Herald*, 18 December 1912.
26   Vincent (ed.), *The Crawford Papers*, p. 293.
27   Text of 'Memorial' in Adams, *Bonar Law*, p. 90.
28   Alfred Gollin, *The Observer and J. L. Garvin* (Oxford: Oxford University Press, 1960), p. 384.

Chapter 9: Odd Man Out

1   Aitken to Bennett, 28 July 1914, BBK/A/221.
2   Adams, *Bonar Law*, p. 114.
3   Aitken to Goulding, 3 March 1913, BBK/C/317.
4   Aitken to Clarke, 14 May 1913, BBK/H/322.
5   *Ashton Reporter*, 31 May 1913.
6   Ibid.
7   Ibid.
8   Gladys Aitken to Coop, telegram undated, BBK/B/83a.
9   Müller to Aitken, 19 August 1913, BBK/B/9.
10   Lord Crewe to Asquith, quoted in Roy Jenkins, *Asquith* (London: Collins, 1964), p. 286.
11   Robert Blake, *The Unknown Prime Minister: The Life and Times of Andrew Bonar Law, 1858–1923* (London: Eyre & Spottiswoode, 1955), p. 161.
12   Rev. William Aitken to Aitken, 9 November 1912, BBK/K/1/62.
13   Aitken to Davidson, 2 December 1913; Davidson to Aitken, 2 December 1913, 6 December 1913 and 13 December 1913, BBK/A/230.
14   Quoted in Adams, *Bonar Law*, p. 146.
15   Beaverbrook to Lady Rugby, 9 December 1963, BBK/B/676.
16   Giles to Aitken, 7 April 1914, BBK/H/348.
17   Doble to Aitken, 4 July 1914 and 6 July 1914, BBK/H/368.
18   Asquith to Venetia Stanley, 24 July 1914, in Michael Brock and Eleanor Brock (eds), *Letters to Venetia Stanley* (Oxford: Oxford University Press, 1982), p. 122.
19   Bennett to Aitken, 27 July 1914; Aitken to Bennett, 28 July 1914, BBK/A/221.
20   Lord Beaverbrook, *Politicians and the War, 1914–1916* (London: Oldbourne Book Co., 1960), pp. 29–30.
21   Cited in Adams, *Bonar Law*, p. 170.
22   Beaverbrook, *Politicians and the War*, p. 31.
23   House of Commons, Official Report, 3 August 1914, col. 1810.

Chapter 10: The Empire at War

1   From Bonar Law's 'Introduction' to *Sir Max Aitken, Canada in Flanders: Vol. I* (London: Hodder & Stoughton, 1916), p. viii.
2   Kathleen Hale, quoted in Sandra Gwyn, *Tapestry of War* (Toronto: Harper Collins, 1992), p. 43.
3   Quoted in ibid., p. 54.
4   Aitken to Kipling, 10 December 1914, BBK/C/198.
5   Aitken to Doble, 19 August 1914, BBK/H/368.
6   Gwyn, *Tapestry of War*, p. 231.
7   Aitken to Davidson, 23 September 1914, BBK/A/230.
8   Ronald G. Haycock, *Sam Hughes* (Waterloo, Ont.: Wilfrid Laurier University Press, 1986), p. 131.
9   Beckles Willson diary, quoted in Gwyn, *Tapestry of War*, p. 242.
10   Aitken to Hughes, 28 December 1914, BBK/E/1/2.
11   Aitken to Hazen, 30 December 1914, BBK/A/234.
12   Aitken to Hughes, 31 December 1914, BBK/E/1/2.
13   Order in Council (Canada), 6 January 1915, BBK/E/1/9.
14   Gwyn, *Tapestry of War*, p. 98.
15   Ernest Sackville Turner, *Dear Old Blighty* (London: Michael Joseph, 1980), p. 204.

16 Gwyn, *Tapestry of War*, p. 234.

17 Ibid., p. 233.

18 Aitken, *Canada in Flanders: Vol. I*, p. 49.

19 Quoted in Gwyn, *Tapestry of War*, p. 235.

20 Aitken to Hazen, 26 February 1915, BBK/A/234.

21 Aitken to Hazen, 21 April 1915, ibid.

22 Aitken to Hazen, 6 May 1915, ibid.

23 Hazen to Aitken, 12 May 1915, ibid.

24 Quoted in Adams, *Bonar Law*, p. 183.

25 Beaverbrook, *Politicians and the War*, p. 118.

26 Bonar Law to Borden, 5 June 1915, BL/50/2/2.

27 Bonar Law to Asquith, 2 June 1915, BL/53/6/21.

28 Aitken to Bonar Law, 2 June 1915, ibid.

29 Aitken to Perley, 2 June 1915, BL/118/9/9.

30 'Report of the Establishment of the Canadian Representative at the Front and Canadian War Records', Aitken to Borden, 1916, BBK/E/1/20.

31 Borden to Aitken, 14 September 1915, BBK/C/50.

32 Aitken to Carrie Kipling, 1 September 1915, BBK/C/199a.

33 Martin Gilbert, *Winston S. Churchill: Companion Vol. III, Part 2, May 1915–December 1916* (London: Heinemann, 1972), p. 1338.

34 Martin Gilbert, *Winston S. Churchill, Vol. III: The Challenge of War, 1914–1916* (London: Heinemann, 1971), pp. 619–20.

Chapter 11: 1916

1   The Duke of Connaught to Beckles Willson in January 1916, quoted in Gwyn, *Tapestry of War*, p. 243.

2   Aitken to Borden, 1 January 1916, BBK/E/1/10.

3   Willson's grandson quoted in Gwyn, *Tapestry of War*, p. 241.

4   Ibid., p. 242.

5   Willson diary, quoted ibid., p. 244.

6   *Sunday Times, Sunday Pictorial* and *Reynolds News* of 30 January 1916.

7   Beckles Willson, *From Quebec to Piccadilly* (London: Jonathan Cape, 1929), p. 201.

8   Haycock, *Sam Hughes*, p. 262.

9   Aitken to Borden, 3 December 1915, BBK/C/50.

10 Alderson to Gwatkin, quoted in Gwyn, *Tapestry of War*, p. 251.

11 Haycock, *Sam Hughes*, p. 250.

12 Willson diary, quoted in Gwyn, *Tapestry of War*, pp. 251–2.

13 Willson, *From Quebec to Piccadilly*, p. 213.

14 Willson diary, quoted in Gwyn, *Tapestry of War*, p. 252.

15 Haig diary entry for 21 April 1916, in Robert Blake (ed.), *The Private Papers of Douglas Haig: 1914–1919* (London: Eyre & Spottiswoode, 1952), p. 140.

16 Haig diary entry for 23 April 1916, ibid.

17 Willson, *From Quebec to Piccadilly*, p. 211.

18 Haig diary entry for 23 April 1916, in Blake (ed.), *The Private Papers of Douglas Haig*, p. 140.

19 Ibid.

20 Aitken to Haig, 27 April 1916, BBK/E/1/44.

21 Aitken to Haig, 28 April 1916, ibid.

22 Quoted in Gwyn, *Tapestry of War*, p. 257.

23 Ibid., p. 258.

24 Beaverbrook, *Politicians and the War*, p. 208.

25 Margot Asquith diary entry for 26 June 1916, in Michael Brock and Eleanor Brock (eds), *Letters to Venetia Stanley*, p. 268.

26 Borden to Governor General, 17 May 1916, BL/118/9/21.

27 Quoted in Gwyn, *Tapestry of War*, p. 173.
28 Hughes to Aitken, 21 October 1916, BBK/E/1/6.
29 Creelman diary entry for 19 September 1916, quoted in Haycock, *Sam Hughes*, p. 310.
30 Aitken to Hughes, 12 November 1916, BBK/E/1/6.
31 Aitken to Hughes, 16 November 1916, ibid.
32 Aitken to Hughes (2), 16 November 1916, ibid.
33 Vincent (ed.), *The Crawford Papers*, diary entry for 2 August 1916, p. 358.
34 Quoted in Travis Crosby, *The Unknown Lloyd George: A Statesman in Conflict* (London: I. B. Tauris, 2014), p. 211.
35 Aitken's 'History of the Crisis', probably written (ghosted) in January 1917 can be found in BBK/G/2/31.
36 Bonar Law's account of the fall of the Asquith government, 30 July 1916, BBK/85/A/1, p. 3.
37 Vincent (ed.), *The Crawford Papers*, p. 366.
38 BL/85/A/1, p. 3.
39 Ibid., p. 5.
40 Cecil Harmsworth diary entry for 3 December 1916 quoted in Crosby, *The Unknown Lloyd George*, p. 215.
41 BL/85/A/1, p. 5.
42 Vincent (ed.), *The Crawford Papers*, p. 372.
43 BBK/G/2/31, p. 55a.
44 Vincent (ed.), *The Crawford Papers*, p. 370.
45 Ibid.
46 Adams, *Bonar Law*, p. 231.
47 BL/85/A/1, p. 10.
48 Ibid., p. 11.
49 Asquith to Lloyd George, 4 December 1916, LG/E/2/23/14.
50 Balfour to Asquith, 5 December 1916, British Library, Balfour Papers, Add MS 49692, ff. 184–6.
51 Vincent (ed.), *The Crawford Papers*, p. 374.
52 Ibid.
53 Balfour to Asquith, 5 December 1916, Add MS 49692, ff. 192–5.
54 BL/85/A/1, p. 12.
55 Memorandum of the 1916 government crisis by Balfour, 7 December 1916, Add MS 49692, ff. 198–9.
56 Asquith to Bonar Law, 6 December 1916, BL 81/1/1.
57 Balfour Memorandum, Add MS 49692, ff. 204.
58 Ibid., ff. 208.
59 Beaverbrook, *Politicians and the War*, p. 491.
60 Lloyd George to Aitken, 9 December 1916, BBK/K/1/13.
61 Aitken to Lloyd George, 9 December 1916, LG/F/4/5/1.

Chapter 12: The Lord Beaver
1   Robert Rhodes James (ed.), *Memoirs of a Conservative: J. C. C. Davidson's Memoirs and Papers 1910–37* (London: Weidenfeld & Nicolson, 1969), p. 29.
2   Beaverbrook, *Politicians and the War*, p. 506.
3   Bonar Law to Aitken, 9 December 1916, BBK/K/1/13.
4   Excerpt published in J. Andrew Ross, 'All this Fuss and Feathers', in Colin Coates (ed.), *Majesty in Canada: Essays on the Role of Royalty* (Toronto: The Dundurn Group, 2006), p. 127.
5   Rodolphe Lemieux in Canadian House of Commons, quoted in ibid., p. 128.
6   Stamfordham to Lloyd George, 14 December 1916, LG/F/29/1/2.
7   House of Lords Journal, Die Mercurii, 14 February 1917.
8   Rhodes James (ed.), *Memoirs of a Conservative*, pp. 27–9.
9   Unpublished fragment originally intended for *Politicians and the War*, BBK/G/5/5.
10 Lord Beaverbrook, *Men and Power, 1917–1918* (London: Hutchinson, 1956), p. 43.

11   Rhodes James (ed.), *Memoirs of a Conservative*, p. 58.

12   Ibid., p. 60.

13   Diary of C. P. Scott, entry for 29 August 1917, quoted in Adams, *Bonar Law*, pp. 255–6.

14   Sanders Diaries, entry for 15 June 1917 in John Ramsden (ed.), *Real Old Tory Politics: The Political Diaries of Robert Sanders, Lord Bayford, 1910–1935* (London: Historians' Press, 1984), p. 87.

15   Beaverbrook to Lloyd George, 10 July 1917, LG/F/4/5/9.

16   Beaverbrook to Lloyd George, undated, LG/F/4/5/10.

17   Quoted in Adams, *Bonar Law*, p. 261.

18   Blumenfeld to Beaverbrook, 7 September 1917, BBK/C/45b.

19   CWRO Report, Beaverbrook to Sir Edward Kemp, 30 March 1918, BBK/E/1/20, pp. 6–7.

20   Ibid., p. 9.

21   *Sunday Express*, 29 March 1931.

22   Ibid.

23   Beaverbrook's account, undated, BBK/G/5/17.

24   Guest to Lloyd George, 23 January 1918, LG/F/21/2/11.

25   Beaverbrook to Lloyd George, 20 January 1918, BBK/C/218a.

26   *The Globe, Evening Standard, The Times*, 6 February 1918; *Westminster Gazette*, 7 February 1918.

27   Stamfordham to Guest, 8 February 1918, LG/F/29/2/6a.

28   Lloyd George to Stamfordham, 9 February 1918, LG/F/29/2/6.

29   House of Commons, Official Report, 19 February 1918, col. 657.

30   A copy of the Resolution of Unionist War Committee, dated 19 February 1918, can be found in BBK/C/203b.

31   Taylor, *Beaverbrook*, p. 140.

32   Milner to Lloyd George, 27 February 1918, LG/F/38/3/16.

33   Beaverbrook, *Men and Power*, p. 288.

34   *Sunday Times*, 4 August 1918.

35   'Need for Intelligence Department of Ministry of Information', 20 February 1918, National Archives (hereafter NA), CAB 24/43/2.

36   'Home Propaganda', 22 February 1918, NA, CAB 24/43/3.

37   'Intelligence Requirements of the Ministry of Information – Memorandum by the Secretary of State for Foreign Affairs', 28 February 1918, NA, CAB 24/43/88, G. T. 3788.

38   'Intelligence Bureau of the Department of Information – Memorandum by General Smuts', 15 March 1918, NA, CAB 24/45/39.

39   Lord Robert Cecil to Beaverbrook, 22 March 1918, BBK/E/3/3.

40   'Memorandum of a meeting in First Lord's Room', 12 April 1918, BBK/E/3/3.

41   Davies to Lloyd George, 18 April 1918, LG/F/29/2/21.

42   Cabinet Minute of 18 March 1918, NA, CAB 23/5/58, WC 366.

43   'Memorandum to the War Cabinet on the subject of the Japanese mission', 10 May 1918, NA, CAB 24/51/30, G. T. 4530.

44   Davies to Lloyd George, 28 May 1918, LG/F/29/2/32.

45   Beaverbrook to Lloyd George, 13 June 1918, LG/F/4/5/21.

46   Beaverbrook to Lloyd George, 24 June 1918, LG/F/4/5/25.

47   Balfour to Lloyd George, 12 July 1918, LG/F/3/3/17.

48   Lloyd George to Bonar Law, 29 August 1918, LG/F/30/2/45.

49   Beaverbrook to Lloyd George, 21 October 1918 BBK/C/218a.

Chapter 13: All Change

1   Stanley Salvidge, *Salvidge of Liverpool: Behind the Political Scene, 1890–1928* (London: Hodder & Stoughton, 1934), p. 225.

2   Quoted in Taylor, *Beaverbrook*, p. 168.

3   Lord Beaverbrook, *Politicians and the Press* (London: Hutchinson, 1926), p. 14.

4   Beaverbrook to Churchill, 26 November 1918, BBK/C/85.

5   Beaverbrook, *Politicians and the Press*, p. 14.
6   Artemis Cooper (ed.), *A Durable Fire: The Letters of Duff and Diana Cooper, 1913–1950* (London: Collins, 1983), p. 131.
7   Venetia Montagu to Beaverbrook on various dates, BBK/C/246.
8   Rider to Beaverbrook, 24 January 1919, BBK/H/44.
9   'Circulation Report by J. L. Reeves', January 1919, BBK/H/44.
10   'Memorandum for Mr Blumenfeld from Mrs Alexander', 1 April 1919, ibid.
11   House of Lords, Official Report, 29 October 1919, cols. 74–82.
12   Wm Grogan & Boyd to Beaverbrook, 1 March 1920, BBK/J/55.
13   Healy to Beaverbrook, 13 December 1919, BBK/C/162.
14   Healy to Beaverbrook, 19 November 1920, ibid.
15   Healy to Beaverbrook, 30 November 1920, ibid.
16   Healy to Beaverbrook, 19 November 1920, ibid.
17   Healy to Beaverbrook, 27 April 1921, BBK/C/163.
18   Bonar Law to Lloyd George, 17 March 1921, BL/101/5/58.
19   Beaverbrook, *The Decline and Fall of Lloyd George*, p. 18.
20   Bonar Law to Lloyd George, 19 March 1921, LG/F/31/1/56.
21   Beaverbrook, *Politicians and the Press*, p. 36.
22   Beaverbrook to Bonar Law, undated, BL/107/3/3.
23   Bonar Law to Beaverbrook, 30 April 1921, BBK/C/204b.
24   Quoted in Taylor, *Beaverbrook*, p. 184.
25   Beaverbrook to Bonar Law, dated May 1921, BBK/C/204b.
26   Quoted in Beaverbrook, *The Decline and Fall of Lloyd George*, p. 71.
27   Healy to Beaverbrook, 9 May 1921, BBK/C/163.
28   Healy to Beaverbrook, 28 May 1921, ibid.
29   Keith Middlemas (ed.), *Thomas Jones: Whitehall Diary, Vol. I: 1916–1925* (Oxford: Oxford University Press, 1969), p. 76.
30   Ibid., p. 147.
31   Healy to Beaverbrook, 17 November 1921, BBK/C/163.
32   Healy to Beaverbrook, 1 December 1921, ibid.
33   Beaverbrook to Carrington, 8 December 1954, BBK/B/480.
34   Salvidge, *Salvidge of Liverpool*, p. 225.
35   Beaverbrook, *The Decline and Fall of Lloyd George*, p. 128.
36   Beaverbrook to Foster, 19 April 1922, BBK/A/260.
37   Churchill to Clementine Churchill, 9 August 1922, in M. Gilbert, *WSC Companion, Vol. IV, Part 3*, p. 1952.
38   Beaverbrook, *The Decline and Fall of Lloyd George*, p. 150.
39   Kidd, *The Beaverbrook Girl*, p. 48.
40   *Sunday Express*, 8 October 1922.
41   Rhodes James (ed.), *Memoirs of a Conservative*, p. 120.
42   Beaverbrook, *The Decline and Fall of Lloyd George*, pp. 189–90.
43   Ibid., p. 192.
44   Rhodes James (ed.), *Memoirs of a Conservative*, p. 123.
45   Beaverbrook, *The Decline and Fall of Lloyd George*, p. 198.
46   Vincent (ed.), *The Crawford Diaries*, p. 454.

Chapter 14: From Bonar to Baldwin
1   Beaverbrook in *Daily Express*, 21 May 1923.
2   Beaverbrook, *The Decline and Fall of Lloyd George*, p. 208.
3   Beaverbrook to Bonar Law, 21 October 1922, BBK/G/4/79.
4   *Sunday Express*, 5 November 1922.
5   Guest to Beaverbrook, 5 November 1922, BBK/C/147.
6   Beaverbrook to Guest, 7 November 1922, ibid.

7 Rothermere to Beaverbrook, 26 June 1923, BBK/C/283a.
8 Beaverbrook (unpublished), *The Age of Baldwin*, Chapter 3, p. 2, BBK/G/5/11.
9 Beaverbrook (unpublished and undated), *Bonar Law: The Last Phase*, p. 1, BBK/G/4/75.
10 Austen Chamberlain to Ida Chamberlain, quoted in Adams, *Bonar Law*, p. 356.
11 Neville Chamberlain to Austen Chamberlain, quoted in ibid., p. 357.
12 Beaverbrook, *Bonar Law: The Last Phase*, p. 10, BBK/G/4/75.
13 Rhodes James (ed.), *Memoirs of a Conservative*, p. 149.
14 Middlemas (ed.), *Thomas Jones: Whitehall Diary, Vol. I*, diary entry for 10 June 1923, p. 242.
15 Davidson to Beaverbrook, 11 May 1923, BBK/C/204b.
16 Beaverbrook, *Bonar Law: The Last Phase*, p. 12.
17 Royal Archives, GV K1853/4, quoted in Adams, *Bonar Law*, p. 365.
18 Middlemas (ed.), *Thomas Jones: Whitehall Diary, Vol. I*, diary entry for 5 November 1923, p. 254.
19 Beaverbrook, *Politicians and the Press*, p. 75.
20 Beaverbrook to Morison, 4 May 1951, BBK/C/251.
21 Beaverbrook to Rothermere, 14 November 1923, BBK/C/283a.
22 Beaverbrook to Borden, 16 November 1923, BBK/C/51.
23 Ibid.
24 *Sunday Express*, 17 February 1924.
25 *Sunday Express*, 16 March 1924.
26 *The People*, 18 May 1924.
27 Baldwin to Beaverbrook, 19 May 1924, BBK/C/19.
28 Beaverbrook, *Politicians and the Press*, p. 63.
29 Kenneth Young (ed.), *The Diaries of Sir Robert Bruce Lockhart* (hereafter *RBL Diaries*), *Vol. I, 1915–1938* (London: Macmillan, 1973), diary entry for 11 May 1931, p. 165.
30 William Gerhardie quoted in Dido Davies, *William Gerhardie* (Oxford: Oxford University Press, 1990), p. 151.
31 Lyndsy Spence, 'Doris Delevingne: The Constant Courtesan', in Lyndsy Spence (ed.), *The Mitford Society, Vol. II* (CreateSpace Independent Publishing Platform, 2014), p. 52.
32 Young (ed.), *RBL Diaries, Vol. I*, diary entry for 22 June 1931, p. 175.
33 Quoted in Chisholm and Davie, *Beaverbrook*, p. 251.
34 J. H. Thomas, quoted in Middlemas (ed.), *Whitehall Diary, Vol. I*, p. 299.
35 Beaverbrook to Rothermere, 30 October 1924, BBK/C/283b.
36 Kenneth Young, *Churchill and Beaverbrook: A Study in Friendship and Politics* (London: Eyre & Spottiswoode, 1966), p. 72.
37 Beaverbrook to Gwynne, 15 May 1925, BBK/C/148.
38 Beaverbrook, *Politicians and the Press*, p. 108.
39 Beaverbrook to Brisbane, 30 November 1925, BBK/C/64.
40 Beaverbrook to Healy, 24 May 1926, BBK/C/165.
41 Ibid.
42 Ibid.
43 NA, CAB 23/52/29, CC 29(26), 11 May 1926.
44 Beaverbrook to Churchill, 11 May 1926, BBK/C/85.
45 Beaverbrook to Brisbane, 24 May 1926, BBK/C/64.
46 Churchill to Beaverbrook, 28 December 1926, BBK/C/85.
47 Wood, *The True History of Lord Beaverbrook*, p. 180.
48 Kidd, *The Beaverbrook Girl*, p. 97.

Chapter 15: Gladys and Other Women
1 See Victoria Glendinning, 'Afterword', in Rebecca West, *Sunflower* (London: Virago Press, 2008), p. 270.
2 Quoted in Chisholm and Davie, *Beaverbrook*, p. 55.
3 *Daily Express*, 2 December 1927.
4 Ibid.

5   Gwyn, *Tapestry of War*, p. 338.
6   Quoted in ibid., p. 339.
7   Alfred Shaughnessy (ed.), *Sarah: The Letters and Diaries of a Courtier's Wife, 1906–1936* (London: Peter Owen, 1989), diary entry for 20 July 1918, p. 73.
8   Ibid., diary entry for 21 July 1918.
9   Wolfgang Saxon in *New York Times*, 28 December 1987.
10   Rebecca West to Beaverbrook, 6 September 1918, BBK/E/3/44.
11   Ziegler, Diana Cooper, p. 58.
12   Tallulah Bankhead, *Tallulah: My Autobiography* (London: Gollancz, 1952), p. 156.
13   Ibid., p. 166.
14   Maxwell Beaverbrook in conversation with the author.
15   John Pearson (writing under the pseudonym 'Henry Cloud'), *Barbara Cartland: Crusader in Pink* (London: Weidenfeld & Nicolson, 1979), p. 239.
16   Maximillien De Lafayette, *Louise Brooks: Her Men, Affairs, Scandals and Persona* (New York: Times Square Press, 2011), p. 20.
17   Ibid., p. 23.
18   Louise Brooks speaking in BBC *Arena* documentary, 18 February 1986.
19   *New York Times*, 22 June 2012.
20   http://www.dorothysebastian.com/newyorkcity.
21   Barry Paris, *Louise Brooks* (New York: Knopf, 1989), p. 72.
22   Ibid.
23   Quoted in Victoria Glendinning, *Rebecca West: A Life* (London: Weidenfeld & Nicolson, 1987), p. 91.
24   Rebecca West biographical note, 28 January 1928, quoted in Lorna Gibb, *West's World: The Extraordinary Life of Dame Rebecca West* (London: Macmillan, 2013), p. 92.
25   Gibb, *West's World*, p. 92.
26   Ibid.
27   Ibid.
28   Glendinning, 'Afterword', p. 272.
29   Ibid., p. 273.
30   Rebecca West to Beaverbrook, both undated, BBK/C/322.
31   Glendinning, 'Afterword', p. 273.
32   Glendinning, *Rebecca West*, p. 89.

Chapter 16: Tilting at Windmills

1   *Sunday Express*, 30 June 1929.
2   Newman Flower (ed.), *The Journals of Arnold Bennett, Vol. III: 1921–1928* (London: Cassell, 1933), p. 244.
3   Wood, *The True History of Lord Beaverbrook*, p. 181.
4   Churchill to Beaverbrook, 9 February 1928, BBK/C/86.
5   Beaverbrook to Davidson, 27 May 1928, BBK/C/111.
6   Beaverbrook to Wise, 6 June 1928, BBK/B/34.
7   Lyndsy Spence, 'Doris Delevingne', p. 51.
8   H. G. Wells to Beaverbrook, 9 November 1928, BBK/C/321a.
9   Beaverbrook to H. G. Wells, 3 December 1928, ibid.
10   Quoted in Chisholm and Davie, *Beaverbrook*, p. 263.
11   Young (ed.), *RBL Diaries, Vol. I*, diary entry for 1 September 1928, pp. 70–71.
12   *Daily Express*, 31 December 1928.
13   Beaverbrook to J. M. Patterson, 24 March 1929, BBK/B/112.
14   Beaverbrook to Borden, 26 March 1929, BBK/C/52.
15   Beaverbrook to Lord Daryngton, 28 May 1929, BBK/B/97.
16   *Manchester Guardian*, 5 June 1929.
17   Birkenhead to Beaverbrook, 6 June 1929, BBK/C/41.

18   Beaverbrook to Birkenhead, 7 June 1929, ibid.
19   Birkenhead to Beaverbrook, 11 June 1929, ibid.
20   *Morning Post*, 27 June 1929.
21   *Sunday Express*, 30 June 1929.
22   Beaverbrook to Rothermere, 3 July 1929, BBK/C/284a.
23   *Daily Express*, 6 August 1929.
24   Beaverbrook to Ferguson, 9 August 1929, BBK/B/100.
25   Beaverbrook to Wise, 21 June 1929, BBK/B/121.
26   Jean Norton's Diary – Russia Trip, BBK/K/2/180.
27   Professor Irina Bystrova email to author, 27 March 2015.
28   Jean Norton's Diary – Russia Trip, BBK/K/2/180.
29   Young (ed.), *RBL Diaries, Vol. I*, diary entry for 1 September 1929, p. 106.
30   Beaverbrook to Fielding, 1 November 1929, BBK/B/101.
31   Beaverbrook to Gwynne, 19 February 1930, BBK/C/149.
32   Gwynne to Beaverbrook, 22 February 1930, ibid.
33   *Daily Express*, 28 February 1930.
34   *Daily Express*, 5 March 1930.
35   Beaverbrook to Lord Queenborough, 11 March 1930, BBK/B/171.
36   Davidson to Beaverbrook, 5 March 1930, BBK/C/111.
37   *Daily Express*, 8 March 1930.
38   *The Times*, 25 March 1930.
39   Neville Chamberlain to Beaverbrook, 17 April 1930, BBK/C/80.
40   Beaverbrook to Neville Chamberlain, 20 April 1930, ibid.
41   Rhodes James (ed.), *Memoirs of a Conservative*, p. 342.
42   Baldwin to Beaverbrook, 7 May 1930, BBK/C/19.
43   Beaverbrook to Cravath, 14 May 1930, BBK/K/1/68.
44   Beaverbrook to Ashley, 13 June 1930, BBK/B/125.
45   Beaverbrook to Amery, 12 July 1930, BBK/C/5.
46   Beaverbrook to Bowker, 8 August 1930, BBK/B/132.
47   *Evening Standard*, 16 October 1930.
48   *Daily Express*, 1 November 1930.
49   Beaverbrook to Borden, 7 January 1931, BBK/C/52.
50   Beaverbrook to Brisbane, 13 January 1931, BBK/C/64.
51   Thelma Cazalet statement to Press Association, 5 February 1931, BBK/B/189.
52   Rothermere to Beaverbrook, 2 February 1931, BBK/C/285a.
53   Young (ed.), *RBL Diaries, Vol. I*, diary entry for 5 February 1931, p. 151.
54   *Daily Express*, 17 and 18 February 1931.
55   Beaverbrook to Brisbane, 3 March 1931, BBK/C/64.
56   *Daily Express*, 28 February 1931.
57   Beaverbrook to Duff Cooper, 5 March 1931, BBK/C/257.
58   *The Times*, 18 March 1931.
59   Neville Chamberlain to Beaverbrook, 23 March 1931, BBK/C/80.
60   Neville Chamberlain to Beaverbrook, 26 March 1931; 'Stornoway Pact', 27 March 1931, both in ibid.
61   Young (ed.), *RBL Diaries, Vol. I*, diary entry for 22 November 1930, p. 135.
62   William Gerhardie, *Memoirs of a Polyglot* (London: Duckworth, 1931), p. 249.

Chapter 17: No More War

1   *Daily Express*, 18 October 1935.
2   *Daily Express*, 30 March 1931.
3   Beaverbrook to Rothermere, 30 March 1931, BBK/C/285a.
4   Beaverbrook to Elizabeth Healy, 2 September 1932, BBK/C/166b.
5   Beaverbrook to Sister Bernard (Healy), 14 September 1932, ibid.

6   *Sunday Express*, 29 March 1931.

7   Nigel Nicolson (ed.), *The Harold Nicolson Diaries, 1907–1964* (London: Weidenfeld & Nicolson, 2004), diary entry for 29 April 1931, p. 78.

8   Beaverbrook to von Mueller, 12 May 1931, BBK/B/202.

9   Beaverbrook to Thannhauser, 2 June 1931, BBK/B/205.

10   Young (ed.), *RBL Diaries, Vol. I*, diary entry for 26 May 1931, pp. 168–9.

11   Ibid., 27 July 1931, p. 179.

12   Ibid., diary entry for 24 June 1931, p. 176.

13   Ibid., diary entry for 28 July 1931, p. 180.

14   Ibid., diary entry for 31 August 1931, p. 182.

15   *Daily Express*, 4 September 1931.

16   Ibid., 15 September 1931.

17   Ibid., 18 September 1931.

18   Ibid., 7 October 1931.

19   'The Nation's Duty: Stanley Baldwin's Election Message', http://www.conservativemanifesto.com/1931/1931-conservative-manifesto.shtml.

20   Beaverbrook to Bridgeman, 12 November 1931.

21   Lord Beaverbrook, *Friends: Sixty Years of Intimate Personal Relations with Richard Bedford Bennett* (London: Heinemann, 1959), pp. 69–70.

22   Beaverbrook to Brisbane, 20 October 1932, BBK/C/64.

23   Ibid.

24   *Daily Express*, 18 February 1933.

25   Ibid., 27 March 1933.

26   Beaverbrook to Cox, 27 December 1933, BBK/A/272.

27   *Daily Express*, 26 June 1933.

28   Ibid., 9 October 1933.

29   Young (ed.), *RBL Diaries, Vol. I*, diary entry for 3 July 1934, p. 299.

30   Beaverbrook to Glover, 7 September 1934, BBK/B/279.

31   Gabriel Gorodetsky (ed.), *The Maisky Diaries: Red Ambassador to the Court of St James, 1932–1943* (Yale University Press, 2015), diary entry for 7 October 1937.

32   Ibid., p. 50.

33   Churchill to Clementine Churchill, 2 March 1935, quoted in Martin Gilbert, *Churchill: A Life* (London: Heinemann, 1991), p. 540.

Chapter 18: 'God Save Our King from Baldwin'

1   Beaverbrook to Churchill quoted in Taylor, *Beaverbrook*, p. 370; see also Beaverbrook's *The Abdication Crisis* (draft dated 16 December 1936), p. 53, BBK/G/6/10.

2   R. A. Butler, *The Art of the Possible* (London: Hamish Hamilton, 1971), p. 57.

3   Quoted in John Charmley, *Churchill: The End of Glory* (London: Hodder & Stoughton, 1993), p. 202.

4   *Daily Express*, 27 September and 30 September 1935.

5   *Daily Express*, 29 June 1935.

6   Beaverbrook to Samuel, 2 November 1935, BBK/B/285.

7   *Daily Express*, 7 November 1935.

8   Beaverbrook to Doidge, 25 November 1935, BBK/C/117.

9   Beaverbrook to Hoare, 14 December 1935, BBK/C/307b.

10   NA, CAB 23/90B/10, CM 56(35), 18 December 1935.

11   *Daily Express*, 20 December 1935.

12   Beaverbrook to Dennis, 13 June 1936, BBK/B/287.

13   Beaverbrook, *The Abdication of King Edward VIII* (New York: Atheneum, 1966), p. 19.

14   Adrian Phillips, *The King Who Had To Go: Edward VIII, Mrs Simpson and the Hidden Politics of the Abdication Crisis* (London: Biteback Publishing, 2016), p. 8.

15   Beaverbrook to Bergen, 9 March 1936, BBK/B/287.

16   *Sunday Express*, 15 March 1936.

17   *Sunday Express*, 22 March 1936.

18   Beaverbrook to Viscount Chaplain, 25 March 1936, BBK/B/287.

19   Gorodetsky (ed.), *The Maisky Diaries*, diary entry for 8 March 1936, p. 66.

20   MI5 report on Ribbentrop's organisation, quoted in Karina Urbach, *Go-Betweens for Hitler* (Oxford: Oxford University Press, 2015), p. 184.

21   Ribbentrop to Beaverbrook, 14 June 1936, BBK/C/275.

22   Ribbentrop to Beaverbrook, 24 July 1936, ibid.

23   Urbach, *Go-Betweens for Hitler*, pp. 167–8.

24   Beaverbrook to Ribbentrop, 12 August 1936, BBK/C/275.

25   Beaverbrook to Lloyd George, 6 October 1936, BBK/C/218b.

26   *Daily Express*, 6 November 1936.

27   *Daily Express*, 14 November 1936.

28   Quoted in Philip Ziegler, *King Edward VIII* (London: Collins, 1990), p. 292.

29   *The Abdication Crisis*, pp. 1–2, BBK/G/6/10.

30   *The Times*, 28 October 1936.

31   *The Abdication Crisis*, p. 6, BBK/G/6/10.

32   Quoted in Michael Bloch, *The Reign and Abdication of King Edward VIII* (London: Bantam Press, 1990), p. 68.

33   Whelan to Beaverbrook, 17 November 1936, BBK/G/6/4.

34   Monckton to Beaverbrook, 18 November 1936, ibid.

35   Quoted in Bloch, *The Reign and Abdication of King Edward VIII*, pp. 70–71.

36   Duchess of Windsor, quoted in ibid., p. 75.

37   *The Abdication Crisis*, pp. 19–20., BBK/G/6/10.

38   John Julius Norwich (ed.), *The Duff Cooper Diaries, 1915–1951* (London: Weidenfeld & Nicolson, 2005), p. 234.

39   Duke of Windsor, quoted in Bloch, *The Reign and Abdication of King Edward VIII*, p. 126.

40   *The Abdication Crisis*, pp. 28–9, BBK/G/6/10.

41   Robert Rhodes James (ed.), *Chips: The Diaries of Sir Henry Channon* (London: Weidenfeld & Nicolson, 1967), diary entry for 1 December 1936.

42   Quoted in Bloch, *The Reign and Abdication of King Edward VIII*, p. 142.

43   Ibid., p. 135.

44   Ibid.

45   *The Abdication Crisis*, pp. 33–4, BBK/G/6/10.

46   Leo Amery, quoted in Bloch, *The Reign and Abdication of King Edward VIII*, p. 167.

47   *The Abdication Crisis*, p. 43, BBK/G/6/10.

48   Ibid., p. 45.

49   Ibid., p. 48.

50   Ibid., p. 49.

Chapter 19: Jean and Other Women

1   Harriet Cohen to Beaverbrook, 5 December 1928, BBK/B/27.

2   The description by Sir Anthony Havelock-Allan appears in http://www.artwarefineart.com/gallery/portrait-richard-henry-brinsely-6th-lord-grantley-baron-markenfield-1892-1954.

3   Alastair Forbes in *The Spectator*, 3 October 1992.

4   Lady Pamela Hicks, *Daughter of Empire: Life as a Mountbatten* (London: Weidenfeld & Nicolson, 2012), pp. 11–12.

5   Duff Hart-Davis (ed.), *End of an Era: Letters & Journals of Sir Alan Lascelles from 1887 to 1920* (London: Hamish Hamilton, 1988), p. 86.

6   Jane Mulvagh in *Daily Telegraph*, 1 June 2008.

7   Arnold Bax to Harriet Cohen, 9 March 1919, quoted in Helen Fry, *Music and Men: The Life and Loves of Harriet Cohen* (London: The History Press, 2008), p. 83.

8   Harriet Cohen to Beaverbrook, various letters written in autumn 1928, BBK/B/27.

9   Jeffrey Potter, *Men, Money & Magic: The Story of Dorothy Schiff* (New York: Coward, McCann & Geoghegan, 1976), p. 81.
10 Ibid.
11 Ibid., p. 84.
12 Ibid., p. 85.
13 Ibid., p. 86.
14 Jean Norton diary entry for 29 September 1931, BBK/K/2/182.
15 Jean-Noël Liaut, *The Many Lives of Miss K: Toto Koopman – Model, Muse, Spy* (New York: Rizzoli Ex Libris, 2013), p. 24.
16 Ibid., p. 59.
17 Ibid., p. 67.
18 Quoted in Chisholm and Davie, *Beaverbrook*, p. 344.
19 Ibid.
20 Lily Ernst to Beaverbrook, 14 April 1937, BBK/B/291.
21 Lily Ernst to Beaverbrook, 1 May 1938, BBK/B/293.
22 Ibid.
23 Quoted in Chisholm and Davie, *Beaverbrook*, p. 346.
24 Ibid.
25 Kidd, *The Beaverbrook Girl*, p. 171.

Chapter 20: From Isolation to Treason and Back

1   Gorodetsky (ed.), *The Maisky Diaries*, diary entry for 15 November 1939, p. 239.
2   Beaverbrook to Matthews, 15 May 1937, BBK/B/291.
3   Nicolson (ed.), *The Harold Nicolson Diaries*, diary entry for 27 May 1937, p. 175.
4   *Daily Express*, 29 May 1937.
5   Whelan to A. J. Cummings, 27 March 1937, BBK/C/104.
6   Beaverbrook to Robertson, 20 August 1937, BBK/H/109.
7   *Daily Express*, 5 November 1937.
8   *Daily Express*, 7 January 1938 and 9 May 1938.
9   *Daily Express*, 8 March 1938.
10 Rhodes James (ed.), *Chips: The Diaries of Sir Henry Channon*, diary entry for 26 February 1938, p. 147.
11 Beaverbrook to Swope, 9 March 1938, BBK/B/294.
12 Beaverbrook to Governor Cox, 7 March 1938, BBK/B/292.
13 Nicolson (ed.), *The Harold Nicolson Diaries*, diary entry for 6 June 1938, p. 189.
14 *Sunday Express*, 13 March 1938.
15 Beaverbrook to A. J. Cummings, 16 March 1938, BBK/C/104.
16 Beaverbrook to Dr Cox, 1 June 1938, BBK/A/276.
17 *Daily Express*, 23 June 1938.
18 *Daily Express*, 1 September 1938.
19 Beaverbrook to Gannett, 7 September 1938, BBK/B/293.
20 Beaverbrook to Neville Chamberlain, 16 September 1938, BBK/C/80.
21 Henderson to Foreign Office, 6 September 1938, NA, FO/371/21737.
22 *Daily Express*, 22 September 1938.
23 *Daily Express*, 29 September 1938.
24 *Daily Express*, 1 October 1938.
25 Beaverbrook to Agate, 5 October 1938, BBK/B/292.
26 Beaverbrook to Gannett, 9 December 1938, BBK/B/293.
27 Michael Wardell quoted in Martin Gilbert, *Finest Hour: Winston S. Churchill, 1939–1941* (London: Heinemann, 1983), pp. 14–15.
28 Beaverbrook to Patterson, 23 February 1939, BBK/B/268.
29 Gorodetsky (ed.), *The Maisky Diaries*, diary entry for 9 March 1939, p. 162.
30 Ibid.

31   Beaverbrook to Macdonald, 15 March 1939, BBK/A/277.
32   Ribbentrop to Beaverbrook, 15 March 1939, BBK/C/275.
33   Beaverbrook to Ribbentrop, 28 March 1939, ibid.
34   *Sunday Express*, 2 April 1939.
35   Quoted in Chisholm and Davie, *Beaverbrook*, p. 356.
36   Taylor, Beaverbrook, p. 393.
37   Beaverbrook to Hoare, 30 October 1939, BBK/C/308a.
38   Roosevelt to Beaverbrook, 14 December 1939, BBK/C/277.
39   Gorodetsky (ed.), *The Maisky Diaries*, diary entry for 15 November 1939, p. 239.
40   British Library, Harvey papers, Peake to Harvey, 26 January 1940, Add MS 56402.
41   Robert Self (ed.), *The Neville Chamberlain Diary Letters, Vol. IV: The Downing Street Years, 1934–1940* (Aldershot: Ashgate, 2005), pp. 492–4.
42   Beaverbrook to Stern, 2 March 1940, BBK/B/302.
43   John McGovern, *Neither Fear nor Favour* (London: Blandford Press, 1960), p. 2.
44   Liddell Hart Centre for Military Archives, King's College, London: LH 11/1940/15, 'Sundry Notes, March 6th, 7th & 8th'.
45   Beaverbrook to Lloyd-Jones, 17 April 1940, BBK/A/278.
46   Beaverbrook to Lord Davies, 7 May 1940, BBK/B/300.
47   *Daily Express*, 6 May 1940.
48   Neville Chamberlain to Beaverbrook, 6 May 1940, BBK/C/80.
49   Beaverbrook to Neville Chamberlain, 8 May 1940, ibid.
50   Nicolson (ed.), *The Harold Nicolson Diaries*, diary entry for 8 May 1940, p. 244.
51   Sir Alexander Cadogan diary entry for 9 May 1940 quoted in Martin Gilbert, *The Churchill War Papers: Volume 1, At the Admiralty, September 1939–May 1940* (New York: W. W. Norton & Co., 1993), p. 1259.
52   Randolph Churchill 'recollection' in ibid., p. 1266.
53   *Daily Express*, 10 May 1940.
54   Neville Chamberlain to Beaverbrook, 10 May 1940, BBK/C/80.
55   John Wheeler-Bennett, *King George VI: His Life and Reign* (London: Macmillan, 1958), p. 443.

Chapter 21: Die Luftschlacht um England

1   Churchill to Beaverbrook, 3 December 1940, BBK/D/415.
2   Quoted in Gilbert, *Finest Hour*, p. 316.
3   Taylor, *Beaverbrook*, pp. 413–4.
4   Winston S. Churchill, *The Second World War, Vol. II: Their Finest Hour* (London: Cassell, 1949), pp. 286–7.
5   Quoted in Taylor, *Beaverbrook*, p. 415.
6   Lord Tedder, *With Prejudice* (London: Cassell, 1966), pp. 14–16.
7   Sir John Slessor, *The Central Blue* (London: Cassell, 1956), p. 308.
8   M. M. Postan, *British War Production* (London: HMSO, 1952), p. 116.
9   J. D. Scott and Richard Hughes, *Administration of War Production* (London: HMSO, 1955), p. 389.
10   A. J. Robertson, 'Lord Beaverbrook and the Supply of Aircraft 1940–1941', in Anthony Slaven and Derek H. Aldcroft (eds), *Business, Banking and Urban History: Essays in Honour of S. G. Checkland* (Edinburgh: John Donald 1982), p. 87.
11   Ibid.
12   Ibid., p. 88.
13   Scott and Hughes, *Administration of War Production*, p. 389.
14   Sebastian Ritchie, *Industry and Power: The Expansion of British Aircraft Production, 1935–1941* (London: Frank Cass, 1997), p. 229.
15   Kenneth O. Morgan, *Michael Foot: A Life* (London: HarperCollins, 2007), p. 75.
16   Ibid.
17   Ibid., p. 77.
18   Churchill, *The Second World War, Vol. II: Their Finest Hour*, p. 286.
19   Gilbert, *Finest Hour*, p. 534.

20 Ibid., p. 539.
21 Ibid.
22 Ibid., p. 547.
23 Ibid., p. 548.
24 Draft Report to the War Cabinet, 18 June 1940, BBK/D/362.
25 Beaverbrook to Churchill, 30 June 1940, BBK/D/414.
26 Churchill to Beaverbrook, 1 July 1940, ibid.
27 Beaverbrook to Churchill, 1 July 1940, ibid.
28 Beaverbrook to Churchill, 29 July 1940, ibid.
29 Alex Danchev and Daniel Todman (eds), *Field Marshall Lord Alanbrooke: War Diaries 1939–1945* (London: Weidenfeld & Nicolson, 2001), p. 98.
30 Ibid., p. 100.
31 Beaverbrook to Churchill, 2 December 1940, BBK/D/415.
32 Churchill to Beaverbrook, 3 December 1940, ibid.
33 Churchill to Beaverbrook, 15 December 1940, ibid.
34 Beaverbrook to Churchill, 3 January 1941, BBK/D/416.
35 Churchill to Beaverbrook, 3 January 1941, ibid.
36 Beaverbrook to Churchill, 6 January 1941, ibid.
37 Churchill to Beaverbrook, 7 January 1941, ibid.
38 Beaverbrook to Churchill, 15 April 1941, ibid.
39 Beaverbrook to Churchill, 1 May 1941, BBK/D/417.

Chapter 22: Enter the Bear

1   Following the end of the Second World War, David Farrer wrote a narrative entitled 'The Second Front' based upon material he had collected in consultation with Beaverbrook. It was intended that it would be published as a book, but for unknown reasons it never progressed beyond an unedited typescript. A copy can be found in BBK/D/451. This quote appears on p. 19.
2   John Colville, *The Fringes of Power: Downing Street Diaries, 1939–1955* (London: Hodder & Stoughton, 1985), p. 405.
3   Gorodetsky (ed.), *The Maisky Diaries*, diary entry for 21 June 1941, p. 364.
4   Ibid., p. 367.
5   'The Second Front', p. 1.
6   Gorodetsky (ed.), *The Maisky Diaries*, diary entry for 22 September 1941, p. 366.
7   'The Second Front', p. 4.
8   Beaverbrook to Churchill, 2 June 1941, BBK/D/417.
9   Gorodetsky (ed.), *The Maisky Diaries*, diary entry for 3 June 1941, p. 357.
10 Beaverbrook to Churchill, 27 June 1941, BBK/D/417.
11 Beaverbrook to Duncan, 27 June 1941; Duncan to Beaverbrook, 27 June 1941; Churchill to Beaverbrook, 28 June 1941, ibid.
12 Beaverbrook to Churchill, 17 July 1941, BBK/D/418.
13 NA, CAB 66/18/26, WP (41) 203, telegram 24.
14 NA, CAB 65/19/23, WM (41) 87, 28 August 1941; Eden to Churchill, 28 August 1941, NA PREM 3/401/7.
15 Churchill to Beaverbrook, 30 August 1941, BBK/D/94.
16 Churchill to Beaverbrook, Ismay and Cadogan, 3 September 1941, NA CAB 120/36.
17 Gorodetsky (ed.), *The Maisky Diaries*, diary entry for 4 September 1941, p. 384.
18 Ibid., p. 385.
19 NA, CAB 65/23/14, WM (41) 90, 'Confidential Annex', 5 September 1941.
20 Gorodetsky (ed.), *The Maisky Diaries*, diary entry for 4 September 1941, p. 385.
21 NA CAB 65/23/14, WM (41) 90, 'Confidential Annex', 5 September 1941.
22 Gorodetsky (ed.), *The Maisky Diaries*, diary entry for 2 June 1941, p. 356.
23 Peter Padfield, *Hess, Hitler and Churchill* (London: Icon Books, 2013), p. 206.
24 Hess to Beaverbrook, 4 September 1941, BBK/D/443.

25 W. Averell Harriman and Elie Abel, *Special Envoy to Churchill and Stalin, 1941–1946* (London: Hutchinson, 1976), p. 78.

26 Ibid.

27 Ibid.

28 Ibid.

29 NA, CAB 65/23/18, WM (41) 94, 'Confidential Annex', 18 September 1941; NA, CAB 69/3, DO (41) 11, 'Conference on British-United States Production and Assistance to Russia', report by the chairman of the British representatives, 22 September 1941; for the minutes of the Defence Committee meeting see NA, CAB 69/2, DO (41) 62, 19 September 1941.

30 Harold Balfour, 'Moscow Diary', diary entry for 26 September 1941, BAL/1.

31 'Guide For Lord Beaverbrook', 19 September 1941, NA, PREM 3/401/7.

32 Churchill to Stalin, 21 September 1941, ibid.

33 *Daily Express*, 20 September 1941.

34 Balfour, 'Moscow Diary', diary entry for 21 September 1941, BAL/1.

35 'The Second Front', p. 19.

36 Harriman and Abel, *Special Envoy*, p. 85.

37 Gabriel Gorodetsky (ed.), *Stafford Cripps in Moscow 1940–1942: Diaries and Papers* (London: Vallentine Mitchell, 2007), diary entry for 18 September 1941, p. 162.

38 Macfarlane to Maj-Gen F. H. Davidson, 22 September 1941, BBK/D/90.

39 Harriman and Abel, *Special Envoy*, p. 84.

40 Ibid.

41 Gorodetsky (ed.), *Stafford Cripps in Moscow*, diary entry for 29 September 1941, p. 168.

42 Harriman and Abel, *Special Envoy*, p. 86.

43 The 'Moscow Narrative', 28 September 1941, p. 26, BBK/D/100.

44 Harriman and Abel, *Special Envoy*, p. 88.

45 Gorodetsky (ed.), *Stafford Cripps in Moscow*, diary entry for 29 September 1941, p. 169.

46 Harriman and Abel, *Special Envoy*, p. 89.

47 'Moscow Narrative', 28 September 1941, p. 35.

48 Harriman and Abel, *Special Envoy*, p. 89.

49 Ibid., p. 90.

50 Ben Pimlott (ed.), *The Second World War Diary of Hugh Dalton, 1940–45* (London: Jonathan Cape, 1986), diary entry for 29 January 1942, p. 357.

51 'Moscow Narrative', 30 September 1941, p. 43.

52 Ibid., p. 50.

53 Gorodetsky (ed.), *Stafford Cripps in Moscow*, p. 171.

54 'Moscow Narrative', 30 September 1941, p. 56.

55 Gorodetsky (ed.), *Stafford Cripps in Moscow*, diary entry for 1 October 1941, p. 175.

56 Harriman and Abel, *Special Envoy*, pp. 100–101.

57 Ibid.

Chapter 23: The Yanks Are Coming

1   Beaverbrook in conversation with Maisky in Gorodetsky (ed.), *The Maisky Diaries*, diary entry for 12 November 1941, p. 405.

2   Churchill to Beaverbrook, 3 October 1941, NA CAB 120/38.

3   Kenneth Young (ed.), *The Diaries of Sir Robert Bruce Lockhart: Volume II, 1939–1965* (London: Macmillan, 1980), diary entry for 19 October 1941, p. 123.

4   Gorodetsky (ed.), *The Maisky Diaries*, diary entry for 12 October 1941, p. 394.

5   *The Listener*, 16 October 1941.

6   NA, CAB 69/2, DO (41) 65, 17 October 1941; 'Assistance to Russia', memorandum by Lord Beaverbrook, NA, CAB 69/3, 19 October 1941.

7   David Dilks (ed.), *The Diaries of Sir Alexander Cadogan OM, 1938–1945* (London: Cassell, 1971), diary entry for 20 October 1941, p. 409.

8   NA, CAB 69/8, DO (41) 67, 20 October 1941.

9   Beaverbrook to Churchill, 25 October 1941, BBK/D/419.
10 Beaverbrook to Churchill, 25 October 1941, CHAR 20/20/61.
11 Young (ed.), *RBL Diaries, Vol. II*, 19 and 20 October 1941, pp. 123–4.
12 *The Times*, 29 October 1941.
13 Foreign Office telegram No. 4915, Washington to Foreign Office, 30 October 1941, BBK/D/419.
14 Beaverbrook to Churchill, 10 November 1941, BBK/D/419.
15 Beaverbrook to Sir John Anderson, 4 December 1941, BBK/D/82.
16 'The American-British Production Programme 1942', 27 December 1941, BBK/D/117.
17 Dorling to Beaverbrook, 10 January 1942, BBK/D/113.
18 Churchill to Beaverbrook, 12 January 1942, BBK/D/419.
19 Harriman and Abel, *Special Envoy*, pp. 125–6, f20.
20 Beaverbrook to Hoare, 17 February 1942, BBK/C/308b.
21 Beaverbrook's account of his resignation in February 1942, 28 February 1942, p. 14, BBK/D/448.
22 Ibid.
23 Ibid.
24 Ibid., p. 15.
25 John Bew, *Citizen Clem* (London: Quercus, 2016), p. 282.
26 Beaverbrook to Churchill, 18 February 1942, BBK/D/419.
27 Beaverbrook to Churchill, 26 February 1942, BBK/D/420.
28 Churchill to Beaverbrook, 27 February 1942, ibid.
29 Quoted in Bew, *Citizen Clem*, p. 283.
30 *The Times*, 20 February 1942.
31 Churchill to Hopkins, 19 March 1942, BBK/D/420.
32 'The Second Front', p. 33, BBK/D/451.
33 *Daily Express*, 31 March 1942.
34 White House Usher's Log, entry for 31 March 1942, see www.fdrlibrary.marist.edu/daybyday.
35 Roosevelt to Beaverbrook, 3 April 1942, BBK/C/277.
36 Roosevelt to Churchill, 1 April 1942, Roosevelt Archive, Map Room Papers, 1941–1945.
37 Speech to the American Newspaper Publishers Association, 23 April 1942, p. 4, BBK/F/47.
38 Ibid., p. 10.
39 Lord Halifax Diary, diary entry for 24 April 1942. The diary can be accessed via the University of York's Digital Library.
40 Danchev and Todman (eds), *Alanbrooke*, p. 249.
41 P. M. H. Bell, *John Bull and the Bear* (London: Edward Arnold, 1990), p. 77.
42 *The Times*, 12 June 1942.
43 'The Second Front', pp. 52–3, BBK/D/451.
44 Beaverbrook to Hoare 2 February 1943, BBK/C/308b.
45 James Stuart, *Within the Fringe* (London: The Bodley Head, 1967), p. 157.
46 House of Lords, Official Report, 3 February 1943.
47 House of Lords, Official Report, 23 February 1943.
48 Roosevelt to Beaverbrook, 24 March 1943, BBK/C/277.
49 John Harvey (ed.), *The War Diaries of Oliver Harvey, 1941–1945* (London: Collins, 1978), diary entry for 13 April 1943, p. 244.
50 White House Usher's Log for 12 May 1943.
51 Churchill to Attlee, 13 May 1943, CHAR 20/128, in Martin Gilbert and Larry P. Arnn (eds), *The Churchill Documents, Vol. 18: One Continent Redeemed, January–August 1943* (Hillsdale College Press, 2015), p. 1289.
52 David Farrer, *G – for God Almighty* (New York: Stein and Day, 1969), p. 115.
53 Ibid., p. 116.
54 Roosevelt to Beaverbrook, 17 June 1943, BBK/C/277.
55 Harriman and Abel, *Special Envoy*, pp. 216–7.
56 House of Commons, Official Report, 21 September 1943, col. 97.
57 'The Second Front', pp. 75–6, BBK/D/451.

Chapter 24: Keeper of the Seal

1   Beaverbrook to Lady Diana Cooper, early in 1945, quoted in Chisholm and Davie, *Beaverbrook*, p. 452.
2   Sir Peter Masefield and Bill Gunston, *Flight Path* (Shrewsbury, Airlife Publishing, 2002), p. 89.
3   Beaverbrook to Baring, 2 October 1943, BBK/B/314.
4   Rhodes James (ed.), *Chips: The Diaries of Sir Henry Channon*, diary entry for 3 February 1943, p. 349.
5   Jonathan Schneer, *Ministers at War: Winston Churchill and His War Cabinet* (London: Oneworld Publications, 2015), p. 176.
6   Beaverbrook to Morrison, 23 November 1942, BBK/C/253.
7   Schneer, *Ministers at War*, p. 176.
8   Masefield and Gunston, *Flight Path*, p. 89.
9   Ibid., p. 91.
10 Ibid., p. 108.
11 Lord Moran, *Winston Churchill: The Struggle for Survival 1940–1965* (London: Constable, 1966), p. 150.
12 Harold Macmillan, *War Diaries: The Mediterranean, 1943–1945* (London: Macmillan, 1984), p. 338, f13.
13 Colville, *Fringes of Power*, p. 458.
14 Moran, *Churchill: The Struggle for Survival*, p. 156.
15 Ibid.
16 Masefield and Gunston, *Flight Path*, p. 107.
17 House of Lords, Official Report, 19 January 1944, col. 461.
18 Ibid., col. 467.
19 Beaverbrook to Churchill, 20 January 1944, BBK/D/421.
20 Sir Ronald Lindsey quoted in Albin Krebs's obituary of Berle, which appeared in the *New York Times* on 19 February 1971.
21 Alan P. Dobson, *FDR and Civil Aviation* (London: Palgrave Macmillan, 2011), p. 165.
22 Foot to Beaverbrook, undated but probably June 1944, BBK/C/136.
23 Dobson, *FDR and Civil Aviation*, p. 194.
24 Masefield and Gunston, *Flight Path*, p. 130.
25 House of Lords, Official Report, 12 October 1944, col. 514.
26 NA, CAB 65/44/19, WM(44)148, 8 November 1944.
27 Masefield and Gunston, *Flight Path*, p. 137.
28 Roosevelt to Churchill, 21 November 1944, FDR Archive: Map Room Papers, Box 7.
29 NA, CAB 65/44/24, WM(44)153, 22 November 1944.
30 Roosevelt to Winant, 24 November 1944, FDR Archive: Map Room Papers, Box 7.
31 Beaverbrook to Keynes, 10 March 1944, BBK/D/138.
32 Beaverbrook to Churchill, 7 December 1944, BBK/D/422.
33 Beaverbrook to Eden, 26 August 1944, BBK/D/427.
34 Attlee to Churchill, 19 July 1945, quoted in Kenneth Harris, *Attlee* (London: Weidenfeld & Nicolson, 1984), pp. 242–3.
35 Churchill to Attlee quoted in ibid., p. 244.
36 Beaverbrook to Lady Diana Cooper, as in note 1 above.
37 Ibid., p. 451.

Chapter 25: Lily and Other Women

1   Lily Ernst to Foot about Beaverbrook, quoted in Simon Hoggart and David Leigh, *Michael Foot: A Portrait* (London: Hodder & Stoughton, 1981), p. 85.
2   Foot, quoted in ibid.
3   As in note 1 above.
4   Beaverbrook to Millar, undated but certainly July 1943, BBK/J/66.
5   Sally Bedell Smith, *Reflected Glory: The Life of Pamela Churchill Harriman* (London: Simon & Schuster, 1997), p. 75.
6   Ibid., p. 78.

7   Ibid.
8   Ibid., p. 76.
9   J. Littlewood, *My Lady Vine*, p. 195.
10 Alastair Forbes in *The Spectator*, 3 October 1992.
11 Josephine Yorke (née Rosenberg) in interview with the author, 23 June 2017.
12 Anne Sharpley, 'The Enchanter', in Gourlay (ed.), *The Beaverbrook I Knew*, p. 220.

Chapter 26: Farewell to Politics
1   Beaverbrook made the remark during the course of a radio broadcast in which he reviewed Stanley Morison's *History of The Times* for the BBC Home Service on 25 May 1952. A copy of the talk, which had originally been delivered as a television lecture transmitted from the BBC's Lime Grove Studios on 14 May 1952, can be found in BBK/K/2/35.
2   *Manchester Guardian*, 23 May 1945.
3   Winant to Secretary of State, 1 July 1945, quoted in Bew, *Citizen Clem*, p. 345.
4   *Manchester Guardian*, 13 June 1945.
5   *Daily Express*, 5 June 1945.
6   *The Times*, 6 June 1945.
7   Michael Newman, *Laski: A Political Biography* (Pontypool: Merlin Press, 2009).
8   *Daily Express*, 16 June 1945.
9   Ibid.
10 *Daily Express*, 21 June 1945.
11 Bew, *Citizen Clem*, p. 345.
12 *Daily Express*, 28 June 1945.
13 *Daily Express*, 11 June 1945; *Manchester Guardian*, 12 June 1945.
14 Beaverbrook to Joe Paterson, 15 June 1945, BBK/B/326.f15.
15 *Daily Herald*, 15 June 1945.
16 *Reynolds News*, 10 June 1945.
17 *Manchester Guardian*, 21 June 1945.
18 *Manchester Guardian*, 23 June 1945.
19 Beaverbrook to Churchill, 4 July 1945, BBK/D/423.
20 Beaverbrook to Bickell, 31 July 1945, BBK/A/227.
21 Robertson to Beaverbrook, 6 October 1945, BBK/H/117.
22 Beaverbrook to Assheton, 1 February 1946, BBK/C/96.
23 Beaverbrook's 'Declaration of Intent' to take up residence in Canada can be found in BBK/H/400.
24 Beaverbrook's evidence to the Royal Commission on the Press of 18 March 1948 can be found in BBK/H/37.
25 Morison to Beaverbrook, 27 June 1948, BBK/C/251.
26 Quoted in Taylor, *Beaverbrook*, p. 591.
27 Beaverbrook, quoted in Moran, *Winston Churchill*, p. 333.
28 A copy of the agreement for Beaverbrook to acquire the Lloyd George Papers, dated 15 June 1950, is found in BBK/G/14/2.
29 Beaverbrook speech from Lime Grove Studios, 14 May 1952, BBK/K/2/35.
30 Beaverbrook speech from Broadcasting House, 25 May 1952, BBK/K/2/35.
31 Driberg to Beaverbrook, 10 June 1952; Beaverbrook to Driberg, 16 June 1952, BBK/C/122.
32 Beaverbrook to Driberg, 14 July 1954, BBK/C/123.
33 Millar to Driberg, 3 June 1955, ibid.
34 Colville, *The Fringes of Power*, p. 668.
35 Ibid.
36 Ibid., p. 669.
37 Gilbert, *Churchill: A Life*, p. 913.

Chapter 27: Sunset
1   Beaverbrook to Gordon, undated, BBK/H/195.

2   Ann Moyal, *Breakfast with Beaverbrook: Memoirs of an Independent Woman* (Sydney: Hale and Iremonger, 1995), p. 54.

3   Ibid., pp. 56–7.

4   Ann Moyal, 'The History Man', *History Today*, Vol. 61, No. 1 (2011), p. 17.

5   John Reid, 'A Conversation with Ann Moyal, Lord Beaverbrook's Researcher', *Journal of New Brunswick Studies*, Vol. 7, No. 2 (2016), p. 50.

6   Moyal, *Breakfast with Beaverbrook*, p. 69.

7   Ibid., p. 72.

8   Ibid., p. 83.

9   Robin Esser was speaking during a Symposium of former Express Newspaper journalists chaired by the author at the House of Lords on 29 July 2015.

10   Josephine Yorke in interview with Joanna Stephens, 23 June 2017.

11   Josephine Yorke in interview with author, 29 May 2018.

12   *The Observer*, 28 October 1956.

13   *The Listener*, 13 July 1972.

14   Beaverbrook to Eden, 23 January 1957, BBK/C/17.

15   Beaverbrook to Bracken, 2 December 1956, BBK/C/58.

16   Bracken to Beaverbrook, 7 December 1956, BBK/C/58.

17   Beaverbrook to Howard, 16 January 1957, BBK/C/179b.

18   Churchill to Beaverbrook, 18 September 1955, quoted in Martin Gilbert, *Winston S. Churchill: Never Despair, 1945–1965* (London: Heinemann, 1988), p. 1162.

19   Churchill to Beaverbrook, 6 October 1955, ibid.

20   Anthony Montague Browne, *Long Sunset: Memoirs of Winston Churchill's Last Private Secretary* (London: Cassell, 1995), p. 216.

21   Beaverbrook to Millar, 27 October 1955, BBK/C/89.

22   Beaverbrook, *Courage* (London: Collins, 1962).

23   Richard Cockett (ed.), *My Dear Max: The Letters of Brendan Bracken to Lord Beaverbrook, 1925–1958* (London: Historians' Press, 1990), p. 188.

24   Beaverbrook to Bevan, 4 December 1958, BBK/C/37.

25   Francis Williams, *Nothing So Strange: An Autobiography* (London: Cassell, 1970), pp. 301–3.

26   Christiansen to Beaverbrook, 29 June 1959, BBK/H/202.

27   Harry Fieldhouse, 'Man of Surprises', in Gourlay (ed.), *The Beaverbrook I Knew*, p. 217.

28   Peter Grosvenor, 'The Seeds of Discord', in ibid., p. 245.

29   Montague-Browne, *Long Sunset*, p. 190.

30   Hugh Cudlipp, 'The Rage', in Gourlay (ed.), *The Beaverbrook I Knew*, p. 2.

31   Sharpley, 'The Enchanter', in ibid., p. 219.

32   Geoffrey Bocca, 'Mentor and Tormentor', in ibid., p. 169.

33   Robert Edwards, *Goodbye Fleet Street* (London: Cape, 1988), p. 141.

34   Beaverbrook to Bidlake, 26 June 1962, BBK/F/101.

35   Beaverbrook to Paul, undated, BBK/C/269.

36   Taylor to Beaverbrook, p. 652.

37   Taylor to Beaverbrook, 19 February 1963, BBK/C/305.

38   *The Observer*, 3 March 1963.

39   *Daily Telegraph*, 4 March 1963.

40   Chapman Pincher, *Dangerous to Know: A Life* (London: Biteback Publishing, 2014), p. 196.

41   Quoted in Chisholm and Davie, *Beaverbrook*, p. 522.

42   *Daily Express*, 26 May 1964.

43   *Daily Express*, 10 June 1964.

44   Junor to Beaverbrook, 26 May 1964, BBK/H/231.

45   Beaverbrook to Churchill, 29 May 1964, BBK/C/90.

46   Beaverbrook to Blackburn, 5 June 1964, BBK/H/232.

47   Taylor, *Beaverbrook*, p. 669.

ACKNOWLEDGEMENTS

M y first thanks go to Maxwell Beaverbrook (the 3rd Baron Beaverbrook) for agreeing to read through my final version of the book and point to errors of fact (while, wisely, refraining from giving an opinion). Peter Hennessy (Lord Hennessy of Nympsfield) and Giles Radice (Lord Radice) have been kind enough to read through the book in draft and make, as always, helpful suggestions. For my research I have been amply blessed: Dr Andrew Ross of the University of Guelph has been an unfailing source of both comprehensive information, as well as deep insight, on Canada's social and political history; Scot Peterson of Balliol College, Oxford, has been good enough to share with me his thoughts, particularly on the abdication; Professor Irina Bystrova has delved for me into the Soviet archives; and Paul Bew (Lord Bew) has cast his magisterial eye over the material on Ireland. On the ground, a number of people have helped, but the palm must go to my three redoubtable musketeers, Matt Lyus, Joanna Stephens and Sophia Gibb. Matt has carried the burden of sustained archival and literary research with the greatest of patience, perception and good humour (except when Tottenham Hotspur lose); Joanna has diligently unearthed new material about Beaverbrook's private life; and Sophia has shown me what skilful and dedicated picture research can turn up. My humble thanks to all three.

Libraries, of course, play a large part in a project such as this. I am particularly grateful to the House of Lords library (although I have much missed Shorayne Fairweather) and the speed with which they operated the inter-library loan system. Special praise must also go to the staff at the Parliamentary Archives, whose unfailing courtesy and assistance have made it a tranquil haven in which to conduct research over the past four years; Simon Gough, its Archives Officer, and Claire Batley, its Senior Archivist, deserve particular thanks for their guidance, good humour and perceptive advice. Graeme Morton, Alan MacDonald and Jim Livesey based at the University of Dundee provided valuable insight into the Disruption of 1843 within the Church of Scotland and the resulting emigration to Canada of young ministers who remained loyal to the established church, one of whom was Beaverbrook's father, William. Bonnie McQuarrie and Jan Fuller supplied important genealogical information concerning Beaverbrook's mother, Jane Noble. A debt of gratitude must also be acknowledged to those who assisted in locating many of the pictures used in this book: Jennifer Jeffrey at akg-images; Marc Cutler of News Syndication Licensing; Colin Panter of PA Images; Julia Schmidt at the Churchill Archives Centre, Cambridge University; Gillian Shaw at the City of Vaughn Archives; Patrick F. Fahy of the Franklin D. Roosevelt Library and Museum; Lucinda Walker and Eva Bryant at Historic England; Heather McNabb and Anne-Frédérique Beaulieu at the McCord Museum, Montreal; Garry Shublak and Jessica Kilford of the Nova Scotia Archives; and Joshua Green of the Provincial Archives of New Brunswick.

There have been many conversations, some random and some not so random, with many friends and chance acquaintances, about Beaverbrook himself, the newspaper industry, the Conservative Party and so on. It has not been possible to record them all, but all deserve and receive my thanks. I would, however, single out those who have made a significant addition to my understanding of Beaverbrook's character: Jonathan Aitken, Penny Junor, Aurelia Young (Oscar Nemon's daughter), Alan Frame and his merry men (former Beaverbrook employees who joined me in a symposium about the Beaver and his works) and Josephine Yorke (née Rosenberg), who worked as Beaverbrook's secretary in the 1950s.

On the production side, my thanks go to Olivia Beattie and her team at Biteback and to Tracy Bohan at the Wylie Agency. On a more personal note, I am immensely grateful to those who saw me through successive bouts of ill health: Ana, Haylene, Murray, the two Johns, Llinos, Meghnad, Jean, Elystan and, of course, Marva. Finally, I have dedicated the book to my most perceptive and pointed critic (and self-styled 'ordinary reader'), my beloved wife Jane, without whose love, patience and support I would, to borrow Beaverbrook's memorable phrase, lose my moorings.

INDEX